AF594504

TRAILBLAZING WOMEN PRINTMAKERS

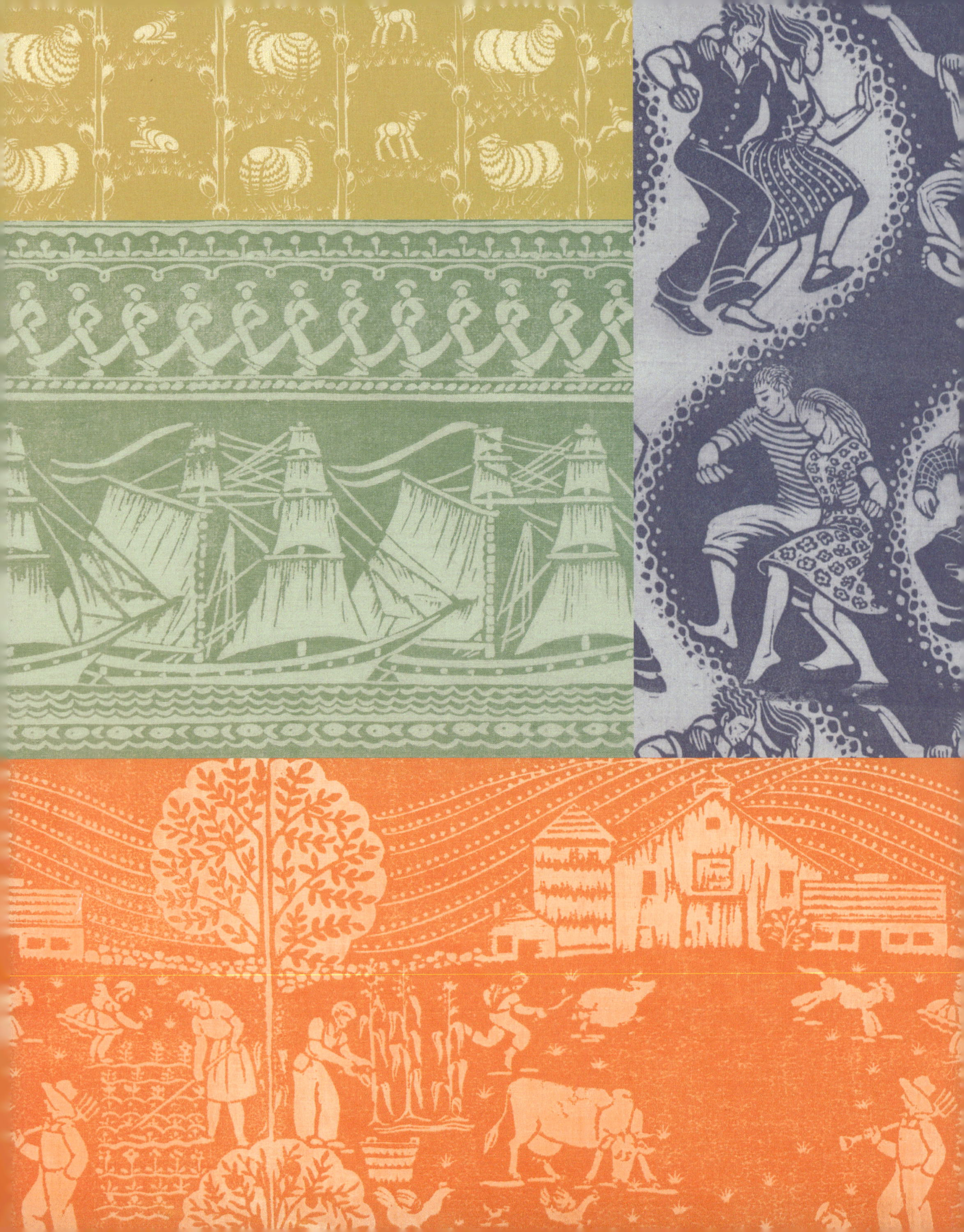

TRAILBLAZING WOMEN PRINTMAKERS

VIRGINIA LEE BURTON DEMETRIOS AND THE FOLLY COVE DESIGNERS

ELENA M. SARNI

PA PRESS
PRINCETON ARCHITECTURAL PRESS · NEW YORK

DEDICATION

To my parents, Nancy and John Sarni...I am forever grateful for your many sacrifices over the years, generosity, love, and support.

To the Folly Cove Designers for their incredible artistry and enduring inspiration. I hope that I have done your legacy justice.

The photography for this book was generously underwritten, in large part, by Speedball Art Products Company. Visit them at www.speedballart.com.

Published by
Princeton Architectural Press
A division of Chronicle Books LLC
70 West 36th Street
New York, NY 10018
papress.com

Printed and bound in China

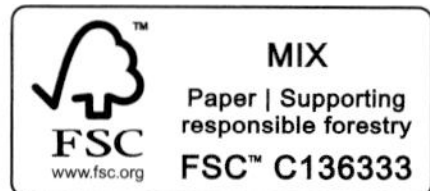

26 25 24 23   4 3 2

ISBN 978-1-7972-2428-2

Editor: Jennifer Thompson
Designer: Natalie Snodgrass

Library of Congress Control Number: 2022951307

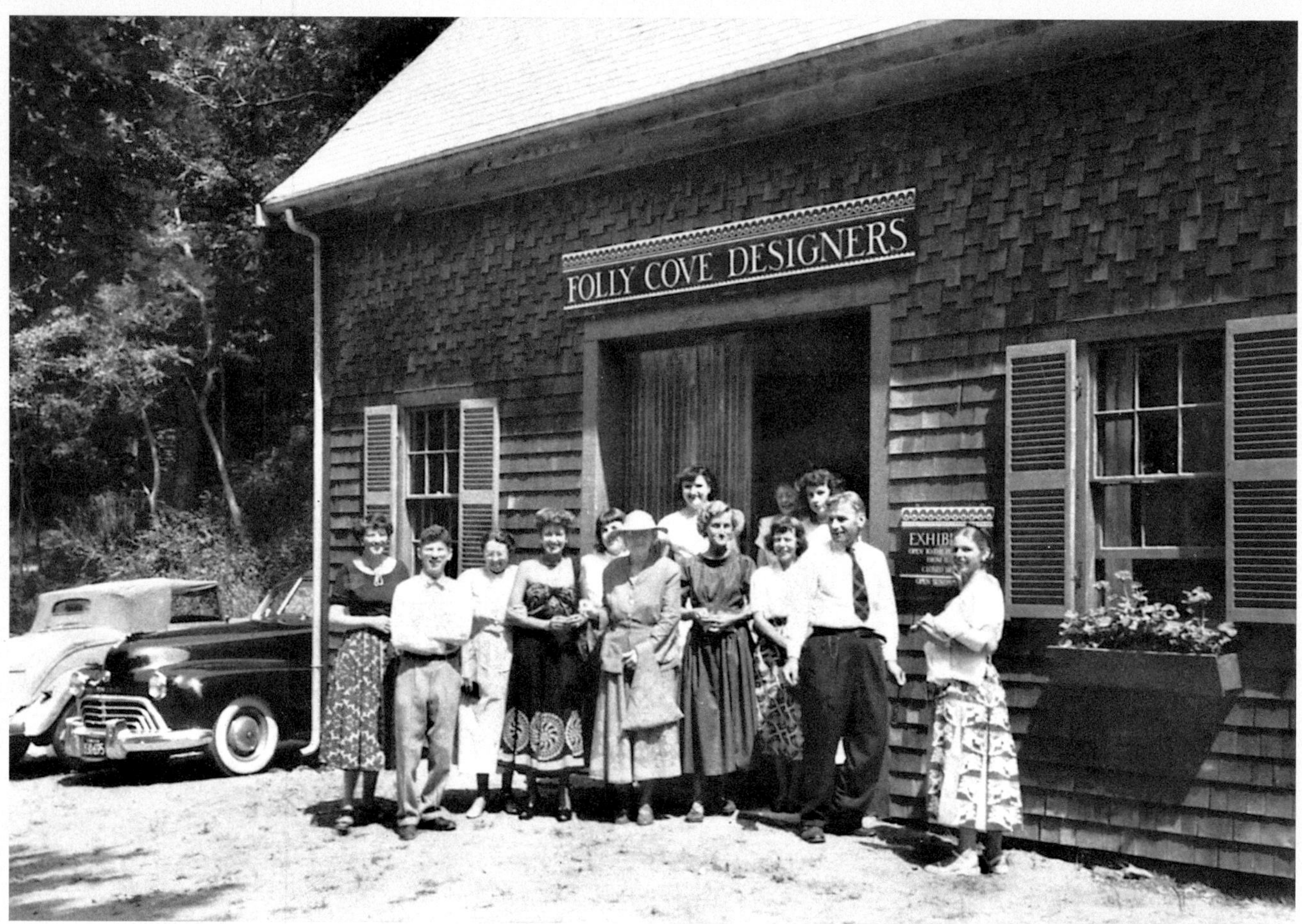

The Folly Cove Designers at their retail barn, ca. 1949. This was likely taken before a seasonal exhibit opening since they are wearing their designs. Virginia is on the far right. This photograph was in the collection of designer Margaret Nelson.

PREFACE

I fell in love with the work of the Folly Cove Designers in 2006 while working as the assistant curator at the Cape Ann Museum in Gloucester, Massachusetts. I was immediately drawn to the intricacy of the designs, the narrative nature of the work, and the stories of the group and the community. Even after leaving the museum, I remained enamored of the topic. In 2010 I submitted a paper on the Folly Cove Designers to the Dublin Seminar for New England Folklife. The success of the presentation and publication of my paper in the conference's annual proceedings encouraged me to write a book on the group and their body of work.

After many years of driving the three-hour trip back and forth to Gloucester to conduct research, I finally started to prepare a book proposal. As with most books by first-time authors, my path to publication was a long one and I was grateful when Princeton Architectural Press offered to publish the book. They expressed a genuine love of the topic and publish gorgeous books, so it seemed like an ideal fit. I am particularly grateful to executive editor Jennifer Thompson for her faith in the project.

Despite many years and *many* obstacles, my love for the topic has never waned. When I would get discouraged, I would receive what I started referring to as "cosmic reminders," such as randomly meeting an artist whose work reminded me of the Folly Cove Designers and learning that her sister-in-law was the granddaughter of one of the early designers.

Since the project has spanned so many years, material continued to become available and hopefully will continue to. Although this is the first book dedicated solely to the work of the Folly Cove Designers, I am grateful for the original research conducted by former curators Deborah Goodwin and Sharon Worley of the Cape Ann Museum in the museum's catalog on the designers (*The Folly Cove Designers: 1941–1969*) and Barbara Elleman for her thorough research into the life and work of Virginia Lee Burton Demetrios and the Folly Cove Designers (*Virginia Lee Burton: A Life in Art*). I am also thankful to Sinikka Nogello for her televised interview (*The Folly Cove Designers*) with some of the designers and Linda Brayton and David Masters for their series "Toward an Oral History of Cape Ann." I am hugely indebted to Bowdoin College professor Theodora Martin for the extensive interviews she conducted with members of the Folly Cove Designers during the 1990s. I have quoted from them heavily. They provide wonderful insight into the lives of the members and offer a clear sense of the community and group dynamics. I also had the pleasure of interviewing several of the original designers myself over the years. I am grateful to all of the family members of the Folly Cove Designers who patiently answered my questions and shared items, as well as to the many private individuals who let me photograph pieces from their treasured collections.

This book is the culmination of thirteen years of work. I have been told that my writing journey and the obstacles I faced could be the subject of a book itself, but I certainly never expected to be writing the book during a global pandemic. I thought I had completed most of my primary research but discovered that the Demetrios family donated about thirty boxes of material to the Cape Ann Museum in fall 2019, which became available to the public just before lockdown. COVID-19 restrictions made library and archival research impossible for many months. I was finally able to access this material after Christmas in 2020. Due to research limitations, the book's focus definitely changed over 2020 and 2021, but other discoveries opened up new avenues.

While I was not able to conduct as much secondary research as I originally planned in order to write about the group's work in the larger context of printmaking and textile design history, I did discover many "lost" Folly Cove designs. By "lost" I mean never-before-seen designs (ones where the name may have been known, but the design itself had never been seen by the public, or at least not in several decades) and in some cases, never-before-heard-of designs, which were completely new discoveries. I was also able to write detailed biographies of a select group of members. Of course, word count limitations prevented me from writing biographies on all forty-plus members of the group, but the contributions of those members are no less remarkable. Through my biographies I was able to flesh out the lives and work of some of the core members of the group, specifically those who were part of the Folly Cove Designers for many years and produced the most designs. I also wrote biographies for several members whom I was able to personally interview, or whose work represented a special aspect of the group (like the only mother/daughter duo to be members), members with "lost" designs to showcase, and one member whose biography has never been shared.

Primary research materials include interviews with some of the designers, drafts and sketches of designs, "homework" binders, business records and correspondence, newspaper and magazine articles, exhibit catalogs, snapshots, scrapbooks, and more. I encourage readers to read the image captions and skim the endnotes, as there are hidden gems of information throughout the entire book: bread crumbs for future researchers.

At times I felt like it might be impossible to complete the book and that history would repeat itself (Virginia worked on an unpublished design manual for nearly three decades). I can definitively say that completing this book has been the most challenging undertaking of my life during what turned out to be one of the most difficult periods of my personal life. But being a writer has been my dream from an early age and writing nonfiction became my goal as an undergraduate when I received fellowships to

Peony **by Mary Maletskos**

conduct research. I am grateful for the opportunity to pursue my dreams and I encourage everyone to do so. Ultimately I hope that my decade plus years of work will satisfy Folly Cove fans (or "deep nerd Folly Cove fans" as a friend of mine refers to us) and at the same time expose a whole new audience of pattern lovers to the Folly Cove Designers and their incredible work, thus furthering the legacy of this dynamic but often historically underrepresented group.

I am, of course, grateful to the many individuals, archivists, and organizations that have helped me out along the way, and I have attempted to thank them all on page 197. Sincere apologies to anyone I may have missed.

INTRODUCTION

A simple Yankee swap in 1938 between neighbors in the quaint neighborhood of Folly Cove, in Gloucester, Massachusetts—design lessons in exchange for music instruction—became the foundation of the Folly Cove Designers, one of the longest running and most successful juried artist guilds in American history. Renowned children's book author and illustrator Virginia Lee Burton (of *Mike Mulligan and His Steam Shovel* fame) traded design lessons in exchange for violin lessons for her sons, leading to community-wide design classes and, ultimately, the formation of the famed eponymous block-printing collective, which operated from 1941 through 1969. As a Folly Cove designer Virginia used her married name, Virginia Lee Demetrios. Over time at least forty people became members. Several husband-and-wife couples joined the group, as well as a few male members, but women dominated the membership. Ultimately the group produced over three hundred distinct designs conveying personal and regional narratives through the use of shared design principles taught to them by Virginia.[1]

Within the first ten years of organizing, the Folly Cove Designers were propelled to international fame through commercial contracts with major retailers (Lord & Taylor and F. Schumacher & Co.) and articles about the group in national periodicals such as *Life*. Despite this success (and their connection with some of the most powerful people in the fields of craft and design during World War II and the postwar period), over time the story of the Folly Cove Designers has in large part receded into the annals of local history.

The inspiration for the Folly Cove designs originated from the flora and fauna of Cape Ann. After a rail line connecting Boston and Gloucester was built in the middle of the 1800s, Gloucester emerged as an artist destination. Folly Cove in particular, located on Gloucester's north shore, with its rugged beauty, has inspired generations of artists. By the late 1930s, Folly Cove was an established artist community. Cape Ann's roots as an artist community are intertwined with printmaking. Gloucester native Fitz Henry Lane's artistic career began with lithography in the 1830s. The women artists of Folly Cove who preceded the Folly Cove Designers, including Gabrielle de Veaux Clements, had established themselves in the field of etching in the late 1800s.

American art in the late 1930s, printmaking and textile design specifically, was undergoing a movement toward modernism. Prior to, during, and following World War II, artists fleeing Europe settled in the United States and brought with them a bold, new aesthetic. Abstract Expressionism, an emotive, spontaneous form of art, evolved during World War II and cemented New York City as a center for international art. In contrast, the Folly Cove Designers were trained to draw subjects from life and as realistically as possible. One of the other primary differences between the Folly Cove Designers and other printmaking groups at the time was that they were a juried group. Most of the members were not full-time artists, but working another job and/or taking care of a family. The goal of the Folly Cove Designers was purely to produce "good design."[2] While there are some similarities between the Folly Cove Designers and other printmaking groups, they are generally unlike any of their contemporaries in style or subject matter. This individuality was part of their appeal.

Virginia made it clear from the start that you didn't have to be an artist to join the group—you just had to be willing to do the work. That meant months of "homework" (for more on that, see chapter 2), culminating in the submission of a design to the Folly Cove jury; approval brought membership to the Folly Cove Designers.

The Folly Cove Designers continue to inspire contemporary—particularly women—printmakers. There is a vast and active printmaking community on Instagram. Many women printmakers, much like many of the Folly Cove Designers, are raising their children by day and working in their studios (or often at their kitchen tables) at night. Among these printmakers, printmaking on fabric is very popular.

This book will underscore the inspirational legacy of the Folly Cove Designers. Many of the women in the group were college-educated, professional, working mothers at a time when research indicates that most women spent fifty hours a week on housework.[3] Like other women, they did set the table for their families every night, only they did so while wearing aprons that they had personally designed, carved into linoleum blocks, printed, and sewn themselves. The women of the Folly Cove Designers forged their own roles in the world, something that today's female printmakers find highly relatable.

As an illustrated history, this book will detail the group's formation, the design principles of Virginia that guided them, as well as the inner workings of the group, the exhibitions in which they participated, and their business dealings. It will explore the lives and work of a select group of designers and the interconnectedness between their lives and art. It will highlight the group's continuing relevance for today's printmakers and textile designers. Finally, the book showcases several never-before-seen (maybe only the title had previously been known) and in some cases never-before-heard-of "lost" designs as well as the most designs published in color to date.

This book examines the community, personal lives, and work of the Folly Cove Designers in an attempt to understand how the designs of this local art movement ended up having such tremendous national appeal, transcending the rolling fields and ocean views of Folly Cove to find favor on New York's Fifth Avenue and beyond.

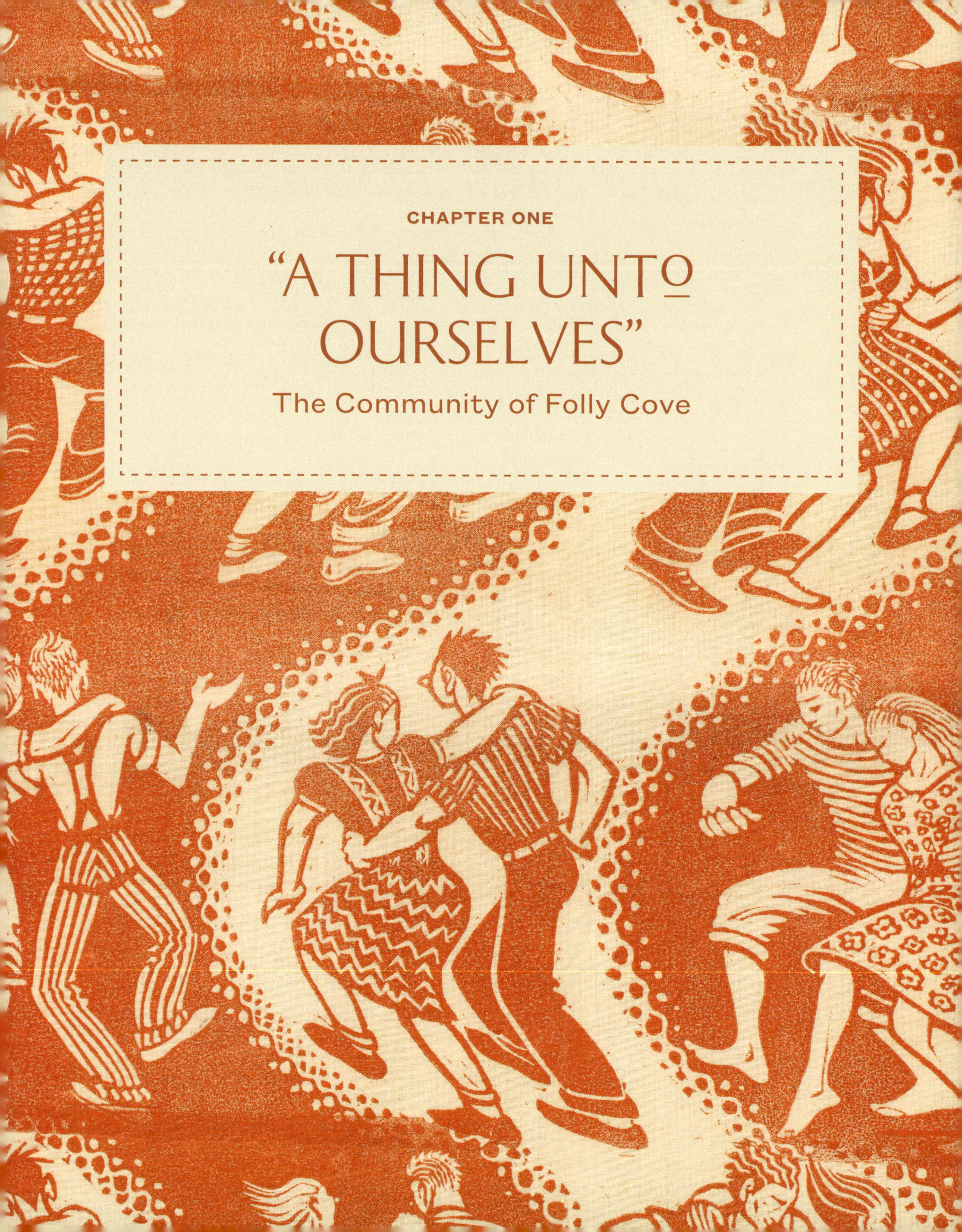

CHAPTER ONE

“A THING UNTO OURSELVES”

The Community of Folly Cove

The freshly scrubbed shingled barn that served as the group's headquarters would be bursting at the seams with the season's colorful inventory of new designs for the Folly Cove Designers' summer exhibition opening. Cars sporting license plates from across the nation would be lined up along Route 127, nearly causing a traffic jam. A policeman was on hand to guide customers to the festive tent set up on the lawn alongside the barn. Salt air would blend with the aromas of nisu, *a traditional Finnish braided cardamom-flavored sweet bread, and steaming coffee set out on tables covered in bright block-printed linens. Women in block-printed aprons served the refreshments. The servers' names, as well as the new designs, would be announced in the* Gloucester Daily Times. *The Folly Cove Designers would mingle with the customers and neighbors and proudly "don themselves with Folly Cove apparel from head to toe" in celebration of the new exhibition season.*[1] *The women designers would model an array of dress styles or pair the Folly Cove Designers' signature peasant blouses with pleated dirndl skirts. The men would wear block-printed vests, while children would run across the lawn in block-printed pinafores. Their outfits had been produced over the long, cold winter and meticulously sewn by hand.*

The above scene was an annual tradition for the Folly Cove Designers (an organized group from 1941 to 1969) as they debuted their new designs, resulting from the previous winter's work. This picturesque opening was part of the appeal of this juried group of block printers that grew out of informal design lessons given by children's book author and illustrator Virginia Lee Burton Demetrios. The opening was a time for the community to gather and celebrate the group's achievements and to admire their new designs, many of them inspired by the flora, fauna, people, and places of Folly Cove. As one member described the group's genesis, it "grew out of the granite of Cape Ann."[2]

FOLLY COVE

Located on Massachusetts's North Shore, approximately thirty miles northeast of Boston, Cape Ann is made up of the towns of Essex, Gloucester, Manchester-by-the-Sea, and Rockport. The region was known as Wonasquam to generations of Indigenous residents prior to European contact in the early seventeenth century when Samuel de Champlain was mapping the coast for the French king Henry IV.[3] In 1623 a fishing outpost called Gloucester was established on behalf of a group of English merchants that organized under the name of the Dorchester Company. It became a flourishing colonial port and fishing center, due to its deep harbor and abundance of cod. Folly Cove, Lanesville, Bay View, and Annisquam are some of the villages that comprise the rocky, northern outer shore of Gloucester on Cape Ann that overlook Ipswich Bay.

In the middle of the nineteenth century, a rail line connecting Boston and Gloucester was built. It was a huge factor in Gloucester's emergence as a destination for both artists and tourists. Fitz Henry Lane and Winslow Homer are two of many iconic American artists who were inspired by Gloucester's ocean views.

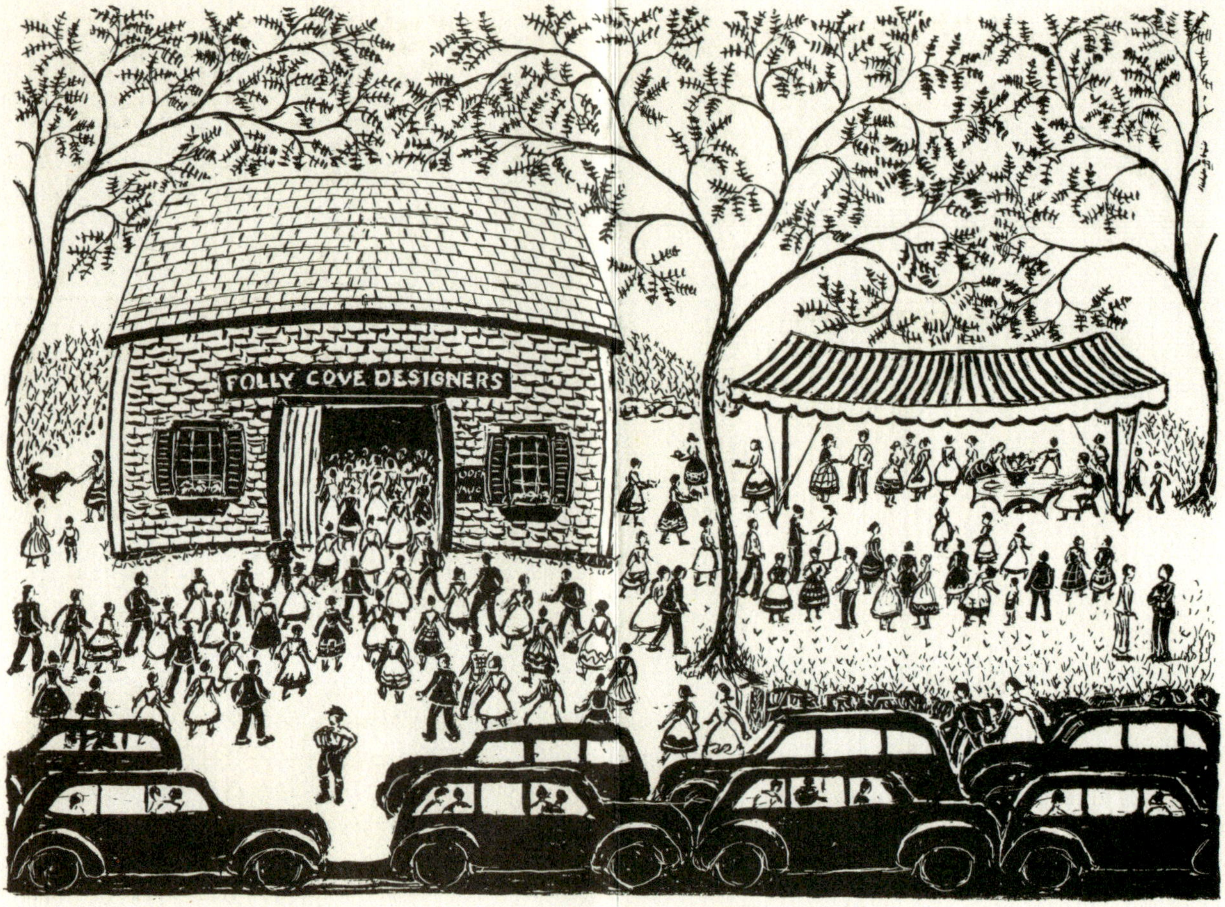

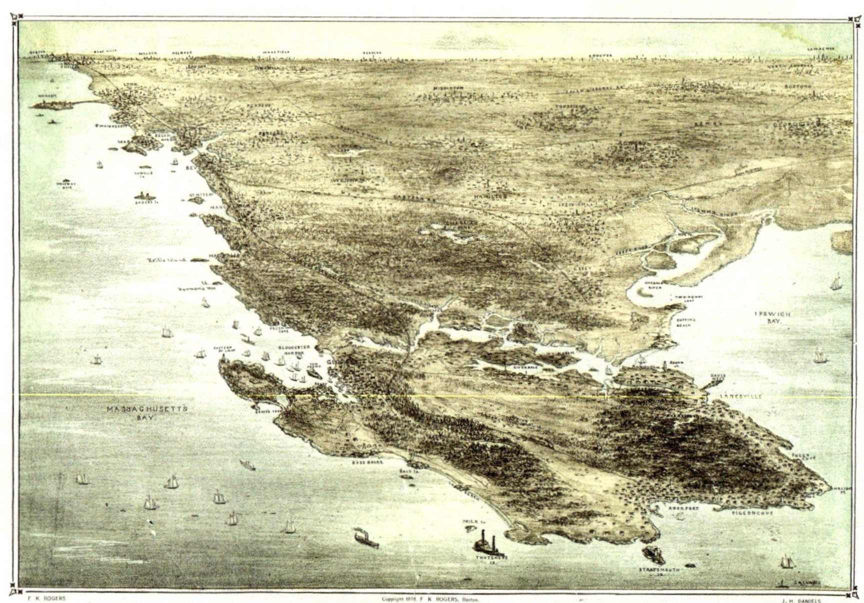

BALLOON VIEW—CAPE ANN TO BOSTON.

FIG. 1 (OPPOSITE TOP)
Eino Natti depicted an exhibition opening for the cover of the group's fifteenth annual exhibition invitation. Notice the barn bursting with people, the women wearing block-printed skirts, and the crossing guard. (Ink on paper.)

FIG. 2 (OPPOSITE BOTTOM)
The northern tip of Cape Ann. *Balloon view, Cape Ann to Boston.* Map by F. Kimball Rogers. Published by J.H. Daniels, Boston, Mass., c. 1879. (Map digitally edited to include additional location names by Cape Ann Museum.)

The granite industry was active on Cape Ann from 1798 through the 1920s and drew many to this remote area to work in the quarries, including a wave of Finnish immigrants in the 1870s. Many had fled Finland to escape Russian imperialism and conscription in the Russian army.[4] Along with the quarries, fishing and art were the primary industries of the region at the turn of the twentieth century.[5] As the artist community grew with the advent of cars, so did the seasonal summer tourist trade and the need for inns and shops.

Twentieth-century artists in the Folly Cove area included the painter and etcher William Meyerowitz, his wife and fellow artist, Teresa Bernstein, and in the 1930s painter Leon Kroll. Earlier artists included painter Ellen Day Hale (who first came to the area to study with William Morris Hunt) and Gabrielle de Veaux Clements (who was introduced to the area by her teacher, etcher Stephen Parrish from Philadelphia).[6] Hale and Clements became good friends and bought homes in the area. Clements's home in Folly Cove was named "The Thickets," while Hale's was "Howletts."[7] Here they entertained many of their contemporaries.

Some of their guests went on to join the community and made Folly Cove their own retreat, including two students of Clements's, Margaret Yeaton Hoyt and Lesley Jackson. Clements frequently used locals as models. She, Hale, and Hoyt worked collaboratively on commissions for large murals. All three, along with Jackson, explored soft-ground etching (*vernis mou*), a French process of color etching that was new to the United States at the time. They employed Uno Seppala, brother to an early Folly Cove designer, Vera Seppala, to help with the press.[8]

One local historian stated that "Miss Hale was a leader in Folly Cove's art colony, composed mostly of women like herself who had stuck 'to their own guns' and studied art despite family traditions of becoming decorative hostesses while men achieved their own goals."[9] Hale, Clements, and their friends set the stage for the largely female Folly Cove Designers who followed.

The Folly Cove area was also a mecca for sculptors in the early twentieth century, due in large part to the presence of renowned portrait sculptor and professor at the Pennsylvania Academy of the Fine Arts in Philadelphia, Charles Grafly. Charles, who also taught at the School of the Museum of the Fine Arts in Boston, established a summer home and studio in Lanesville in the early 1900s and his students followed him; Walker Hancock, Paul Manship, and George Demetrios eventually settled in the area.

VIRGINIA LEE BURTON AND GEORGE DEMETRIOS

George Demetrios immigrated to the United States from Greece in 1911 and made his first visit to Folly Cove while studying with Charles. Charles died in 1929 and bestowed the lifetime use of his studio to George. By this time, George had established his own drawing school, holding classes in Boston

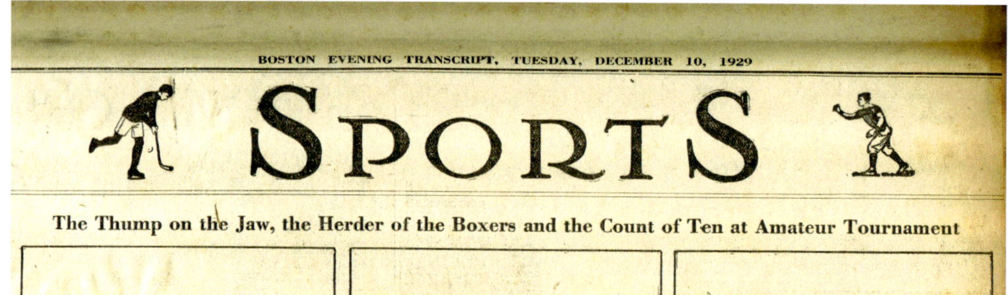

BOSTON EVENING TRANSCRIPT, TUESDAY, DECEMBER 10, 1929

SPORTS

The Thump on the Jaw, the Herder of the Boxers and the Count of Ten at Amateur Tournament

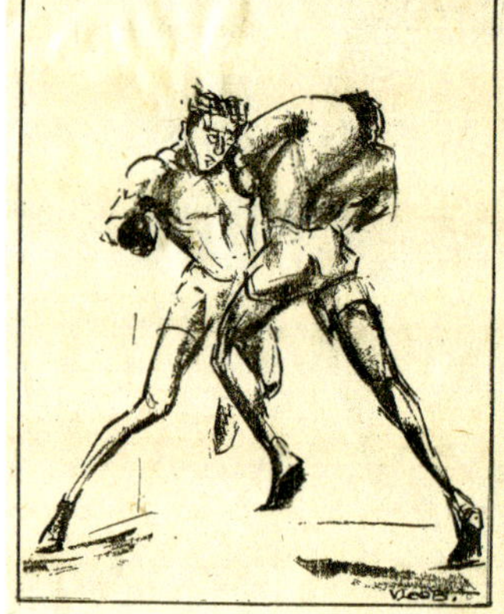

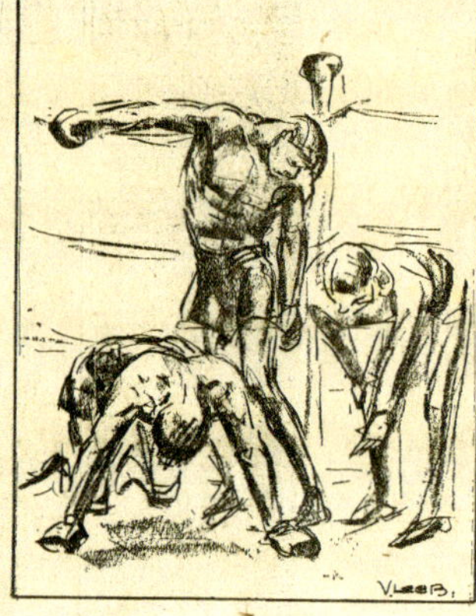

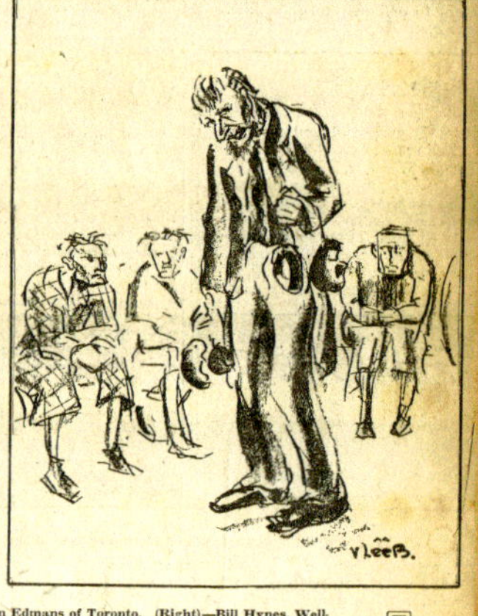

Miss Virginia Lee Burton Pictures (Left) Cataclysmic 126-Pound Final Between Edward Sullivan of Walpole and Ruben Edmans of Toronto. (Right)—Bill Hynes, Well-Known Herder of the Boxers, in the Act of Demanding That "That New York Guy Get Into the Ring." (Middle—George Carthew of Toronto, Taking the Count of Ten in the Second 160-Pound Bout. Jack McCarthy, Savage Roxbury Middleweight, Was Carthew's Opponent

FIG. 3 (LEFT)
Virginia Lee Burton's work for *Boston Evening Transcript* (December 10, 1929), which she signed "VLeeB." Some of the self-consciousness she may have felt sketching public events, particularly prizefights, might have stemmed from the fact that she was probably one of few women in attendance at that time.

FIG. 4 (BELOW)
Virginia returned to the ring for *Double Knockout*. Like many early works, this narrative piece reads from top to bottom, left to right. The men and their hats create a border, but in the final scene their hats are off and their arms raised in excitement at the unexpected outcome. (Ink on fabric.)

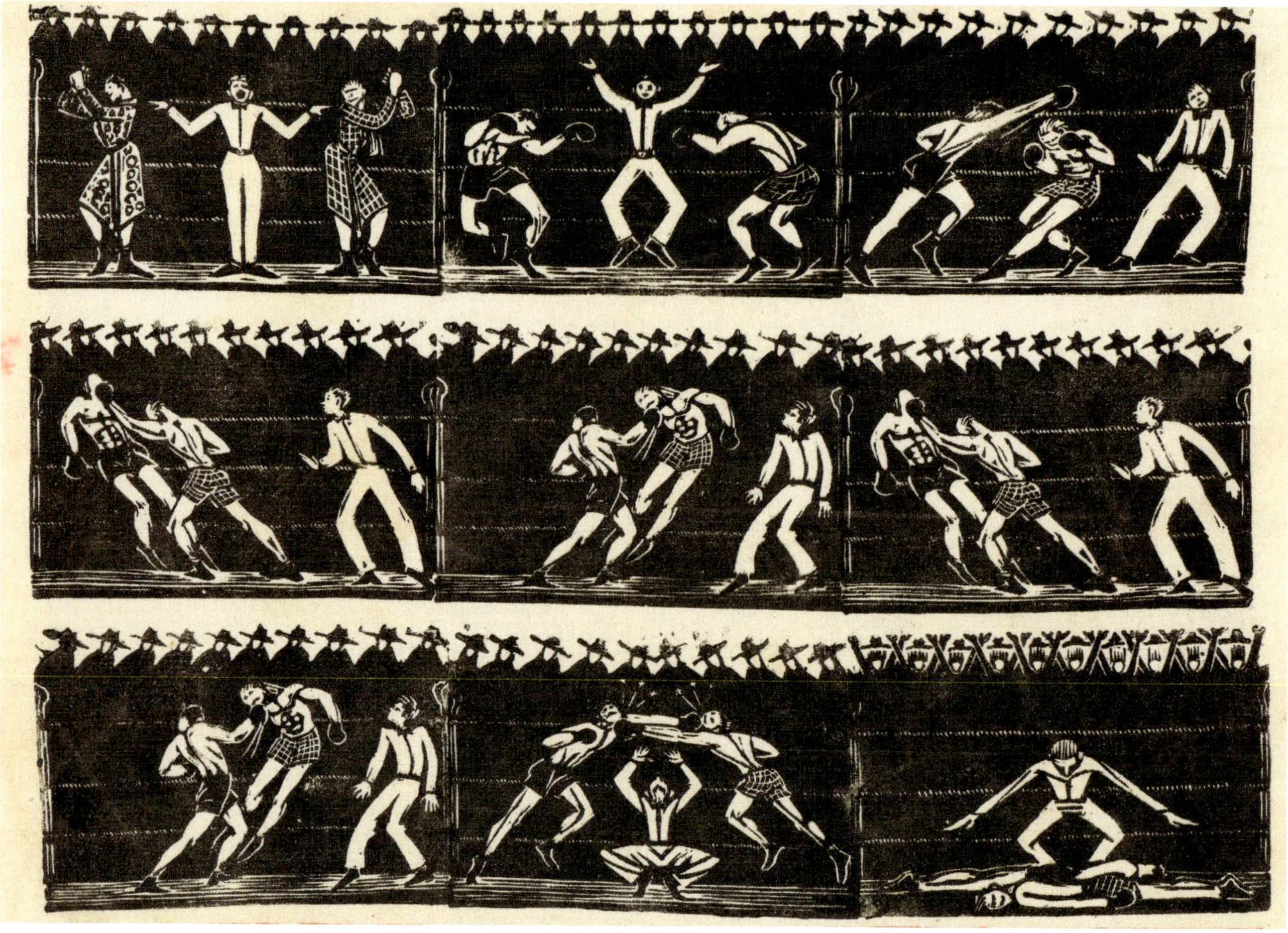

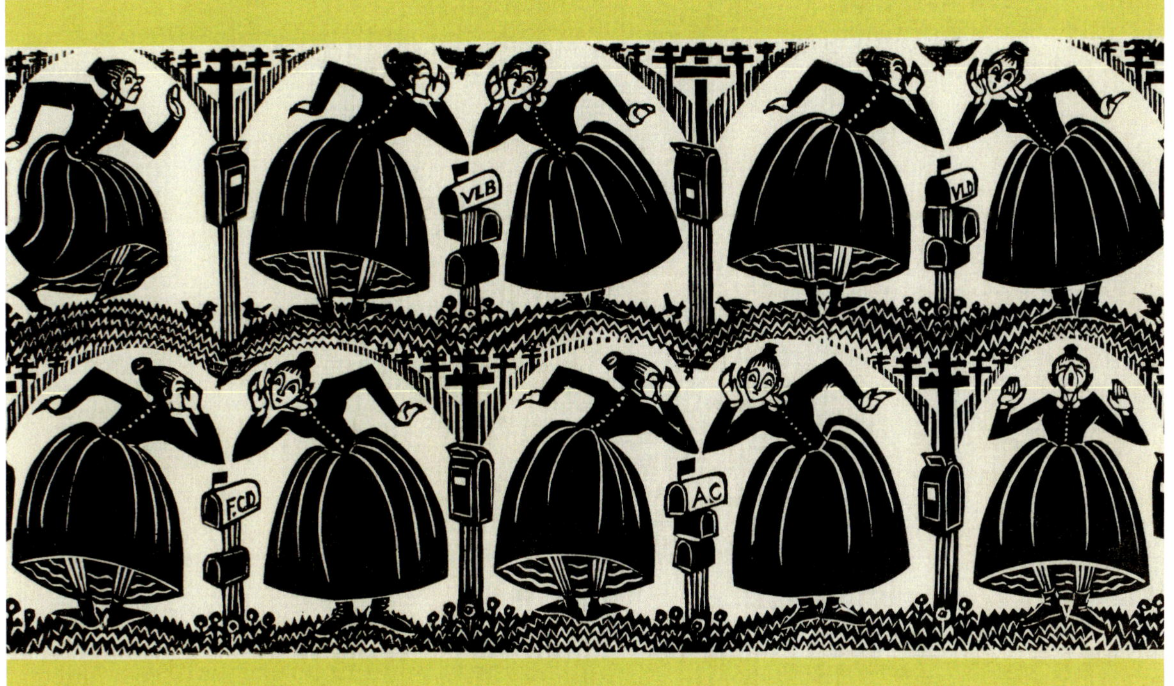

FIG. 5
Gossips **is one of Virginia's most iconic designs and depicts "typical small town gossips," as Dorothy Norton once described it. Virginia personalized the humorous design with the mailbox initials. The telephone poles are reminiscent of the illustrations for many of her children's books. (Ink on fabric.)**

during the winter and Folly Cove during the summer. Virginia Lee Burton (affectionately called Jinnee by loved ones and friends) worked as an illustrator for the *Boston Evening Transcript* from the late 1920s to the early 1930s, her assignment being to create "visual profiles," as she had proven herself gifted at capturing action and motion, including prizefights (though she said that she felt self-conscious sketching at them).[10] She signed her work during this time as "VLeeB."[11]

In 1930, Virginia enrolled in one of George's drawing classes. They fell in love and married a year later. George and Virginia moved to Folly Cove full-time in 1932 with their newborn son, Aristides (Aris); Virginia gave birth to their second son, Michael (Mike), in 1935.[12]

George continued teaching and sculpting in Folly Cove; Virginia began to write and illustrate children's books. *Choo Choo,* published in 1937, was the first book that she both authored and illustrated. She published under her maiden name, Virginia Lee Burton, and went on to gain tremendous distinction, especially for *Mike Mulligan and His Steam Shovel* (1939); her Caldecott Medal winner, *The Little House* (1942); and *Katy and the Big Snow* (1943).

In the late 1930s, Virginia was mother to two young sons as well as a children's book author and illustrator. Despite the demands of an already full life, Virginia took on yet another endeavor, offering design lessons to her neighbors, which would lay the foundation for the formation of the Folly Cove Designers.

An early design by Virginia titled *Gossips* references her dual identities as author and designer by humorously illustrating two women swapping secrets over their mailboxes, which bear four different sets of initials in a

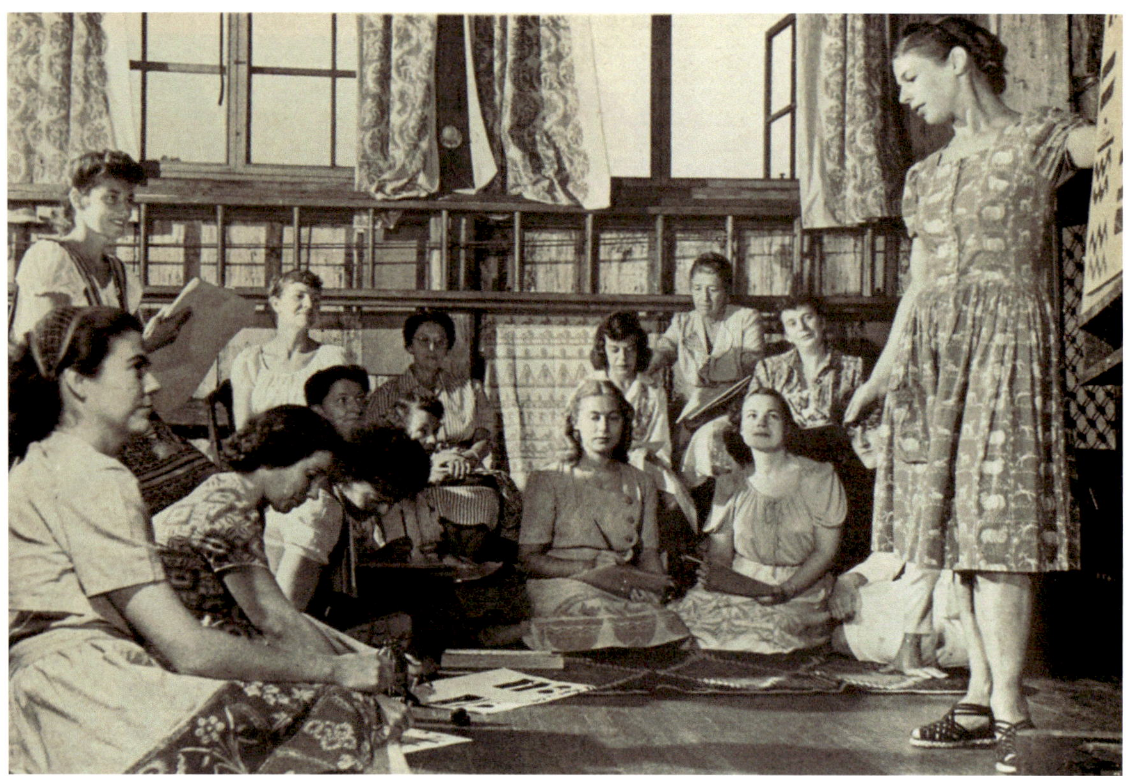

Malmi, Ilmari Natti, Robert Natti, Helen Pistenmaa, Pauline Pistenmaa, Hilda Ross, and Vera Seppala.[16] Only one class member, Jean Berkenbush, was not from the immediate area. (The Berkenbush family was friends with Virginia and one family member was integral to the plot of *Mike Mulligan and His Steam Shovel*.)[17]

Many members of the original design class were descendants of Finnish families who had moved to the area to work in the quarries. Out of the initial class, it appears that only two students weren't Finnish, Hetty Beatty and Jean Berkenbush. Eleanor Malmi was employed by the Demetrios family as a housekeeper and babysitter. Later in life she remembered the block-printing lessons as a bright spot at the end of the Depression: "It was something that brought everybody together—those years—so that you weren't thinking about the poverty."[18]

When interviewed decades later, other early class members couldn't pinpoint the reason Virginia started the classes. Vera Seppala acknowledged that it might have been a way to pass the time, but added, "We weren't teenagers. We were really adults at this point, and I think we were also ready for something different than just walking in the woods on Sunday."[19] Irja Jacobson, who also worked for the Demetrios family, marveled at her inclusion. "Why would she [Virginia] make such a big deal out of me? I was just a little Finnish girl out of high school. But she must have seen something there that she wanted to nurture..."[20]

THE FINNISH COMMUNITY

Lanesville was a predominantly Finnish community at this time, as was nearby Folly Cove. "During the years from 1892 to 1920 the Finns were drawn to Lanesville as a place to live simply in a group and enjoy their social activities much as they had done in Finland."[21] A community center was built in 1897 and was maintained by the Temperance Society of Lanesville, which was an important part of the Finnish community. Besides hosting plays, dances, and athletic programs, the hall was where the women held their rag-cutting parties in preparation for weaving rugs. Coffee socials were also held and *nisu* was served.[22] Church services at the Lutheran church were conducted in both English and Finnish until the early 1950s.[23]

Finnish Americans remember speaking Finnish at home while learning English at school and picking it up from their Yankee friends and neighbors. Their parents would speak a mixture of English and Finnish, what the children referred to as "Finnglish."[24] The Finns in the area retained a lot of cultural pride despite the eventual assimilation of the first and second generations. Early Finnish members of the Folly Cove Designers often credited their skill in music and art to their Finnish heritage, of having, as one Finnish designer described it, "brains in their hands," when it came to art and handicrafts.[25]

Saunas were prevalent in the neighborhood, as it was a Saturday custom for Finnish people to take their baths. "To those early Finnish quarrymen, the sauna was so important that many times the bathhouse was built before the house was begun."[26] There were both private and public bathhouses throughout the twentieth century and these were "quite a center for the community."[27] Along with running a dairy farm, the Seppala family operated a public sauna and charged fifteen cents per head.[28]

FIG. 7 (OPPOSITE)
Aino Clarke's *Sauna*, debuted in 1940. She and Virginia took them regularly. Just as bathers moved from top to bottom, this design reads from top to bottom. Buckets of water and birch switches were provided to increase circulation. A cold-water rinse concluded the bath. (Ink on paper.)

THE FOLLY COVE DESIGNERS' PROCESS

Design lessons would start each fall and span the long winter months. The lessons centered on design principles that could be applied to many art forms. Initially the group considered applying their designs to pottery but ultimately chose linoleum block printing, primarily because the equipment and supplies were inexpensive and accessible to all members. Virginia had studied with printmaker Robert Hestwood in her teens, which may have further influenced the decision to concentrate on block prints. The group also elected to print on fabric because it afforded them the opportunity to create practical pieces like clothing and decorative textiles for their homes.[29]

The design process started with each designer selecting a subject of study for that year's class, which would become the basis of a new design. The winter was spent sketching the subject repeatedly, refining the design, then carving the block and, finally, printing the design onto fabric. Students were encouraged to find inspiration for their subjects from the natural world around them. To aid in this process, Ilmari (called Jimo) Natti, a member of the first design class, gave lectures on tree identification and other nature-related subjects.[30] Collectively the group's designs could be seen as a naturalist's guide to Cape Ann.

Finnish culture and Scandinavian design aesthetics were also apparent in many Folly Cove designs; Ilmari most clearly demonstrated this with his block prints depicting the *Kalevala*, a nineteenth-century epic poem compiled by Elias Lönnrot from Finnish folklore.[31]

At the outset, to transfer the designs to fabric, the carved linoleum blocks would be inked, then set on the fabric and jumped on by the designer to imprint the image. This practice was physically challenging and may have been responsible for at least one broken ankle, so it was likely a relief to most members when the group began upgrading to hand-operated proof presses in 1943.[32]

In general, the designers worked alone in their homes, except for the design lessons and monthly meetings where the designers convened to critique one another's work. Until the late 1940s, when most of the members had acquired their own presses, members who had them would often share their presses with those who didn't.[33] Throughout the group's history, only Ruth Hendy and Barbara Bisbee Souza Hoffmann seemed to be the exception to this solitary style of working. As close friends, they would work on their designs at one or the other's kitchen table, placing their young children in a playpen together.[34]

In 1941 the group officially organized under the name Folly Cove Designers and named officers. Virginia refused the title of president, but everyone recognized her as the group's leader.[35] In 1943 they decided that

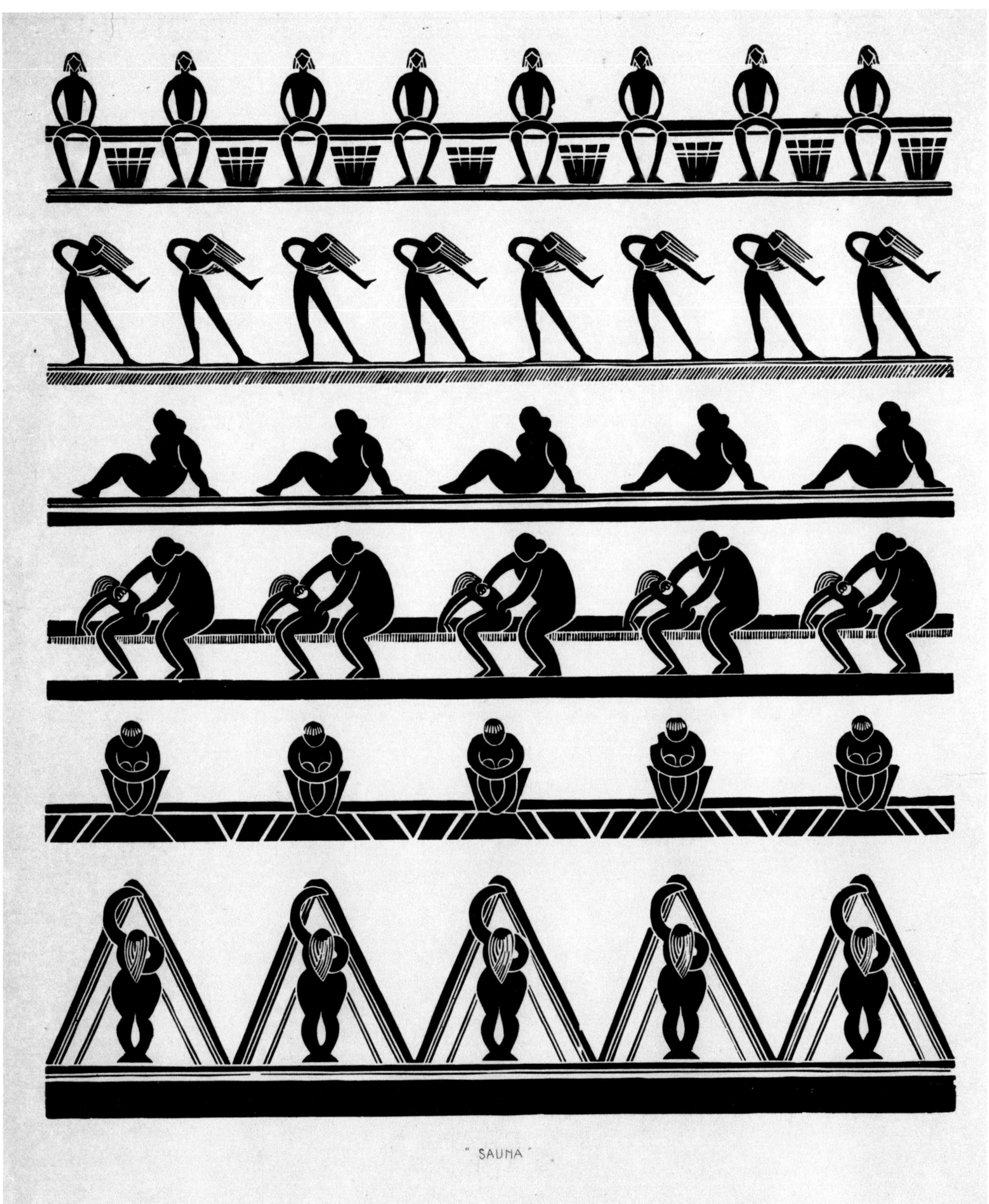
" SAUNA "

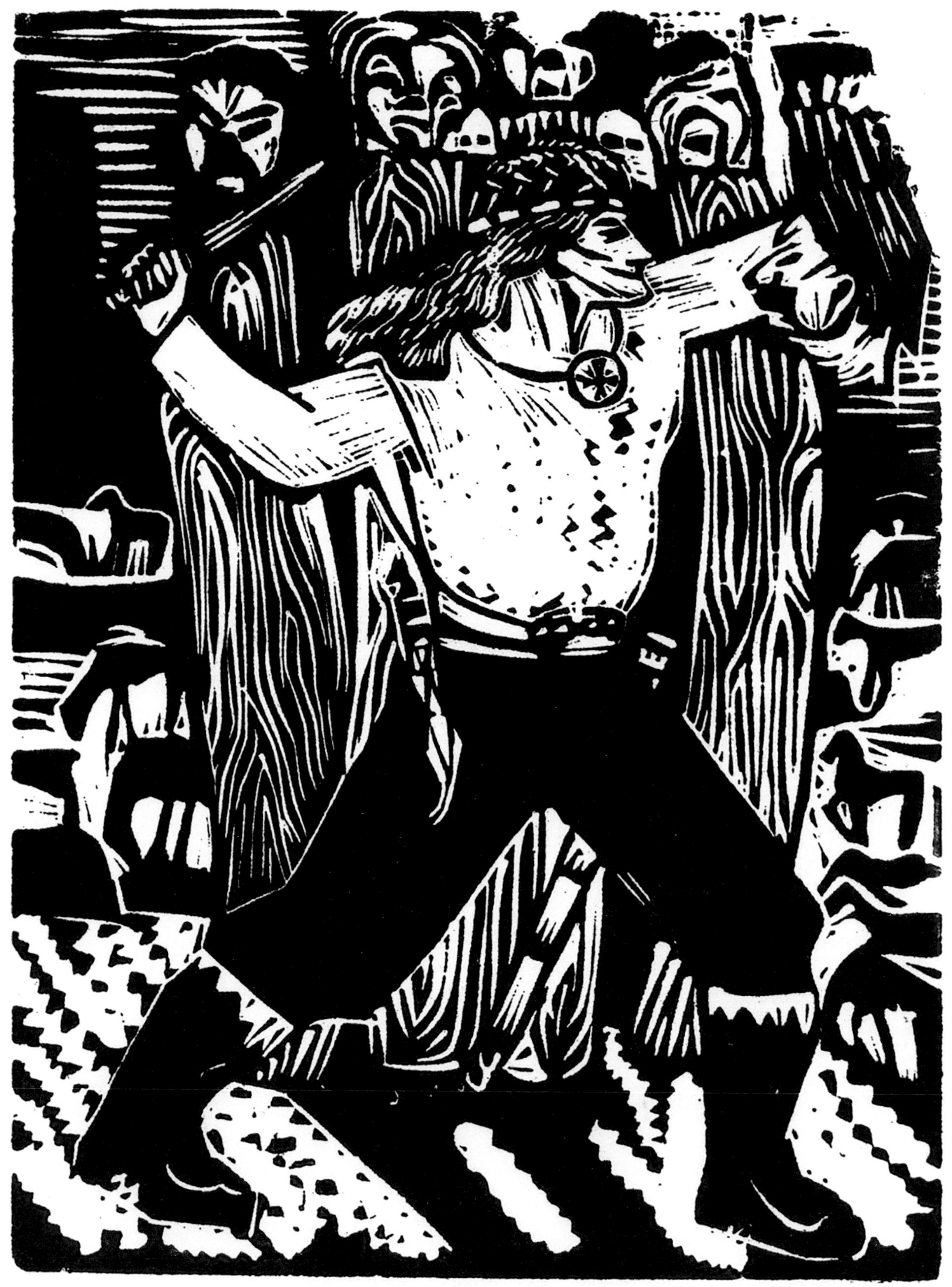

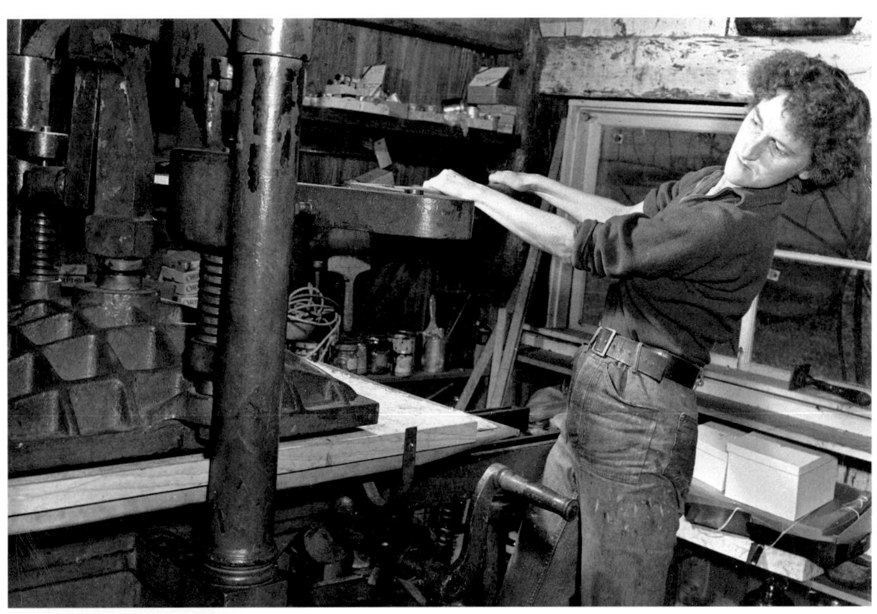

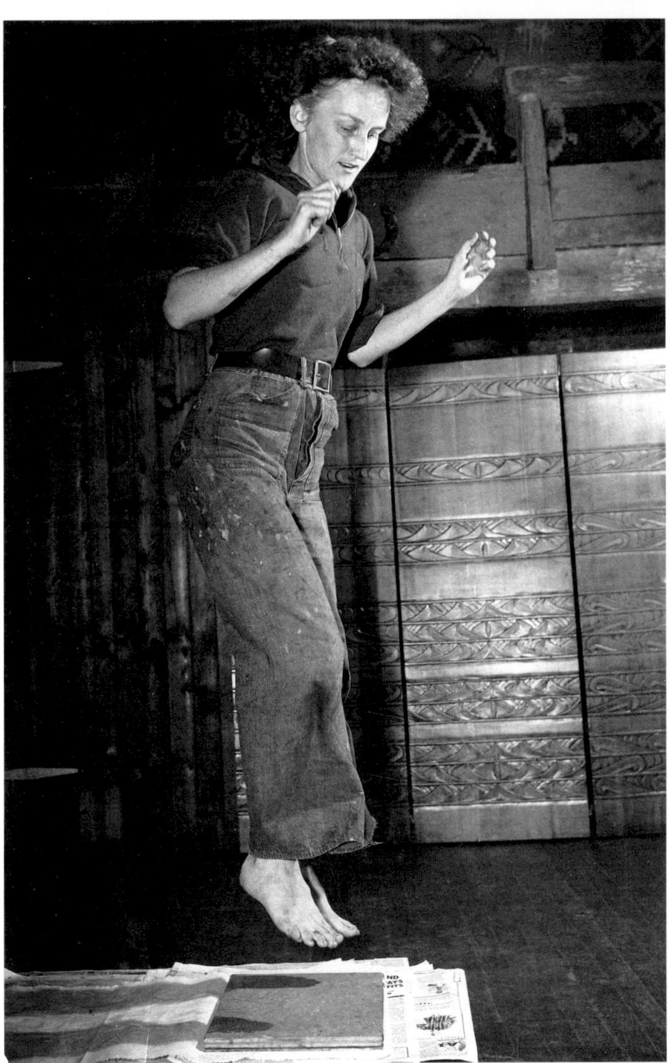

FIG. 8 (OPPOSITE)
Ilmari (Jimo) Natti produced prints based on the Finnish *Kalevala* in 1940. This image features his depiction of the folk hero Lemminkäinen. This piece was printed by his daughter, Isabel Natti, using her father's block.

FIG. 9 (ABOVE)
Aino Clarke using one of the group's hand presses.

FIG. 10 (LEFT)
Aino Clarke getting a full-body workout as she imprinted an image by jumping on a linoleum block. (A wood carving by Virginia is in the background.)

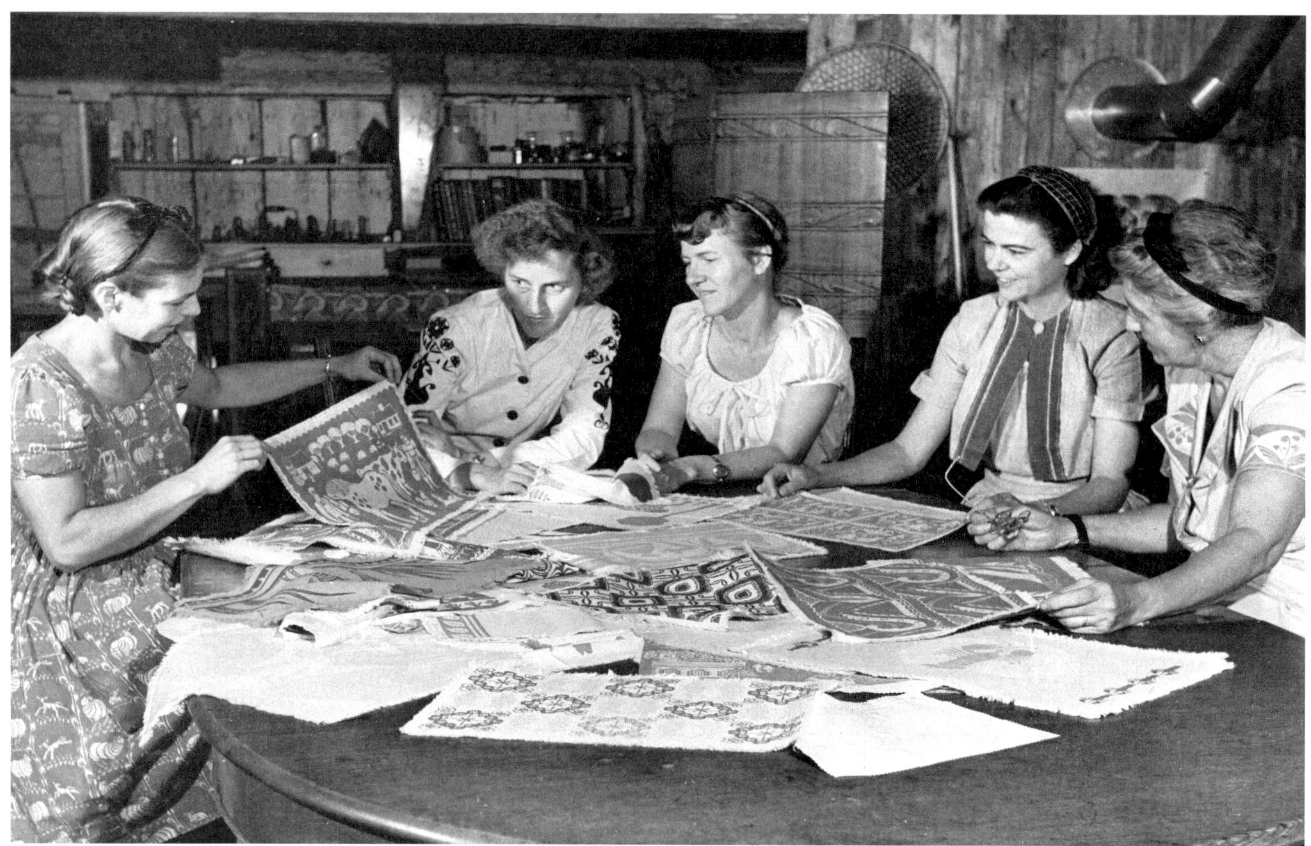

they would operate in the same way that craft guilds dating back to medieval times had: they would form a jury and only upon its approval could a design be considered an official Folly Cove design.[36] Upon completion of their first juried design, students were awarded a block-printed diploma featuring Virginia's design *The Making of a Block Print* and became official members of the Folly Cove Designers.[37]

The group wrote formal "Rules and Regulations" by the mid-1940s to ensure the quality of the product, the standard of their brand, and also possibly to comply with the requisites for trademarking their name and logo. Members were considered designer-craftsmen, which meant that they each were responsible for his or her own work from start to finish—from design to print. Only the sewing of clothing items and the signature fringing of their table linens could be farmed out. The rules stated clearly that the goal was for each designer to create at least one new design per year.[38]

Those who joined the Folly Cove Designers after the first group of students, for the most part, came with some degree of art or craft experience. The annual class size varied but averaged about twelve designers. Over the group's lifespan, it wasn't unusual for people to be members for only one to three years, but by the mid-1940s a core group of designers was established. These individuals remained part of the group until it disbanded and included Virginia, Aino Clarke, Libby Holloran, Louise Kenyon, Eino Natti, Lee Natti, Dorothy Norton, and Peggy Norton.

FIG. 11
Jury members rotated, but they typically consisted of four to seven of the most experienced designers. From left to right, Virginia Lee Demetrios, Aino Clarke, Louise Kenyon, Hetty Beatty, and Ida Bruno. Virginia's carving in the background features a wave pattern, which she often incorporated in her work as a Folly Cove designer.

FIG. 12 (OPPOSITE)
***The Making of a Block Print* depicts the design process from struggling to think of an idea to revealing the design. The lines that move your eye from level to level act as a parallel story line and feature printmaking tools. The final design is the group's circular logo. (Ink on fabric.)**

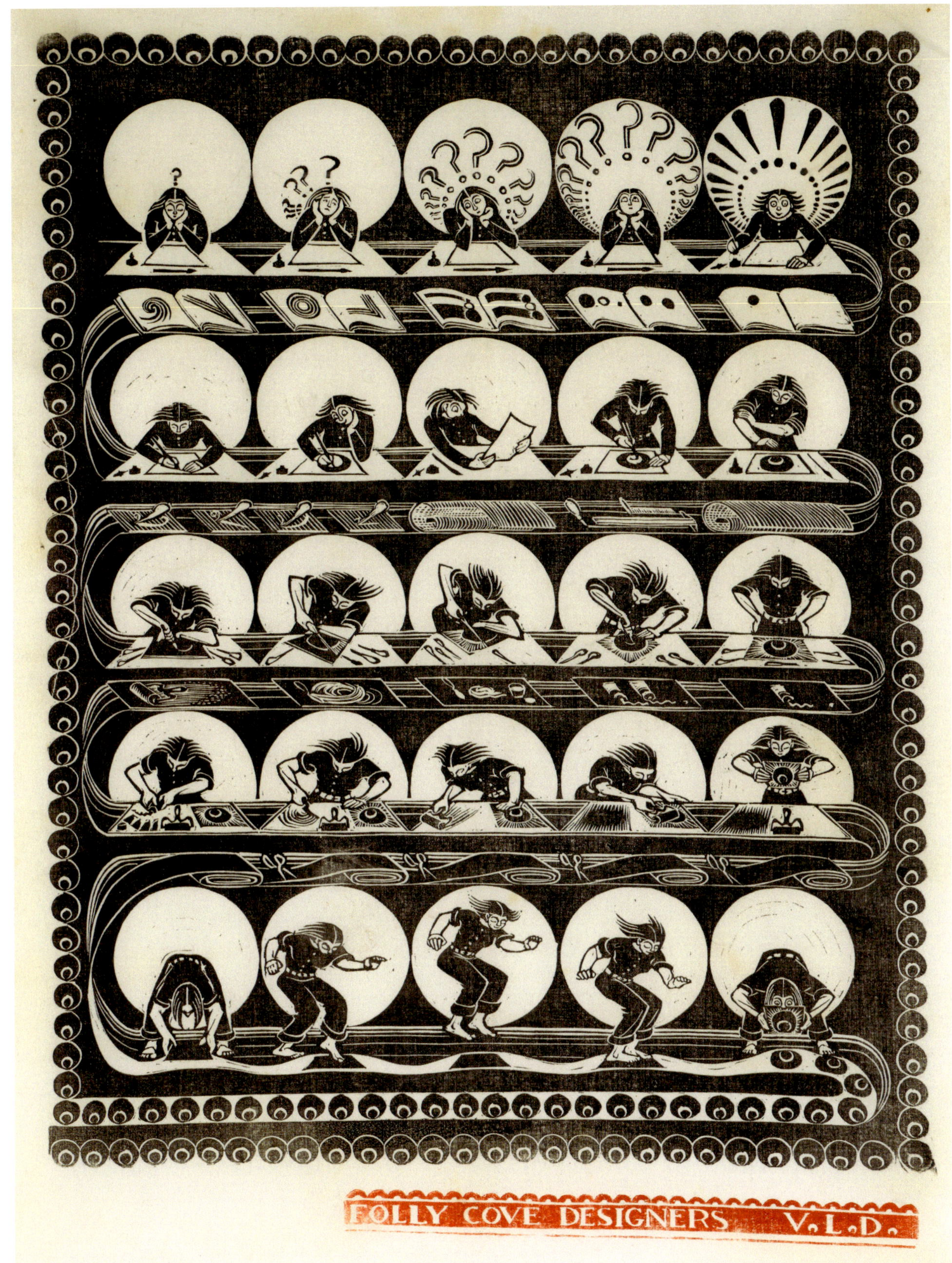
FOLLY COVE DESIGNERS V.L.D.

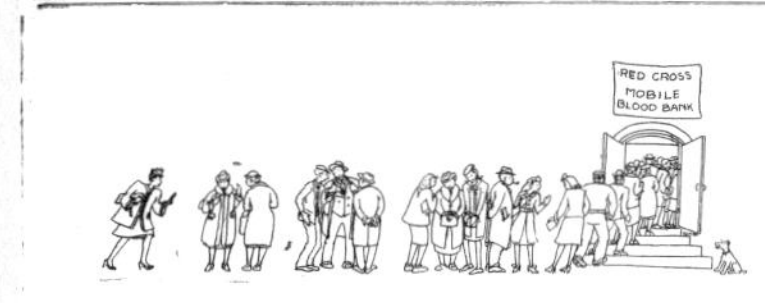

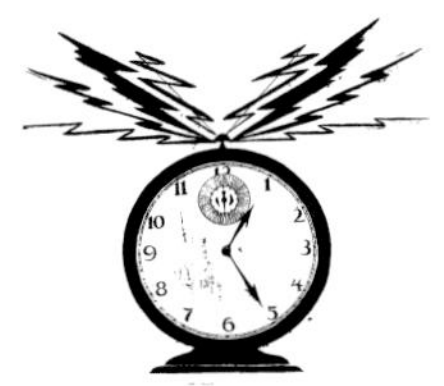

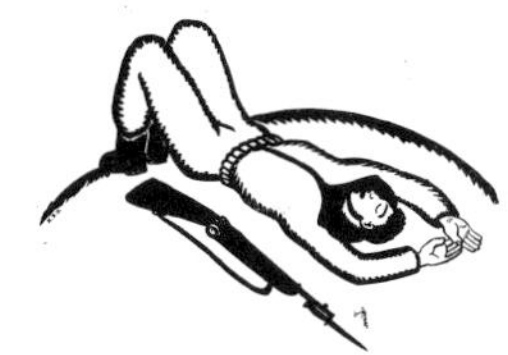

"Hurry Up! Sign Up! Our Wounded Cannot Wait!": World War II and the Folly Cove Designers

FIG. 13 (LEFT)
Virginia's illustration of a line for a blood bank is reminiscent of her beloved depictions of the townspeople of Popperville from *Mike Mulligan and His Steam Shovel* and Geoppolis from *Katy and the Big Snow*. January 5, 1944, *Gloucester Daily Times*.

FIG. 14 (MIDDLE)
Employing Virginia's design principles, Aino Clarke used lines to show the motion of a ringing alarm clock. January 14, 1944, *Gloucester Daily Times*.

FIG. 15 (RIGHT)
A wounded soldier reminds potential donors of what is at stake in this illustration by Hetty Beatty. Hetty seemed particularly devoted to veteran causes. In a 1945 *Magazine Digest* article it was mentioned that she taught whittling to wounded veterans. January 15, 1944, *Gloucester Daily Times*.

Even in their remote corner of Cape Ann, Folly Cove residents were growing victory gardens and dealing with ration books like the rest of the nation.[39]

Virginia's editor at Houghton Mifflin wrote in a 1943 article that while Virginia was writing *The Little House* (published in 1942), "As the work progressed, World War II also progressed and there was one moment when Jinnee began to have doubts about her work—stirrings of conscience over her war effort."[40] During the war, George Demetrios used his art skills to sculpt heads for MIT as models for universal heads to aid in the design of gas masks.[41] But the editor reassured Virginia of her book's value, adding, "I felt then, as I do now, that if *The Little House* does nothing more than reaffirm the realities, the peace and security of a little child's world, it is building for a future in which these realities may be unquestioned."[42]

So it is not surprising that when an opportunity arose to create artwork to promote a blood drive in January 1944 for the local chapter of the Red Cross, the group produced eight designs.[43] Three are featured here. *The Gloucester Daily Times* noted: "The full-page and half-page messages are unusually dynamic in their attention-getting qualities, as illustrated and laid out by members of the Folly Cove Designers..."[44] The ad designs and illustrations were created by Hetty Beatty, Aino Clarke, Virginia Lee Demetrios, and Louise Kenyon.

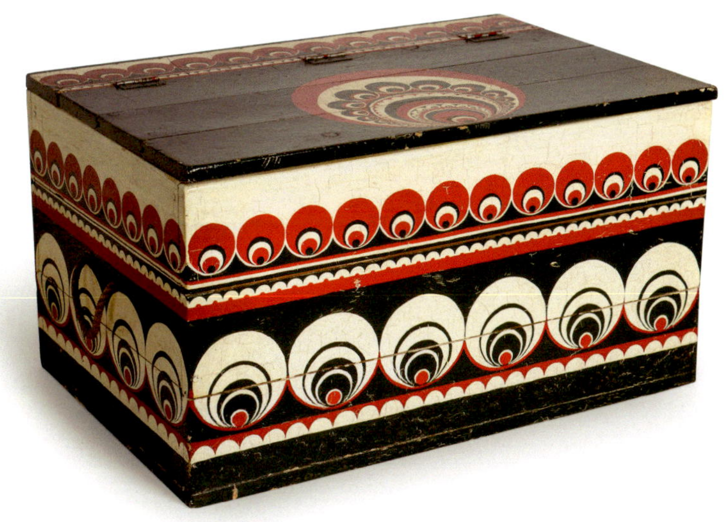

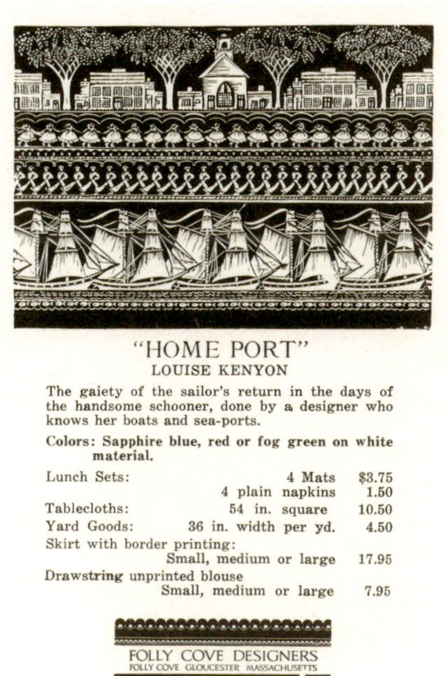

"HOME PORT"
LOUISE KENYON

The gaiety of the sailor's return in the days of the handsome schooner, done by a designer who knows her boats and sea-ports.

Colors: Sapphire blue, red or fog green on white material.

Lunch Sets:	4 Mats	$3.75
	4 plain napkins	1.50
Tablecloths:	54 in. square	10.50
Yard Goods:	36 in. width per yd.	4.50
Skirt with border printing:	Small, medium or large	17.95
Drawstring unprinted blouse	Small, medium or large	7.95

FOLLY COVE DESIGNERS
FOLLY COVE GLOUCESTER MASSACHUSETTS

FIG. 16 (LEFT)
The group initially considered applying their designs to other mediums. This circle design became part of the Folly Cove Designers' logo and was printed by the figure in *The Making of a Block Print*. This was likely painted by Virginia.

FIG. 17 (RIGHT)
Louise Kenyon created *Home Port*. These inserts served as the group's catalog and were included with an invitation to the annual opening at the barn. They listed items and colors the design was printed in, which were decided by the individual designer, but discussed with class members and the jury.

THE ANNUAL EXHIBITION

Every year, from the inception of the Folly Cove Designers, there was an annual exhibition of that year's designs. The first year, in 1940, Virginia's students exhibited their work at her home studio (as they did the next year's work) to an audience of 150 people. *The Gloucester Daily Times* gave the exhibition a glowing review.[45]

In 1942 the annual exhibition moved to Old 'Squam Mill in Annisquam and following that to the Home Industries shop in Rockport (owned by husband-and-wife Folly Cove Designers).[46] In 1948 the Demetrios family started renting the group their barn on Washington Street (Route 127), in the heart of Folly Cove; it eventually became the group's retail outlet.[47]

The annual exhibition openings grew in size, especially after the group established their own retail space in the Demetrioses' barn. The group began extending their exhibition season until it ran from March through early December.[48] Members took turns working at the barn, including holding printing demonstrations open to the public several days a week.[49] The local hotels advertised these demonstrations to their guests and in 1950 the group began to produce a catalog, consisting of a packet of inserts that featured an image of each of the season's designs with written descriptions.[50]

Each year a new design was selected for the cover of the exhibition invitation (or designed specifically for it) and mailed to the group's mailing list. "Opening day was always very joyous," reminisced one designer.[51] The exhibit openings were the social event of the season, not just for the designers, but for local residents, summer people, and loyal customers. "Everybody came—all the artists and the people from New York who spent the summer up there. They all came."[52]

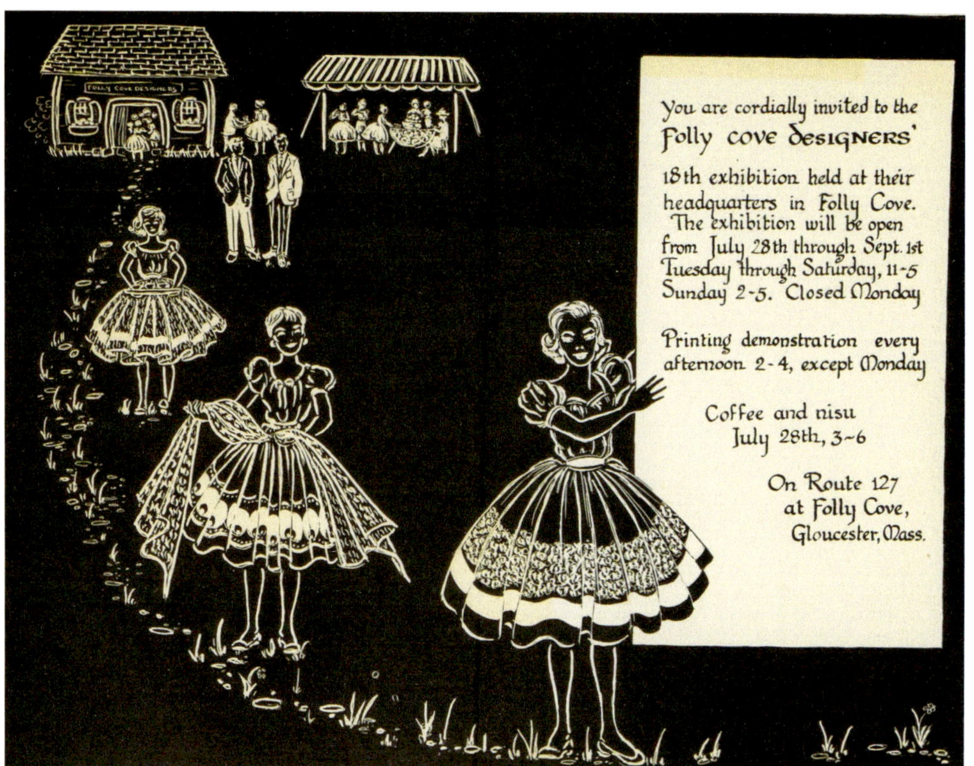

FIG. 18 (LEFT)
The eighteenth annual exhibition invitation, designed by Libby Holloran with lettering by Aino Clarke, focuses on the group's block-printed clothing since members were encouraged to make themselves an outfit for the opening out of their most recent design. Libby made beautiful opening exhibition outfits (see page 67).

FIG. 19 (BELOW)
The designers, likely in the 1950s, celebrating at the Demetrioses'. Aino sips a beer wearing *Musicale*. Peggy Norton is in the center wearing *Hearts and Flowers*. Dorothy Norton is in front of Aino, wearing *Ivy*. Lee Natti, standing beyond Peggy with a sweater, wearing *Underbrush* and facing Louise Kenyon.

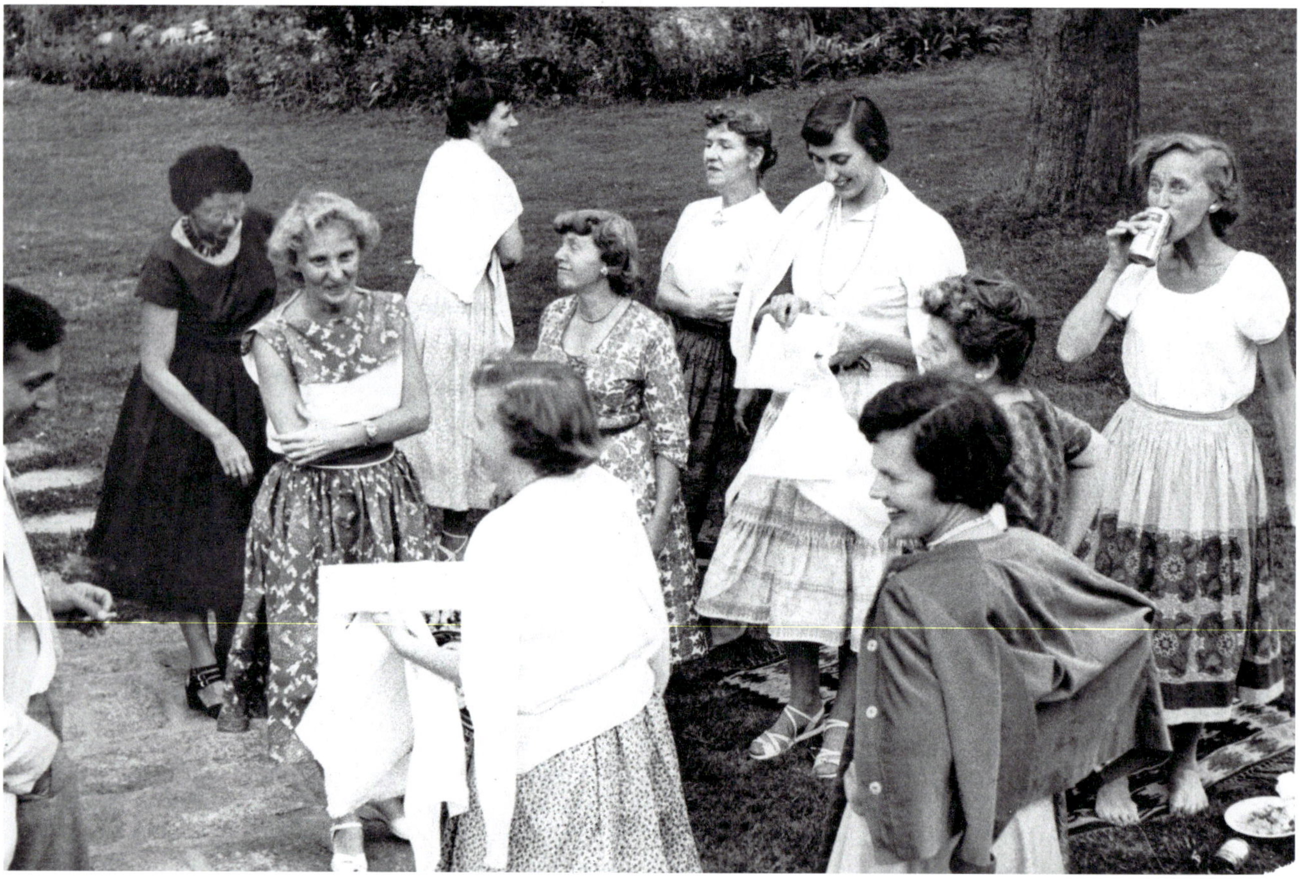

Following the opening, Virginia and George would host an after-party, which consisted of a lobster bake and dancing and was remembered fondly by the designers. "She had these great big polished granite tables outdoors—gorgeous. And salad bowls like this [gesturing for huge] and lobster...it was a nice, friendly, friendly gathering."[53] Others recalled the dancing. "There'd be dancing—Greek dances—[we'd] drink beer, and everybody had a wonderful time..."[54]

During this party, new designers were awarded their "diplomas."[55] Once a student member had graduated and became an official designer, the other designers would often give the graduate one of their own designs to celebrate the accomplishment.[56] This process of exhibiting and graduating was meaningful to members. For most of the Folly Cove Designers, seeing their year's work exhibited served as a major incentive to continue producing new designs throughout the year. One designer explained, "You looked at it [the exhibit] with...breathlessness, thinking of the total hours that each designer had put into it—on the creation of their idea and then the printing of it, cutting the block and all—it just totaled up to an aggregate beyond what anyone could imagine."[57]

For one member, the opening day of the exhibition was especially meaningful to her as a recent immigrant. "The feeling of actually belonging, really belonging to a significant group of people in this country—because everything seemed incredibly alien for so long. It seemed as though everything was just perfect that day..."[58]

THE FOLLY COVE SOCIAL SCENE

Virginia and George Demetrios were renowned for entertaining. Community members shared fond memories of Virginia, Aino Clarke, and Eino Natti playing their recorders on Saturday nights during the winter (or Aino might play her violin or the harpsichord) while George and his friends played poker in the kitchen. The Demetrioses' sons and many neighbors reminisced years later about the Finnish hops, square dances, and polkas their parents hosted in the barn.[59]

George loved to entertain and tell stories. He also enjoyed a lively debate and discussing art and is said to have had a wonderful singing voice.[60] Lee Natti remembers that people would sing songs in different languages at the parties. "It was such an eye opener to me because it was totally different."[61] Both Lee Steele and Lee Natti remarked on how amazing it was that these events included multiple generations.[62]

Over the years, the members' entertainments became the subjects of designs. Aino Clarke's *Fiddle Dee Dee* (see page 104) design depicts the violin sessions and dances held in the Demetrioses' barn. Virginia had three designs that featured dancing, an early one entitled *Finnish Dancers,* as well as *Grand Right and Left* (see page 113) and *Finnish Hop* (see page 32), in which she depicted fellow designers Robert and Lee Natti and other neighborhood couples, several of whom had met through George and Virginia.

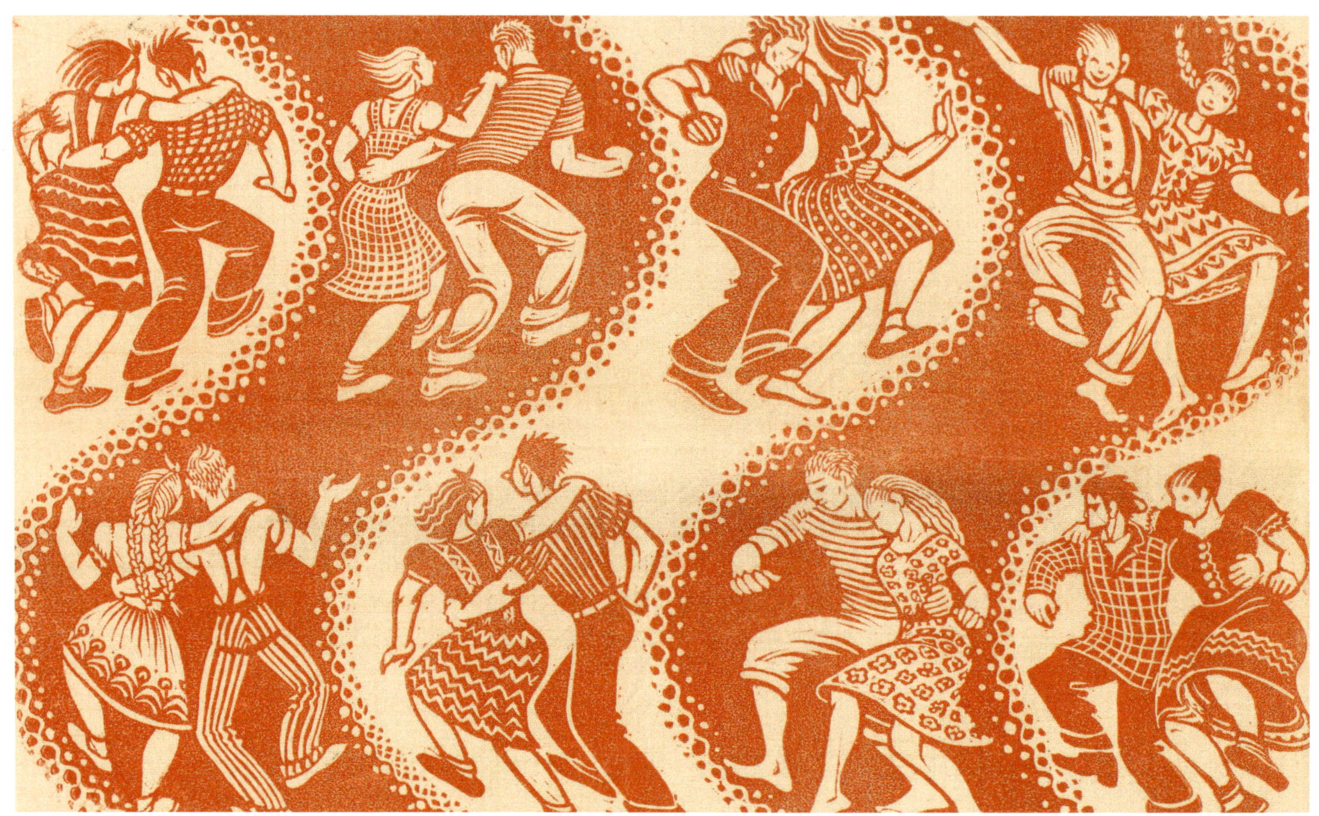

FIG. 20
Lee Natti's pigtails swing in the breeze in the top right as the dancers (many Folly Cove Designers) move throughout this design. Virginia's early training as a newspaper illustrator of dance and theater subjects is evident in the way she was able to capture movement. (Ink on fabric.)

The Demetrios family hosted barbecues for art students, other area artists, Folly Cove Designers, and neighbors on their beautifully landscaped property in the summer. Irja Jacobson remembers learning the art of seating arrangement from Virginia when she worked for the family, to never seat husbands and wives next to or across from one another. She recalled that everyone would sit "for hours with good wine and good conversation."[63] There were also Sunday afternoon walks and softball games that the painter Leon Kroll would umpire.[64]

BLOCKS AND BEES

Folly Cove was a cooperative community. The Demetrioses' younger son, Mike, remembered building bees to clear land for neighbors' homes. The "able-bodied" men would gather for a day to do the work, he said, adding that his father would oversee the work crew, "of course."[65] He went on to explain, "If you had to hire people to do it—would probably take a couple of weeks and be extremely costly, so they have everybody helping everybody else out."[66] Mike's brother, Aris, remembers there being between seventy and eighty people at these bees.[67]

Mike, Aris, and their dad were all working at one of these bees in 1948, shingling their cousin Costa Maletskos's house, when they got word that their own house was on fire.[68] Aris remembers neighbors jumping in to help remove items from the house.[69] This philosophy of helping neighbors was ingrained in the Demetrios boys. Mike, in particular, recalls that he once got in trouble for taking payment from Leon Kroll for mowing his lawn all summer. When George found out, he made Mike return the money.[70]

Given the tales of high-spirited dancing, barbecues, afternoon swims, nature walks, and cooperative projects, it is hard not to view Folly Cove as an idyllic community. Aris acknowledged that many people moved there due to the sheer "magnetism of [my] parents" and added, "I mean it really was a marvelous kind of social agenda that went with it."[71] Designer and neighbor Lee Steele described Virginia and George as deliberately, but not consciously, creating an intellectually stimulating community in which to raise their boys. She called their home "a social center for the area."[72] But she felt strongly that the members of the Folly Cove Designers and the people who were allowed into George and Virginia's inner circle were definitely chosen.[73]

Aris Demetrios described the Folly Cove Designers as having their own belief system, and he noted the fact that they "created their own culture."[74] Lee Steele agreed, explaining that the community was "a thing unto ourselves."[75] This community brought together a mix of diverse people and transcended class in many ways. Lee felt that, in terms of class, it was a "non-class class."[76] People took pride in "not recognizing class."[77] As designers, they were equals. To be a member of the Folly Cove Designers, you just had to be willing to do the work and create "good design."[78] It was a democratic approach to art anchored in a belief that anyone could be taught.

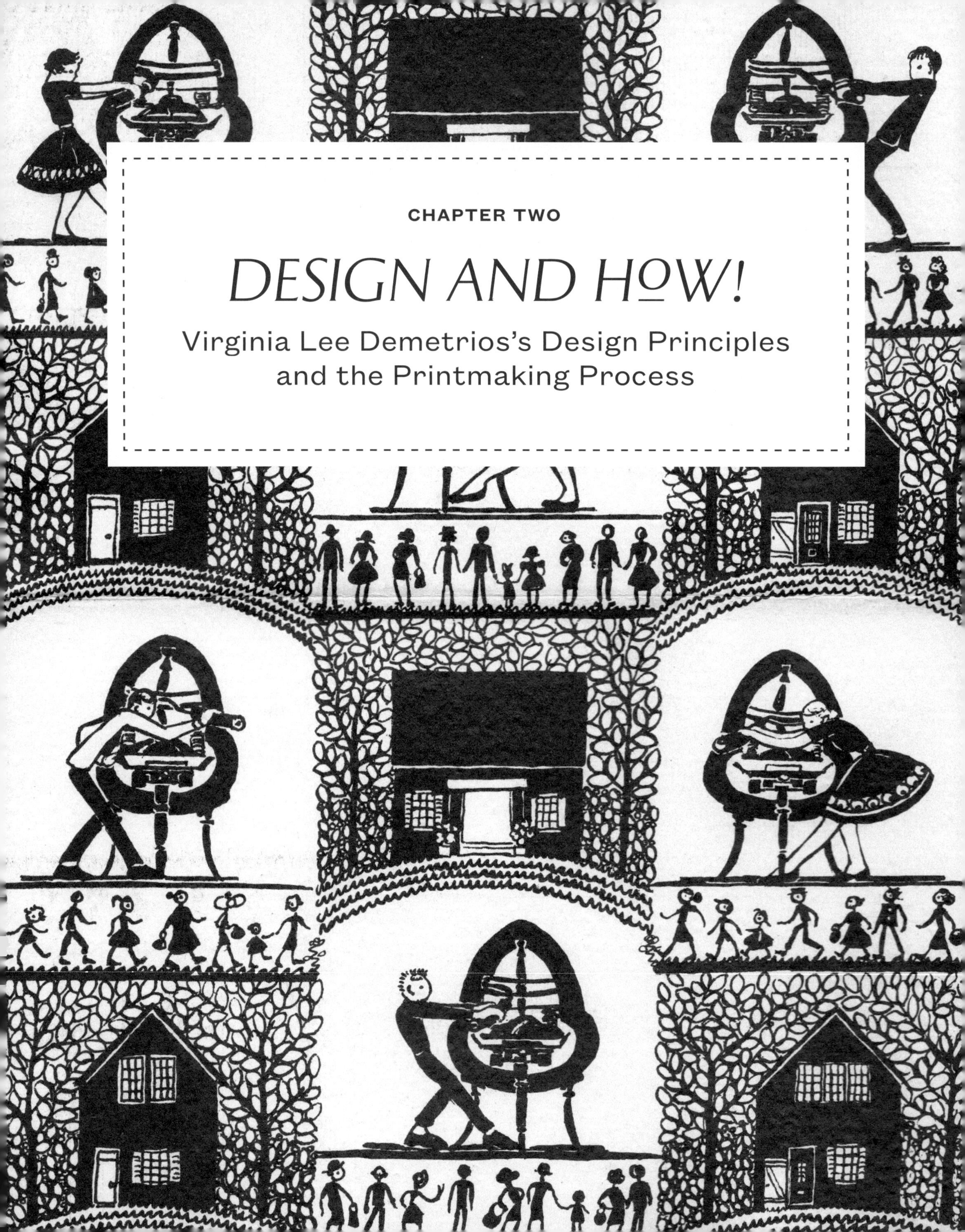

CHAPTER TWO

DESIGN AND HOW!

Virginia Lee Demetrios's Design Principles and the Printmaking Process

The work of the Folly Cove Designers is proof of Virginia Lee Demetrios's successful teaching methodology and ability to turn even artistic novices into competent printmakers. Peggy Norton studied art with many teachers over the years but recalled, "I learned much more from her than I did from any other design teacher I ever met."[1]

Virginia's method of teaching informed the structure and content of the design lessons and she intended to publish the material in a manuscript titled *Design and How!* Virginia worked on it over the span of nearly twenty-five years but it was never completed, despite the prodding of her editors at Houghton Mifflin.

In the unfinished manuscript Virginia described her process:

> Many have asked me how I go about writing a book and where I find the material...Writing is very difficult for me and only a necessary evil... I draw my books first...telling the story...without putting down words... and anything I can put in a picture and take out of the text I do. After all I only do picture books...[2]

The design course was demanding and included extensive homework assignments, about which Virginia's students lovingly complained.[3] Aino Clarke recalled joking with Virginia that the best place to teach the course would be in jail since students would have the time necessary to complete the homework.[4] But there was an appreciation of the process. Peggy Norton said of it, "There is something about working within a rather strict discipline—you have to make it conform to the problem you are trying to solve."[5] Students were expected to start work on the assignments in class and complete them at home. Looking at the work of designers who kept their homework, it is interesting to see the evolution of their designs.

This chapter highlights the main tenets of Virginia's design theories supplemented with examples of her lessons excerpted from the numerous drafts of *Design and How!*, as well as homework assignments from members of the Folly Cove Designers. Her illustrations and sketches have been included so that readers may visualize how *Design and How!* might have appeared in published form.

VIRGINIA LEE DEMETRIOS'S DESIGN BACKGROUND

In drafts of the dedication page for *Design and How!*, Virginia identified printmaker Robert Hestwood as her "first teacher in design," studying with him in California when she was a teenager.[6] She attended the California School of Fine Arts (now the San Francisco Art Institute), where she was enrolled for at least one year and took several painting courses as well as a class in costume design and one in commercial art.[7] Robert appears to be the only printmaker with whom she studied.

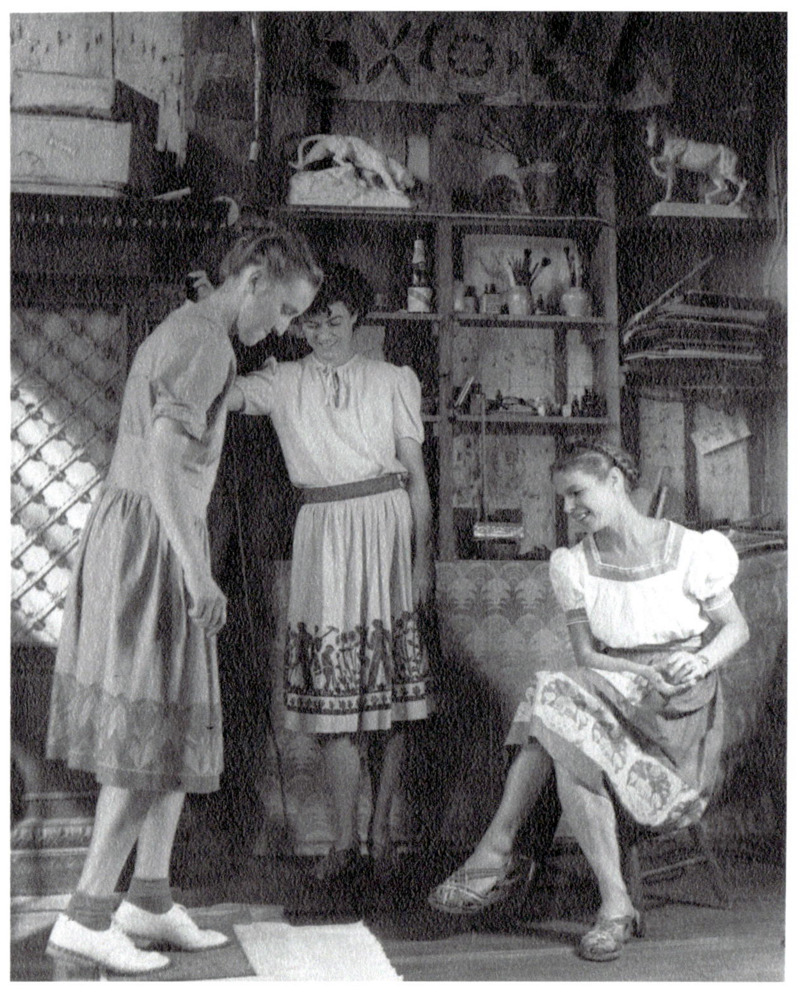

FIG. 21 (LEFT)
From left to right, Aino Clarke, Hetty Beatty, and Virginia Lee Demetrios. Virginia, wearing a skirt in her *Little House* design, watches as Aino (wearing a dress with her *Geometric I* design) jumps on a block. Hetty (in the middle) wears a skirt with her *Victory Garden* design.

FIG. 22 (BOTTOM LEFT)
A draft of Eino Natti's *Violets* with a completely different arrangement than the final design. This draft included a circular design and two horizontal border patterns. (Ink on paper.)

FIG. 23 (BOTTOM RIGHT)
Eino Natti's final *Violets*, which became an example of an allover pattern in a square format. This print on paper was signed by the artist and notarized as a kind of self-copyrighting (although not legally binding). (Ink on paper.)

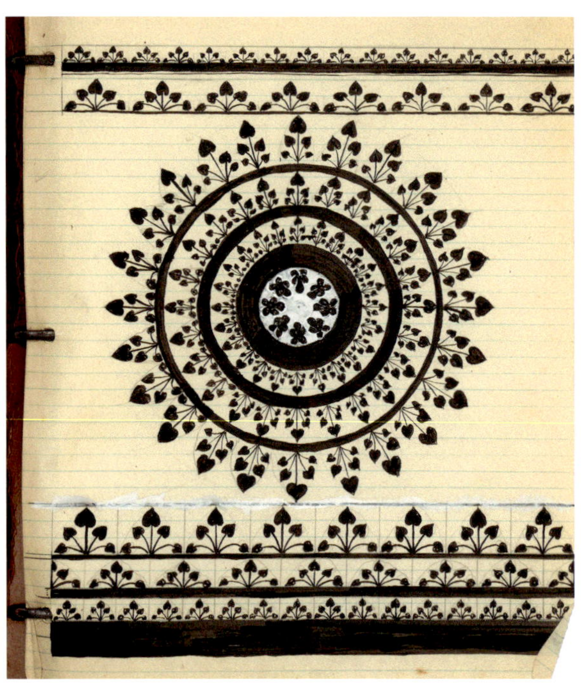

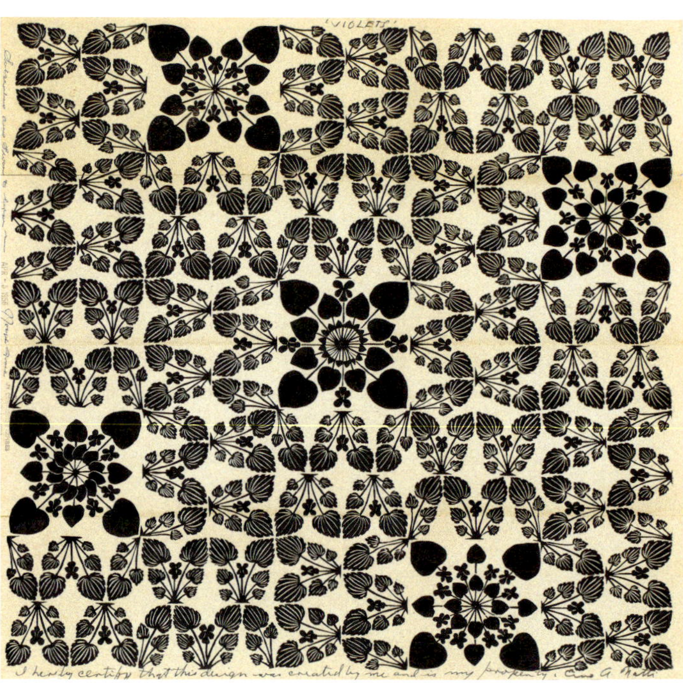

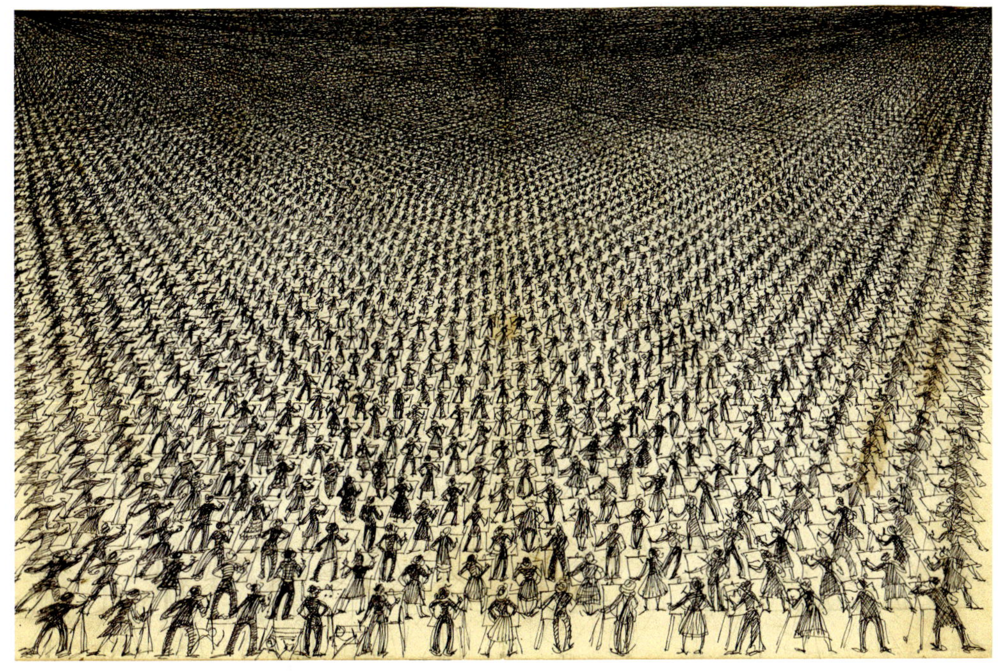

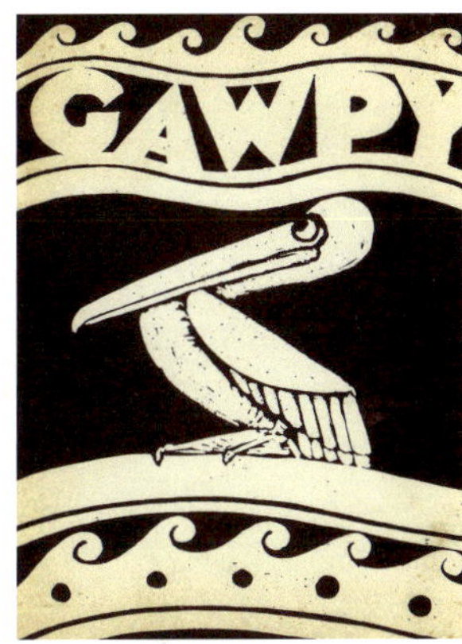

FIG. 24 (LEFT)
Virginia's detailed sketches of men and women at easels were the endpapers for one of her mock-ups for *Design and How!* (Ink on paper.)

FIG. 25 (RIGHT)
The wave pattern of Robert Hestwood's *Gawpy* cover became a signature motif for Virginia and the Folly Cove Designers.

Years after the group disbanded, Folly Cove designer Mary Maletskos recalled having been gifted a book that Virginia had given to a fellow designer, *A Method for Creative Design*, by Mexican artist Adolpho Best-Maugard. Maletskos noted the similarities between some of the book's teachings (particularly the border patterns) and Virginia's methods and wondered if the book had been used in Virginia's own education with Robert.[8] Robert did spend time in Mexico City prior to 1926, the year that the book was published, so it is possible he met Best-Maugard while there and was influenced by his teaching methodology.[9] In an interview, Robert described his own teaching style as less structured and more focused around students figuring things out on their own and using design to express themselves. Like Virginia, he encouraged students to look to natural forms for inspiration.[10] Aino Clarke recalled that Robert's teachings on the importance of the contrast between dark and light (negative and positive space) in design, which Virginia also stressed, were inspired by Mexican pottery.[11]

Virginia also studied with her husband, George Demetrios, and continued to do so throughout her career. Lee Natti recalled that "Jinnee studied with George whenever she could."[12] Virginia's work at the newspaper had already instilled in her the practice of capturing the essentials and big movements first, then going back and adding detail, which was what George taught his students.[13] She encouraged her students to study with him as well. Many students did, as drawing was the foundation for successful designs.[14]

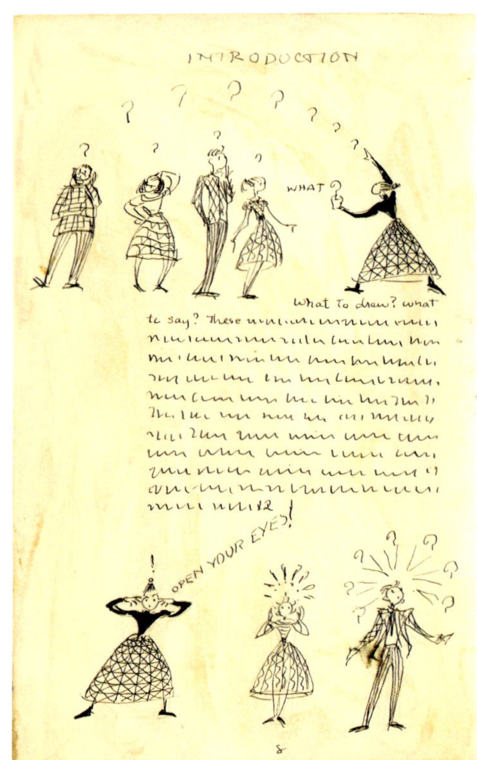

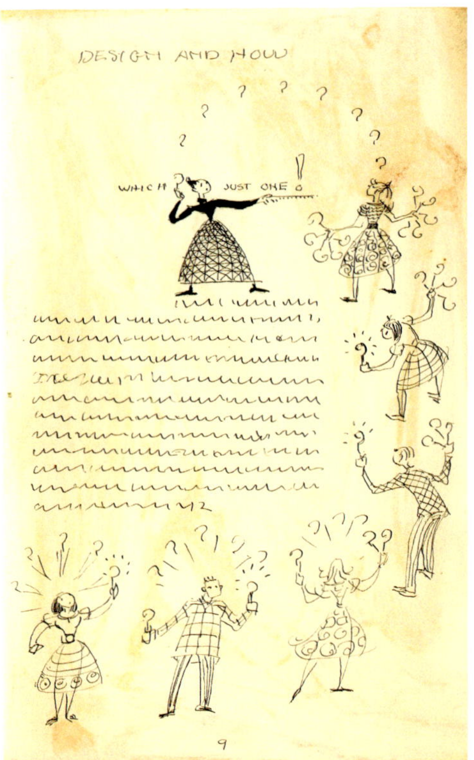

FIG. 26
An illustration from a draft of the introduction of *Design and How!* The teacher stresses "Just one!" to her students as they search for a subject. In the other corner, she shouts, "Open your eyes!," encouraging her students to take inspiration from the world around them. (Ink on paper.)

OPPOSITE (CLOCKWISE FROM TOP LEFT)

FIG. 27
A page from Peggy Norton's homework for *Apple Pie*, c. 1951, where she sketched apples from different angles, with stems and without, sliced and whole. (Ink on paper.)

FIG. 28
Peggy put her apple homework to good use, also creating *Apple Pie (small)*, which would have been used to print items like cocktail napkins. Here the three-leaf pattern that was in the inner circle of *Apple Pie* serves as the outer border. (Ink on fabric.)

FIG. 29
Peggy Norton's homework culminated in *Apple Pie*, showing apples in various stages from growing on trees to being baked in pies. There is a rolling pin border. (Ink on fabric.)

VIRGINIA'S TEACHING METHODOLOGY

In drafts of *Design and How!* Virginia dedicated the book to "Aino Y. Clarke my first student in design," who, beginning in 1941, would often teach Virginia's design course over the winter.[15] Virginia also dedicated *Design and How!* to the Folly Cove Designers, "without whom I never could have done this book."[16] The designers jokingly referred to themselves as her "guinea pigs" and Demetrios called them so in drafts of the book.[17]

Drafts of homework exercises, the poster boards from which the course was taught, and Virginia's unpublished manuscript provide insight into her teaching methods. The subject chosen was extremely important. "It must be taken or drawn (literally) from life. You will be allowed only *one* for the whole course...so choose something you like and which is available for study."[18] "By the time you have completed this course you will be able to draw that subject of yours with ease and skill...frontwards and backwards... right side up and up side [*sic*] down."[19]

Since designers were expected to produce one new design per year, they would often work on a subject as part of the homework and turn it into a design. Dorothy Norton's homework binder included exercises with ducks, which yielded her design *Ducks* (see page 157). For Eino Natti, it was roosters, leading to *Cockerels* and his many rooster-inspired designs. Occasionally the subject of homework assignments would be abandoned, as in the case of a fish design by Lee Natti (see page 150).[20]

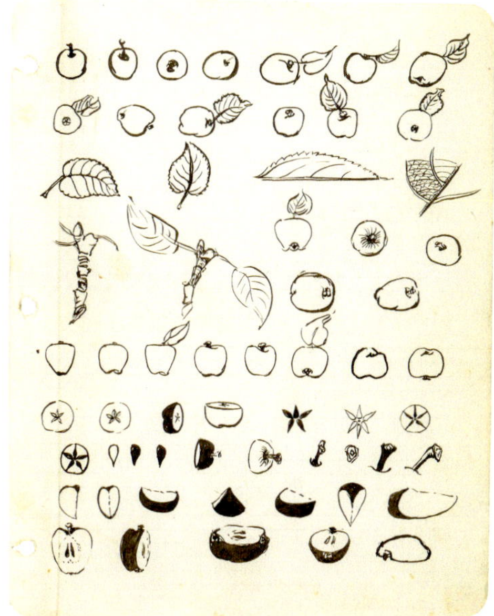

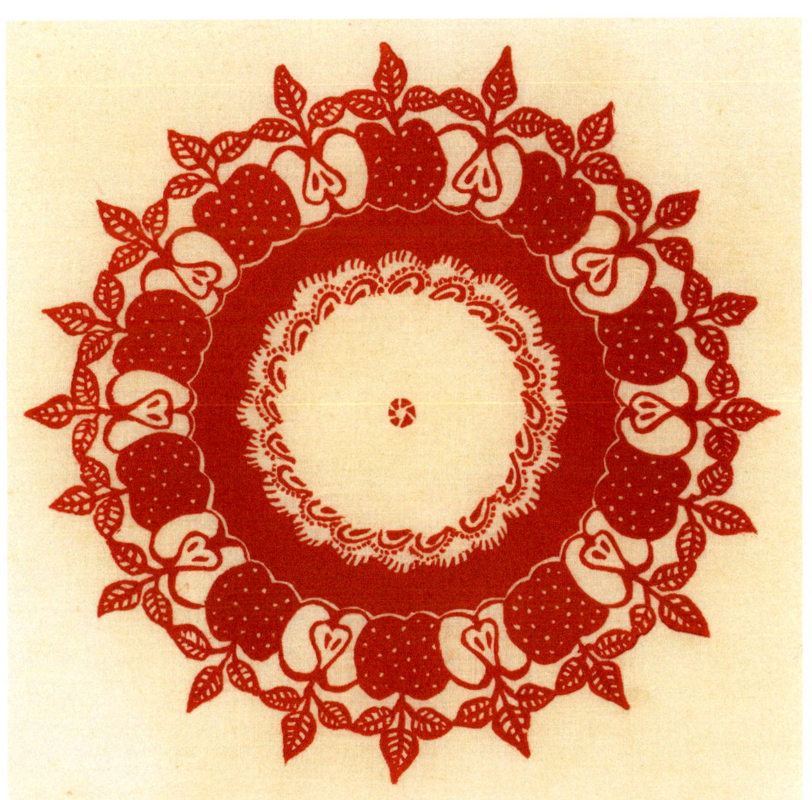

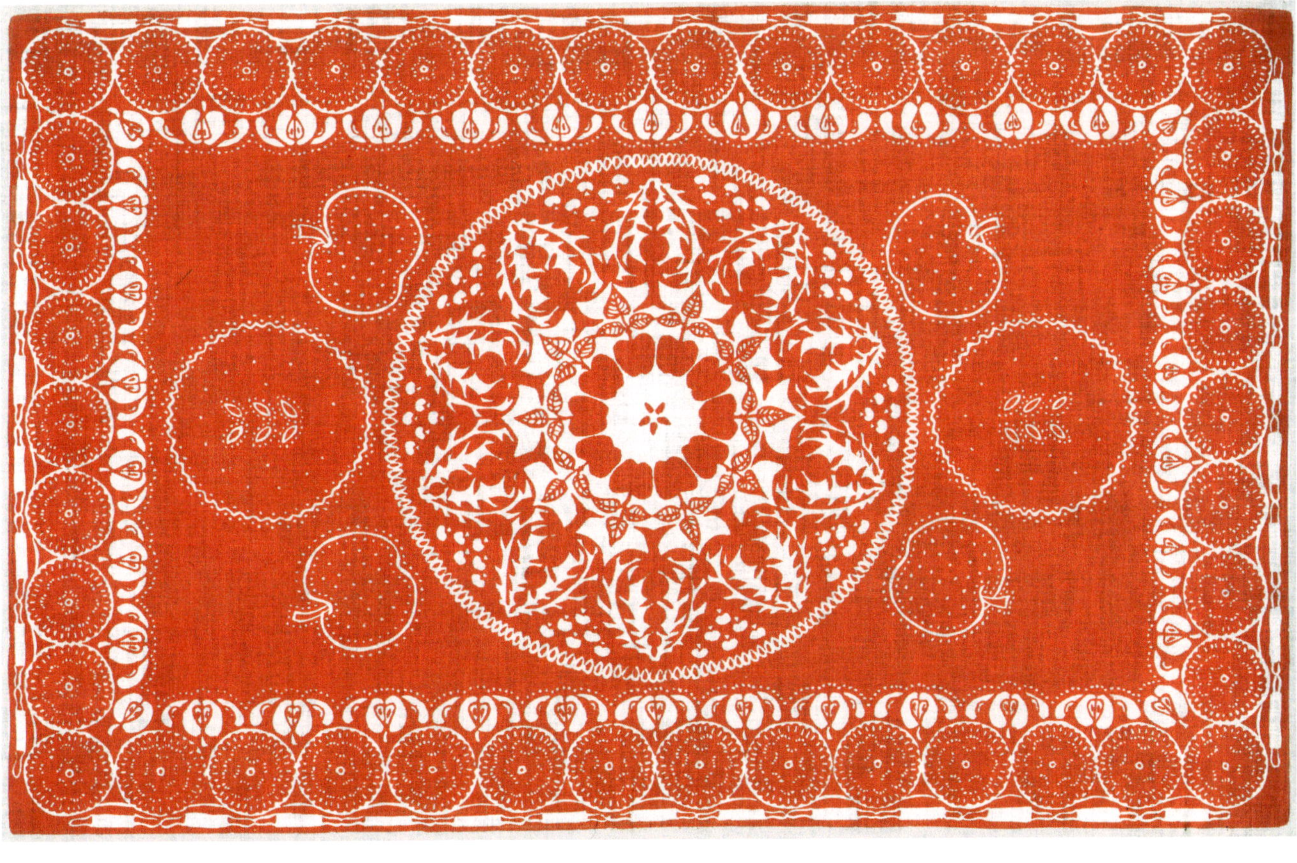

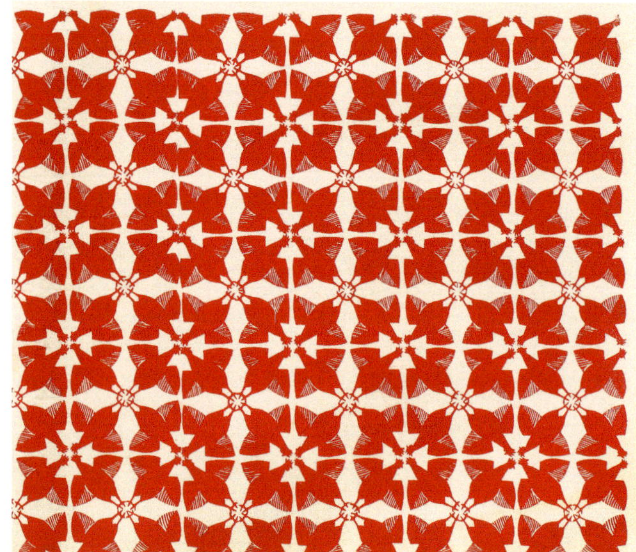

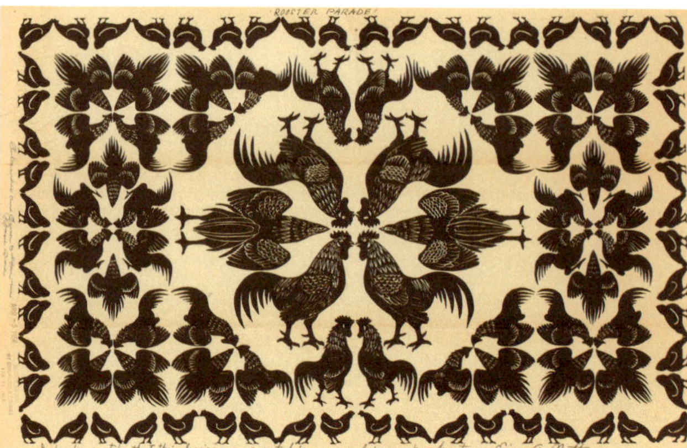

Since Virginia encouraged her students to draw from life—at least initially—rather than to rely on photographs, it led to some interesting stories about designers struggling to get animals to hold poses. Aino Clarke supposedly admitted that this caused her to have difficulty drawing roosters, while Peggy Norton described feeding a mouse sunflower seeds so that she could observe it for *Cranberry Bog*.[21] In her own work, the subject was so vital to the design that Virginia "examined it and she drew it, she drew, she drew it again until it was hers."[22] The designers followed suit. In Peggy Norton's design of an apple, she prepared by drawing an apple "in every possible way," adding that if Virginia had been doing it you would have known what variety of apple it was.[23] This pattern of extensive study often led students to produce multiple designs on a subject.

Virginia was not concerned when students chose the same subject, as she knew they would each have their own original approach. Dorothy Norton explained, "that's the beauty of designing. There can't be too much competition because no two people see any one thing with the same perspective. My idea of an onion [referring to her design *Onions* (see page 67)] isn't yours..."[24] Although Eino Natti returned to the subject many times, several designers chose roosters or chickens as their subject matter as well.

As students developed their designs, Virginia instructed, "Your subject becomes easier to draw and you will be forced to simplify it because of the many times you repeat it."[25] She did this herself in her two *Fish Story* designs.[26] She produced pages and pages of sketches that included complex backgrounds of aquatic life and rounded fish. In the end, she released two versions, *Fish Story* and what the author refers to as *Fish Story II*, a design which until now has been "lost" to the public and not recognized as part of her oeuvre.[27] In both she reduced the schools of fish to simple geometric forms, perhaps inspired by the pattern of fish scales. She eliminated the backgrounds, following her own rule of making sure that "everything in your design must contribute" to the design.[28]

FIG. 30 (LEFT)
Aino Clarke's *Little Roosters* was a smaller-scale version of her early design *Big Roosters*. The feet of the birds connect to make a pattern in the surrounding negative space and their outspread wings create another pattern. (Ink on fabric.)

FIG. 31 (RIGHT)
Eino Natti's *Rooster Parade* is similar to Aino's design in the formation of roosters meeting at their heads. But Eino's design is realistic and depicts roosters from different perspectives. This is another print on paper, signed by the artist and notarized as a type of self-copyrighting. (Ink on paper.)

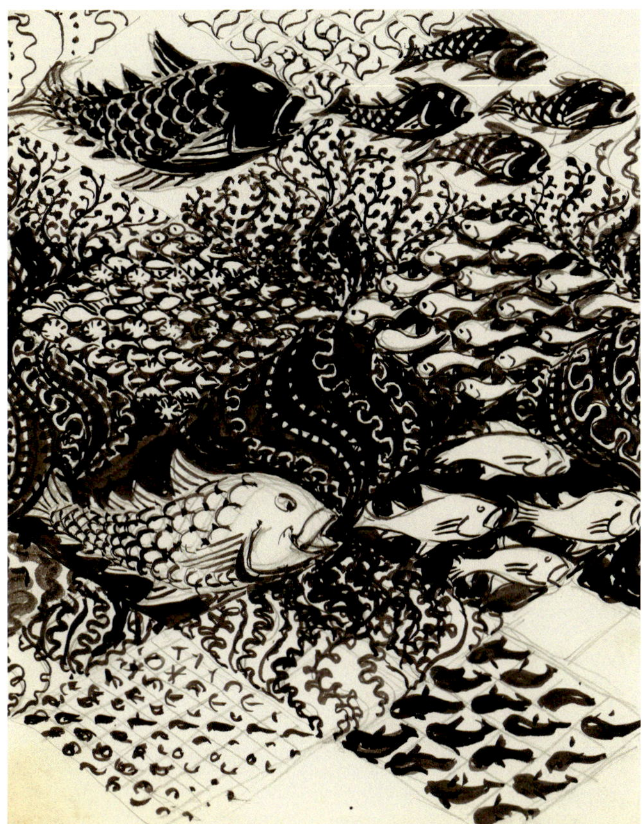

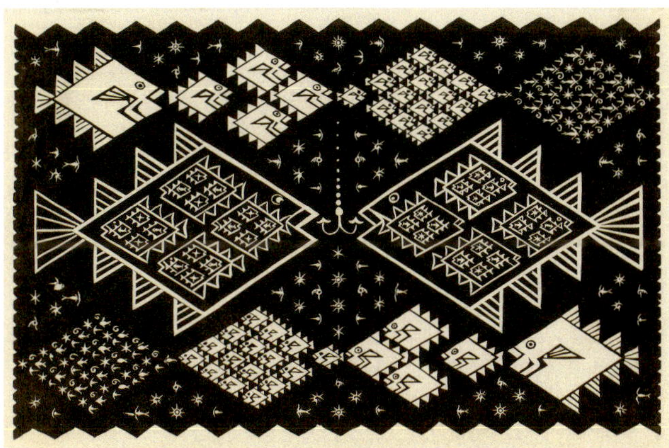

FIG. 32 (TOP LEFT)
Virginia's fish were initially rounded and the background a complex pattern of seaweed. This sketch also shows how she began to triangulate the design. (Ink on paper.)

FIG. 33 (TOP RIGHT)
Virginia's final version of *Fish Story* is a Pac-Man–esque, bold, simplified, triangulated design of larger fish swimming after smaller fish and the smallest fish swimming after plankton. (Ink on fabric.)

FIG. 34 (BOTTOM RIGHT)
This version of *Fish Story* is a "lost" design. A 1957 newspaper article referenced this design as depicting "schools of fish in a diagonal style." The plankton background can be seen in some panels of the skirt, but not in others. (Ink on fabric.)

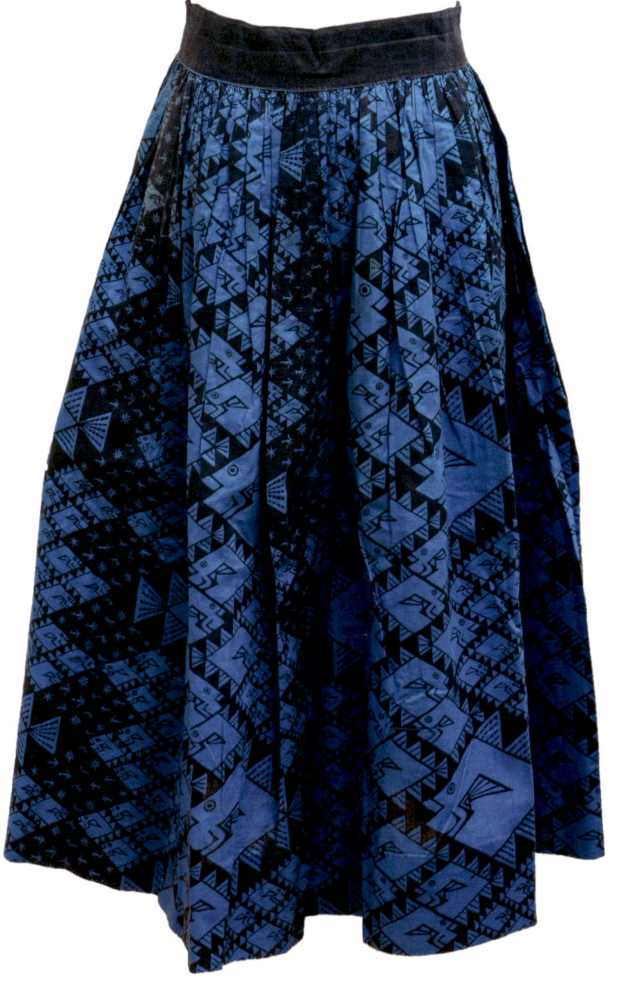

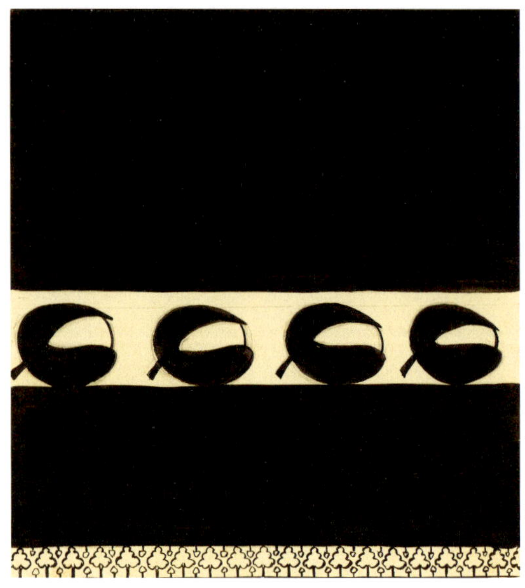

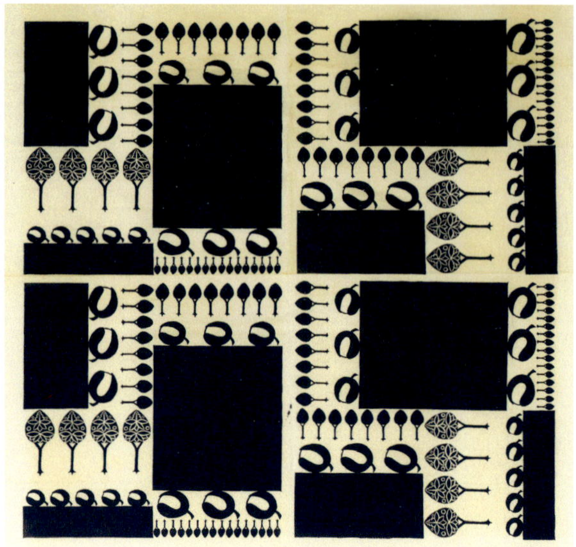

FIG. 35 (LEFT)
An early draft of Elizabeth Iarrobino's *Horse Chestnut* features three motifs: horse chestnuts, trees, and rectangles. Each motif was one size. The nut was shown at different stages of ripening. The intended orientation of this draft is unknown. (Ink on paper.)

FIG. 36 (RIGHT)
A second draft of Elizabeth's *Horse Chestnut* featured more horse chestnuts and trees in multiple sizes. The final printed version (seen here) is similar, but is printed four times in two different directions to make a grid and features more horse chestnuts and two tree styles. (Ink on fabric.)

Size was a central part of Virginia's lessons. She believed that "Equals are static...they do not move..." but that "Unequals give movement...They are more interesting."[29] She was able to capture movement in *Fish Story* by representing her subject in multiple sizes. The design visually tells the story of plankton being eaten by a school of fish, then those fish being eaten by progressively larger fish until the largest fish are caught by hooks—to be eaten by humans. *Fish Story II* "shows schools of fish" but there is less negative space in portions of this composition; the arrangement is different and the largest fish are not caught by hooks, so it has less of a narrative quality.[30]

Elizabeth Iarrobino experimented with size as well in her design *Horse Chestnut*. Virginia's goal was to teach students to train their eyes to be able to judge size, scale, and proportion, without the need of a ruler. To this end, she frequently required students to draw their subjects in various sizes. The varied sizes in the final version of Elizabeth's design made it more visually "interesting," as Virginia would say.[31]

Another focus of Virginia's lessons was the use of tone (white to black and all of the gradations of gray tones in between). She felt that working in black and white (as engravers do) would act as a "springboard for your imagination."[32] She wanted students to focus on the white in the pattern as much as the black (the negative space was as important as the positive space). She encouraged students to complete the homework assignments in black ink, applying it with a brush to white paper.[33] Some designers used scratchboard or made scratchboard using ink on board as a way to work out the darks and lights of their designs before carving.

Each lesson (and chapter in her unpublished design manuscript) was devoted to a different topic, such as "the horizontal" or "the vertical."[34] The lessons built upon one another and culminated in arranging designs in a pattern based on the arrangement of subjects in varying orientations. Some drafts of her book refer to triangles, squares, and other formations,

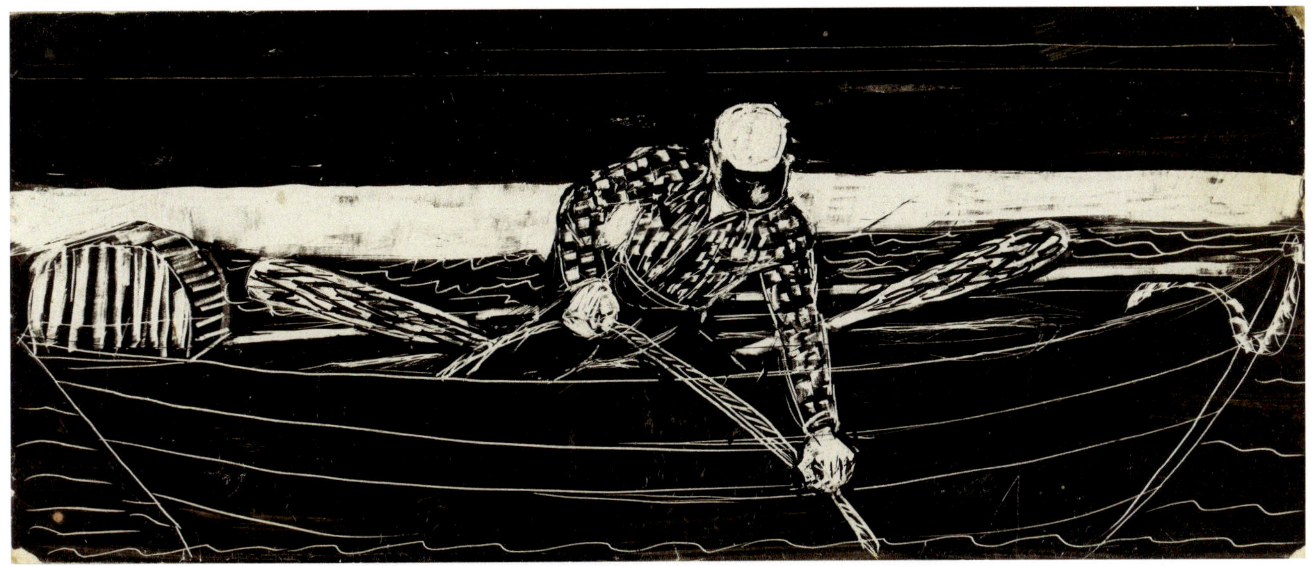

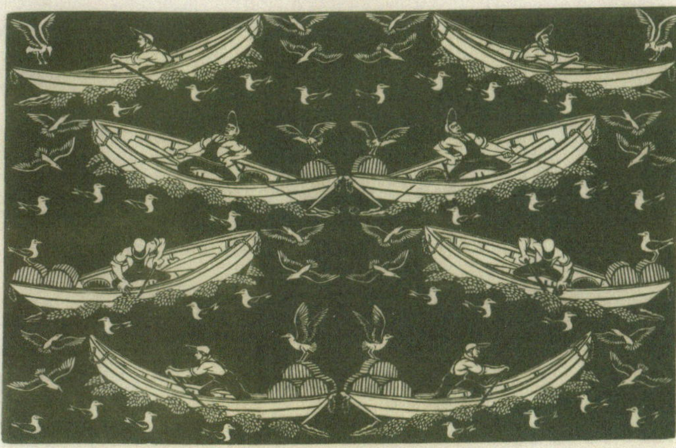

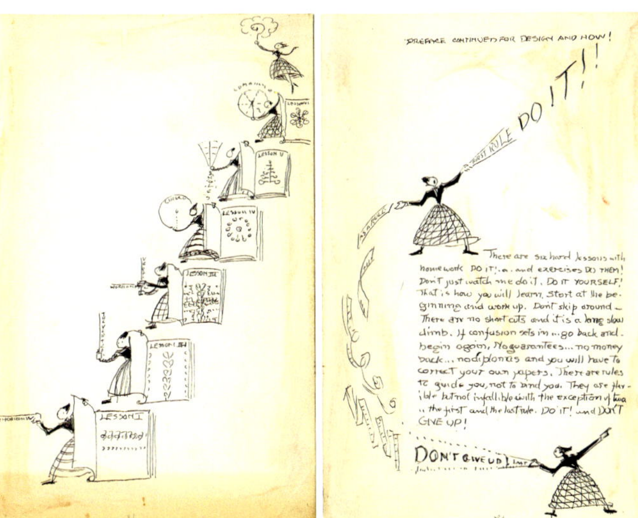

FIG. 37 (TOP)
Eino Natti used scratchboard before carving his *Yo Heave Ho* design. It appears that he initially considered a different shirt for the lobsterman.

FIG. 38 (MIDDLE)
Eino's final *Yo Heave Ho* design highlights the use of symmetry. (Ink on fabric.)

FIG. 39 (BOTTOM)
This version of Virginia's *Design and How!* table of contents contained chapters on horizontal, vertical, vertical and horizontal, circle, angles, and possibly "compass" (radial symmetry). She used the mantras "Do it!" and "Don't give up!," which she lived by, working on *Design and How!* for decades. (Ink on paper.)

FIG. 40 (LEFT)
Peggy Norton shows the use of tones in this homework for her *Story and a Half* design, which was based on her seventeenth-century house. (Ink on paper.)

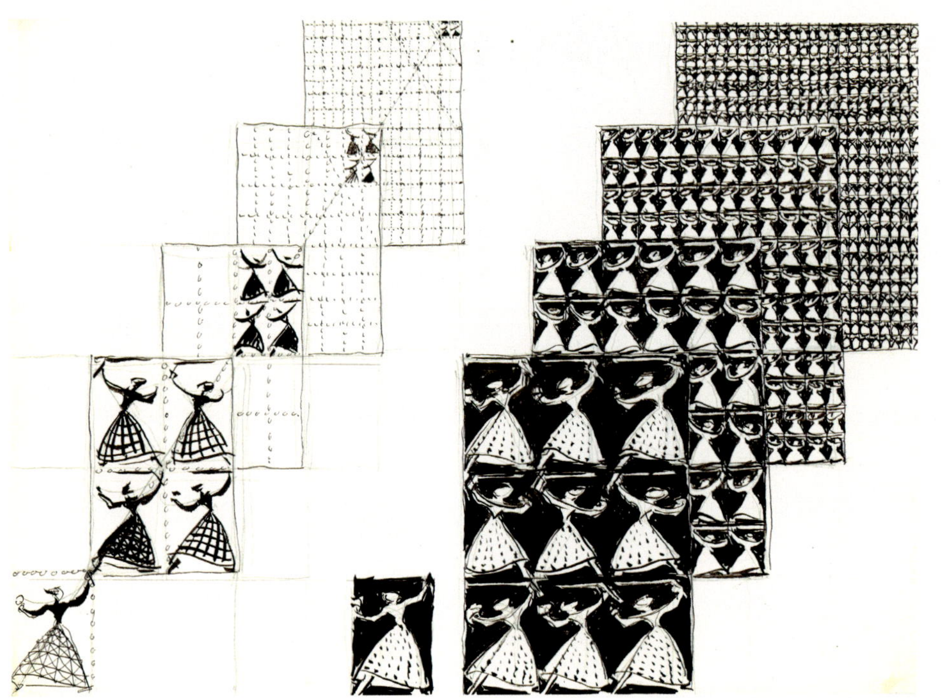

FIG. 41 (LEFT)
This manuscript example shows the horizontal arrangement of Virginia's subject (the woman motif). Since each lesson was multifaceted it exemplifies sizing, arrangements, and positive and negative space. (Ink on paper.)

FIG. 42 (BOTTOM LEFT)
This is an example of an angle and progression in Peggy Norton's homework for her *Story and a Half* design. (Ink on paper.)

FIG. 43 (BOTTOM RIGHT)
Virginia described this design as an all-over pattern. The subject seems to be the woman motif from her manuscript. It employs right angles and borders. The reverse of black and white is shown in this proof print. (Ink on paper.)

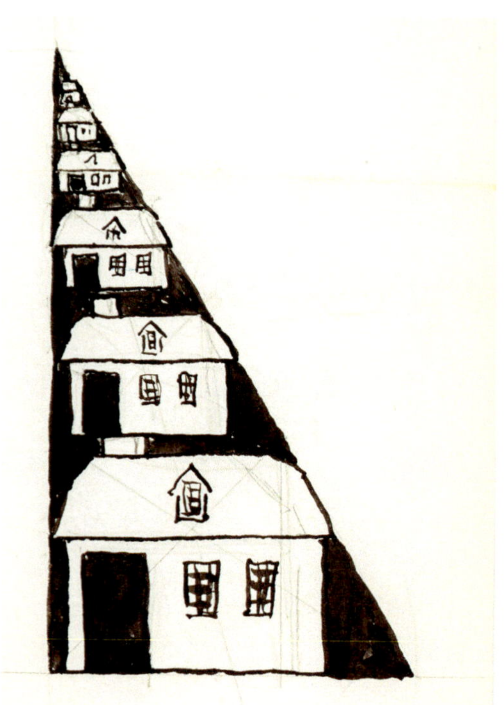

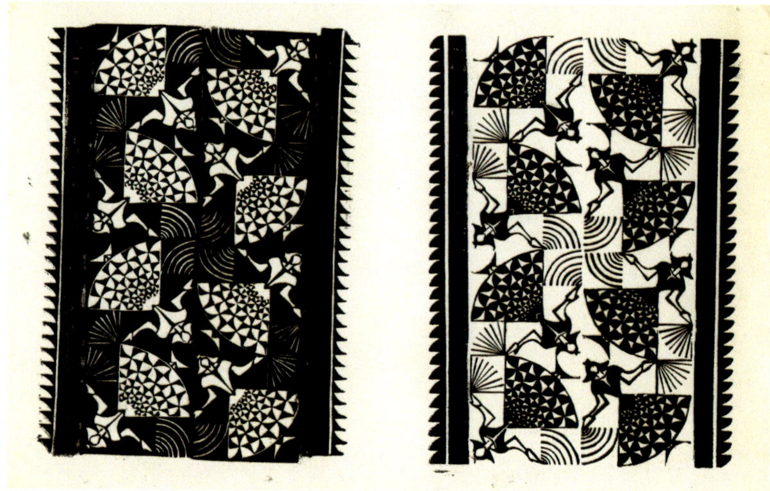

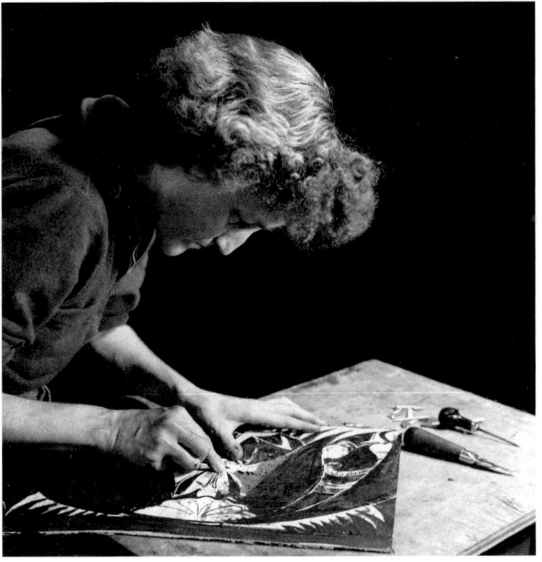

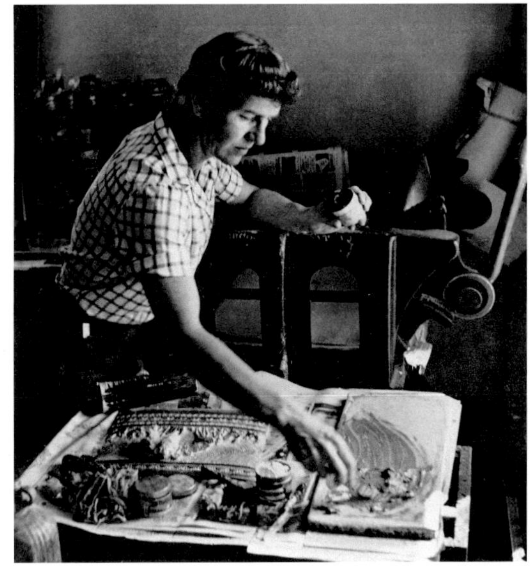

FIG. 44 (LEFT)
Aino Clarke was known as a wonderful carver and is seen here carving her *Geometric I* design. She taught many of the designers how to carve.

FIG. 45 (RIGHT)
Louise Kenyon was admired for her sense of color and ability to mix inks. Here she is mixing colors to print the block for her design *Farmer's Daughter*.

indicating that she seemed to continue to expand her teachings, likely contributing to her inability to complete the book.[35] This chapter includes visual examples of Virginia's lessons on the creation of a pattern through the arrangement of the subject.

While Virginia acknowledged that the homework was hard work, she felt it should be fun. "The more you do it and the more you understand the more fun it can be" and that "there is nothing more satisfying than when you get it just right and you know it..."[36]

Critique was another important skill to be mastered. Designers needed to be able to evaluate their own work and offer constructive advice to others. Peggy Norton explained, "[Virginia] gave us the ability to do our own work and to criticize our own work, which is very important."[37] "Anyone had to be able to take criticism as well as give it."[38]

Although only one set of designers seemed to ever work together regularly outside of meetings, members, like those of other printmaking studios, did work collaboratively.[39] Each designer had special skill sets and generously shared them. Members often said that Aino Clarke was a wonderful carver, Louise Kenyon had a great sense of color and the ability to mix inks, while Peggy Norton was a skilled printer.[40]

SLINGING INK: THE PRINTMAKING PROCESS

After hours of sketching, the final design would be transferred to a lineoleum block. The usual process was to trace it over carbon paper that had been placed in between the sketch and the block, which had been primed with white shoe polish or gesso to make the design transfer lines stand out more and aid in carving. Other designers applied their design in india ink directly to the primed block.[41] It was encouraged by Virginia to draw designs "freshly each time[,] in that way you will develop your skill and technique."[42]

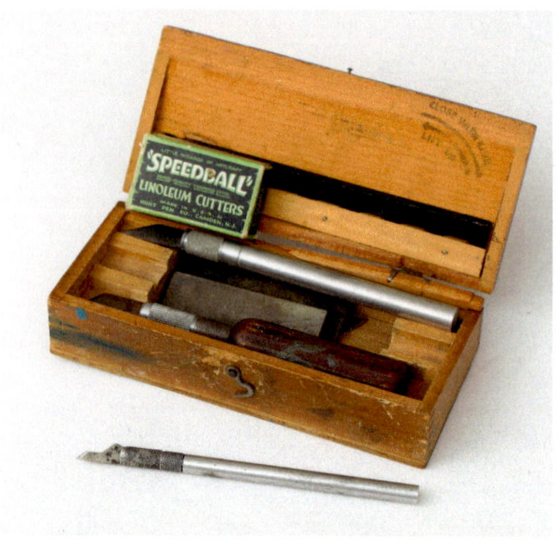

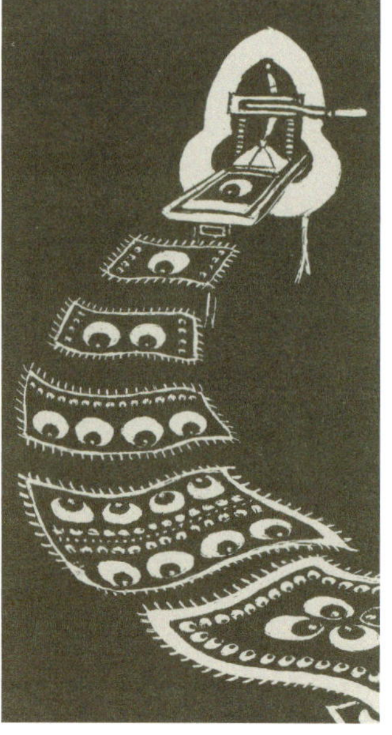

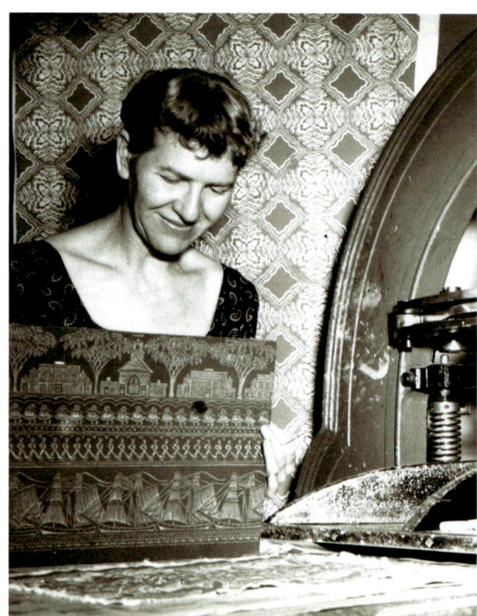

The group used sturdy battleship linoleum. Members made the linoleum more malleable by carving in the sun or by heating the block.[43] Norton said that warming the linoleum would allow it to "cut almost like butter."[44] The blocks would be carved using various V-shaped tools and simple mat knives (similar to X-acto knives).[45] They settled on a standard 11×17–inch size (unless the block was for cocktail napkins) and started mounting their blocks on plywood in order to take the pressure of the hand presses and many years of reuse.[46]

Ink color selections were made by the designers, although the group provided feedback during meetings. All the designers used the three primary colors (blue, red, and yellow) to mix their colors, as well as a white base.[47] Virginia was partial to a particular dark green that the group called "Jinnee's green."[48] Aino Clarke felt that "the warm greens and browns of seaweed" were the inspiration behind Virginia's favorite printing colors.[49] Louise Kenyon also preferred earth tones.[50] Most of the designers did not use a standard black, but mixed their own.[51] Oil paint was mixed with printer's ink purchased from Boston Printing Ink Company to make the colors permanent and washable.[52] (Lee Natti mentioned that they chose printer's ink instead of silk-screen ink because after World War II the silk-screen ink had a "potent" smell. Printer's ink did smell when ironed, but it did not need to heat-set as required of silk-screen ink.)[53]

The mixture was applied to the block with a roller. The fabric was prepared to absorb more ink by adding a few drops of wetting agent to water and sponging that onto the fabric. The damp material would then be placed on a thick pad of newspapers and the block pressed onto the fabric, either by stepping on it (as was the case in the early days of the Folly Cove Designers) or using a press.[54]

FIG. 46 (LEFT)
Some of Eino Natti's tools, specifically mat knives. Speedball linoleum cutter blades are also featured. Speedball is still a favorite brand among printmakers.

FIG. 47 (MIDDLE)
Virginia's depiction of an acorn press, which served as the group's 1956 exhibition invitation. Notice that it is printing the group's circle logo in various arrangements. The invite included lettering by Aino Clarke. (Ink on paper.)

FIG. 48 (RIGHT)
Louise Kenyon "revealing" her *Home Port* print. Her *Conventional Flower* design is in the background.

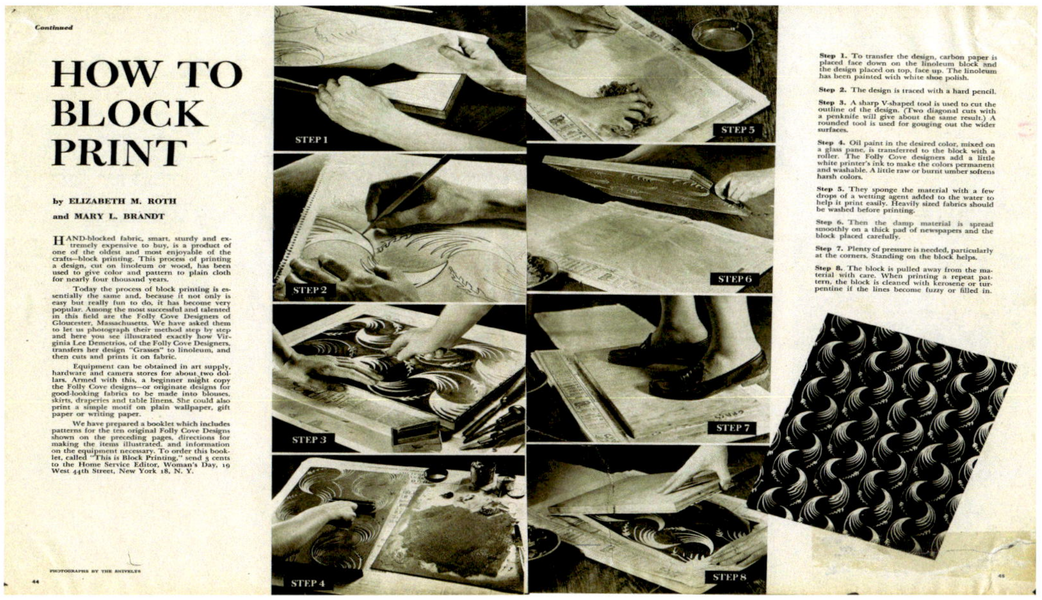

Continued

HOW TO BLOCK PRINT

by ELIZABETH M. ROTH and MARY L. BRANDT

HAND-blocked fabric, smart, sturdy and extremely expensive to buy, is a product of one of the oldest and most enjoyable of the crafts—block printing. This process of printing a design, cut on linoleum or wood, has been used to give color and pattern to plain cloth for nearly four thousand years.

Today the process of block printing is essentially the same and, because it not only is easy but really fun to do, it has become very popular. Among the most successful and talented in this field are the Folly Cove Designers of Gloucester, Massachusetts. We have asked them to let us photograph their method step by step and here you see illustrated exactly how Virginia Lee Demetrios, of the Folly Cove Designers, transfers her design "Grasses" to linoleum, and then cuts and prints it on fabric.

Equipment can be obtained in art supply, hardware and camera stores for about two dollars. Armed with this, a beginner might copy the Folly Cove designs—or originate designs for good-looking fabrics to be made into blouses, skirts, draperies and table linens. She could also print a simple motif on plain wallpaper, gift paper or writing paper.

We have prepared a booklet which includes patterns for the ten original Folly Cove Designs shown on the preceding pages, directions for making the items illustrated, and information on the equipment necessary. To order this booklet, called "This is Block Printing," send 3 cents to the Home Service Editor, Woman's Day, 19 West 44th Street, New York 18, N. Y.

PHOTOGRAPHS BY THE SNIVELYS

44

Step 1. To transfer the design, carbon paper is placed face down on the linoleum block and the design placed on top, face up. The linoleum has been painted with white shoe polish.

Step 2. The design is traced with a hard pencil.

Step 3. A sharp V-shaped tool is used to cut the outline of the design. (Two diagonal cuts with a penknife will give about the same result.) A rounded tool is used for gouging out the wider surfaces.

Step 4. Oil paint in the desired color, mixed on a glass pane, is transferred to the block with a roller. The Folly Cove designers add a little white printer's ink to make the colors permanent and washable. A little raw or burnt umber softens harsh colors.

Step 5. They sponge the material with a few drops of a wetting agent added to the water to help it print easily. Heavily sized fabrics should be washed before printing.

Step 6. Then the damp material is spread smoothly on a thick pad of newspapers and the block placed carefully.

Step 7. Plenty of pressure is needed, particularly at the corners. Standing on the block helps.

Step 8. The block is pulled away from the material with care. When printing a repeat pattern, the block is cleaned with kerosene or turpentine if the lines become fuzzy or filled in.

FIG. 49

This article from *Woman's Day* in January 1945 showed the group's process. The design is *Grass* by Virginia, which was also included in the foreground of the Lord & Taylor window display on Fifth Avenue (see page 54).

The group began to acquire hand-operated presses as early as 1943.[55] Louise Kenyon was the first to have one.[56] In 1945 Dorothy Norton wrote to staff at *Life* that "Most of the designers have abandoned the foot printing for the less picturesque hand presses" because "you get more pressure and a better print with a press."[57] Although decades later Dorothy described her press as "beautiful."[58] Peggy also recalled that Dorothy "had a particularly beautiful" press and that it had been used to print racing forms in its day, adding that she would have loved "to have known what the history was of some of them."[59]

The presses worked by pulling a lever, which would release a heavy plate that would "squash" the inked block and imprint the design into the fabric.[60] The presses were not intended to be used with fabric and Peggy added that "we ask[ed] quite a lot of them."[61] Group members had their own presses or shared them and completed their printing outside of meetings.[62] When the group opened their retail barn in 1948, Eino Natti moved his to the barn for public demonstrations.[63] Eino's press was an acorn press, named for the shape of the metal frame.[64] This type of press became popular "particularly in the Boston area, beginning in the early 1820s" and were made by a number of companies.[65]

Whether imprinting by foot or by hand press, it was important to apply a lot of pressure to imprint the image onto the fabric properly, especially at the edges.[66] The block was then carefully removed. It "was an exciting thing" to see what contemporary printmakers refer to as the "reveal peel," when the first print is unveiled (today's printmakers generally use softer linoleum so it is more of a peel-away process than was the case with battleship linoleum).[67]

When printing repeats of a pattern, the block would often need to be cleaned with kerosene or turpentine and rerolled if the lines became fuzzy or filled with ink where there shouldn't have been any.[68]

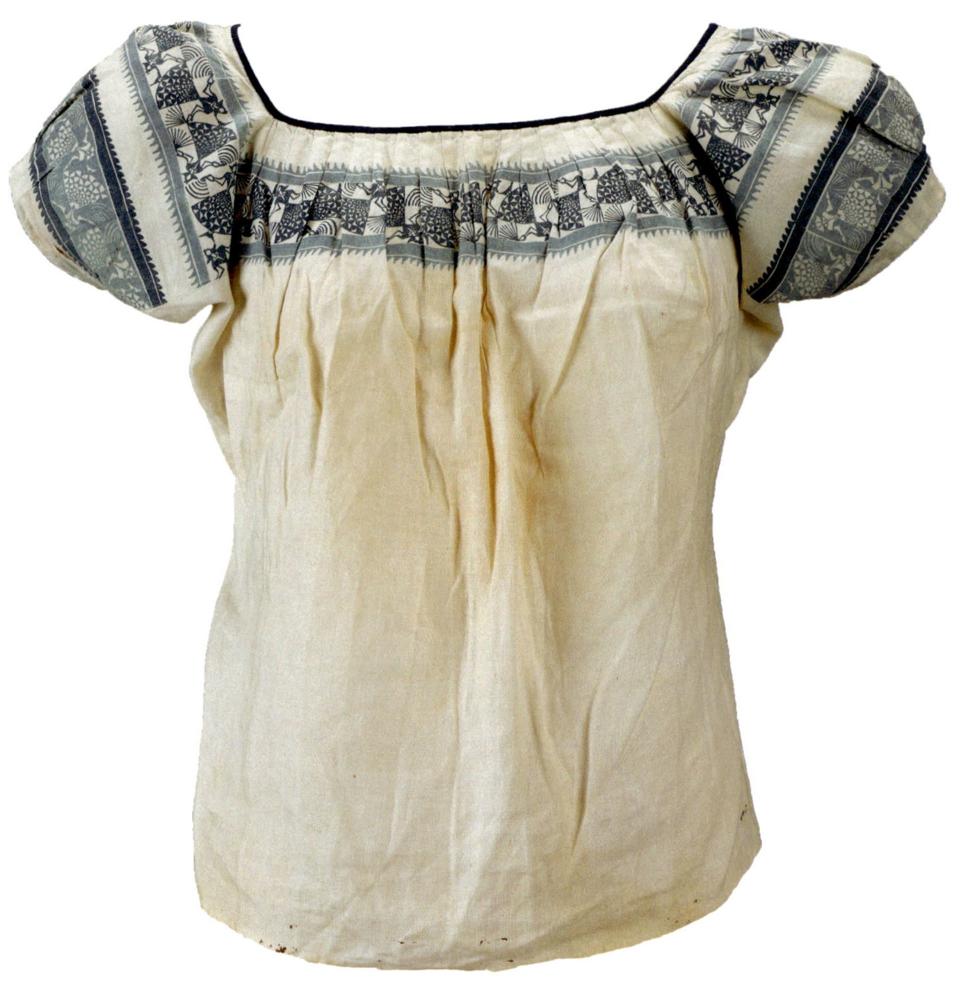

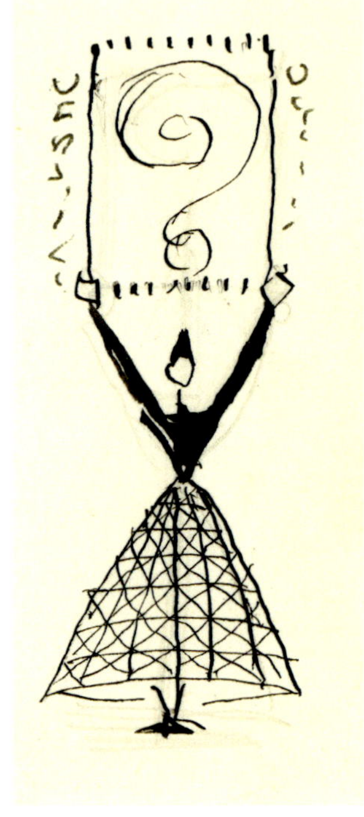

THE JURY PROCESS

Designs were drawn on the blocks and submitted to Virginia Lee Demetrios at least five days in advance of the scheduled jury meeting.[69] Blocks could only be carved upon majority jury approval. A print needed to be submitted again for "final approval" prior to the exhibition in case changes needed to be made.[70] The jury rotated, but it typically consisted of four to seven of the most experienced designers.[71] Over time the jury would rotate approximately twice per year. The jury meetings were closed sessions, although non-jury members were given opportunities to attend sessions throughout the year.[72] Lee Natti felt that "by the time something got to the jury, it had been pretty much shown and discussed and developed, and in some cases that last step was pretty much a formality."[73] Dorothy Norton agreed, with the exception of "premature submissions."[74] During the class meetings, designs had already undergone informal critiques. Designers would present their design homework on the table or floor.[75] Peggy Norton recalled that often if there was an element you were struggling with, that once you laid it out "before anyone

FIG. 50 (LEFT)
Virginia used the block she carved on page 44, featuring what appears to be the *Design and How!* woman teacher motif, to print this blouse for herself. (Ink on fabric.)

FIG. 51 (RIGHT)
Virginia started writing *Design and How!* with a question mark motif, then switched to a woman motif, but still incorporated the question mark in a lot of her illustrations. (Ink on paper.)

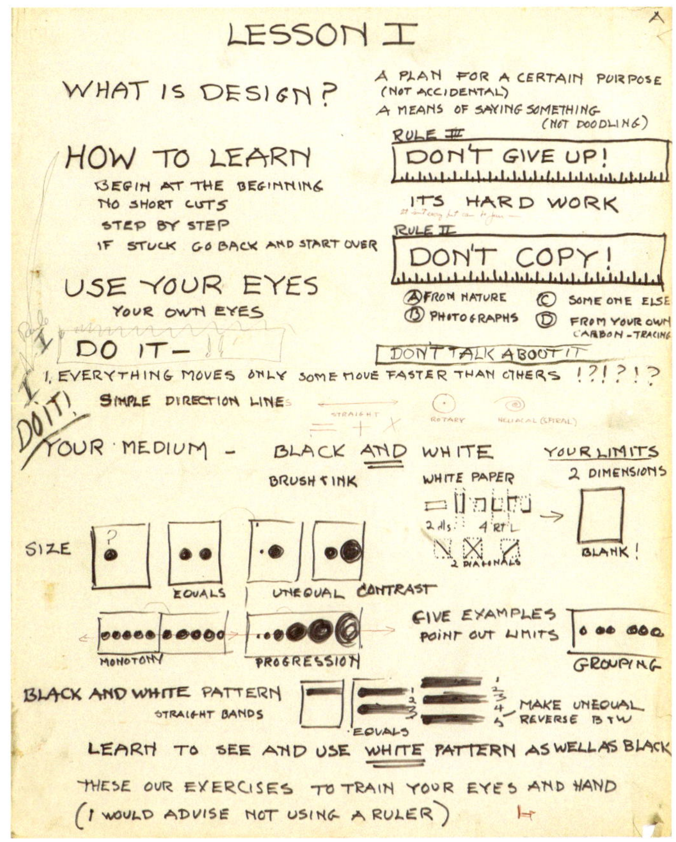

FIG. 52
Virginia taught from large poster boards that she created, as featured in *Life* (see page 20). (Ink on paper.)

said anything…you knew it right away" and you solved your own issue, but added that the criticism was "very valuable."[76] Feedback about size and emphasis and colors was discussed ahead of time.[77] It was mandated that designs "turned down by the jury either because of inferior design, color or workmanship should be destroyed and not sold or given away, either under the name of the Folly Cove Designers or that of the individual."[78] The jury also made decisions regarding policy and what would be sent as submissions for exhibitions that stipulated a limited number.[79]

DESIGN AND HOW!

Virginia amassed boxes of resource materials for the book, including sketchbooks, handwritten index cards delineating each section of the book, notebooks of page layouts with exquisitely detailed illustrations, as well as countless drafts of the preface and introduction. At some point she changed her illustrated motif, which runs throughout the book, from a question mark to a woman, causing her to redraw the manuscript, which undoubtedly played a part in the delay of the book.[80]

Although one of her sketchbooks includes a to-do list for "H.M.Co." and references "Design Book—finish Sept. '45," it is unclear when Virginia first started working on the book.[81] Completing the manuscript in 1945 was an ambitious goal, as the Folly Cove Designers were embarking on some of their largest commercial contracts around this time and exploded onto the national stage with the publication of an article about the group in *Life* in fall 1945.[82]

It appears that there was a push to finish it in the mid-1950s, as numerous copies of letters regarding the book date from this era. A letter from Virginia to her editor in 1954 expressed her renewed desire to get the book done. She responded to his gentle nudge by proclaiming, "I shall practice the first rule in the book and 'Do it! Don't Talk About it!'"[83]

Virginia submitted at least her introduction to the publisher because her editor wrote back to say, "This is the most purely seductive opening to a book that I have ever read. You tell them it's going to be work, but by the end of the Introduction they're running out to buy paper and ink."[84] While countless drafts of the preface and introduction exist, it does not appear that the text for the other sections was ever completed, despite Virginia having received samples of typeset and fonts from Houghton Mifflin's production department in 1955.[85]

In 1963, Virginia's editor, Paul Brooks, wrote her with a copy of a valentine that she had previously sent him asking him to "have a heart and give me some more time."[86] The illustration featured her at her desk, with a huge pile of material to her left marked "unfinished" and her signature wastebasket full of cast-offs. The editor wrote, "The Valentine is undated, but the other masterful depiction of the author at work goes back more than eight years. You must agree that my heart has proved soft to the point of senility."[87] He pointedly added:

> Can't you combine gull-watching with the completion of this book? I gather that you are giving another course in design, so this would seem to be the time to get it finished once [and] for all. How can I persuade you that this is your duty, your pleasure and a future source of profit for both of us and our grandchildren?[88]

Although the following letter excerpt is undated, it appears to be a response to her editor's plea as it features a drawing of Virginia seated on the cliffside at Folly Point, outside of her writing cottage, overlooking the ocean and working on the book while gulls carry pages away. Virginia wrote:

> Thank you for your good letter and gentle reminder—I have not forgotten my book on design—and I fully intend to get at it—But my last book was such a struggle and took so long I didn't feel the urge or need to tackle another. I am playing around painting a large screen I had planned to do over 25 years ago.[89]

Virginia Lee Burton published *Life Story,* a history of life on earth presented as an illustrated play, in 1962.[90] It was her last published book and, like *Design and How!,* was likely a long-term project as a note in an early notebook listed "next juvenile" as "planet evolution" with the date 1946.[91] Additionally, her health had begun to decline.[92] Her editor remained

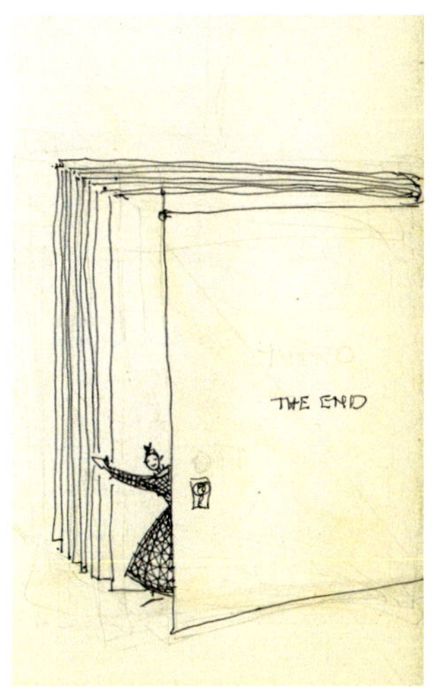

FIG. 53
"The end" from one of Virginia's mock-ups for the manuscript. (Ink on paper.)

undeterred, as he seemingly followed up his 1963 valentine referencing missive with a Christmas card and a separate sketch of a Christmas tree that had a copy of the future *Design and How!* book nestled underneath it with the presents and the caption "and anticipating Christmas 1965."[93]

The introduction to *Design and How!* touched upon the purpose of design and the potential for its application. Virginia wrote in many drafts that "Design is a language of signs and symbols" as well as "Design is selection and arrangement in order for a certain purpose."[94] She was adamant that "design was not doodling."[95] Her own work bore this out, her designs having a narrative quality that were key to the story being told.

Drafts of the preface state that the book's intended audience is everyone who wants to "make their own Designs...from what they see around them."[96] She specifically mentions the housewife "who wants to decorate her home... and express herself in her curtains or dresses or table linen."[97] She considered the book "a primer and very elementary...However, if you can master the first few steps...and build a solid foundation on which to work there is no limit to which you can learn."[98]

Virginia had an amusing formula that shifted slightly from draft to draft, which she attributed to a professor:

Intellect + work – emotion = drudge
Emotion + work – intellect = screwball
Emotion + intellect – work = dilettante
Emotion + intellect + work = genius, good designer[99]

Virginia admitted that the work of design was hard and that one needed persistence in order to be successful. She acknowledged that much of a designer's work ends up in the wastebasket, especially in the beginning.[100] In one of her many drafts of *Design and How!* she characteristically advised readers to "never be satisfied" with their work.[101] She felt that the more one practiced, the more one learned. She believed strongly that one got out what one put in.[102]

Peggy Norton said that Virginia had the manuscript "almost done" but that she kept "pruning it."[103] Aino Clarke explained that, in the writing process, Virginia discovered "how difficult it was to try to teach by a book" and that "it seemed much simpler to teach a class."[104] Lee Natti, a fellow designer and former Houghton Mifflin editor, speculated that Houghton Mifflin would probably have been happy to publish it as it was, although it seems likely that Virginia's perfectionism never allowed for the completion of the book.[105] In terms of scholarship, it is a shame that it was never published, as "what has been documented about printmaking instruction in the United States tends to emphasize male figures."[106]

Thankfully, what we do have are over three hundred designs completed by the Folly Cove Designers, evidence of Virginia's successful teaching methodology.[107] Virginia Lee Demetrios should certainly be included as one of the printmakers who "played key pedagogical roles in forming printmaking programs," having taught more than forty students over the course of nearly three decades.[108]

CHAPTER THREE

DOROTHY'S DOMAIN

The Business Dealings of the Folly Cove Designers

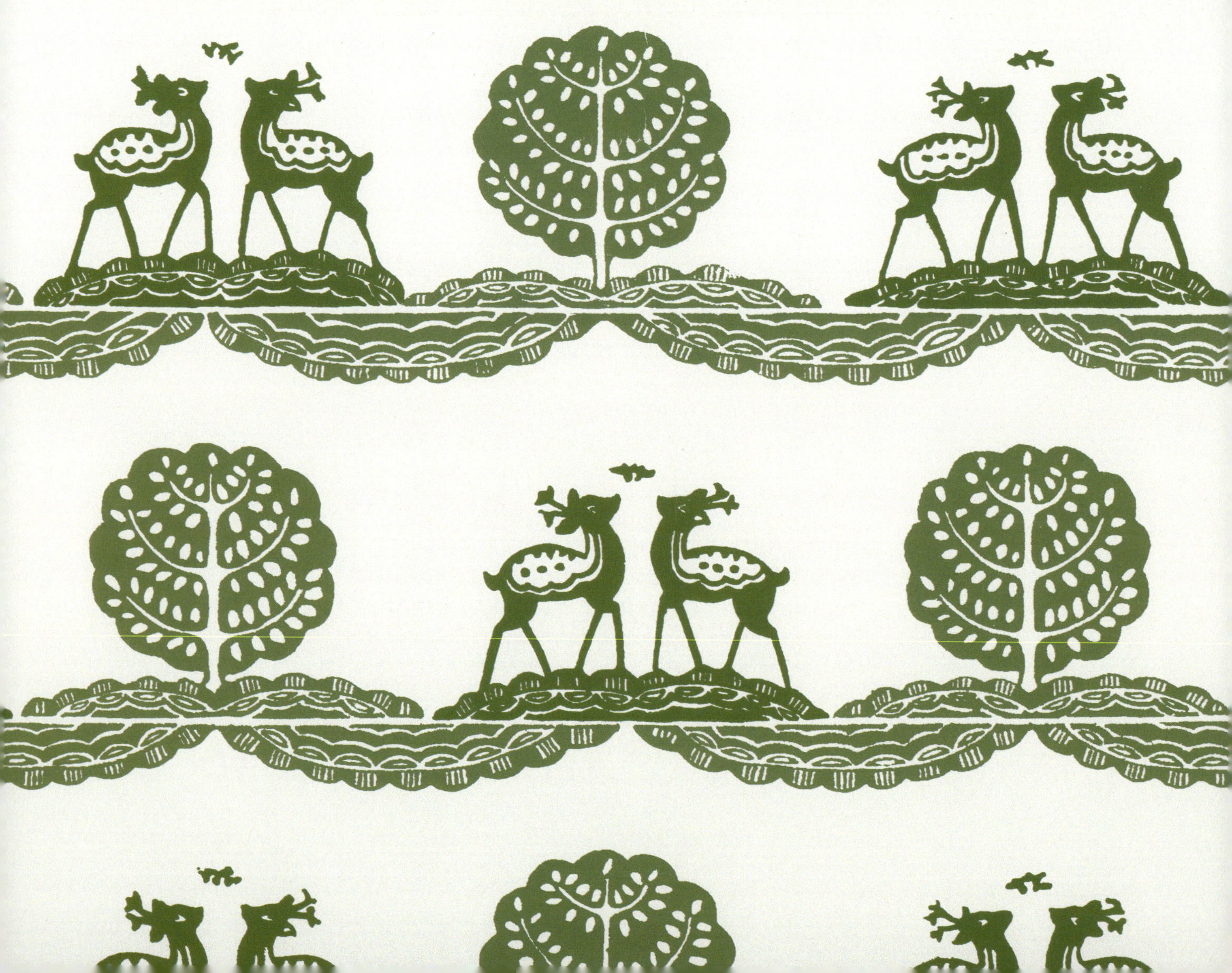

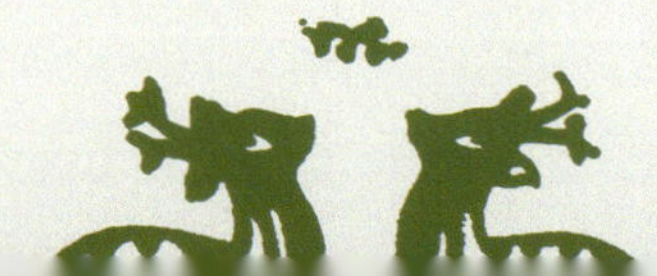
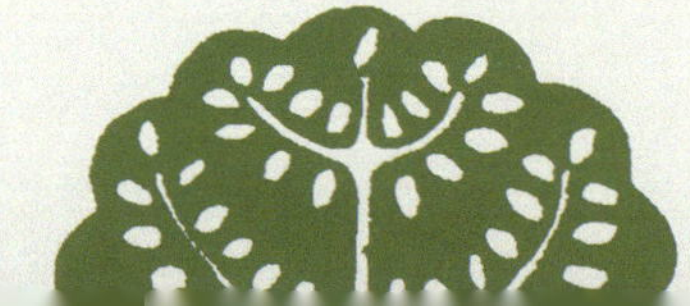
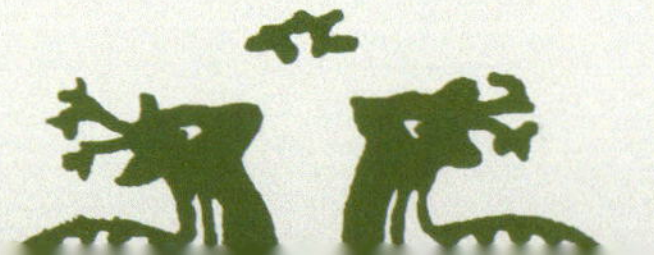

By 1944, the Folly Cove Designers entered their most commercial phase. Business inquiries were pouring in and they began negotiating with major retailers to have their designs mass produced as yard goods. The group decided to hire designer Dorothy Norton as their secretary. Her business acumen was essential to the group's success and longevity.

Dorothy was a secretarial school graduate and had worked as an interior designer. She skillfully took charge of the business and became the main point of contact for the group. Dorothy often invited executives to visit them in Folly Cove, especially for the summer exhibition openings, so that clients could experience firsthand the inspiration behind the designs. Most companies gladly sent representatives and developed friendly relationships with the group. She handled all business offers, publicity, and accounting tasks, including paying each designer. Dorothy made the fabric purchases both to ensure a standard for the group and to allow them to buy in bulk, cutting down on overhead. She also set wholesale and retail prices for the work, which had previously fluctuated.[1]

Dorothy also sought out new accounts and encouraged the group to trademark their name, which was finalized in 1948. She had an eye for marketing—for instance, telling her sister, Peggy Norton, to change the name of one of her designs, featuring an arrangement of leaves, from *Compost Pile* to *Deciduous,* because it was more appealing.[2] She began to record the release of new designs in 1950. Her record keeping has significantly contributed to the safeguarding of the group's history.

LORD & TAYLOR

By 1944, the group had begun talks with Lord & Taylor. The retail store had become aware of the group's work through its inclusion in the New England handicrafts exhibit at the Worcester Museum of Art in 1943 and the sale of their work at America House in New York City.[3] The work of the Folly Cove Designers was a good fit; under the leadership of Dorothy Shaver, Lord & Taylor had a "big push for American design."[4] Shaver had promoted American fashion designers with the launch of the "American Look" program in the 1930s. She continued to do so after she became president of the company in 1945, becoming one of the industry's first female presidents. She also helped form the Museum of Costume Art, now the Costume Institute at the Metropolitan Museum of Art.[5]

The group initially corresponded with the linen, rug, and upholstery departments. While it does not appear that the rug department ever produced their designs, the upholstery department produced their designs as yardage for decorating fabrics and the group hand-printed table linen orders.[6]

From the beginning of their business dealings, the group requested that the selvedge bear the name Folly Cove Designers.[7] Lord & Taylor ultimately purchased six designs: Virginia Lee Demetrios's *Gossips*; Louise Kenyon's *Fish and Bubbles, Head of the Cove, New England (Wild) Flowers,* and *Trees*

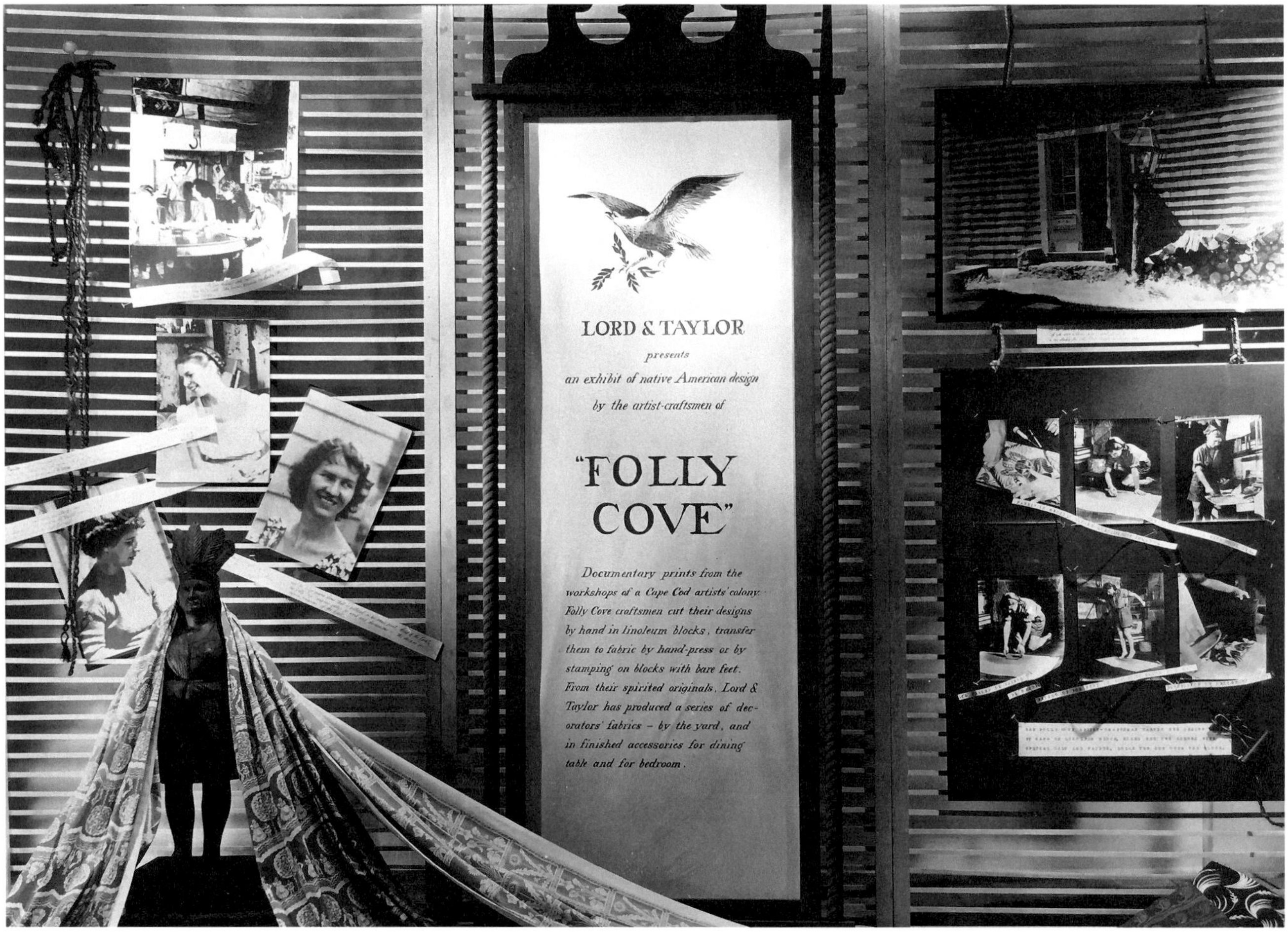

FIG. 54 (ABOVE)
To the left are photos of Virginia (center), Bettine Nichols (left), and Louise Kenyon (right). On the right are images of Virginia carving, inking, and jumping on her design *Ocelot* to print it. Above these is a photo of Virginia's studio door. Yardage from Louise's designs are draped in the foreground.

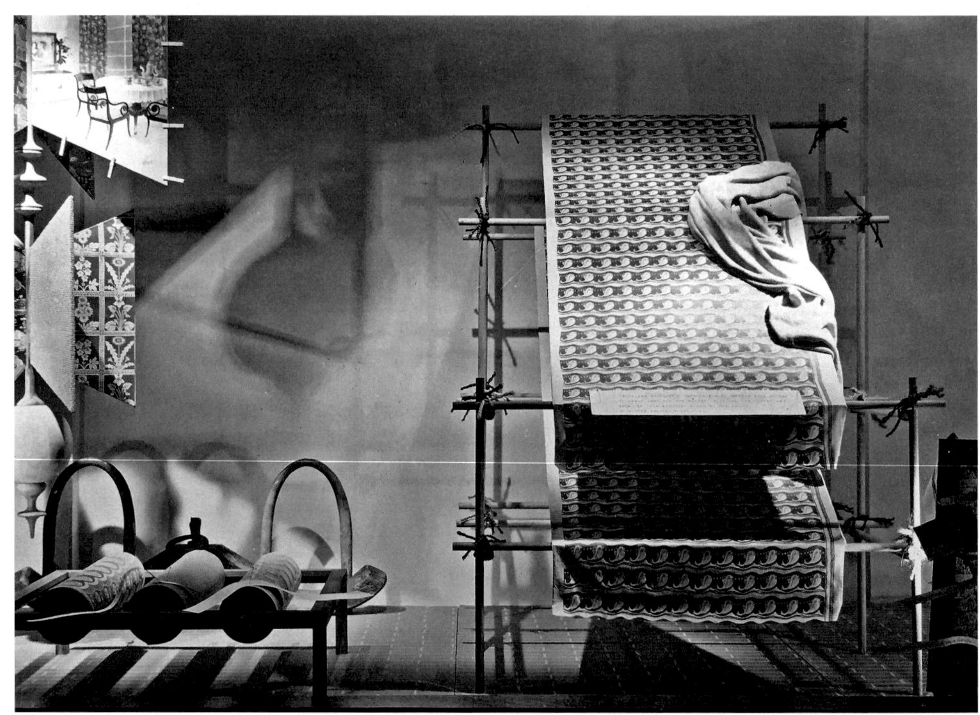

FIG. 55 (RIGHT)
The window display included Louise's design *Head of the Cove*, as well as photographs that she used of family members (see page 134) since the design was based on her neighborhood. Louise and her husband visited New York City to see the windows in-person, which must have been exciting.

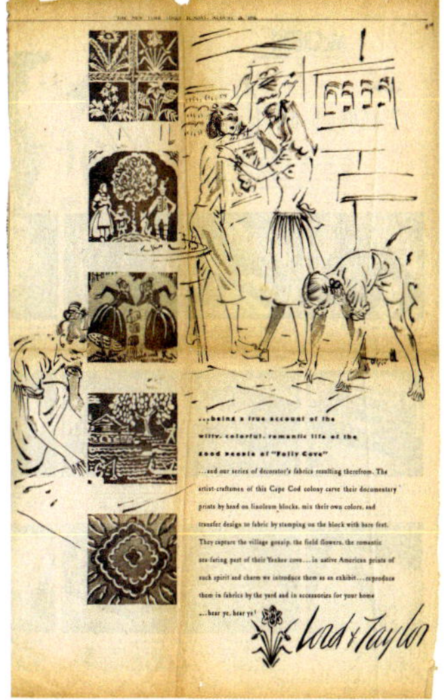

FIG. 56

This August 1945 *New York Times* ad describes the Folly Cove Designers' work as "documentary prints" and states, "They capture the village gossip, the field flowers, the romantic sea-faring [*sic*] part of their Yankee cove..."

FIG. 57 (OVERLEAF)

***Gossips* by Virginia. Cotton twill, screen-printed by Lord & Taylor. Dorothy Norton wrote that the group felt this version "lost some of its original charm," but didn't elaborate. It is unclear whether the initials say "VLD" or "VLB." Perhaps she had not added the VLD at this point. (Ink on fabric.)**

and People; and Bettine Nichols's *Bayleaf* (see page 183).[8] In August 1945, Lord & Taylor devoted "a full bank" of their legendary Fifth Avenue store windows to the Folly Cove Designers. There were also "room-like groupings" installed in the main fabric and bedroom ensembles departments.[9]

The Lord & Taylor store windows were designed by Karl Bissinger and blended Americana style with mid-century accessories.[10] Karl went on to become a stylist for the Condé Nast photography studios and then a famous portrait photographer, making his mark photographing celebrities like Truman Capote, Marlon Brando, Katharine Hepburn, James Baldwin, and the Duke and Duchess of Windsor.[11]

The main Folly Cove window display prominently featured an eagle with an olive branch, a sign of peace in the days leading up to the end of World War II. The main window also included the Folly Cove Designers' printing blocks and tools and photographs of individual designers as well as a photo of members working together around the table in Virginia's studio.[12] The other window featured a mid-century–style hanging display of Louise Kenyon's *Head of the Cove* and *New England (Wild) Flowers*. A large drying rack was used to display her *Red Bubbles* design.[13]

The Lord & Taylor ad campaign and window displays erroneously described the Folly Cove Designers as a Cape Cod group, which elicited many phone calls from disgruntled Cape Ann residents. David Williams, Lord & Taylor's upholstery buyer, wrote Dorothy Norton to apologize for the error. He added, "I hope that it did not hurt local pride too much and I can assure you that those who made the error were corrected by the public about every fifteen minutes with telephone calls."[14]

A trade magazine described the display of prints as seeming to "fill a long felt want. Their nostalgic flavor has appealed not only for country and suburban houses, but orders have been taken for apartments in town as well."[15] Lord & Taylor's window displays prompted tremendous publicity, which led to an article in *Life* and other magazines, propelling the group to international fame.[16]

Dorothy Norton referred to David Williams as "sort of a fairy godmother."[17] She wrote him that "We feel that Lord & Taylor's sponsorship of our designs will have a great deal to do with any future success which we may have in this field, and we want to tell you again how much we appreciate what you have done for us."[18]

F. SCHUMACHER & CO.

In September 1945, after the success of the window displays at Lord & Taylor and before the *Life* article was published, the Folly Cove Designers were approached by the design powerhouse F. Schumacher & Co. Initially, the wallpaper department inquired about converting the six designs that Lord & Taylor had produced as upholstery fabric into wallpaper.[19] The group was agreeable to licensing the designs but requested that "Folly Cove Designers" be printed in the selvedge. They also specified that "If it is necessary to re-draw the original design these changes shall be made by the designer"[20];

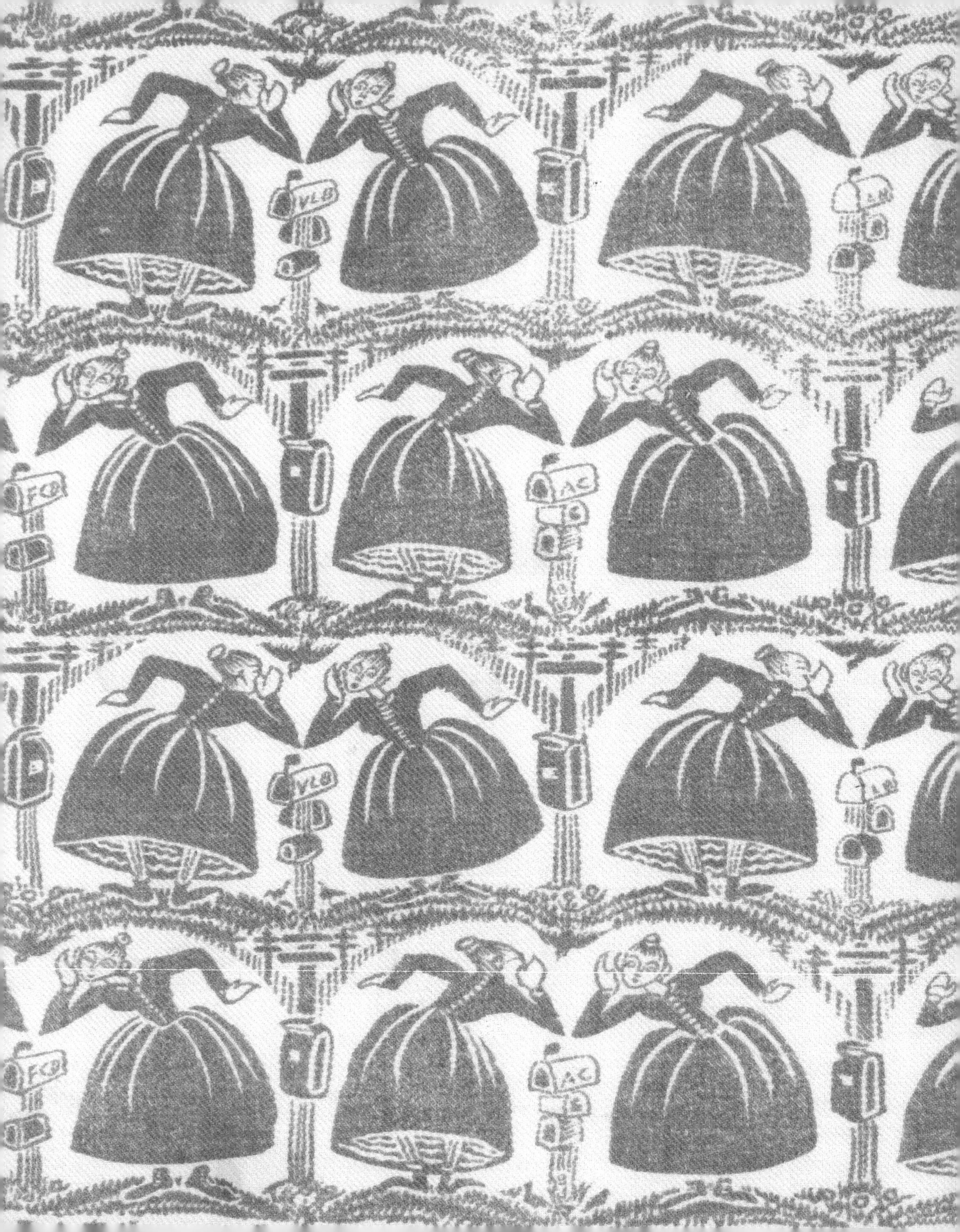

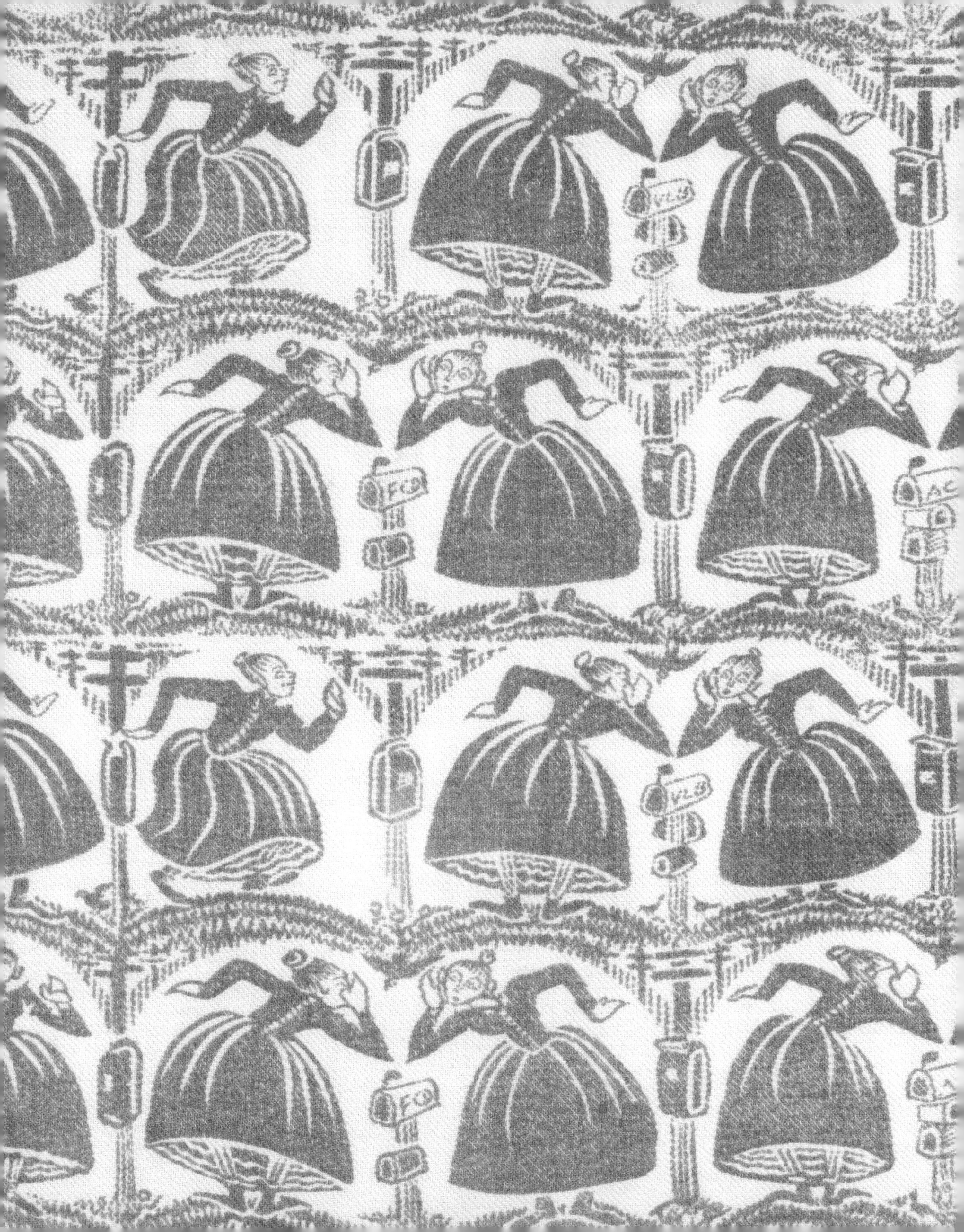

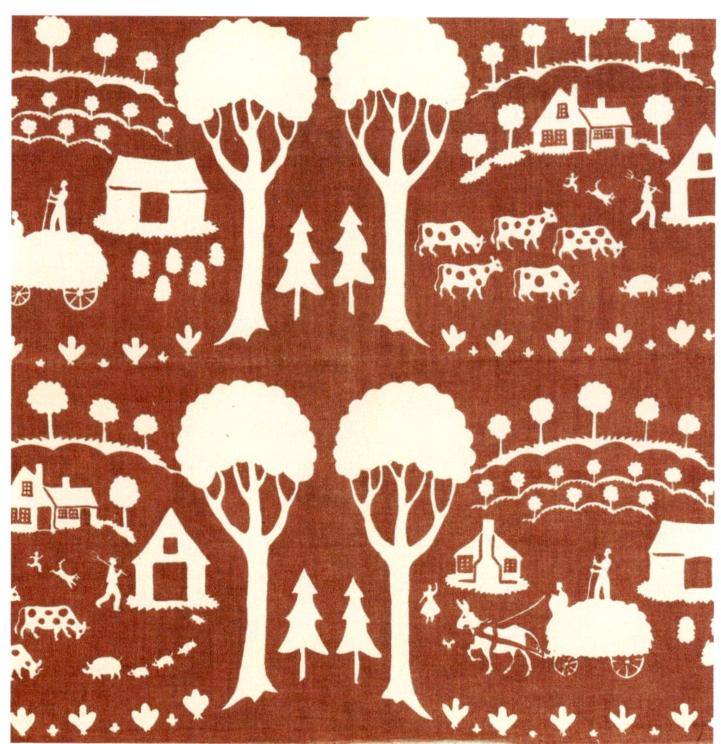

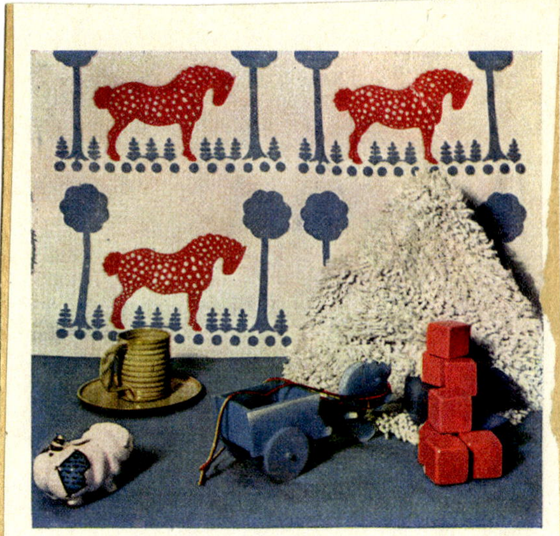

Lively colors in the nursery

Blue Grass, Rugged Rose, white in a polka dot pony print—a Folly Cove design, Schumacher. Matching wallpaper border available. Solid-color poplin, Jofa. Shag rug, Lawrence Products. Mug, plate, America House. Bank, El Futuro, blocks, F. A. O. Schwarz.

FIG. 58 (LEFT)
***Farm Scenes* by Hetty Beatty. Hetty completed several farm-based designs. This "lost" design was not previously recognized as part of her oeuvre. (Ink on fabric.)**

FIG. 59 (RIGHT)
***Polka Dot Pony* ad in *House and Garden*, September 1946. Hetty's design was promoted for nursery decor.**

they had not been pleased with how *Gossips* had been redrawn by Lord & Taylor, feeling it had "lost some of its original charm."[21] They also requested to "reserve the right to print these same designs by hand," later explaining "this is a steady source of income for some of our members who may not sell as many designs."[22] The group asked for royalty advances on their designs, with *Gossips* being the most expensive at $200 and *Head of the Cove* at $150. The other four were either $75 or $100.[23]

In November 1945, F. Schumacher representative Peter Leavitt visited the group in Folly Cove to discuss an exclusive two-year agreement for drapery and upholstery textiles, both printed and woven, wallpapers, and carpets and picked out several additional designs for the company's consideration.[24] F. Schumacher agreed to pay $75 "in advance royalties."[25] Royalties of 3 percent of the wholesale price of screen prints and 1.5 percent on machine prints were to be paid to the designers.[26]

The group decided to enter into a contract with F. Schumacher to "produce and distribute all new designs of ours for a limited time."[27] Dorothy described their reasoning for doing so in a letter to their trusted Lord & Taylor executive, David Williams:

> We have had a great many requests for our designs from people who wish to promote them, inspired by your introduction of our designs. Since our experience in this field is limited and we have no way of making intelligent decisions as to which offers to accept and which to reject, we feel that the present arrangement should keep us out of trouble.[28]

At the end of that November, Rene Carrillo returned from the service and took over the Folly Cove account from Peter Leavitt at F. Schumacher. Rene had sold his family's business (Carrillo Fabrics) to F. Schumacher in the early 1930s.[29] He had an eye for talent and "must have known every arists [*sic*] and designer in the New York textile and art world."[30] Rene is credited with "discovering" Vera Neumann for F. Schumacher, signing Frank Lloyd Wright to design a line for them, and working with the interior designer Dorothy Draper.[31]

One of the first designs F. Schumacher printed was *Polka Dot Pony* (originally submitted as *Spotted Pony)* by Hetty Beatty, which has a more modern, graphic look, which may have represented Rene's personal style preference.[32] It proved to be one of the most popular Folly Cove designs released by the company and was featured in several advertisements and ultimately in a 1953 episode of *I Love Lucy* in the upholstery of a child's chair ("The Ricardos Change Apartments," where Lucy filled the living room with children's furniture and toys to convince Ricky that they needed a bigger apartment after the arrival of Little Ricky.)[33]

The designers expressed initial concerns about color upon receiving the sample for *Polka Dot Pony* in April 1946.[34] In June the group was still debating the coloration. After complimenting Rene on F. Schumacher having "retained the feeling of hand blocking very successfully with the screen print process," Dorothy reminded him that their contract stipulated that the designers retained the right to okay any color changes and that, "We are not as enthusiastic about the colors."[35] She continued, "The color can so easily make or break a design, and we feel very strongly about this... Miss Beatty was particularly distressed about the chartreuse. She thinks it is much too sharp and should have been a mixed color instead of 'right out of the can.'"[36] Rene responded diplomatically:

> We appreciate that your conception of colorations and ours will probably differ from time to time but we do feel that we know our market and we hope that you will have confidence in any original colors we put in even tho [*sic*] they may not be as pleasing to your eyes as we hope they will be to our consuming public.[37]

F. Schumacher resolved the situation by suggesting that the Folly Cove Designers submit five colorations with each design submission.[38]

Due to incomplete business records, it is difficult to discern which designs F. Schumacher ultimately printed. But the designers' financial records indicate that F. Schumacher produced the following seven designs: *Farm Scenes* and *Polka Dot Pony* by Hetty Beatty; *Finnish Hop* by Virginia Lee Demetrios; *Clover, Georgia Builds* or *Plantation Pattern, Georgia Wildflowers,* and *Tree & Fawns* by Louise Kenyon.[39] These were produced as textiles printed on Aralac, a synthetic fiber developed in the 1930s from milk protein to mimic wool since wool was scarce during the war years. Fabrics made from this fiber became popular, but its popularity was fleeting.[40] Schumacher blended the Aralac with rayon and cotton.[41]

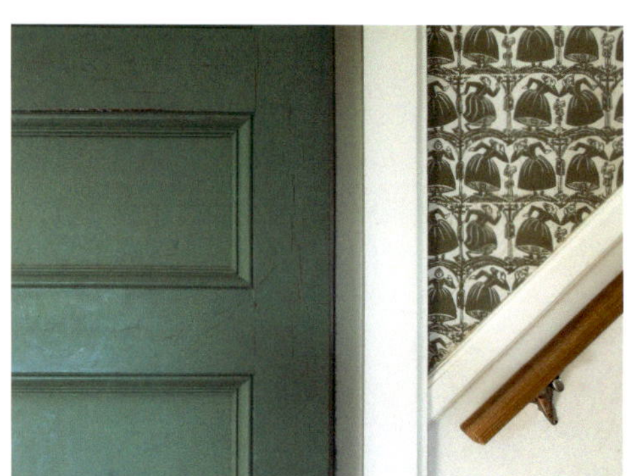

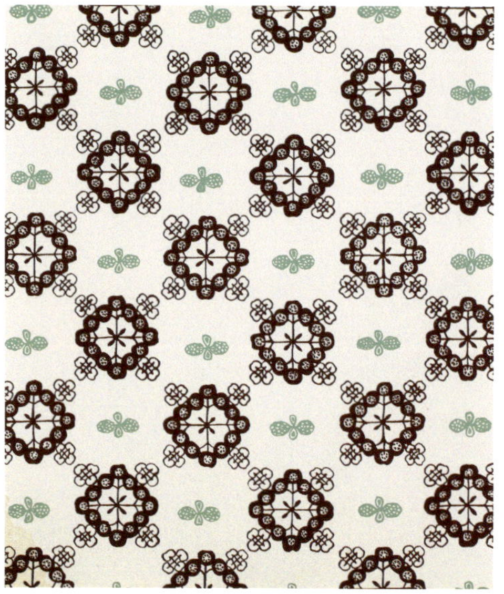

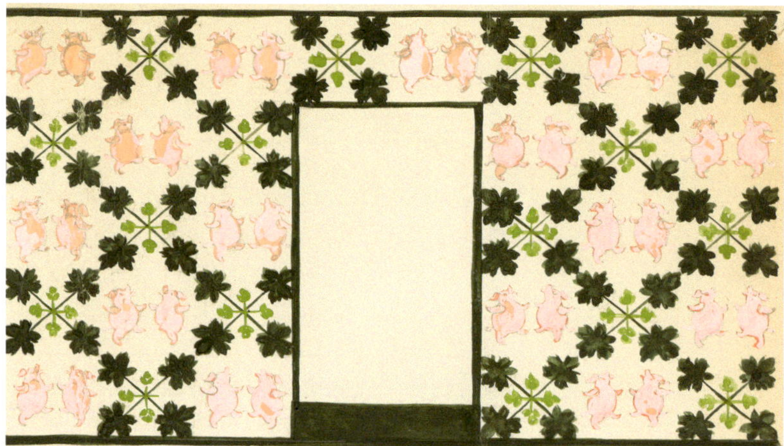

FIG. 60 (TOP LEFT)
F. Schumacher *Gossips* wallpaper in a Gloucester home. *Gossips* was part of the initial group of designs that F. Schumacher purchased. The wallpaper seems to have been popular in the area, as designer Lee Steele said that her home originally had it when she purchased it from a fellow designer.

FIG. 61 (BOTTOM)
A draft of this design for Bakon Yeast and a letter from Pickwick, Ltd., dated April 1945, were in the papers of Louise Kenyon. It likely prompted the creation of her design *Pigs in Clover* (not shown). (Ink on paper.)

FIG. 62 (TOP RIGHT)
F. Schumacher *Clover* wallpaper. An executive requested "the pattern with the Cloverleaf in the middle" that he saw on wallpaper at the Kenyon home (presumably *Pigs in Clover*). The request seems to have led to *Clover*, another "lost" design.

In addition to the six Lord & Taylor designs, F. Schumacher records suggest that the following designs were printed as wallpaper: *Clover*, *Farm Scenes*, *Finnish Hop*, *Polka Dot Pony*, and *Tree & Fawns*.[42]

The group's contract ran from January 1946 through January 1948.[43] It does not appear that it was renewed. There was some correspondence in 1949 and the last letter in Dorothy Norton's business files was one from Carrillo in 1950 welcoming design submissions by the group.[44]

The association with F. Schumacher raised the Folly Cove Designers' profile, leading to other opportunities. In the case of Louise Kenyon, it possibly prompted her to redraw *Head of the Cove* (due to some printing logistics) to appear as the design we know today, as you'll see described in Louise's biography in chapter 5.[45] It may have also inspired her to create *Clover*, which appears to be a "lost" design by Louise and one not recognized as part of her oeuvre. Letters suggest that clover was just one element in a larger design, *Pigs in Clover*, but a Schumacher executive requested that it be made the focus of a new design.[46]

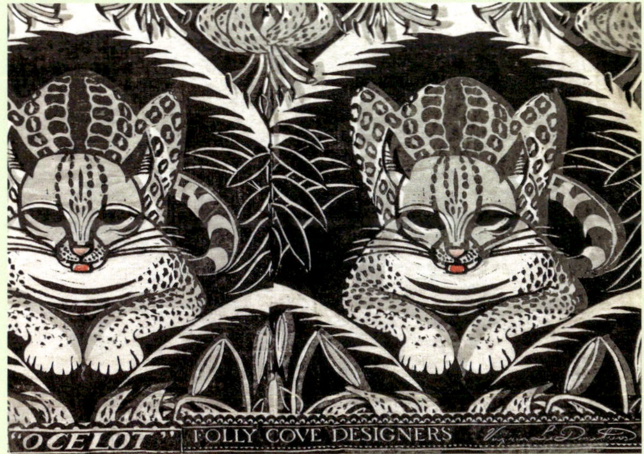

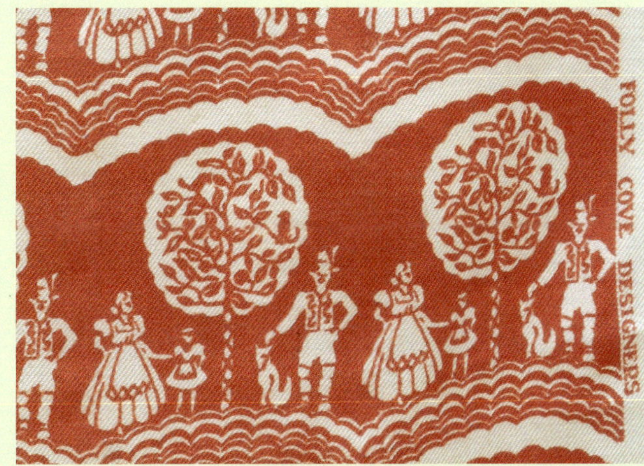

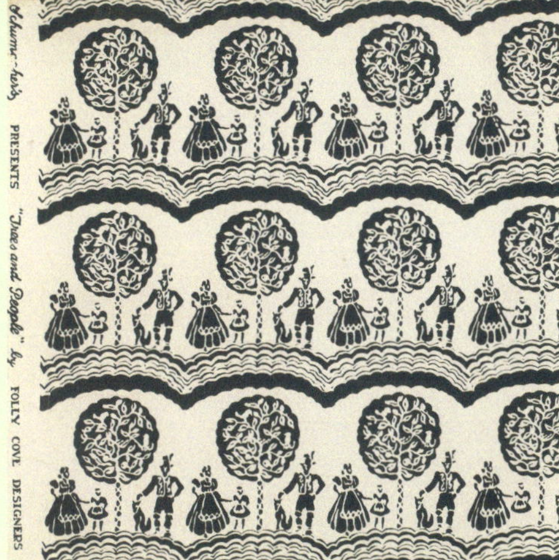

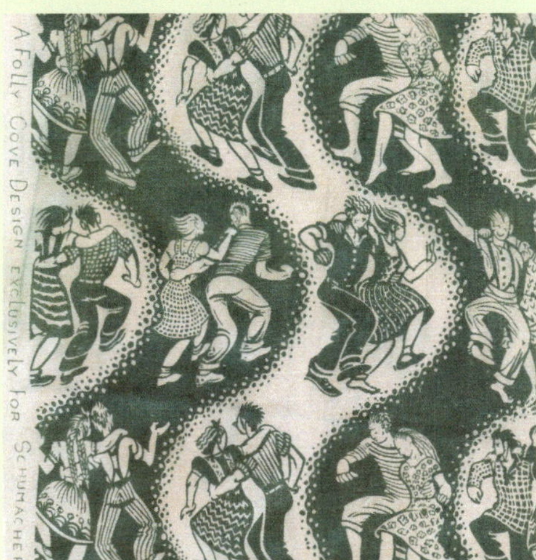

CLOCKWISE FROM TOP LEFT

FIG. 63
Ocelot **by Virginia is an example of hand-printed selvedge. It includes the design name, "Folly Cove Designers," and the designer's name (sometimes the full name, sometimes initials, sometimes as a signature).**

FIG. 64
Louise's ***Trees and People*****, printed by Lord & Taylor. As their first commercial contract, the Lord & Taylor pieces simply listed "The Folly Cove Designers" in the selvedge. (Ink on fabric.)**

FIG. 65
Finnish Hop **by Virginia exemplifies the typical F. Schumacher selvedge. The group would have preferred "Folly Cove Designers" instead of "A Folly Cove Design." Other F. Schumacher yardage examples also include the design name and the designer's initials. The group had advocated for the designers' full names. (Ink on fabric.)**

FIG. 66
An alternative F. Schumacher ***Trees and People*** **selvedge. This was either an early sample or produced after Schumacher agreed to change the selvedge from "A Folly Cove Design." Schumacher also reversed the lights and darks in this wallpaper sample. (Ink on paper.)**

Know Your Selvedge

Above are images of the most common Folly Cove Designers' selvedges, including examples of hand-printed yardage as well as work printed by Lord & Taylor and F. Schumacher. Each of them credits the group in the selvedge, and the hand-printed work and some of the F. Schumacher selvedges also list the designer, unusual for the time, as scholars Pat Kirkham and Lynne Walker have pointed out, because individual textile designers did not typically get credit for their work.[47]

Most of the extant F. Schumacher fabric and wallpaper samples have selvedges that list "A Folly Cove Design Exclusively for Schumacher." Some wallpaper samples (and at least one fabric sample in a private collection) include the name of the design and the designer's initials, with one wallpaper sample carrying the credit "Schumacher's Presents 'Trees and People' by Folly Cove Designers" (fig. 66).[48]

RICH'S INC.

In late September 1945, about a month after Lord & Taylor's Fifth Avenue store window display, the Folly Cove Designers were approached by the department store Rich's Inc. in Atlanta, Georgia. Rich's sought custom, southern-inspired designs for their store, with plans for a promotion launch similar to that of Lord & Taylor's. Mary Brandt had written an article on the group for *Woman's Day*, then taken a job at Rich's and made the connection with the Yankee block printers.[49]

Mary knew that Virginia preferred the members to draw from life, so had a "cotton plant, pine branch, holly branch, pine cones and peanut stalk," in addition to photographs and prints of Georgia scenery, architecture, and iron grill work, shipped up to the group to convey "a little of Georgia's local color."[50]

Within roughly a month and a half, the group submitted seven designs.[51] Rich's promptly responded that they would be purchasing at least five designs and "We are really thrilled with the feeling of Georgia that is so evident."[52] Designs by Aino Clarke, Virginia Lee Demetrios, Louise Kenyon (two), and Eino Natti were chosen. A letter confirmed the agreement, granting Rich's exclusive rights to print the designs as decorating fabric yard goods for six months and payment of an advance against royalties of $200 for the more detailed and architectural of Louise's designs and $150 for each of the others.[53] Again, the group requested that any changes to the designs be made by the designer "in order to preserve the original character of the design."[54]

As they had done for the Lord & Taylor window displays, the group furnished Rich's with props for their promotion of the Georgia designs, including a wall hanging of Virginia's *Making of a Block Print*, the print every member received when they completed their first design.[55] Rich's described the rollout as "very gratifying" and said they had "been besieged by every trades publication for information and photographs."[56] Hostesses of the event wore outfits made from fabric printed with one of the group's designs to greet customers.[57]

FIG. 67 (OPPOSITE TOP)
Georgia Pine **by Virginia. (Ink on fabric.)**

FIG. 68 (OPPOSITE LEFT)
Georgia Wildflowers **by Louise Kenyon. Rich's had hoped from the outset for a southern version of her** ***New England (Wild) Flowers*****. When the Rich's contract expired, this design was purchased and produced by F. Schumacher. This is an example of the F. Schumacher version with color swatches. (Ink on fabric.)**

FIG. 69 (OPPOSITE RIGHT)
Georgia Peanuts **by Aino Clarke. Aino was able to study peanuts in person because a local man raised them. She incorporated varying sizes and radial symmetry. (Ink on fabric.)**

WILLIAM SKINNER & SONS

The Folly Cove Designers' most significant foray into the fashion world was with textile manufacturer William Skinner & Sons. In March 1947, George Gibson wrote the group to say that the company was making a line of prints to celebrate its centennial anniversary.[58] In later correspondence, George wrote Dorothy Norton that they typically paid advance royalties of $60 to $85 for designs "from the local studios," but that Mrs. Demetrios had informed the company that the Folly Cove Designers had already sold designs for $150 to $200.[59] He acknowledged that "from the workmanship that obviously has gone into these designs, there is no question but that they are worth more than the standard type of designs that are submitted by New York studios."[60]

Skinner was so taken with the Folly Cove Designers that they initially expressed hopes of "developing a special fabric for Folly Cove designs" and

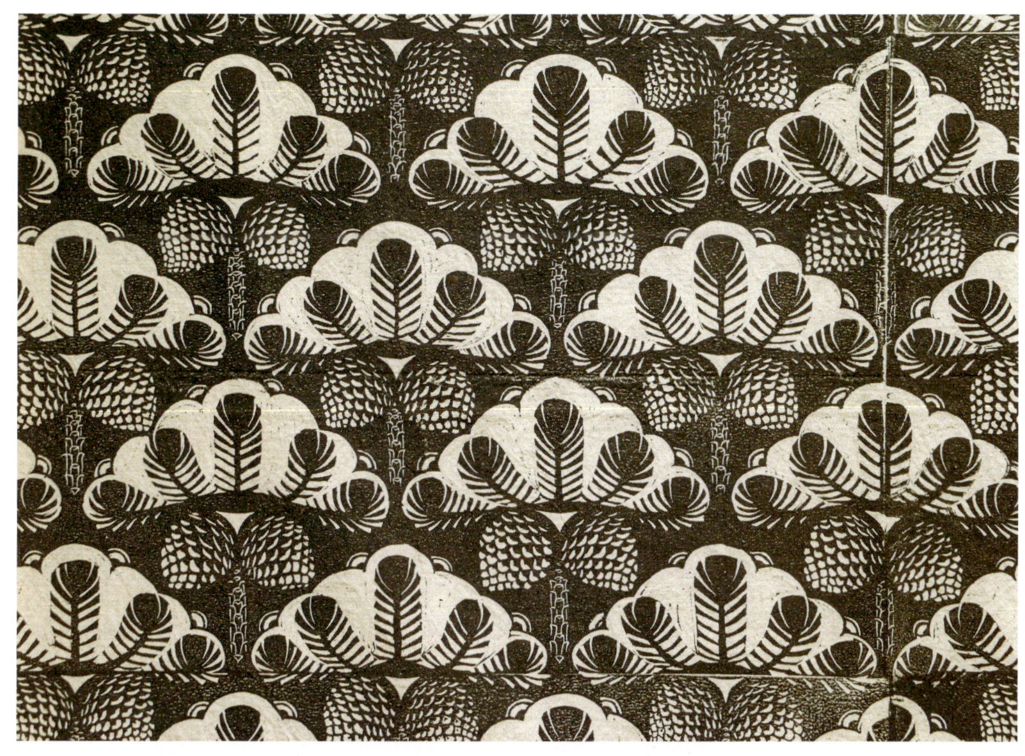

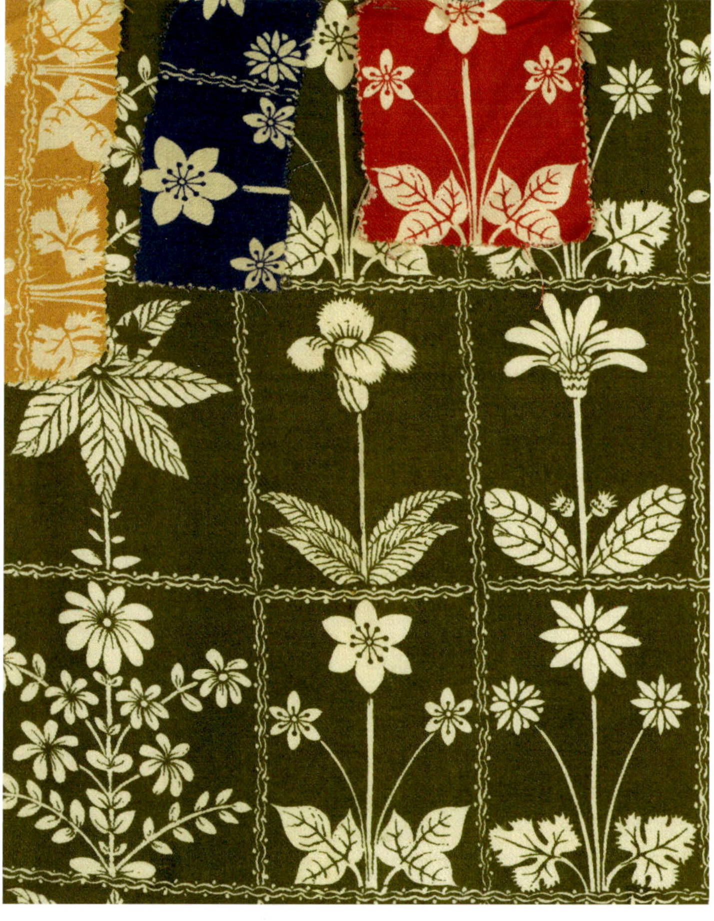

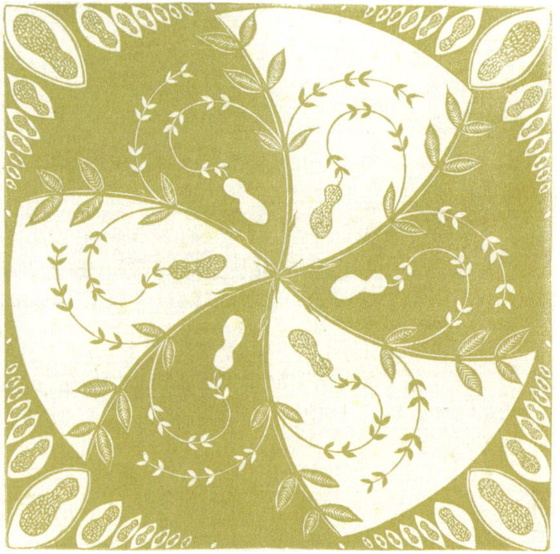

envisioned acquiring "the exclusive Folly Cove franchise for the piece goods and dress industries" in the United States.[61] Although this never came to fruition, five designs were included in the company's group of ten Centennial Prints.[62] In a 1964 newspaper article on the designers it was said that the group "executed the designs, cut the blocks, and suggested colors, but the company [Skinner] took care of the actual production."[63]

Among the designs were *Mill Valley* (originally titled *Connecticut Valley*) by Lee Natti, *A Stitch in Time* by Virginia Lee Demetrios, and *Village Green* by Dorothy Norton.[64]

Out of these Centennial Print designs, two dress manufacturers purchased designs by the Folly Cove Designers, one of which was Virginia's *A Stitch in Time*.[65] Yard goods of the same designs were sold at R.H. Stearns, an upscale Boston-based department store.[66]

While the Centennial Print fabrics were in production, Skinner had solicited from the group designs that celebrated the California Gold Rush and other historic events of that time period in the West for inclusion in a resort line to be produced by West Coast manufacturers.[67] When this project fell through, George wrote Dorothy in September 1948 that he remained "optimistic about the possibility of our using your designs in the sports fabric about which I have talked to you in the past."[68] The group sent designs based on these themes in spring 1948, but Skinner ultimately chose not to produce the Gold Rush theme.[69] They did however purchase a design titled *Tiger* by Hetty Beatty.[70]

In February 1950, George wrote Dorothy to pass along feedback from some of their customers regarding additional designs sent to them for review in December of 1949.[71] He explained that everyone admired the "tremendous amount of power and motion inhererent [*sic*] in them [the designs], but that the set patterns in which these ideas are conveyed do not lend themselves to a dress fabric."[72] George acknowledged that he understood "that the symmetrical theory is one that is close to the heart of the Folly Cove designers [*sic*]," but added that "We wish that a little more freedom in spacing could be used by your designers so that their really creative and talented artistry could be put to use in the fields to which we supply our materials."[73] He added that "Dress manufacturers and piece goods buyers of retail stores normally avoid buying a pattern, the repeats of which come out in set forms: squares, stripes or diagonals. This, of course, is just a reflection on their part of their customers who usually cannot wear prints of this type."[74]

George ended the letter by saying that he hoped "there is a possibility of resubmitting some of these designs in a more fluid over-all effect, or maybe some new designs with this general feeling."[75] But this letter appears to be the end of the three-year-long correspondence between Skinner and the Folly Cove Designers.

While the group seemed to have had an interest in seeing their designs reproduced in the fashion industry on a greater scale, they were not interested in changing their style of design to conform with the needs of large dress manufacturers. They did continue to produce and sell their own block-printed dirndl skirts and dresses at smaller Boston-area stores and their own retail shop.

FIG. 70 (OPPOSITE TOP LEFT)
This blouse was made by Lee Natti in her *Mill Valley* design for William Skinner & Sons. It was one of Lee's first designs for the group, if not her first.

FIG. 71 (OPPOSITE TOP RIGHT)
Skinner Centennial ad, *The Boston Herald*, March 30, 1948. All five of the Folly Cove Designers' prints were sold at R.H. Stearns in Boston. Dorothy Norton wrote to an executive that the designers were looking forward to buying dress-lengths of their fabrics.

FIG. 72 (OPPOSITE BOTTOM LEFT)
***A Stitch in Time* by Virginia shows women's apparel over the decades. Crisscrossing thread and thimbles connect the women and an hourglass represents time. Swirling bolts of fabric, dressmaking patterns, and scissors add a secondary story line.**

FIG. 73 (OPPOSITE BOTTOM RIGHT)
***Village Green* by Dorothy, which features villages surrounded by lines representing roads. Covered wagons, trains, and steamships represent the industrial revolution and the passage of time for Skinner's Centennial anniversary.**

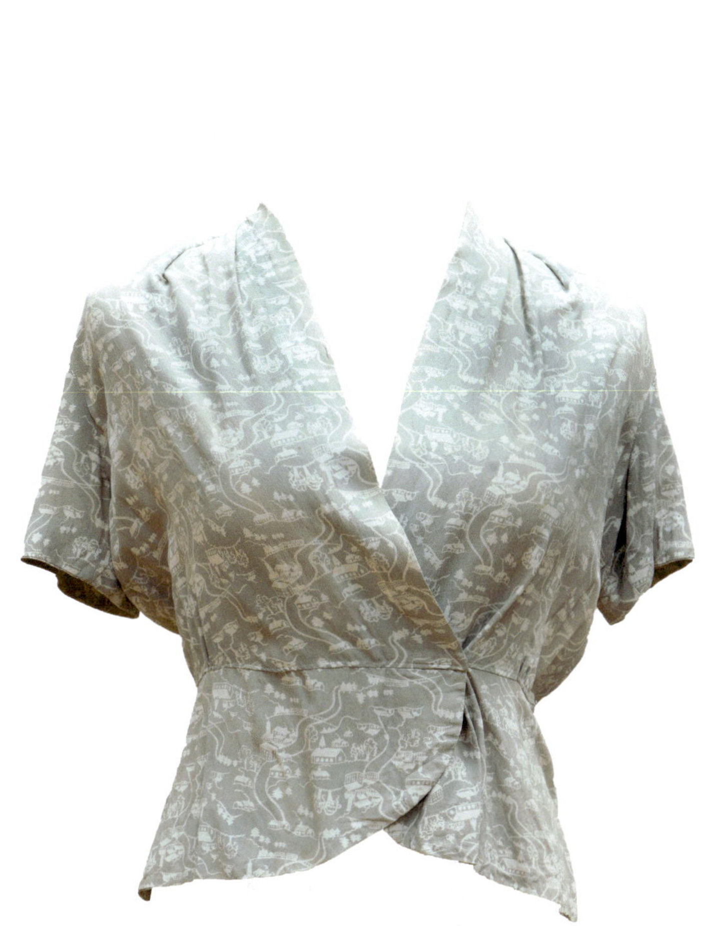

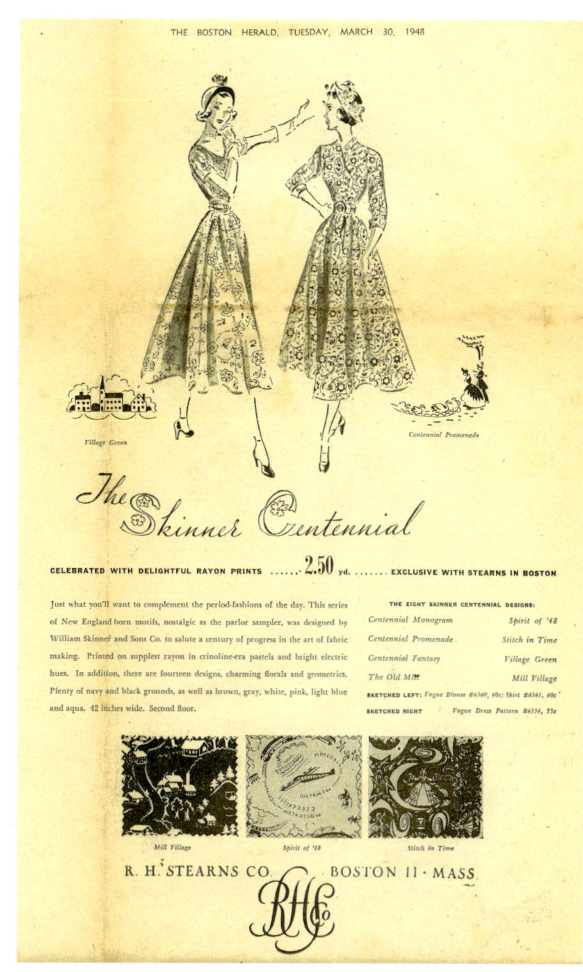

THE BOSTON HERALD, TUESDAY, MARCH 30, 1948

Village Green

Centennial Promenade

The Skinner Centennial

CELEBRATED WITH DELIGHTFUL RAYON PRINTS .... 2.50 yd. .... EXCLUSIVE WITH STEARNS IN BOSTON

Just what you'll want to complement the period-fashions of the day. This series of New England born motifs, nostalgic as the parlor sampler, was designed by William Skinner and Sons Co. to salute a century of progress in the art of fabric making. Printed on supplest rayon in crinoline-era pastels and bright electric hues. In addition, there are fourteen designs, charming florals and geometrics. Plenty of navy and black grounds, as well as brown, gray, white, pink, light blue and aqua. 42 inches wide. Second floor.

THE EIGHT SKINNER CENTENNIAL DESIGNS:

Centennial Monogram	*Spirit of '48*
Centennial Promenade	*Stitch in Time*
Centennial Fantasy	*Village Green*
The Old Mill	*Mill Village*

SKETCHED LEFT: *Vogue Blouse #6360, 40c; Skirt #6361, 40c*

SKETCHED RIGHT *Vogue Dress Pattern #6354, 75c*

Mill Village

Spirit of '48

Stitch in Time

R. H. STEARNS CO. BOSTON 11 · MASS.

RHCo

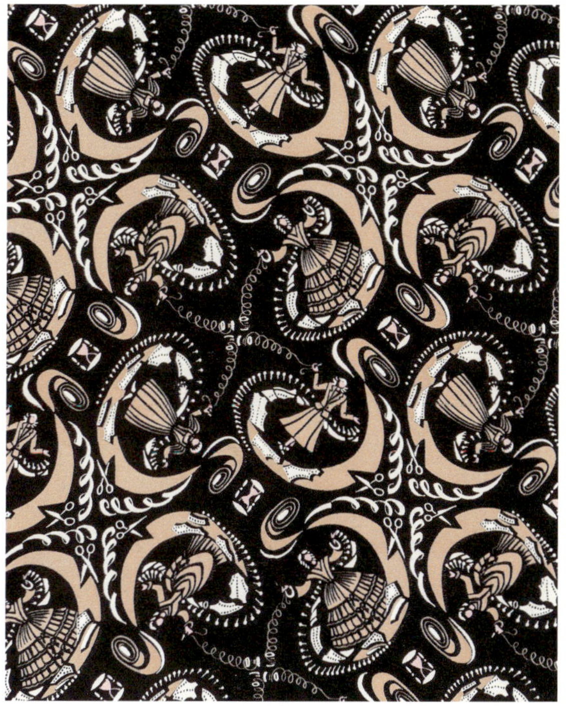

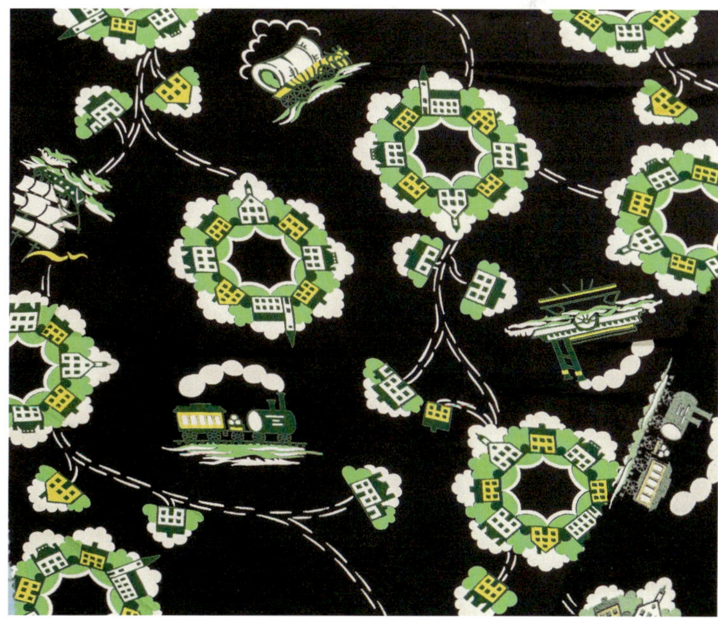

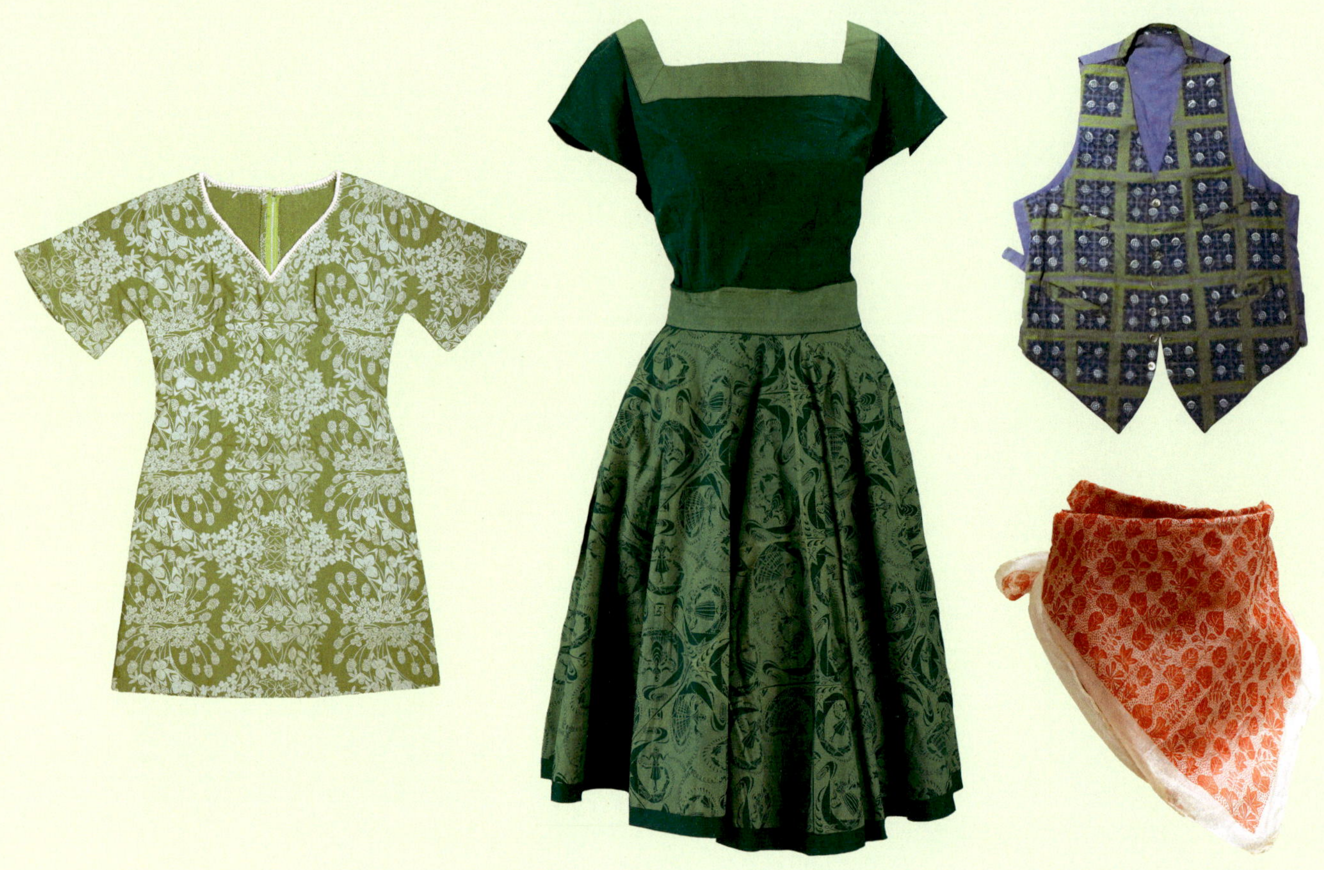

Hand-printed Fashion

The straightforward styles of the designers' in-house clothing items easily lent themselves to block printing. The write-up in the *Gloucester Daily Times* of the group's first exhibition in 1940 tells us that they had already started to produce clothing. The article specifically mentioned handkerchiefs, kerchiefs, scarves, and block-printed dresses with designs on "neck line, cuff, and borders, while a few girls successfully printed the whole dress."[76]

Over time the group printed dresses, skirts, peasant blouses, and bathing suits (see page 139) as well as bags and aprons. For children they printed skirts, pinafores, and bibs. One article mentioned "minor grumblings" among husbands that "the Covesters have never produced a male sports shirt, or even pajamas scalloped with shark's teeth."[77]

An in-house history states that, along with fringing, "only sewing can be farmed out."[78] Presumably, this rule was instituted because some of the members were more skilled with the needle than others, or for those who accepted a lot of clothing orders it would have been too time consuming to do all of the sewing. The group also sold packaged sets of block-printed fabric pieces for items such as skirts, children's pinafores, and dresses, which the customer would sew.[79]

CLOCKWISE FROM LEFT

FIG. 74
Shift dress made by Lee Natti, printed in her 1964 *In Clover* design. (Ink on fabric.)

FIG. 75
Virginia designed *A Stitch in Time* (see page 65) for William Skinner & Sons, but printed this outfit for herself on cotton, seeming to prefer cotton over the rayon that the company used. (Ink on fabric.)

FIG. 76
A rare example of men's clothing, printed in Peggy Norton's multicolored *Mulberry Maze*. (Ink on fabric.)

FIG. 77
An untitled, "lost" design by Peggy. She printed cards in the same design. (Ink on fabric.)

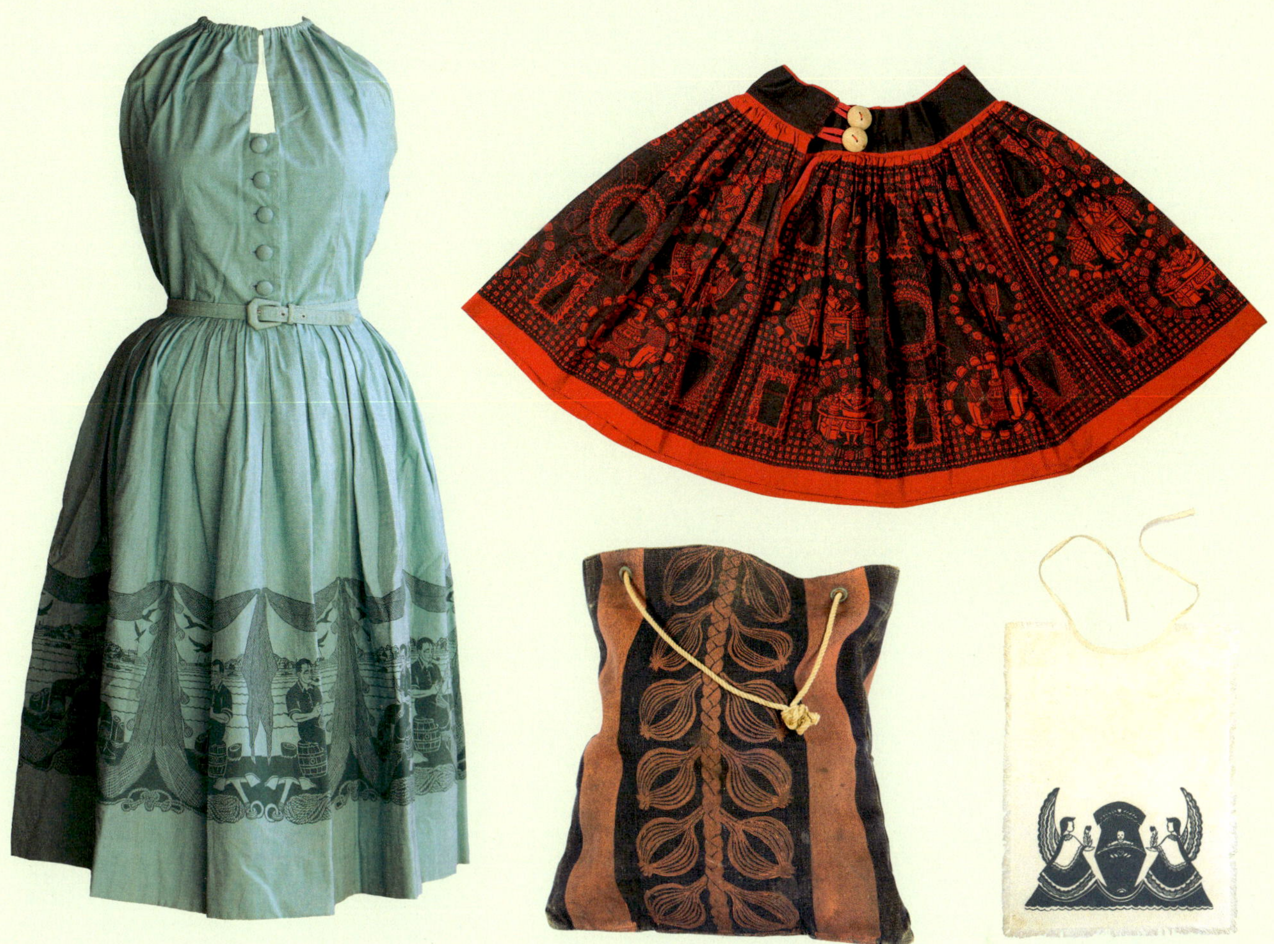

CLOCKWISE FROM LEFT

FIG. 78
This dress was made by Libby Holloran in her *Fisherman* design, likely for an exhibition opening. Her husband was the model for the male figure. (Ink on fabric.)

FIG. 79
***Baked Bean Supper* by Peggy as a children's skirt. The wooden buttons were a charming detail. (Ink on fabric.)**

FIG. 80
Lee Natti collected angels and designed *Little Angels*. (Ink on fabric.)

FIG. 81
A tote-style bag in Dorothy Norton's *Onions* design. The group had a few different styles of bags. (Ink on fabric.)

By 1945, a separate clothing jury was established. The clothing jury met "twice a year to decide on the models [styles], materials and prices for the coming season."[80] The rules stated that: "If a new model is introduced during the season the price should be approved by the clothes jury. If one designer introduces a model, the other designers should get her permission before using this same model."[81] For the most part the styles did not change, except for the addition of a shift dress in the 1960s.[82]

Designer Lee Steele commented that no one in their neighborhood would have been caught dead reading a fashion magazine.[83] World War II had brought about a more relaxed style of clothing for women and the style of the Folly Cove Designers was casual and practical. In the fall of 1945 Dorothy Norton wrote to staff at *Life* that "during the war years…" most of their clothing had been "printed on rayons but are more effective when printed on cotton."[84] Even when negotiating with William Skinner & Sons regarding a possible clothing line, the group wrote, "We are still hoping that you will be able to obtain a cotton-like fabric as we feel that the type of design which we like to do is better suited to this kind of fabric."[85] The dirndl skirt was a personal favorite of Virginia's; Lee Natti recalled how she loved spinning around in them.[86]

THE EDWIN M. KNOWLES CHINA COMPANY

In July 1950, the Edwin M. Knowles China Company telephoned the Folly Cove Designers. In a follow-up letter, Frederick Lawrence summarized that the company had contacted them in the hopes of adapting their designs as "dinnerware decoration."[87]

It was suggested that the group "make whatever distinction you feel proper between prices for existing designs merely adapted to dinnerware and prices for new designs made expressly for dinnerware."[88] Since the group used horizontally oriented 11x17–inch blocks, for the most part, even existing designs would have required a fair amount of reworking to conform to dinnerware. The company also indicated they were looking for designs that had mass appeal.[89]

The group promptly submitted twenty-six table linen samples of existing designs, but Dorothy told the company that the group members all had other employment and designed "because they like it, not because they are trying to turn out the biggest number of saleable designs possible."[90] She wanted to make sure that Knowles knew this since the group didn't necessarily work at the same speed as those devoted "to this kind of work on a purely commercial basis."[91]

After receiving samples of the intended plate style in order to get a sense of scale, the group submitted sixteen sketches in November 1950, which included Virginia's *Grand Right and Left* and *Dance of the Hours*. Both of these designs were circular, so the conversion would have been easier. Among the submissions were three versions of Aino Clarke's *Ash Tree* (a "lost" design), Louise Kenyon's *New England (Wild) Flowers*, Dorothy Norton's *English Daisy*, two versions of Hetty Beatty's *Little Farm* ("lost" designs, but similar to her farm-related designs as seen on pages 58 and 187), and Eino Natti's *Hen Party*.[92]

The company was quick to tell the designers that the initial sketches "have convinced us that you can produce designs that are well suited to dinnerware," but an issue with the company's stamping machine delayed production.[93] Ultimately the company only chose Eino Natti's *Hen Party*, introducing it at the Pittsburgh Pottery and Glass Show in January 1952 with samples in green and brown. They wrote the group that the other submissions "are either not adaptable to our technique of printing (chiefly because they involve too many large solid areas of color) or do not appear to be suitable subjects for volume sales on dinnerware."[94]

A formal contract does not exist in the group's business records, but it was the group's standard practice to request that changes to the design be made by the designer. As the group waited to receive the prototype, they wrote the company that "As we told you when you were here, we always make the necessary changes in any of our designs ourselves,"[95] but Knowles hired "a local artist" to make tweaks to the design.[96] The company felt "the final effect we achieved is a satisfactory one," but admitted that it was "different from the original rough sketch."[97] Upon receiving the prototype,

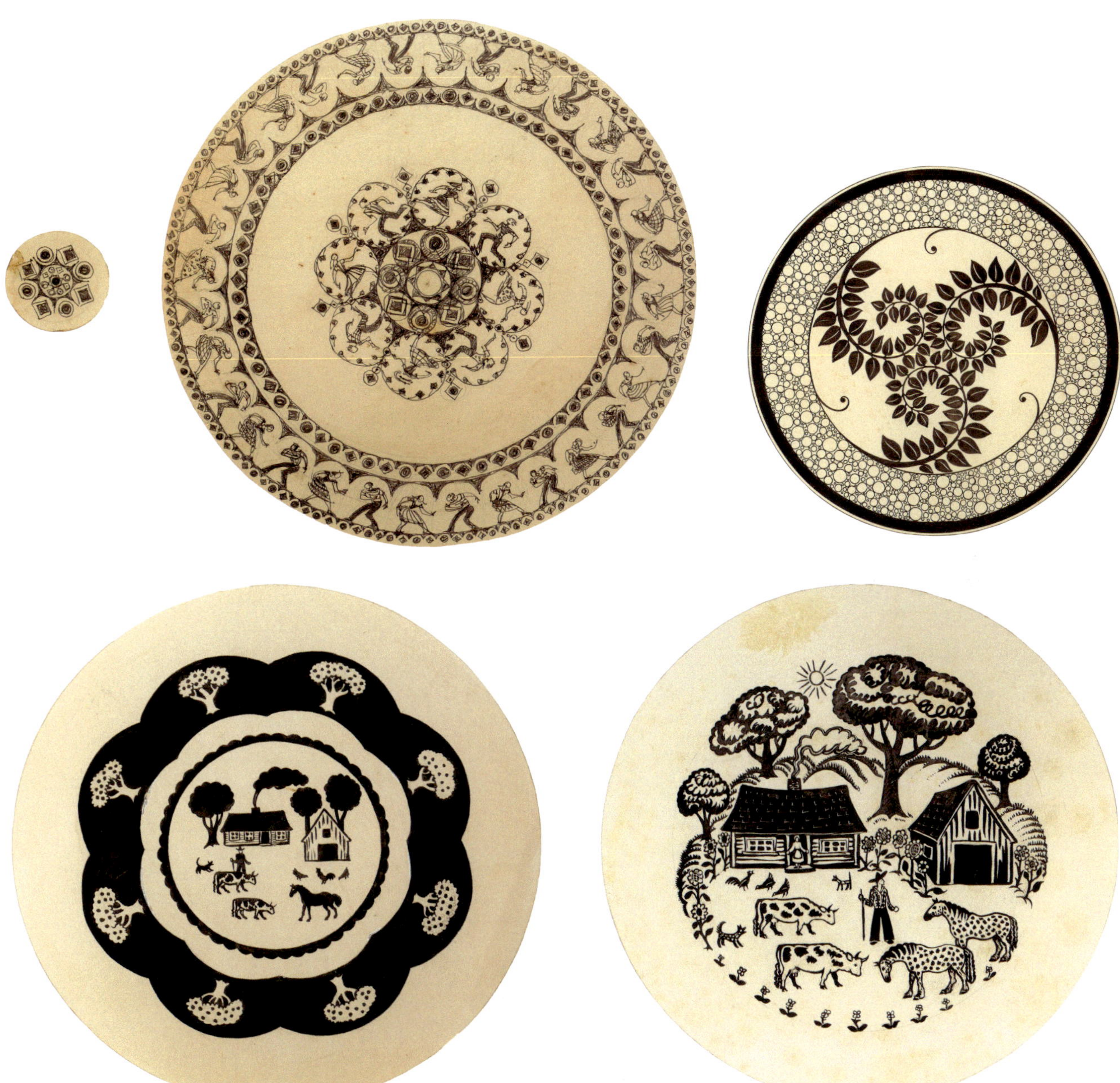

FIG. 82 (TOP LEFT)
Virginia submitted two versions of *Grand Right and Left*. One was the center of the existing design (see page 113). In this version she included two options for center artwork. She left white space in the center of the plate and added a more populated outer border. (Ink on paper.)

FIG. 83 (TOP RIGHT)
Aino Clarke's *Ash Tree* design is another "lost design." In an interview later in life she mentioned that Virginia displayed an *Ash Tree* design of hers in her studio, suggesting that Aino might have had another version of the design on which she based this plate design. (Ink on paper.)

FIG. 84 (BOTTOM LEFT)
Hetty Beatty submitted two versions of *Little Farm*. Although she created other farm- and horse-related designs, these two, along with *Farm Scenes* on page 58, which she created for F. Schumacher, are "lost" designs. This version looks similar to one section of *Farm Scenes*, though the house differs. (Ink on paper.)

FIG. 85 (BOTTOM RIGHT)
This design by Hetty hints at Virginia's *Little House* with bowed roof, trees, and sun. The least folklike of her work, the refinement might stem from her career illustrating children's books at this point, but still shows Virginia's influence. Hetty's signature spotted (polka dot) ponies are featured. (Ink on paper.)

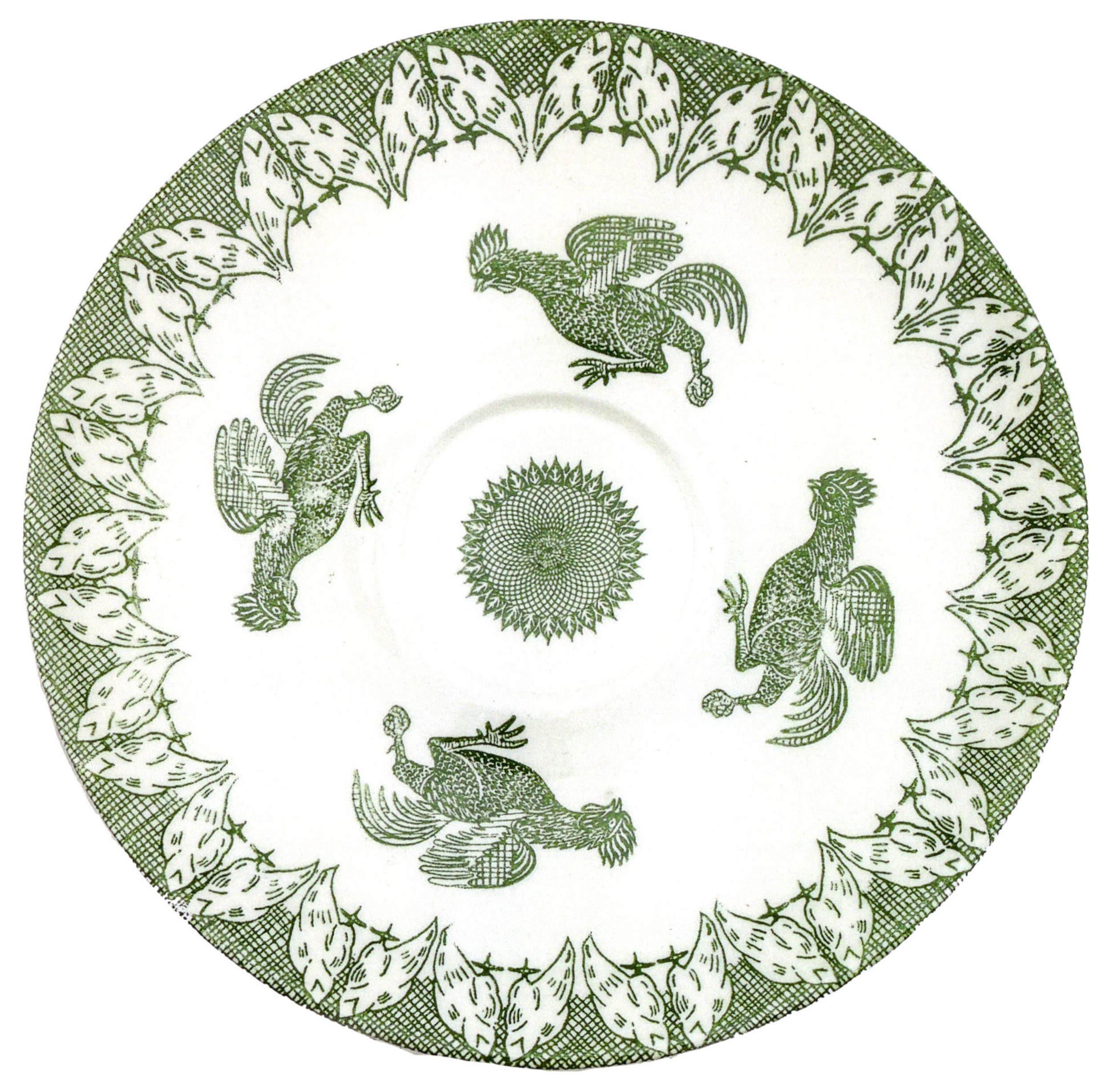

FIG. 86
A prototype saucer of Eino Natti's *Hen Party*, produced for Edwin M. Knowles China Company. A sketch of the original design does not exist, so it is difficult to compare the final results. The rim looks similar to the border of Eino's *Chanticleer* design (see page 143), but less crisp.

the designers decided that while "the sets are attractive... in view of the rather extensive changes to the design we do not wish to have the Folly Cove name on the dishes."[98]

Dorothy softened the response by saying that the sample gave them an idea of what the process entailed design-wise. She wrote that potential designs would "have to be very small in scale, but with a little time, this fine detail could be carefully and interestingly designed."[99] Members of the group used magnifying glasses to carve some of their designs, so this level of detail was certainly achievable; however, it does not appear that they submitted any other designs.[100]

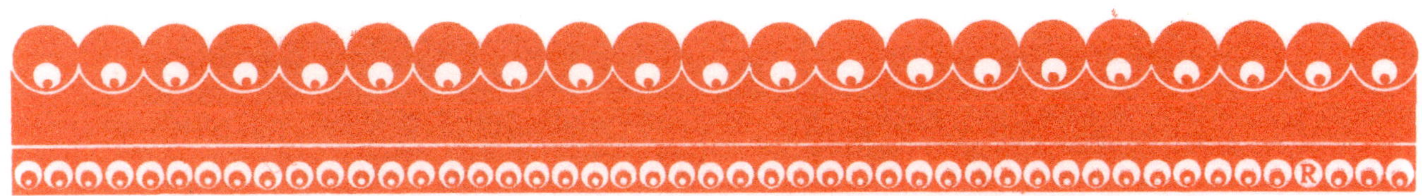

FIG. 87
The Folly Cove Designers' trademarked logo. Dorothy Norton said that Aino Clarke designed the labels and stationery, although perhaps she assisted with the lettering since Virginia seemed to have instituted the use of the circle motif.

TRADEMARKING FOLLY COVE DESIGNERS

The group began the process of trademarking their name in 1946, employing a Boston attorney to assist them. They chose to trademark both the name Folly Cove Designers and their signature circle border logo for added protection.[101] The group filed for trademark in 1947, ultimately receiving them in 1948.[102]

The issue of copyrighting individual designs had been discussed over the years with executives at both Lord & Taylor and F. Schumacher. They had been advised that it would offer them little protection, that subtle changes made to a design would allow someone to legally use it. Even their attorney seemed to feel that it wouldn't offer much protection.[103]

In 1947 the Folly Cove Designers felt that Louise Kenyon's *Head of the Cove* (see page 135) had been copied by a dress manufacturer and in 1955 Peggy Norton's *Potpourri* (see page 160).[104] Libby Holloran recalled that the group became aware of one possible infringement when a local woman showed up at one of the group's annual exhibition openings in one of the knock-off dresses.[105] In a letter to the offending company regarding Peggy Norton's design, Dorothy Norton wrote:

> We are... gravely concerned with the increasing number of cases in which our designs are being "adapted" and appearing as commercial prints without our authorization. In each instance, the subject matter is so peculiar to the experience of the artist that designed it that even the long arm of coincidence could not account for the similarity in the designs.[106]

Peggy's design was inspired by her herb garden and Louise's depicted her family and neighborhood. Unfortunately, the designers did not have any legal recourse as they had not registered their designs.[107] Due to these instances members began implementing a form of self-copyrighting where they printed their designs on paper, signed them and had them notarized, and kept copies in a safe-deposit box (although this is not a legal form of copyrighting).[108]

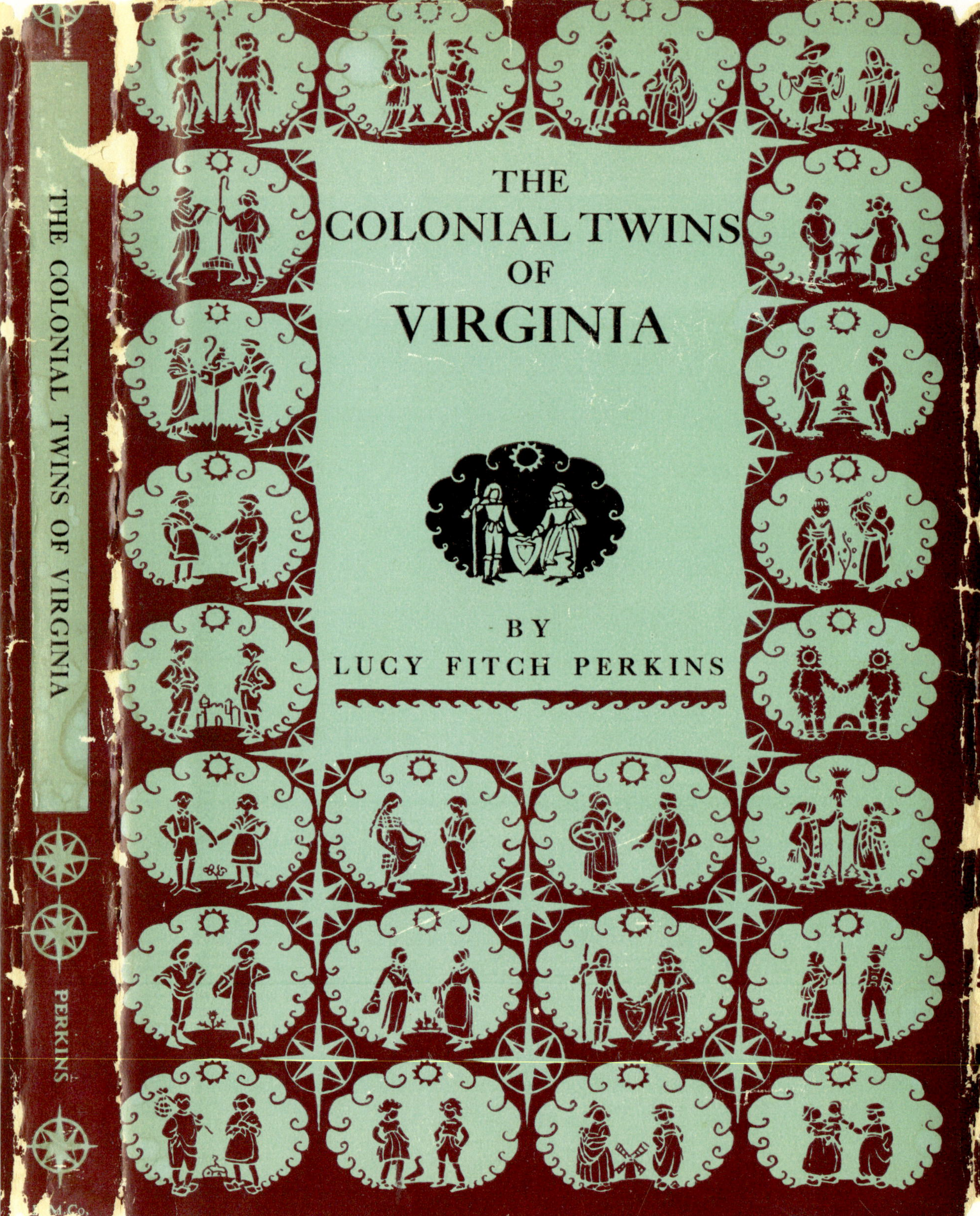
THE COLONIAL TWINS OF VIRGINIA
BY
LUCY FITCH PERKINS
THE COLONIAL TWINS OF VIRGINIA
PERKINS

PUBLISHING

FIG. 88 (OPPOSITE)
One of the Twins series by Lucy Fitch Perkins, cover illustrations attributed to Virginia. The covers vary in color schemes, but feature two people framed within a design, each cover representing a culture or historical time period. The signature Folly Cove Designers' wave pattern underlines the author's name.

There are two letters in the business records between Houghton Mifflin and Dorothy Norton from fall 1947 that make reference to cover artwork and lettering being done for book titles, including an edition of *Rebecca of Sunnybrook Farm*.[109] One letter mentions that "Mrs. Clark [*sic*] has been doing an excellent job on the lettering for the TWINS."[110] The group was paid $300 in December 1947.[111]

While a copy of *Rebecca of Sunnybrook Farm* with a cover designed by the Folly Cove Designers has not been located, the Cape Ann Museum has examples of the popular Twins series of books by Lucy Fitch Perkins that were illustrated by the designers.[112] It is thought that the illustrations might be those of Virginia Lee Demetrios, as they bear a strong resemblance to illustrations she completed under the name Virginia Lee Burton for a 1949 edition of Hans Christian Andersen's *The Emperor's New Clothes*. The inclusion of the sun is also reminiscent of Virginia's *Little House* design and her book *The Little House*.[113]

The group is credited on the inside of the back covers of each book in the Twins series ("Here are the Twins, printed again with attractive new covers and jackets, designed by the Folly Cove Designers").

COMMISSIONS

The group also took on special projects doing custom designs. Each commission was opened to the group and members were encouraged to submit designs, which often required extensive research. Usually the commissioning entity would ask for exclusive rights to the design for a specific period of time, after which the designer was free to use the design.

In 1959 Sturbridge Village (a living history museum in Sturbridge, Massachusetts) purchased two designs to be printed as table linens, *Old Sturbridge Country Store* by Lee Natti and *Old Sturbridge Stars and Lanterns* by Peggy Norton.[114] Peggy's design was one of her simplest and featured antique lanterns of different sizes arranged horizontally and symmetrically. Lee's was one of her more detailed designs. She said she was interested in the historic items, including barrels, baskets, teakettles, bottles, spice drawers, candleholders, spoons, jugs, and bed warmers.[115]

The Alumni Society of Smith College (Northampton, Massachusetts) purchased designs by Lee Natti (a Smith alumna) and Louise Kenyon in 1954 and 1955 for sale as coordinating napkins and place mats, respectively.[116] In an unusual decision for the group, they paid a Smith alumna 10 percent of the profits from this sale for acting as their sales agent.[117] Both items were first advertised by Smith College in 1955.[118] Lee's design *Grecourt (Smith College)* featured graduates pouring through the school's ornate gates and linking hands. Louise's *Smith College* highlights her architectural and figurative drawing skills, representing both the buildings and the women of Smith. Louise said that the design "was a very intricate cut, but I enjoyed doing it," including the research, which involved visiting the campus.[119]

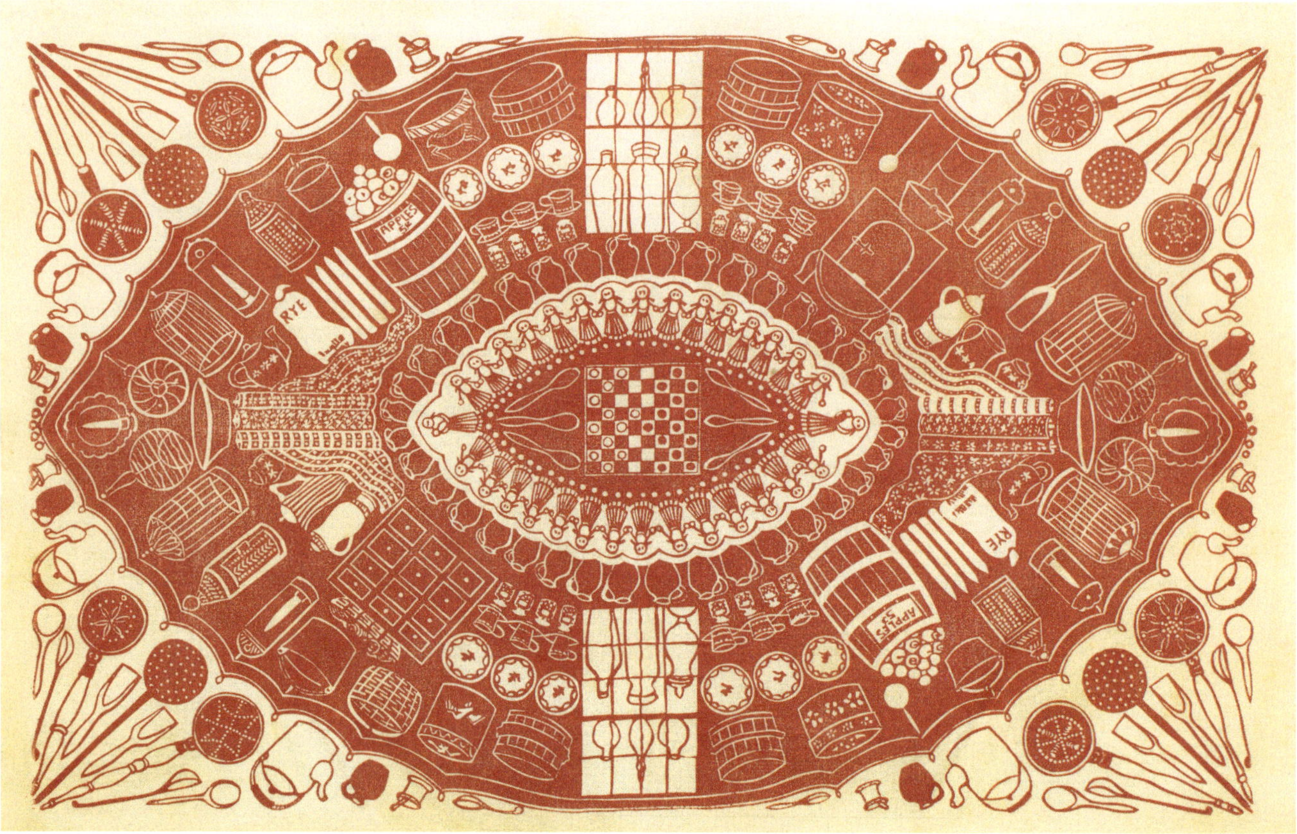

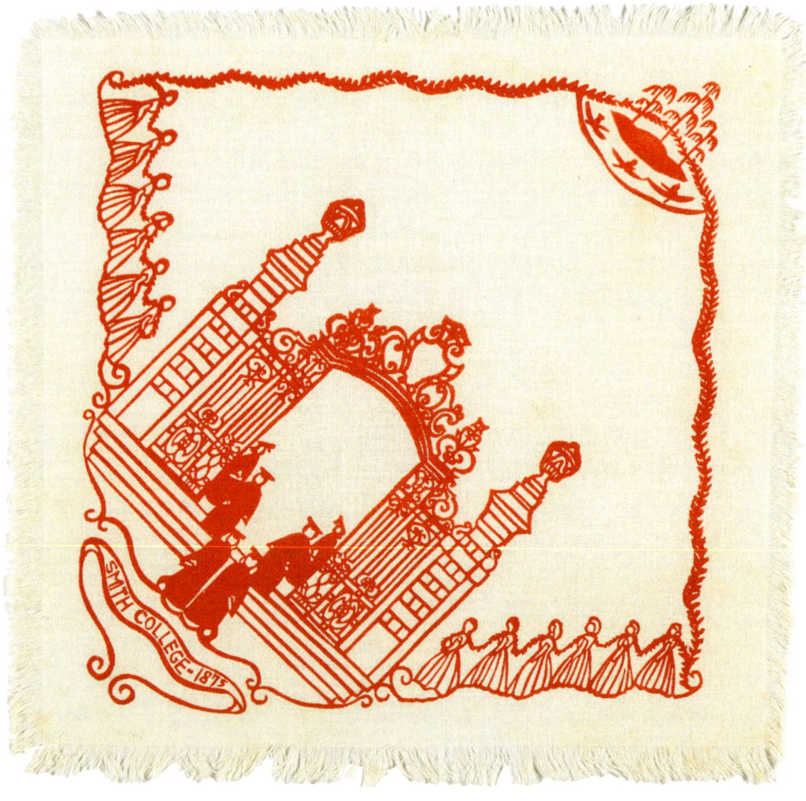

FIG. 89 (ABOVE)
Lee Natti's *Old Sturbridge Country Store* features historic items. Having an assigned topic was probably welcome since Lee said in an interview that she sometimes felt constrained in choosing a topic by time and her drawing skills. Lee used some of the same items for *Collector's Items*. (Ink on fabric.)

FIG. 90 (LEFT)
***Grecourt (Smith College)* was designed by Lee, who was a Smith alumna. It sold as printed napkins to coordinate with Louise Kenyon's *Smith College* place mat design. (Ink on fabric.)**

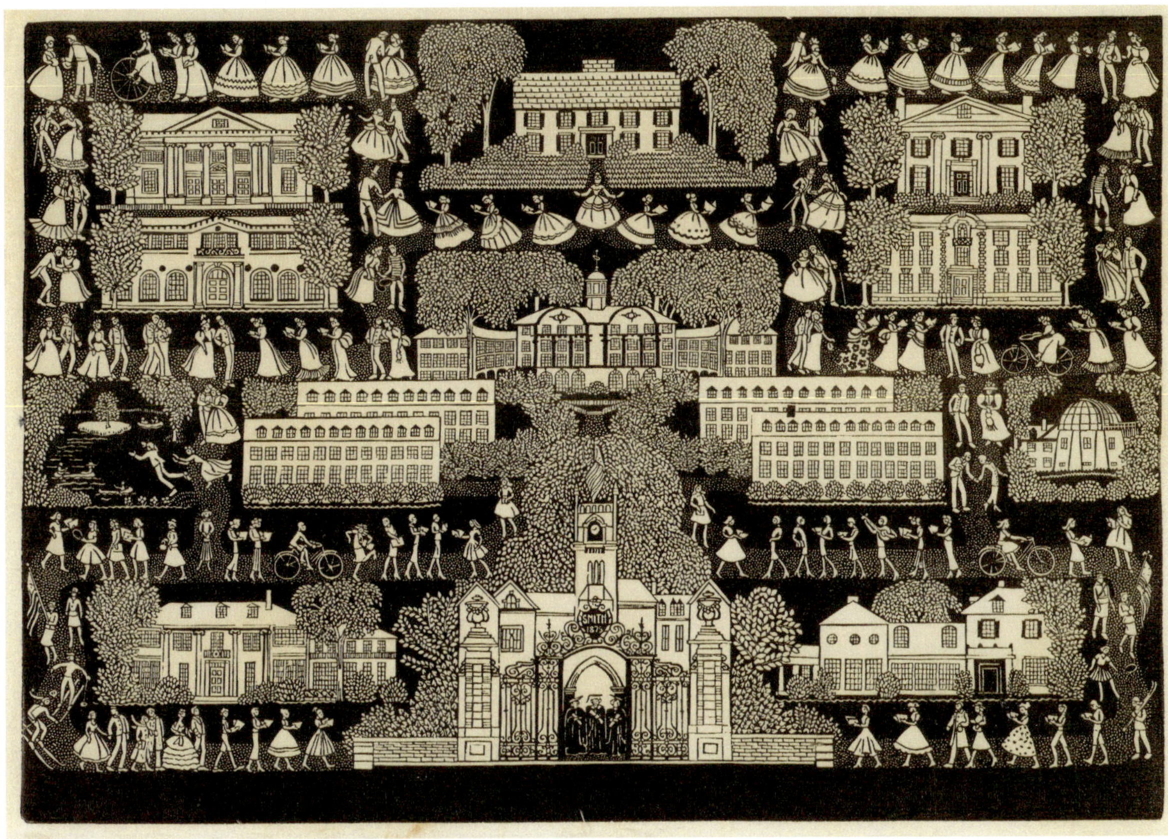

FIG. 91
Louise particularly enjoyed the research process for the costumes in her detailed *Smith College* design. Notice that she included the Smith tradition of women pushing their fiancés into the pond.

FIG. 92 (OVERLEAF)
Peggy Norton's thorough research for the intricate *Guernsey* made her want to visit the island.

As a lover of fashion, she particularly enjoyed drawing students from the various decades and their different styles of dress.[120] She also included some of the iconic campus traditions of Smith. Louise said that Lee Natti might have given her a few suggestions as well as another Folly Cove Smith alumna, Mary Maletskos.[121] Lee's and Louise's designs were advertised as "Smith College—Past and Present" and described as "The campus and students of today and yesterday, hand-blocked in fascinating detail by the Folly Cove Designers of Gloucester…Whether you did the Charleston or paddled on Paradise, wore knee socks or bustles—you'll enjoy these delightful designs."[122]

In another commission, Peggy Norton and Louise Kenyon submitted designs for place mats to the American Guernsey Society in Peterborough, New Hampshire, and Peggy's was chosen for use for the organization's one-hundredth anniversary.[123] *Guernsey* is a highly detailed design, the result of a great deal of research. Through a local veterinarian, Peggy located a Guernsey cow in nearby Hamilton, Massachusetts, and spent an afternoon sketching the animal since Demetrios encouraged her students to draw from life. She also visited the Boston Public Library to study the history of the island of Guernsey and to be able to infuse other historical details into her design.[124]

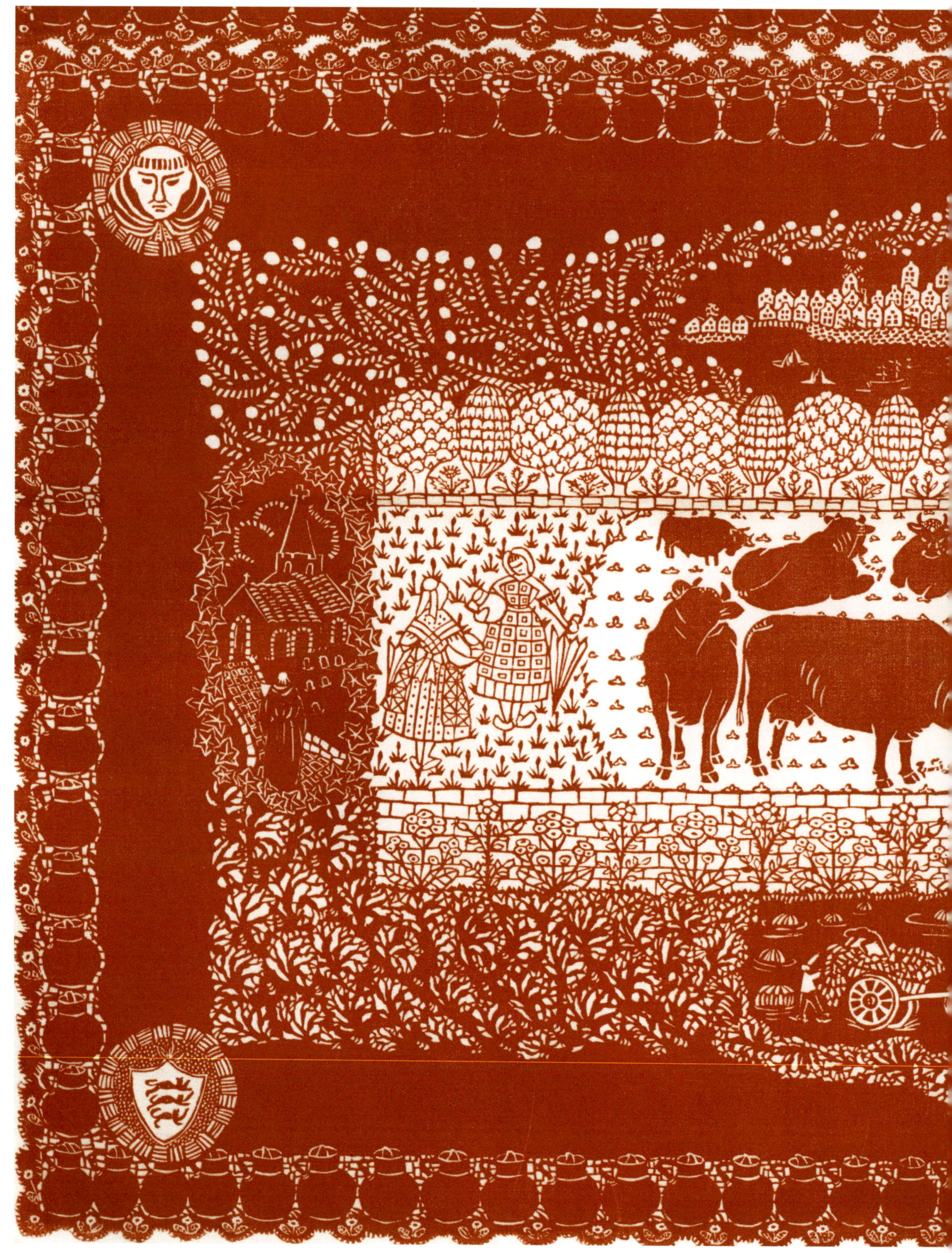

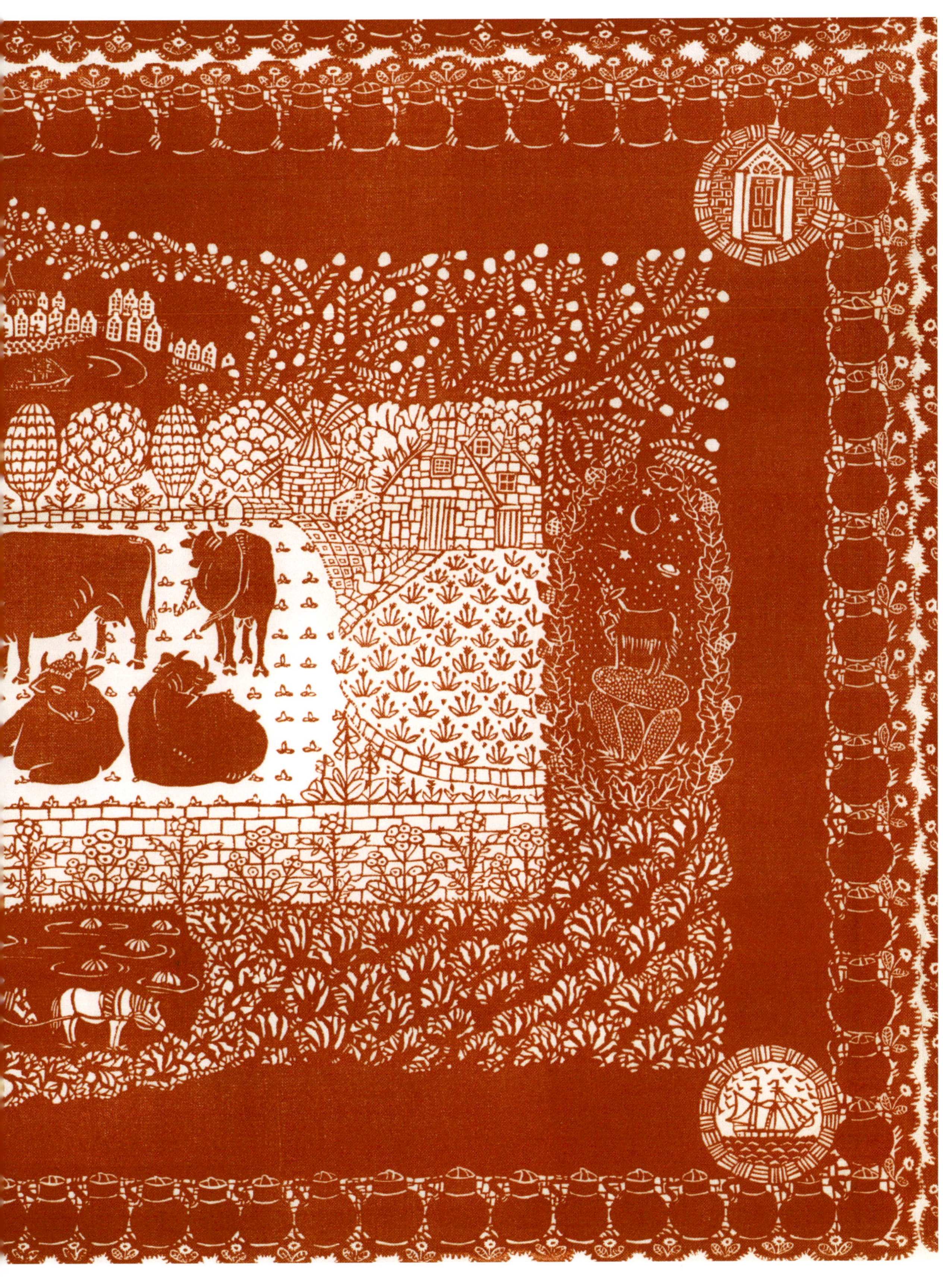

FOLLY COVE DESIGNERS FINANCES AND PRICING

Despite having "compromised with the age of the machine," even when the group licensed their designs, they retained the right to sell hand-block-printed versions of their designs.[125] At their peak, their work was sold at dozens of retail stores throughout the United States.[126] Two of their biggest wholesale clients were New York City–based America House (operated by what is now the American Craft Council) and Johnny Appleseed's.[127] Lee Natti recalls Johnny Appleseed's ordering a hundred sets of her work at a time for their catalog business.[128]

When Dorothy Norton became secretary, rules and regulations were set for the group, along with wholesale and retail prices for these hand-blocked pieces.[129] In 1945, the group stipulated that members would be paid the wholesale price for items sold and out of their profits members would contribute 1.5 percent toward a general fund for the group's operating expenses (postage, office supplies, etc.) and Dorothy Norton's salary. The difference between retail and wholesale prices went to "the Folly Cove Fund," and designers also contributed 5 percent of advance royalties from any designs sold.[130] In addition each member paid $2 per year as dues.[131] By 1950 the percentage that the Designers paid to the general fund seems to have increased to 3 percent (but their operating expenses had also increased).[132] Dorothy would order fabric for the group. Designers purchased fabric from her, but they were responsible for ordering their own printmaking supplies.[133]

Prices for their hand-blocked work remained modest throughout the group's tenure. Even though it would seem logical that hand-printed items would cost more, printmaker and craft writer Florence H. Pettit, wrote in 1955 that "Block printers cannot hope to make fabrics to sell at prices comparable to those of silk-screened or machine-printed fabrics. However, hand blocked textiles have always been valued as among the finest and most personal expressions of craftsmanship in the field of fabrics."[134] Lee Natti felt that since they were selling mostly utilitarian items that weren't meant to last forever that it made sense to keep prices low.[135] She felt that if they had come along after "the Marimekko impact" in the 1960s this might have changed things as Marimekko fabric was often bought to be framed or stretched and hung on the wall.[136]

Yet despite their pricing, the group's overall earnings were not insignificant. Total income (after the percentage paid to the Folly Cove Designers) ranged from about $1,700 to $4,000 per year for the top four earners, the equivalent in 2022 of approximately $20,300 to $47,800.[137] The group grossed approximately $16,000 in retail and wholesale sales in 1950, the equivalent of roughly $191,400 in 2022.[138] In 1960 individual earnings fell within the same general range for the top earners and the group generated almost $22,000 in gross retail and wholesale sales, or approximately $200,000 in 2022.[139] By the group's last year of operation in 1969, their busiest due to the announcement of their impending closure, the group grossed $42,000 in

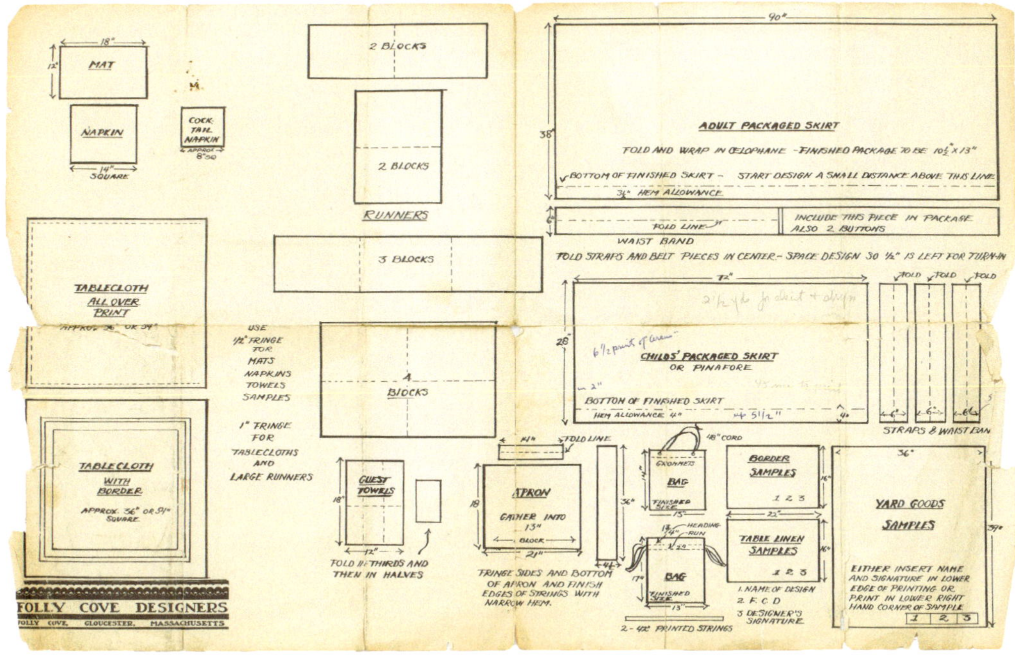

FIG. 93
An undated pattern for the group's product line with items ranging from packaged clothing to table linens, guest towels, and bags. The pattern dictates fringing and branding practices. (Ink on paper.)

retail and wholesale sales, the equivalent of approximately $330,000 in 2022, with the top earner taking in about $6,000 (or $47,300 today).[140] Despite paying for fabric and supplies, as one designer plainly stated, "financially it helped."[141] While most of the designers did not rely on the money as their sole source of income, the money was surely welcome.

THE UP AND DOWN SIDES OF BIG BUSINESS

The Folly Cove Designers derived more than just a financial benefit from their commercial contracts; they also received valuable advice that further supported their success. One of the first retailers in New York City to carry the work of the Folly Cove Designers was America House. Frances Wright Caroe (Frank Lloyd Wright's daughter), director of America House, helped the group settle on the 11x17–inch block size, which made economical use of the 36-inch-wide bolts of cloth they purchased.[142] Frances also likely encouraged their signature fringing (see page 74), as that was a popular style of table linens that America House sold at the time.

The support of Lord & Taylor's David Williams helped the group learn how to navigate the mostly male-dominated commercial business world.[143] (In some instances, initial correspondence to the group was addressed to "Gentlemen.")[144] The publicity that resulted from these business affiliations, particularly the 1945 feature in *Life* magazine, skyrocketed the group to international fame.[145] Over the years they were featured in *Woman's Day*, the *New Yorker*, the *New York Times*, *Christian Science Monitor*, *Better Homes and Gardens*, *Yankee*, and more. The Folly Cove Designers were often praised for their low-overhead business model.[146]

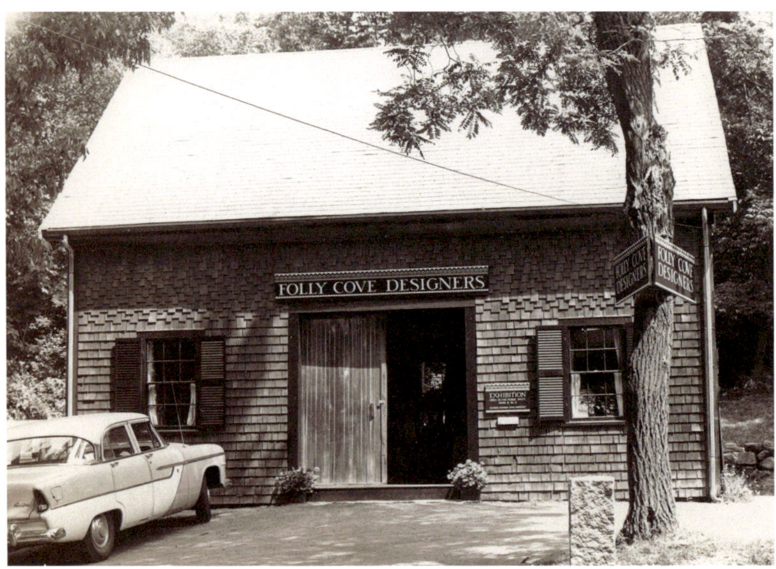

FIG. 94
The exterior of the barn. Likely that is Dorothy Norton's car out front. The sign over the door now graces the Cape Ann Museum's Folly Cove Designers' display.

FIG. 95 (OPPOSITE)
Mary Maletskos depicts the group preparing the barn for their seasonal opening in this 1955 exhibition invitation. The woman on the roof is fearless. (Ink on paper.)

Though the Folly Cove Designers embarked on numerous commercial ventures in their first decade, they did not sell their designs to everyone who contacted them. In an oft-repeated story, a Macy's representative told Virginia Lee Demetrios that if the group were to sign with Macy's and let them handle production, she could be driving a Rolls Royce instead of a Ford, to which she is said to have replied that she liked her Ford.[147]

And even if a particular business relationship was a positive one, the group was sometimes displeased with the results because of their incredibly high standards. Or in some cases, their rigid design principles did not lend themselves to the all-over patterns and repeats that worked well with commercial printing. They were also working with companies as the country tried to rebound from World War II, which meant they had to deal with fabric shortages or poor-quality ink and fabric. Lack of full creative control was also difficult for a group that wanted to be responsible for their designs from creation to printing.

Yet perhaps the most defining experience of this period involved Virginia. Walt Disney adapted Virginia's book *The Little House* as an animated short film and released it in 1952. The company used her storyline but employed other artists for the animation. Lee Natti described the film as "almost a travesty of the spirit of the book" and "one of the things that upset Jinnee most in her productive career."[148] This incident might have shaped Virginia's views regarding commercial contracts as the group seemed to stop seeking commercial work in the early 1950s.

THE RETAIL BARN

The establishment of their own headquarters and retail outlet in the Demetrios family barn in 1948 provided a steady source of income and made the group less reliant on commercial contracts and commissions. Dorothy

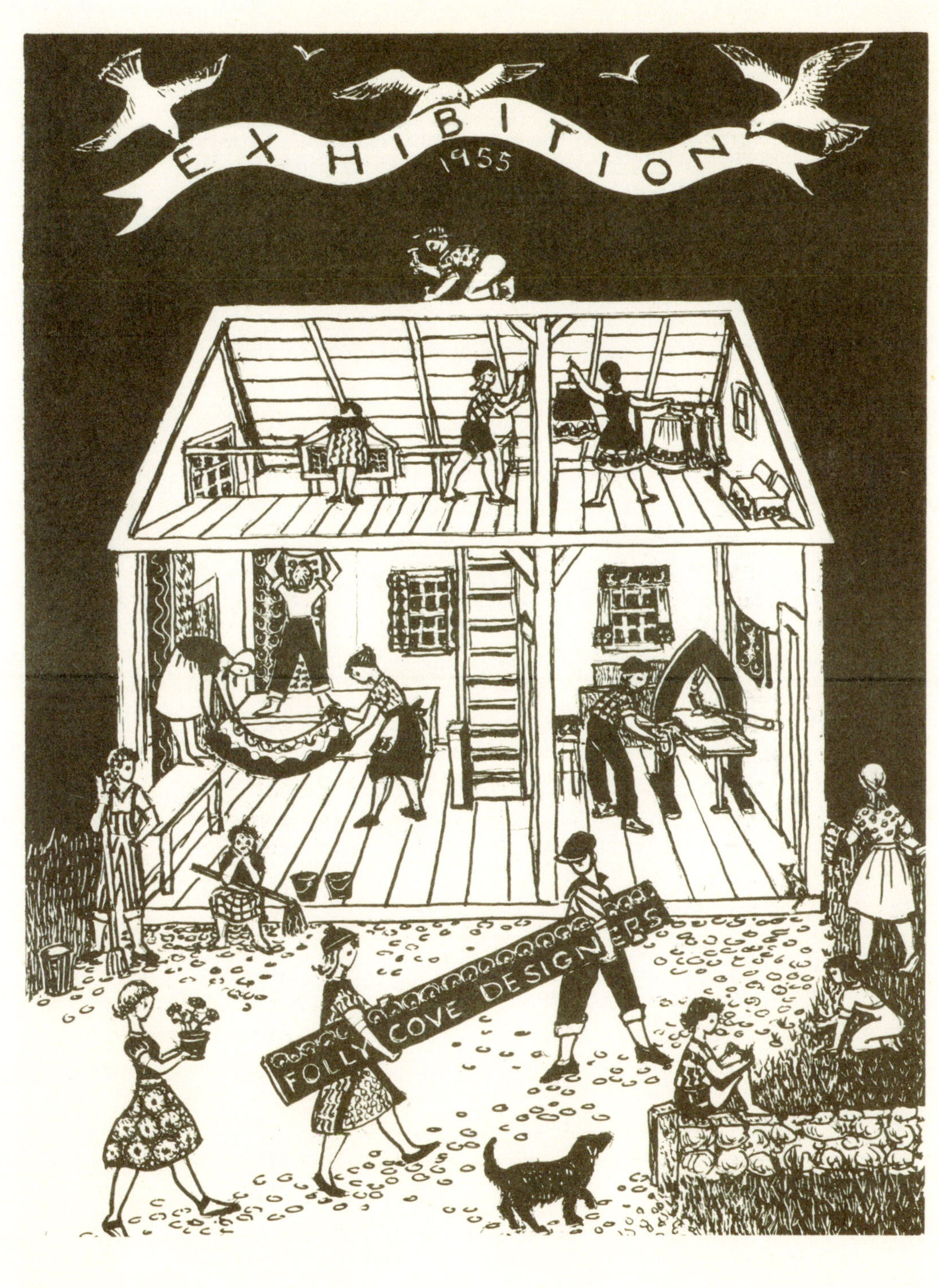
EXHIBITION
1955
FOLLY COVE DESIGNERS

Norton probably would have continued to pursue commercial contracts, but Virginia was against it. They respected one another but did not see eye to eye on this matter.

In 1957 Dorothy approached the group and, while not explicitly asking for a raise, she explained that she was still making what she was when she was hired in 1944 and had taken another part-time job to supplement her income.[149] She acknowledged the fact that while "some of the Designers still feel that 'Business' is a dirty word," that she had been hired for her business skills and reminded them that "no one in the group has more consistently and sincerely stressed the paramount importance of the design and the method in which the group operates to our friends, our customers and to the press" than herself. She outlined her specific contributions and explained that although it was still a part-time position, she was averaging forty plus hours during the months the barn was open. She suggested dividing tasks or to make it "a regular place of business, on a year round [*sic*] basis."[150] The group appears to have chosen the regular business option, as they expanded their hours and season at the barn, hired Eino Natti to help out part-time, and Dorothy stayed (seemingly exclusively) with them.[151] By 1960 retail sales were three times the income from wholesale accounts.[152]

From the outset the retail outlet was a success.[153] Eino Natti installed his press in the barn so that the designers could offer printing demonstrations. Interacting directly with their customers helped sales. While the group printed on fabric and did not sign their work, each designer personally labeled and signed the hang tags attached to all of their items. The group put a lot of hard work into preparing the barn to become their exhibition space and gave it a thorough cleaning each year in preparation for opening day. Lengths of fabric were hung to display the designs and a section of the barn housed their clothing inventory. Dorothy created tablescapes with the linens and added bouquets of flowers.[154]

The group had gained international fame but ultimately were happiest hand-printing their work and selling it through their own retail store, "the building, itself a gem of New England architecture" in the heart of Folly Cove, often welcoming hundreds at their annual openings.[155] As Virginia explained, "Our main interest is not commercial...we are more concerned with good design than anything else; but we always have more orders than we can fill."[156]

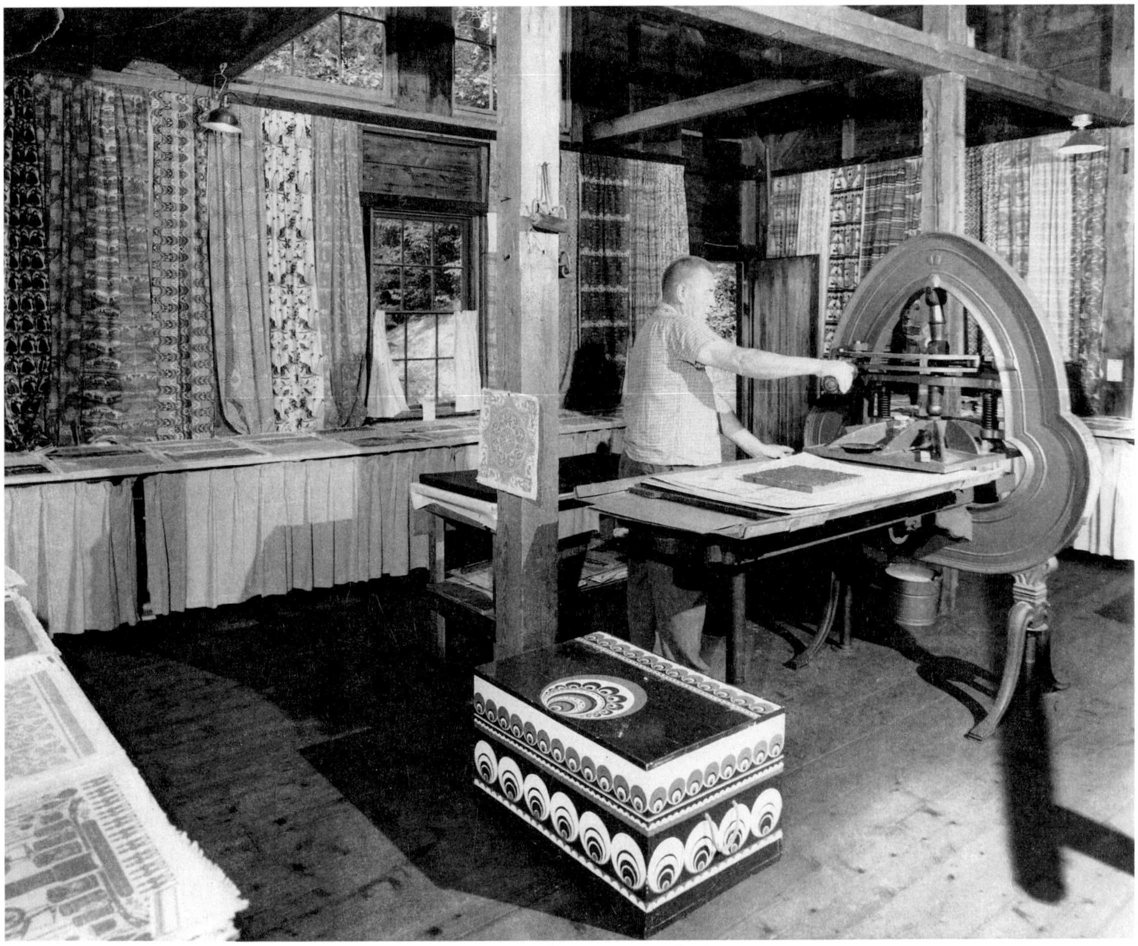

FIG. 96 (ABOVE)
Eino Natti using his acorn press in the barn with fabric swatches and textile displays in the background. Place mats were laid out on the countertops. (After the Folly Cove Designers disbanded, Libby Holloran used Eino's press in her eponymous shop.)

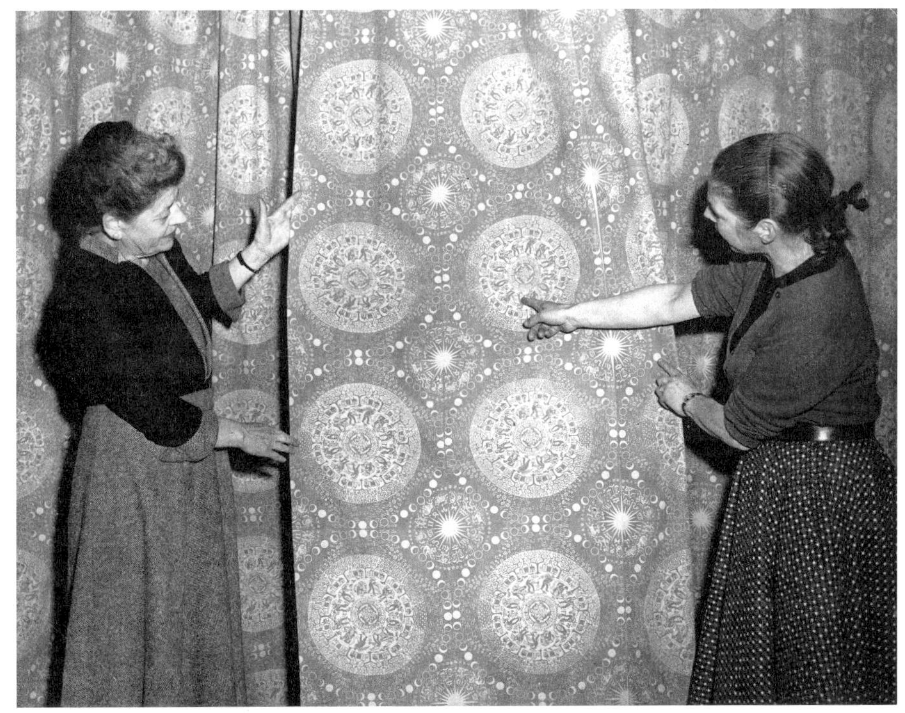

FIG. 97 (RIGHT)
Dorothy Norton and Virginia admire Virginia's *Farmer's Almanac* design.

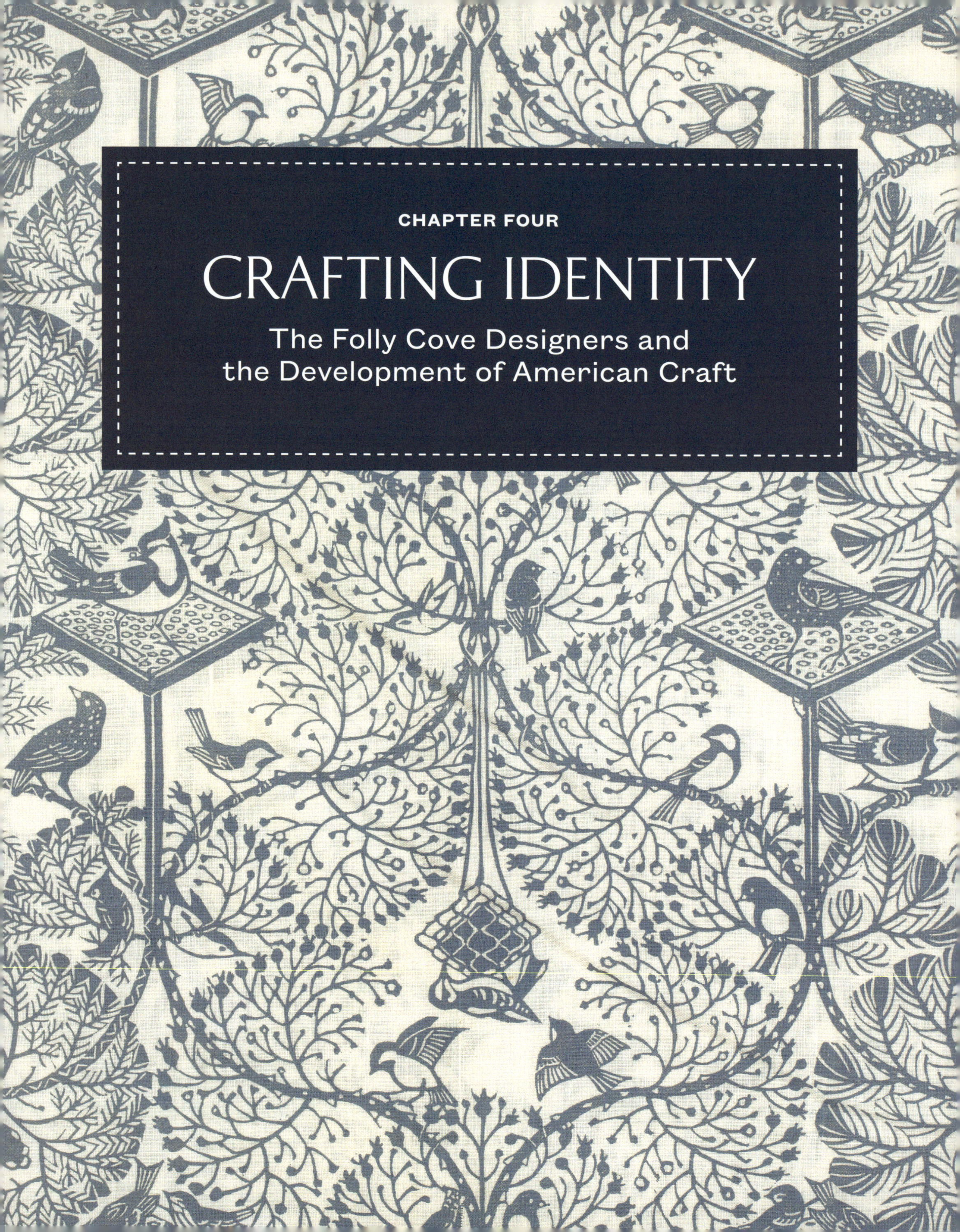

CHAPTER FOUR

CRAFTING IDENTITY

The Folly Cove Designers and the Development of American Craft

It is important to analyze the work of the Folly Cove Designers in the larger context of craft history. This chapter examines several of the craft exhibitions in which they participated. Although they were printmakers, because they printed on fabric, their work was often exhibited alongside that of textile designers at these events.

PRINTMAKING AND THE WPA

While the 1929 stock market crash plummeted the United States into the Great Depression, it also triggered a significant period in American craft history. As the country's financial situation worsened, Franklin Delano Roosevelt enacted the New Deal. As part of this initiative, several federally funded art projects were established between 1933 and 1943 that employed artists and provided arts training to unskilled workers.

Directors and administrators of these programs, as well as many of the artists who received aid and employment from them, became leaders of the United States arts scene and remained so for decades thereafter. The Federal Art Project (1935–1943) is one of the era's most well known and ambitious programs. Under the larger umbrella of the Works Progress Administration (WPA), it employed thousands of artists to create public murals, many still in existence today, as well as other artworks. Holger Cahill, an experienced curator and writer who had curated some of the first folk art exhibits in the field, was appointed its director.

The Federal Art Project included craft programs that varied in scope and focus from state to state. "Crafts were seen as a democratization of art, a program for fruitful leisure activity, as well as an antidote to the dehumanization of the machine age. Indeed, a kind of national therapy was pursued through these programs."[1] Linoleum block printing was a medium of choice for many federally funded programs during the Great Depression due to the inexpensiveness of its equipment. Milwaukee's block-printing program, part of the Milwaukee Handicraft Project (MHP), became one of the country's most well-regarded printmaking programs.

> Milwaukee led the country in textile block-printing workshops. This Wisconsin program, sponsored in part by Milwaukee County and the Milwaukee State Teachers College, was developed specifically for women interested in becoming self-supporting. Several examples of their work were shown at the 1939–40 World's Fair. The highest accolade for any of the programs was inclusion in the World's Fair; there, regional and local products, arts and crafts from the states, were displayed—visual paens to the American work ethic.[2]

The MHP drew upon significant support from the art education department at Milwaukee State Teachers College, led by faculty member Elsa Ulbricht and select students. From 1935 to 1942 the program "employed over 5,000 women and minorities."[3] Participants were of varied nationalities and many did not speak English. The WPA also sent many African American women to participate. Skilled and unskilled workers and minorities worked together, which distinguished this particular WPA program.[4] MHP included units in book binding, block printing, screen printing, weaving, rugs, appliqué, doll making, cloth toys, costumes, wood, and furniture.[5]

The MHP's block-printing unit grew out of its book-binding unit, which produced illustrated books and decorative endpapers. Like the Folly Cove Designers, the Milwaukee women printed wall hangings and draperies, but their intended market was public institutions such as schools and hospitals so as not to compete with the private sector. Unlike the Folly Cove Designers, who were "designer-craftsmen" and responsible for their work from design through printing, the Milwaukee block printers divided their work into stages and by skill levels. The patterns were designed by "designer-foremen" who were experienced artists (art students), while the design transfer, carving, and printing were executed by the workers, who initially had little or no experience in printmaking.[6]

"The MHP also gained public exposure as many high profile people visited the project, including Eleanor Roosevelt and Frank Lloyd Wright."[7] While there is no direct connection between the Folly Cove Designers and WPA-era craft programs, news surrounding the success of block-printing programs such as the one in Milwaukee must have made its way to Folly Cove.

While the MHP was a work program designed for unskilled women and minorities during the Great Depression, the financial effects of the Great Depression were also felt in Folly Cove, as they were compounded by the closing of the granite quarries so central to the area's economy. Virginia Lee Demetrios's design class created an avenue for creative expression for her community and a new source of income at the tail end of the Great Depression when most of the people in the neighborhood could benefit from such an opportunity. Beyond providing a source of income, Elsa Ulbricht designed MHP to educate participants and to make products that contributed culturally.[8] Working on a much smaller scale, Virginia had similar goals of imparting art education and upholding standards of design. Although it is likely that Virginia chose block printing primarily because she had studied printmaking in her youth, the low cost of the medium was one of the factors in the Folly Cove Designers' decision to focus on printmaking.[9] But in contrast to MHP, Virginia did not break up the work into skilled and unskilled tasks, but instead taught even the most inexperienced members to create original designs, which they would transfer, carve, and print as "designer-craftsmen."

THE 1940S: AMERICAN CRAFT ORGANIZES

An outgrowth of the Great Depression was Aileen Osborn Webb's Handcraft Cooperative League of America, established in 1939. Its goal was to serve as a national craft organization as the nation sought to create its own identity in the field of craft.[10] Aileen was an affluent woman with strong connections to the art world. Both her grandfather and father were supporters of the

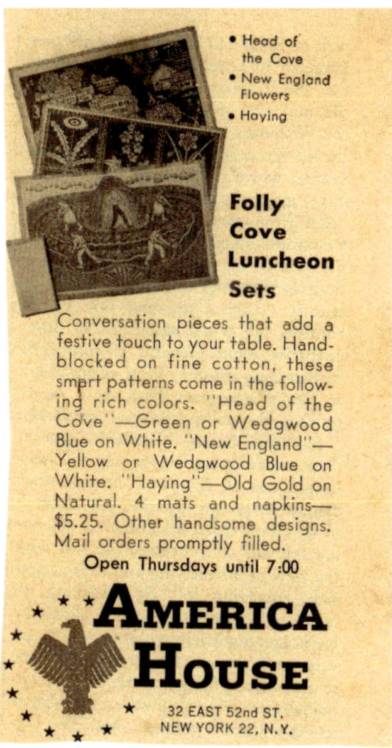

FIG. 98
This America House ad appeared in the *New Yorker* in 1952. It features three designs by the Folly Cove Designers. The ad refers to the luncheon sets as "conversation pieces that add a festive touch to your table."

Metropolitan Museum of Art. Her father served as the board of trustees' president from 1941 to 1948, and the family had amassed quite a remarkable art collection.[11] Webb's particular passion was handicrafts. Prior to establishing the League, Aileen had marketed the work of a New York–based group called Putnam County Products, including "agricultural products, quilts, pottery, and other handmade, traditional wares produced in rural areas to urban centers in the northeast."[12] She believed in the beauty of the handmade object and wanted to share it with the average citizen.

Aileen sought to "earn a position for craft within the art world."[13] As she had aspired to with Putnam County Products, Aileen's goal for the Handcraft Cooperative League of America was to make handicrafts available to the masses and offer "distribution channels for rural crafts in metropolitan centers."[14] In 1940, the Handcraft Cooperative League of America opened a retail store in New York City, America House.[15] Frances Wright Caroe, daughter of architect Frank Lloyd Wright, was named director.[16] As his daughter, Frances represented "an important link to established cultural capital in the United States."[17] Frances solicited work from artists and was the point of contact between them and the shop. She often provided advice on how to improve production and make items more saleable. In an unpublished autobiography, Aileen praised Frances and wrote that her "vision of the future of crafts was far ahead of mine."[18] Working together, Aileen and Frances ensured that America House carried only the best in the craft field.

From its inception, America House was one of the first retail outlets to carry the work of the Folly Cove Designers. Virginia wrote that in 1941 members, including herself, Hetty Beatty, Aino Clarke, and Louise Kenyon, met with Frances in New York.[19] The relationship between the group and America House was decades-long and prosperous, and established them as professional craftsmen.

The American Handicraft Council was founded in 1939 by Anne Morgan, daughter of finance magnate John Pierpont Morgan, a friend and neighbor of Aileen Osborn Webb. While the goal of Aileen's organization was to promote rural craftsmanship and create a marketplace for artists' work, Anne Morgan's group focused on the study of craft. The two groups merged in 1942, becoming the American Craftsmen's Cooperative Council, Inc.[20] In 1955 it became what we know today as American Craft Council and it played a pivotal role in professionalizing craft in America. "Under Webb's leadership the American Craft Council established the first of each type of North America's professional institutions for craft, including the retail outlet America House (1940), the journal *Craft Horizons* (1942), the School for American Craftsmen (1946), and the Museum of Contemporary Craft (1956)."[21] (*Craft Horizons*, which remains one of the preeminent publications in the field of craft, was renamed *American Craft* in 1979.)[22]

The Field of Craft During WWII and Postwar America

Just as was the case in the field of fashion, the onset of World War II in Europe presented American craftsmen with an opportunity to take center stage. America House was not just patriotic in name, but intention. For many years, and at two or more locations, the interior of America House was decorated in bold red, white, and blue, with the America House's emblem, an eagle, hanging over the door.[23] The red-white-and-blue theme was fitting, since during World War II, "America House was partially motivated by the patriotic idea of supporting through purchase goods and objects that were made by Americans, using traditional methods, local materials and historical techniques."[24]

Fashion designers, artists, and craftsmen were acutely aware of the importance of this window in time. In 1944 Hetty Beatty, on behalf of the Folly Cove Designers, was cited in an issue of *Craft Horizons*, assumingly in a response to a previous article: "We are glad you feel as we do, that the postwar influx of European crafts will not spell the end of the American craftsman. You are right though that he will have to work both hard and well to keep his present standing."[25]

To ensure this, during this same time Aileen Osborn Webb established a new branch of the American Craftsmen's Cooperative Council, the American Craftsmen's Education Council, in 1943. Aileen wanted to create opportunities for would-be craftsmen to receive training at American universities. In 1941, Webb's brother, Brigadier General Frederick H. Osborn, helped develop the U.S. Army's Arts and Crafts Program with the objective of "boosting morale and inspiring creativity in soldiers."[26] Aileen supported her brother's work and wanted to create craft programs for returning veterans. She quickly set about to establish the School for American Craftsmen in 1944.[27] The school was initially part of Dartmouth College in New Hampshire; it relocated in 1946 to Alfred University in New York State, then moved to its permanent home at Rochester Institute of Technology in 1949. The move to Alfred was precipitated by an offer to be part of a degree-granting program within their College of Liberal Arts and Sciences. "This affiliation with the university milieu was considered to be important for the status of crafts in the United States."[28]

Opportunities for American craftsmen expanded after World War II due in large part to the Servicemen's Readjustment Act, familiarly known as the G.I. Bill. Passed in 1944, it offered returning servicemen, many of whom had left for the war right out of high school, the opportunity to attend college or a vocational program. While university enrollments doubled and tripled in some cases, "few fields were changed as much, however, as craft."[29] Schools had to hire faculty and "returning GIs and other interested students increasingly had access to degree-granting institutions as well as a number of smaller residential programs of a shorter duration that were also instrumental in training craftspeople and propagating techniques in the postwar period."[30] Many veterans sought out the study of craft as the antidote to

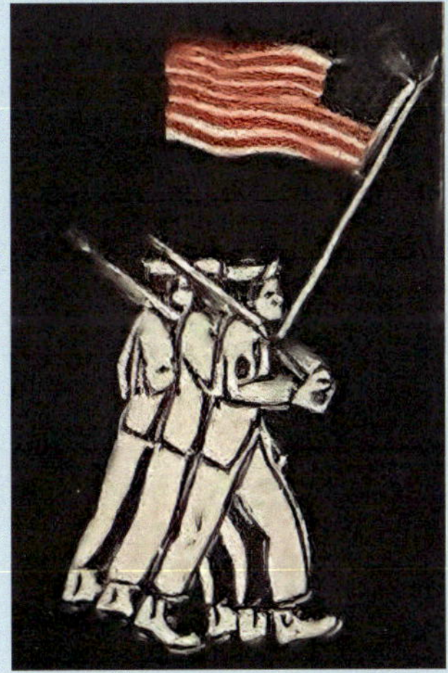

FIG. 99

An element from Eino Natti's *Pass in Review* design, this one with a colored flag. Eino produced several military-inspired pieces. *Pass in Review* is featured on the cover of Alexander Ross Burton's book *GI: World War II*, which Eino illustrated.

their battle-scarred minds and bodies.[31] It "allowed those who had gone through years of following orders in a rigid, compartmentalized military system to explore their creativity."[32] Folly Cove Designers Ross Burton and Eino Natti both pursued this path by enrolling at the School of Museum of Fine Arts (now part of Tufts University) upon returning from World War II.[33]

In 1945 the Folly Cove Designers were asked to participate in an international traveling exhibit organized by the U.S. Office of War Information. It is not known which designs were chosen for exhibition, but veteran Eino Natti submitted a military-inspired piece.[34] Upon receipt of their work the designers were told that "We think your designs are very swell, and as good a projection of 'Americana' as we have seen."[35] In later interviews Dorothy Norton recalled the exhibition as representing "what was being done in the crafts in America."[36]

Another positive postwar effect on craft was that Americans had more disposable income than they had before, enabling the average family to buy items based not just on utility but on beauty. National pride resonated and led to more interest in American-made products. An example of this was Dorothy Shaver of Lord & Taylor, who also served on Aileen's board of directors, with her dedication to American designers and her promotion of the Folly Cove Designers in the store windows of the flagship Fifth Avenue location at the end of the war in 1945.[37]

THE ROLE OF CRAFT EXHIBITIONS AND THE FOLLY COVE DESIGNERS' RISING REPUTATION

After 1941, when the Folly Cove Designers officially organized, they began to participate in exhibitions. A July 1941 newspaper clipping cites that they had exhibited at the Boston Garden for the 1st Annual Handicraft Show, at the Addison Gallery of American Art (Phillips Academy, Andover, Massachusetts), and at the University of New Hampshire (Durham, New Hampshire).[38] They also had a show at the Philadelphia Art Alliance in April 1942. A write-up reported that the group felt "that the creation of useful objects is as much as part of art as the modeling of figures or painting of landscapes."[39]

The first major fine crafts exhibit in which the Folly Cove Designers participated was the 1943 *Exhibition of Contemporary New England Handicrafts* at the Worcester Art Museum in Massachusetts. The works of Virginia Lee Demetrios (*Gossips*), Louise Kenyon (*Conventional Flower*), and Eino Natti (*Cockerels*) were exhibited alongside several artists listed as WPA Crafts Project members. Their names appear in the catalog, as well as "Folly Cove Designers."[40] The catalog introduction was written by author, speaker, and curator Allen Eaton, who became known as "the Dean of American Crafts."

In his introduction, Eaton stressed that the Worcester exhibition represented a second wave of the Arts and Crafts movement.[41] The history of American craft was greatly influenced by ideals espoused by the Arts and Crafts movement of the late 1800s when it made its way to the U.S. from England, where it originated. The movement was both a social and an aesthetic one that "aspired to reform not only the appearance of useful art objects...but also the process by which these objects were made, the environment of their making, and the way in which they were taught, thought about, exhibited, and discussed."[42] It opposed mechanization and promoted the unity of designer and maker. It encouraged the creation of communities of craftsmen that reflected their ideals. "Some advocated a return to medieval craft systems; others retreated to utopian communities; and still others established schools of design, sought new ways to organize industry, and initiated crafts philanthropies."[43]

According to Eaton, this second wave was more "democratic in the sense of much wider participation."[44] He also stated that "the present handicraft movement is largely rural, its materials and patterns are more local or regional, and its workers are a cross section of our citizens, old and new."[45] In order for the revival to really flourish, and for artisans to be able to make money, the rural craftsman needed to find a way to access the urban marketplace. Aileen Osborn Webb was determined to make that happen with America House.

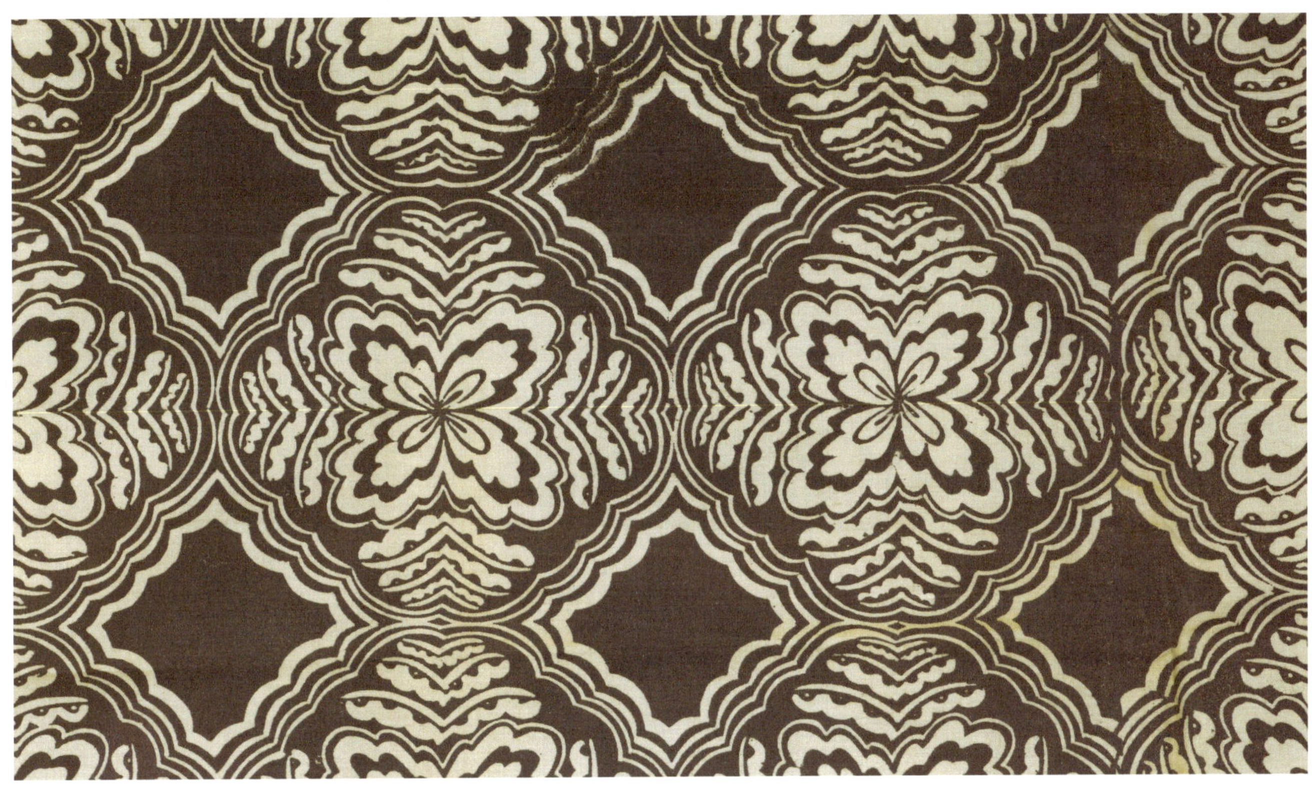

FIG. 100
Conventional Flower **by Louise Kenyon was displayed as wall fabric in an installation at the** ***Exhibition of Contemporary New England Handicrafts*** **at Worcester Art Museum. Here is the design in hand-printed yardage.**

The American Craftsmen's Cooperative Council expanded its offerings to include workshops "that would raise awareness and also train new craftsmen."[46] In March 1946, the work of the Folly Cove Designers was included in an exhibit titled *Print Workshop*. A write-up in *Craft Horizons* states:

> The gallery space was transformed into a working studio with the tools and materials needed for woodblocking, stenciling, and silk screening well arranged on working tables. The walls were hung with fabrics designed by Ruth Reeves, M. Wallach, Wesley Simpson, Inc., Folly Cove Designers, and Nini Turcotte. The graphic arts were represented by artist members of the Serigraph Society.[47]

It was an honor for the Folly Cove Designers to have their work exhibited with Wesley Simpson, Inc., and Ruth Reeves. Wesley Simpson, Inc. (more commonly referred to as Wesley Simpson Custom Fabrics) was one of the largest textile converters in post–World War II America. They produced their own designs, either in-house or by contract, outsourcing the printing. They gained a reputation for partnering with contemporary artists and had their fabrics carried in over three hundred stores nationwide. Illustrator and painter Marcel Vertes and surrealist painter Salvador Dalí were some of the artists with whom they partnered.[48]

Ruth Reeves was an American painter, graphic designer, academic, and textile designer who received major commissions and awards throughout her career. She co-spearheaded the creation of the Index of American

Design, which was an effort funded by the Federal Arts Program to document folk and decorative art in the United States. Reeves studied the textile arts of other countries and incorporated historical and global influences in her designs. She successfully partnered with many commercial companies and was regarded as one of the most successful textile designers of her time.[49]

The Folly Cove Designers had previously exhibited at the *Annual International Textile Exhibition* at Weatherspoon Art Gallery, Woman's College of University of North Carolina, in 1944 where Ruth Reeves served as a judge. The exhibition was described as "a significant event" that aimed, among other goals, to bring "the finest textiles in the world to a central place."[50] Hetty Beatty, Virginia Lee Demetrios, and Louise Kenyon had work in this show, although it is not known which designs.[51]

Dorothy Liebes was involved with the exhibition, although in what capacity it is not clear, beyond writing text for the catalog, suggesting that she played a part in the curation of the show.[52] Dorothy was an American weaver and designer whose "highly characteristic use of color, materials, and textures was so influential that by the end of the Second World War it was known throughout the country as 'The Liebes Look.'"[53] Wesley Simpson was also in this exhibition, along with weaver Marianne Strengell, a Finnish-born textile designer who was serving as head of the Weaving and Textile Design department for Cranbrook Academy of Art (Bloomfield Hills, Michigan) at the time.[54]

In 1949 the Council opened a gallery space within America House purely for exhibitions. The first exhibition featured the work of embroidery artist Mariska Karasz, including hooked rugs. Prior to this show textiles were "relatively unchartered [*sic*] territory for an art exhibition."[55] In February of 1951, America House hosted another printmaking exhibition similar to the one in 1946, titled *Recording Your Design*.

> In this showing, fine examples of wood and linoleum blocked materials, stenciled lengths and silk-screened draperies were hung on the walls, as were the blocks, stencils and silk screen equipment used. Among these some of M. Wallach's famous wood blocks, materials from the Folly Cove Designers, silk-screened lengths from the School for American Craftsmen, silk-screened pictures and cards supplied by the National Serigraph Society. Each week saw four mornings devoted to demonstrations with observer participation for which an admission of $1.00 was charged. These demonstrations were conducted by E. Natte [*sic*] of the Folly Cove Designers, blocking. Bernard Steffen of the National Serigraph Society, in silkscreen on paper. Mrs. Edith Roberts, silk-screening on materials, and Miss Mary Frances Burns, a representative of the American Craft Council.[56]

Following the exhibition, Eino Natti published an article in *Craft Horizons* titled "Folly Cove Blockprinting," where he outlined the group's process.

In 1947 the Folly Cove Designers participated in an exhibition of hand-printed textiles at the Print Club in Philadelphia (now the Print Center) along with three other groups. Given Folly Cove's long history with Philadelphia artists, including George Demetrios's association with Charles Grafly (his daughter, Dorothy Grafly, wrote a history of The Print Club in 1929), it is not surprising that they exhibited here.[57]

The Print Club, which was founded in 1915, describes its mission as building "understanding and appreciation for marginalized media. Until the 1940's [*sic*] printmaking was not regarded with equal importance as painting and sculpture."[58]

In his seminal 1949 text *Handicrafts of New England*, Allen Eaton recognized the Folly Cove Designers as printmakers. The book is based on the survey of New England crafts that Allen conducted from 1941 to 1948. His work has been posthumously criticized for including "folk arts and hobbies."[59] Despite this, Allen's scholarship remains the most extensive documentation of individual craftsmen and craft groups in America through the late 1940s. In his survey, Allen sang the praises of the Folly Cove Designers, writing, "Among the best-known blockprinters of our country are the Folly Cove Designers."[60]

THE 1950S: THE RISE OF CRAFT IN POSTWAR AMERICA

Post–World War II America became home to many European artists, who introduced the use of new materials and pushed the boundaries of their mediums. During this time "organizations and benefactors began to connect these disparate actors into a unified community of craftspeople."[61]

In 1953 the American Craftsmen's Council (it would change its name to American Crafts Council in 1969) hosted *Designer-Craftsmen, U.S.A.*, a major national exhibit that featured "the work of top craftspeople from across the United States."[62] The show traveled to ten major U.S. museums, making its debut at the Brooklyn Museum, then continuing on to the Art Institute of Chicago and the San Francisco Museum of Art. After these venues, the exhibition traveled for one year under the umbrella of the American Federation of the Arts.[63] The exhibit was "considered the first national survey of contemporary crafts in the United States" and "was intended to impress the U.S. public with the highest quality of crafts available in the United States."[64] It featured the work of 203 craftsmen, including the Folly Cove Designers.[65]

An open call to all craftsmen was broadcast throughout the country since the purpose of the exhibit was to gain an understanding of the regional development of crafts in the United States. Representatives from museums in each region of the United States assisted in the screening process, along with the members of the executive committee, of which Aileen Osborn Webb was one.[66] *Winter Boarders* by Virginia Lee Demetrios and *Cranberry Bog* by Peggy Norton were selected for inclusion in the exhibition and listed for

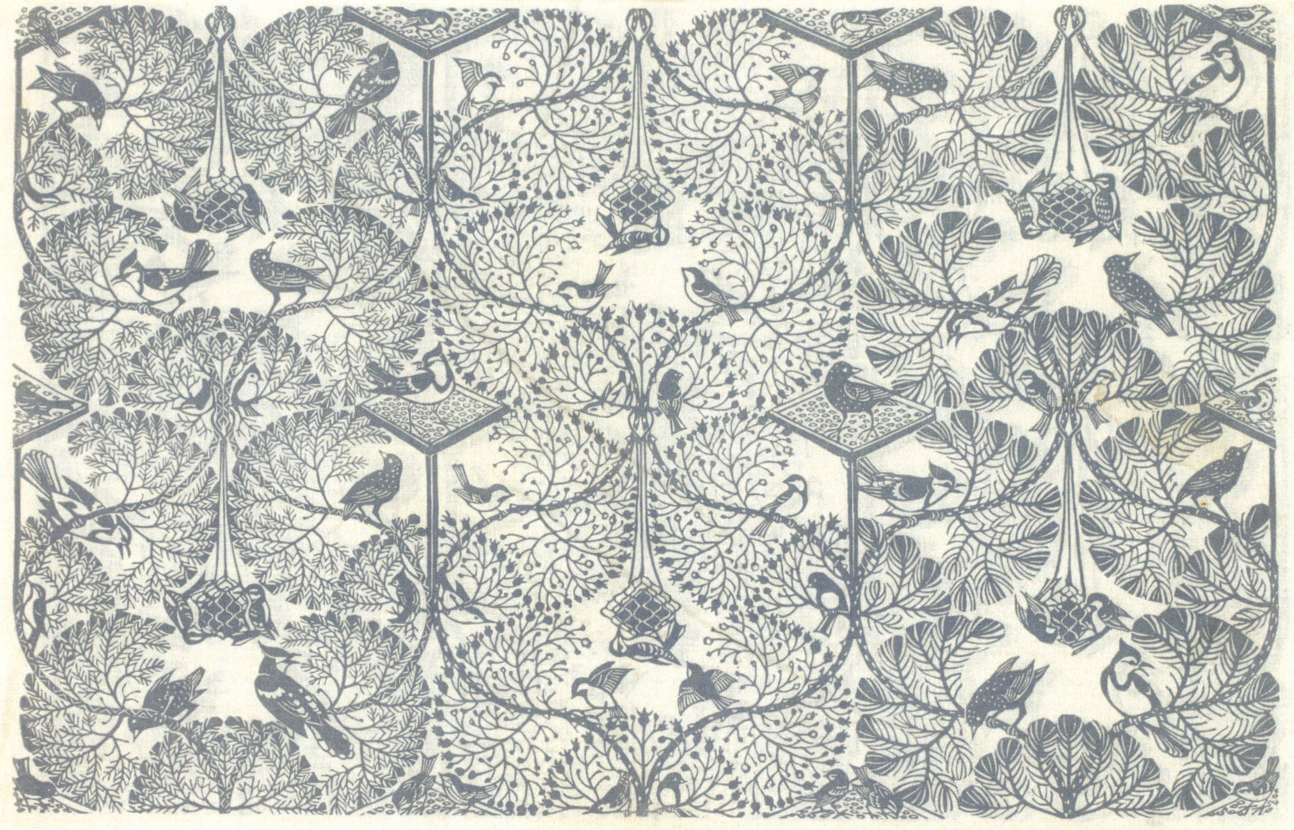

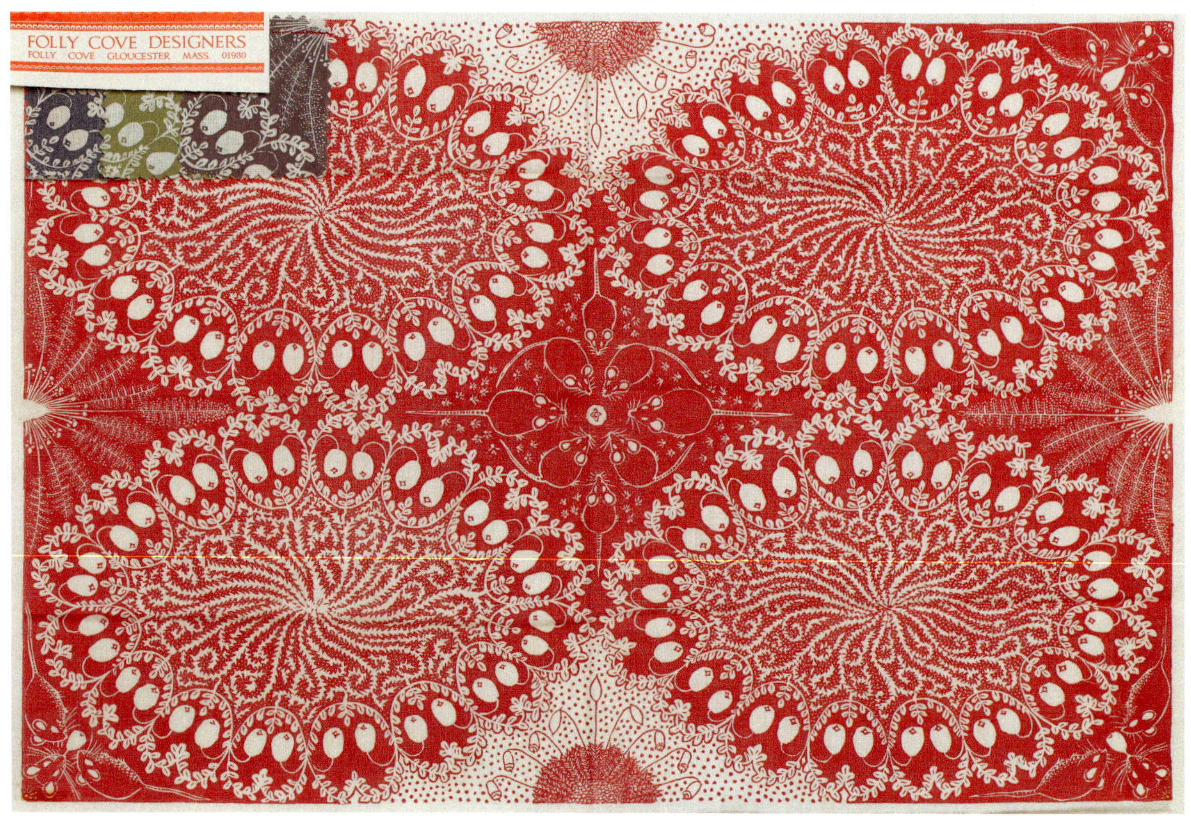
FOLLY COVE DESIGNERS
FOLLY COVE GLOUCESTER MASS. 01930

FIG. 101 (OPPOSITE TOP)
Virginia did extensive research on birds and winter foliage. She created many drafts before completing the intricately carved *Winter Boarders*.

FIG. 102 (OPPOSITE BOTTOM)
Peggy Norton's *Cranberry Bog* is extremely detailed. Peggy said that she fed mice sunflower seeds in order to be able to sketch them properly. The oval shape of their ears is reflected through the patterning of the design. The swatches show the colors in which the design was printed.

sale. Their work was exhibited alongside other major names in the textile field, such as Ruth Reeves and Ruth Adler-Schnee, who began her career as a screen printer and transitioned to weaving. She was one of the first women to graduate from Cranbrook Academy of Art with an MFA in design.[67]

The main catalog essay, titled "The Craftsman in America," used the popular term *designer craftsmen* and defined it as representing "those workers in a craft who design their own pieces."[68] This was a term with which the Folly Cove Designers identified. The essay dealt with many issues regarding contemporary crafts, such as what constituted mass production and how craft could improve the quality of daily life. It stressed that the craftsman must be a part of the community because "the presence of the craftsman enriches the community life, and the craftsmen themselves are invigorated by contact with men and women of other professions and occupations," which was happening in Folly Cove.[69] This essay was representative of many of the issues with which the Folly Cove Designers dealt, such as the group's decision to cut back on mechanization and commercial contracts, their desire to make items for everyday use, and their belief that community was at the heart of their enterprise.

As the first national craft exhibition of its scale, and an innovation of Aileen Osborn Webb, the exhibit was designed to foster discussion and interaction between artists, because "if the solitary craftsmen across the country were spokes in need of a hub, they found it in Aileen Osborn Webb."[70] This hub extended to the creation of national craft conferences beginning in 1957. The second annual conference was titled "Dimension of Design" and discussed "discipline and freedom, vision and individual response and external pressures on creativity."[71] The Folly Cove Designers were mentioned at this conference by panel moderator, author, and printmaker Florence H. Pettit as the "one well-known studio" that used block printing over silk-screen printing for large orders.[72] Florence's own work during the 1950s resembled that of the Folly Cove Designers. She was correct that the group was exclusively hand block printing at this point.

The group submitted work for a 1954 exhibit hosted by the Massachusetts Association of Handicraft Groups.[73] Virginia Lee Demetrios's *Winter Boarders* and Dorothy Norton's *Signs of Spring* were requested in the form of place mats. The final exhibition also included Elizabeth Iarrobino's *Turtles* and Eino Natti's *Yo Heave Ho*. Only two other printmakers were included in the textile section; the balance were weavers.[74]

Eight members of the group took part in the New England craft exhibition of 1955 at Worcester Art Museum. The jury selection committee chose from a total of 451 entries submitted by 165 New England–based craftsmen.[75] The Folly Cove designs that were selected included: Aino Clarke's *Little Rooster*s; Virginia Lee Demetrios's *Dance of the Hours*, *Farmer's Almanac*, *Reducing*, and *Zaidee and Her Kittens* (*Zaidee and Her Kittens* was also featured in the catalog); Elizabeth Iarrobino's *Horse Chestnut* and *Sandpipers*; Louise Kenyon's *Smith College*; *New England Farm*, *Polyphemus,* and *Rooster Parade* by Eino Natti; *Snow Storm* by Lee Natti; Dorothy Norton's *Onions*, *Vegetables*, and *Ad Infinitum;* and Peggy Norton's *Potpourri* and *Busy Bee*.

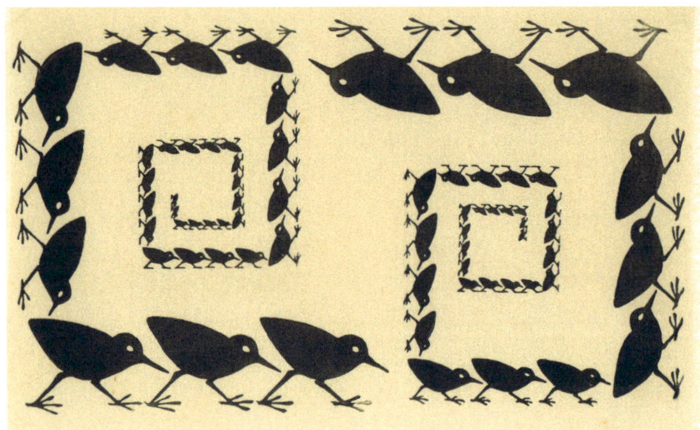

FIG. 103
Elizabeth Iarrobino, an avid bird watcher and beach lover, emphasizes Virginia's lessons in size in *Sandpipers*, which features the bird in ten different sizes.

Selections from the exhibition traveled with the Smithsonian Institution Traveling Exhibition Service throughout the U.S.; representing the Folly Cove Designers were *New England Farm*, *Horse Chestnut*, *Onions*, and *Zaidee and Her Kittens*.[76] The items that were part of the exhibit were also for sale. Dorothy's *Onions* sold and she had to send another set of place mats and napkins to replace it.[77]

The group also participated in the annual exhibition of the Massachusetts Association of Handicraft Groups in 1956, which was installed at the Society of Arts and Crafts in Boston. Virginia Lee Demetrios's *Winter Boarders*, Eino Natti's *Flora and Fauna,* and Peggy Norton's multicolored *Hearts and Flowers* were included.[78]

THE 1960S: EXPERIMENTATION IN CRAFT AND THE END OF AN ERA

As more opportunities for exhibiting emerged, a new type of artwork, called "exhibition work," developed, in contrast to purely utilitarian pieces. The craft field entered a phase of "intense experimentation."[79] The term *designer-craftsman* was replaced by *artist-craftsman* or *object maker*.[80] Technology propelled this period of rapid change. Equipment became smaller and more affordable, allowing more access to craft and an overall democratization of the field. "Miniaturization [of tools] could make any space a craft studio, from garage or workshop to a table in the living room."[81]

Despite being one of the older members of the group, Peggy Norton was one of the most adventurous. Peggy had previous experience screen printing, but she and her sister, Dorothy, experimented with silk-screening together in the 1940s.[82] In a letter to a Lord & Taylor executive, Dorothy wrote, "Inspired by your enthusiasm, my sister and I have been struggling with screen printing. I think if anyone stuck to it they could work up a technique as interesting as block printing."[83] Peggy submitted a silk screen–printed version of her design *Cucumber Vine* to William Skinner & Sons for consideration in 1949.[84] But Peggy later stated that silk screening was

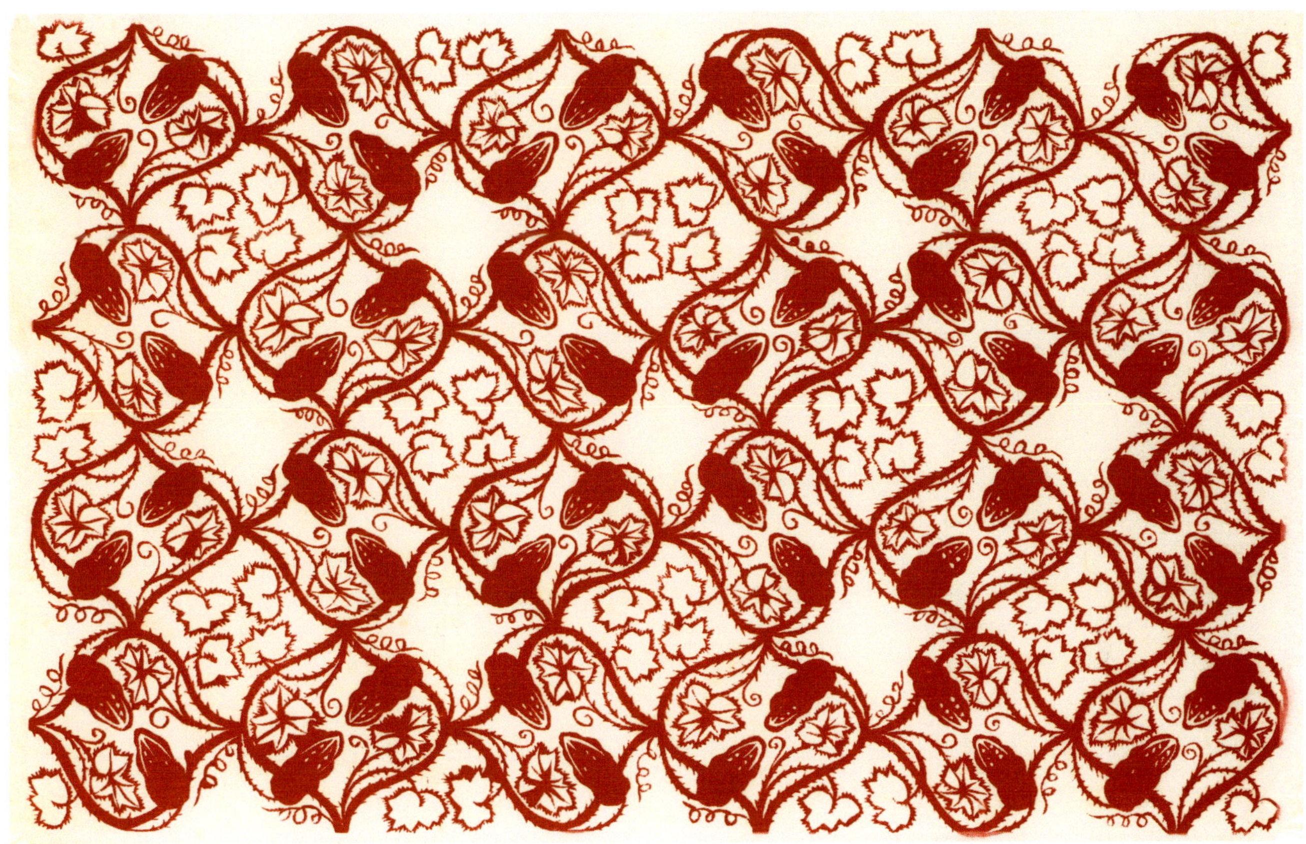

FIG. 104
This print of *Cucumber Vine* appears to be a block print, but Peggy Norton submitted a silk screen–printed version of it to William Skinner & Sons for consideration in 1949.

"nowhere near as much fun."[85] By the 1960s Peggy was experimenting as a Folly Cove designer with transparent inks in block printing. This allowed for overprinting, with the base layer colors showing through. She stated that she had set herself the challenge to "get as many colors out of three printings as I possibly could" for the printing of *Small Fruit*. She ultimately used the primary colors red, yellow, and blue mixed with transparent inks but printed dozens of strips to test the color combinations of her overlays with the transparent inks to figure out how the colors would come through one another. To Peggy, "every one [print] was an experiment."[86]

Eino Natti experimented with copper etching.[87] A native of Folly Cove, he grew up near the region's first group of printmakers, led by etchers Gabrielle de Veaux Clements—who had been introduced to the area by her teacher, etcher Stephen Parrish—and Ellen Day Hale, and may have had some exposure to etching early in his life.[88] Mary Maletskos and Anthony Iarrobino, both art school graduates, explored monoprinting and collographs, respectively.[89]

The Folly Cove Designers began to scale back in the 1960s. A core group remained, most of them in their fifties or sixties; only one or two younger women had joined the group in the late 1950s and early 1960s. The group was still utilizing hand presses, which were physically taxing to operate. When Virginia Lee Demetrios passed away in 1968, the group decided to only operate for one more season, closing their doors in 1969.

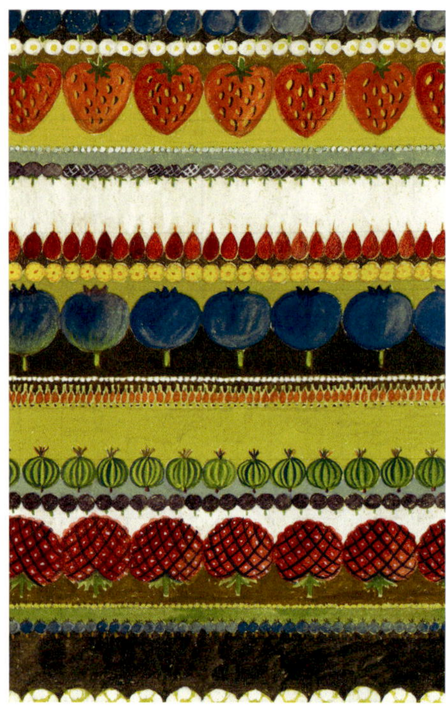

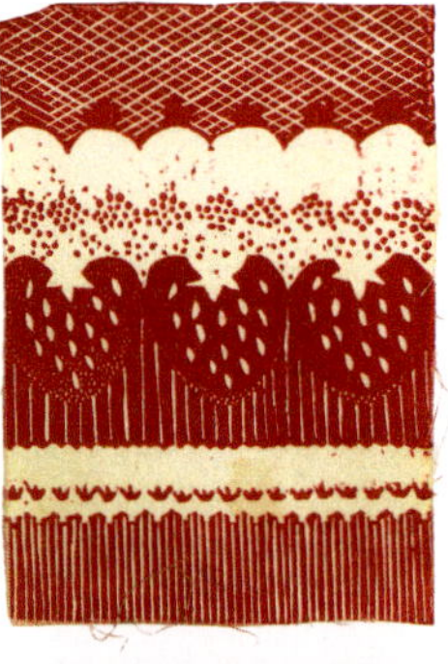

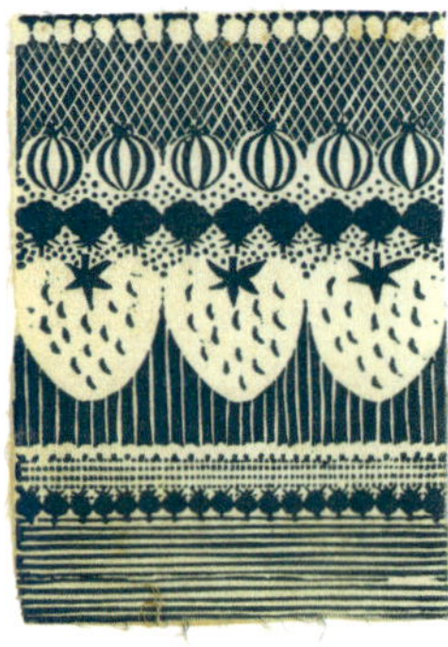

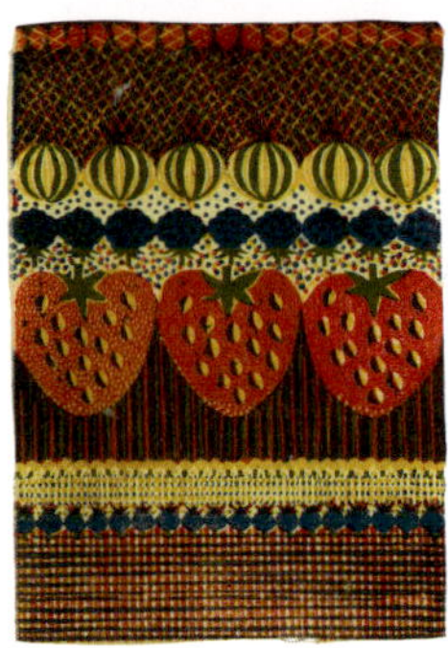

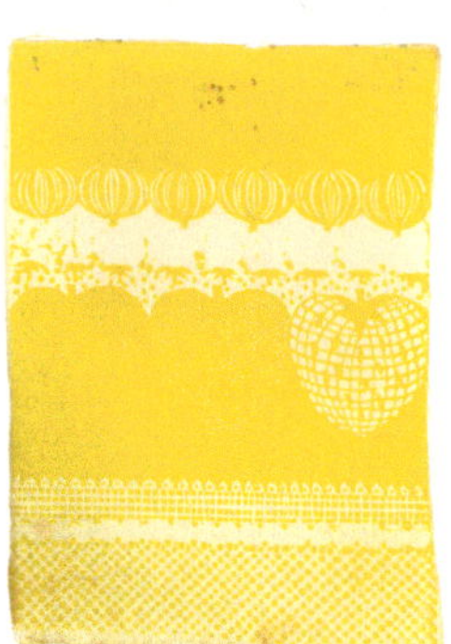

Virginia's son Michael, a businessman, recognized that many in the group did not want to continue without his mother. He attributed the group's decision to close to its unwillingness to make changes that would have allowed them to continue, such as training younger members, outsourcing the parts of the printmaking process that were physically demanding, and/or hiring additional personnel to work in the retail barn so that they could concentrate on designing.[90] Dorothy Norton shared Michael's feelings on these points.

But the philosophy of designer-craftsmen was central to the group. Virginia explained in a 1949 interview that "Back at the beginning of the Machine Age the designer and the craftsman got separated. The designer went white-collar. The craftsman became a superior sort of mechanic."[91] She added that the Folly Cove Designers "set out to follow the job straight through" and that "nobody is afraid to be a craftsman as well as a designer."[92]

Dorothy Norton was proud of the group's thirty-year run, stating that it "was a long time for a craft group."[93] Virginia's son Aristides, who became a sculptor, was amazed at the level of quality that they were able to sustain. "Usually you see entropy, but you didn't."[94]

The designers continued to sell their work at America House until they disbanded in 1969, just a few years shy of when America House closed its doors in 1971. As for the craftsmen represented by America House over the years, "The roster of artists who sold through America House reads like a who's who in American Crafts."[95] The Folly Cove Designers were a part of that history, standing shoulder to shoulder with the best craftsmen and some of the biggest names in textile design.

FIG. 105 (ABOVE LEFT)
Usually designers worked strictly in black and white when drafting a design but Peggy Norton painted *Small Fruit* in preparation of making this multicolored print.

FIG. 106 (ABOVE RIGHT)
Peggy used three primary colors as her base for *Small Fruit*. These swatches show her color separations for red, blue, and yellow, with a swatch of the final results. A block was carved for each color.

FIG. 107 (OPPOSITE TOP)
Yellow and red mixed with transparent ink. This was part of a series of samples for the printing of *Small Fruit* that Peggy had labeled and presumably displayed in the retail barn to show the process.

FIG. 108 (OPPOSITE BOTTOM)
The final version of *Small Fruit* using all three primary colors and the transparent inks to create multiple colors.

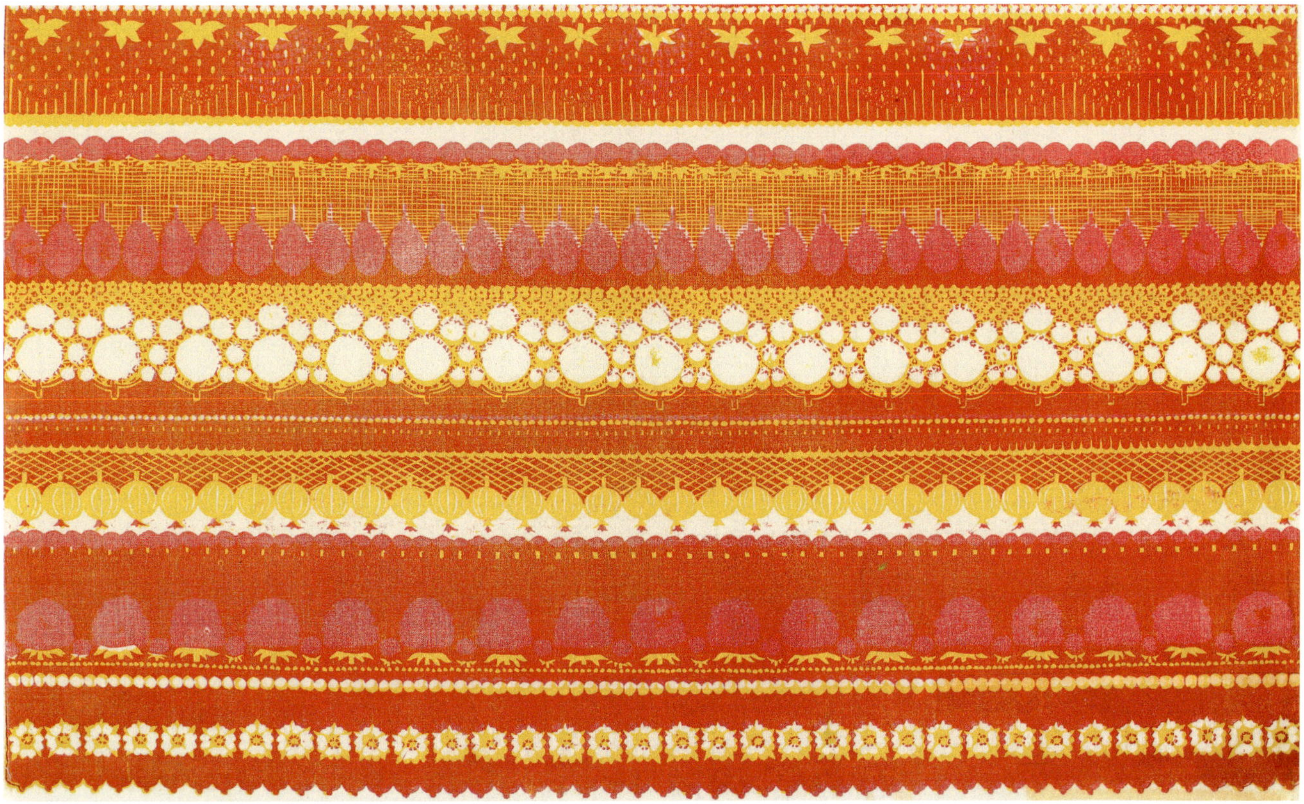

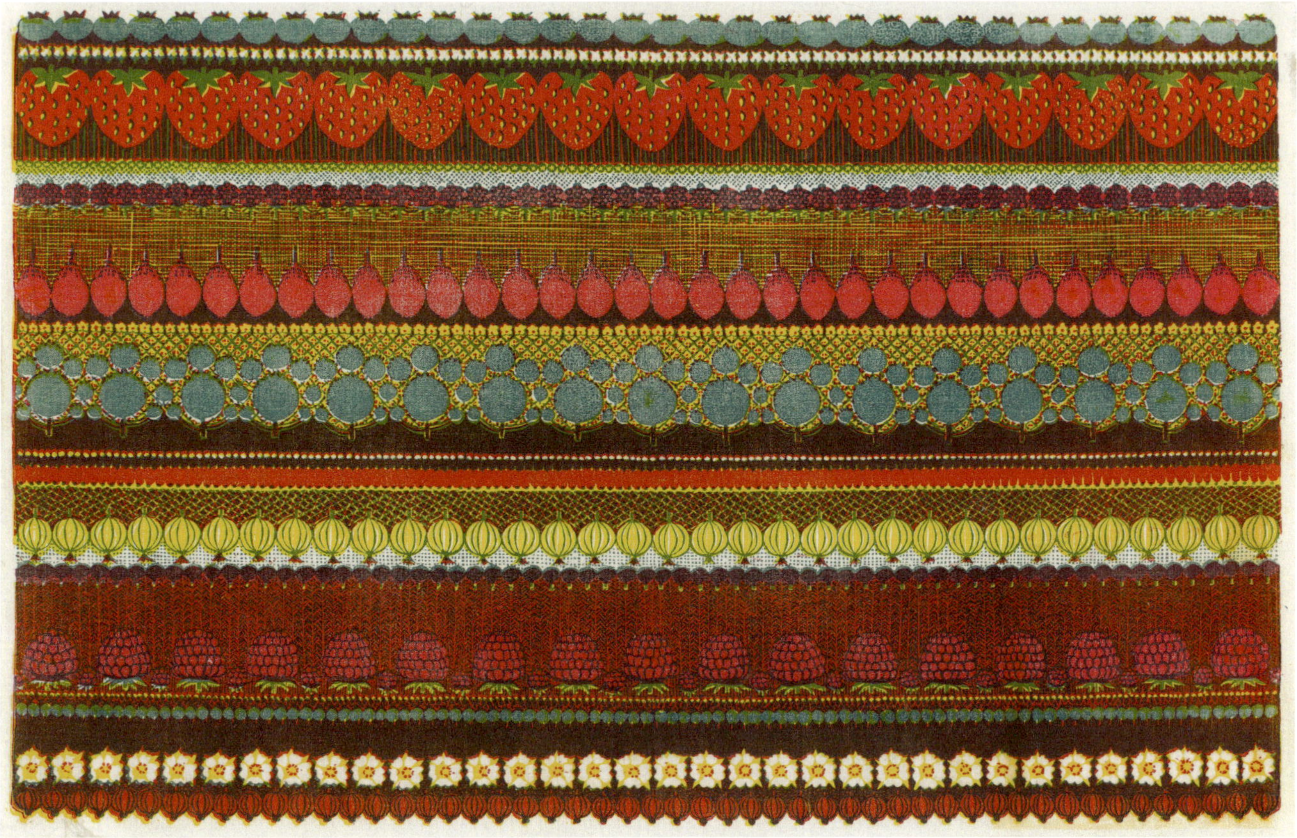

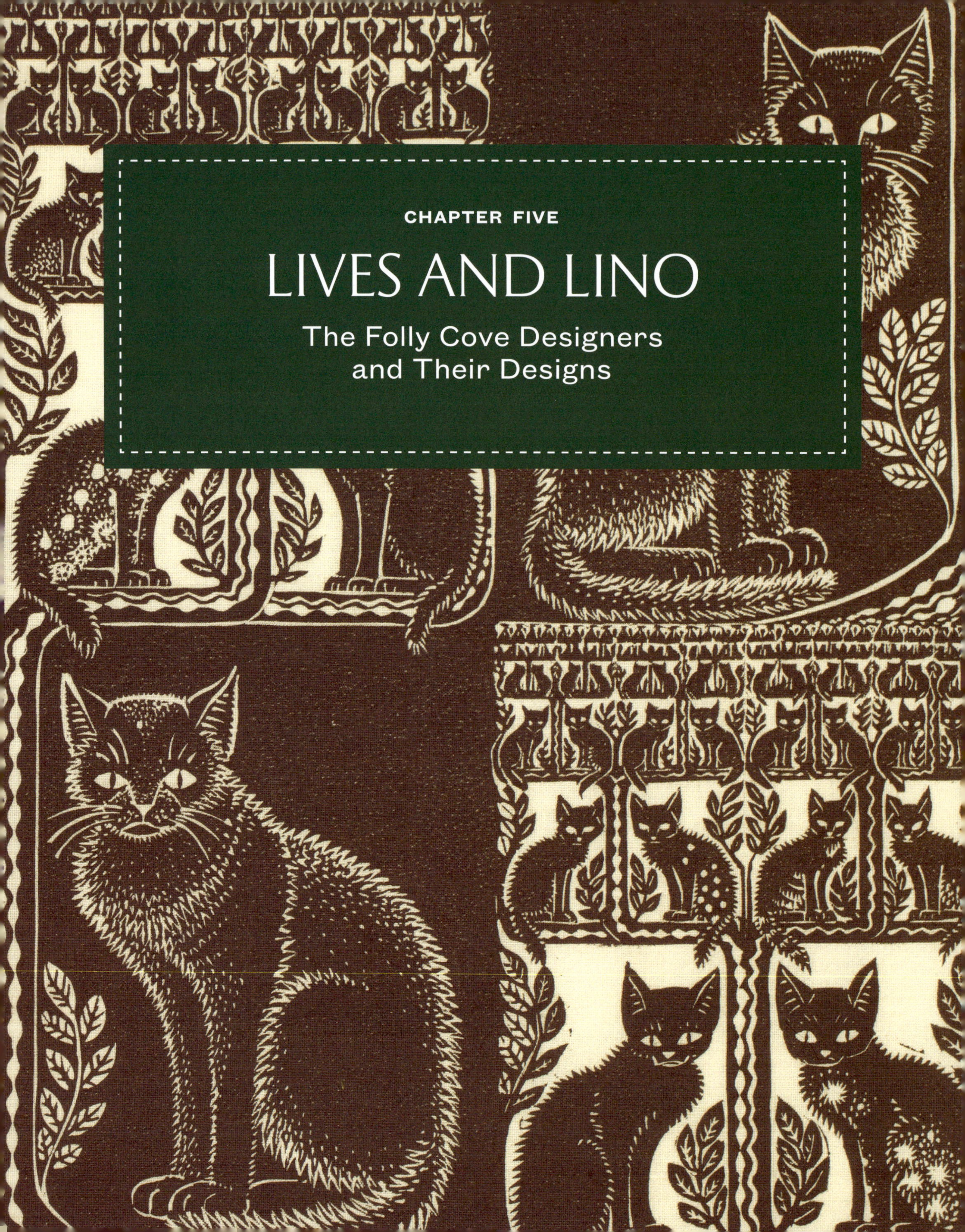

CHAPTER FIVE

LIVES AND LINO

The Folly Cove Designers and Their Designs

Over the nearly three decades the group operated, more than forty designers were part of the Folly Cove Designers.[1] This chapter includes select biographies, beginning with the eight designers considered most core to the group (arranged alphabetically by last name): Aino Clarke, Virginia Lee Demetrios, Libby Holloran, Louise Kenyon, Eino Natti, Lee Natti, Dorothy Norton, and Peggy Norton. This determination was based on three factors: length of involvement with Folly Cove Designers, extent of involvement (whether they were part of the jury at any point), and the number of designs they produced.

This chapter also includes a select group of designers, chosen for a particular contribution they made to the group, a newly discovered work, or, in a few instances, because they are or were still alive during the research stage and participated in interviews. The designation of core designer by no means diminishes the role of other designers. A strong case could be made that Anthony and Elizabeth Iarrobino and Mary Maletskos were core members, as all three were active for many years and produced a sizable number of designs, though it does not appear that any of them served on a jury. But this book is meant to be a celebration of the group as a whole.

A note on names: Since many of the women in the group used their maiden names in their professional lives, the maiden names of the women members appear in parentheses. Over the years members would print their names or signatures in the selvedge of hand-printed yardage. The manner in which they labeled their work changed; sometimes it included initials only, sometimes first and last names, sometimes maiden or middle names; such details have been included in their biographies wherever available.

The goal of this chapter is to give insight into the personalities of some of the Folly Cove Designers and highlight how their designs reflected their personalities. In the process of researching this book, many never-before-seen designs were discovered that there was either no record of or that previously only the name of the design was known. These pieces are referred to as "lost" designs throughout the text.

CORE DESIGNERS

Aino (Yrjola) Clarke (1914–1995)

Aino Clarke initiated the formation of the Folly Cove Designers with Virginia Lee Demetrios and was a central member, often teaching the design course.[2] Born in Roxbury, Massachusetts, Aino grew up in Gloucester. Aino's father passed away when she was five and it was likely after this that her mother moved them to her native Gloucester.[3]

Music was Aino's first love and she credited her mother with her musical inclination. At age twelve she asked for violin lessons and continued with them for many years. Her teacher willed her his violin upon his death and she played at his funeral.[4] She copyrighted an arrangement for voice and piano of "The Twelve Days of Christmas" in 1948, a collaboration with a fellow member of the Folly Cove Designers.[5] She based many of her designs on music.

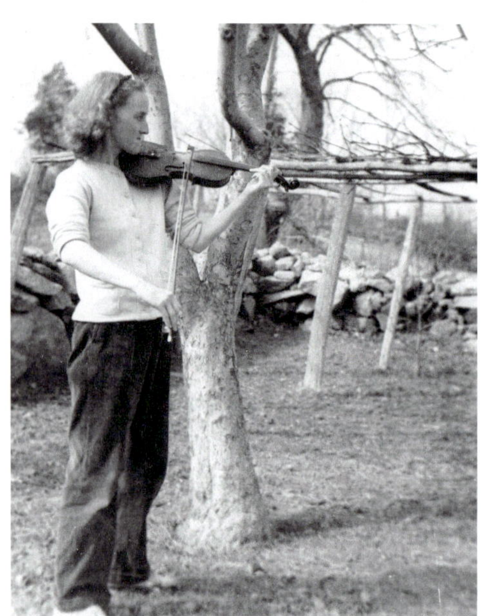

FIG. 109 (LEFT)

Aino Clarke learned violin as a child and continued to play throughout her life.

FIG. 110 (BELOW)

***Elephants* by Aino. Despite there being several mothers in the Folly Cove Designers, *Elephants* is one of the few maternally themed designs, along with one scene in *Sauna* (see page 23), which was also by Aino. Aino was a mother herself. (Ink on paper.)**

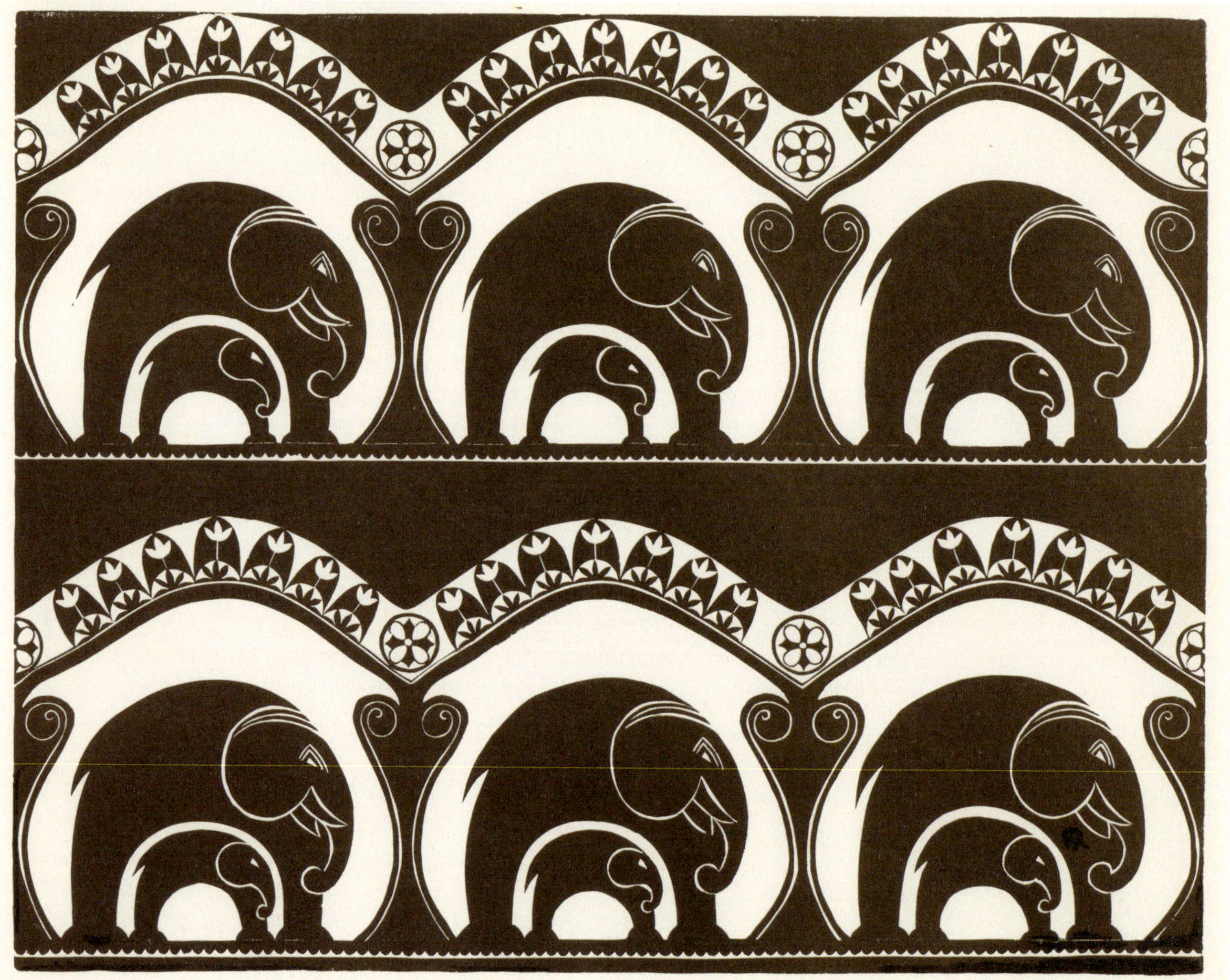

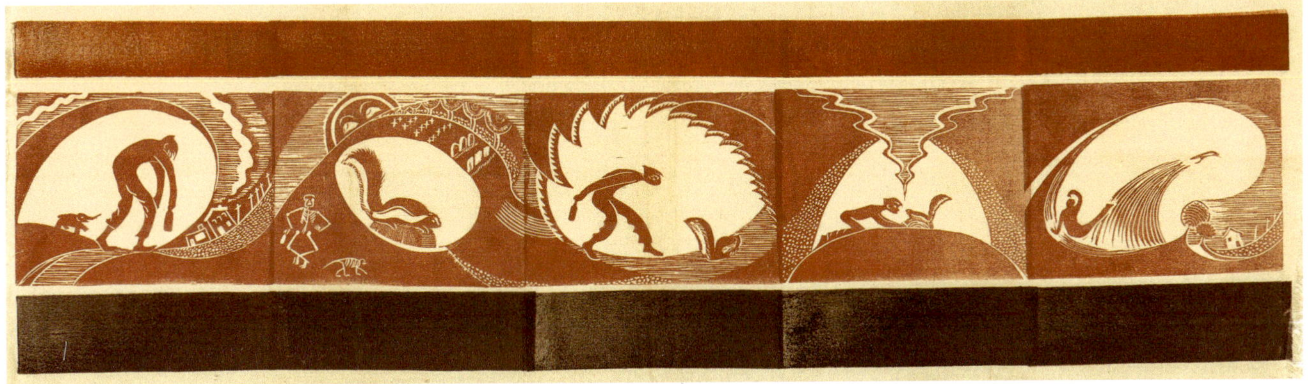

FIG. 111
Skunk and Drunk by Aino. The plume of chimney smoke and the skunk spray frame the action and reflect signature Folly Cove Designer border patterns. An elephant appears in the first frame, possibly to suggest how drunk the man is and that he is hallucinating. (Ink on fabric.)

Music was a bond she shared with Virginia.[6] Aino spoke of Saturday nights at the Demetrioses' house; they would play Bach on the piano while the men played poker. Eino Natti joined their music-making when he returned from World War II. Virginia and George also had a harpsichord, which Aino learned to play, along with the recorder. But she modestly said that she didn't play any of them well.[7]

Aino and Virginia were close friends, so much so that George referred to them as the Mutual Admiration Society. They took traditional Finnish saunas together and sunbathed in the summer, lathering themselves with so much oil that they nearly slid off the rocks.[8]

Skunk and Drunk was one of Aino's early designs. It is a narrative design, telling the story of a drunken man's interaction with a skunk in five scenes. The man is making his way home when he meets a skunk as he is passing a graveyard. He gets sprayed and the final frame shows him kicking the skunk. The lines in this design move the eye from left to right, frame by frame. This piece, although not as refined as some of her later work, captures the shapes and motion of the man and the skunk.

Aino had taken art in high school, but the design lessons with Virginia were a turning point for her artistically.[9] In hindsight she felt her early blocks were "childish looking."[10] Choosing a subject was one of the most important of Virginia's lessons, as was drawing from life, so that when Aino chose an elephant as her subject, she hopped on the train to visit the zoo. Though it was closed to the public that day, she was allowed a look at an elephant and then referenced photographs to finalize the design. She learned that baby elephants walk under their mothers for protection, which became the basis for *Elephants*, often printed in pink.[11]

Fiddle Dee Dee features the violin and was likely inspired by the dance sessions she, Virginia, and others would have in the barn and and for which Aino provided the music. Virginia suggested Aino redo *Fiddle Dee Dee* because originally the figures were the same size as the ash trees. Even looking at the design in the 1990s, Aino critiqued the design, commenting that she placed the clouds "too close to the top" edge of the design.[12]

Aino designed one of the group's most personal designs with *My Friday*, which depicts the activities of her typical Friday. Lee Natti described Aino as being the "most adventuresome" with her subjects.[13] George Demetrios had

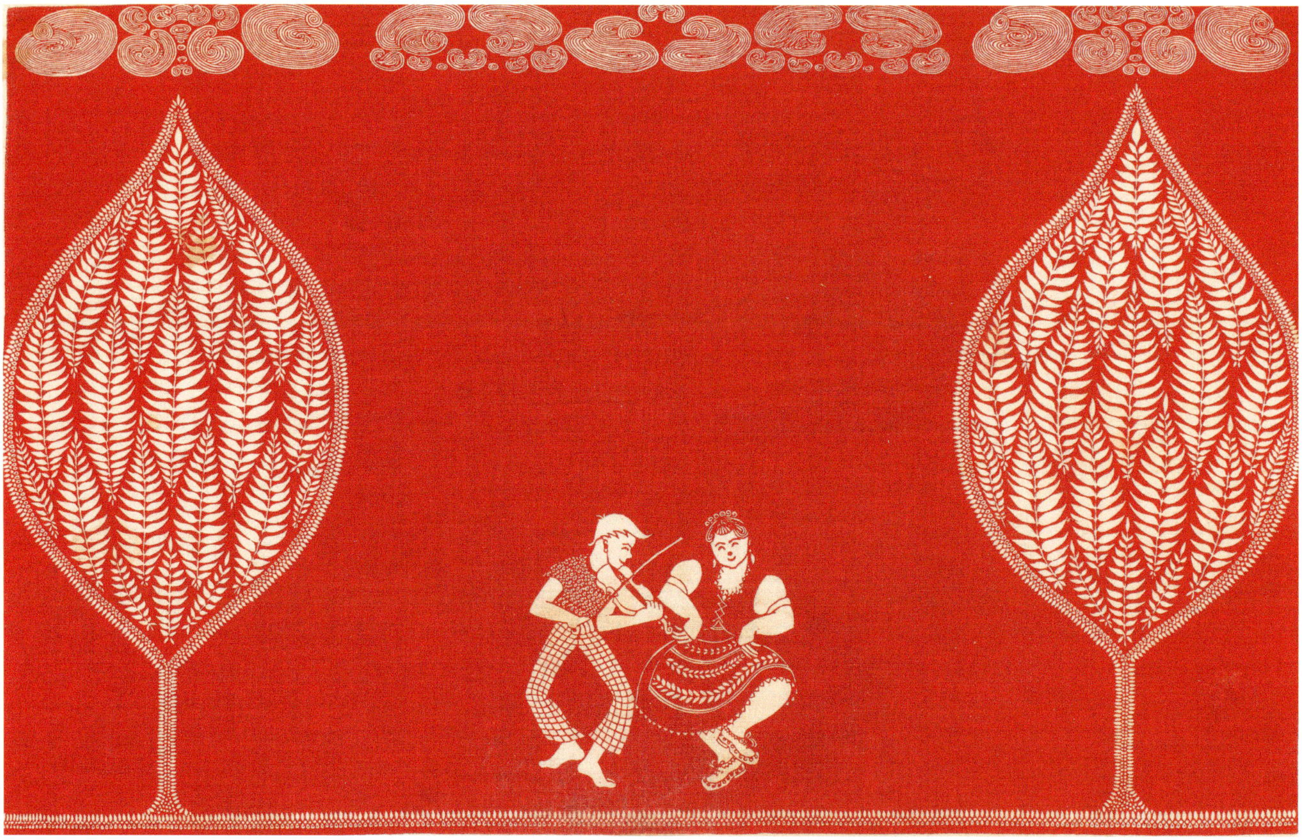

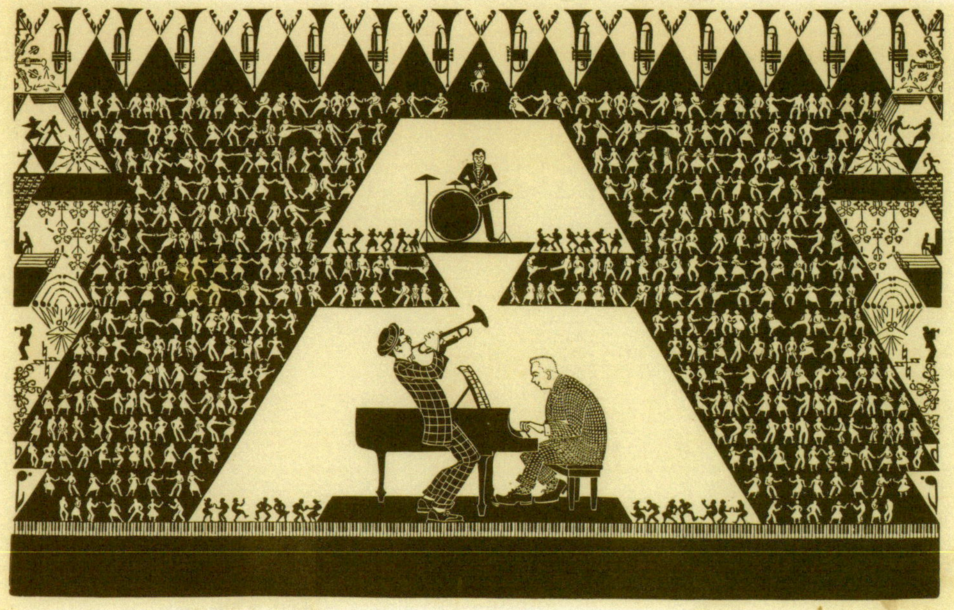

FIG. 112 (ABOVE)
Fiddle Dee Dee **by Aino Clarke. The female figure was based on a Finnish woman who worked for the Demetrios family. Aino also drew ash trees for her submission to the Edwin M. Knowles China Company (see page 69). (Ink on fabric.)**

FIG. 113 (LEFT)
Jazz **is a fun design filled with geometric shapes and figurative work, with piano keys as the bottom border. (Ink on fabric.)**

warned her of the challenge involved with the drawing-heavy composition. She admitted, "I hadn't had that much drawing—I practically had to teach myself how to draw."[14] The completed design is impressive, lively, and engaging. But Aino was still critical, explaining that she had "started it in this corner and I tried to make six sided shapes the way I did in *Geometric I* and instead I ended up just putting them anywhere, scattered."[15] In this respect the design did not follow the group's standard design principles. Lee Natti admired Aino's ability to express originality. "She could take the structure and twist it to suit her ideas."[16] Aino worked on the design over the course of two years and conceded that, by the second year, maybe "I was not staying true to the idea and just wanted to get the darn thing carved, which can happen."[17] She felt that one corner was better design- and spacing-wise.[18]

Aino created another unique design in *Atomic Age*, one of the group's few topical designs.[19] Here she used a geometric design and infused it with personal meaning and statement on current events.

Perhaps because of her *Elephants* experience, Aino generally chose subjects she had easy access to, such as *Schooners*.[20] She wasn't sure how to "treat the clouds" in the piece, ultimately using the lines of the mast to form donut-shaped clouds since Virginia taught her students that lines conveyed motion.[21]

Aino had her mother sew the skirts she printed.[22] She said that skirts sold well, but that she didn't produce as many as other designers such as Louise Kenyon. Virginia took a few of Aino's skirts in the *Musicale* design out to California for her mother to use in Carmel for an event that she hosted.[23]

Aino did the capital lettering of the ballads in the edition of *Song of Robin Hood* that Virginia illustrated. She credited Virginia with helping her and recalled initially doing the lettering on scratchboard.[24] Aino also did the lettering for the Twins series book covers (see page 72), as well as the lettering for some of the Folly Cove Designers' annual exhibition invitations.[25]

Aino had other employment; she worked at the Museum of Fine Arts gift shop in Boston for twenty years. Commuting didn't leave her with a lot of time to practice her violin (she was part of a quartet for many years and, according to her obituary, a member of the Cape Ann Symphony) or work on her designs. She would designate a day to work on her designs, breaking at midday to take a nap after lunch and recharge enough to return to her work.[26] Aino remained in the group until it disbanded.

Even though Aino was the impetus for the formation of the group and taught many members the design lessons, she never spoke about her role within the group in later interviews. Yet she recalled her friend Virginia warmly and shared that her life changed from knowing her.[27]

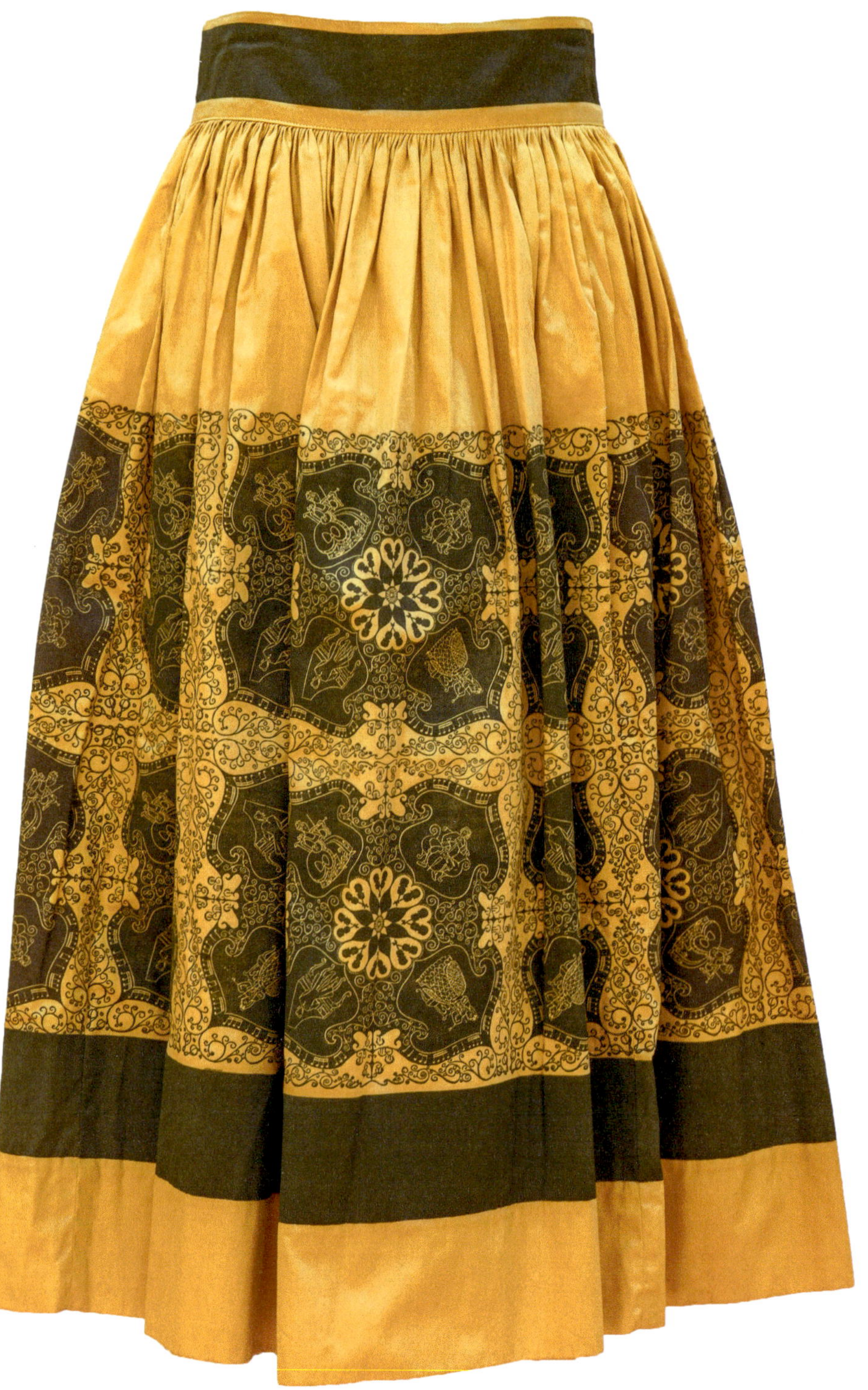

FIG. 114 (LEFT)
A skirt in Aino Clarke's *Musicale* design. Several designers recalled that Aino had used a magnifying glass to carve the fine lines in this design. Violins are at the center, with music notes framing the musicians as a border. (Ink on fabric.)

FIG. 115 (OPPOSITE TOP)
In *Atomic Age*, Aino employed radial symmetry. (Ink on fabric.)

FIG. 116 (OPPOSITE BOTTOM)
***Schooners*, printed on paper by Aino. This design was inspired by a local schooner and Aino was proud that people could recognize the ship from her print. (Ink on paper.)**

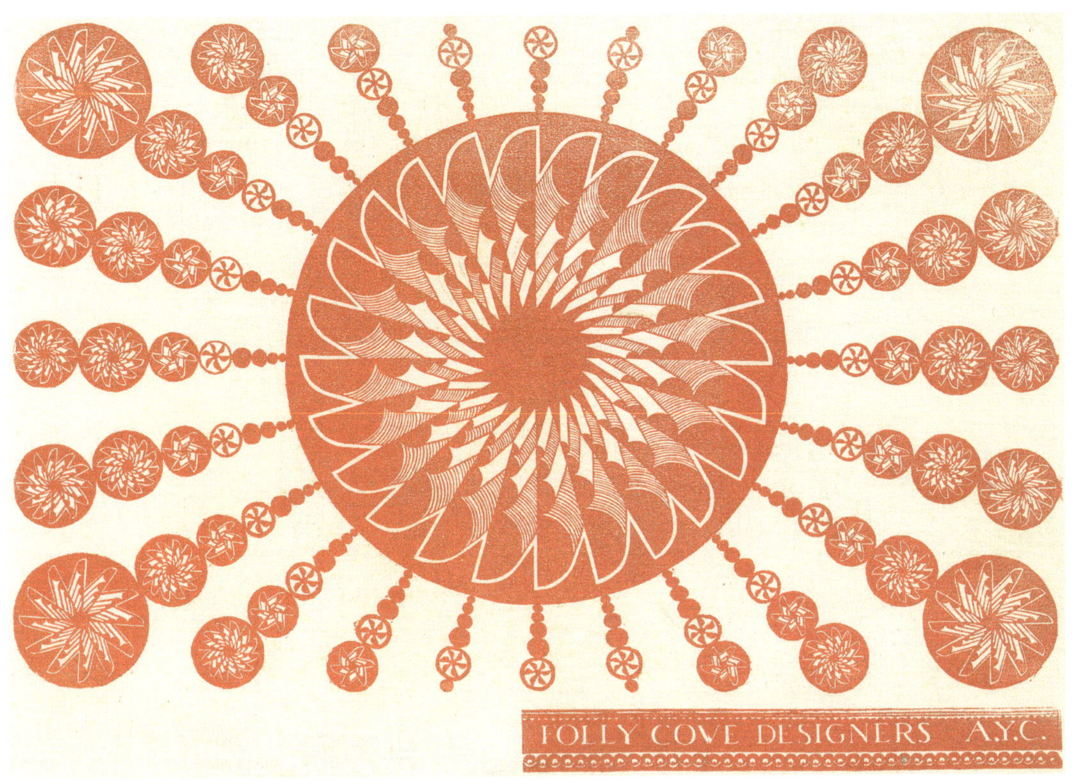

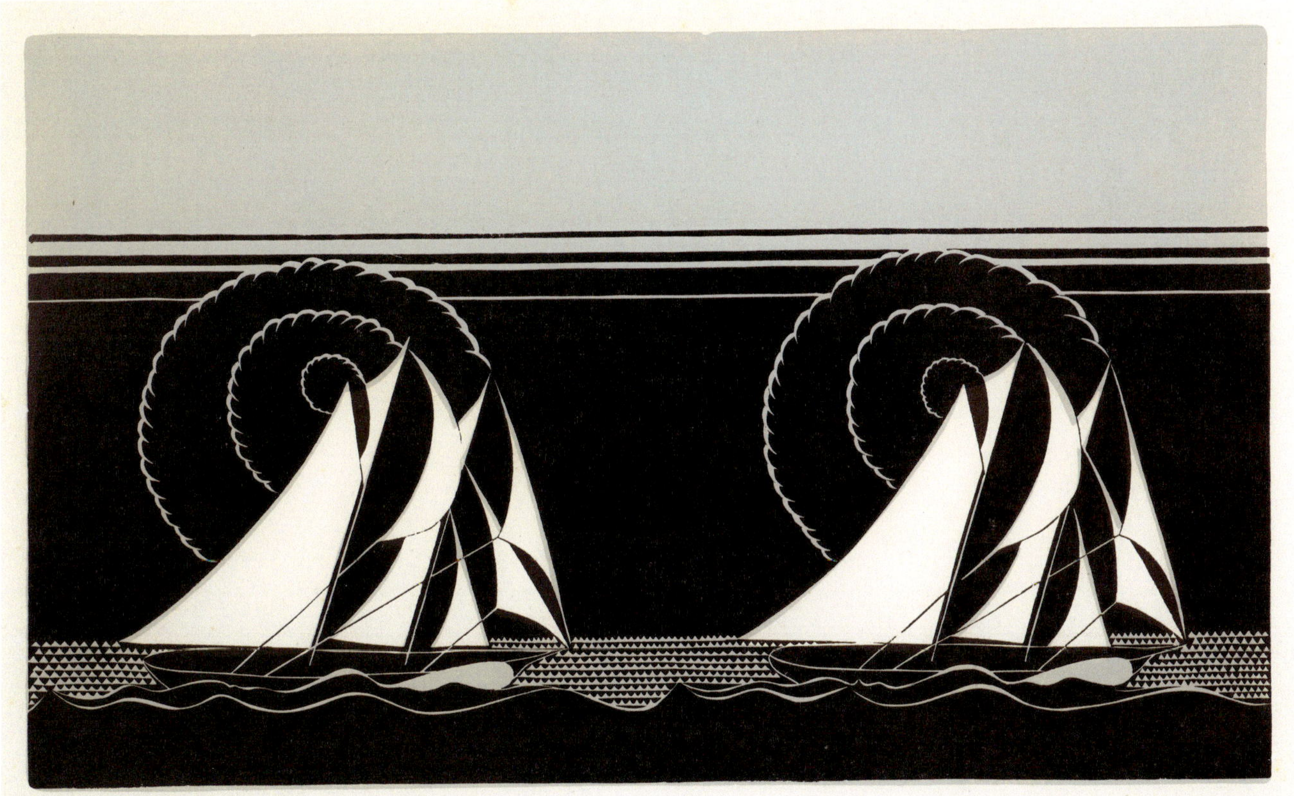

" SCHOONERS "

FIG. 117

Aino's *My Friday*. Aino later said in an interview that her mother had wondered who would be interested in her Fridays, but it proved to be one of her most fascinating designs. Although she certainly did a lot of housework! (Ink on fabric.)

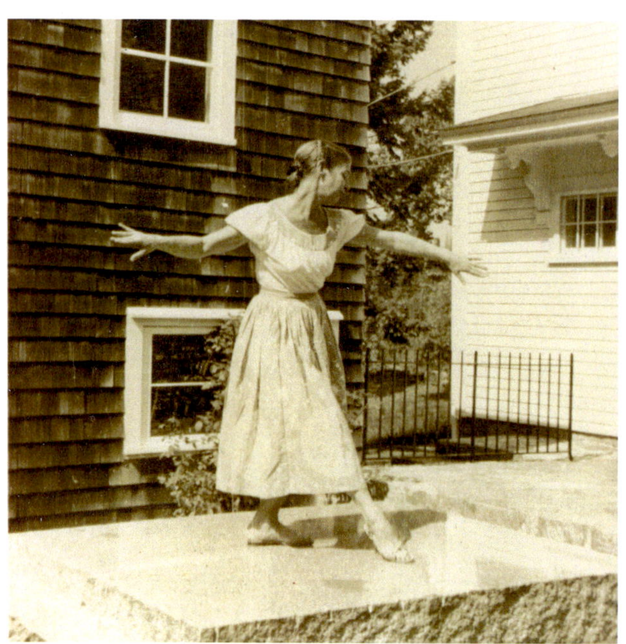

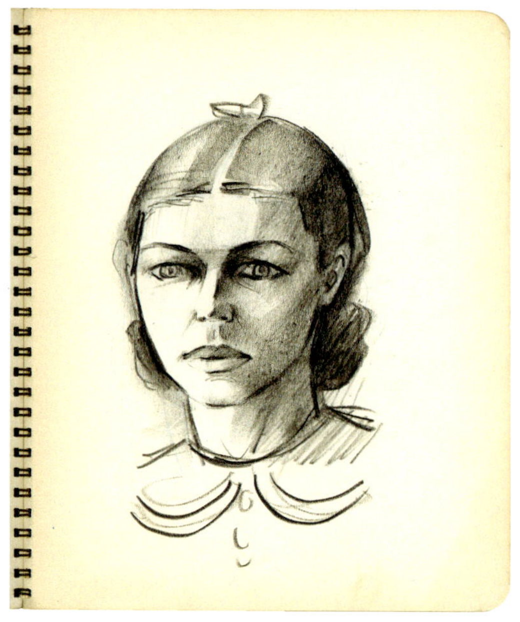

FIG. 118 (LEFT)
Virginia dancing in a skirt printed with her *Farmer's Almanac* design on one of the large granite tables in her yard.

FIG. 119 (RIGHT)
Charcoal self-portrait of a young Virginia, undated.

Virginia Lee (Burton) Demetrios (1909–1968)

Virginia Lee Demetrios was a writer, illustrator, and designer. By all accounts she was also a talented dancer, expert swimmer, generous teacher, beloved friend, and loving mother. From her notebooks, sketchbooks, and countless drafts—even for Christmas cards—her perfectionism is immediately apparent. But reflections by friends and family highlight another side of Virginia (known as Jinnee to her friends and family)—the playful side—capable of being fully present in the beautiful moments of the life she created in Folly Cove.

Virginia was born in 1909 in Newton Center, Massachusetts. Her father, Alfred Burton, was a professor and the first dean of the Massachusetts Institute of Technology in Cambridge. Her mother was Lena D. Yates, an artist and writer.[28] Virginia was the middle of Lena and Alfred's three children. She had two older half brothers from her father's first marriage.[29] Lena moved the three younger children to California in 1920, ultimately settling in Carmel-by-the-Sea.[30] Virginia thrived there, enjoying the artistic community and lifestyle and performing in plays and dance performances with her sister.[31] Upon retiring from MIT in 1921, her father rejoined the family. He also participated in the theater and community life, but the family was abruptly pulled apart when Lena left him in 1924 for a much younger man, a former MIT student named Carl Cherry, whom she would later marry.[32]

As an artist, Lena had started going by the name Jeanne D'Orge while in Carmel.[33] The divorce and remarriage were scandalous for that time.[34] Virginia was only sixteen and was sent to live with friends of Lena's, Virginia's printmaking teacher Robert Hestwood and his wife, Anita, who taught at Sonora High School.[35] There Virginia was active in dance, drama, and music, graduated with the highest honors, and received a scholarship to the California School of Fine Arts (now San Francisco Art Institute), where the Hestwoods taught Saturday children's classes. Virginia enrolled and attended for a year.[36] She also studied dance privately with an instructor who had been a student of the celebrated Russian ballerina Anna Pavlova.[37]

Virginia was deeply influenced by Robert's work, with its strong use of black and white, acknowledging his influence in her unpublished *Design and How!* manuscript by crediting him as being her first design teacher.[38]

By 1928 Virginia had returned east to help care for her father after he had broken his leg. She was passionate about dance and is said to have given up a spot in her sister's dance troupe to care for him.[39] While in Boston she took a job as an illustrator at the *Boston Evening Transcript*, which included creating illustrations to accompany articles by the renowned theater and music critic Henry Taylor Parker, who went by his initials.[40] During this time Virginia signed her work as VLeeB. Working for the newspaper, she learned to sketch quickly to capture the essentials and fill in the details later, training herself "to work mainly from memory."[41] While in Boston a friend of Virginia's recommended a teacher named George Demetrios, who taught drawing in a similar vein, having models switch poses every two minutes.[42] She enrolled in his class at the Boston Museum School in 1930 and they were married in March of 1931.[43] The couple lived in Lincoln, Massachusetts, for the first year of their marriage and the birth of their eldest child, Aristides, in 1932.[44] In 1935 a second son, Michael, was born, completing their family.[45]

In 1929 George had inherited his teacher Charles Grafly's studio, located in Lanesville, Massachusetts, upon Charles's death. After the birth of Aris, the couple decided to move there year-round, first renting a house for a year before purchasing a several-acre property in nearby Folly Cove. The home was on a busy main road, so they had the house moved back to the apple orchard, which became fodder for Virginia's book *The Little House*. The property ultimately included a barn-like studio for Virginia and an actual barn for the animals. George maintained Charles's studio on Woodbury Street for classes and another studio closer to the house.[46]

George enjoyed gardening and landscaping. Virginia honored his green thumb in her design *George's Garden*, which featured his vegetable garden. He also created a rock garden and artfully installed sculptures throughout the property.[47] There was a meadow for sheep, which inspired *Spring Lambs I* and *Spring Lambs II*.[48]

Virginia and George loved entertaining. "Stony Brook ran through the property and George formed a small pool and surrounded this with a granite settee and fireplace for barbeques. In the center of the pool was a natural oval stone on which George sculptured a sleeping boy in a curled position."[49] George and Virginia were renowned for their summer barbecues (George would often serve lamb) and lobster bakes and held regular Saturday evening square dances during the winter.[50] It was through them that many local couples met, including Ross and Hilja Burton, Robert and Lee Natti, and George's nephew Costa Maletskos and his wife, Mary.[51]

Virginia was a hard worker, getting up early to work in her studio, then taking a break to wake the boys for school and returning to work after they left.[52] Designers recalled the sign on her studio door (as seen in *Life* on page 54), which listed her work hours and essentially said, "If you have nothing

FIG. 120 (RIGHT)
Aino said that Virginia displayed some of her original sketches for this 1930 write-up of Lillian Gish in Anton Chekhov's *Uncle* in her studio in Folly Cove. Lillian was given some of the sketches and sent a thank you, writing "I think it [the original drawing] and its caption charming."

FIG. 121 (BELOW)
Virginia's ornate *Dance of the Hours* combined her love of dance and design. (Ink on fabric.)

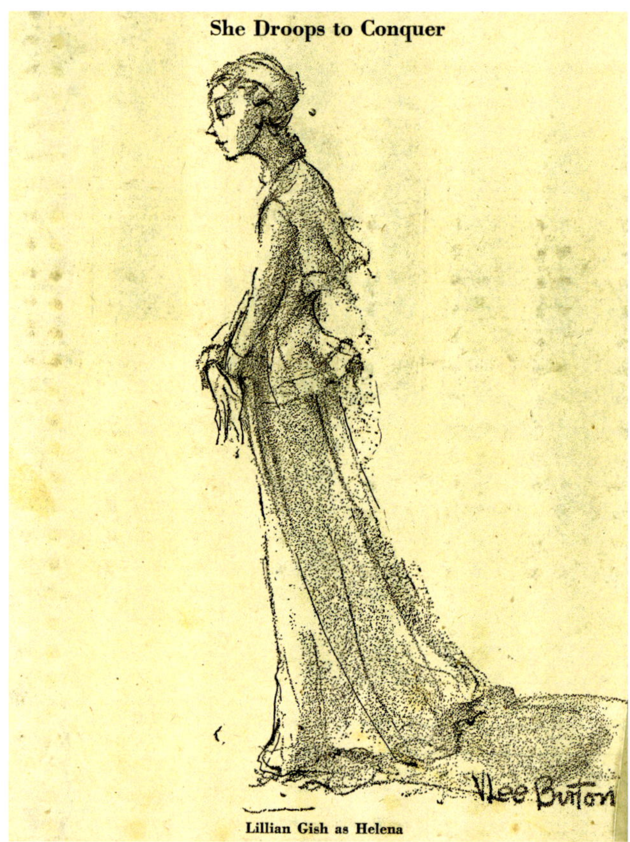

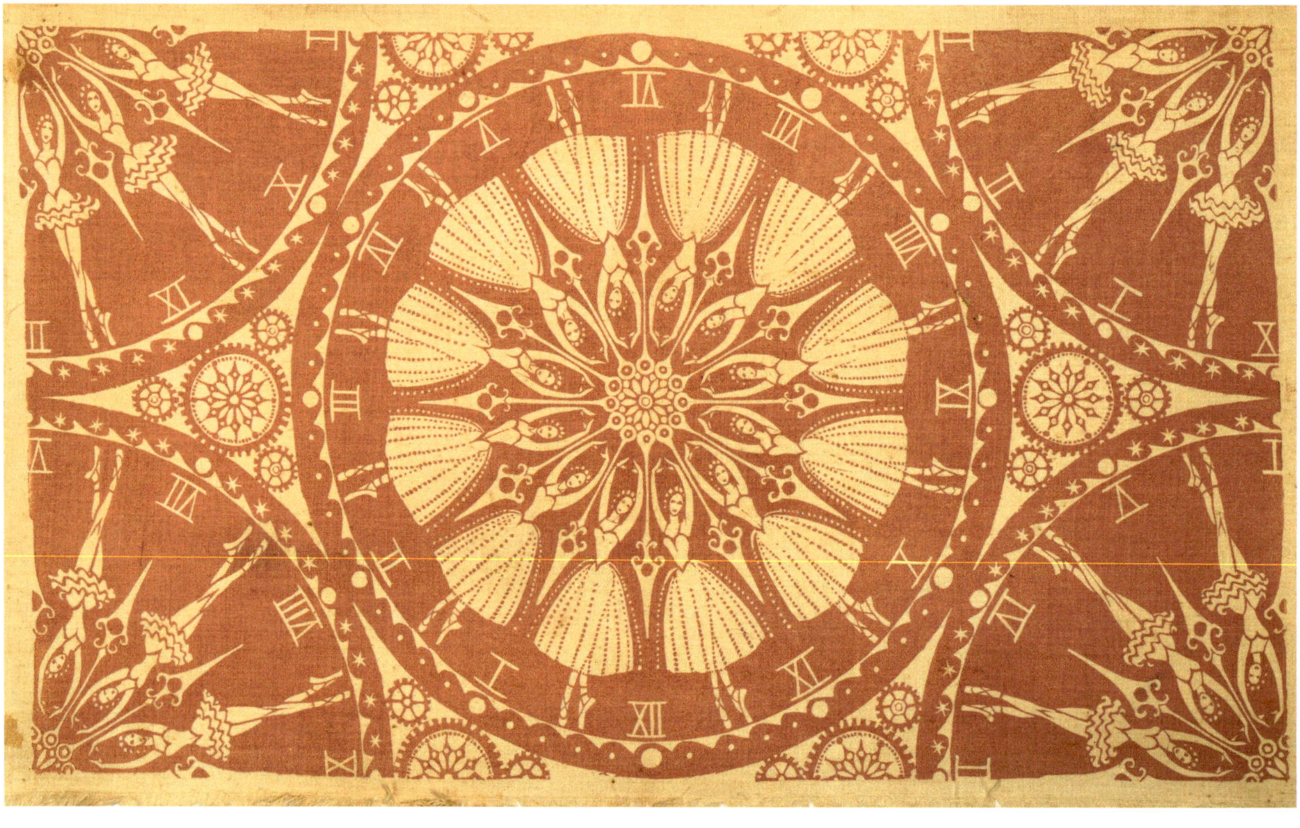

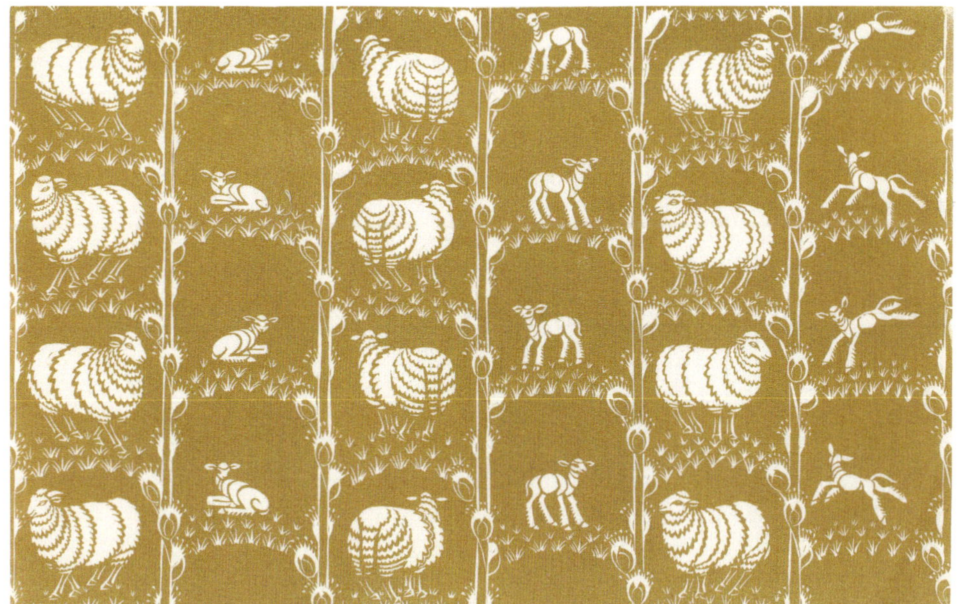

FIG. 122 (LEFT)
Spring Lambs I **by Virginia. Virginia wore a dress in this pattern in *Life* (see page 20). (Ink on fabric.)**

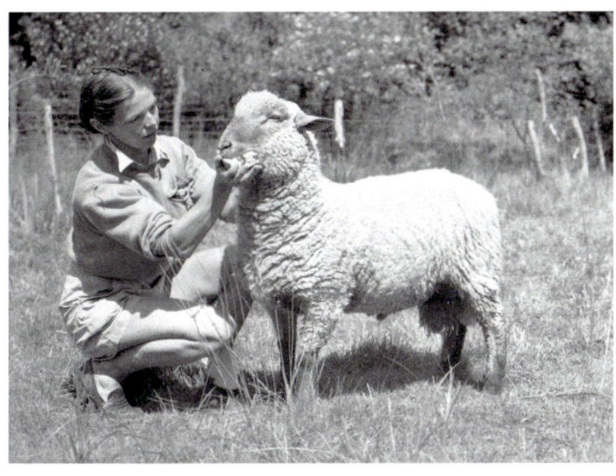

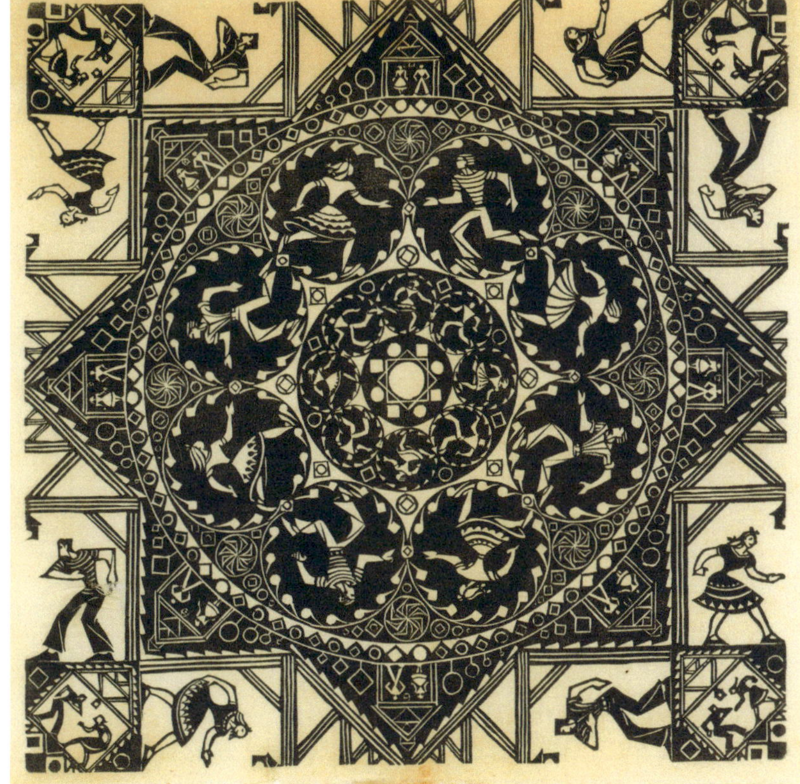

FIG. 123 (ABOVE)
Virginia feeding a sheep. Dorothy wrote Lord & Taylor in 1946, "Right now the meadow in front of her [Virginia's] house is full of spring lambs and looks like an animated version of her design [*Spring Lambs II*]." It does not appear that Lord & Taylor released this design.

FIG. 124 (RIGHT)
Virginia's love of square dancing inspired *Grand Right and Left*, with the barn beams framing the dancers on the outer edge. The trees serve more as elements of the pattern and geometric shapes rather than realistic depictions, which is different from most of Virginia's designs. (Ink on fabric.)

to do—don't do it here," which successfully kept interruptions at bay but some designers found initially intimidating.[53] By day's end there would be mounds of perfectly good sketches in the wastebasket.[54] The Cape Ann Museum's archive houses countless manuscript drafts and multiple reworkings of her designs—first as pencil sketches, then ink on paper or india ink on Bristol board (a type of thick illustration paper).

Virginia would switch back to her role as mother and housewife, though, and her sons remembered the time after dinner as being particularly special. She would read to the boys and enjoyed having fun, laughing and engaging in silliness and pranks. One fellow designer described the appeal of Virginia's personality as being based in the "child's curiosity that she never lost."[55] She painted murals on the walls of her sons' rooms.[56] Aris and Mike, whom she referred to as her "two alert little critics," inspired her books, which were lovingly written for and dedicated to them.[57]

Despite having a blossoming career as an author/illustrator and two young sons, Virginia found the time to start the design lessons in 1938. She had already published *Choo Choo* (1937); *Mike Mulligan and His Steam Shovel* (1939) was published as the design lessons expanded. She went on to author and illustrate five more books: *Calico the Wonder Horse: Or the Saga of Stewy Slinker* (1941; republished in 1950 with the revised subtitle of *Or the Saga of Stewy Stinker*), *The Little House* (1942; a Caldecott Medal winner, it was made into a Disney animated short film), *Katy and the Big Snow* (1943), *Maybelle the Cable Car* (1952), and *Life Story* (1962). All of them were published under her maiden name, Virginia Lee Burton.[58]

The consummate teacher, even through her books, Virginia strove to instill an understanding of "good design" in her young readers.[59] In her Caldecott Medal speech for *The Little House,* Virginia stated, "If the picture is well drawn and finely designed they [children] learn more than literal definition. They acquire a sense of good design, they learn to appreciate beauty, and they take the first step in the development of good taste."[60]

Virginia's design work influenced her books and her books influenced her designs. Everything in her life was intertwined.[61] Designs such as *Robin Hood, Little House, Choo Choo,* and *Steam Shovel* were block prints of her book illustrations.[62]

Editor, friend, and Folly Cove designer Lee Natti felt the influence of Virginia's design work was most evident in her illustrations for an edition of *Song of Robin Hood,* executed in striking black and white.[63] Virginia felt that her design work made her a better illustrator. In 1950 she decided to redraw her book *Calico the Wonder Horse*. "She felt that she had progressed so much in her Folly Cove design and discovered so much more that could be done with shades of black, white, gray and what have you that she just felt compelled to do the whole book over again."[64] Her work on *Song of Robin Hood* inspired other designs, as she had studied plants native to England for the book and was pleased to find that many were found in New England as well, allowing her to study them firsthand. Her intense plant, flower, and tree research likely inspired the design *A Rose Is a Rose* and the weeping willows in *Sentimental* (see page 169)—both of which she mentions in the

FIG. 125 (OPPOSITE LEFT)
One of Virginia's many *The Little House* drafts, featuring a child on a swing, which Virginia would use in her *Swing Tree* designs. This exact illustration is not in the book, but the house and trees became the cover art, along with some of Virginia's signature birds and a sun.

FIG. 126 (OPPOSITE RIGHT)
Virginia's design *Little House*, which emphasized the anthropomorphized sun. Virginia is wearing a skirt printed in this design on page 36. (Ink on fabric.)

FIG. 127 (OPPOSITE BOTTOM)
Virginia's design *Robin Hood* is the same design as the endpapers for the edition of *Song of Robin Hood* that she illustrated. She included similar-looking birds in flight in her design *Early Bird*. (Ink on fabric.)

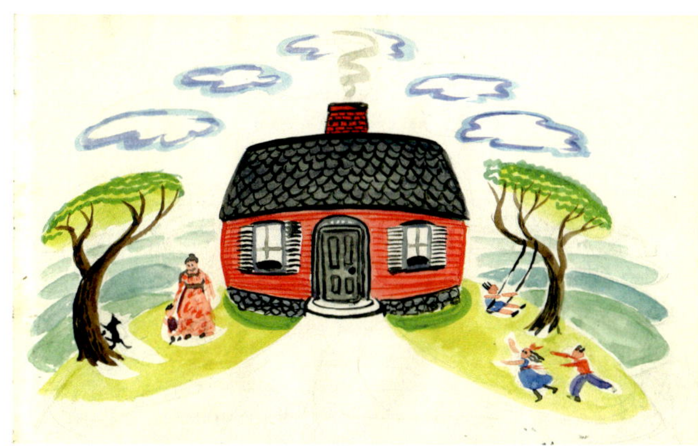

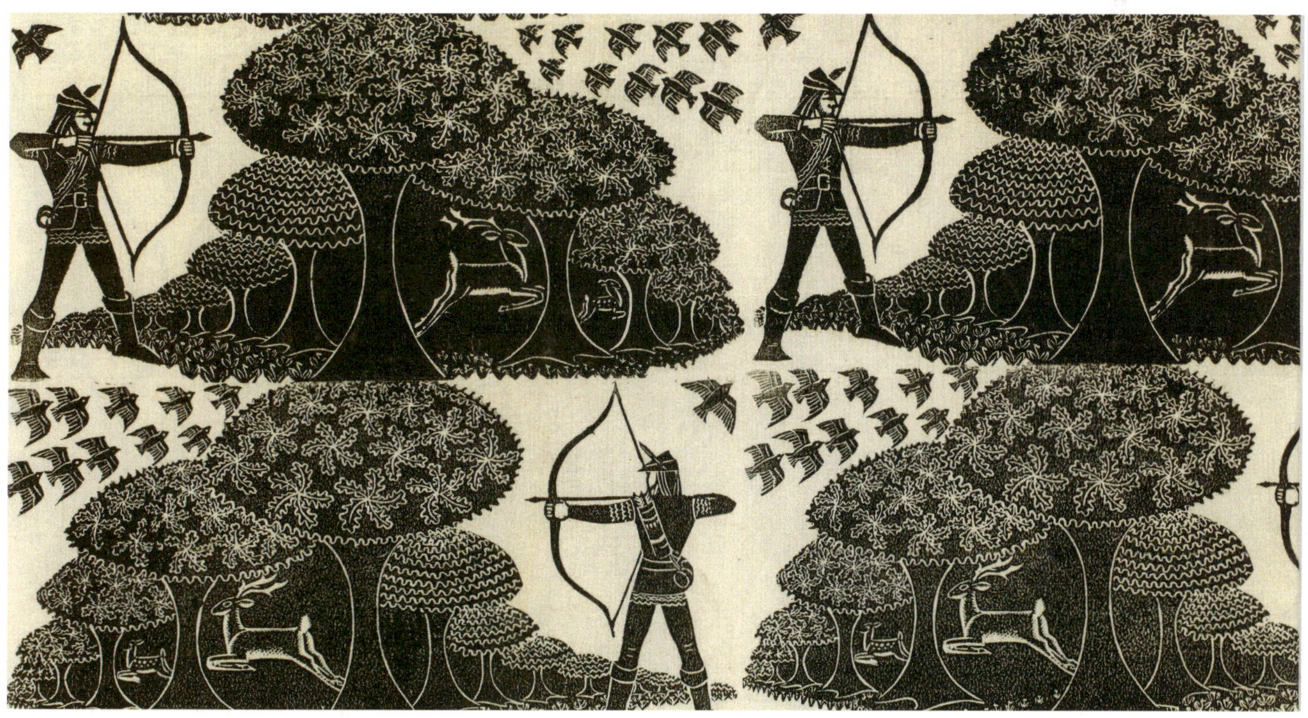

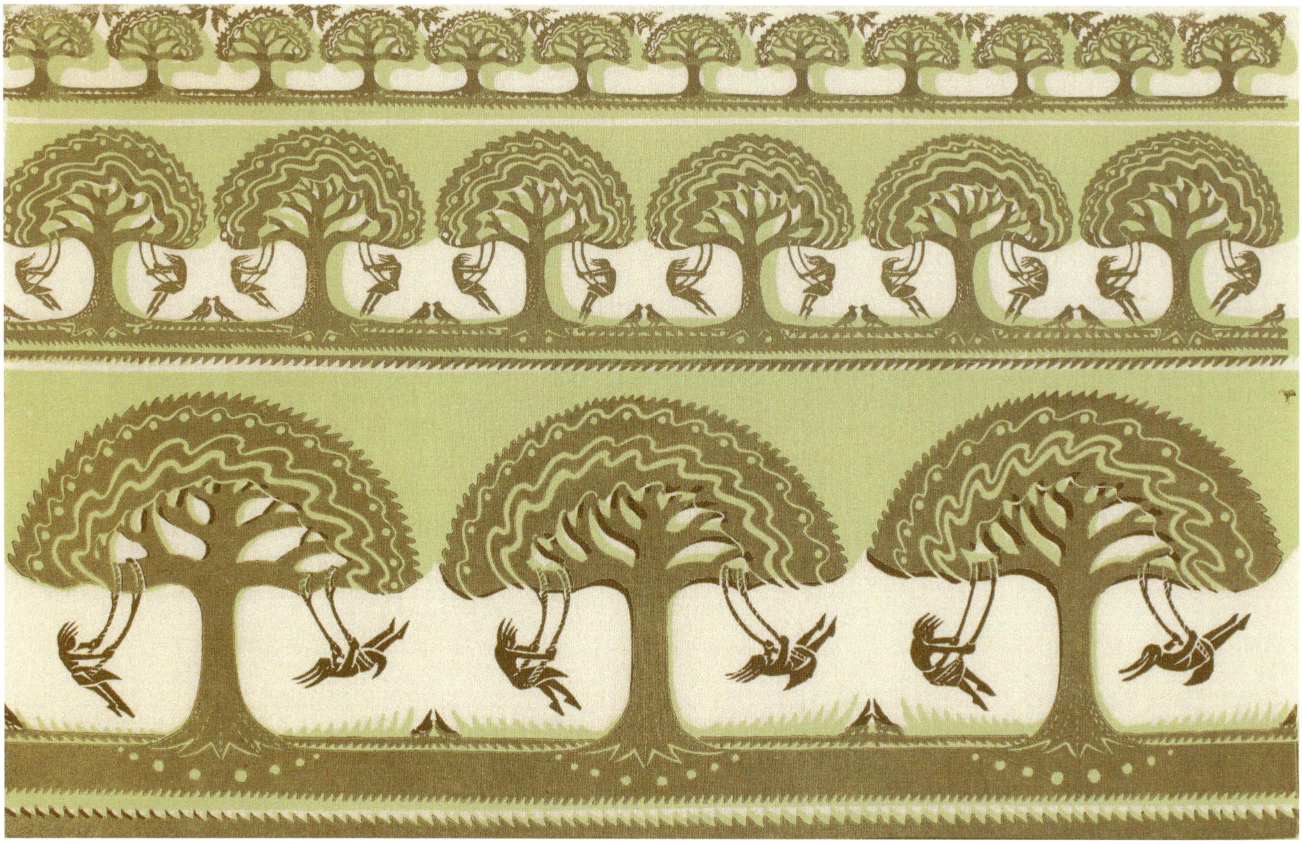

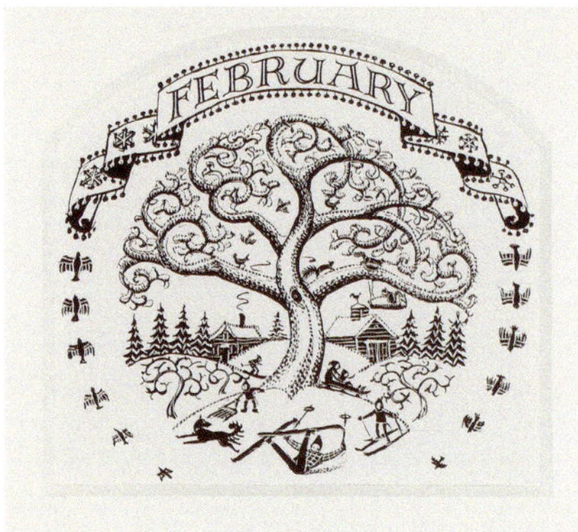
FEBRUARY

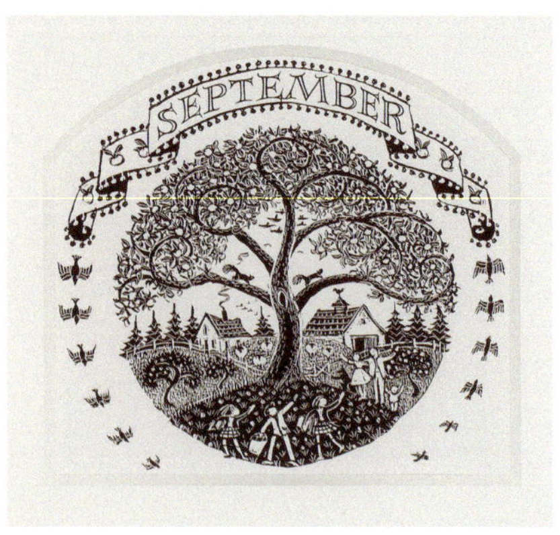
SEPTEMBER

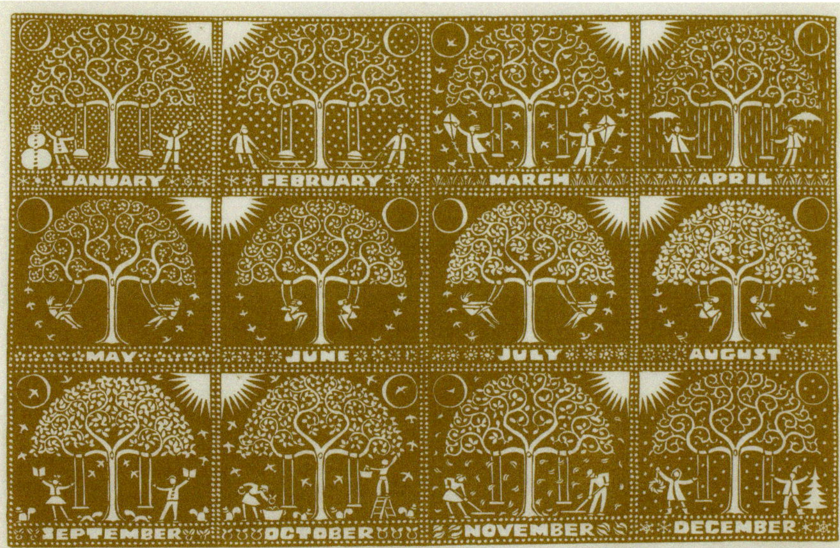
JANUARY
FEBRUARY
MARCH
APRIL
MAY
JUNE
JULY
AUGUST
SEPTEMBER
OCTOBER
NOVEMBER
DECEMBER

FIG. 128 (OPPOSITE TOP)
Swing Tree I **was a motif in her book *The Little House*. This design was featured in a 1945 edition of *Woman's Day*, though it featured only the row of large trees, suggesting that there might be an earlier version of this design. (Ink on fabric.)**

FIG. 129 (OPPOSITE RIGHT)
Swing Tree II **features monthly depictions of activities revolving around the swing tree as well as seasonal changes of the sun and moon. Notice the snow on the seats of the swings during the winter months. (Ink on fabric.)**

FIG. 130 (OPPOSITE MIDDLE)
One of The Horn Book, Inc., calendar illustrations (1965), feature the addition of her house and the basic activities of *Swing Tree II*, but in much greater detail.

FIG. 131 (OPPOSITE BOTTOM)
Another Horn Book, Inc., calendar illustration (1965), including filigreed tree branches and the birds that she incorporated into her book *Song of Robin Hood* and her designs *Robin Hood* (see page 115) and *Early Bird*.

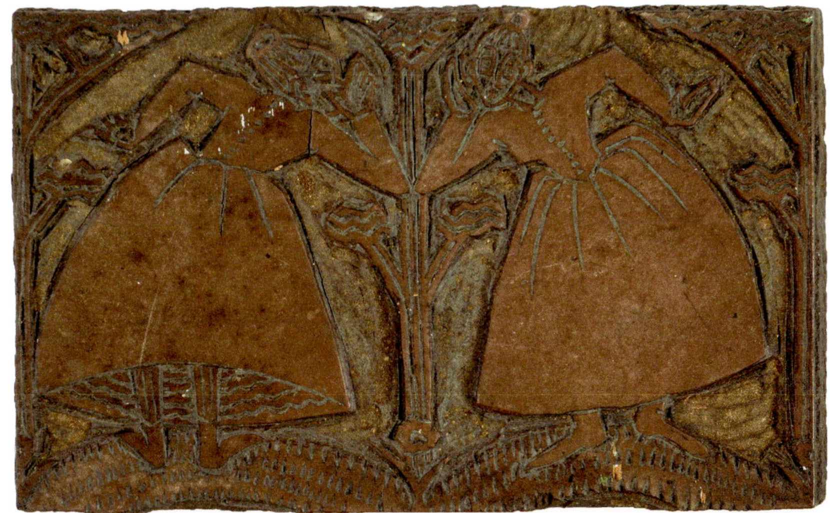

FIG. 132 (TOP)
Presumably the original *Gossips* block, date unknown. This version only includes two women, not the mailboxes, telephone poles, birds, and additional flowers in the final design.

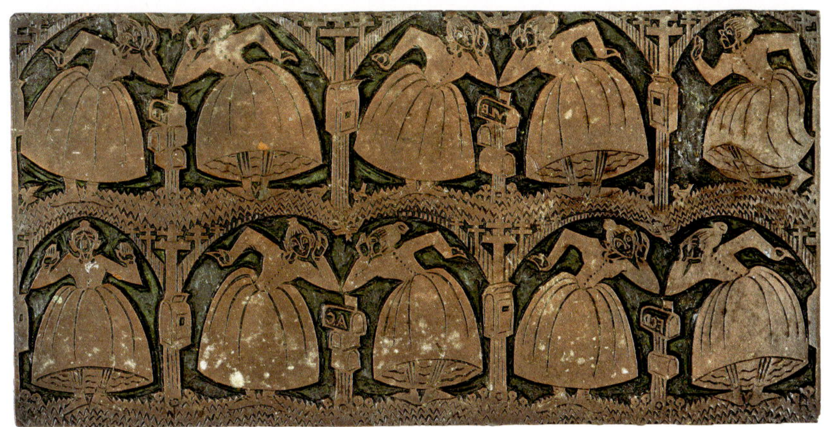

FIG. 133 (BOTTOM)
The block for the design most people recognize as *Gossips*. The two women's positions are reversed and it includes the woman racing to spread the news and shouting the gossip to the world. The telephone poles are very similar to those featured prominently in her books. But in this design they likely reference the children's game telephone, where stories get twisted the more they are repeated.

illustration description of *Song of Robin Hood*.[65] Similarly, a 1966 newspaper article stated that it was during Virginia's research for her book *Life Story* that she became inspired to create a design based on the subject of ferns, *Pterydophyta*.[66]

Lee Natti explained, "She would get a lot of material for her books and then she would feed it into her designs or she would start doing a design and then somehow something or other would trigger an idea for a book."[67] Lee recalled Virginia's *Swing Tree* design, which Virginia used to print curtains for her home. It depicted an old apple tree that sat on a little knoll outside of her house. "Possibly she had done the swing tree design first and then that led into the idea of the house by the swing tree and all of the idea from the book [*The Little House*] was created from that. But she certainly went back and forth from textile design to book and each sort of grew from the other."[68] *The Little House* was published in 1942 and *Swing Tree I* existed by January 1945 as it was included in a *Woman's Day* article.[69] Virginia designed *Swing Tree II* (also referred to as *Swing Tree Calendar)* in 1964, which led to additional swing tree illustrations she completed in 1965 for a calendar published for the Horn Book, Inc.[70]

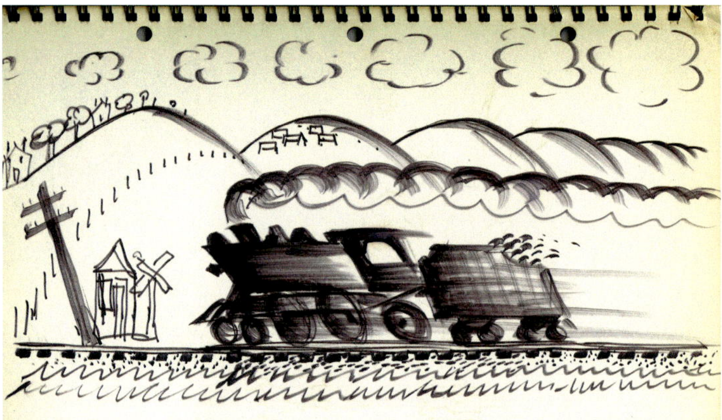

FIG. 134 (TOP)
***Gloucester Branch*. The bottom row features a city station; each of the other rows becomes more suburban, with the top row featuring farmland. Trains played prominent roles in her book *Choo Choo* and other designs; Virginia also included one in *Katy and the Big Snow*. (Ink on fabric.)**

FIG. 135 (MIDDLE)
An ink drawing for Virginia's book *Choo Choo*. Notice the telephone poles, which she also included in *Gossips* as well as the cover of *Katy and the Big Snow*.

FIG. 136 (BOTTOM)
***Commuting*. The train is the focus of this design, featuring the most rural of the stations from *Gloucester Branch*. The plume of smoke leads the viewer's eye. Virginia followed her own rule of using a slight angle to convey motion. (Ink on fabric.)**

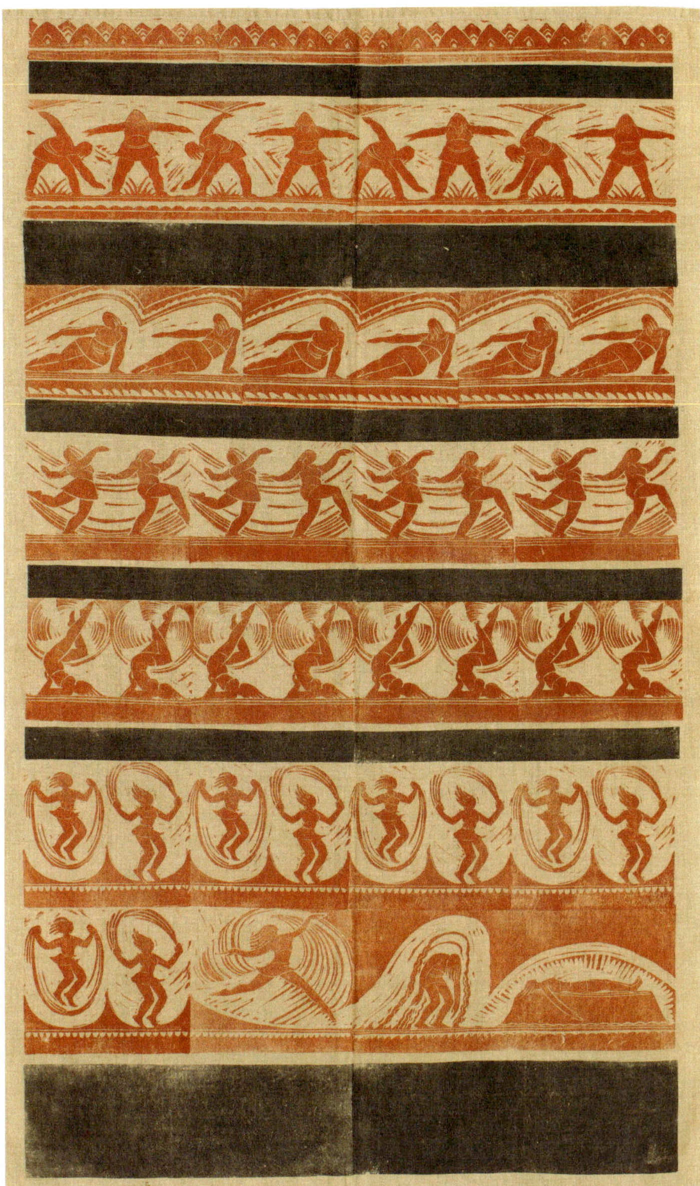

FIG. 137 (LEFT)
The presumably original *Reducing* is a "lost" design. The lines show movement. The borders and more primitive figures (similar to those in Aino's *Sauna*, page 23) make it understandable that sometimes the two women's work was mistaken for one another's early on. The slimmer but exhausted woman collapses into bed in the final scene. (Ink on fabric.)

FIG. 138 (BELOW)
A sketch by Virginia, with the figures on the top row confirming that the "lost" *Reducing* was done by her. (Pencil and on paper.)

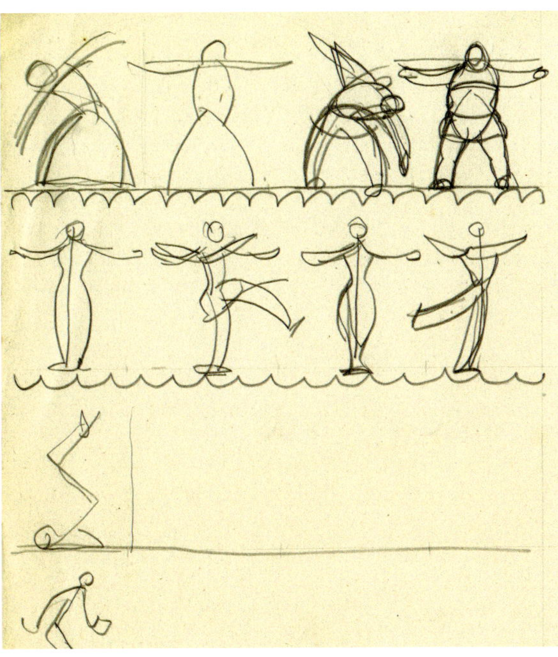

Similarly, train-related designs such as *Commuting* and *Gloucester Branch* were tangentially related to her book *Choo Choo*. *Gloucester Branch* and *Commuting* are nearly identical, although *Commuting* focuses more on the train. *Commuting* debuted in 1952 according to one accounting ledger kept by Dorothy Norton but *Choo Choo*, *Commuting*, and *Gloucester Branch* are all listed as new designs debuting in 1961 according to another ledger kept by Dorothy.[71]

Just as she redrew *Calico the Wonder Horse*, Virginia recarved designs. *Gossips*, for which she is perhaps the most well known, does not appear to be her first version. A smaller block and a proof print exist of two women animatedly gossiping.[72] It is not known whether this was a draft or whether it was printed beyond the one proof print on paper that exists in the Cape Ann Museum archives (although blocks could not be carved until the designs were approved by the jury). In this version, the women are framed by borders, similar to the framework of another of her early designs, *Finnish Dancers*. *Gossips* existed by 1942, but it is not known whether the reference is to this version or the final design.[73] By 1943 the design had been finalized to the version we recognize today as *Gossips* with mailboxes and telephone poles and was chosen for exhibition at the Worcester Art Museum.[74]

Another design that she appeared to redo was *Reducing*. The iteration presumed to be the original recalls the primitive figures in Aino Clarke's *Sauna* (see page 23) and the motion of Aino's *Skunk and Drunk* (see page 103).[75] The early *Reducing* also features the signature Folly Cove Designers' border, which many of them employed. But a sketch by Virginia clearly shows that the block-like figures in the top row were done by her.[76] Both versions of *Reducing* are narrative pieces that tell a story from top to bottom and left to right. The later version is more refined and representative of Virginia's figurative work.

The alternate versions of *Gossips* and *Reducing* are both "lost" designs by Virginia, as is what is referred to as *Fish Story II* in chapter 2 on page 42. In addition to discovering different versions of existing designs, some designs by Virginia were discovered that prior to now had only been known by name, including *Kittens and Knittin'*, which was submitted to William Skinner & Sons in 1949.[77] It is not clear if it was ever produced by the company, although a display board with swatches of the printed fabric featuring a Folly Cove Designers' label exists for the design in a private collection.[78]

Similarly, *Zodiac* is listed in Cape Ann Museum's catalog on the Folly Cove Designers but not accompanied by an image of the design. However, Virginia's homework collection includes notes on astrological signs, moon phases, and countless sketches that Virginia made.[79] One of the two ink on paper/boards shown might be the missing design. Usually when Virginia had progressed to the heavier weight paper (Bristol board) she was finalizing a design. A ledger lists that she debuted *Farmer's Almanac* and *Zodiac* in 1954 and both of these designs share design elements with *Farmer's Almanac*.[80] Additionally, Virginia used elements of *Zodiac* for one of her block-printed Christmas cards. Due to the depth of her research and numerous sketches, *Zodiac* and *Farmer's Alamanac* are likely a similar situation as

FIG. 139 (OPPOSITE)
***Reducing* is recognized as part of Virginia's oeuvre with its streamlined narrative and the clever addition of the measuring tape as border art. (Ink on fabric.)**

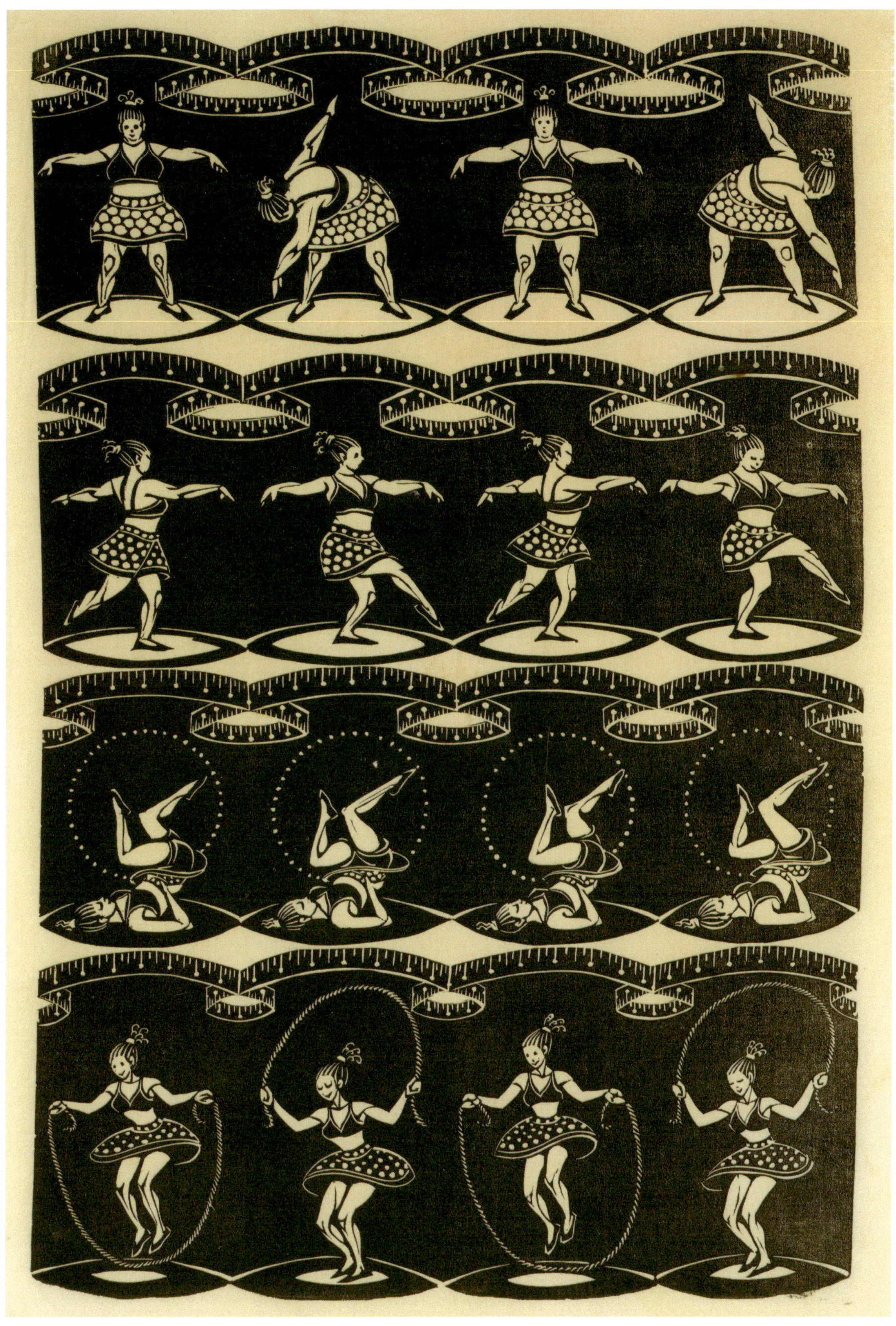

FIG. 140 (RIGHT)
Virginia's *Kittens and Knittin'* is a "lost" design emanating from a sample board bearing a Folly Cove Designers' label and multiple colorways. Yet Virginia didn't usually print multicolored designs and the colorways are similar to those that William Skinner & Sons used for her *A Stitch in Time* design (see page 65), making it plausible that this was printed by the company.

FIG. 141 (BELOW)
***Zaidee and Her Kittens* was one of Virginia's best sellers so she had the block made into zinc. A commercial company would have been hired to convert the linoleum block into zinc.**

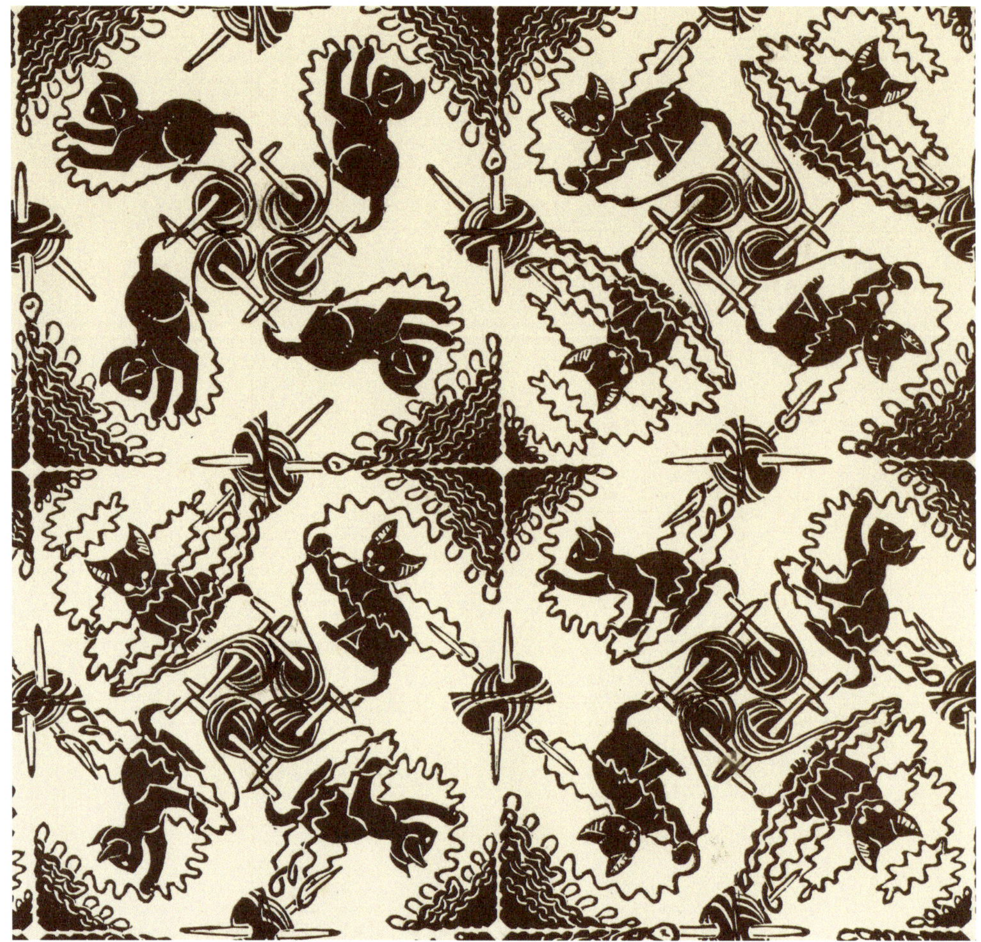

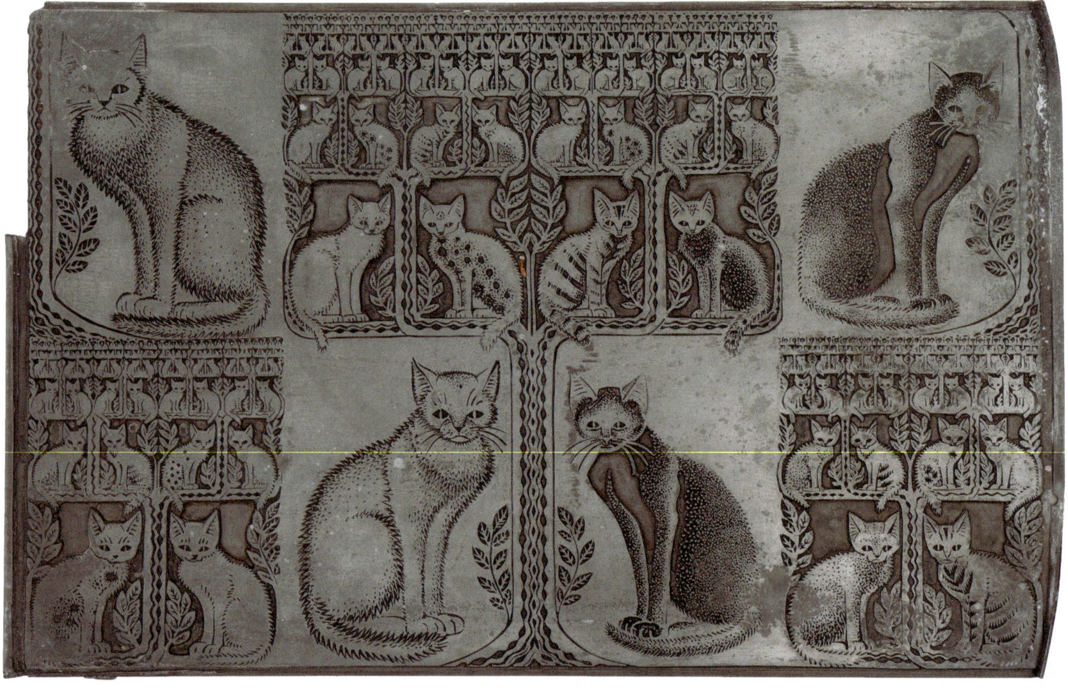

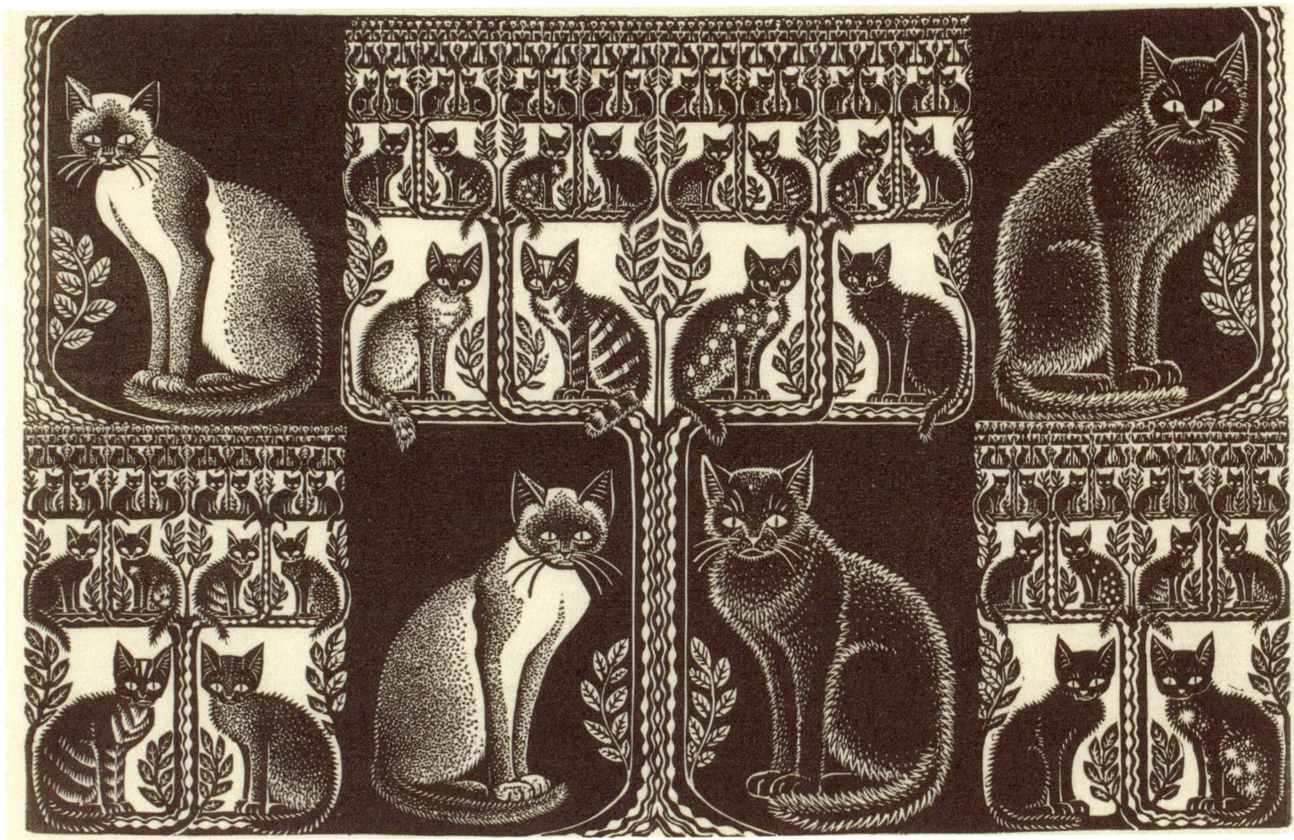

FIG. 142
It was said that *Zaidee and Her Kittens* was printed exclusively in this color, matching the color of a Siamese cat. Virginia said in an interview that the design featured the fur variations of all the kittens Zaidee ever had. (Ink on fabric.)

the two *Fish Story* versions and *Commuting* and *Gloucester Branch,* where she produced similar designs based on the same subject and ultimately was unable to choose between them, so she released both (or all) at the same time.[81]

Virginia again took inspiration from her own life for designs such as *Zaidee and Her Kittens*, which was based on the family's cat.[82] To incentivize people to take a kitten from one of Zaidee's many litters, Virginia would offer a place mat set to anyone who would take one.[83] *Zaidee* was one of her most laborious designs.[84] Lee Natti remarked on its many halftones and the multitude of painstakingly carved dots, an effort by Virginia to represent the range of colors of all of Zaidee's kittens in the design.[85] *Zaidee and Her Kittens* was one of Virginia's most popular designs.[86] It was so in demand that instead of recarving the block in linoleum when it became too worn to print, Virginia had it made in zinc so that the block would be more durable. Being less flexible, the zinc block yielded a sharper image of the fine details.[87] She also had *Spring Lambs II* made out of zinc.[88]

The enduring popularity of Virginia's books and her designs reflects how even people from "over the bridge" (as they say in Gloucester) were drawn to the magnetism of Virginia's life in Folly Cove. Her life extended beyond the pages of her books and the fabric of her designs, capturing the hearts of generations.

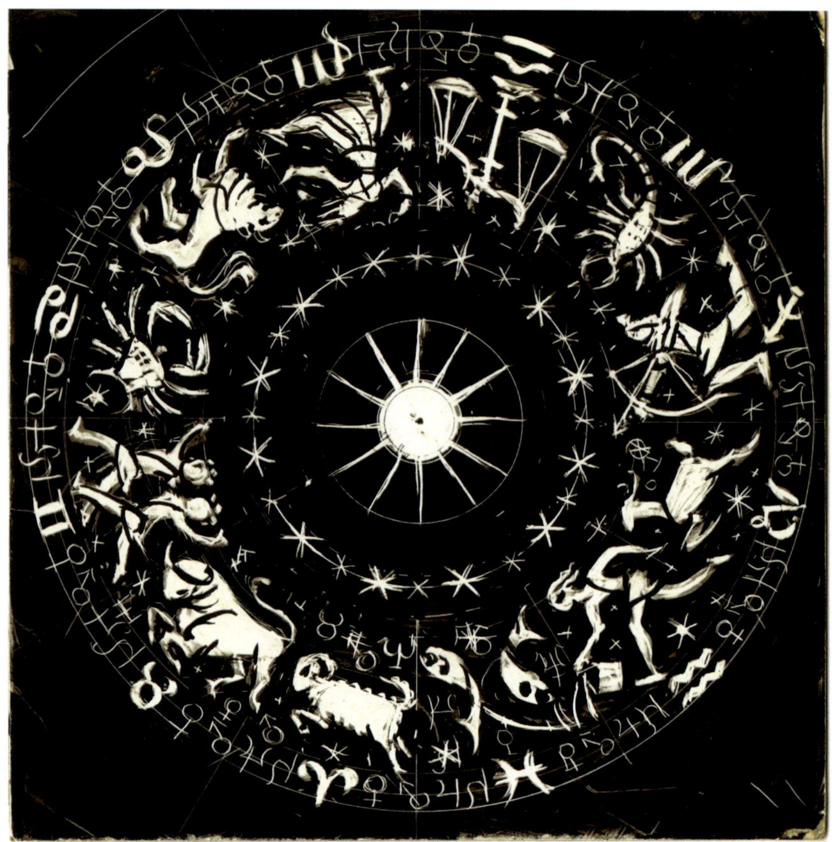

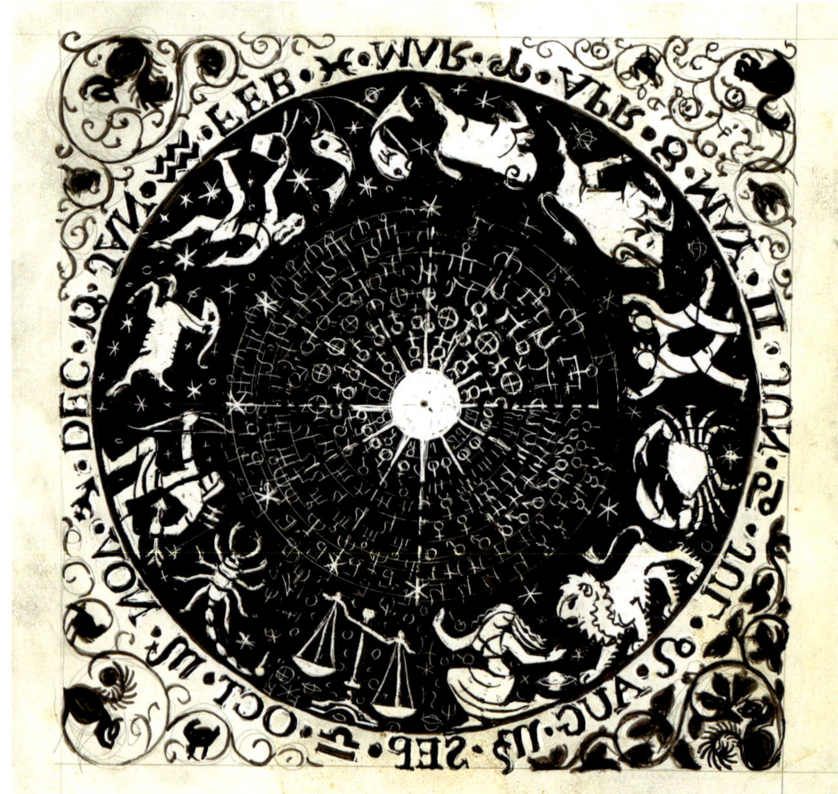

FIG. 143 (LEFT)
Possible version of *Zodiac*. This is very similar to a section of *Farmer's Almanac* but the focus is on the stars and the sun is simplified. (Ink on cardboard.)

FIG. 144 (BELOW)
Another possible version of *Zodiac*. This seems to be more of a stand-alone finished design, with squirrels in the corners. The months are listed in Latin and English along the outer edge of the circle. (Ink on cardboard.)

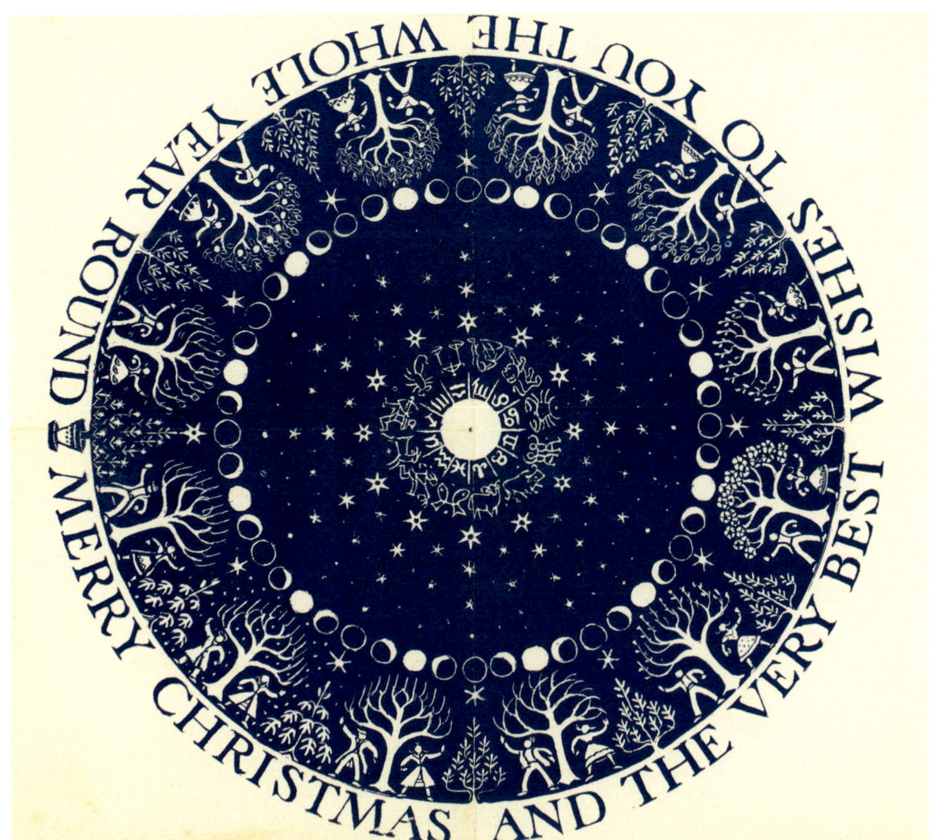

FIG. 145 (RIGHT)
Folly Cove Designers often converted their designs, or elements of them, into Christmas cards, for personal use or to sell. This card incorporates moon phases, stars, and zodiac symbols and was folded into a smaller square, allowing it to fit into an envelope. (Ink on paper.)

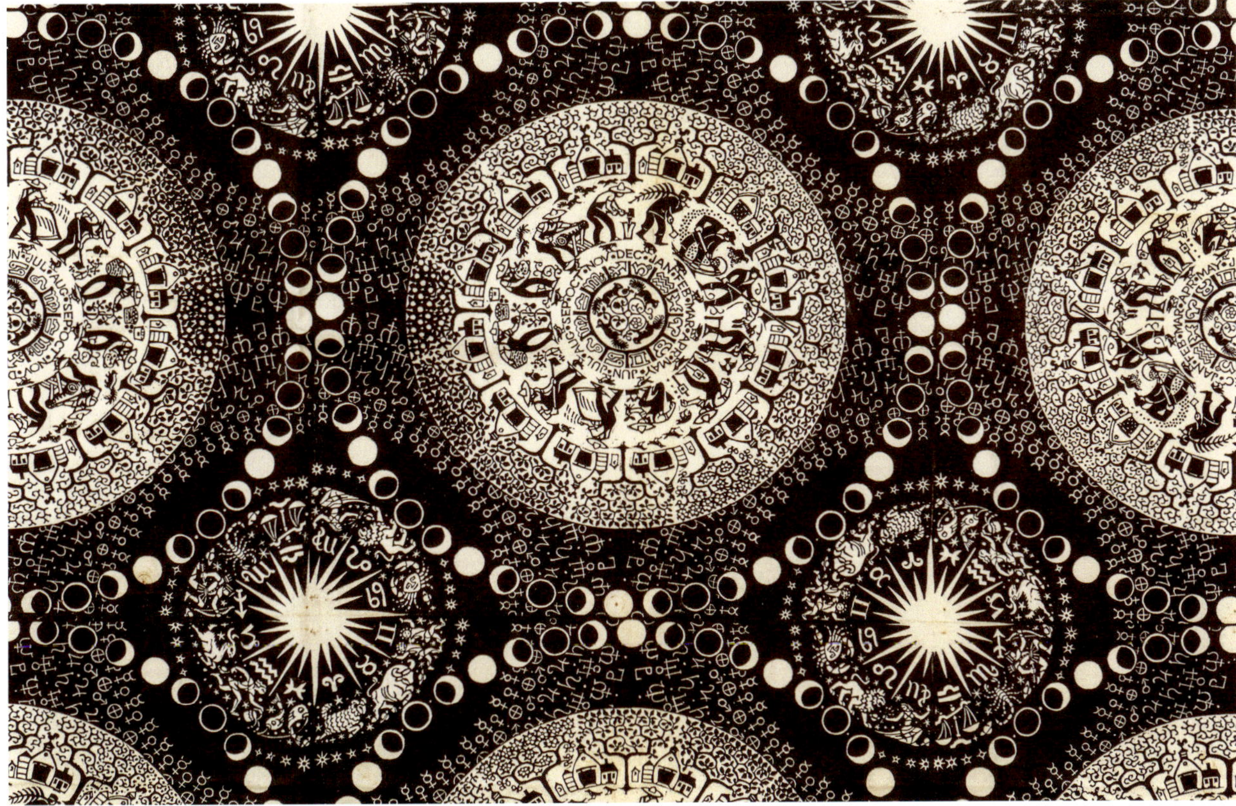

FIG. 146 (BELOW)
Virginia's *Farmer's Almanac* features monthly farm activities, moon phases, and zodiac symbols. The smaller circles are simplified versions of the possible *Zodiac* designs. The bowed barn recalls *The Little House*. The squirrels in the center of the white circle are reminiscent of the possible *Zodiac* design with squirrels in the border. (Ink on fabric.)

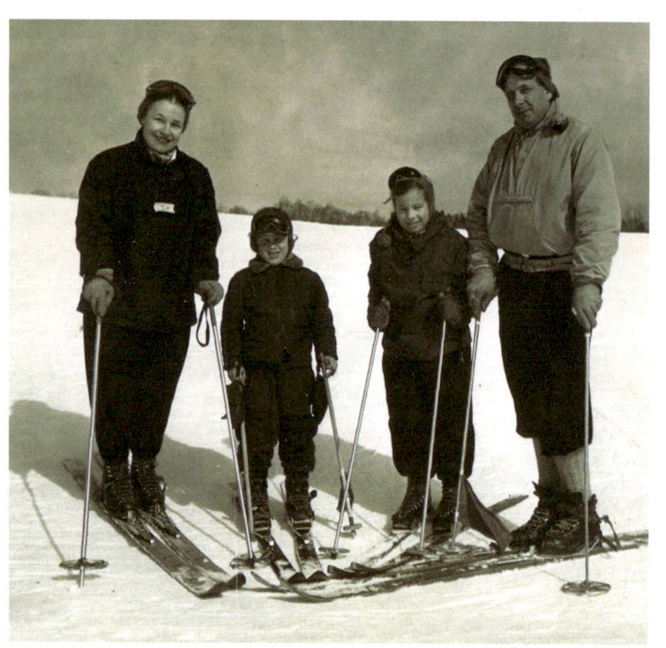

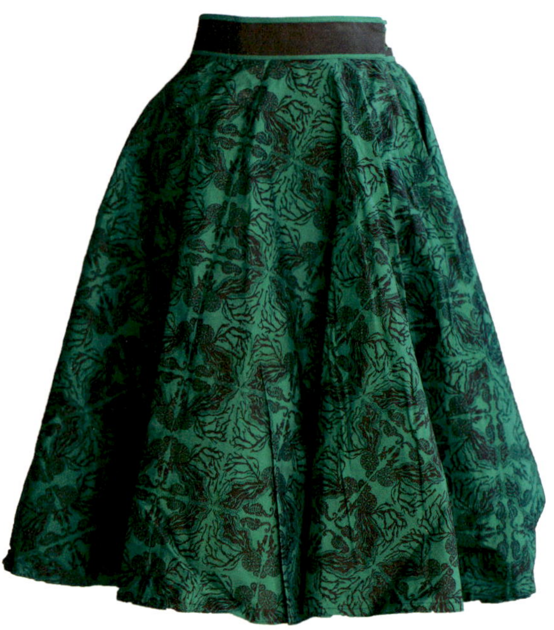

FIG. 147 (LEFT)
Libby Holloran, her husband, Robert (also a Folly Cove designer), and their children, Beth (right) and Timothy (left), February 1956, Jackson, New Hampshire. Many of Libby's designs were based on skiing.

FIG. 148 (RIGHT)
Libby was inspired to join the Folly Cove Designers after seeing one of their block-printed skirts. She recalled thinking, "I'm going to learn to make those skirts myself." This dirndl skirt with wooden button is printed in her *Seafare* design, which features seahorses surrounded by seaweed. (Ink on fabric.)

Sarah Elizabeth (Johnson) Holloran (1917–2009)

Sarah Elizabeth Holloran was born and raised in Gloucester. Elizabeth (or Libby as she was more familiarly called, and the name she used in her design work) was interested in art from childhood. Her parents fostered her interest and enrolled her in Saturday art classes in nearby Rockport. After high school she attended Bradford Junior College (now Bradford College in Haverhill, Massachusetts) for two years, where she took some studio art courses and graduated in 1937. She then attended Vesper George School of Art in Boston to study costume design and illustration, graduating in 1940.[89] She originally wanted to go into advertising but found it to be "an awful hard thing to break into."[90] She returned to Gloucester and married in 1942 because as she said "in those days, we didn't work—we were married."[91] She was only married a few months when her husband, Robert (Bob) Holloran (see page 171), was shipped to the South Pacific to serve in World War II for eighteen months. Wanting to keep busy, Libby took a job as a substitute children's librarian at Sawyer Free Library in Gloucester, where she conducted story hours on Saturdays, drawing while she told the stories.[92]

In the fall of 1942 Libby saw a skirt for sale by the Folly Cove Designers. Near it was a placard with contact information for anyone interested in design and block printing. Libby followed up, becoming a member until the group disbanded twenty-seven years later.[93] "I fell in love with it. When I saw those skirts down there, the whole thing, I just loved it."[94]

Libby credits Dorothy Norton with being her mentor. Libby did not have her own press initially, but Dorothy was a night owl and Libby would go over to her house at night to print. "I'd call up and say 'can I come down tonight, Dorothy?' I'd have my blocks and all of my stuff ready in a basket. And when my husband got home I'd put his dinner on the table and I ran out the door. And so he'd take care of the kids and I would go down and print. Sometimes

FIG. 149
Dog-Tooth Violet **features a flower bud in a design that is more of a geometric pattern than a realistic likeness of the flower. The swatches indicate the other colors in which she printed it. (Ink on fabric.)**

I'd work till midnight. Oh, when I think of the time I put in on that press."[95] Later on she bought a press from a member who was retiring and had it installed in her basement to accommodate its weight.[96]

Balancing family life with her design work was difficult. "I used to joke about it because I said I'd be cutting a block and there'd be linoleum in the mashed potatoes. And I took the blocks to the beach with me, in the sun—I'd cut down at the beach. Everywhere I'd go I'd take a block with me."[97] Members were expected to create one new design per year and being a young mother of two made that challenging. She recalled Dorothy Norton once defending her to Virginia, reminding her that Libby had young children.[98] Like other designers, she also designated one day a week for her design work. "I would either be designing or printing or sewing or fringing. Which you always had to do—fringe those mats—they were always hanging over your head—so I just took that day and I said to heck with the house, and that was my Folly Cove Designer day and I just devoted it to that."[99]

Dog-Tooth Violet was one of her first designs, a very simple, bold pattern. Her designs became much more intricate. *Fisherman* (see page 67) in 1951, which was a portrait of her husband, is particularly detailed.[100] The fine lines of the netting the fisherman is mending is a prominent feature of the design in this portrait, as is the rope in the foreground.

Like other Folly Cove designers, Libby's interests were an inspiration for her designs. *Slalom* and *Skiers* reflect her love of skiing.[101] *Skiers* depicts skiers making their way down the slope, with one skier in the center climbing back up the mountain (in the days before there were as many ski lifts).[102] She designed *Slalom* with the purpose of printing the draperies for the cabin she and her husband built in Jackson, New Hampshire.[103] It is much more detailed than *Skiers* and features skiers racing around poles with plumes of

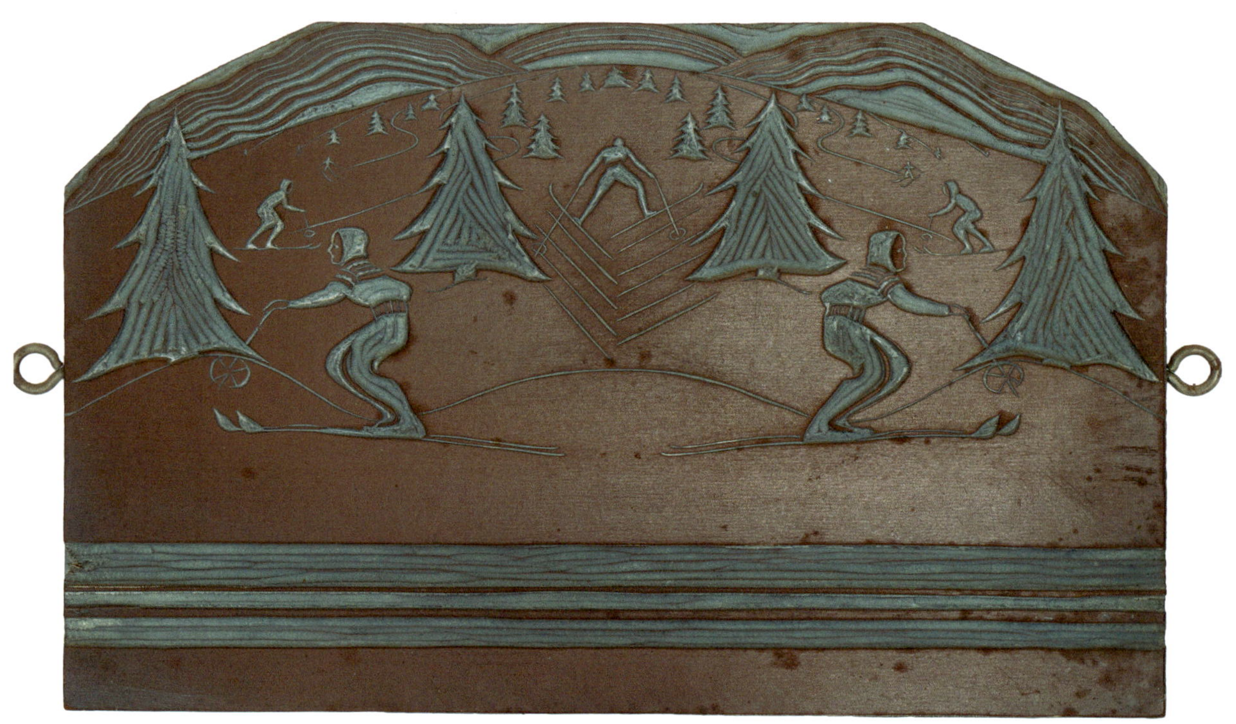

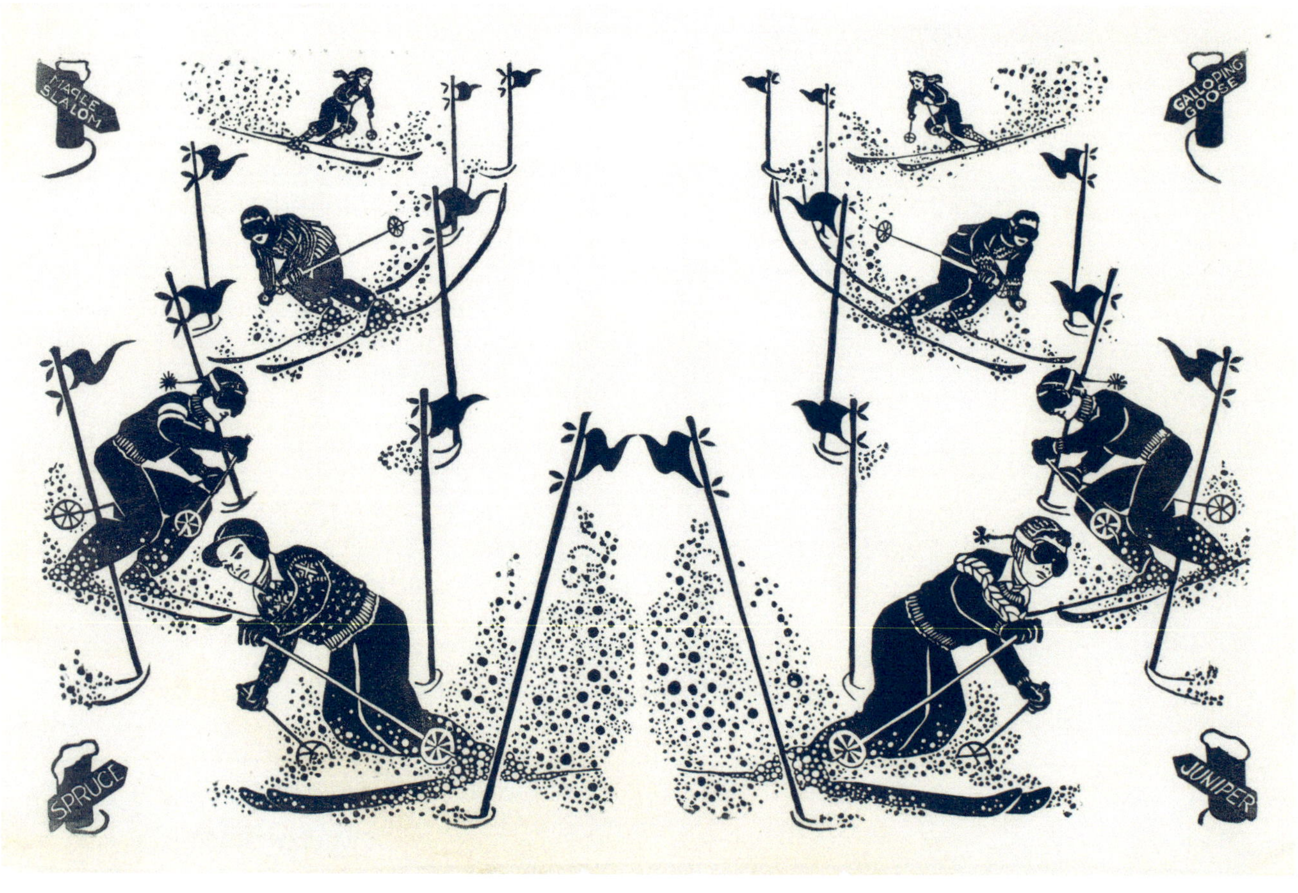

MAPLE SLALOM
GALLOPING GOOSE
SPRUCE
JUNIPER

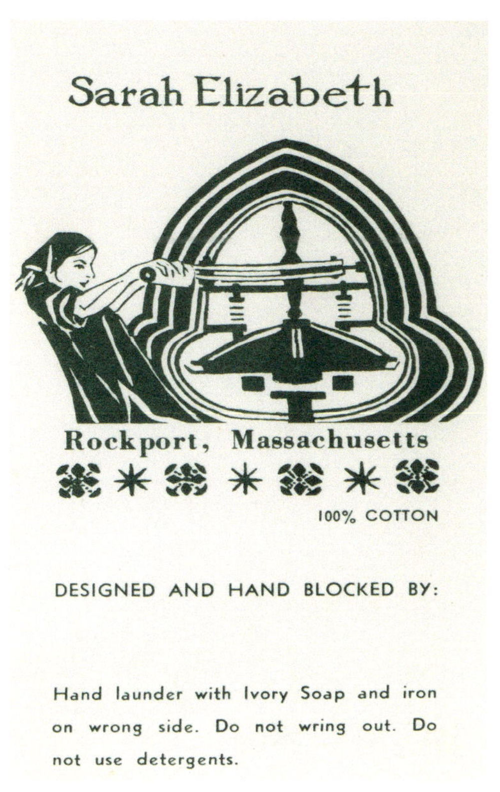

FIG. 150 (OPPOSITE TOP)
Libby Holloran's *Skiers* (1950) is one of her two ski-themed designs. The skier in the middle is returning up the mountain using the herringbone technique. According to Libby's daughter, before there were many ski lifts, skiers would climb back up using this technique. The design reflects Virginia's lessons in size and symmetry. (Linoleum block.)

FIG. 151 (OPPOSITE BOTTOM)
***Slalom* (1956) by Libby. Despite there being an error in the "Maple" trail marker in the top left, it doesn't appear that the block was ever recarved. The figurative work in this second skiing themed piece of hers is particularly detailed. (Ink on fabric.)**

FIG. 152 (LEFT)
The logo for the eponymous printmaking shop that Libby opened after the Folly Cove Designers disbanded features Eino Natti's press, which had once been in the Folly Cove Designers' barn. (Ink on paper.)

FIG. 153 (BELOW)
***Sugar Bush* by Libby entailed a lot of detailed carving, particularly the little trees, the cut wood, and stone wall in the top row. The sugarhouse it portrays was located on the Sugarbush Trail in Jackson, New Hampshire, on Black Mountain. (Ink on fabric.)**

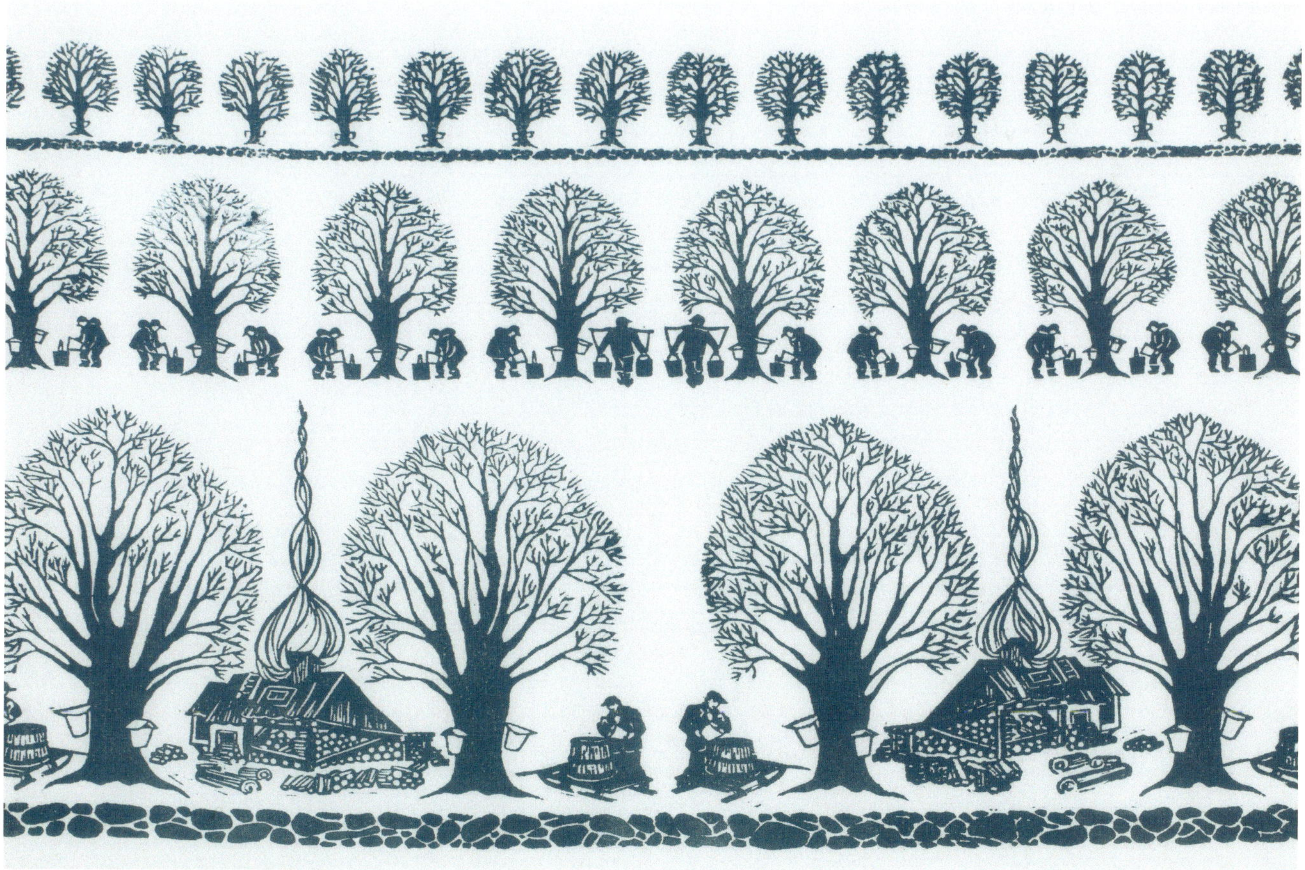

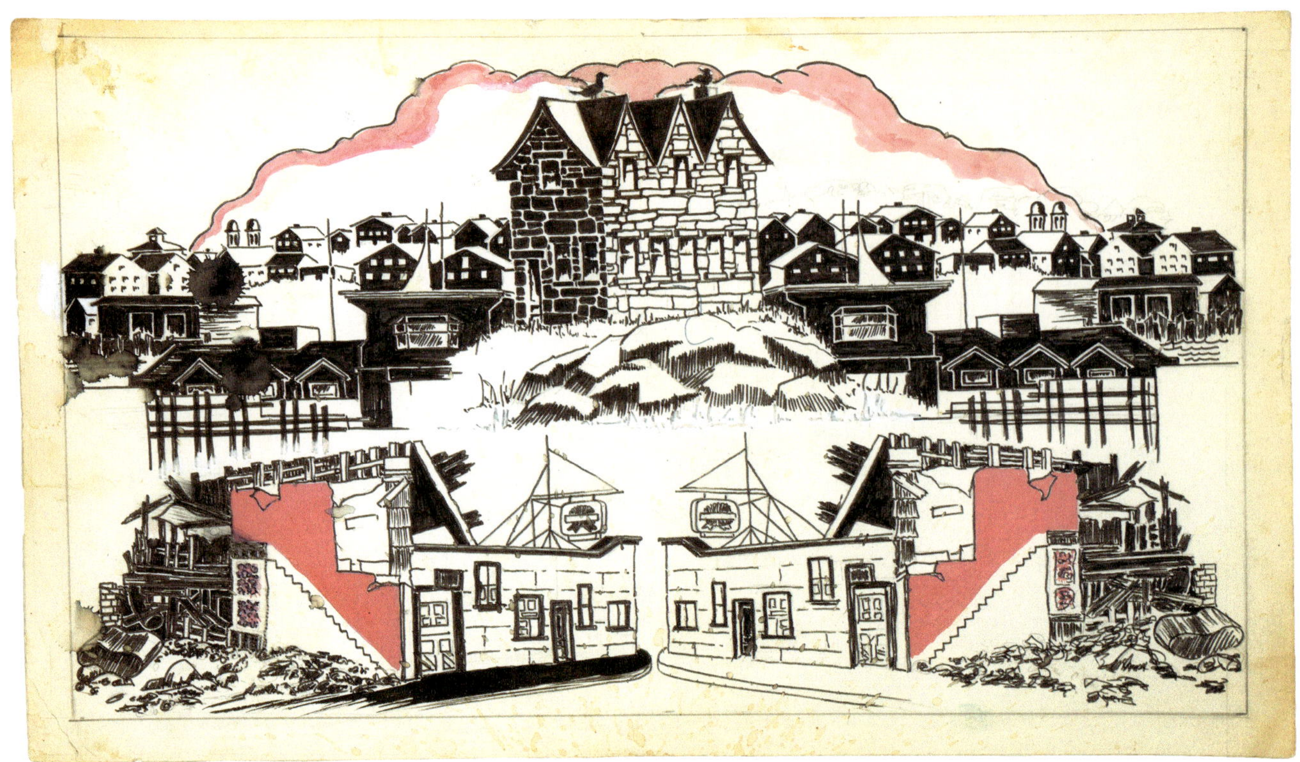

FIG. 154
Libby Holloran's detailed sketch for *Urban Removal*. She started working on this design as a Folly Cove designer, but finished it after the group disbanded (upon the encouragement of her daughter, Beth) and sold it in her shop. Artist Fitz Henry Lane's home is in the center. (Ink, pencil, and watercolor on paper.)

snow flying up behind them. It is interesting to note that *Slalom* contains a tiny error—the trail name "Maple Slalom" has a reversed "P" in the trail marker, a common carving error with letters, but a rare mistake that slipped past the jury.

Libby's last design as a Folly Cove designer (and one of her personal favorites) was *Sugar Bush* in 1961, based on her friend Ken Davis's sugarhouse.[104] While she did not produce as many designs as some Folly Cove Designers, Libby remained an active part of the group and continued printmaking professionally after the group disbanded in 1969. She opened an eponymous storefront and studio, The Sarah Elizabeth Shop, in Rockport in 1974 and ran it until 2001 when she gave up printmaking in her mid-eighties.[105] Despite the rule that retired members would not use their blocks to print anything other than for personal use, she was granted permission by former Folly Cove Designers and Michael Demetrios to sell items using her designs and those of her then ex-husband, Bob (at his suggestion).[106] Bob had been a member of the Folly Cove Designers, as well. Libby also created new designs and worked alongside Eino and Lee Natti's niece Isabel for many years. When interviewed at the age of seventy-four, she said, "I just can't conceive of myself without doing this. And I just love it—to come here every day and work."[107]

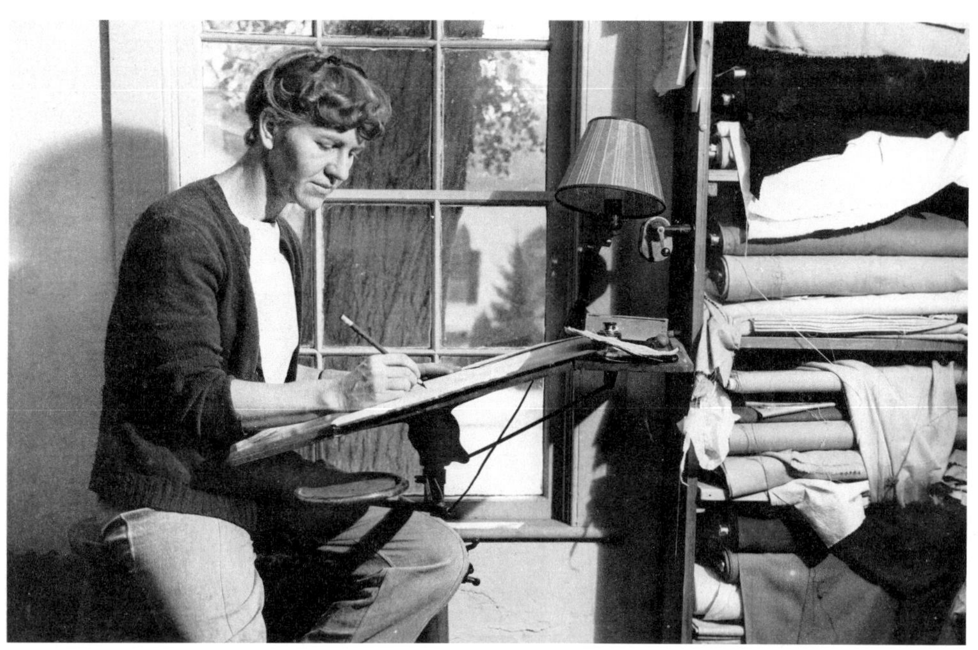

FIG. 155
Louise Kenyon sketching by bolts of fabric.

Louise (Tomlinson) Kenyon (1906–1998)

Louise Kenyon was one of the most prolific of the Folly Cove Designers. She was especially known for her architecture-based designs. Growing up, Louise (or Weezie, as her friends and family called her) summered with her large family of three brothers and four sisters in the Long Beach neighborhood of Gloucester. But her family's year-round residence was Newton, Massachusetts; it was also where she met her husband, Paul Kenyon, a fellow Newtonian who had survived polio as a child and regained the ability to walk. Louise initially attended Skidmore College (Saratoga Springs, New York) but transferred to Vesper George School of Art in Boston to focus on drawing and painting. After graduation she moved to New York City to pursue her passion for fashion design. She worked at Henri Bendel and considered taking a job at Bergdorf Goodman, but in the end returned to Massachusetts to be with Paul. She later said that she had no regrets about leaving New York City since she was "madly in love" and that "I've had such a happy time to be back here."[108] Paul was working at the *Boston Evening Transcript* (where he met Virginia Lee Burton) in 1930 when he married Louise.[109] Louise admired her husband's tenacity in facing adversity and his efforts to regain as much mobility as possible, stating, "Handicap's a word that doesn't exist in Paul's vocabulary."[110]

Layoffs at the *Boston Evening Transcript* during the Depression led the couple to move to her family's beach cottage on Cape Ann for the summer. Paul intended to write the great American novel. Louise spent her days caring for their young son, Paul, and enjoying the beach. In the fall they moved to Pigeon Cove in Rockport, where they lived for several years. After the birth of their second son, Peter, the family moved to their home in Annisquam (an area of Gloucester). Paul found a position at the *Gloucester Daily Times,* where he rose to the level of editor.[111]

Louise had been carving and block printing linoleum cards for their family since "the first year of [their] marriage—little ones—and they got more and more interesting."[112] After the boys entered school, she was able to return to her art. One summer her husband suggested they go see Virginia Demetrios's exhibition, the work of what Louise believed was Virginia's first class, which included Aino Clarke, Eino Natti, and Jimo Natti. Virginia asked her to join and Louise recalled her being "very compelling."[113] She felt that Virginia's design theories were "great," but admitted that, unlike some members, she was "rather spasmodic" about doing her homework.[114] She did say that as someone with design experience she felt that she had more "independence" and that "I had done my own thing and continued to do it more or less."[115] She enjoyed the different phases of the work, including designing and sketching, carving, and printing. She recalls printing 50 to 60 pieces at one time.[116] Several designers mentioned Louise's eye for color and skill at mixing inks. Lee Natti said, "Louise was wonderful. She could mix any color and match it."[117] Aino Clarke remembered Louise's preference for earth tones.[118]

Head of the Cove was one of Louise's earliest and most popular designs.[119] It depicts her neighborhood in Annisquam, the title referencing Lobster Cove, which was nearby. Louise printed it onto wall cloth for her home's two-story entryway.[120] It features Louise's house, her older son doing yard work at Peggy Norton's house, her youngest son chasing chickens, her husband rowing, her parents on their way to church, and herself in the garden.[121]

Its original composition—as printed in her entryway and produced by Lord & Taylor and seemingly F. Schumacher—was entirely different than the design most people recognize as *Head of the Cove*.[122] At some point, perhaps due to a worn block or the fact that it makes more sense compositionally, or maybe to make the design fit on an 11x17–inch block suitable for printing place mats, Louise recarved the design.[123] After receiving a wallpaper sample of *Head of the Cove* in 1946, Dorothy wrote F. Schumacher executive Rene Carrillo, "In the enlargement, the jury feels that it has lost a great deal of its charm. When a design is reversed and blown up as this one was, the jury thinks that designers should have an opportunity to redraw the design"[124] But this letter suggests that F. Schumacher may have prompted the redesign. The components of both versions are the same, but the details are changed: Louise moved the church and Norton home to the opposite side of the block; she reversed the direction of the church; she removed the outbuilding from the back of the Kenyon home; she moved the addition on their house to the left side, to reflect how it appears from the street. The clothing on the couple and woman and child were changed, as were the shrubs and trees. Overall, the second version is more refined, with far more detail, and the buildings more symmetrical.

Louise would go on to print many things for her home, including curtains and upholstery fabric.[125] She said she designed *New England (Wild) Flowers* on a larger scale with the purpose of using it for wallpaper in one of her bedrooms. Louise incorporated flowers from her yard, including the dandelions that her husband diligently waged an ongoing but losing battle against.[126]

She also designed more architecturally inspired patterns such as the waterside hillside of *Marblehead* and the classic buildings of *Chestnut Street*

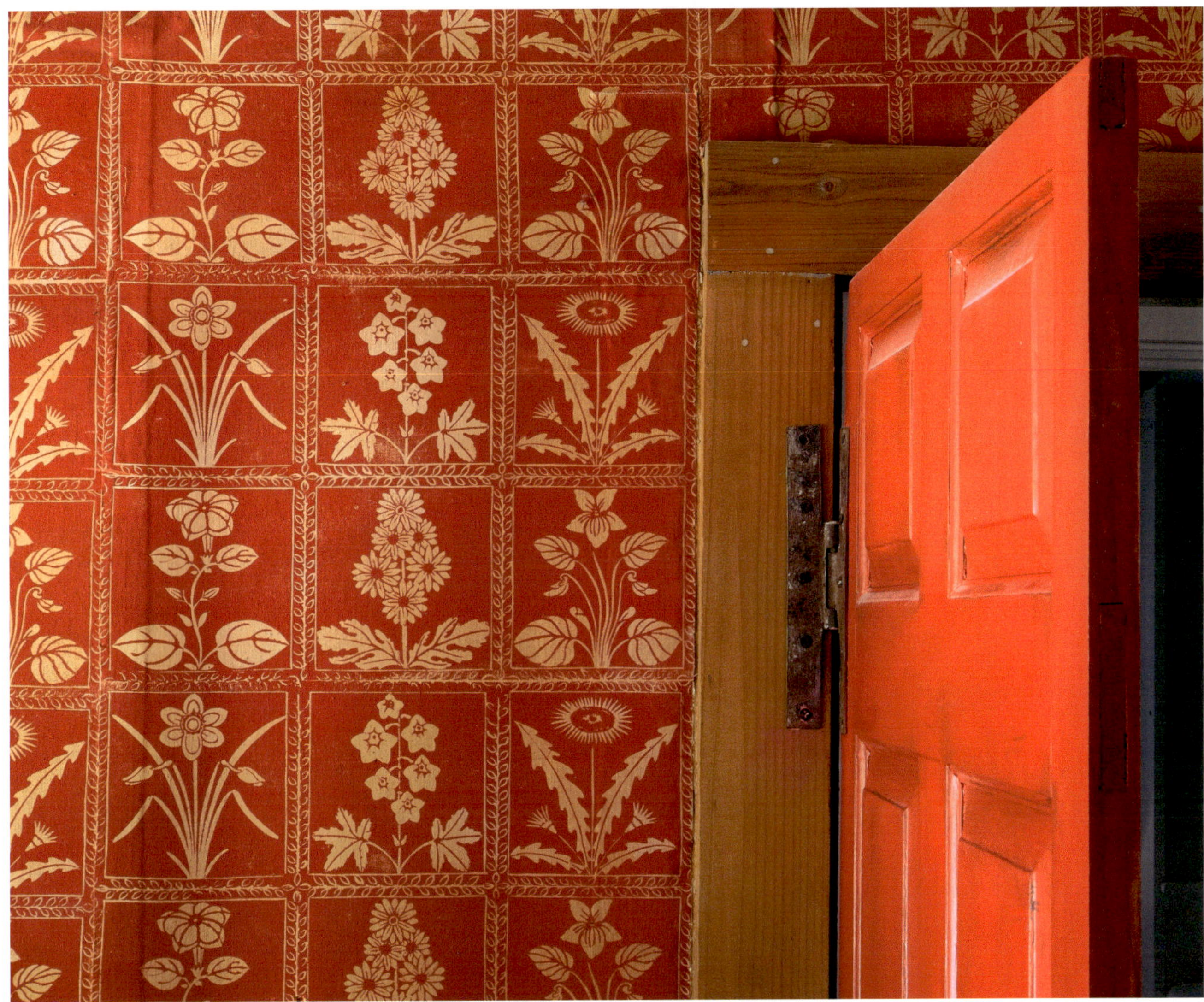

FIG. 156
Louise Kenyon's *New England (Wild) Flowers* as hand-printed wall cloth in the Kenyon home, where it still exists.

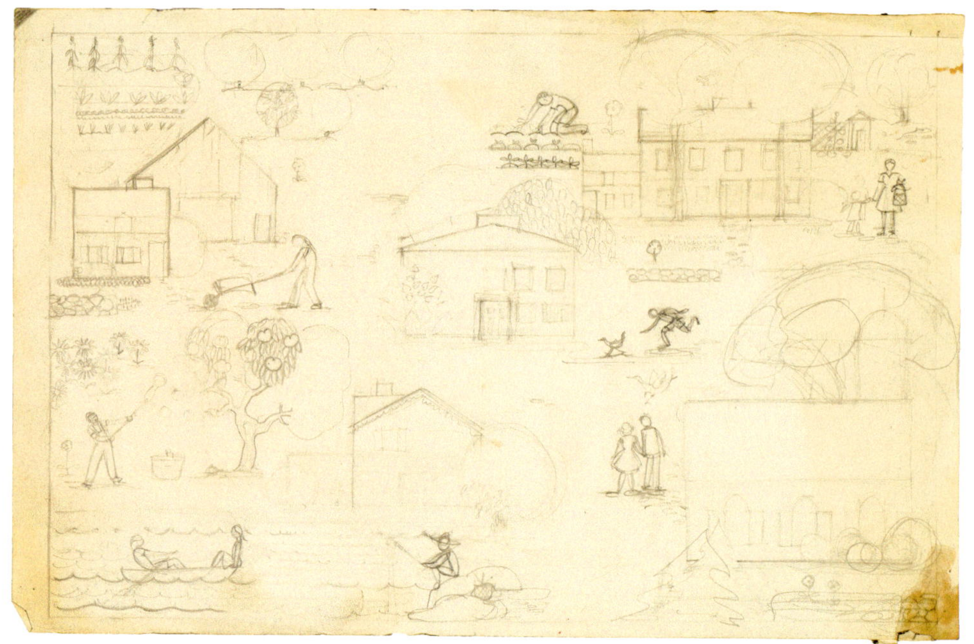

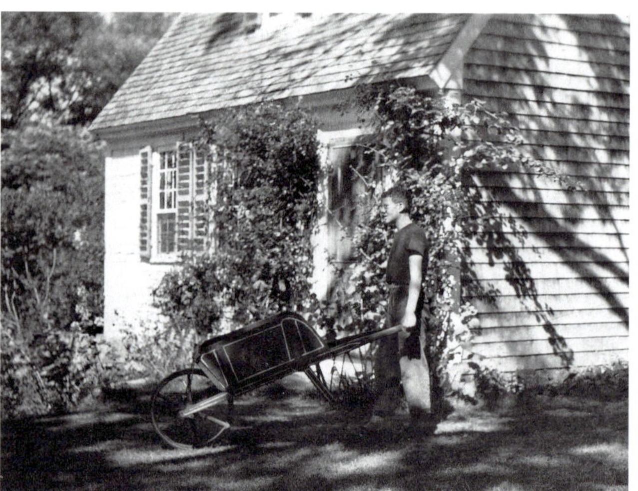

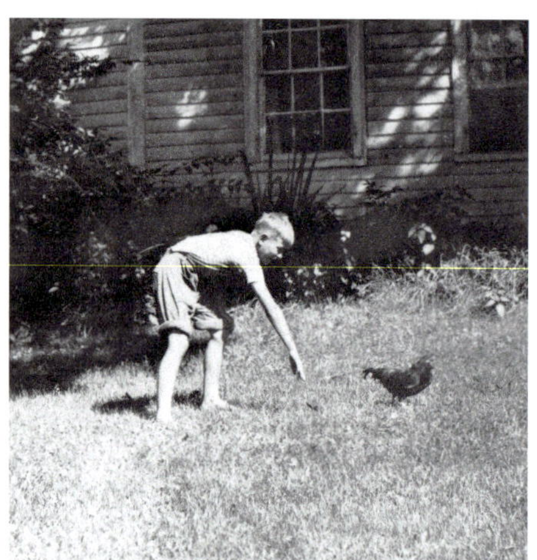

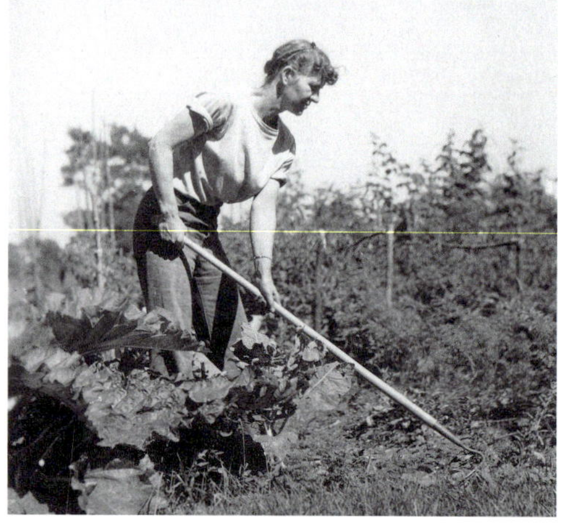

FIG. 157 (TOP)
The sketch for *Head of the Cove*, by Louise Kenyon, which appeared in *Life*. It shows the buildings as they appear if you were looking at them and not as a sketch to transfer. The squared buildings look more like the final *Head of the Cove*, but it includes the outbuilding that appears in the original *Head of the Cove*. (Pencil on paper.)

FIG. 158 (MIDDLE)
Three of the study photos for Louise's *Head of the Cove* as displayed in the Lord & Taylor Fifth Avenue store window with the design. Louise's eldest son, Paul, is shown with a wheelbarrow.

FIG. 159 (BOTTOM LEFT)
Louise's younger son, Peter, chasing chickens in front of their home.

FIG. 160 (BOTTOM RIGHT)
Louise in her garden. She often gardened with her sister Grace Murray, who lived nearby and who fringed place mats for Louise and other designers.

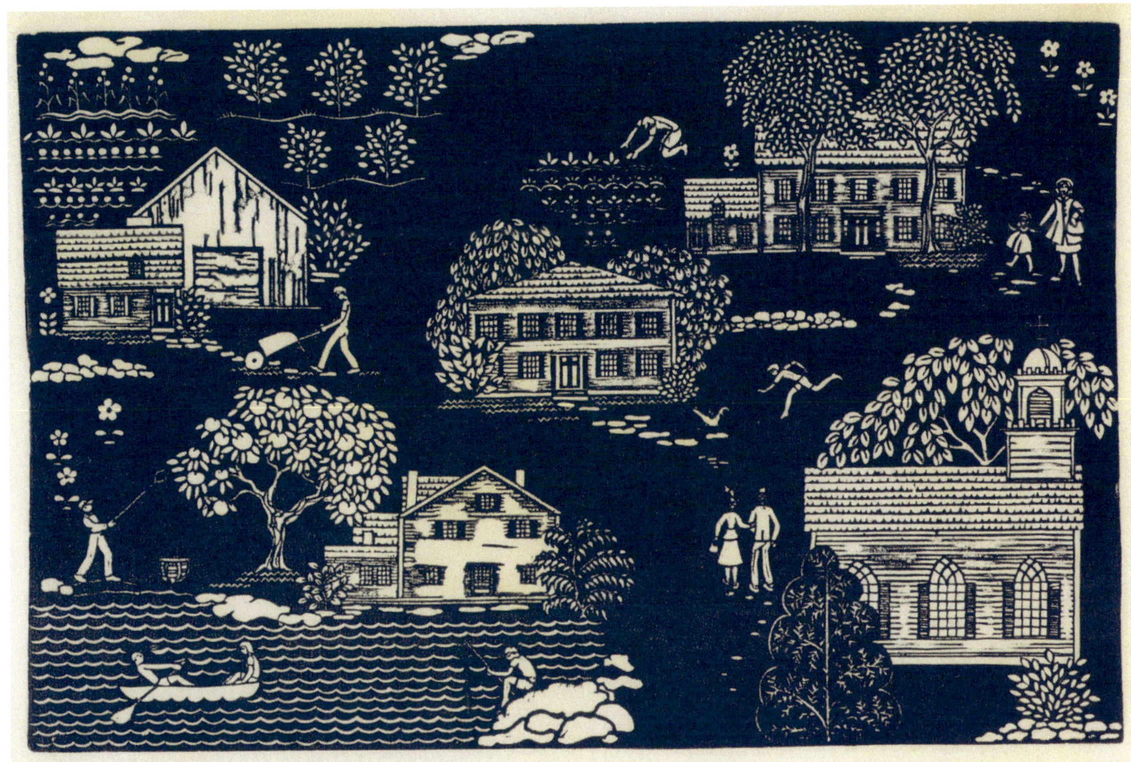

FIG. 161 (ABOVE)

Head of the Cove II **(as the author refers to it) is reversed and has cleaner lines. This is the design that most people recognize as *Head of the Cove*. This version reflects the original sketch and how the buildings are seen from the road. (Ink on fabric.)**

FIG. 162 (LEFT)

The original *Head of the Cove* hand-printed as wall cloth by Louise for her home. The current owners have retained the wall cloth and say that locals still affectionately refer to their home as "the Kenyon house."

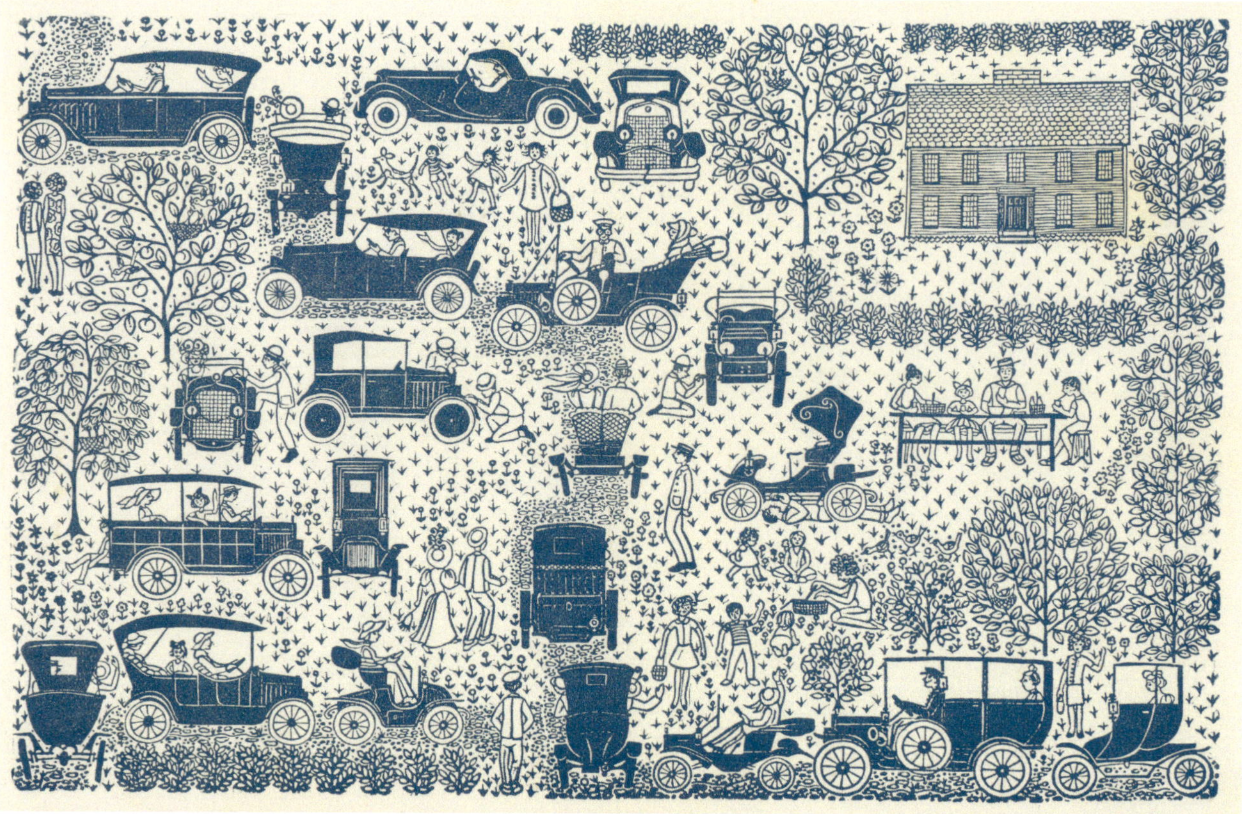

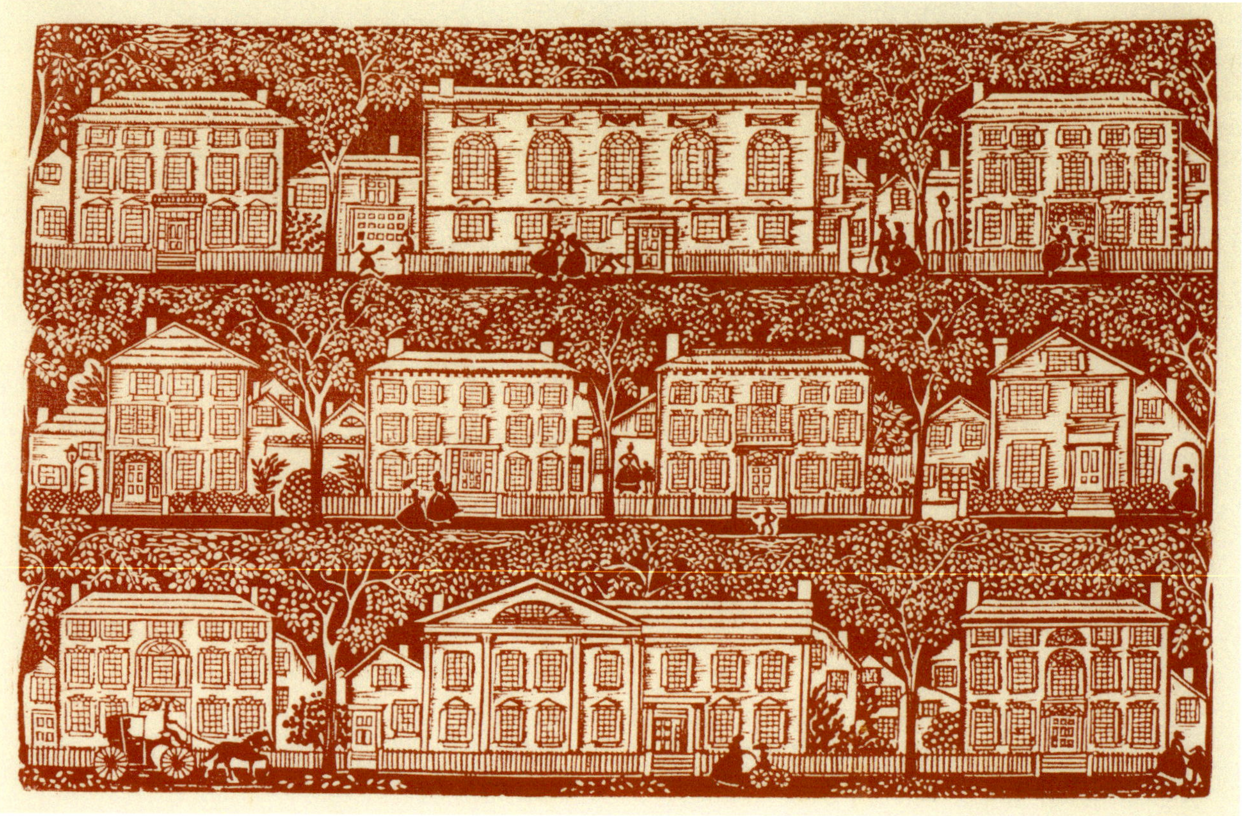

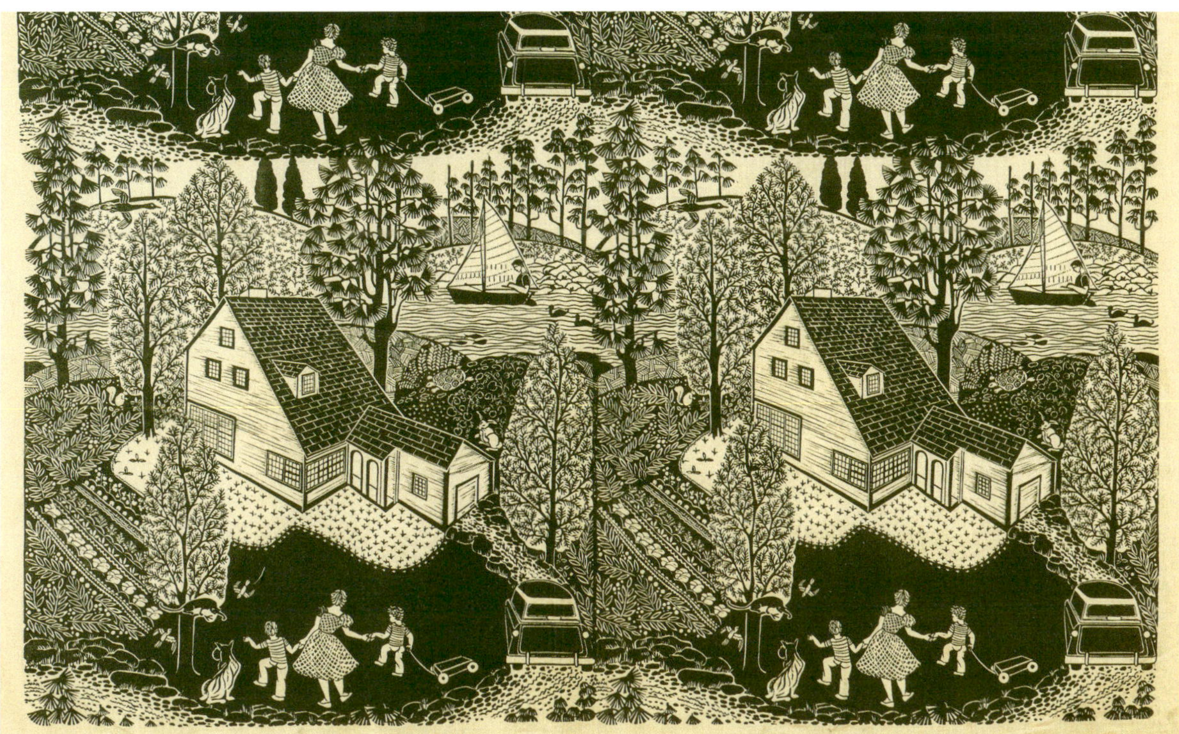

FIG. 163 (OPPOSITE TOP)
Up Country Meet **by Louise Kenyon. Perhaps car afficionados can spot the Chrysler touring car that Louise said that she and her husband, Paul, drove on their honeymoon. (Ink on fabric.)**

FIG. 164 (OPPOSITE BOTTOM)
Chestnut Street **by Louise features the Federal-style mansions of historic Chestnut Street in Salem, Massachusetts, many of them built by architect and carver Samuel McIntire. It also includes people in period outfits, combining Louise's love of both historic homes and clothing. (Ink on fabric.)**

FIG. 165 (ABOVE)
Louise's ***Goose Cove*****, lovingly designed for her sister's fiftieth anniversary. She may have carved two blocks for this, as she mentioned in an interview that she added her sister's two sons for use of the design on the anniversary party invitation. Her sister's garden is prominently featured. (Ink on fabric.)**

in Salem, towns with which she was familiar. *Up Country Meet* was also inspired by items close to home—the antique cars that both her father and her husband collected (and later her son Peter).[127] She designed *Goose Cove* (another nearby cove) for her sister Grace Murray's fiftieth wedding anniversary.[128]

One of Louise's later designs for the Folly Cove Designers was *Garland of the States*. Although it debuted in 1958, prior to Alaska and Hawaii officially becoming states, Louise included them, along with the District of Columbia.[129] The original sketch shows that Louise initially also included the state birds in an elaborate design. It is unknown whether she decided to focus on the flowers or whether her fellow designers advised her to do so.

Many of Louise's designs were printed and sewn as skirts, a large number of which sold through Jays Department Store in Boston.[130] In the group's early days she designed a bathing suit that was also sold by Jays.[131] At one point she had three women sewing for her.[132] So ultimately her love of art and fashion were merged and her dreams of being a fashion designer were executed.

In researching this book, several never-before-seen or "lost" designs by Louise Kenyon were unearthed: the seahorse bathing suit design; *Dogwood Leaf* and *Grapevine* (these two were especially suited for decorating fabrics because of their all-over designs); and a block of a horse and carriage[133]. All four are likely early designs. The Cape Ann Museum also has a block featuring a tree design by Louise in their collection that is undated and untitled. It is another "lost" design, making a total of six recovered designs by Louise, (including the original *Head of the Cove*).

FIG. 166 (RIGHT)
A silk scarf printed with *Garland of the States* by Louise Kenyon. She debuted this design in 1958, including Alaska and Hawaii, even though they did not officially become states until 1959. She also included the District of Columbia. This was a rare square design and so was not available as a place mat.

FIG. 167 (BELOW)
A sketch for Louise's *Garland of the States*, which originally included state birds. It is not known why Louise simplified the design, but perhaps the notation of "month & a half" and the date of June 2 indicates that time might have been an influencing factor. (Ink and pencil on paper.)

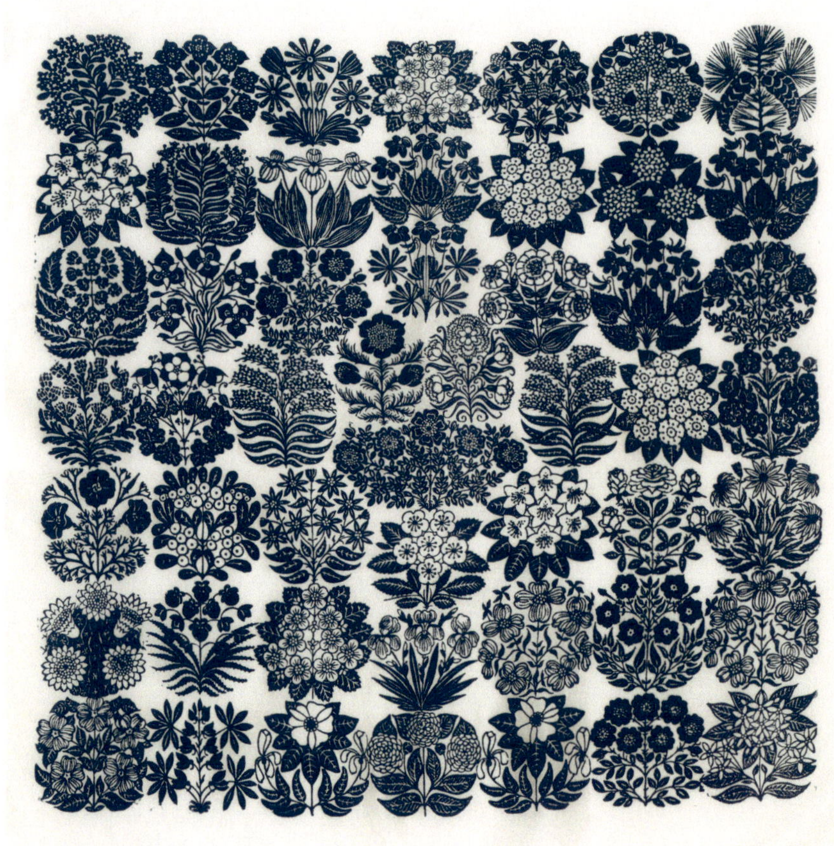

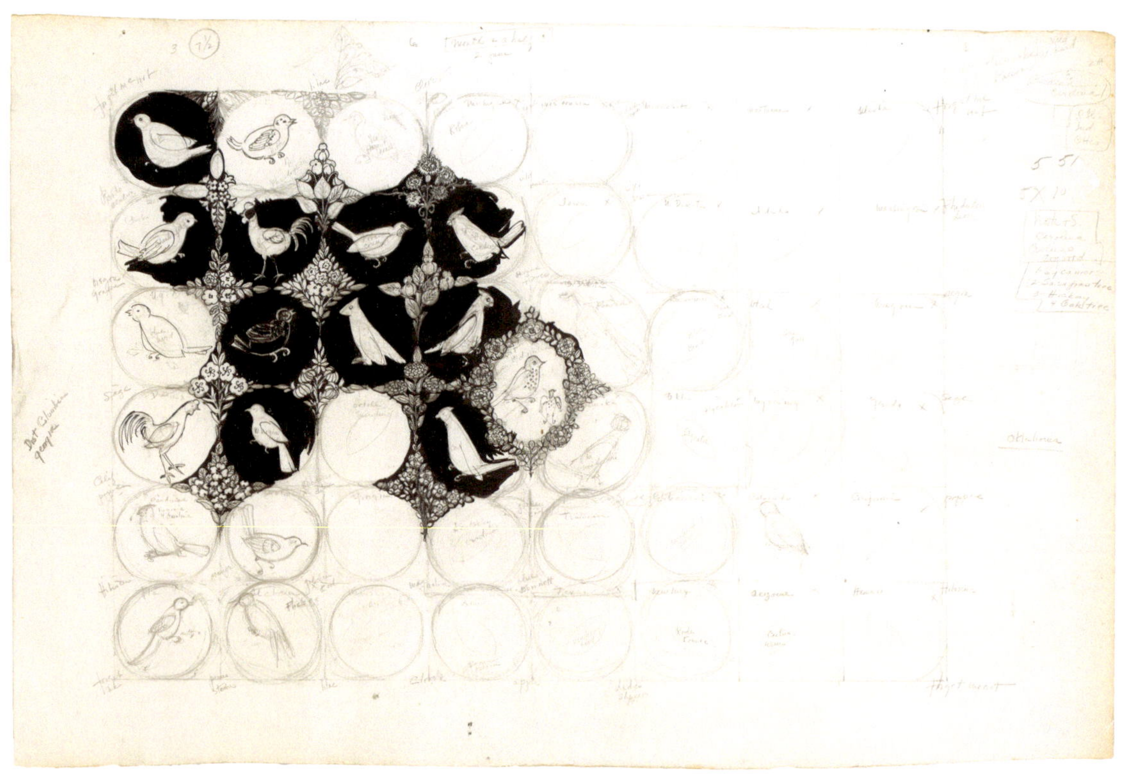

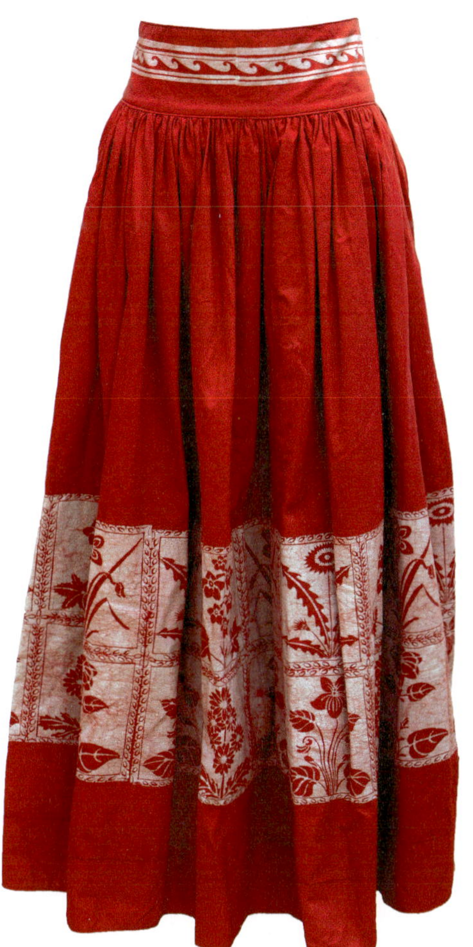

FIG. 168 (LEFT)
Louise's *New England (Wild) Flowers* design as a skirt. Notice the signature wave pattern of the Folly Cove Designers on the waistband.

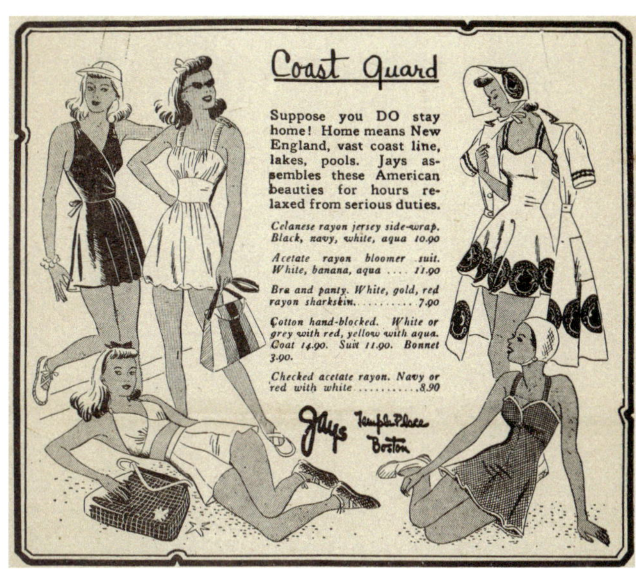

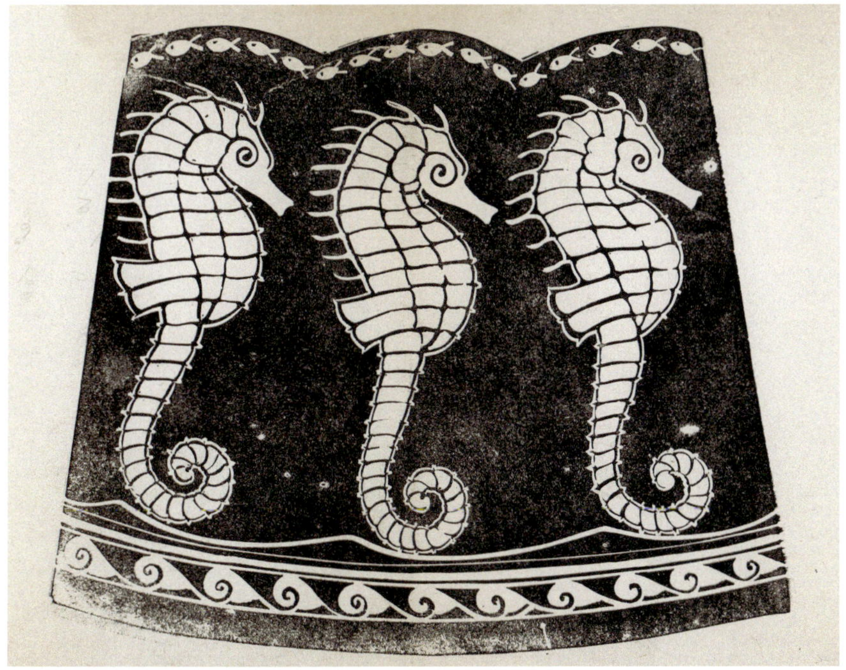

FIG. 169 (ABOVE)
A 1942 Jays bathing suit ad, sent to Louise by the company, featuring a bathing suit, sunbonnet, and a cover-up with a fish design by Folly Cove designer Ida Bruno. Dorothy Norton mentioned that the group sold bathing suits for "around $15" in correspondence with *Life* staff in 1945.

FIG. 170 (LEFT)
This is an undated proof print of one of Louise's bathing suit designs. A photograph of Louise wearing the bathing suit was published in a 1947 *Ladies' Home Journal* that chronicled her family. Notice the wave design on the bottom border. She used the top fish border in *Home Port* (1949), see page 29; designers often recycled elements of their designs. (Ink on paper.)

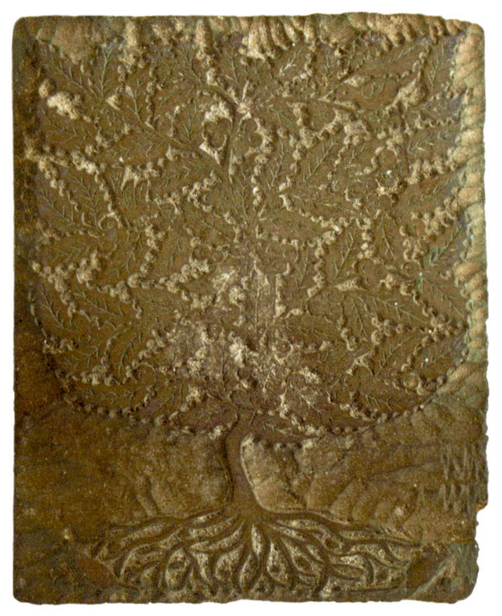

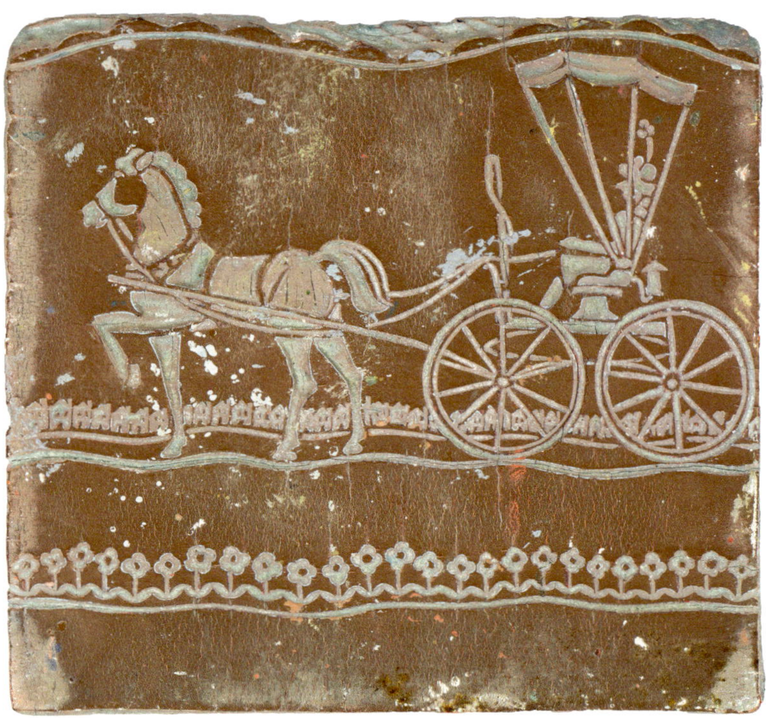

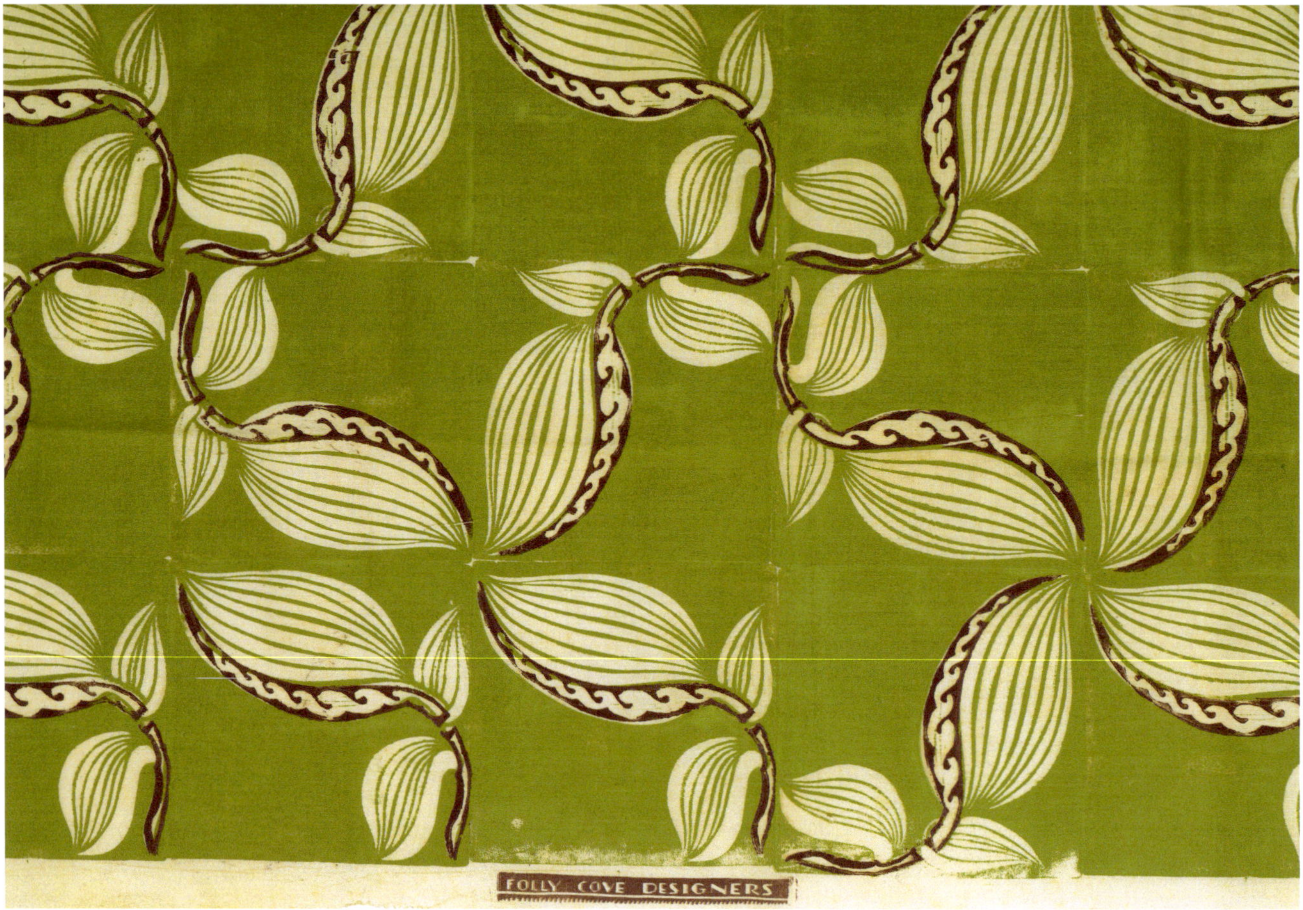

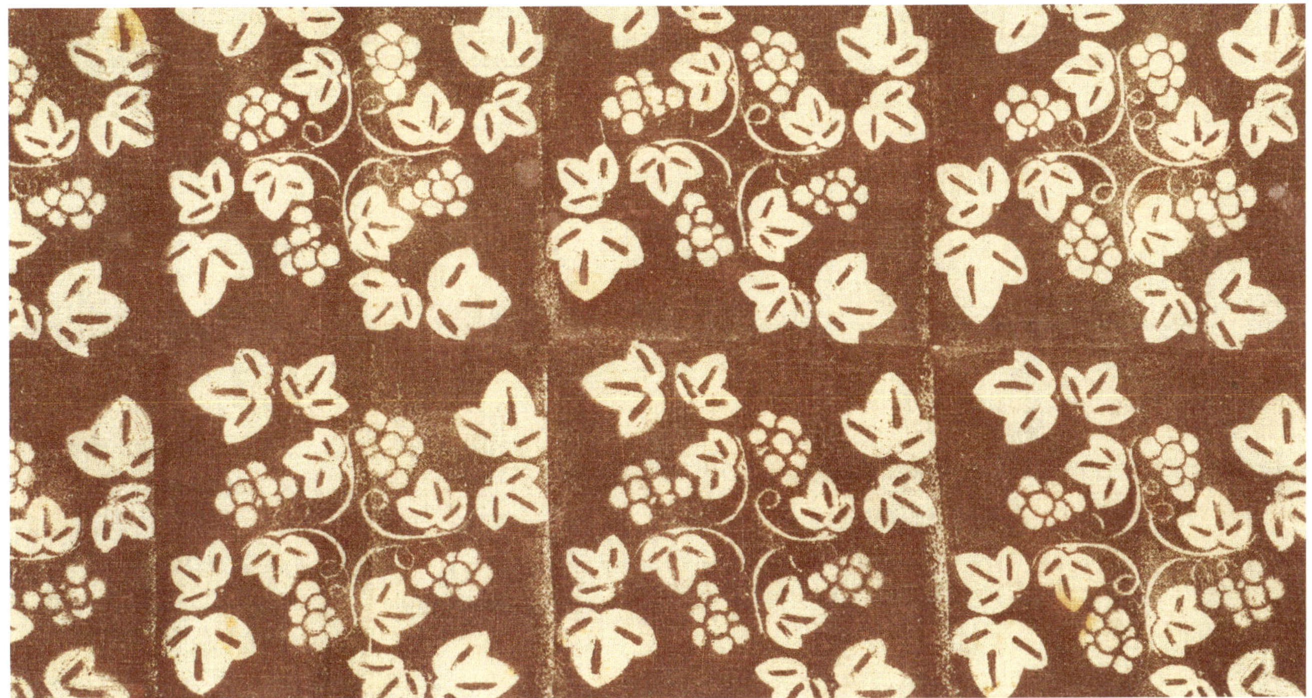

FIG. 171 (OPPOSITE LEFT)
This undated, untitled block features an intricate tree design. It is labeled "practice linoleum block," but if a block was carved it meant that it had passed jury approval, unless this one predated the formation of the jury in 1943.

FIG. 172 (OPPOSITE RIGHT)
This linoleum block featuring a design of a horse and buggy is another "lost" design, presumably an early one due to the size of the block. Louise saved an undated clipping from the *Christian Science Monitor* that featured this design.

FIG. 173 (OPPOSITE BOTTOM)
Hand-printed yardage of *Dogwood Leaf* by Louise. Date unknown, but likely early. (Ink on fabric.)

FIG. 174 (ABOVE)
***Grapevine* by Louise Kenyon. This design appeared in a 1945 *Woman's Day* feature on the Folly Cove Designers. This piece was in the collection of Louise's friend and fellow designer, Bettine Nichols (see pages 182–83). It was likely a gift from Louise. (Ink on fabric.)**

Louise didn't think of her work as a business, although a 1947 *Ladies Home Journal* feature on the Kenyon family lauded her for her "paying hobby" and mentioned that she "contributes solidly to the family income."[134] Her husband's young adult novel *Driftwood Captain*, for which Louise designed the cover and illustrations, even includes a passage where the mother, Weezie, is able to come to her son Peter's rescue with $250 to invest in the son's boat building endeavors because she "just sold a design to a wallpaper company."[135] Yet for Louise, it was not about money, "It was just something I loved to do—I had to do it!"[136]

The *Ladies' Home Journal* article mentioned that Louise's studio was "picturesquely full of the blocky iron press, linoleum blocks and bolts of bright fabrics" and was conveniently located next to the kitchen, allowing her to "alternately print off a few more yards of an order and dart out to see how the pie in the oven is doing."[137] The article may have romanticized the reality of household chores, because Louise recalled, "I would...leave them [the dishes] in the sink and get out my design after the boys got off to school. And [I] did that all day until they came home."[138] Her family was her priority, but one of the incentives of the work for her was that it allowed her to hire a cleaning woman once a week, admitting that "I liked the house but not cleaning it."[139]

Years later Louise thought about the success of the group and its longevity and felt that "it took a person like Jinnee" and "people who could work together."[140] She felt the members "stimulated one another" and one of the things she liked most was the feeling of being with "people who were interested in the same thing."[141]

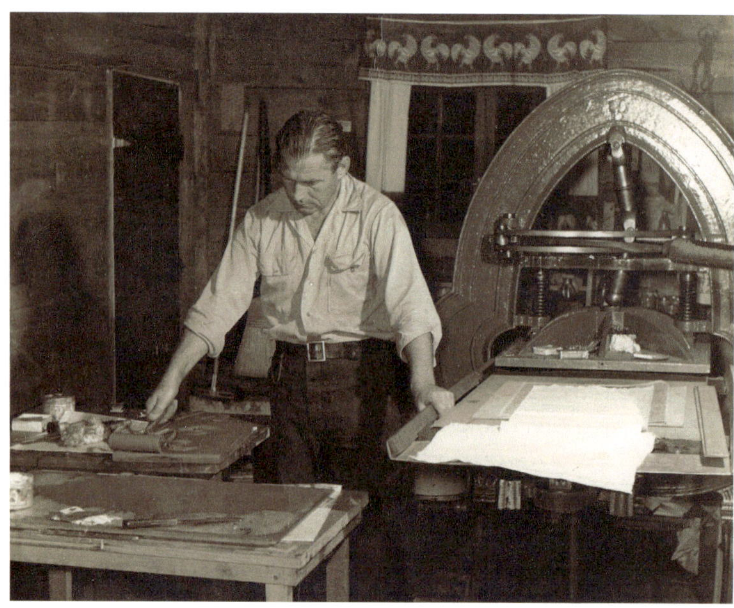

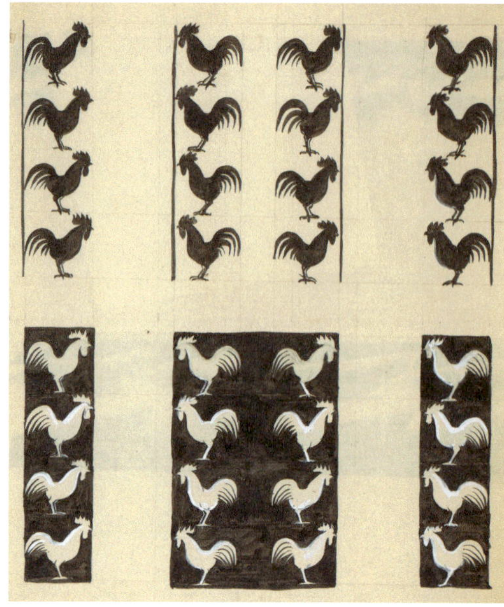

FIG. 175 (LEFT)
Eino Natti printing on his acorn press with *Chanticleer* printed as a valance in the background. This became the press that the designers used in the barn.

FIG. 176 (RIGHT)
Some of Eino's rooster sketches in a vertical arrangement as he worked out the blacks and whites. The arrangement is similar to that of an early rooster design he did titled *Cockerels*. (Ink on paper.)

FIG. 177 (OPPOSITE TOP)
Eino's *New England Farm* features the Natti family homestead. His dog is on the doorstep and there are chickens on the fence. (Ink on fabric.)

FIG. 178 (OPPOSITE BOTTOM)
Eino's *Chanticleer*, featuring two roosters in front of cornstalk rows. He adapted the border of this to become part of his *Hen Party* design for Edwin M. Knowles China Company (see page 70). Chanticleer is the name given to a rooster in one of Geoffrey Chaucer's *Canterbury Tales* and other fables. (Ink on fabric.)

Eino A. Natti (1909–1975)

Eino Natti was one of the few male members of the Folly Cove Designers and one of the group's biggest producers. He grew up in Lanesville in a large Finnish family, the fifth child of twelve.[142] As a young man he played the tuba in Lanesville's Waino Band (a mostly Finnish brass band with which the internationally known musician Sylvester Ahola first performed) and went on to play in an Army band stateside for the duration of World War II where he earned the rank of corporal.[143]

After returning from the war, Eino built a cabin for himself on the Natti family property.[144] Using the G.I. Bill, he attended Northeastern University and graduated from the School of the Museum of Fine Arts in Boston.[145] It is unclear what he studied, but he is most remembered for printmaking. In addition to linoprinting, he did copper etching and in an article in 1951 it is mentioned that he sculpted and painted too.[146] By the mid-1940s he was a member of the Folly Cove Designers.[147]

His sister-in-law and fellow Folly Cove designer, Lee Natti, remembered Eino as someone on whom the community leaned. "Everybody called Eino when they needed something done around their yard, their house—he kept a lot of households together."[148] Designer Mary Maletskos remembered him as being a "fine carpenter and a restorer," which was the main source of his income.[149] She added that he had restored sculptor Paul Manship's Lanesville home and that he moved a large barn from Bay View to the Manship property.[150] Anthony Iarrobino remembered Eino as being a talented artist and carpenter. His wife, Elizabeth, recalled that he would often be invited to dinner at the homes of the wealthy people for whom he did work because he was "such a fascinating conversationalist."[151] Eventually he was hired by the Folly Cove Designers as a part-time staff member.[152] He often represented the group by giving demonstrations and lectures about printmaking to local groups and organizations.[153]

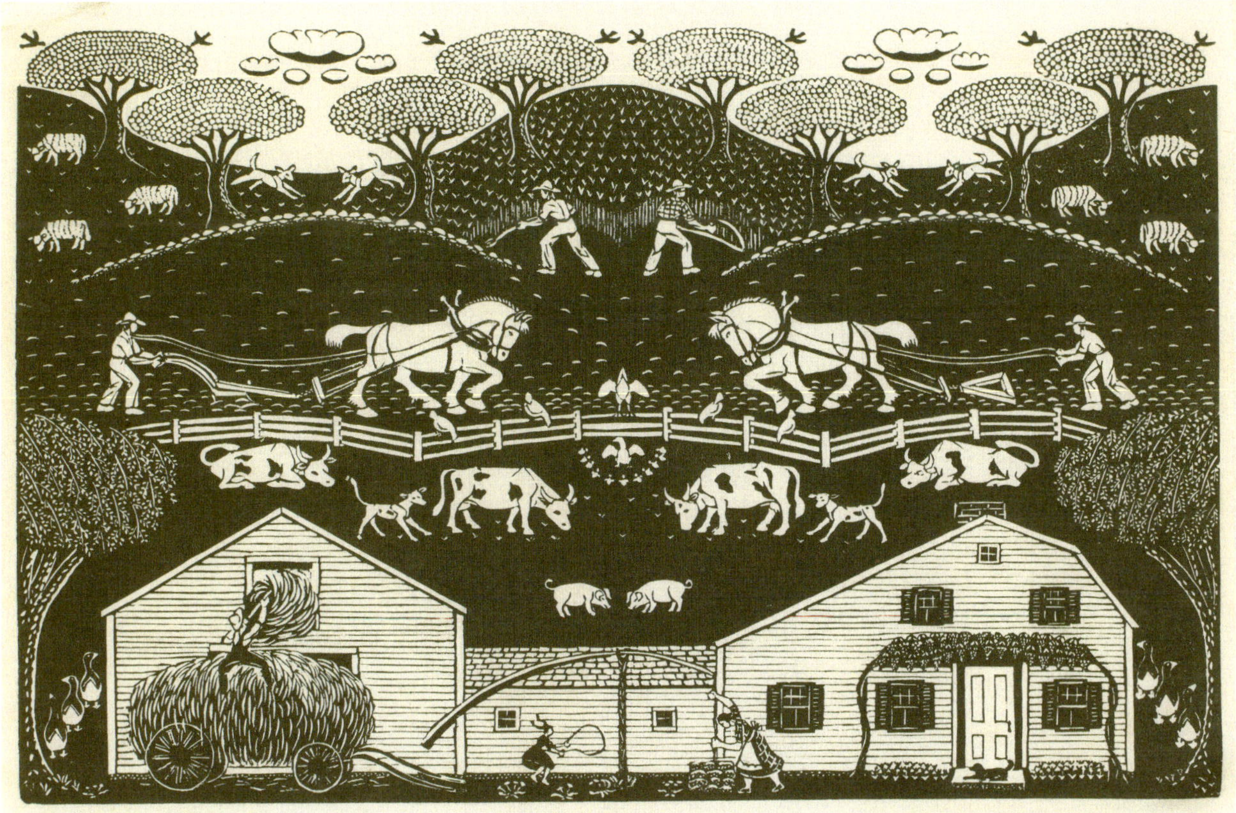

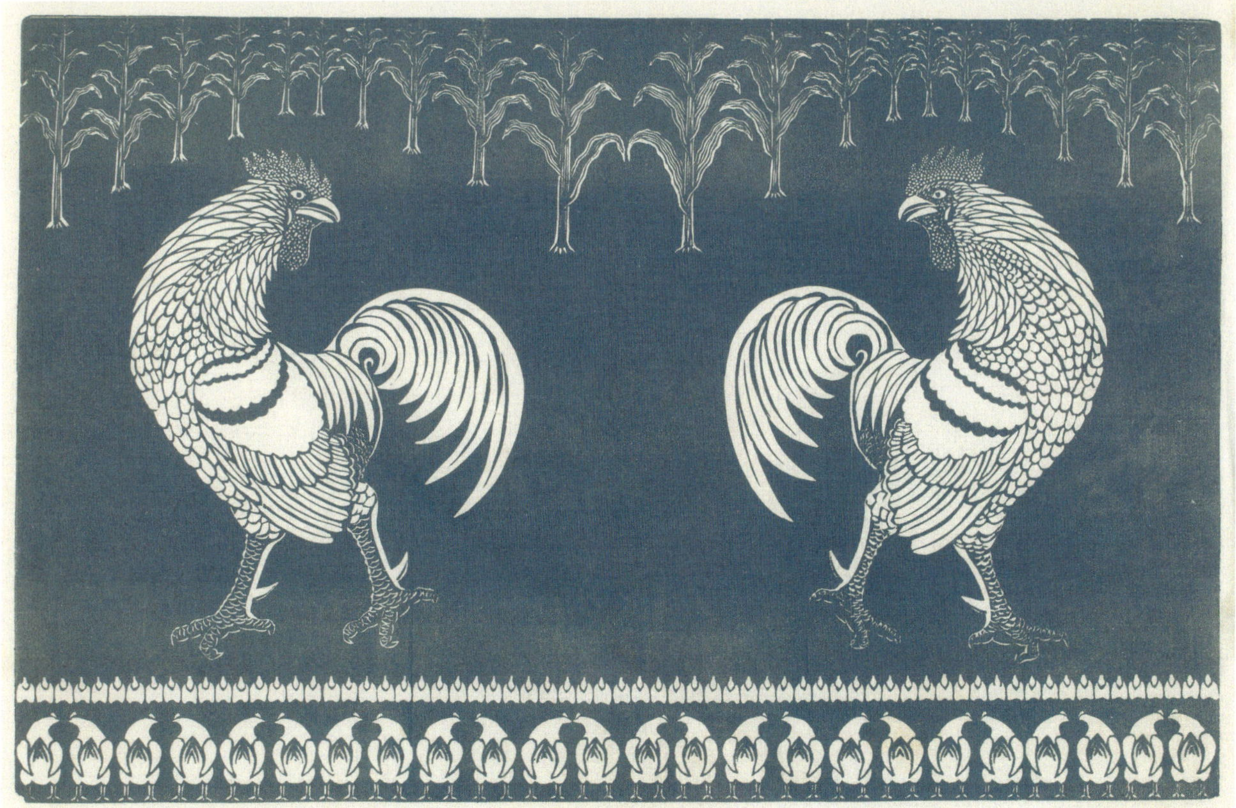

FIG. 179 (RIGHT)
***Winter Waterfowl* by Eino Natti. Eino often printed it as a wall hanging, as seen here. (Ink on fabric.)**

FIG. 180 (BELOW)
A preliminary charcoal sketch by Eino of birds in various stages of swimming and flight appears to be a precursor to *Winter Waterfowl*, although the gulls on the bottom might have been sketched for *Yo Heave Ho*.

FIG. 181 (OPPOSITE TOP)
***Golden Pheasants* was a five-color print, which entailed carving one block for each color with varying detail and registering the prints on top of one another. Along with Peggy Norton, Eino produced multicolored designs. (Ink on fabric.)**

FIG. 182 (OPPOSITE BOTTOM)
***Polyphemus* depicts the locomotive for which Eino was a brakeman, showing the granite being carried from the quarries to the waterfront, where it was loaded onto barges. He marked the railroad car in the design with "FCD RR." (Ink on fabric.)**

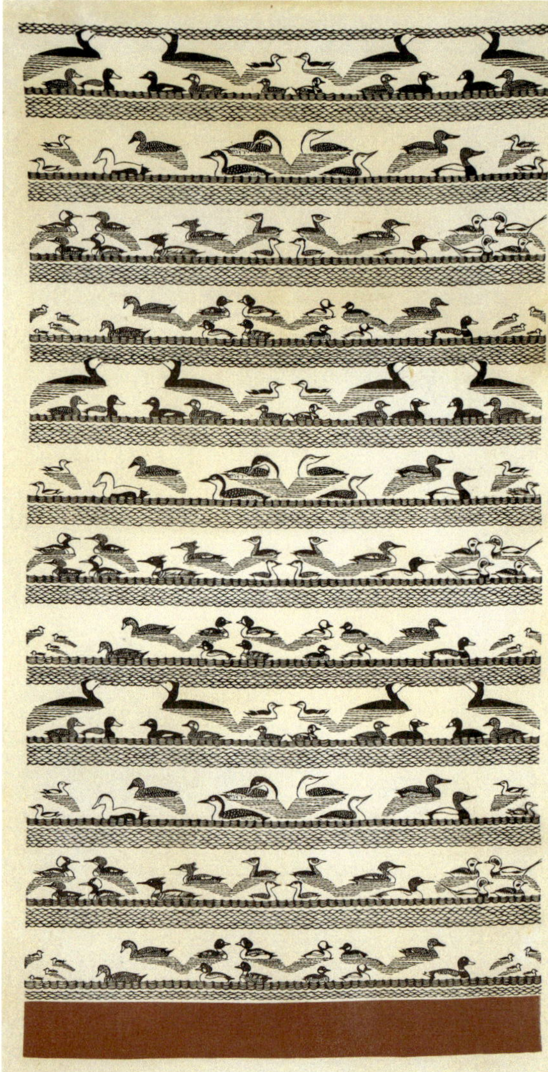

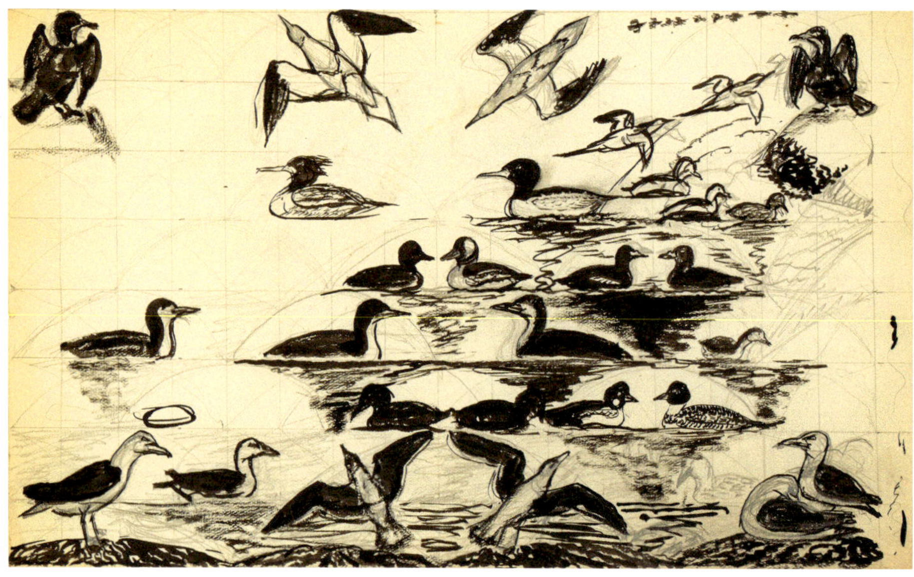

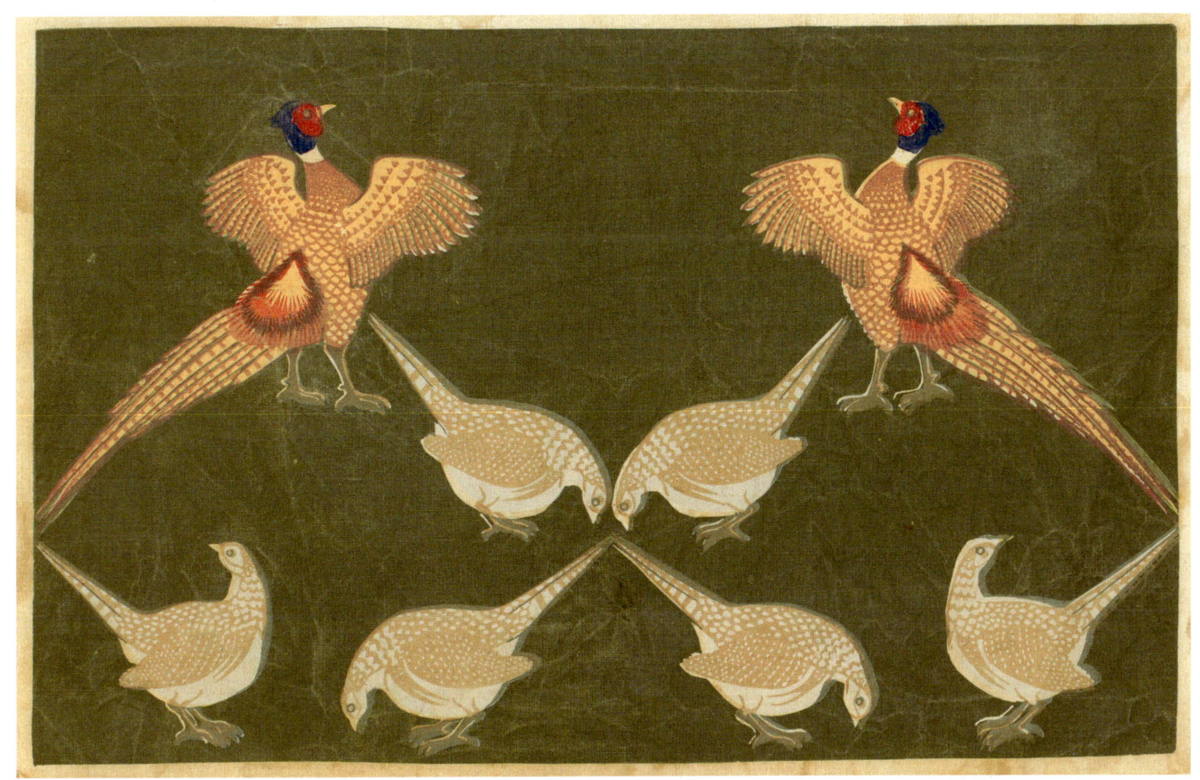

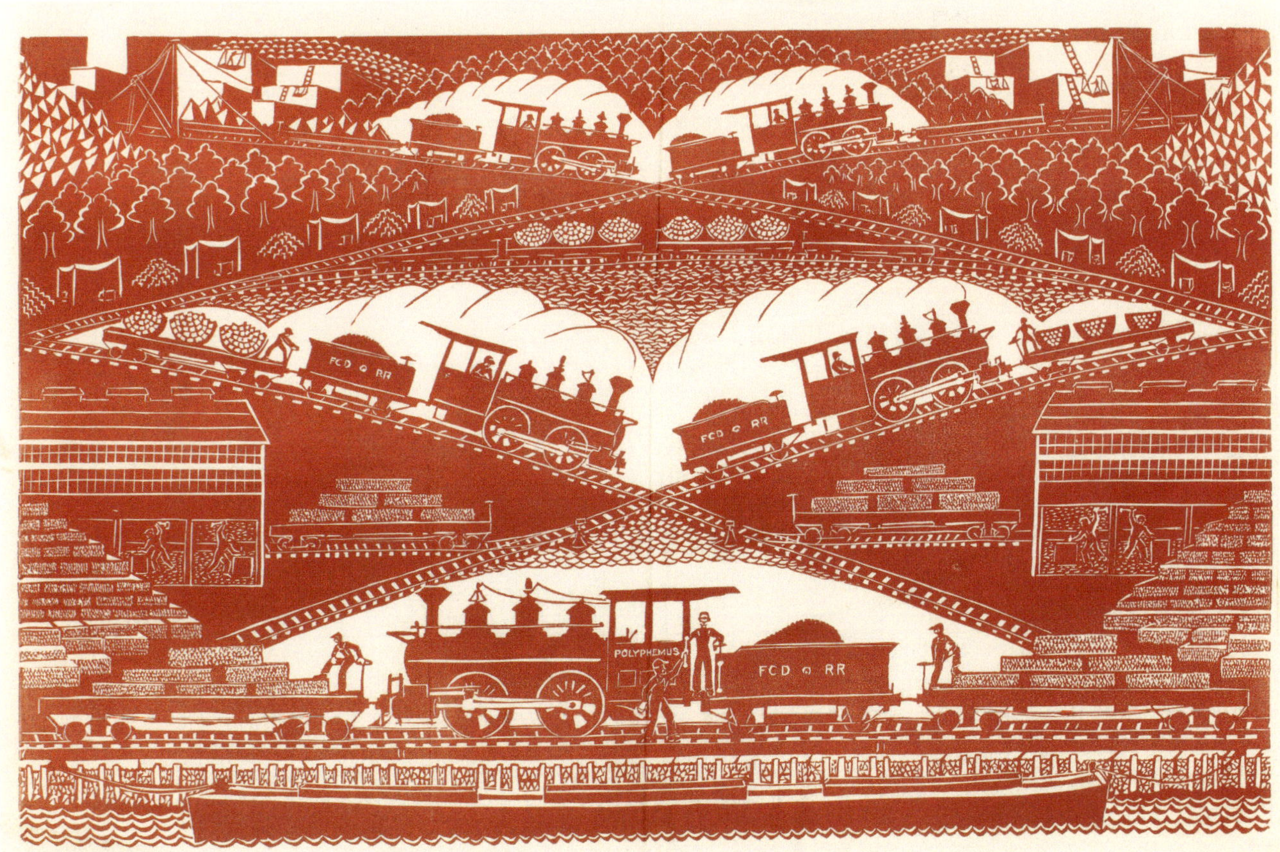

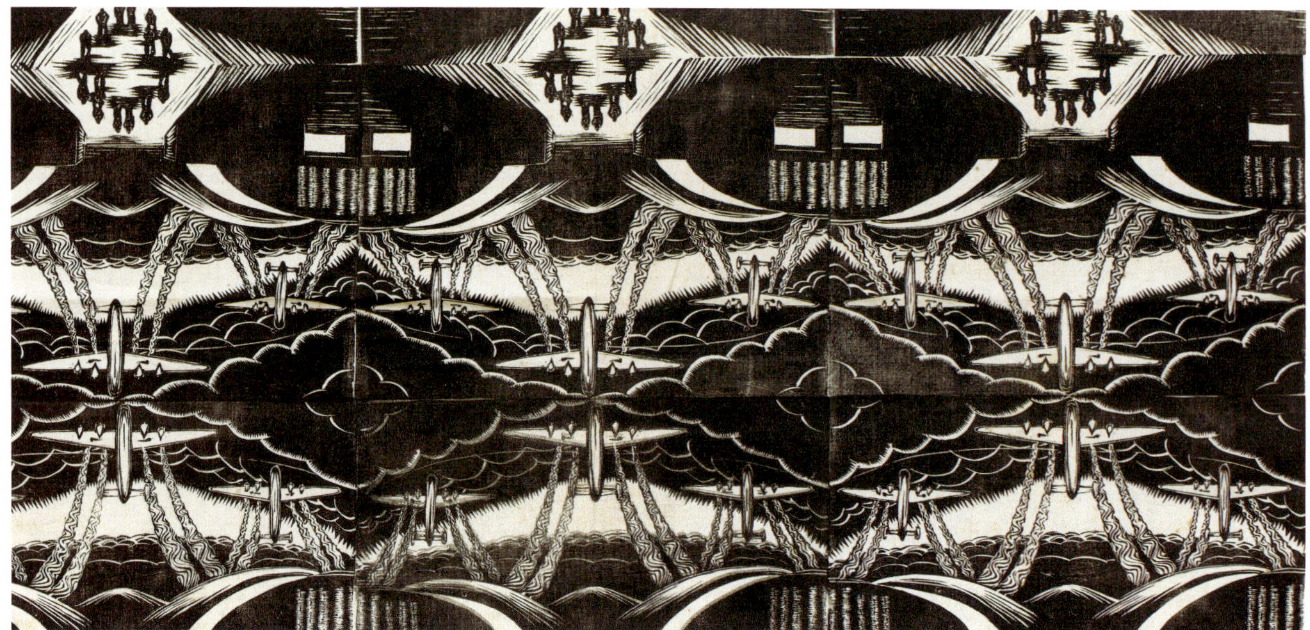

Eino passed away in 1975 and did not give any recorded or written interviews. He was a beloved uncle but never married and had no children, so initially writing a personal biography for him seemed challenging.[154] But one need only to look at his designs to be able to piece together the personal strands woven throughout his work and learn more about his personality.

Undated pages from Eino's homework binder include several ink sketches of roosters, the plumed tail feathers similar to ones in his popular *Chanticleer* design (see page 143).[155] Eino raised chickens, so his subject matter was close at hand for sketching.[156] Eino did four more designs involving roosters.[157] Some have speculated that his many depictions of them may have indicated his role as one of the only male members of the group among a brood of "hens."[158] His submission to the Edwin M. Knowles China Co. bore the name "Hen Party," thus giving weight to this theory.[159]

Eino seemed to be particularly interested in birds, as other designs featured waterfowl and pheasants, including the multicolored print *Golden Pheasants*.

Eino's designs were slightly more masculine since, like all Folly Cove Designers, they were influenced by his life. *Polyphemus* was inspired by his employment at Rockport Granite Company as a brakeman on the locomotive. His obituary noted that it "took every man who could to brake the engine as it puffed down the track to cross Washington Street, pulling tons of granite from the quarries. The flag man at the crossing always gave the engine the right-of-way and Mr. Natti used to tell many stories of braking just in time to avoid collisions."[160] At some point he also did additional granite quarry–inspired pieces that were more realistic depictions.

Similarly, Eino's experience in the Army inspired designs like *P.T.*, *Pass in Review* (see pages 89 and 168), and *Liberators Take Off*. *Pass in Review* depicts an Army band with two tuba players and became the cover for "*GI*":

FIG. 183
Flight **was one of Eino Natti's illustrations for the book** ***"GI"*****. Eino printed this piece on fabric, although it is not clear if he sold it as a Folly Cove designer or just printed it for himself.**

OPPOSITE, CLOCKWISE FROM LEFT

FIG. 184
The numerous mast lines in Eino's ***Gloucester*** **would have required many hours of intense carving. (Ink on fabric.)**

FIG. 185
Eino seated in the barn, next to a wall hanging of his design ***Gloucester*****.**

FIG. 186
These untitled, undated designs by Eino are more realistic versions of quarry work. His niece Susanna recalls these being at her parents' house before the 1960s, which would have meant that Eino completed them while a designer, but they may have been a personal project. (Ink on paper.)

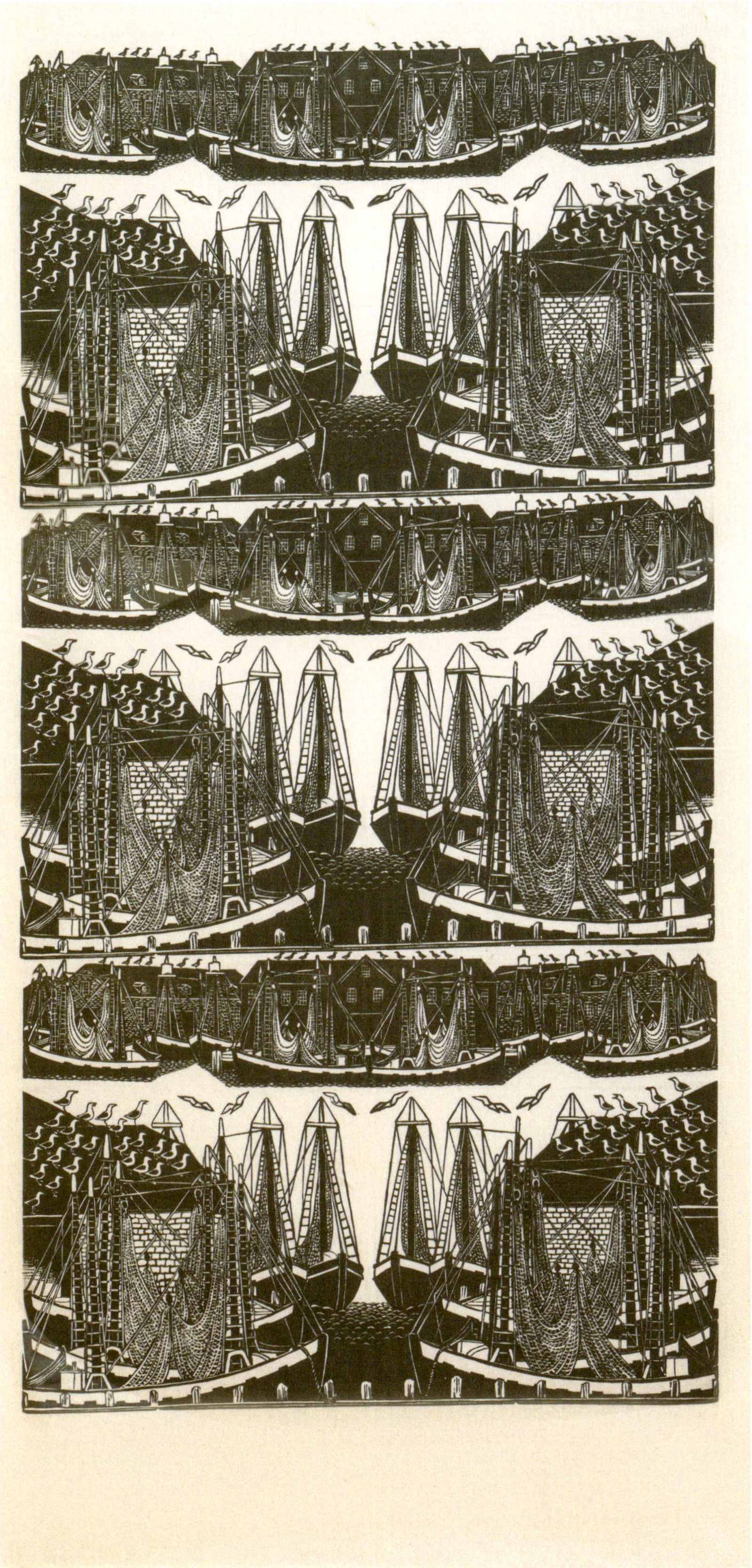

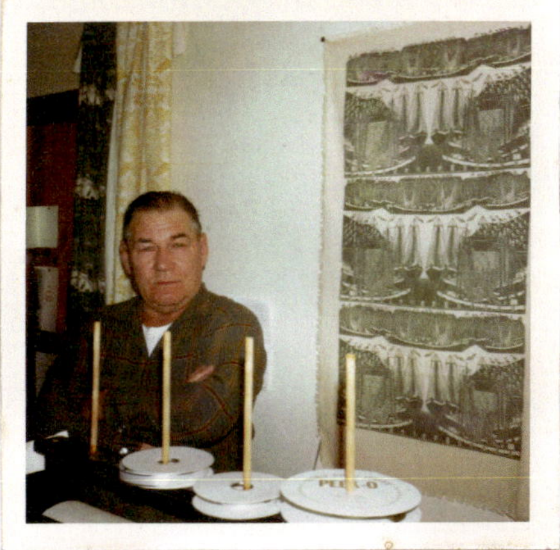

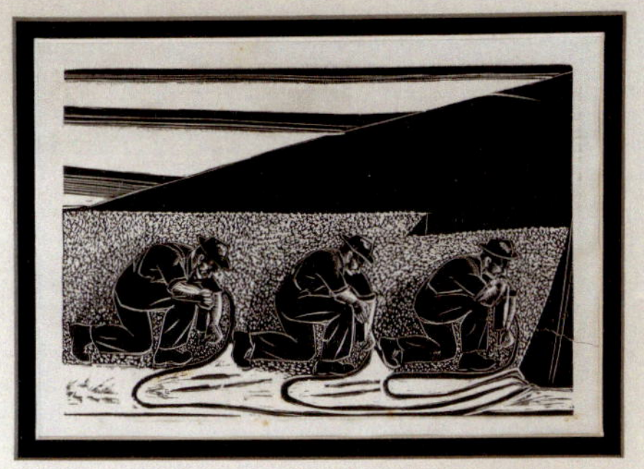

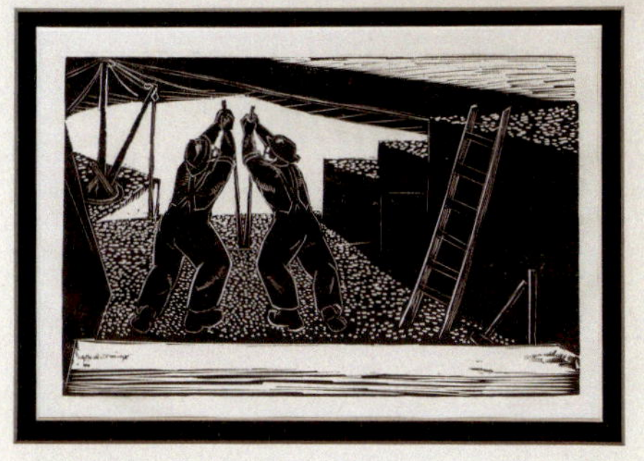

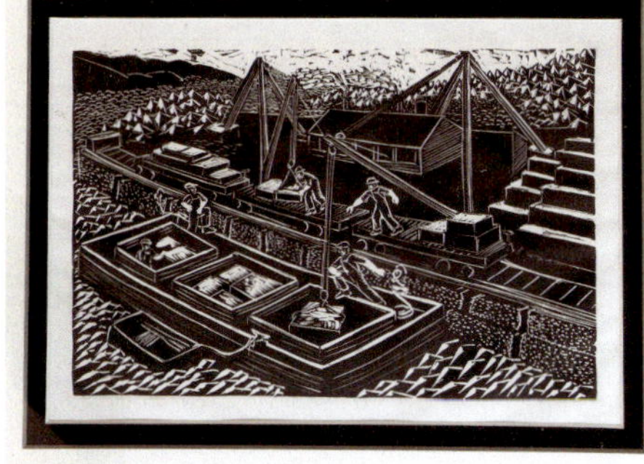

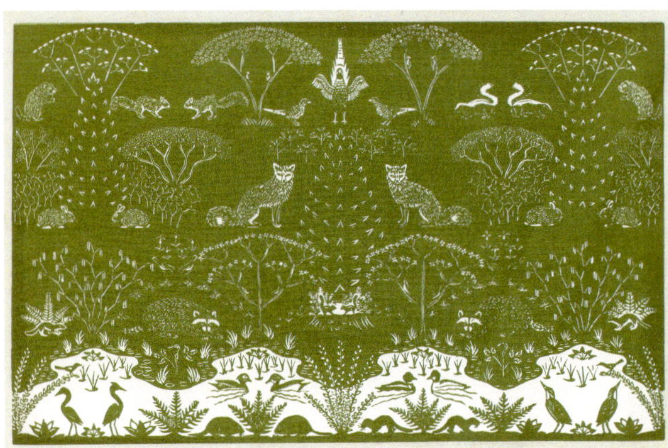

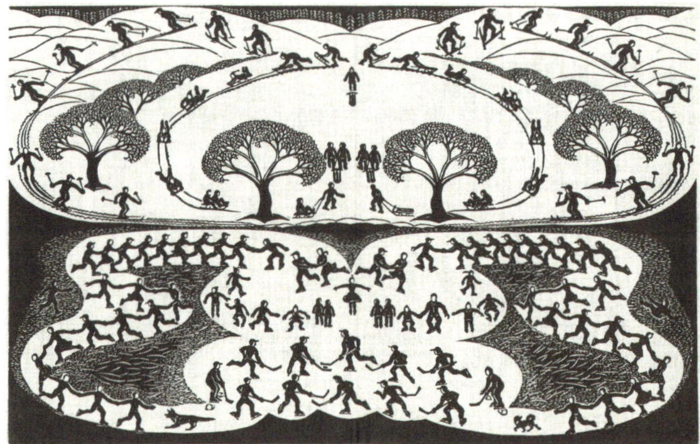

World War II, a book of free verse he illustrated for fellow designer (and Virginia's younger brother) Alexander Ross Burton. It was published locally in 1963 as a limited edition.[161] The interior illustrations depict a soldier's experience through Eino's bold black-and-white prints.

Gloucester is a particularly striking and detailed design, often seen as a wall hanging. Lee Natti recalled that Eino often chose to print his designs on linen as wall hangings.[162]

Other designs were reflective of life on Cape Ann. *Flora and Fauna* features foxes, rabbits, raccoons, woodchucks, otters, pheasant, heron, ducks, and more. *Winter Sports* shows local winter activities of skiing, sledding, and skating.

Eino also created two designs based on dogs and even included a dog in an exhibition invitation design (see page 16). *A Dog Would* (1951) is a smaller-scale design that became a "lost" design. Each of the dogs (in one repeat) holds a different pose. *Tempu* (1952) features Eino's dog, the name being Finnish for "frolicsome."[163]

Eino was a faithful member of the group through to the end. He was particularly devoted to Virginia and thought highly of her and her work. Virginia's son Aris remembers Eino's kindness in helping his mother continue to print her much-in-demand designs when at the end of her life, his mother being too ill to turn the heavy lever of the press.[164]

FIG. 187 (LEFT)
Flora and Fauna **by Eino Natti features the whole spectrum of wildlife on Cape Ann, as well as trees, branches, tree stumps, and animal tracks. (Ink on fabric.)**

FIG. 188 (RIGHT)
Winter Sports **by Eino. Locals often skated on lakes that had been created by the quarrying industry. The linked arms of the skaters highlight the importance of negative space in designs. (Ink on fabric.)**

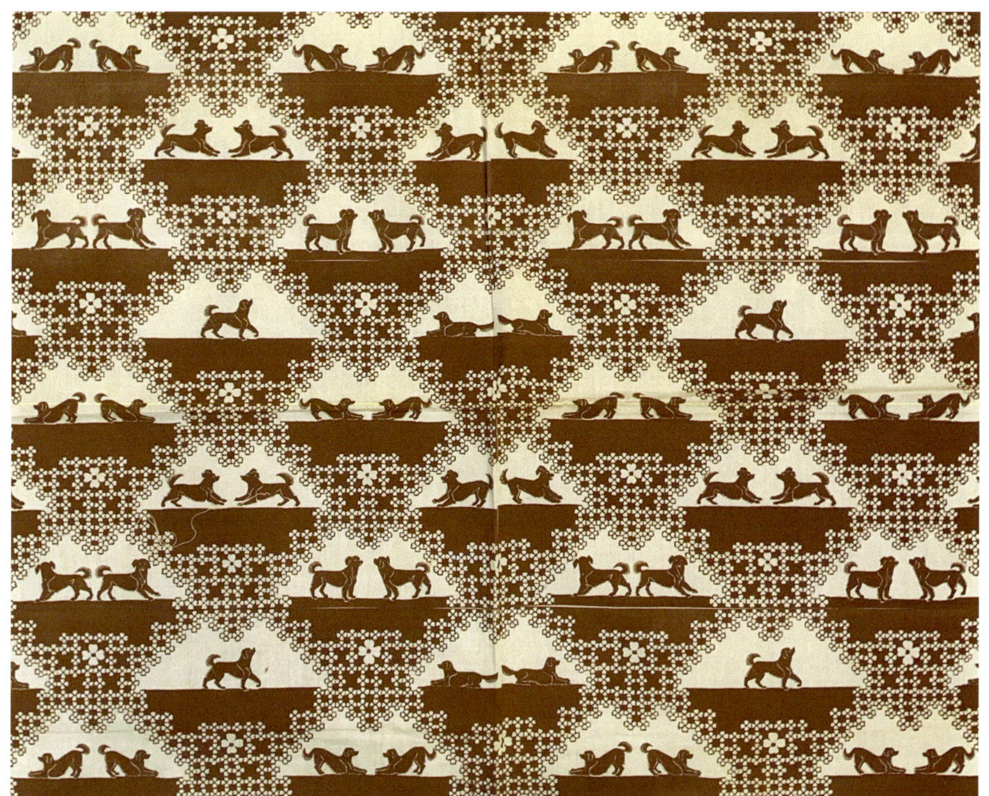

FIG. 189 (LEFT)
A Dog Would **is a "lost" design and has not been recognized as part of Eino's oeuvre. The pattern surrounding the dogs is just as intriguing. (Ink on fabric.)**

FIG. 190 (BELOW)
Tempu **(named for his own dog) by Eino. The intricate floral designs show Eino's versatility and build upon the floral pattern in** ***A Dog Would*** **from the previous year. (Ink on fabric.)**

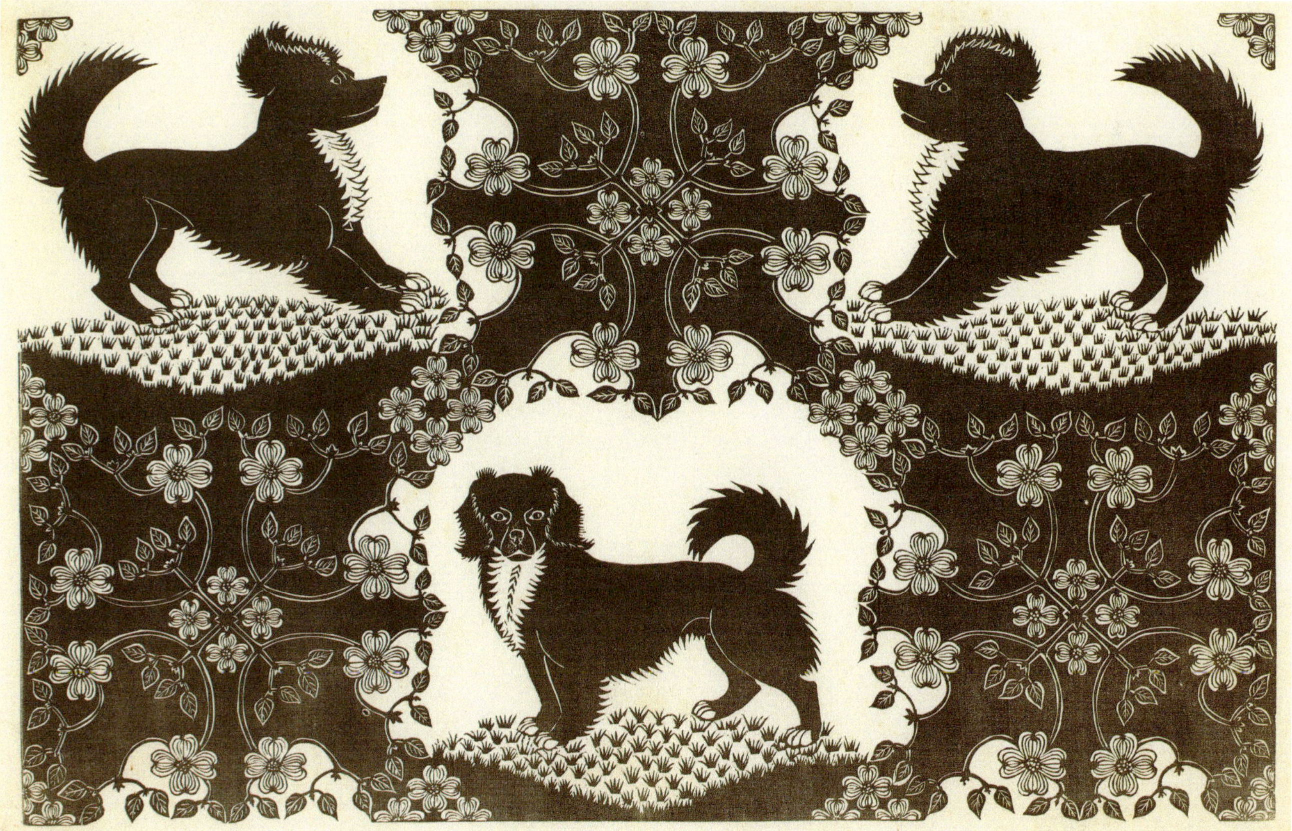

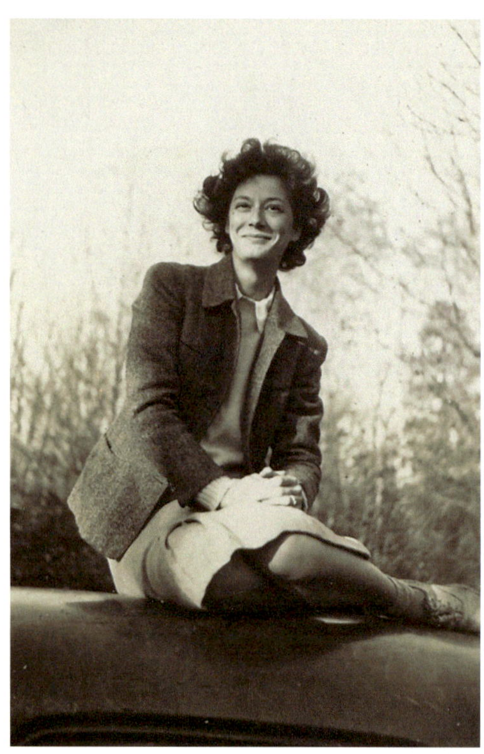

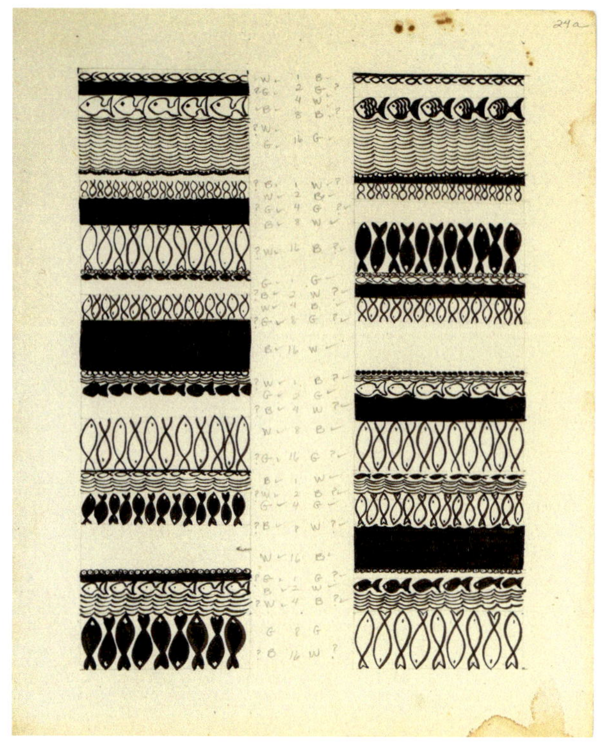

FIG. 191 (LEFT)
Lee Natti, taken shortly after her marriage to Robert Natti in 1945.

FIG. 192 (RIGHT)
A page from Lee's homework. Her subject was fish, although she never completed a fish design. Here she was working in different sizes with black, white, and gray. (Ink on paper.)

Mary Lee (Kingman) Natti (1919–2020)

Lee (as she was called) Natti was born in the Boston suburb of Reading.[165] Her mother had attended art school and her father was the business manager of a boys' camp.[166] An only child, Lee was exposed to art from a young age by her mother and always had an interest in craft, but by high school she knew she wanted to be a writer.[167]

Lee attended Colby Junior College (now Colby-Sawyer College) in New London, New Hampshire, for two years before transferring to Smith College (Northampton, Massachusetts).[168] She met future fellow Folly Cove designer Mary Maletskos during her senior year at Smith and they became good friends.[169] Upon graduating, she enrolled in an eight-week secretarial school at the request of her father.[170] Lee explained, "I needed to know how to earn money."[171] Upon completion she took a job at an insurance company handling a large switchboard. She joked that "Lily Tomlin had nothing on me," although she told a story of spilling coffee on the switchboard and wiping out all the calls.[172] She secretly wished that she'd be fired, but she wasn't and worked there for about two years.[173]

While at the insurance company, Lee channeled her creativity into writing children's plays for a Boston-based magazine.[174] In 1942, she heard through a cousin that an editor at Houghton Mifflin was looking for an assistant.[175] The editor was Grace Hogarth, who had founded the children's department at Houghton Mifflin.[176] Lee got the job and it was while working at Houghton Mifflin that she met Virginia Lee Burton, who was already an established author.[177] Grace sent Lee to Folly Cove to study figure drawing with George Demetrios for two weeks in the summer of 1943. Since she was going to be working with illustrators, Hogarth thought it would be helpful for Lee to study drawing.[178] Lee had done some landscape painting while a student at Colby Junior and had taken a beginning studio course at Smith but described her art experience as limited.[179]

While she was in Folly Cove Lee met her future husband, Robert Natti (see page 181), who was on leave from the Army Air Forces. Robert was from a large Finnish family in Lanesville and was modeling for a bust for George Demetrios.[180] Lee and Robert saw each other as much as possible during the week they had together, wrote letters when they parted, and met up when he was on leave in New York City that September, where he proposed to her.[181] They corresponded for two years while he was serving in Europe, excitedly writing of their plans to purchase land in the Folly Cove area and build a house.[182]

In the meantime, Grace Hogarth, who was married to an Englishman, decided, despite the war, to return to England with her children to be with her husband and Lee became Houghton Mifflin's children's book editor.[183] Lee later described her promotion as "absolutely ridiculous" since she was so young.[184] During her time there, despite her workload, Lee wrote the first two of many books she would go on to author.[185]

Lee and Robert married upon his return from the war in September 1945.[186] Lee remained at Houghton Mifflin for roughly one year after their marriage while Robert worked on his doctorate in education at Harvard.[187] In 1946 the couple moved to Lanesville and rented a house while their home was being built in Folly Cove. After Lee suffered a failed pregnancy, her friend from Smith and maid of honor, Mary Maletskos, came to stay for a couple of months.[188]

Lee would soon take the design course with Virginia and join the group, as would Mary.[189] Lee's first design was likely *Mill Valley*, which contains a remarkable amount of detail and was designed for William Skinner & Sons in 1947 (see page 65).[190]

By the early 1950s, Lee and Robert's family included two children, Susanna (Suzi) and Peter.[191] While the children were young and she was still writing, Lee found it nearly impossible to keep up with her Folly Cove design homework. Like other designers, she developed a work schedule. "I started developing a block during the winter, and then during the summer [I] would hire a babysitter mornings and do my writing."[192] Once the children were in school, she wrote in the mornings while they were at school.[193]

Lee found coming up with ideas and the drawing to be challenging.[194] She explained that "[I]f you don't draw naturally...you really have to struggle to get something that looks like something."[195] Looking back she laughed at one of her early seagull designs and described the gulls as looking like "flying milk bottles."[196] Over the years, she completed three gull-inspired designs.

The evolution of Lee's drawing skills is markedly noticeable. She credited her progression to Virginia's teaching methodology and belief that "the more you draw something, the more you can do with it because you're aware of really all the aspects of the form and how you can use them to advantage."[197] Lee was most pleased with her final gull-related design, *Gulls*. She

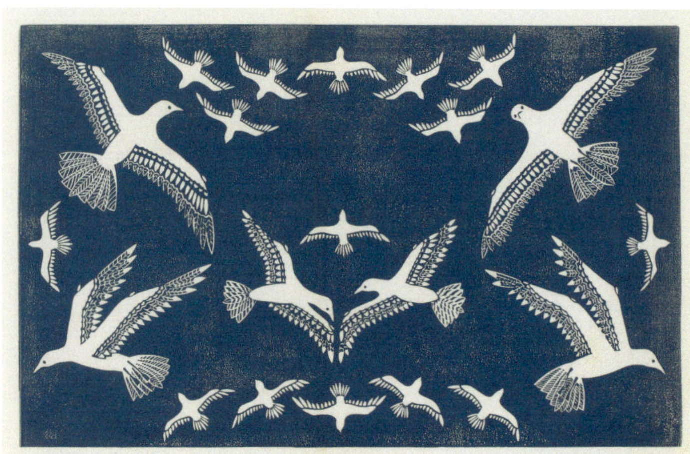

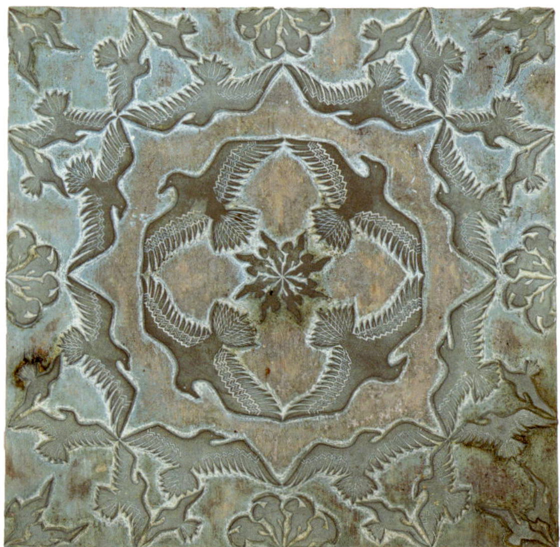

FIG. 193 (TOP LEFT)
***Flight*, by Lee Natti, date unknown, but likely an earlier piece. It was Lee's first gull design. (Ink on fabric.)**

FIG. 194 (TOP RIGHT)
***Cotillion* by Lee (1957). Two blocks exist for this design. There might be a slight difference in scale on some of the gulls, but otherwise they are identical. Perhaps its popularity necessitated a recarving. (Linoleum block.)**

FIG. 195 (ABOVE)
***Gulls* by Lee (1962). Lee was happy with this final piece. She perfectly captured the movement, and the detail, particularly at the very top of the design, is amazing. (Ink on fabric.)**

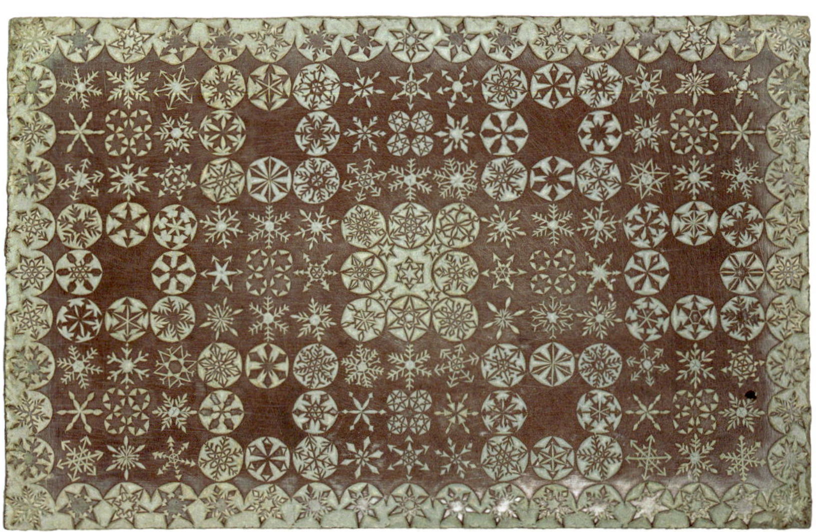

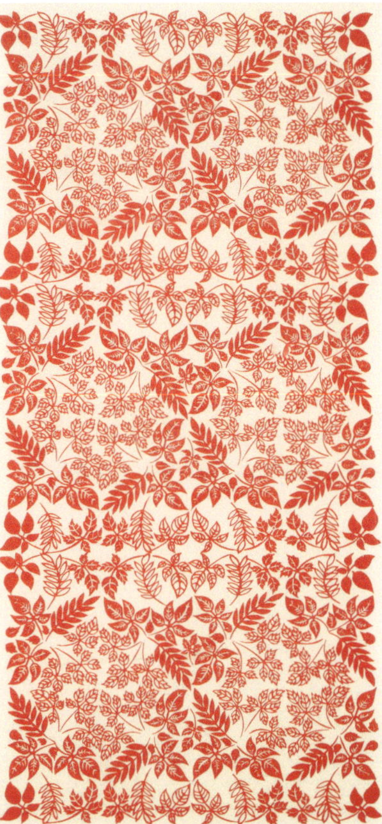

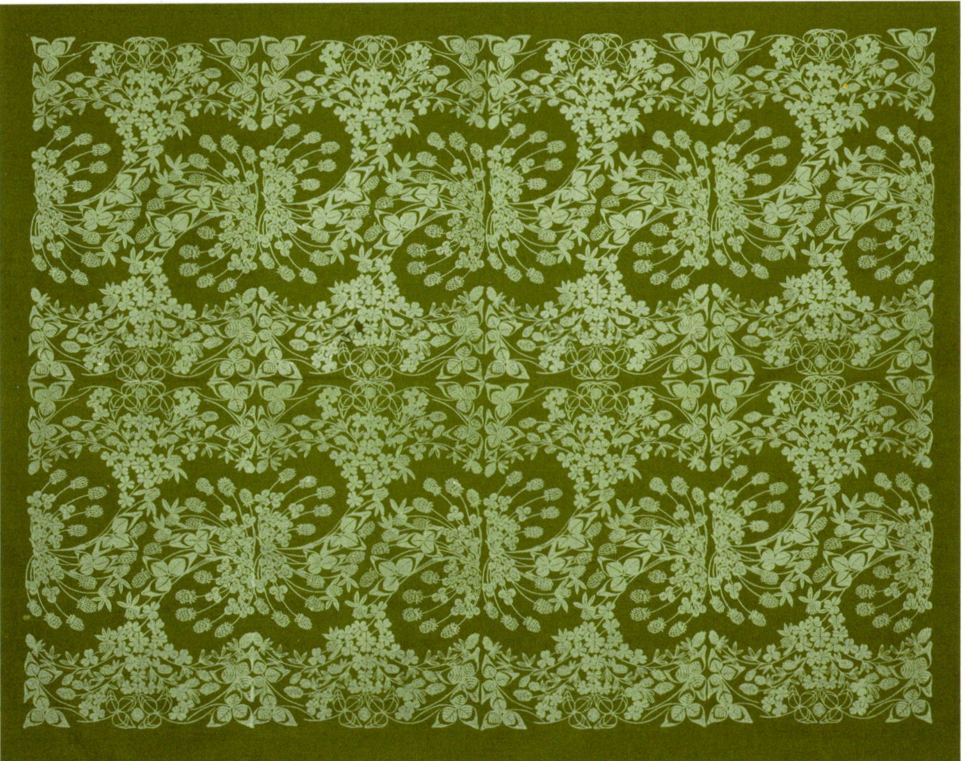

FIG. 196 (ABOVE LEFT)
Snow Storm **took Lee the longest of her designs to carve and was one of her earlier works. It features multiple unique snowflakes requiring fine carving skills. (Linoleum block.)**

FIG. 197 (ABOVE RIGHT)
Underbrush **by Lee is another botanical-inspired pattern. Many of her designs were true all-over patterns and not confined within a border or geometric framework, which lent themselves to printing seamless repeats and yardage. Lee made both a skirt and a dress for herself using *Underbrush* (this may be the skirt Lee is wearing on page 30). (Ink on fabric.)**

FIG. 198 (RIGHT)
In Clover **by Lee. By this point (1964), Lee was so skilled at conveying movement that one can almost see the clover stems swaying in the breeze. The shift dress on page 66 was printed in this pattern. (Ink on fabric.)**

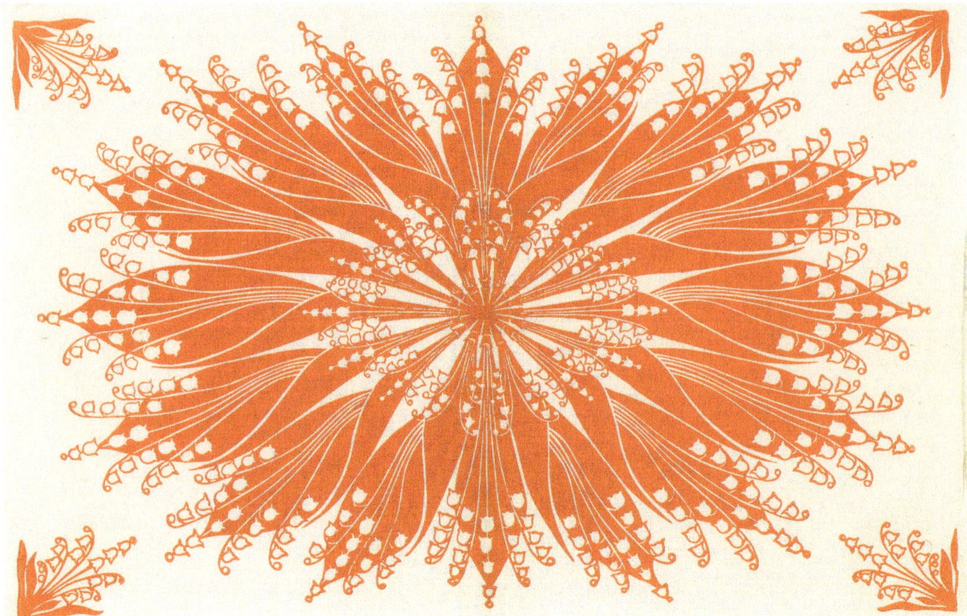

FIG. 199
Lily of the Valley **is one of Lee Natti's most beautiful designs, in which she captured movement with the lines of the twisting stems and curled leaves. Lee made herself a skirt with this design as a border. (Ink on fabric.)**

described seagulls as "about the hardest thing I tried to cope with" in terms of subject matter.[198] She said that *Gulls* was probably the design she printed the most because seagulls were a popular subject and representative of local color.[199]

Another early design, titled *Clover*, was very simple. Lee returned to the subject in 1964 for a more detailed version, *In Clover*. Years later, Lee still joked about her drawing skills and said that "Whereas somebody who couldn't really draw, as I can't really draw, was struggling so hard to come up with something that was recognizable—that's why I did an awful lot with leaves," seemingly referencing both clover designs, as well as her design entitled *Underbrush*.[200]

Lee was a prolific writer, many of her books inspired by her husband's large Finnish family.[201] Like Virginia, she published under her maiden name, in part because she had published her first books prior to marriage. But she drew from other sources of inspiration for her design work. Unlike Virginia, she said that "I really did separate the two parts of my creativity and it was sort of a break to think of myself in two different ways."[202]

Lee said that she didn't produce a lot in the first handful of years of being a member of the Folly Cove Designers and that it took her a while to become a good printer, a skill requiring practice.[203] As was the case with most of the designers, her press was in the basement and she later expressed regret for having spent summers in "the dungeon."[204] Preparing the fabric was also time consuming and involved fringing the edges of the place mats and a lot of ironing. She reported going through three steam irons a year.[205]

Lee kept records of how long it took her to carve each block, saying most required eighty to ninety hours. *Snow Storm* (1952) took her the longest, at ninety hours.[206] Lee said that after five to six years of practice she became quicker at carving and started to enjoy the process more.[207]

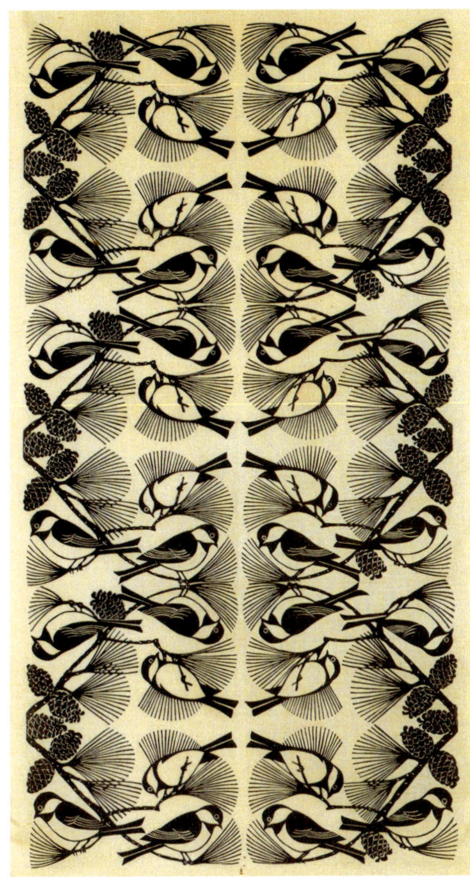

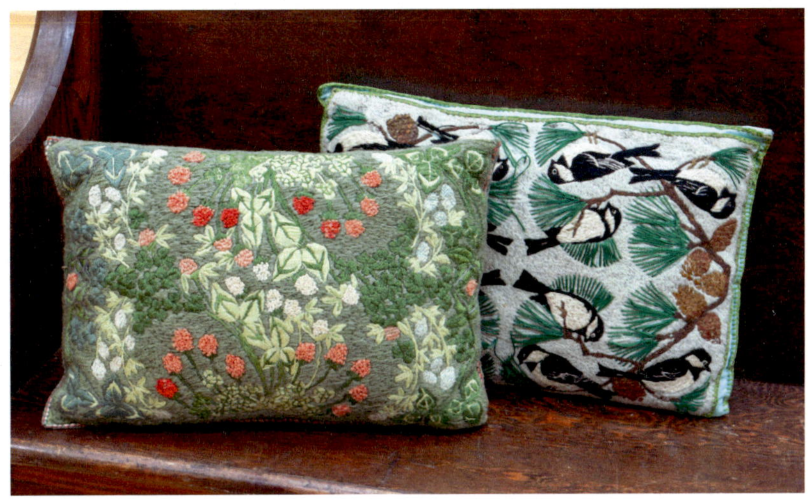

FIG. 200 (LEFT)
***Chickadees* by Lee was another intricate carve and one of her last designs (1967). (Ink on fabric.)**

FIG. 201 (RIGHT)
Lee embroidered her designs *In Clover* and *Chickadees* and sewed them as pillows. The colored thread and added dimension give the designs a whole different look.

Lee's favorite design was *Lily of the Valley*, which she says took her fifty hours to carve. She later said that the subject could have been boring in its simplicity, but that she thought that adding the blossoms along the edge gave it a "lightness."[208] One of her most impressive designs is *Chickadees*. The lines for the pine needles were so fine that she had to be careful printing it.[209]

Lee spoke candidly about the Folly Cove Designers' jury not being a "rubber stamp process."[210] She said it took her several times to pass a cat design (*Etc.*). "[I]t had nothing to do with [Virginia's] *Zaidee and Her Kittens*. I think we [her family] had cats at that point and I was interested in drawing them."[211] She added that "[W]ith somebody who was limited in time and limited in the ability to draw, it was a luxury to take time to do things over and over until you got them to pass."[212]

Lee published twenty-nine books in her lifetime in addition to her designs.[213] She did all of this while working from a desk that she remembers had "always been in the midst of whatever was going on."[214]

Lee also enjoyed embroidery and would sometimes print designs and embroider them as pillows for her home. She also embroidered a wall hanging of Virginia's *Robin Hood* design. Lee treasured this piece and installed it above her bed during the final years of her life.[215] This piece represents Lee's role in Virginia's life "on three different levels" as "her editor, her friend, and a member of the Folly Cove Designers' group."[216]

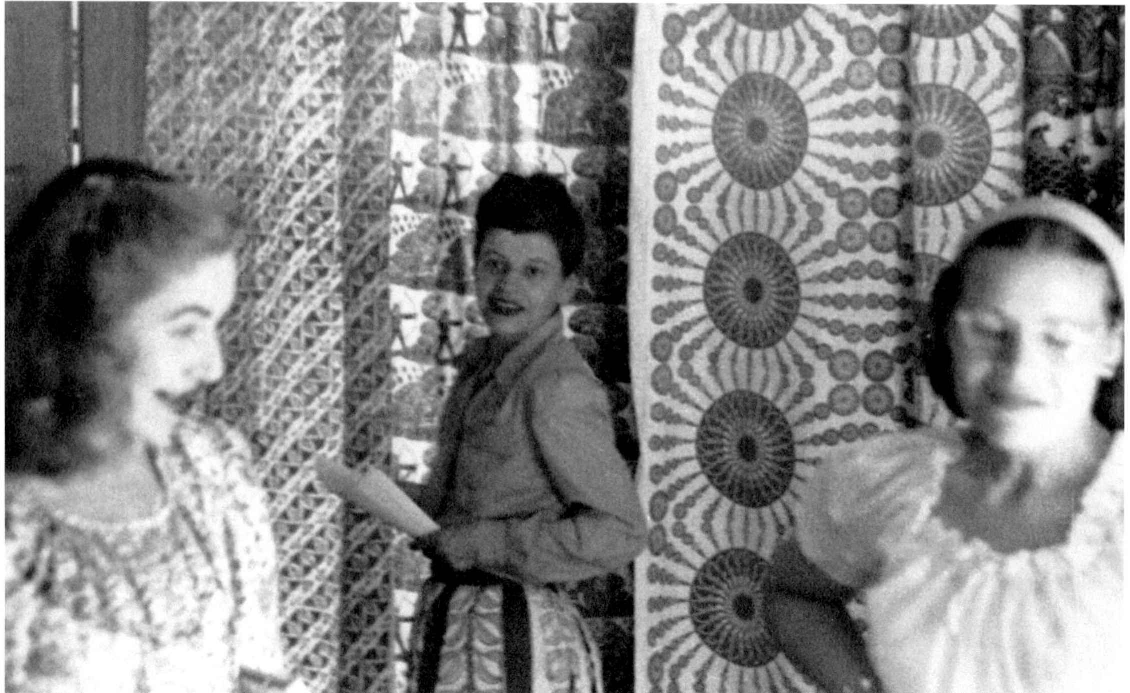

FIG. 202
Dorothy, papers in hand, while wearing a skirt printed in her *Onions* design as she stands in front of a sample of Virginia's *Robin Hood* and Aino's *Atomic Age* to her right. Libby Holloran is on the right.

Dorothy Norton (1900–1989)

Dorothy Norton was another of the group's linchpins. She was born in Manchester, Massachusetts; the family moved to Hudson and then Nashua, New Hampshire, before settling in Boston, where she graduated from Miss McClintock's School for Girls in 1918. She attended the Pierce Secretarial School for two years afterward.[217] Dorothy went on to attend the Sacker School of Design and Interior Decoration, founded by designer, illustrator, teacher, lecturer, and leather worker Amy M. Sacker.[218] She graduated in 1924 and stayed on as an instructor in design and interior decoration from 1925 to 1926. Dorothy also volunteered as a medical illustrator at Massachusetts General Hospital from 1930 to 1932 and took a summer course in microscopic anatomy at Harvard Medical School to aid her. She worked as an interior designer for much of the 1930s and early 1940s. In 1943 she took a job dehydrating vegetables for Gloucester businessman and inventor of frozen foods, Clarence Birdseye.[219] Her family had a summer home in Gloucester, so she was familiar with the area.[220]

It was around the time that she worked for Clarence that Dorothy began her affiliation with the Folly Cove Designers, hired as their first and only (for many years) employee. She became the group's executive secretary in 1944, just a few years after the group had officially organized and as they were starting to explore commercial contracts.[221]

Dorothy was extremely organized, ambitious, and, unlike many members, commercially minded. She kept fastidious records of their correspondence and business dealings and began ordering fabric and supplies for the entire group so they could receive a bulk discount. While the job was meant to be part-time, it became a full-time endeavor for Dorothy.[222]

FIG. 203 (TOP)
Vegetables **reflects Virginia's lessons in symmetry and ratios, with the subject matter radiating out from the center, from small to large. (Ink on fabric.)**

FIG. 204 (MIDDLE)
Signs of Spring **by Dorothy Norton is one of the most detailed designs of the group. Each of the four scenes is framed by intricate carvings. There are tiny structures behind the carpenters; the men planting are framed by a picket fence; there is a curving row of flowers and the iconic Boston Public Garden footbridge and Swan Boats with ducks in the foreground. Finally, laundry arcs in the wind to serve as the top border of the scene of the woman hanging her clothes, while flowers in the foreground complete the frame. (Ink on fabric.)**

FIG. 205 (BOTTOM)
Ducks **seems to be another Boston Public Garden–inspired piece, perhaps preceding *Signs of Spring.* Dorothy used ducks as a subject in her homework binder, indicating that it was an early design or an idea that was germinating for some time. The designers described *Ducks* as a "rhythmic pattern" in their catalog. (Ink on fabric.)**

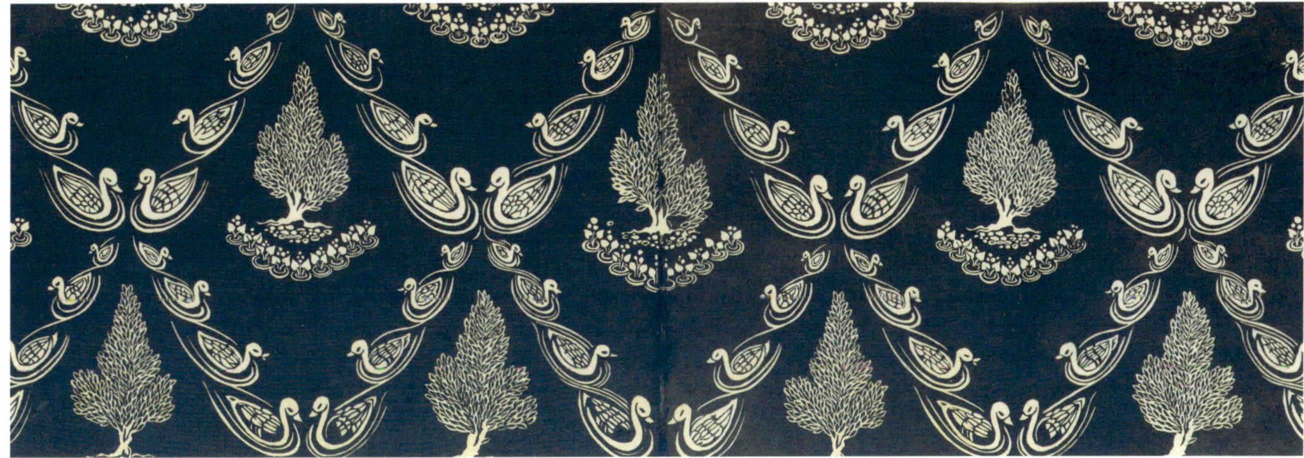

FIG. 206 (OPPOSITE LEFT)
***Ad Infinitum* is a narrative piece and one of the few that Dorothy Norton ever spoke about; she often did not speak of her own work in interviews but rather the group's achievements.**

FIG. 207 (OPPOSITE RIGHT)
***Ivy* by Dorothy is a geometric interpretation of the classic vine plant.**

FIG. 208 (OPPOSITE BOTTOM)
***Mimosa* by Dorothy in the form of hand-printed yard goods.**

Libby Holloran was appreciative of Dorothy taking her under her wing, despite her many responsibilities, and fondly recalled her sense of humor.[223] Lee Natti remembered how kind Dorothy was to her daughter, Susanna (Suzi), who worked at the barn as a teenager in the mid-1960s.[224]

Dorothy was a talented designer in her own right. Despite the demands of her job, she still found time to design, submitting a number of designs for commercial consideration, including *Village Green,* which was accepted by William Skinner & Sons (see page 65).[225] Her work was also accepted for exhibitions.[226]

Signs of Spring is one of Dorothy's narrative designs. Each quadrant depicts springtime activities, including building, planting a garden, the Swan Boats in Boston's Public Garden, and hanging laundry. *Ducks* was another one of her designs, perhaps inspired by the ducks in Boston's Public Garden, made famous by *Make Way for Ducklings* in 1941.

Ad Infinitum depicts a seed pushing up through the earth, starting to sprout and grow roots, working its way past worms and snails, and blooming, with bees swarming around it and pollination beginning, thus starting the process over again. The design is striking in its strong use of black and white. Dorothy said that years before she had wanted to publish a children's book on annuals so she had done a lot of preliminary sketches before it became a design. This design was printed mostly as a wall hanging with a colored border along the bottom to accentuate the black-and-white design. It was also printed as a tablecloth.[227]

Mimosa and *Ivy* are wonderfully intricate all-over patterns, perfect for yard goods. Deceivingly simple at first glance, both designs are very detailed. The carving entailed for both designs required a great deal of skill. *Mimosa* almost reminds one of Dorothy's sketches of cellular structure from the microscopic anatomy course she took at Harvard Medical School.[228]

When speaking of the group, Dorothy was very modest about her own pivotal role.[229] But other designers recalled her contributions and work ethic.[230] Lee Natti described Dorothy as the "the liaison between us and the public."[231] As an expression of gratitude during the group's years together, Lee playfully penned two poems in her honor. One, modeled on Henry Wadsworth Longfellow's "Paul Revere's Ride," began with "Listen, Designers, and you shall hear of the midnight work of Dorothy Dear."[232] (Dorothy was known to be a night owl.)[233] Elizabeth Holloran recalled, "Dorothy ran the place down there and she really did a wonderful job. If it wasn't for Dorothy I think the place would have gone apart."[234] Dorothy's sister, Peggy, felt similarly, saying, "I don't think it could have worked without her—in fact I'm sure it couldn't."[235]

A few years after the group disbanded, Dorothy told an interviewer, "My press still sits quietly in the corner of the living room... I'm full of good intent."[236] But she remained the quintessential group spokesman, rattling off the group's achievements and her pride in the group's business contracts in the 1940s, the exhibitions in which they participated, the widespread press accolades they received, the customer base that came from near and far, and the quality of the designs.[237]

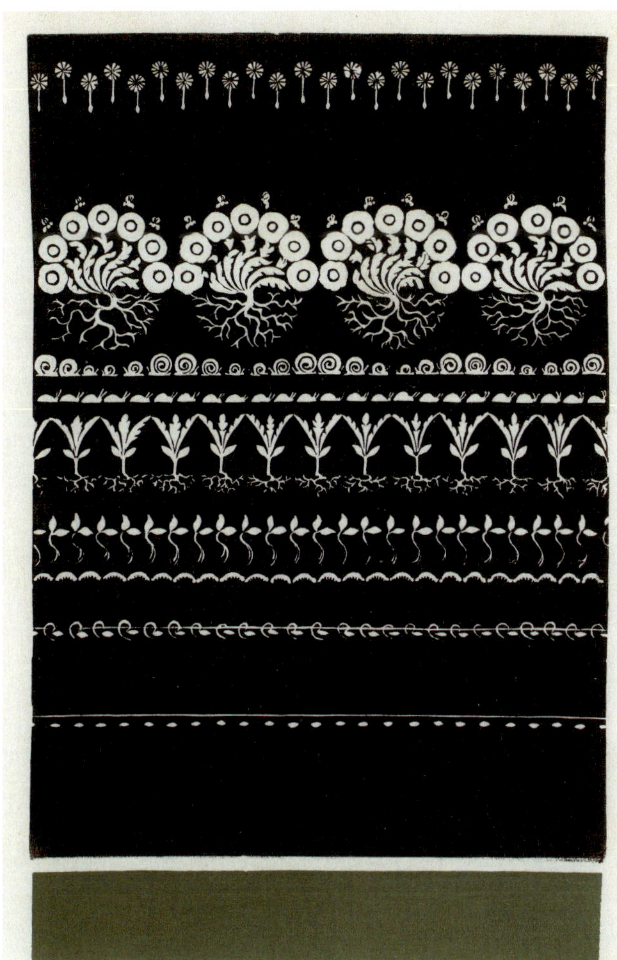

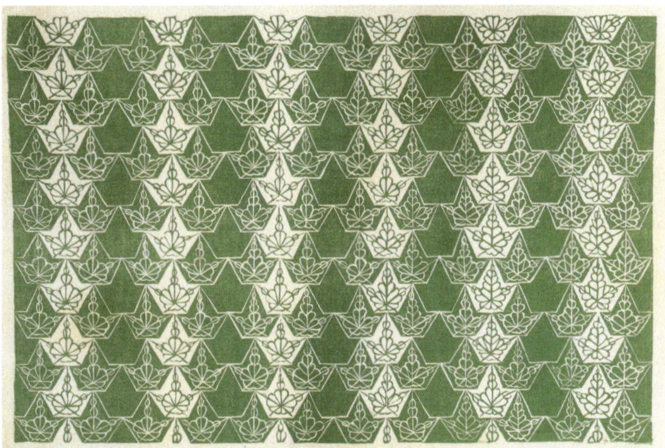

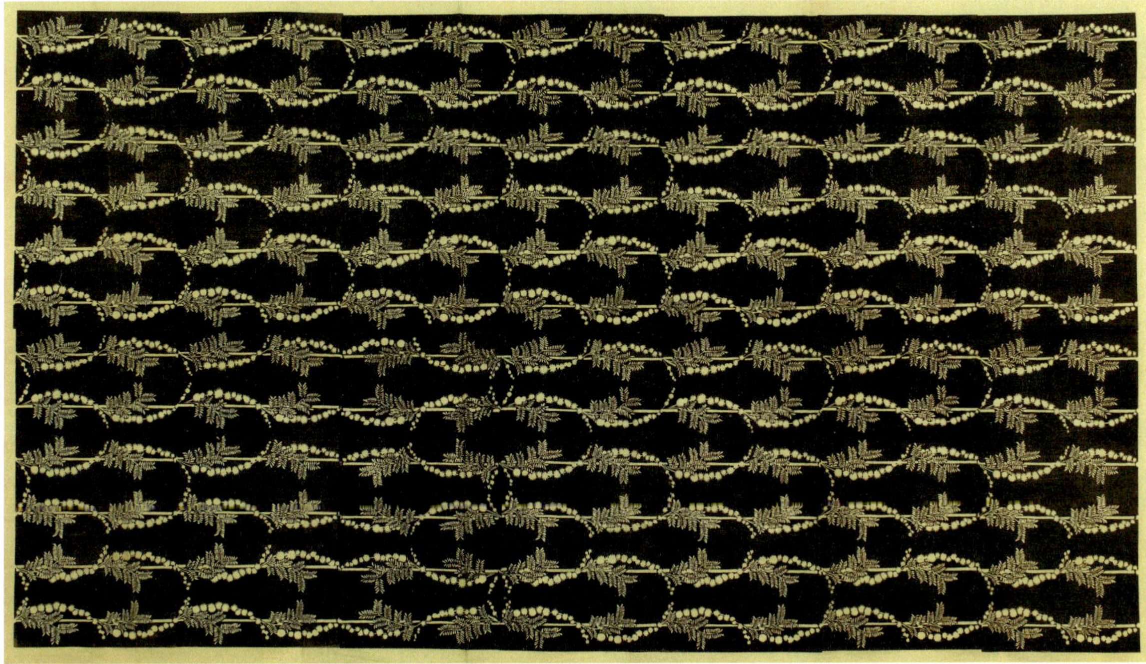

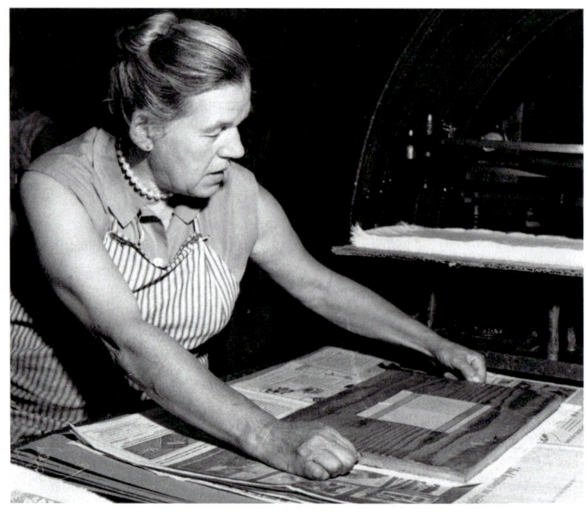

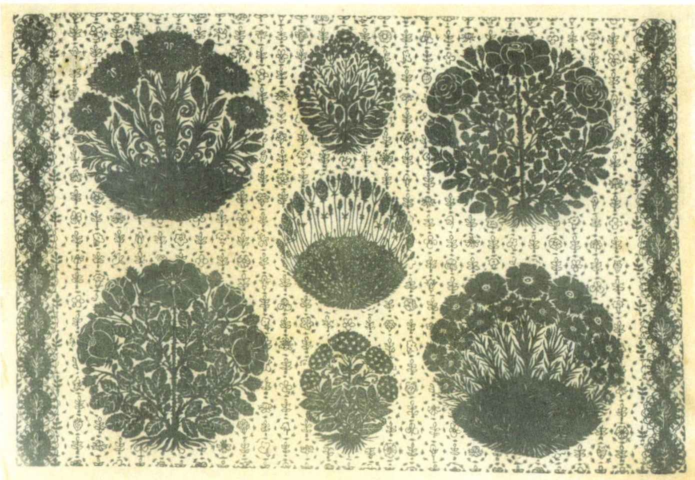

FIG. 209 (LEFT)
Peggy Norton carefully registering a block while printing in the Folly Cove Designers' barn. As she got older, she found that it was easier to print from a sitting position. Even while hard at work, she is wearing a string of pearls.

FIG. 210 (RIGHT)
In a nod to Peggy's herb business, many of her designs incorporated herbs or other plants, such as *Potpourri*. As mentioned in chapter 3, this design was copied by a dress manufacturer. (Ink on fabric.)

Margaret Norton (1905–2000)

Both the Norton sisters were multitalented. Margaret, the younger of the two and known as Peggy, received a bachelor of arts degree in physics at Wheaton College (Norton, Massachusetts) before enrolling in the Sacker School of Design and Interior Decoration to study art and follow in her mother's and Dorothy's footsteps. (Her mother was a portrait painter and studied at the School of the Museum of Fine Arts in Boston.)[238] She worked in interior design and continued to take art courses, including studying with Charles Woodbury.[239] A car accident that Peggy survived but her mother did not resulted in Peggy deciding to move to Gloucester year round in 1939.[240] There she started a mail-order herb business called the Little House, after her own house, again following in her mother's footsteps, since her mother had been a founder of the Herb Society of America.[241] Peggy grew sage, lavender, and all of the "common" herbs in a large field.[242]

With the onset of the war, running the business became impossible. It was around this time that she joined the Folly Cove Designers. She found the work gratifying and much less strenuous than gardening.[243] Peggy joined the group after it had transitioned to mechanical presses, for which she was grateful, given her health limitations.[244]

Peggy was one of Virginia's most dedicated students. She credited her ability to do the homework to having more time than most of the designers, plus she thought the classes were fascinating.[245] Like Virginia, Peggy was a perfectionist. Her homework folders (at the Cape Ann Museum and in private collections) are filled with sketches and completed assignments. As Lee Natti said, Peggy and Virginia had the ability to produce "all these different combinations and permutations and have the great fun of seeing something change and pick the best."[246] Because of the amount of source material she had, Peggy would often create multiple designs based on one subject, such as her designs involving apple pie, her quirky home, and strawberries. After seeing all of her homework for *Apple Pie* and *Apple Pie (small)* (see page 39), an interviewer once asked Norton if she ever tired of apples. She responded, "Never."[247]

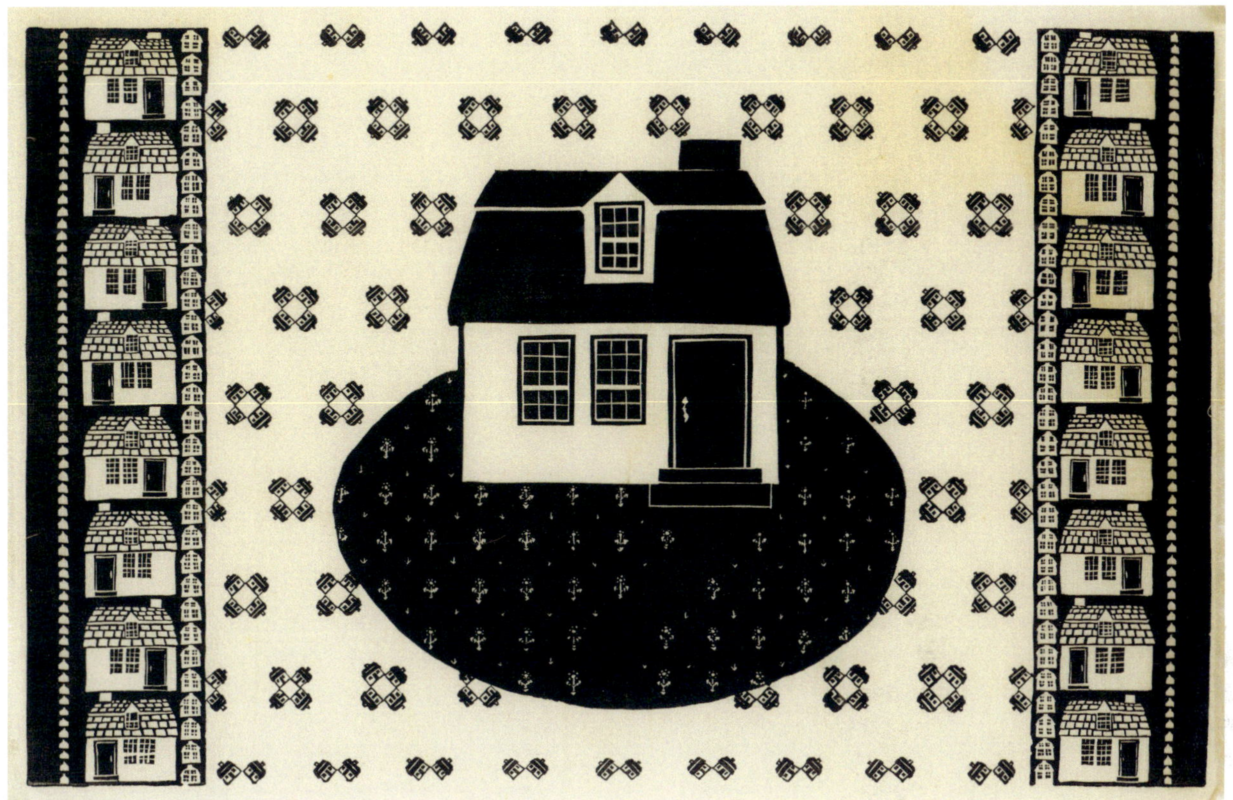

FIG. 211 (ABOVE)
Story and a Half **by Peggy depicts her home. Some of the homework that led to this design is featured in chapter 2. There are multiple sizes of the house in this one design and alternating front door openings in the side borders. The circle highlights the flowers growing around the house and negative space creates a pathway leading to the front door. (Ink on fabric.)**

FIG. 212 (LEFT)
Peggy's *Story and a Half House (small)*. Sizes and repetition are central to this design, as well as radial symmetry. This particular print features one color for each square, while other prints of the same design feature multiple colored squares, suggesting that she was hand-printing the color. (Ink on fabric.)

Peggy's own home inspired her *Story and a Half* design.[248] She kept her press in the barn behind her house and used it as her studio.[249] Likely not wanting to let her homework from the original design go to waste, she also created *Story and a Half House (small)* and several other "lost" variations. Some of the "lost" house-inspired designs are in the Cape Ann Museum collection in the form of linoleum carvings, along with homework related to the designs. If a design was carved, it indicated jury approval. Peggy was a rule follower, although it is possible that she broke the rules and carved some of these designs to test print them.

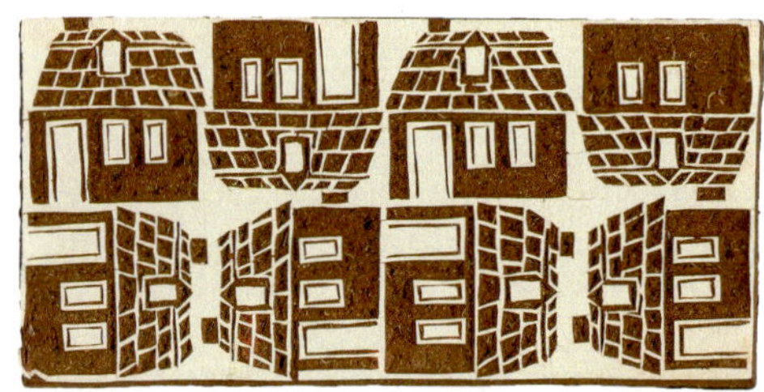

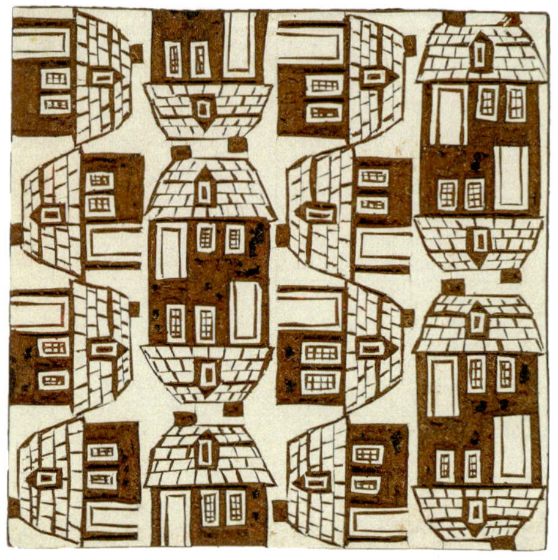

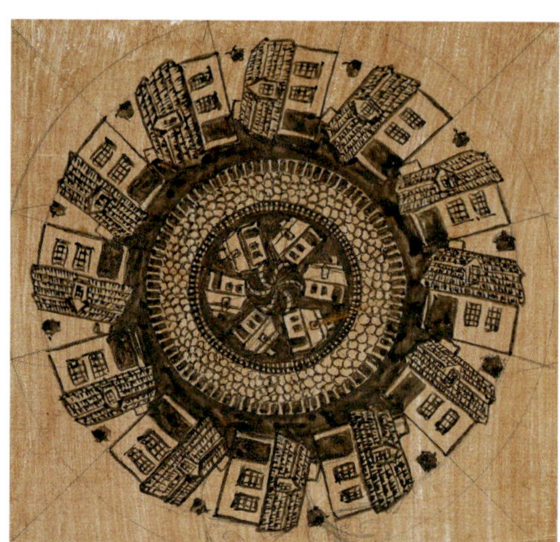

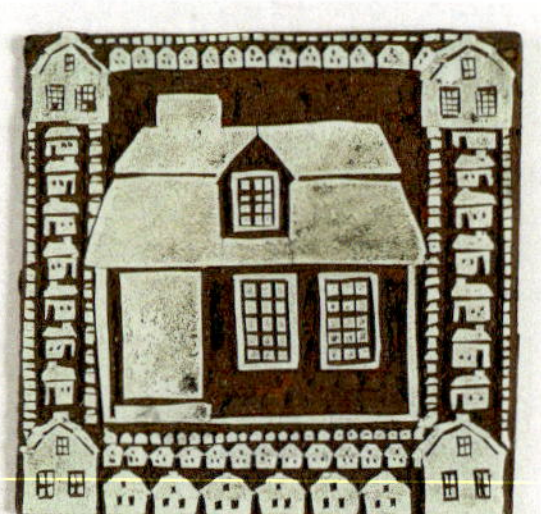

FIG. 213 (TOP LEFT)
This block by Peggy Norton was printed on a piece of cloth, although it was not fringed, suggesting the fabric was a test piece.

FIG. 214 (MIDDLE LEFT)
This block by Peggy was also printed on an unfringed piece of fabric. It is almost identical to the other piece except the space between some of the houses has been eliminated.

FIG. 215 (TOP RIGHT)
This block by Peggy was never carved, but would have been demanding in its detail. Notice the "whirling" pattern in the center and the detail of the tree inner border. The roof in this design is especially textured. Note the penciled compass marks.

FIG. 216 (MIDDLE RIGHT)
This block by Peggy includes a spiral arrangement, or a "whirling" design, as Virginia would have described it. There seems to be a row of trees between the rows of the smallest houses.

FIG. 217 (BOTTOM RIGHT)
This block by Peggy, which is coated with what appears to be white gesso or shoe polish, is another exploration of size and a "lost" design. This is clearly not as clean as some of her other work in terms of carving.

FIG. 218 (BOTTOM LEFT)
Although a block for this design was not found with Peggy's other house-related homework, this design was used for the waistbands of skirts printed with *Story and a Half House (small)*, as well as printed as Christmas cards such as shown here. (Ink on paper.)

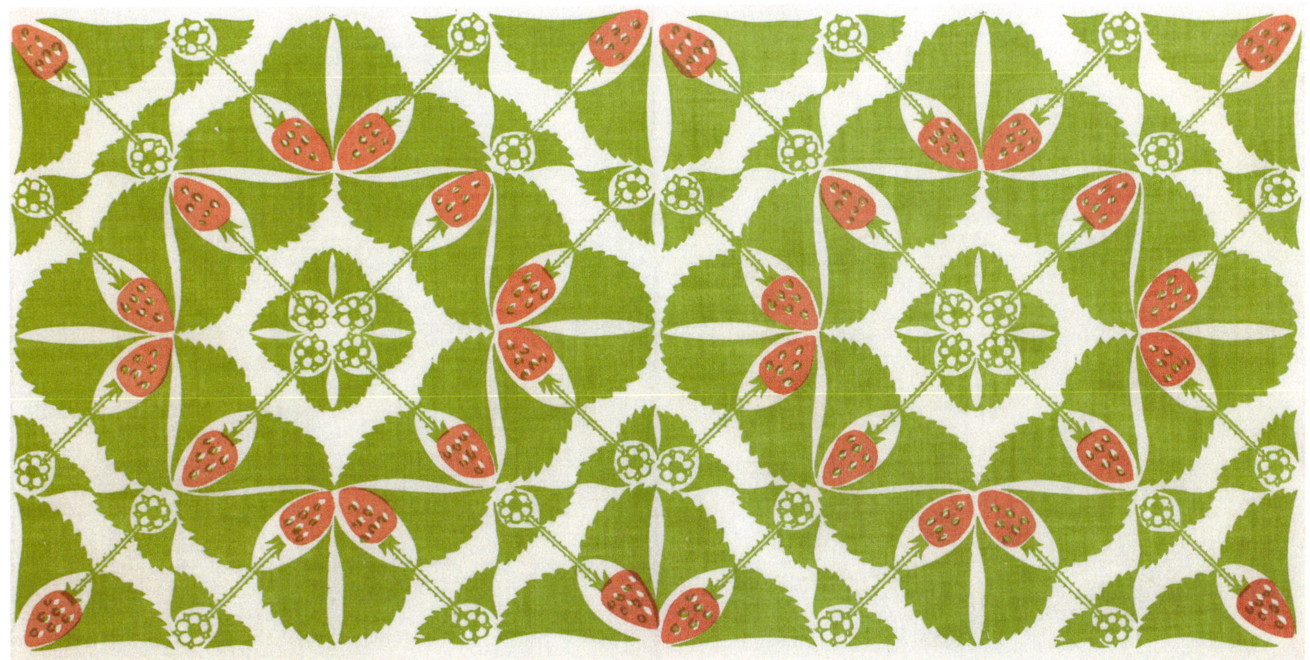

FIG. 219 (ABOVE)
Strawberry Patch **by Peggy Norton is a multicolored print with stylized leaves and a bolder, more graphic look. (Ink on fabric.)**

FIG. 220 (LEFT)
Strawberry **by Peggy is another very detailed design with its delicate vines. At first glance one might think it is a typical floral design, but upon closer inspection you see the detail of the strawberry, the blossoms, and the leaves. (Ink on fabric.)**

Similarly, Peggy created two designs based on strawberries, *Strawberry* and *Strawberry Patch*. A strawberry was also featured on a 1938 copy of one of the herb company catalogs that she designed, so it seems it was a popular motif of hers.[250] Peggy enjoyed experimenting with scale and positive and negative space.

Peggy's printing skills, particularly her registration skills (the precise alignment of the blocks on the printing surface), were admired by fellow members.[251] This made her execution of multicolored designs such as *Mulberry Maze* (see page 66) and *Hearts and Flowers* easier and she was one of the few designers to produce multicolored prints. The gridlike framework of these designs is reminiscent of garden plots or rows of crops. Likewise *African Violets* is arranged in rows. It was likely inspired by her younger sister Frances Norton Batcheller's research. Frances studied horticulture and was known as an expert on the flower.[252]

Deciduous is a remarkably detailed piece depicting Peggy's compost pile, but with artfully arranged leaves. She had planned to call it simply *Compost Pile,* but Dorothy stepped in and suggested it would sell better as *Deciduous*.[253] *Baked Bean Supper* became a top seller, though. It is Peggy's only figurative piece and another detailed one.[254]

Always the overachieving student, Peggy completed two designs in some years.[255] In an interview Peggy indicated that her first design for the Folly Cove Designers was *Bee Skeps*.[256] Peggy returned to the subject on a smaller scale in 1950 with *Busy Bee,* which is notable as one of her only designs to convey motion.[257] Some of her whirling "lost" house-inspired designs also conveyed motion, but were either never released or, in the case of figure 215 on page 162, never carved.

In addition to the many house-inspired designs in the Cape Ann Museum collection, during the research for this book one "lost" design by Peggy was discovered in a private collection. The floral design appears in chapter 3 on page 66 in the form of a printed scarf.[258]

As Peggy got older, printmaking became too physically demanding and she retired a few years before the group officially disbanded.[259] She took up rug weaving in 1971, at the age of sixty-six. She studied at the Haystack Mountain School of Crafts (Deer Isle, Maine) with master weaver Peter Collingwood. (Glass artist Dale Chihuly was an instructor at Haystack at the same time.)[260] In an interview Peggy said that, even in her weaving, "I could still use all the things Jinnee taught me."[261]

Peggy found her design work "fulfilling."[262] She was fascinated by the process. When interviewed she discussed the process rather than the inspiration for her designs.[263] Yet Peggy said that, in terms of subject matter, "You're not aware of it, but what you are comes out in your prints" and for her it was her love of the garden.[264] And even though she experimented with silk-screening and went on to explore weaving, she stated that block printing was "the most satisfying kind of creative work that I'd ever tried."[265]

FIG. 221 (OPPOSITE TOP)
Hearts and Flowers **by Peggy is another detailed, multicolored print. Each heart-shaped leaf consists of intricate patterns made out of lines or dots. The ability to print multiple shades of green is impressive and gives depth to the design. (Ink on fabric.)**

FIG. 222 (OPPOSITE BOTTOM)
In a rare square block, *Deciduous* by Peggy is an example of gradations and conveys negative and positive space. The inner circle gives the effects of grays through the tiny dots in the background. (Ink on fabric.)

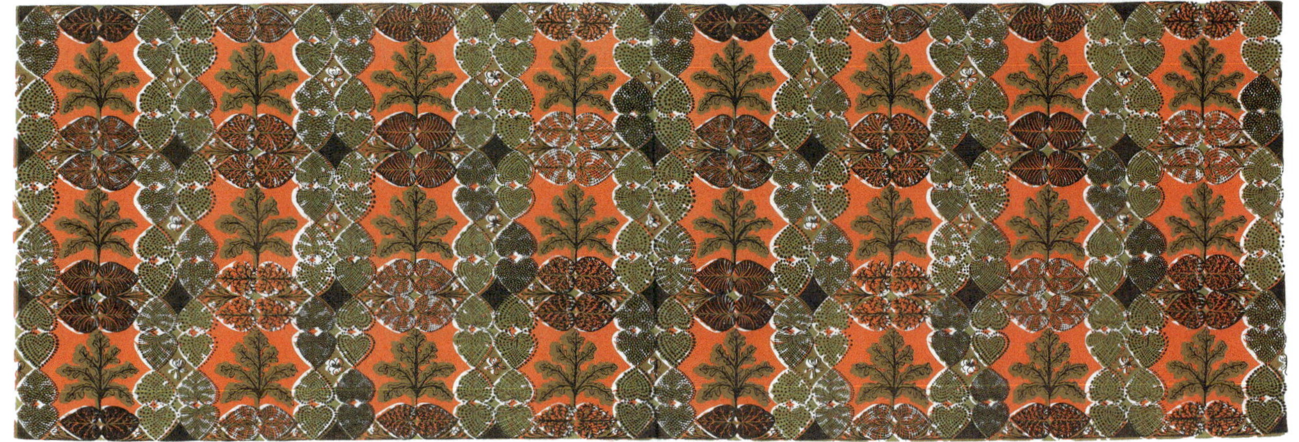

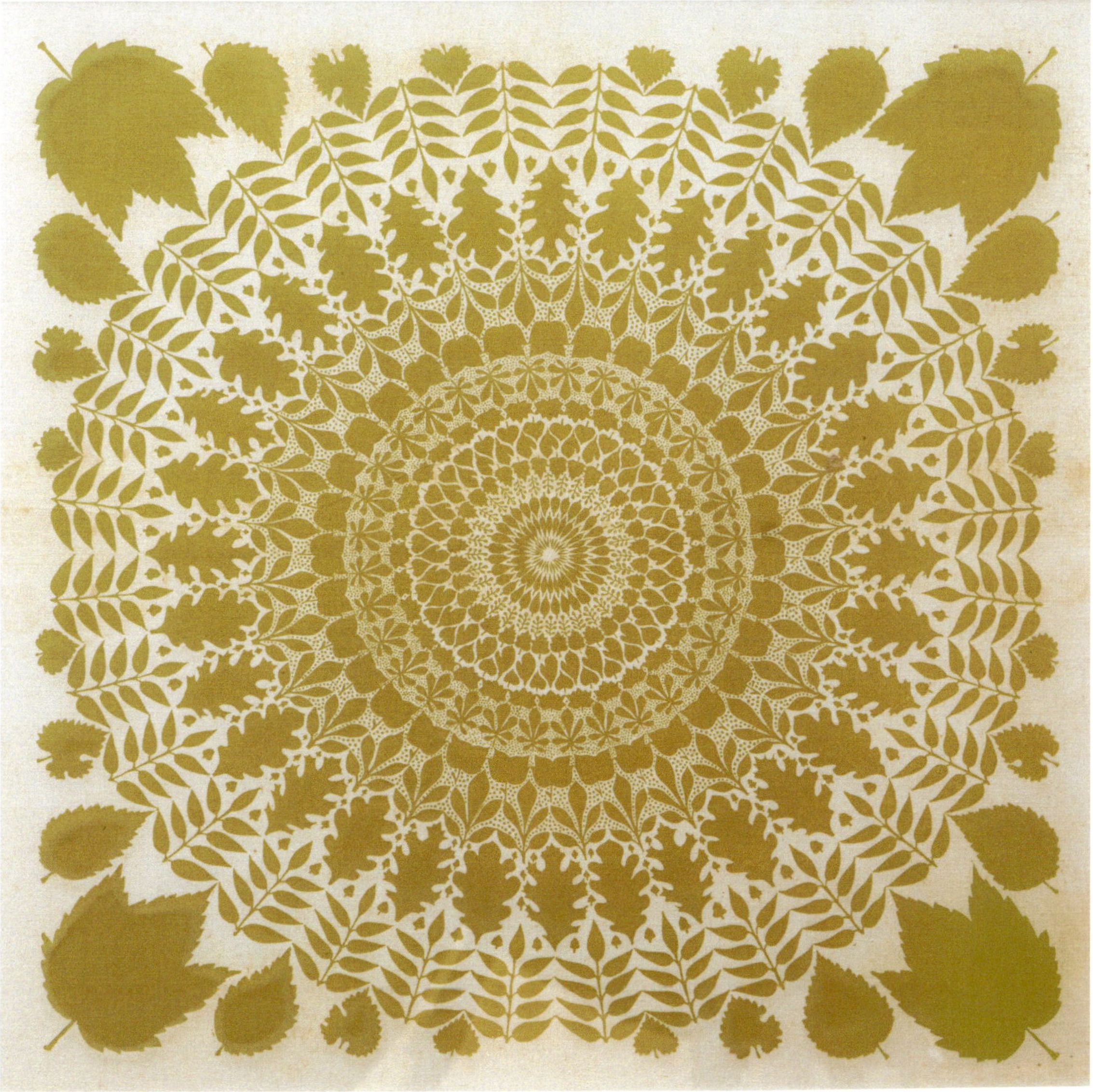

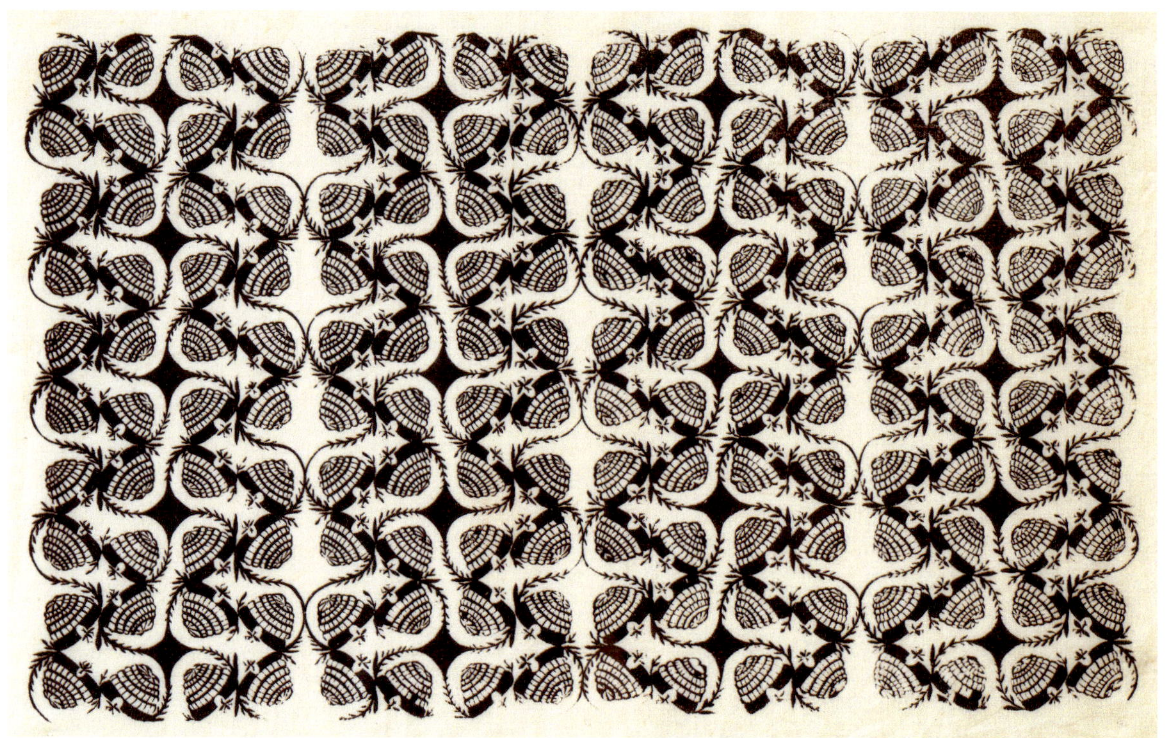

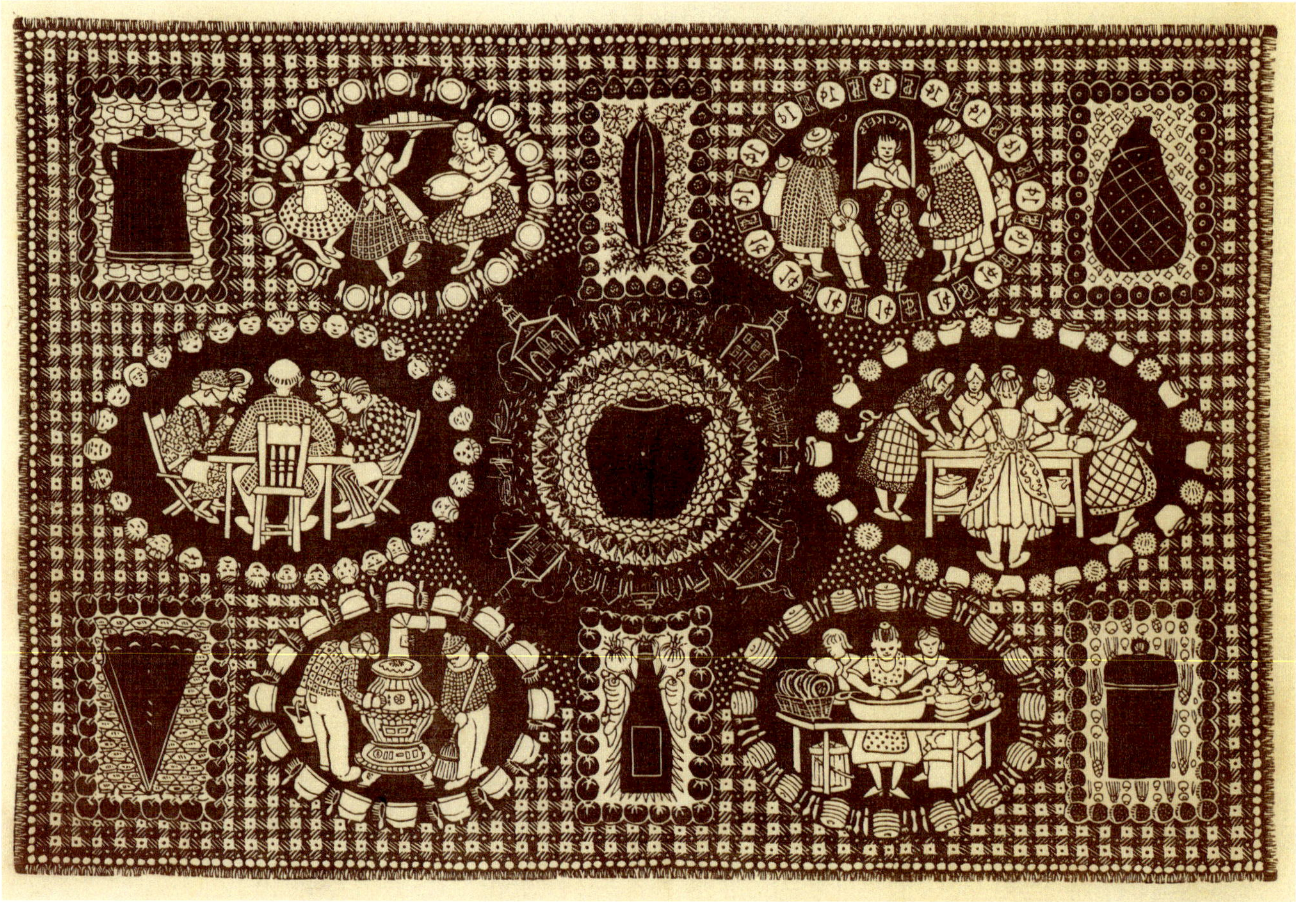

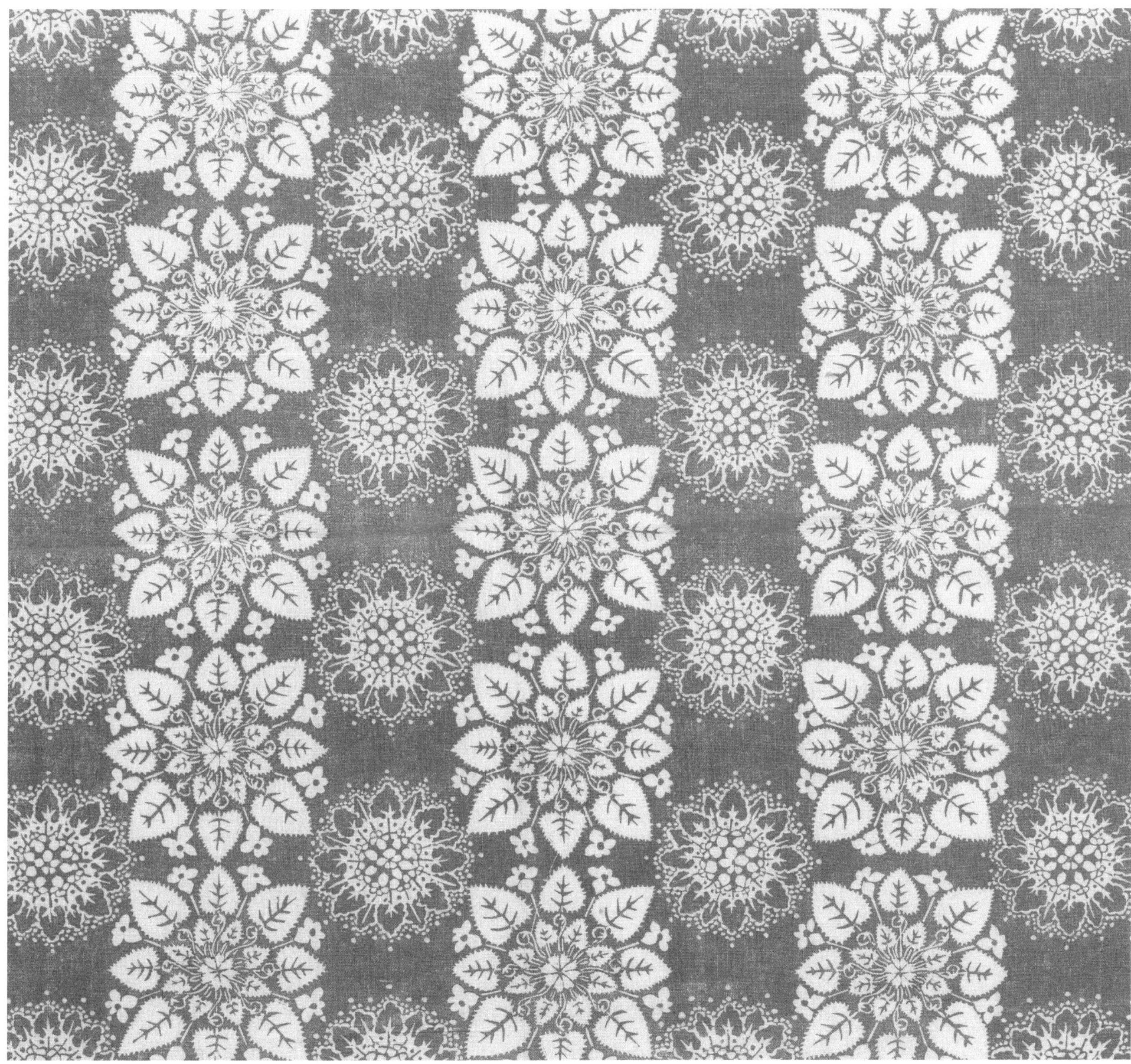

FIG. 223 (OPPOSITE TOP)
Busy Bee **conveys motion through its alternating vertical patterns and lines. (Ink on fabric.)**

FIG. 224 (OPPOSITE BOTTOM)
Baked Bean Supper **is a celebration of this New England tradition. Peggy produced pages of homework for this. Each vignette of this design has a border offering a parallel story line. The intricate checkerboard pattern must have been time-consuming to carve, the design as a whole honoring the concept of patterns within patterns. (Ink on fabric.)**

FIG. 225 (ABOVE)
Peggy Norton's younger sister Frances was an expert on African violets, which likely inspired this design by the same name. The designers stated in their catalog description that Peggy grew the flower on her home's windowsills. (Ink on fabric.)

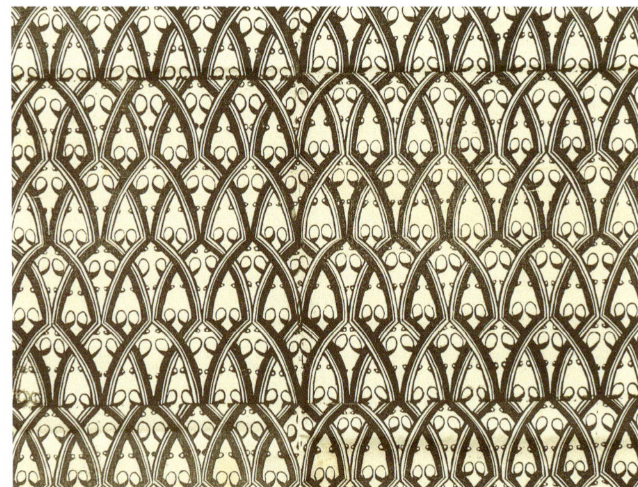

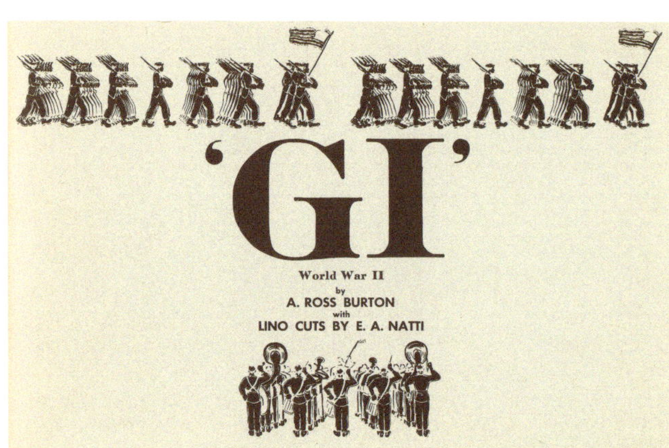

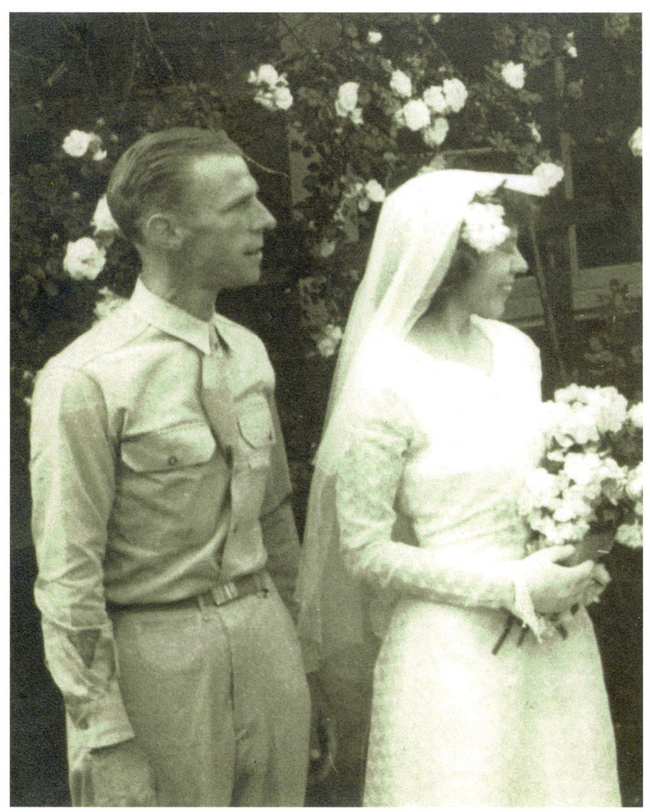

SELECT OTHER DESIGNERS

Alexander Ross Burton (1911–1970)

Ross Burton (as he was called) was the younger brother of Virginia Lee Demetrios. During World War II he served in the Army Air Corps as a pilot and teletype operator in Europe. Upon his return home, he used the G.I. Bill to become a silversmith, studying at the School of the Museum of Fine Arts, Wentworth Institute of Technology, and North Bennett Street School in Boston. He opened his own shop in Rockport.[266]

Gothic Willow is the only known design by Ross. This intricate, architecturally inspired design is seemingly inspired by the pattern of Gothic windows. Ross also wrote poetry and published a book of free verse titled *"GI": World War II* in 1963, based on his Army experience. Fellow Folly Cove designer and Army veteran Eino Natti illustrated the book with block-printed images (see page 142).[267] Virginia praised the draft of his book to her editor at Houghton Mifflin and shared a copy with him, admitting that "I am prejudiced…because the author is my brother and the artist is one of the good Folly Cove Designers."[268] Ross also made sterling silver sculptures.[269]

FIG. 226 (TOP LEFT)
Ross Burton's *Gothic Willow* with the beautiful arches of a Gothic window. (Ink on fabric.)

FIG. 227 (BOTTOM LEFT)
Both Ross and Eino Natti were veterans of World War II. The book cover features Eino's *Pass in Review*.

FIG. 228 (RIGHT)
Ross and Hilja Johnson were married in June 1945 at Virginia and George Demetrios's property. Hilja's dress included her Folly Cove design work and that of other designers.

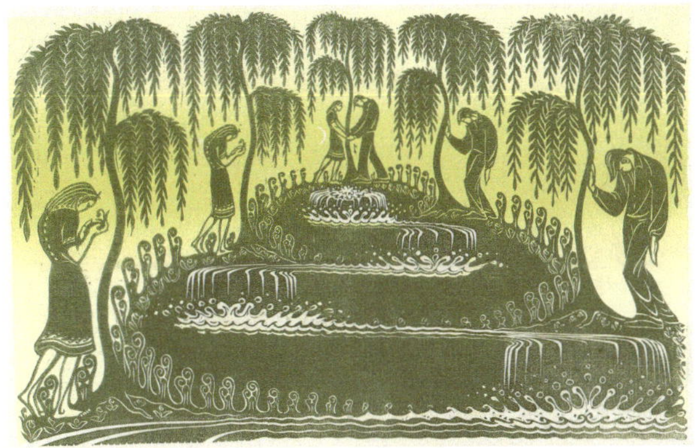

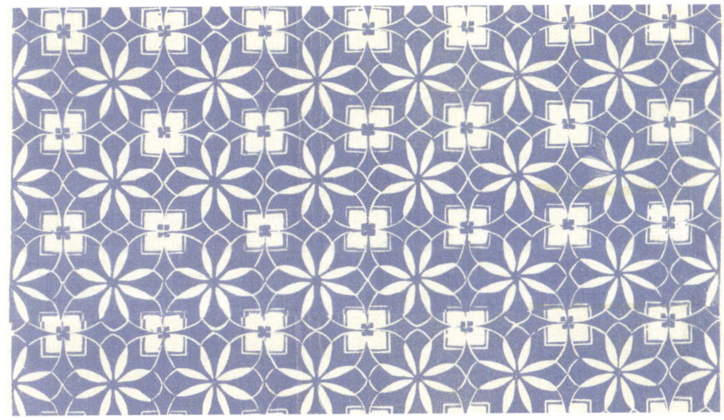

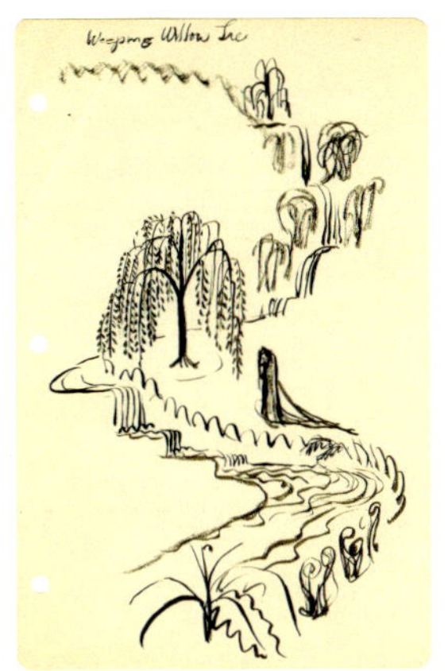

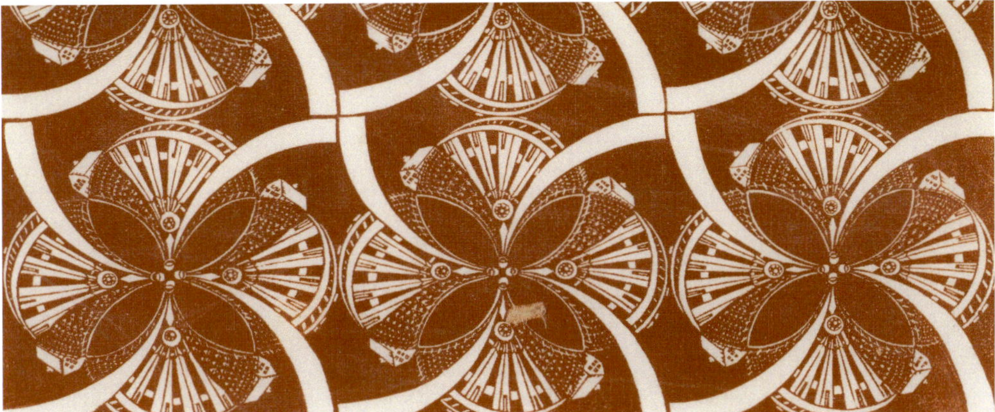

CLOCKWISE FROM TOP LEFT

FIG. 229
Sentimental **was created by Virginia for her sister-in-law and depicts the stream along which Hilja married Ross. (Ink on fabric.)**

FIG. 230
Hilja's wedding dress appears to have been printed with her ***Little Daisy*** **design. (Ink on fabric.)**

FIG. 231
Mill Stream **shows the evolution of Hilja's work. The narrative design conveys motion through "whirling" patterns with technical precision and a sense of dimension in how the waterwheels are angled. (Ink on fabric.)**

FIG. 232
This ink sketch of ***Sentimental*** **depicts Hilja as a bride with a long train and veil, while in the final design Virginia has Hilja wearing a Folly Cove Designers' skirt.**

Hilja (Johnson) Burton (1919–1993)

A native of Gloucester, Hilja Burton was one of the original members of the Folly Cove Designers and participated in the 1940 exhibition.[270] In 1945 she married Virginia's younger brother, Ross Burton. They were married on the grounds of Virginia and George Demetrios's property.[271] In a 1945 *Magazine Digest* article about the Folly Cove Designers it said that the bride wore a dress "which was the joint handiwork of all the Folly Cove Designers."[272] Her gown looks to be printed with her *Little Daisy* pattern.[273] It is unclear which other designs were included in her ensemble, but it is possible that her veil featured designs by fellow members. Virginia created *Sentimental* for her sister-in-law, which shows the brook they got married next to.[274] The weeping willow trees it includes are similar to the ones Virginia used in her illustrations for *Song of Robin Hood*, which she was likley already working on.

Hilja created a handful of designs for the group. *Mill Stream* was particularly intricate, with the waterwheel and mill building incorporated into the geometric pattern. Hilja worked with her husband at the shop, but she was also a painter (watercolor and oil) and a member of the Rockport Art Association. She continued to do block printing after the Folly Cove Designers disbanded.[275]

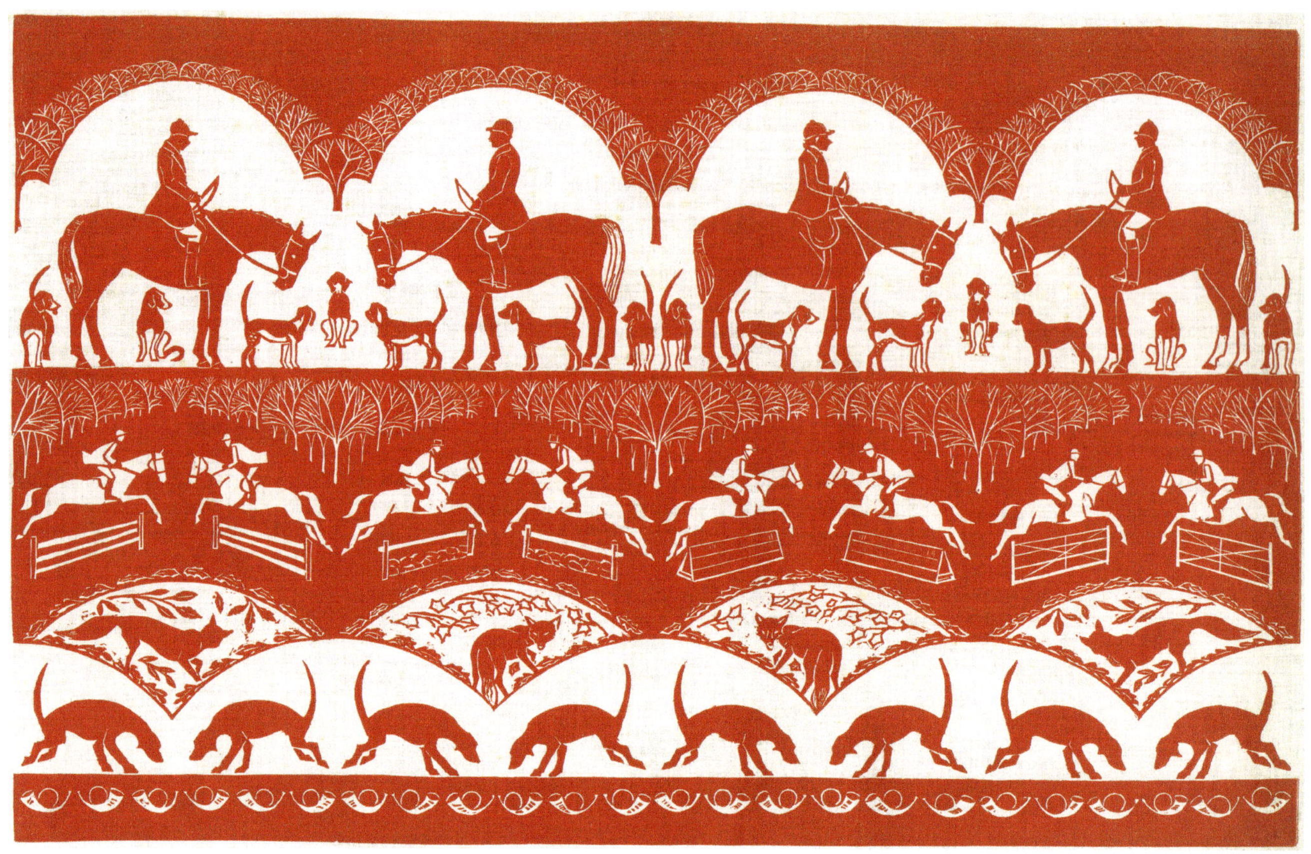

Zoe (Cominos) Eleftherio (1930–)

Zoe Cominos was born in Boston. Her father was Greek and a good friend of George Demetrios, as well as his doctor. She attended what is now Garland Junior College in Boston and took drawing and sculpture lessons with George in the summers of 1948 and 1949 while on Cape Ann with her family.[276] She joined the Folly Cove Designers in the early 1950s and commuted to the design meetings from Groton before she left the group to get married.[277] She recalls being one of the youngest members at the time.[278] Her two designs reflect her love of horseback riding. One was inspired by a performance of the Spanish Riding School. She went on to co-found the Groton Center for the Arts in the early 1970s, and is a watercolor artist.[279]

FIG. 233
Zoe Eleftherio is one of the last living Folly Cove Designers. She based her designs on her love of horseback riding. *Tally Ho* depicts a foxhunt and features lovely details such as the trees as borders and the horns with a strong use of positive and negative space. (Ink on fabric.)

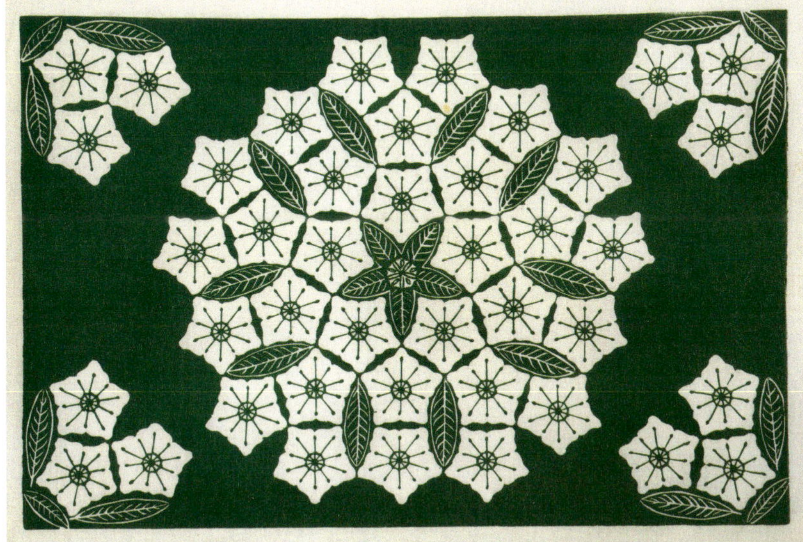

FIG. 234 (LEFT)
Bob Holloran said he was inspired to create *Mountain Laurel* to "prove" that it was possible to create a "five-sided figure." He certainly proved the point by creating an overall five-sided figure consisting of individual five-sided white flowers and a dark five-sided, starfish-shaped element in its center. (Ink on fabric.)

FIG. 235 (RIGHT)
***Anchors* is a "lost" design that has not previously been recognized as part of Bob Holloran's oeuvre. It was inspired by the Navy veteran's lifelong interest in boats and was likely one of his first designs. (Ink on fabric.)**

Robert Timothy Holloran (1919–2008)

Robert (Bob) Holloran was a Gloucester native and married to designer Libby Holloran (see page 126).[280] Following in his father's footsteps, he earned a degree in architecture from the Wentworth Institute of Technology in Boston.[281] He served two tours in the Naval Construction Battalion, known as the Seabees, in the South Pacific during World War II.[282]

Bob joined the Folly Cove Designers after the war, completing three designs: *Anchors, Mountain Laurel*, and *Trumpet Vine*.[283] *Anchors* is a "lost" design and was not previously recognized as part of his oeuvre. Anchors and rope were elements in his wife's design *Fisherman* (see page 67), for which he modeled.

He had a distinguished architectural career that included designing buildings for the Smithsonian Institution. An avid skier, he was one of the founders of Attitash Mountain Resort in New Hampshire.[284]

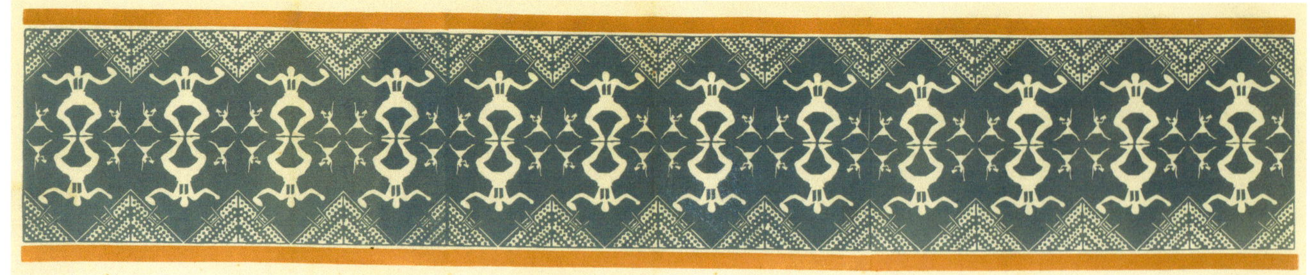

FIG. 236
Anthony Iarrobino's first design was *Football Idols*. He later said that he felt that the group had been "kind" to him by letting it pass. (Ink on fabric.)

Anthony Iarrobino (1913–2006) and Elizabeth (Droney) Iarrobino (1915–2009)

Anthony (Tony) Iarrobino was born in Revere, Massachusetts, Elizabeth (Betty) Iarrobino in Milford.[285] They met at Massachusetts College of Art and Design in Boston, where he earned a master of fine arts and Elizabeth a bachelor of fine arts degree.[286] Anthony took a job at Forbes Lithograph Manufacturing Co. (Chelsea, Massachusetts). The couple married in 1941, settling in the coastal town of Marblehead, north of Boston. Elizabeth gave birth to Anthony, Jr., the first of their two children, before Anthony left for World War II.

Anthony served with the Army 652nd Engineers, where his skills as a mapmaker were utilized.[287] During the war, Elizabeth's aunt moved in to look after their young child so that Elizabeth could take over some of Anthony's duties at Forbes Lithograph.[288] When he returned home, he resumed his job at the company (he printed Virginia Lee Burton's *Life Story* in the 1960s while working there), where he worked in the color correction department.[289] Elizabeth is said to have found the transition from working to full-time homemaking difficult; she joined the Folly Cove Designers within a few years of his return. The couple had their second son, Paul, in 1949.[290]

Anthony became a portrait artist and taught private classes and group classes at Marblehead Arts Association in life drawing and portraiture.[291] In addition to block printing, he began collograph printing (printing with a collaged surface or plate that allows for the impression of different textures and materials) in 1975 and established himself in the medium.[292]

After college and before her marriage, Elizabeth worked as an illustrator for a newspaper and was employed at a print shop.[293] She returned to school at Salem State University and Massachusetts College of Art and Design in the early 1960s to obtain a bachelor of science in education.[294] She taught at Lasell Junior College (now Lasell University) in Newton, Massachusetts, from 1962 to 1983, teaching studio art and design and rising to the level of associate professor.[295]

Elizabeth was inspired to join the Folly Cove Designers in 1948 after reading about them in *Life*. Anthony drove her to the meetings, then he joined two years later.[296] "I had to join—you can't be exposed and not be attracted to it."[297] Elizabeth studied with Aino and Virginia.[298] Anthony, like many of the men in the group, did not recall having taken the course.[299] Both of them also studied with George Demetrios.[300] Despite having two young children and the commute from Marblehead to Gloucester, they were active

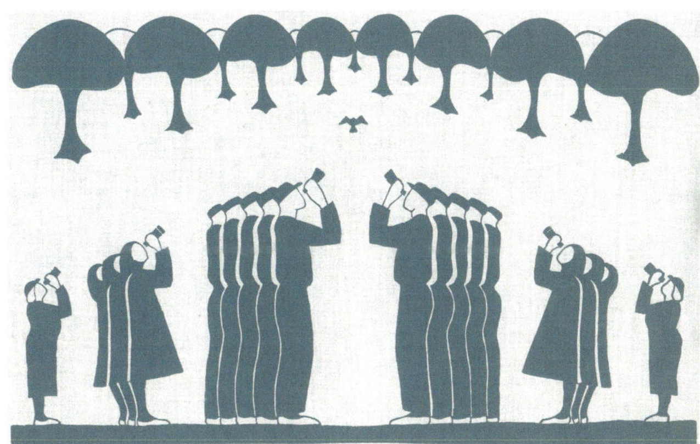

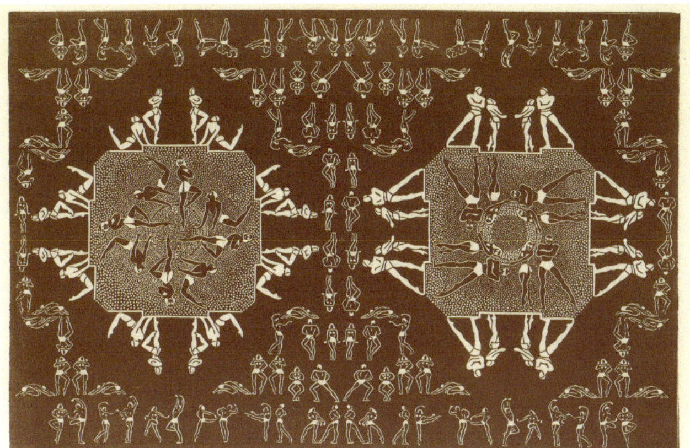

FIG. 237 (LEFT)
Anthony and Elizabeth Iarrobino enjoyed the ballet and the beach and his *Beach Ballet* combined those interests. The detail required him to use a magnifying glass to carve it. The design incorporates a lot of the group's design principles, while still showcasing his figurative skills. (Ink on fabric.)

FIG. 238 (RIGHT)
***Bird Watchers* by Elizabeth. As a bird watcher she saw herself in this design, with the men out front and "one little old lady off to the side." She accentuated the use of positive and negative space as well as strong lines. (Ink on fabric.)**

members and the most enduring couple to participate in the group, remaining members until the early 1960s.[301] Dorothy Norton considered them to be some of "the most important and productive members," citing their retirement as a loss to the group.[302]

In addition to the Folly Cove Designers, Anthony and Elizabeth were active in the Marblehead Arts Association, helping to hang and jury shows.[303] They were founding members of the cooperative Art Guild Gallery in Marblehead.[304] Anthony was also a member of the Sandy Pond Printmakers.[305]

The couple shared an acorn press, which Eino Natti had helped them find and they later donated to the Cape Ann Museum.[306] Anthony had studio space in the home, but Elizabeth often worked on her designs at the kitchen table.[307] The Iarrobinos had mutual respect for one another's art and although they may not have worked together or collaborated per se, they were sounding boards for one another. When interviewed in 1991, Anthony referred to his wife as "my best critic."[308]

Although sharing interests in the theater, ballet, bird watching, and the ocean and thus having similar subject matter in their designs, the two had different styles.[309] Anthony's prints were more detailed, with his work as a portrait artist reflected in his designs featuring dancers and football players.[310] *Football Idols* was Anthony's first design and he later criticized it for the stiffness of its figures.[311]

Elizabeth only did two figurative pieces, *Footlights*, which featured performers on stage, and *Bird Watchers*. Both of her designs integrated Virginia's emphasis on scale. Elizabeth also stressed lights and darks in her work. Both Anthony and Elizabeth returned to the same subjects multiple times. Elizabeth felt their work had humor in it, such as Anthony's *Beach Ballet* (men and women doing ballet in bathing suits) and her *Bird Watchers*, with a group of people observing the same, solitary bird.[312]

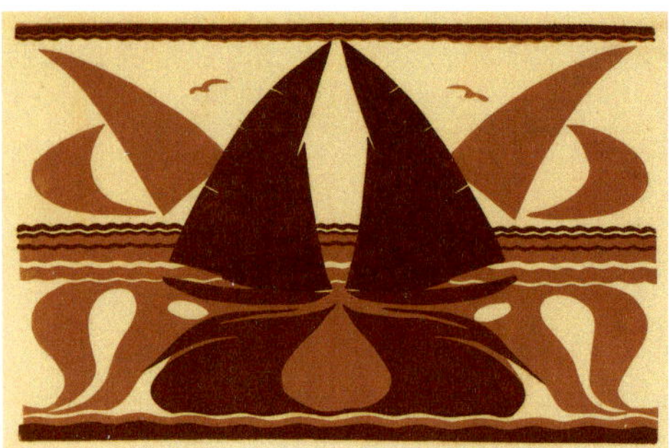

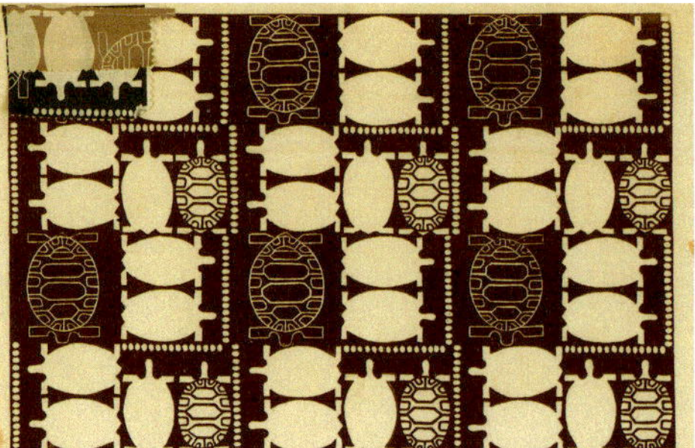

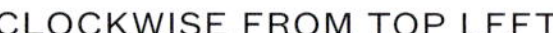

CLOCKWISE FROM TOP LEFT

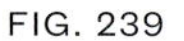

FIG. 239
Sail Boats **by Anthony Iarraobino uses triangular shapes to abstractly depict the boats and lines to show the movement of the water. The reflection of the boats can also be seen in the water. (Ink on fabric.)**

FIG. 240
Turtles **by Elizabeth Iarrobino was chosen for exhibition and is also in the permanent collection of the Cooper Hewitt, Smithsonian Design Museum. The sample swatches show the other colors in which Elizabeth printed this simple but effective design. (Ink on fabric.)**

FIG. 241
Wings **by Elizabeth. Her work had more of a mid-century/abstract feel to it, minimalistic with a focus on pattern through the use of positive and negative space. (Ink on fabric.)**

Several of Elizabeth's designs were chosen for inclusion in major exhibitions and her design *Turtles* is part of the Cooper Hewitt, Smithsonian Design Museum permanent collection.[313] *Wings* was published in the *New York Times* in 1957, alongside many mid-century designs, including work by famed textile artist Alexander Girard.[314] In Elizabeth's designs, the focus was often more on pattern rather than detail.

One of Anthony's simplest pieces and the one that overlapped the most in style with Elizabeth's more geometric and graphic designs was *Sail Boats*. Elizabeth had *Sail Boats* etched into Anthony's tombstone. A few years later, in a eulogy for his mother, Anthony Iarrobino, Jr., recalled her printing and "the smell of turpentine, of ink," that permeated his youth.[315]

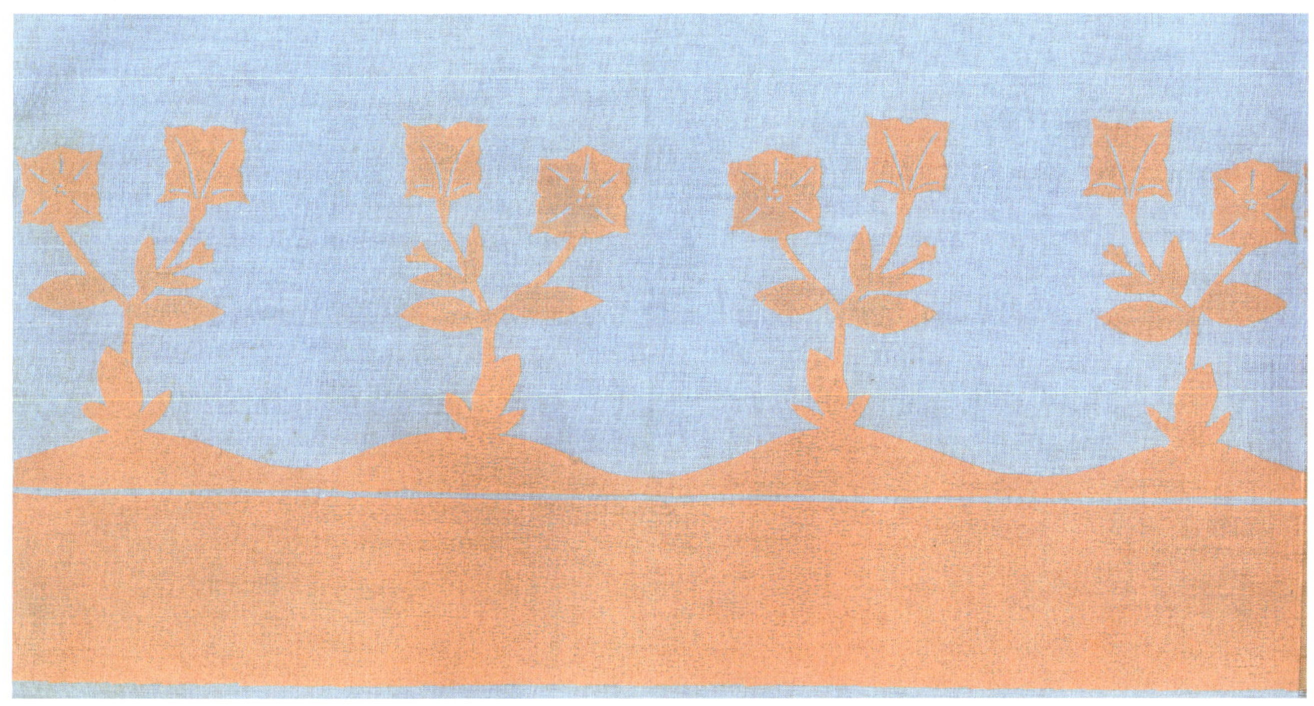

FIG. 242
Flower **by Hilda Kaihlanen. Around 2011 Hilda carved fish under the flowers (presumably alluding to the compost used in the seaside community) and had this design reprinted to sell in her family's gallery. (Ink on fabric.)**

Hilda (Ross) Kaihlanen (1919–2013)

A native of Lanesville, Hilda was one of the original members of the Folly Cove Designers, taking the course with Virginia and completing a single design called *Flower*, which has a folk art feel.[316]

Hilda's true passion was watercolor painting.[317] She designed the cover for *The Night of the Hurricane* by the celebrated author Nancy Hale (niece of Ellen Day Hale), who summered in the area. She later published her own book, *A Finnish Christmas,* based on her heritage, which she also illustrated. Hilda belonged to several art associations, including North Shore Arts Association, Newburyport Art Association, and the Copley Society of Art (Boston). She had two children and ran a gallery with her husband and son, where she sold her folk-style paintings depicting "happy scenes" that celebrated life on Cape Ann and "happy memories."[318] Her son, also an artist, still runs the family gallery on Bearskin Neck in Rockport, Massachusetts.[319]

Although she only completed the one design, Hilda spoke fondly of the group decades later, saying that she felt lucky to have been chosen and adding that she made *nisu* for the designers.[320]

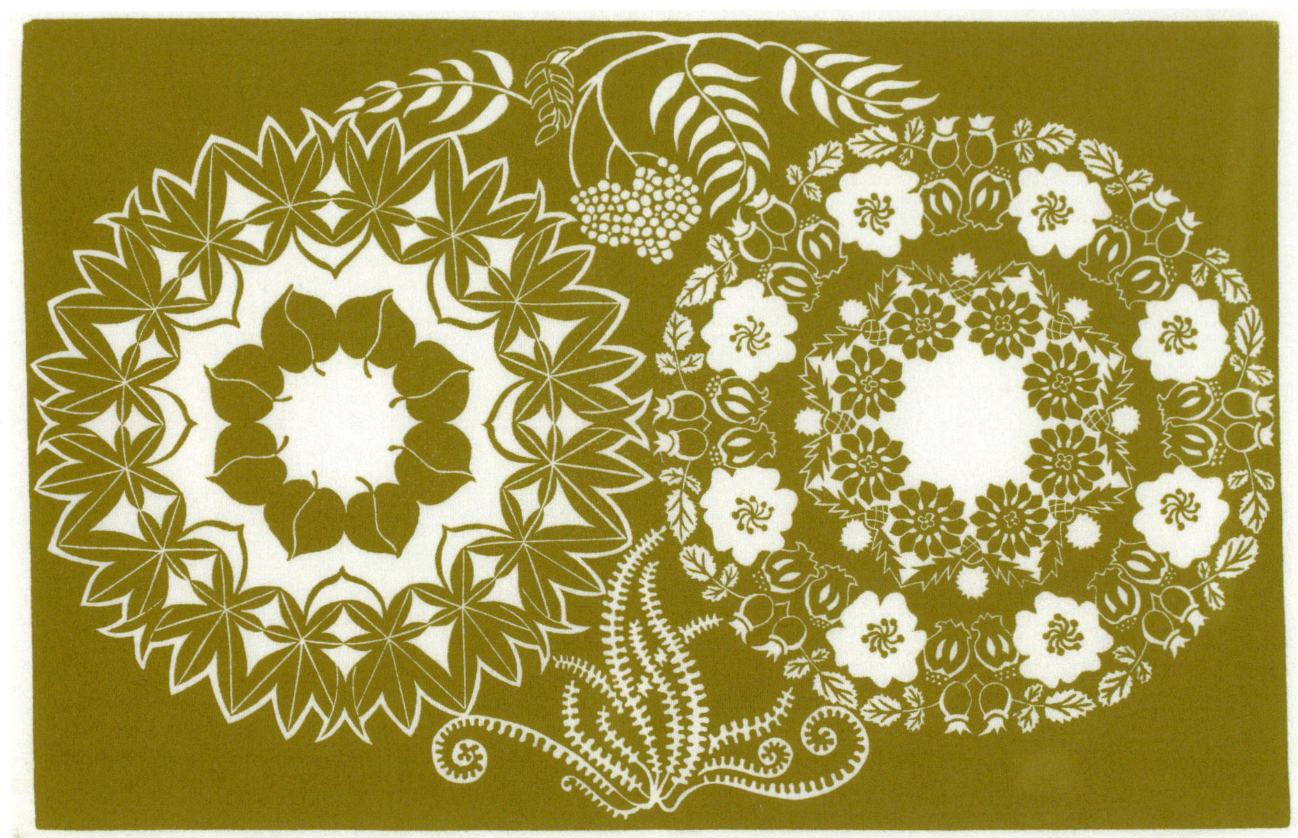

FIG. 243
***Summer Wreaths* was one of Mary Ann Lash's nature-inspired designs. It includes a tremendous amount of detail and a strong use of lights and darks. She is one of the last living designers. (Ink on fabric.)**

Mary Ann (Smith) Lash (1931–)

Mary Ann Lash graduated from Wellesley College (Wellesley, Massachusetts) with a bachelor of arts degree in English literature. A mother to two young children at the time, she was one of the last people to become a member of the Folly Cove Designers, completing three intricate designs in the late 1960s during the group's final years.[321] Her designs were inspired by her interests in nature and gardening.

A writer and illustrator, Mary Ann worked in publishing as an editor, including for Beacon Press and Peter Smith Publisher. She felt that the work of the Folly Cove Designers "represented a certain way of life . . . rooted in the practical but also transcending it."[322]

Mary (Magna) Maletskos (1918–1993)

Mary Maletskos was born in Chicago and raised in Tennessee and Connecticut.[323] Growing up she was encouraged to pursue her passions, art being one of them. Mary attended Smith College.[324] The studio art program there was still in its infancy, so she augmented her studies with a summer at artist Kimon Nicolaïdes's farm in Lyme, New Hampshire, where she studied "drawing, painting, watercolor, and lithography" with the Art Students League alum.[325] As part of her studies, she spent a year in Italy. After graduation, Mary attended Hartford Art School in West Hartford, Connecticut, where she taught children's art classes and assisted sculptor Henry Kreis. She went on to study sculpture with Ossip Zadkine at the Art Students League of New York, working in a ceramic design studio while she was there. During World War II she worked as a draftsman at Pratt & Whitney in West Hartford.[326]

Mary's friendship with Smith classmate Lee Natti led her to Folly Cove. Mary was a bridesmaid in Lee and Robert's wedding in 1945 and she lived with the couple in Lanesville for a few months in 1946.[327] During one of her visits, Mary met Constantine (Costa) Maletskos, nephew of George Demetrios, whom she married in 1947.[328] She took the Folly Cove Designers' course in the late 1940s and went on to complete some of the group's most ornate designs.[329]

Mary and Costa had three children and, like other women members, Mary juggled art with family responsibilities.[330] Outside of her Folly Cove work she explored "sculpture, ceramics, blockprinting [*sic*], watercolors, collages, monotypes."[331] She also studied with George Demetrios.[332]

Aino Clarke felt that working in black and white to create block prints probably felt restrictive to Mary since she was "gifted in other ways as an artist," particularly her use of color.[333] Aino, who had once taught Mary the design lessons, credits Mary with teaching her how to see color.[334] Aino recalled them driving by the Annisquam church and Mary telling her to look at the colors. "It was like a mental awakening for me," Aino said.[335] Mary experimented with multicolored printing with *Nasturtiums* as a Folly Cove designer.

According to Lee, Mary was involved in the group through to the end but wasn't as prolific due to her limited time and other interests. Lee also felt that Mary's "urge to be a painter and go into monotype and all the wonderfully creative things that she did" made it "hard for her to do something over and over and over by rote."[336] Mary said, regarding the design lessons, "I learned a tremendous amount that I could use in my art, in my painting," admitting "my first love would really be painting and printing [monotypes]."[337] She also said that before she studied with Virginia her painting style was "really wild" and she credited Virginia with teaching her how to "have a discriminating eye."[338]

Perhaps because she was a fine artist, Mary tended to print her designs as table runners, in a more decorative format as opposed to utilitarian.[339] The piece featuring a heron (see page 179) is attributed to Mary and may be a "lost design," although, with its single subject and no background elements, it is not typical of the Folly Cove Designers' work. It is not known

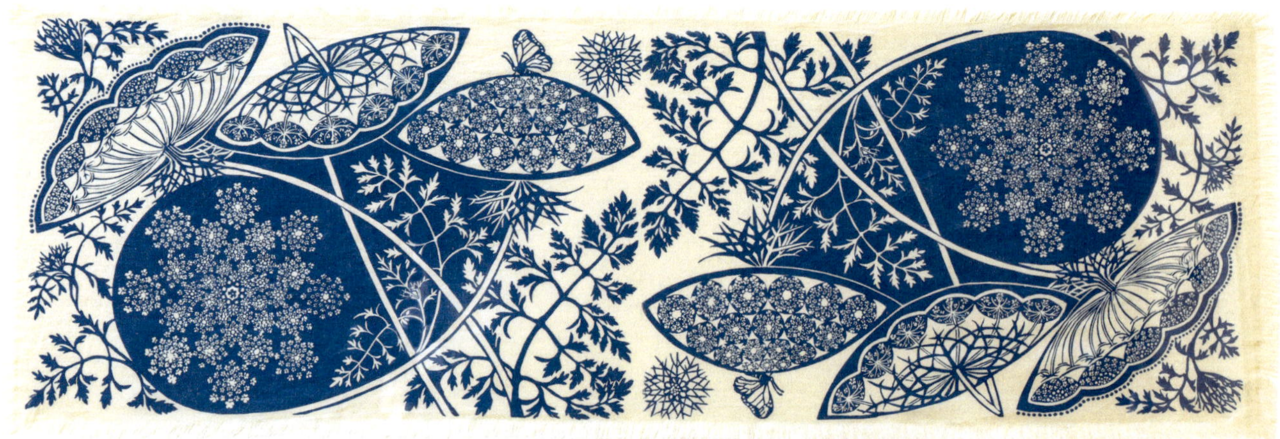

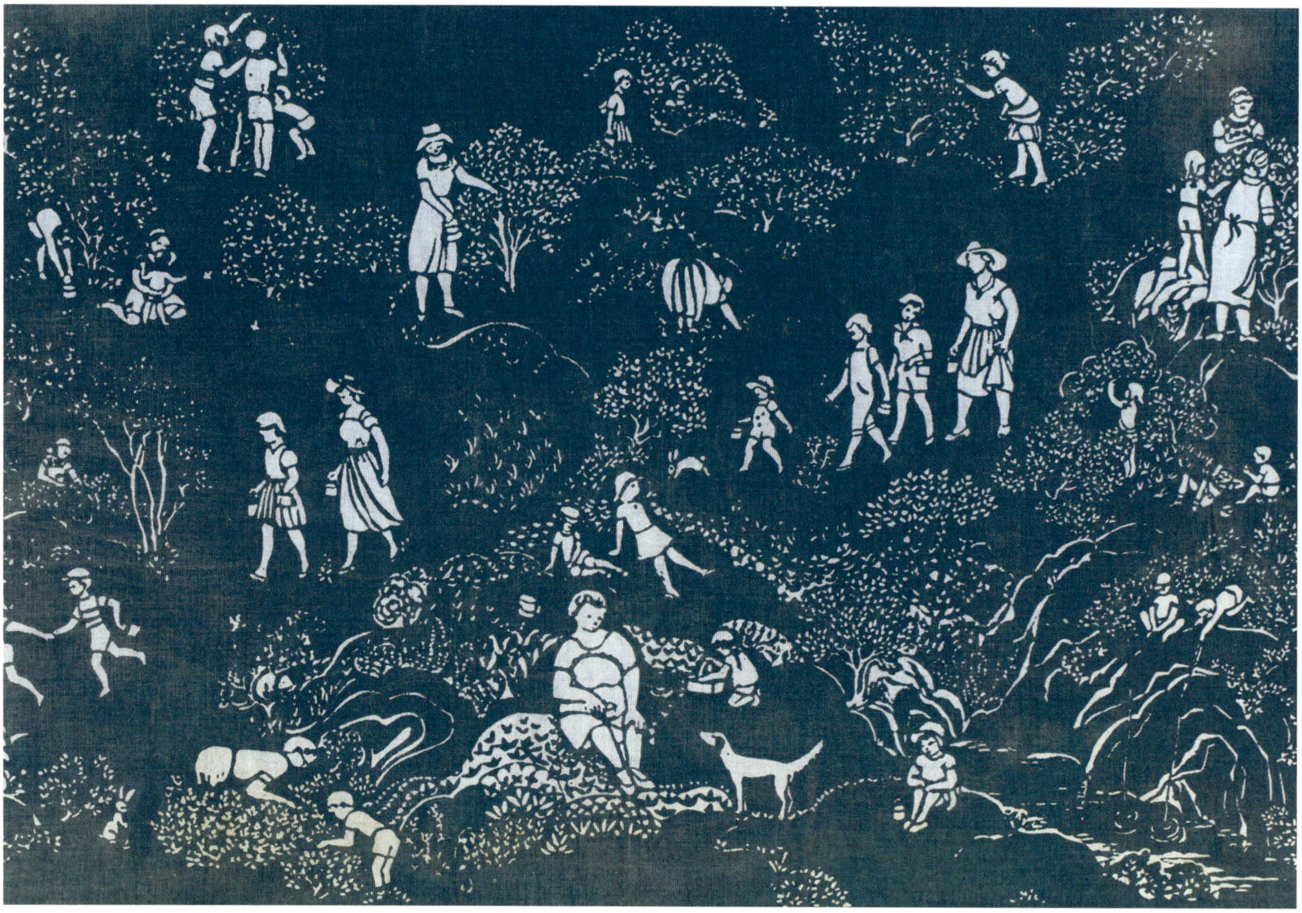

FIG. 244 (TOP)
Queen Anne's Lace **by Mary Maletskos is one of the group's most stunning designs. The intricacy is remarkable. The curving lines convey motion and there is a strong emphasis on darks and lights. Highlighting that she really studied her subject, she chose to depict the back, front, and side views of the flower. (Ink on fabric.)**

FIG. 245 (BOTTOM)
Mary's ***Blueberry Hill*** **featured her mother, children, and neighbors on a blueberry picking excursion. (Ink on fabric.)**

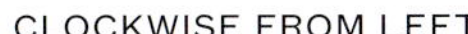

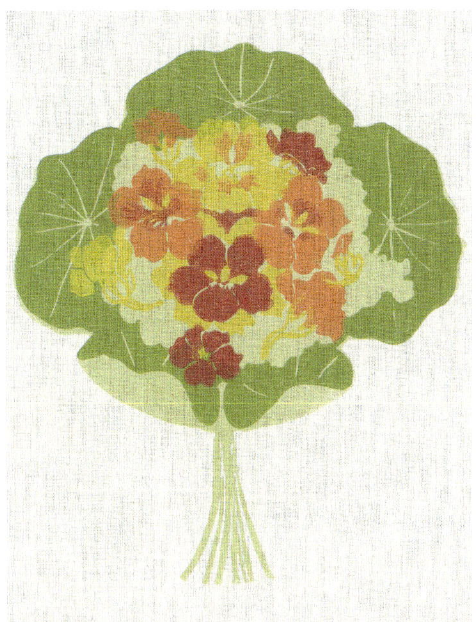

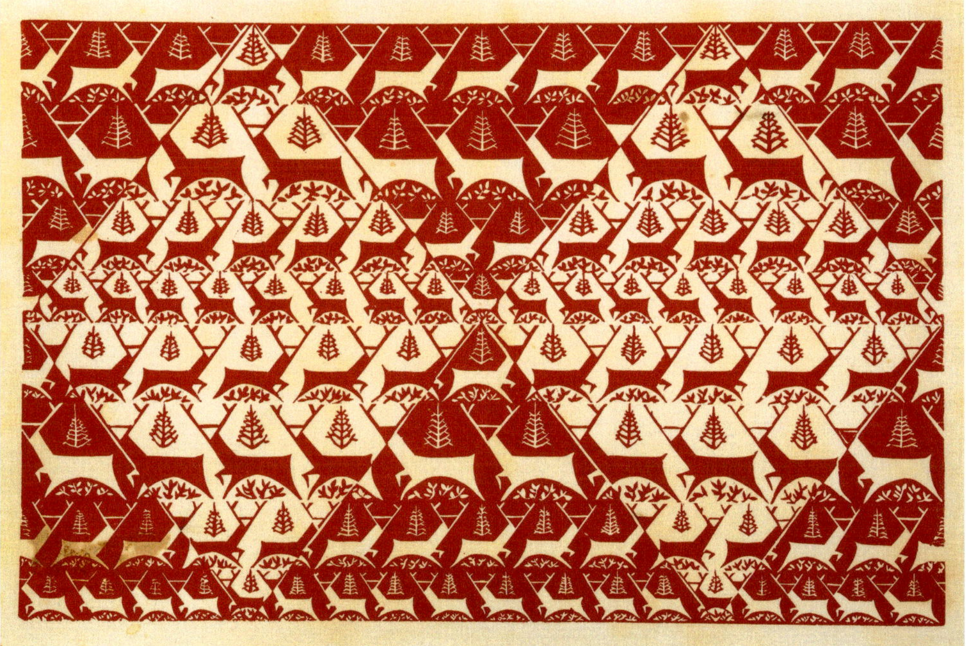

CLOCKWISE FROM LEFT

FIG. 246
This heron was purchased from Mary's estate, so it is attributed to her. It is unclear if it is a "lost" design of hers as a Folly Cove designer or one done independently. With its single subject matter, it is atypical for Folly Cove Designers' work, but *Nasturtiums* also had one subject. (Ink on fabric.)

FIG. 247
The multicolored *Nasturtiums* by Mary is a decorative piece. As with *Queen Anne's Lace*, the furled leaves show the underside of the plant and her mastery of her subject. (Ink on fabric.)

FIG. 248
This *Deer Crossing* place mat belonged to Lee Natti, Mary's best friend from Smith College and fellow Folly Cove designer. Mary employs geometric shapes and emphasizes darks and lights here to create this complex pattern that is almost an optical illusion. Despite the name and the emphasis on deer as the subject, one sees the trees first and you almost have to train your eye to see the deer. It is as if they are camouflaged, as in real life. (Ink on fabric.)

if Mary executed this design as a member of the Folly Cove Designers or whether she explored printing on fabric outside of the group.[340] Designs like *Queen Anne's Lace* and *Peony* (see page 11) show her strength in capturing flowers, while *Deer Crossing* and *Wood Lily* (not shown) show her ability to simplify shapes and build designs based on intricate patterns.

Mary's love for Folly Cove and her life there came through in her exquisite designs. She wrote, "I was one of the lucky ones who crossed over the threshold into the special world of Jinnee and George."[341]

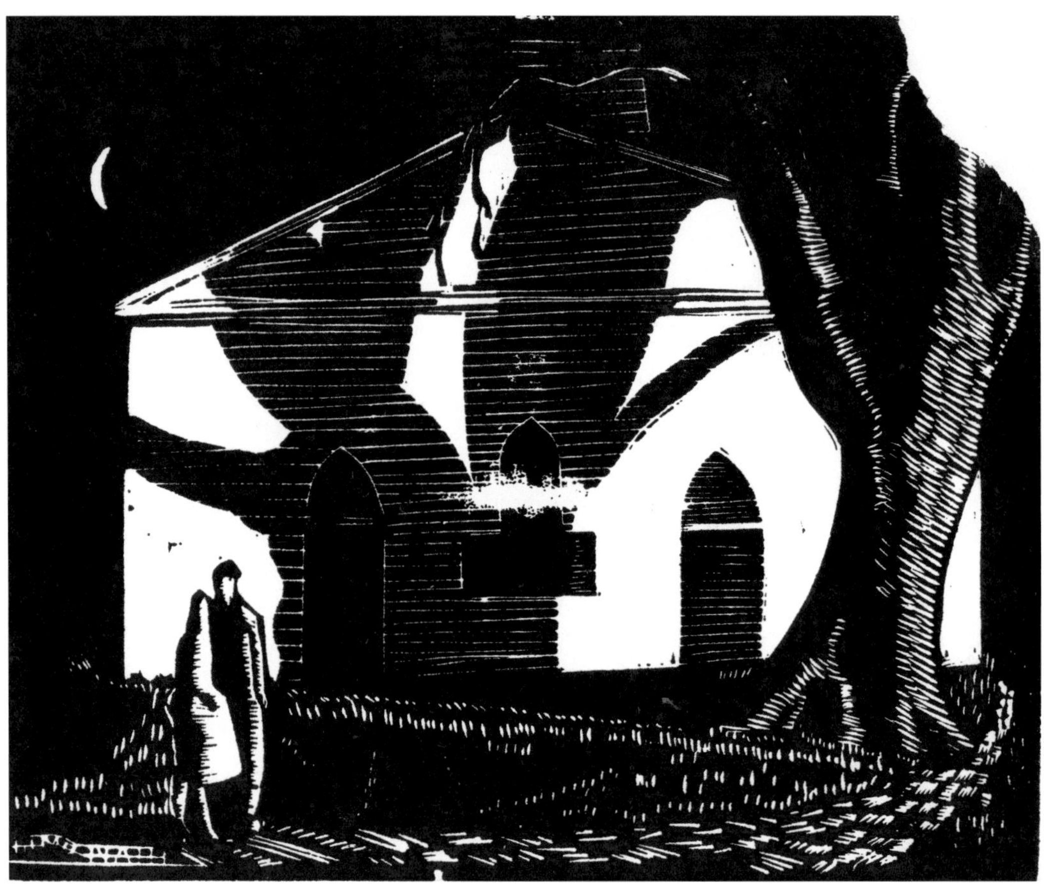

FIG. 249
Dramatic shadows are cast against a church in this untitled, undated print by Ilmari Natti. His work was not representative of Virginia's principles, although it is a masterful example of the use of dark and light. This was printed by Ilmari's daughter, Isabel Natti.

Ilmari Natti (1910–1988)[342]

Ilmari was the sixth child of the Natti family (see Eino Natti, page 142).[343] He joined the Folly Cove Designers before they officially formed.[344] Ilmari (called Jimo) married Pauline Manship, the daughter of sculptor Paul Manship, and they had two children, Erik and Isabel.[345] It is not clear how long Ilmari participated or in what capacity, but he was still involved in 1943; he provided naturalist instruction in the early 1940s.[346]

Ilmari's designs were largely based on the Finnish epic *Kalevala* and were exhibited in 1940 at Virginia's studio (see page 24).[347] Like his older brother Eino, he took as his subjects the family homestead, roosters, and the granite quarry industry. He attended Massachusetts Agricultural College (now University of Massachusetts Amherst) to study landscape architecture but had to suspend his studies due to tuberculosis. He went on to work in landscaping and raise chickens, and was later employed by Medallic Art Company, which designs and produces medals and medallions.[348]

Although they never knew him, Anthony and Elizabeth Iarrobino heard how talented Ilmari was. "He was a legend," Anthony said.[349]

His daughter Isabel worked at the Sarah Elizabeth Shop with Libby Holloran for many years, continuing the tradition of the Folly Cove Designers.[350] Isabel took over the business upon Libby's retirement and worked there until her death in 2011.[351]

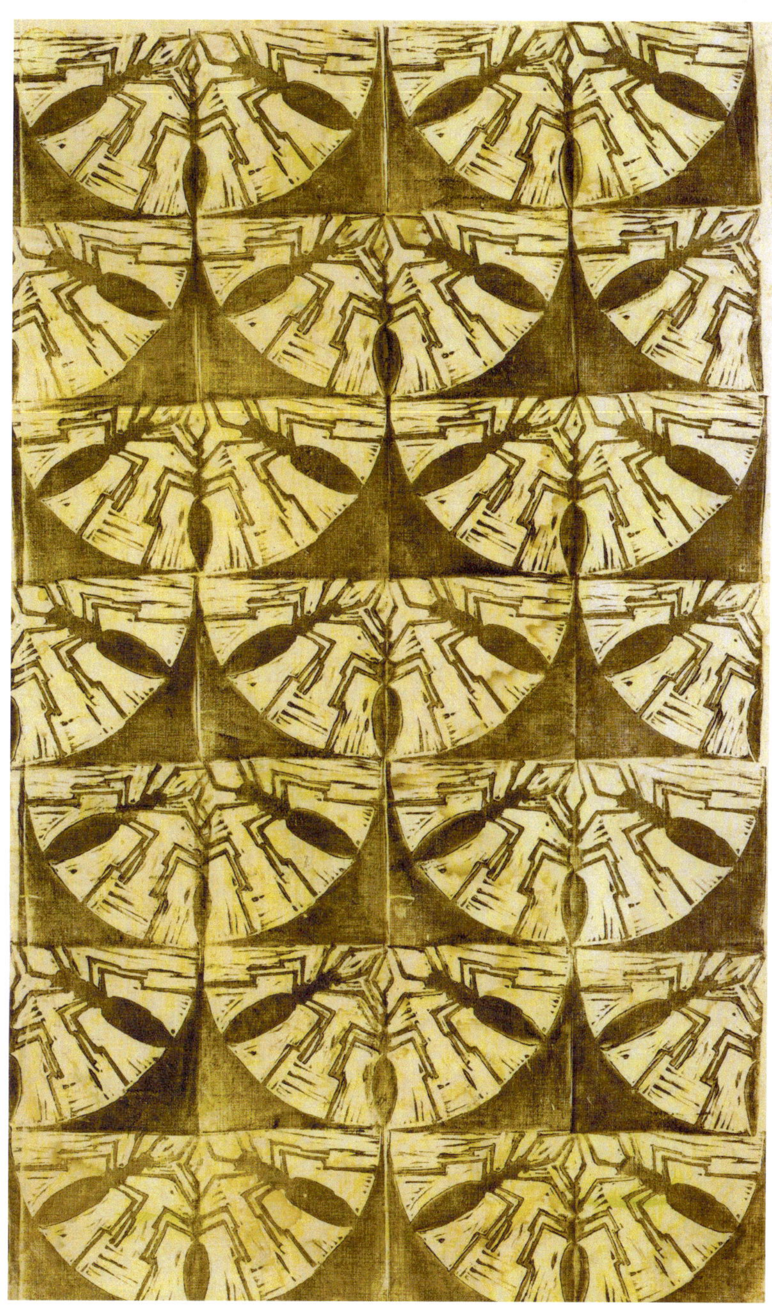

FIG. 250
***Ants* is Robert Natti's one known design. The positive and negative space create a really interesting pattern in this piece. Although Robert did not stay with the group, his understanding of the work was helpful to his wife, Lee, and he was always supportive of her participation. (Ink on fabric.)**

Robert Natti (1916–2000)

The ninth child of the Natti family, like his brother Ilmari (see page 180), Robert took the design class before the Folly Cove Designers became an official group.[352] Robert entered the Army Air Forces and served as a military policeman in World War II.[353]

Upon returning from the war, he married Lee Kingman (see page 150) and they settled in Gloucester.[354] He worked as a teacher, guidance counselor, and principal in the Gloucester school system.[355] He also had an interest in community chorus and theater, as well as pottery.[356]

FIG. 251 (RIGHT)
This is a print of *Punch and Judy* by Bettine Nichols that was made by imprinting the block side by side. The backs of the children's hats make a pattern in the foreground. The balloons must have been carved as a separate block or added by hand, as they are not part of the *Punch and Judy* block. (Ink on fabric.)

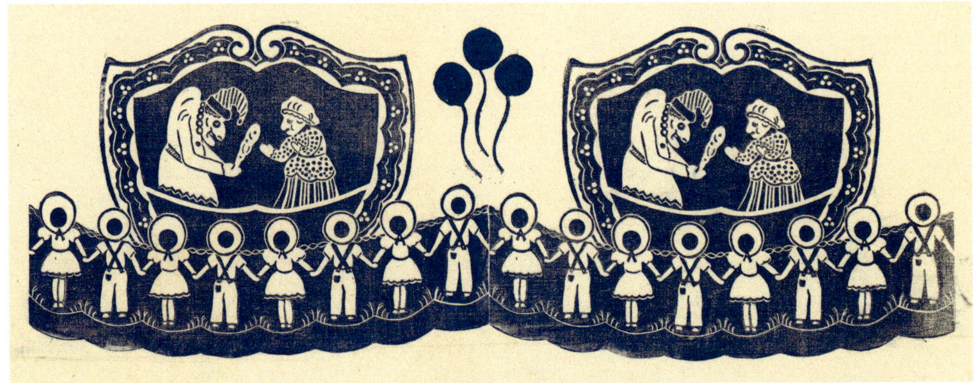

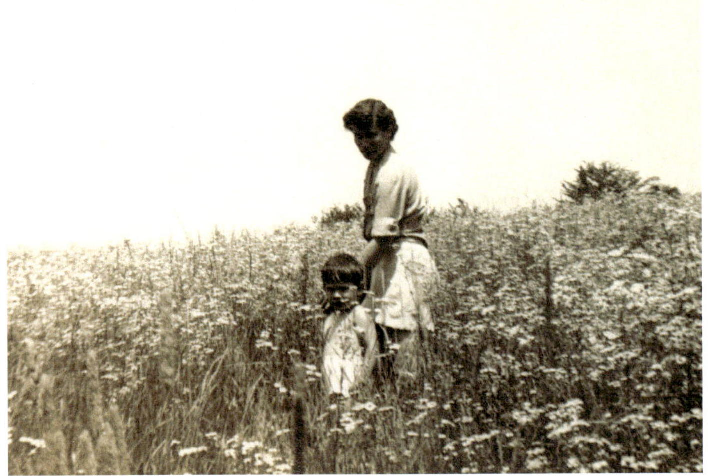

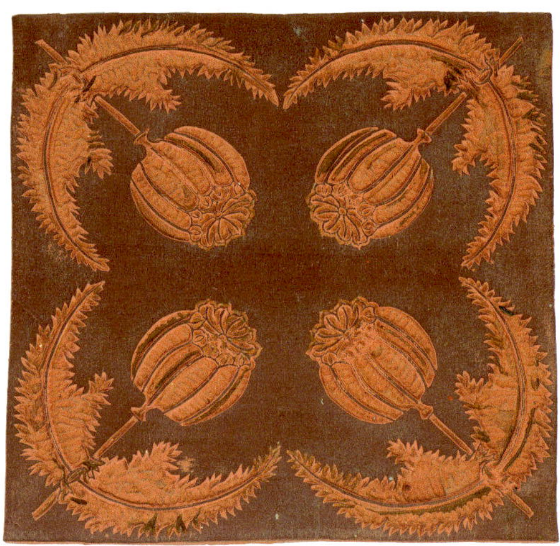

Bettine (Bradish) Nichols (1911–1947)

A member of the Folly Cove Designers for only a few years, Bettine Nichols produced quite a few designs (at least eight). She and her son Peter lived in the addition on the Kenyon family home during World War II while her husband, Dr. Arthur Nichols, served in the Army Medical Corps.[357] Bettine and Peter were living in Gloucester by the summer of 1942.[358] It is unclear how the couple knew the Kenyons, but it appears that they lived in the Boston area prior to the war, so they likely met the Kenyons there.[359]

Bettine's work was featured in *Woman's Day* and she was included in the *Life* magazine group photo. Lord & Taylor produced her design *Bayleaf* and her photo was displayed in their Fifth Avenue windows, along with those of Virginia Lee Demetrios and Louise Kenyon (see page 54).

When Arthur Nichols returned from the war, the family relocated to the small coastal town of Wiscasset, Maine, where Arthur started a medical practice.[360] Not long after the birth of their second son, Joel, Bettine passed away.[361] F. Schumacher had planned to produce *Bayleaf*, but Dorothy Norton wrote her contact there in February 1947 to inform him that "we were all very much distressed" to be informed that Bettine had "died very suddenly."[362] She added that Bettine "did some of the most charming Folly Cove designs."[363]

FIG. 252 (BOTTOM LEFT)
This photo features Bettine and her son Peter in a field, presumably in Folly Cove. Perhaps Bettine sent this to her husband overseas. The photo was labeled on the back: "6/26/42 Peter aged 2 ½."

FIG. 253 (BOTTOM RIGHT)
***Poppy* is another "lost" design by Bettine. Prints of it and a block were found among her things. Due to the varied uses for the blocks and likely before the group had standardized their block size, Bettine had a larger block with four poppies and then a single block with one large poppy. The name of the design is known because of the hand-carved title of the design that she would have used to mark the selvedge of hand-printed yardage. (Linoleum.)**

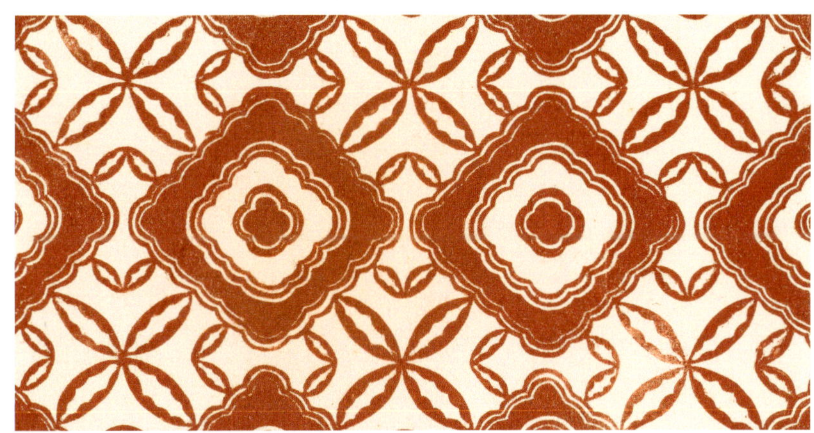

FIG. 254 (ABOVE)
This is a hand-printed example of Bettine Nichols's *Bayleaf* design, which was mechanically produced by Lord & Taylor. It bears resemblance to Louise Kenyon's *Conventional Flower* design (see page 91). (Ink on fabric.)

FIG. 255 (LEFT)
This untitled, "lost" design is attributed to Bettine as it was part of her estate. A block for this design was not located and she did have work by other designers, but this design is similar to *Bayleaf*, with its scalloped borders. It may have been an early version. (Ink on fabric.)

All of Bettine's Folly Cove material (blocks and prints) was kept together by her family, giving us a glimpse into her short but impressive creative life. Two of these designs are "lost" designs. There is no known title for one design, which looks similar to Louise Kenyon's *Bayleaf,* and the other is *Poppy*. An image of her design *Punch and Judy* is featured here. It has not been published since appearing in *Woman's Day* in 1945.[364] There was a tag among Bettine's things that was labeled *Strawberry*. This was likely the original or intended name of the design that has been recognized as *Bird and Berry,* since it depicts strawberry leaves (not shown).[365]

Among Bettine's possessions was her diploma from the Folly Cove Designers. Poignantly, in one of the last entries in the small black notebook that she had kept as a Folly Cove designer she had written how long the drive from Gloucester to Wiscasset had taken.[366] It has been rewarding to document the life and design work of such a promising designer whose story has remained largely untold until now.

FIG. 256
Anna Stephanio's *Woodbine* is detailed and delicate. (Ink on fabric.)

Anna (Natti) Stephanio (1902–1976)

Anna was the firstborn of the Natti family.[367] She trained to be an RN at Addison Gilbert Hospital in Gloucester and met her husband, Edward J. Stephanio, while working as a nurse.[368] She also conducted cancer research at Harvard Medical School. The Stephanios raised their family of five daughters in Lanesville.[369] Their daughters modeled for the artist Leon Kroll.[370]

Anna took the design course and was a member in the late 1940s, joining her brother Eino (see page 142). Her one known design, *Woodbine*, depicts the climbing plant and was likely inspired by her love of gardening.[371]

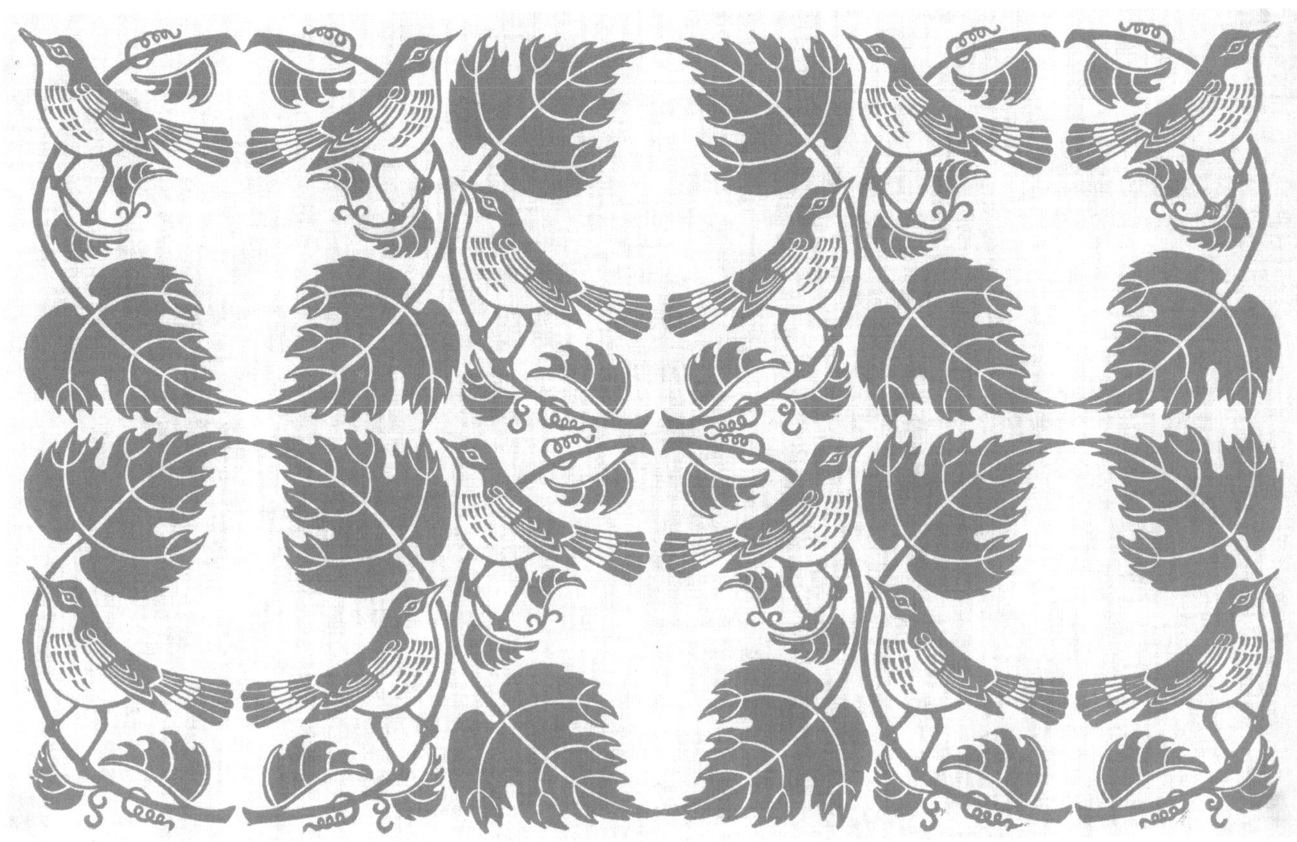

FIG. 257
A bird enthusiast, Mary Ann Mangan featured a magnolia warbler in *Vignette*. The vines are reminiscent of her mother's work. (Ink on fabric.)

Mary Ann (Stephanio) Mangan (1932–1991)

Mary Ann Mangan became involved with the designers in the mid- to late 1960s, following in the footsteps of her mother, Anna Stephanio, and other Natti family members. An award-winning photographer, Mary Ann studied graphic design at UCLA before returning to Lanesville. She was also an avid bird watcher and member of the Audubon Society.[372]

Mary Ann created two designs as a Folly Cove designer, *Plovers* and *Vignette*. Anna and Mary Ann were the only mother/daughter pair to be members of the Folly Cove Designers (although at different times). The similarities between Mary Ann's *Vignette* and Anna's *Woodbine* are striking.

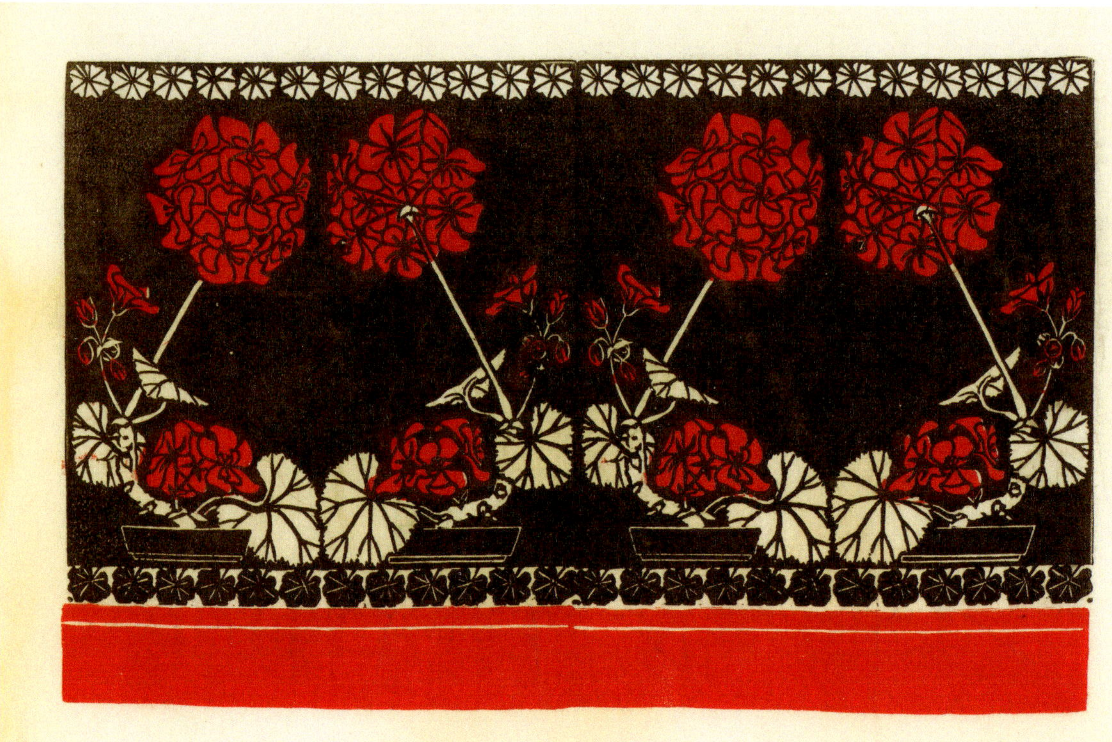

FIG. 258
Lee Steele's *Geraniums*, for which she carved two blocks. This must have been printed with the single, smaller block as it does not have a border like the 11×17–inch block does. The 11x17–inch also features three sets of two geraniums in each row. (Ink on fabric.)

Muriel Lee (Hamilton) Steele (1925–2022)[373]

Muriel Lee Steele (called Lee) was born in Brooklyn, New York, and raised in Newark, New Jersey. She played the cello and graduated from Smith College in 1946 with a degree in music. In 1948 she earned a master's degree in social work from Smith.[374]

Lee moved with her husband, Robert (Bob), to Folly Cove in the early 1950s, purchasing their home from Folly Cove designer Hetty Beatty. At the time the home had *Gossips* wallpaper. As a neighbor, Lee felt welcomed into the Demetrios family and she would often swim on summer afternoons with Virginia. She felt there was a real "sense of community" in Folly Cove and remarked that it felt "incredible to be included."[375]

Lee completed one design, featuring a geranium.[376] She said that her original design was of a passionflower, but she knew Virginia liked geraniums and thought it would be more popular with the jury.[377] In more recent years, Lee explored silk painting, preferring to work in a more abstract style.[378]

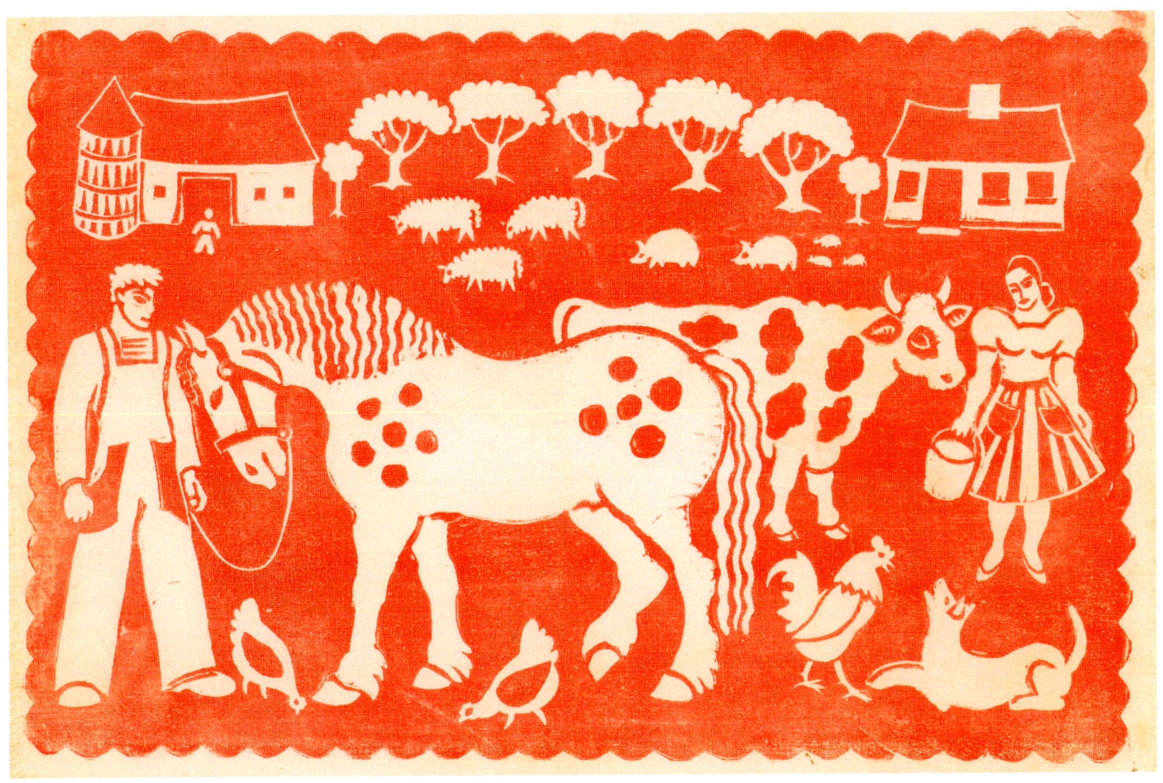

FIG. 259
***Farm* by Hetty Beatty features a farm and a spotted pony, two themes she revisited. It is an early design and the style is more folklike and less refined. (Ink on fabric.)**

Hetty Burlingame (Beatty) Whitney (1907–1971)[379]

Hetty Burlingame Beatty was born in Connecticut and married Rockport pewter artist and sculptor Lewis F. Whitney in 1959.[380] She was no longer a member of the group when she married, but sometimes she is referred to as Hetty Beatty Whitney. Since she seemed to go primarily by Hetty Beatty for most of her career and as a designer, she is referred to simply as Hetty Beatty throughout this book.

Hetty studied sculpture at the School of the Museum of Fine Arts with Charles Grafly and George Demetrios (1924 to 1929), which ultimately brought her to Folly Cove. She returned to school in the 1960s to study at the University of Maryland through extension courses in Bermuda (where she lived with her husband). Her sculptures were exhibited at the Worcester Art Museum, among other venues.[381]

Hetty was one of the original members of the Folly Cove Designers, participating from the early 1940s through the early 1950s.[382] She received acclaim for her *Polka Dot Pony* design (see page 58), produced by F. Schumacher. *Farm Scenes* was another design produced by F. Schumacher (see page 58), previously a "lost" design, along with her farm-themed submissions for Edwin M. Knowles China Company (see page 69). Her early designs had a folk quality to them, although her work became more detailed over time as she dedicated herself to illustration.

She went on to write fourteen children's books, illustrating twelve of them. She published under her maiden name, Hetty Burlingame Beatty.[383]

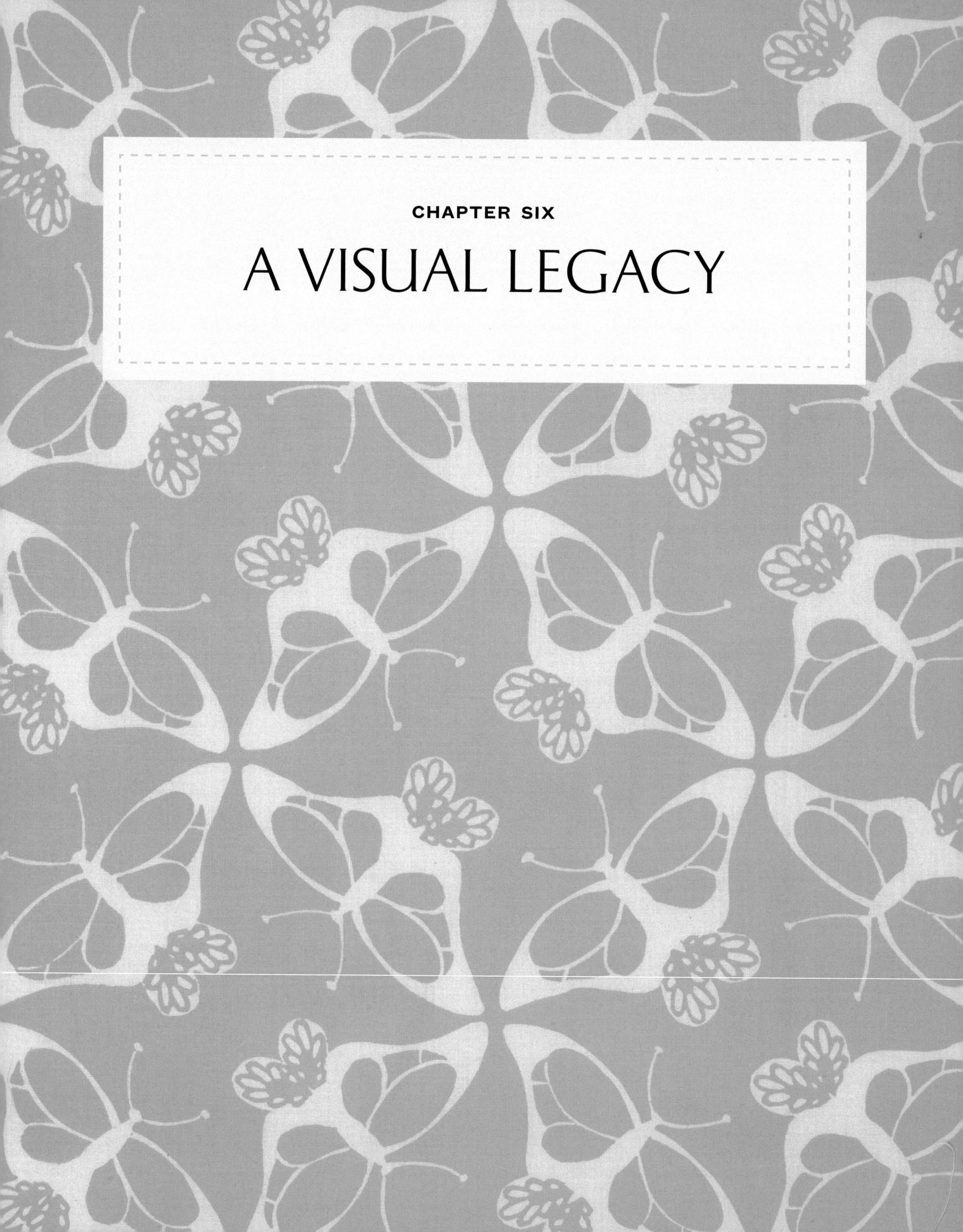

CHAPTER SIX

A VISUAL LEGACY

Virginia Lee Demetrios passed away in 1968. After her death, the Folly Cove Designers decided to disband. Virginia's youngest son, Michael, later said that he felt that his mother would have wanted them to continue, adding, "She started something, and she didn't want it to end with her."[1] But as members aged, there was less availability to teach new members and the group's existing members found it physically difficult to keep up with the orders. Dorothy Norton explained that it would have taken "a radical change" in how the group operated for it to have continued.[2] Maintaining the integrity of the brand and the quality of the work was important to them. Dorothy added that the announcement of their intent to close at the end of the season in 1969 triggered "a tremendous wave of interest, protest and affection."[3] Their work was beloved. The group had a dedicated local fan base, as well as an international one.

Today place mats and table runners are handed down as treasured family heirlooms, particularly by locals, and there is still a devoted collecting base, but in recent years one writer aptly described the Folly Cove Designers as "the best designers you've never heard of."[4] This change in public awareness for a group whose work once graced the pages of *Life* and was displayed in the windows of a Fifth Avenue department store might possibly be a result of choosing to pull back from commercial contracts in the early 1950s or their decision to require that when members resigned or when the group disbanded, that members retire their blocks, allowing them only to print for family and friends. Part of the impetus for this book was to celebrate the group's incredible artistry, document their achievements, and introduce a new audience to their work.

Another goal was to answer the question of what it was about their designs that made them so popular in their time and continues to attract admirers today? There is a timelessness about them, perhaps because the group chose not to address topical issues (with a few exceptions). There is also a relatability to the subject matter. Who hasn't admired Queen Anne's lace growing by the side of the road? Or skated on a pond? Or planted geraniums in a pot and set them on a windowsill?

The designs also have a nostalgic quality that resonates now as well as it did in the 1940s, when the designers came to the attention of national retail stores like Lord & Taylor.[5] In the immediate aftermath of World War II, Americans were attracted to the beauty and simplicity of the designs. Not surprisingly, with author/illustrator Virginia Lee Burton Demetrios as their teacher, the works were often narrative. Some of the most popular designs were the most personal—Virginia's cat and kittens in *Zaidee and Her Kittens* (see page 123) and Louise Kenyon's depiction of her own home, family, and neighborhood in *Head of the Cove* (see page 135).[6]

In large part, the designs depicted the flora and fauna of Cape Ann and reflected the community of Folly Cove in particular. Both then and now the Folly Cove Designers were seen as having an idyllic lifestyle. Virginia's son Aristides Demetrios acknowledged the allure of his parents' life in Folly Cove; he said they "created their own culture."[7] Folly Cove was a dynamic community filled with art, cultural diversity, varied economic classes, and a cooperative spirit that united everyone. Members enjoyed the social aspects of the group, even though they primarily worked alone in their homes outside of the classes and other meetings. It was a collaborative group and members were "mutually quite helpful" to one another and generously shared their skills and time.[8]

But, Dorothy Norton was quick to point out, the Folly Cove Designers were a "working group."[9] Like all people, the designers dealt with health issues (either related to themselves or family members), marriage difficulties, financial stress, hardship, and loss during their tenures with the group, but personal issues remained largely separate. Lee Natti compared her experience with the designers to that of joining a group of writers and editors after the Folly Cove Designers disbanded, commenting, "We [the Folly Cove Designers] all were coping with the kind of things that these writers seem to fall apart over... But we didn't bring that to the group."[10] Membership in the Folly Cove Designers was an opportunity to disconnect from one's everyday realities. As Lee explained, "The group had a goal. It had a structure, and it didn't change, didn't mutate into different kinds of things," which ultimately contributed to the group's longevity and success.[11]

Yet the Folly Cove Designers are rarely (if at all) included in printmaking histories. The publication of Virginia's teaching methodology in *Design and How!* might have altered this outcome if it had come to fruition. Because the group chose to print on fabric, their work was often regarded more as craft than fine art and often exhibited alongside that of textile designers rather than printmakers. But their work can be found in many museum collections and has been recognized in important works published over the last two decades on the history of twentieth-century design, women designers, and specifically textile design.

Even the designers did not always view their work as art. One of the most talented, Louise Kenyon, acknowledged that, if she had printed her designs on good paper, signed them, and had them hanging, she might have considered them art.[12] For her, the utilitarian aspect of the group's work seemed to relegate it to craft. Another designer felt that the medium of linoleum on fabric relegated the work to craft, as opposed to, say, wood-block printing, which he later pursued.[13] Interestingly, Elizabeth and Anthony Iarrobino, both art school graduates and professional artists, were quick to define the Folly Cove Designers' work as art.[14]

Despite the group being mostly female, members did not generally consider themselves a women's group. Dorothy Norton said that "men were welcome if they wanted to come."[15] Yet gender roles undeniably had their imprint. In business dealings, the group was often assumed to consist primarily of men and letters were initially addressed to "Gentlemen." Many of the women were mothers and spoke about the difficulty of balancing their design work and homelife. Finding childcare was an issue for most. The women who remained core members of the group all had supportive husbands, such as Louise Kenyon and Lee Natti. Lee's husband had taken the course early on and knew what it entailed. Likewise Libby Holloran and Elizabeth Iarrobino, whose husbands were also designers, felt supported.

Yet most of the women did not have their own creative spaces (sometimes even if their husbands did) and often worked at the kitchen table or in the midst of family life.[16]

Interestingly many male members of the group could not recall taking a formal design course.[17] Whether they were exempt or opted out is unclear. For at least one male member, the experience was not entirely positive. He felt "completely subjugated when I was within that group."[18] Other male members of the group also felt slightly marginalized, but they attributed it to the fact that they had separate careers and that the group wasn't their main focus. (Although this could be said of many of the female members, as well.) One male member, who was recovering from tuberculosis when he became involved with the group, wondered if this might be because "it was clear that I was doing it temporarily."[19] Anthony Iarrobino attributed his exemption from the lessons simply to the fact that his wife had taken them.[20]

Overall gender doesn't seem to have been reflected in the designs in a definitive way. Both Virginia and Anthony Iarrobino had designs based on ballet, while Eino Natti and Louise Kenyon had farm designs. While Eino gravitated toward more masculine themes, like his preference for military subjects and his iconic roosters, despite all the mothers in the group, only a few designs are overtly maternal. Aino Clarke's *Elephants* depicts mother elephants protectively standing over their young, as well as her design *Sauna*, which includes a mother bathing her child. Additionally both of Virginia Lee Demetrios's *Spring Lambs* designs (ewes with their lambs) are maternal, as is Mary Maletskos's *Blueberry Hill,* featuring women and children blueberry picking, with one woman hugging a child.

Members of this group shared an impulse to create and to learn. "When the group got together the air sparkled with the excitement of creativity... And the personality of the group was remarkable, so unselfish, so free with giving in ideas and everything and enthusiasm..."[21] After the group disbanded, Louise Kenyon continued to create new linoleum carvings as well as to explore painting. Lee Natti continued to write books (twenty-nine in total) and Libby Holloran opened her own shop, creating and printing new designs until 2001.[22] Peggy Norton went on to study rug weaving, while Anthony Iarrobino began exploring collograph printing in 1975.[23]

Members seemed split on whether the group could have existed outside of Cape Ann in a different form. All seemed to agree that Virginia was central to the success of the group. As one designer summarized, "Sometimes people can affect you one way or another, but to actually bring out of you something that's maybe lying dormant—that to me is a special gift..."[24]

Membership was impactful in different ways to each member. Louise Kenyon found the work to be "a means of expressing myself."[25] For others it was the community and shared interests that were meaningful. One member articulated that being in a group that entailed learning and a connection to art "made me aware of the fact that if I wanted to find the sort of people that I liked best, probably I would find them in a group like that."[26] Peggy Norton described it as a "great privilege to be one of the group."[27] For many of the Folly Cove Designers, particularly those who were core members, it was a central part of their identities, as evidenced by their participation being highlighted in their obituaries and eulogies. In Virginia's case, her role as the founder and leader of the Folly Cove Designers is a lesser known but equally important part of her artistic career.

Isabel Natti, niece of Eino Natti and Lee Natti, joined Libby Holloran at the Sarah Elizabeth Shop. In this way many of the principles of the Folly Cove Designers were passed to a younger generation, ending with Isabel's death in 2011. Yet the group continues to inspire printmakers, especially women printmakers. The Folly Cove Designers are standard bearers for today's maker's movement. Over three hundred designs were created during the group's lifespan.[28] The Folly Cove Designers' work represents a permanent visual legacy of this vibrant community, communicated in the compelling language of pattern.

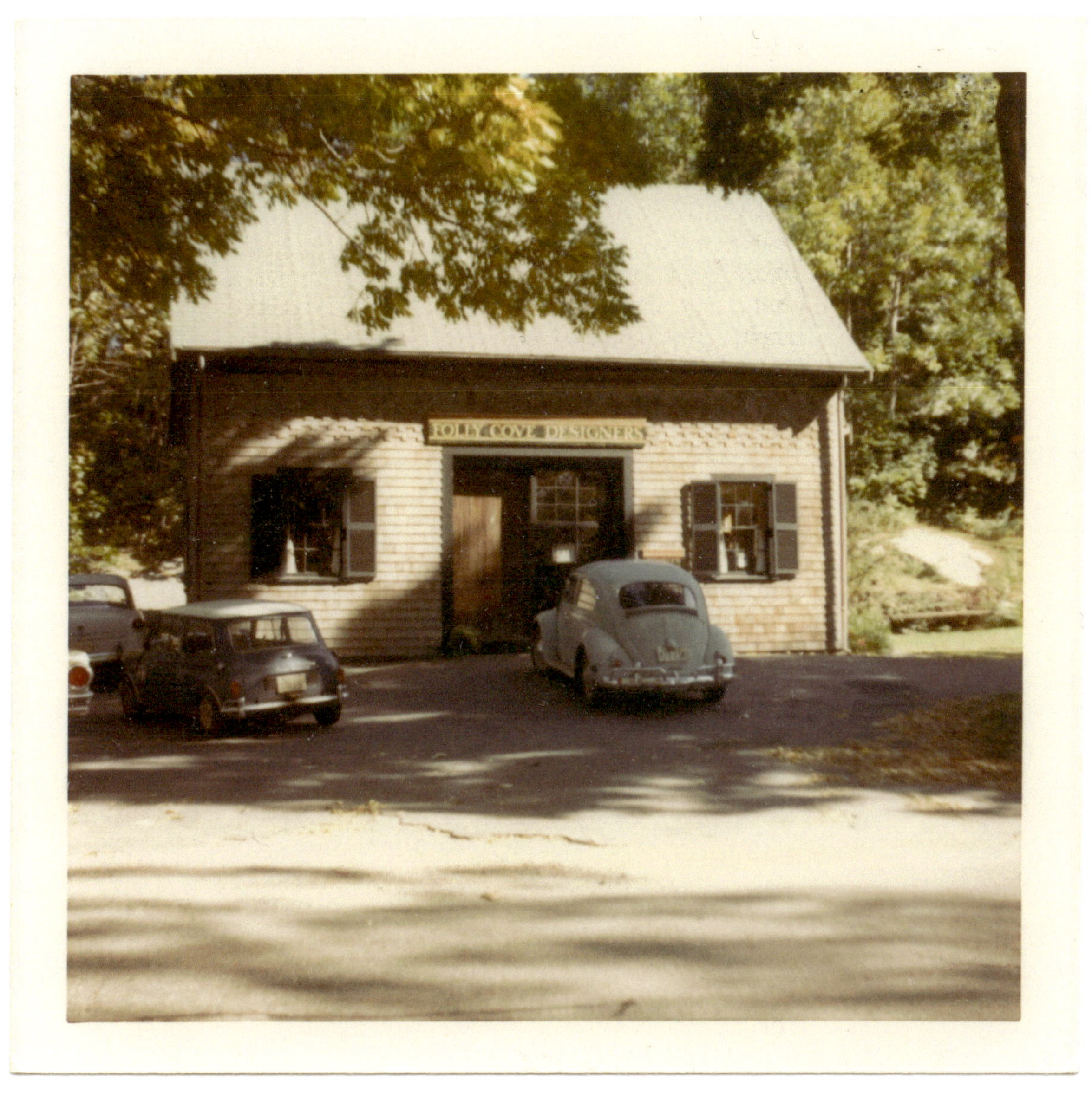

FIG. 260
The Folly Cove Designers' retail barn with a VW bug and Mini car outfront, ca. 1960s.

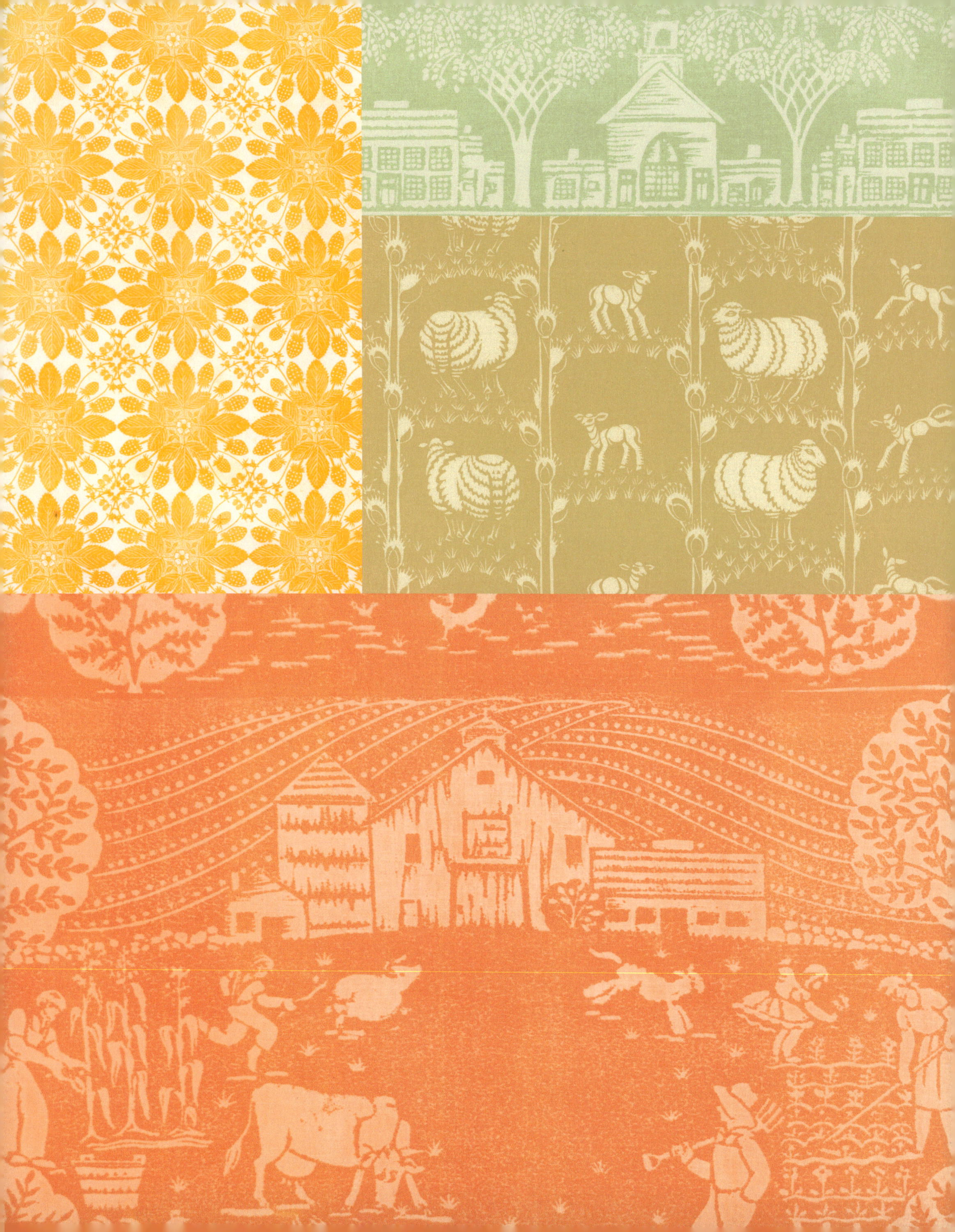

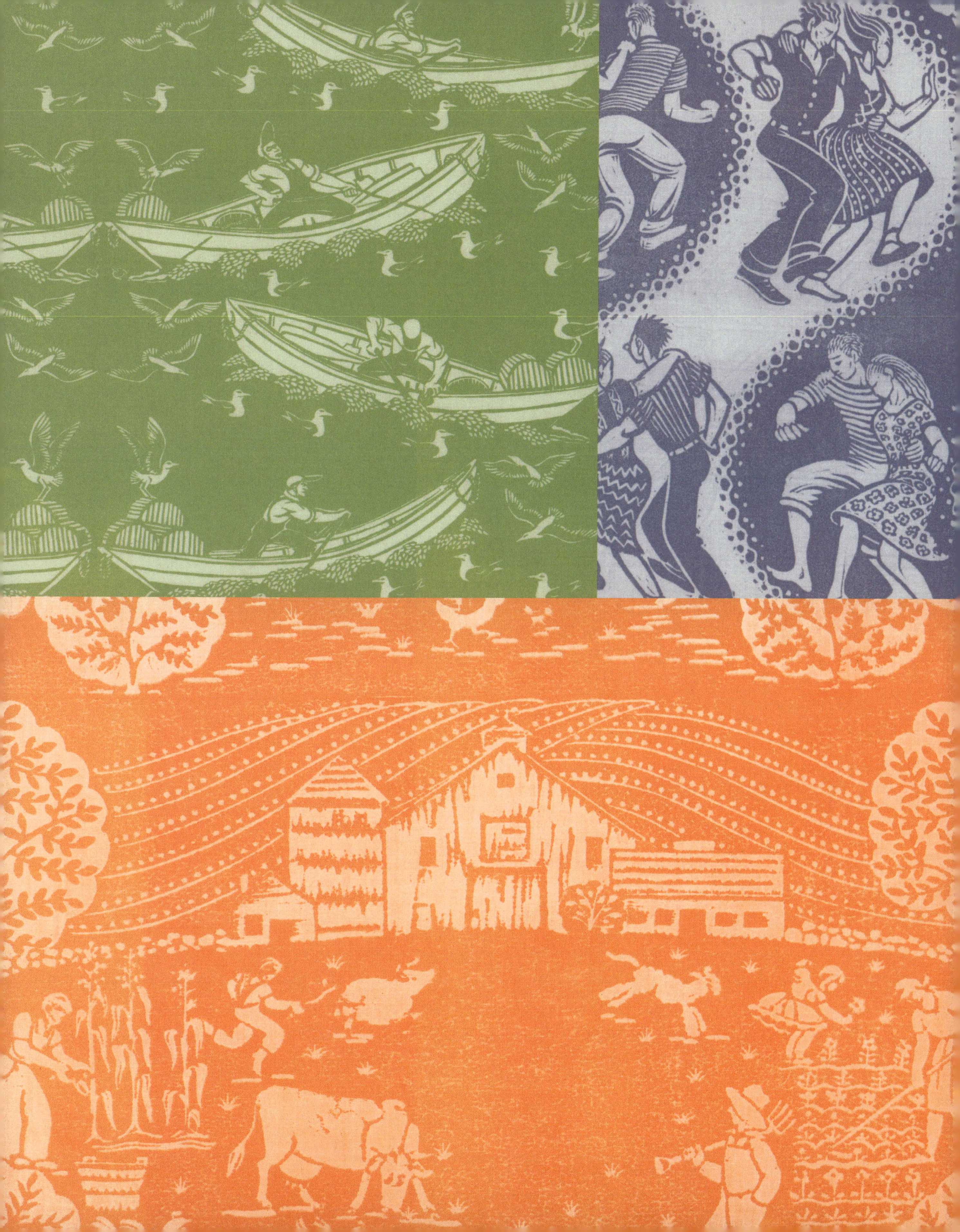

ACKNOWLEDGMENTS

A special thank you to Speedball Art Products Company and your generous support of this book and Kelley Braun (director of brand and marketing operations) for your leadership on this partnership and for Speedball's unparalleled support of printmaking history and contemporary printmakers.

A huge thank you to the Iarrobino Family for also donating to fund the photography for this book.

Special thanks to Sandy Bay Historical Society, Rockport, Massachusetts, for the use of your collection. Ingrid Brown and Gwendolyn Stephenson were particularly helpful.

Designers:

Thank you to designers Hilda Kaihlanen, Lee Natti, and Lee Steele, whom I had the honor of interviewing and getting to know. Lee Natti generously made some wonderful introductions on my behalf and offered sound publishing advice. Years ago, I spent a wonderful afternoon overlooking the beach at Folly Cove with Lee Steele and later had the pleasure of photographing her blocks. In the case of all three women, our interactions are especially meaningful to me as they have since passed away. Also thank you to designers Zoe Eleftherio and Mary Ann Lash for your contributions.

Families of the Folly Cove Designers:

Aristides Demetrios (in memory) and Ilene H. Nagel, Eleanor Demetrios, Ross (Sandy) Burton, Susanna Natti, Erik and Theresa Natti, Janet Natti, Isabel Natti (in memory), Carol Babson, Matthew Babson, Ellie Fleet, Grace Murray (in memory), Ethel Maletskos, Ann and Sue Kenyon (in memory of Peter Kenyon), the Iarrobino Family, Beth (Holloran) Bourguignon, Jane Nichols-Ecker and Chessell (Nichols) McGee, Charles Norton, Marcia Norton (in memory), Dona (Kaihlanen) Shea, and Lauri Kaihlanen.

Heartfelt thank yous to those who have gone above and beyond for me:

Dr. Sandra Yarne for your steadfast support and encouragement.

My sister Angela Sarni for image selection assistance, art and printmaking knowledge, and overall support. Also thank you to my brother-in-law, Alex Subach, for your interest in the Folly Cove Designers and help in finding research leads. And to my wonderful nieces Madelane and Jane Subach. I hope I have inspired you.

Susana McDonnell for your indispensable archival and photography assistance, printmaking knowledge, and friendship. Also thank you to your husband, Angus Smith, for his much-needed technical support and passion for the Folly Cove Designers.

Kathy Soucy. You have been there for me from the beginning of this project, helping in any way possible. You are one of the biggest Folly Cove Designers fans that I know.

James and Katie Craig for your friendship and support throughout this long journey, as well as your help with the photography of private collections.

Mindy Schumacher for image selection assistance, printmaking knowledge, and support.

Rachel Schumacher for designing my book proposal and your continued support throughout the rest of the project.

Heather Dutton for always answering my image-related and textile questions.

My cousin, Xandra Castleton, for reading early book proposal drafts, making introductions, and overall support.

Bridget Quinn for taking time out of your own busy writing schedule to give me advice and encouragement.

My cousin Julie Francis for your enthusiasm and encouragement.

In loving memory of Suzie Goodwin, who supported all of my dreams and photographed Folly Cove Designers pieces for my book proposal. I miss you.

In loving memory of Sandra J. Morong, a true bibliophile.

In loving memory of my grandmothers, who inspired and supported me—Madalene Castleton, Mary Sherman, and Lorraine Morong—all of whom would have made excellent Folly Cove Designers. Grammy, I hope that I made you especially proud.

Love always and forever to my two orange boys, Leland and Ricky.

A special thank you to the following collectors:
Gregory Van Boven and David Beck, Christine Kahane, Peter and Bobbi Kovner, Anne Morin, Mark and Valentine Oldham, the Perry Family, Faith Ronan, Second Glance Thrift Store, Dan and Evan Shay, and Andrew Spindler.

Photographers:
Peter Morse, Gary Lowell, Nicole Gearty, Leslie Bartlett, Esther Pullman, Eric Roth, and Kevin Kerr.

Other Museums, Libraries, Organizations:
Boston Public Library, Boston (reference librarian Katie Devine); Cape Ann Museum, Gloucester, Massachusetts (director Oliver Barker, archivist Trenton Carls, assistant curator Leon Doucette, former archivist Stephanie Buck, former archival assistant Fred Buck [in memory], Cara White, curator Martha Oaks, and former director Ronda Faloon); Carl Cherry Foundation, Carmel, California (executive director Robert Reese); Carmel Public Library, Carmel, California (local history librarian Katie O'Connell); Costume Society of America (Northeastern Region); the Dublin Seminar of New England Folklife (in memory of Peter Benes); Fashion Institute of Technology, New York City (associate professor and head of special collections and college archives Karen Jamison Trivette); F. Schumacher & Co., Boston and New York City (former archivist Avodica Ash, former managing director, New England, Katherine Kalapinski, creative partnerships Manager Katarina

Otsbye, and former creative partnerships manager Meeghan Truelove); Gloucester Lyceum & Sawyer Free Library, Gloucester, Massachusetts (local history librarian Jacklyn Linsky); Historic New England, Boston (senior curator of collections Nancy Carlisle); the Horn Book, Inc., Boston (former editor-in-chief Roger Sutton, acting editor-in-chief and executive editor Elissa Gershowitz, Julie Danielson, and Julie Roach); Houghton Mifflin Harcourt, Boston (senior executive editor Deanne Urmy, archivist Susan Steinway, and executive director of school and library marketing Lisa DiSarro); Marianna Kistler Beach Museum of Art, Kansas State University, Manhattan, Kansas (curator Elizabeth Seaton); Museum of Fine Arts, Boston (assistant curator Jennifer Swope); Museum of Printing, Haverhill, Massachusetts (chairman and executive director Frank Romano); New York Public Library, New York City; Peabody Essex Museum, Salem, Massachusetts (director of curatorial affairs Petra Slinkard and curator Paula Richter); San Francisco Art Institute, Anne Bremer Memorial Library, San Francisco (librarian and archivist Jeff Gunderson); Santa Cruz Public Libraries, Santa Cruz, California (librarian Arturo Villaseñor); Smith College, Northampton, Massachusetts (college archivist Nanci Young); Syracuse University Libraries, Special Collections Research Center, Syracuse, New York; and University of New Hampshire Library, Durham, New Hampshire (associate professor, government information/reference librarian Louise A. Buckley).

Thank you to the following individuals for their expertise and support:
Allen Abend, Aline Ableson, Glenn Adamson, Laura Berman, Professor Libby MacDonald Bischof, Janet Blyberg, Hank Bornhofft (in memory), Maria Buszek, Martha Carlson, Nana Carrillo, Nina Carrillo de Albornoz, Julia Denos, Carol Edwards, Susan Edwards, Barbara Elleman, Melanie Falick, Jeannine Falino, Lynn Felsher, Michelle Finamore, Larry Fuersich, Cora Ginsburg, E.B. Goodale, Kathie Groves, Abigail Halpin, Jon Harari, Ashley Hasty, Jen Hewett, Heidi Horner, Leslie Jonath, Jennifer Judd-McGee, Katy Kelleher, Pam Kingsley, Pat Kirkham, Danielle Krysa, Linda Lear, Ron Longe, Pam Marshall, Linzee Kull McCray, Shawna Mullen, Amanda Nelson, Bridget Watson Payne, Becca Powell, Jessica Skwire Routhier, Susan Schwake, Kirsten Sevig, Anita Silvey, Diane St. Jean, Leslie Stoker, Jessica Swift, Raul Tovar, Janine Vangool, Christopher Volpe, Susan Ward, Lauren Whitley, Brenna Wilson, Alexa Griffith Winton, and Leigh Wishner.

SELECTED BIBLIOGRAPHY

BOOKS

Adamson, Glenn. *Craft*. New York: Bloomsbury Publishing, 2021.

Burton, A. Ross. Special issue, *"GI": World War II*. Gloucester, MA: Richard C. Tarr, 1963.

Burton, Virginia Lee. *Calico the Wonder Horse: Or the Saga of Stewy Slinker*. Boston: Houghton Mifflin, 1941.

Burton, Virginia Lee. *Choo Choo*. Boston: Houghton Mifflin, 1937.

Burton, Virginia Lee. *Katy and the Big Snow*. Boston: Houghton Mifflin, 1943.

Burton, Virginia Lee. *Life Story*. Boston: Houghton Mifflin, 1962.

Burton, Virginia Lee. *The Little House*. Boston: Houghton Mifflin, 1942.

Burton, Virginia Lee. *Maybelle the Cable Car*. Boston: Houghton Mifflin, 1952.

Burton, Virginia Lee. *Mike Mulligan and His Steam Shovel*. Boston: Houghton Mifflin, 1939.

Eaton, Allen H. *Handicrafts of New England*. New York: Harper & Row, 1949, republished by Bonanza Books, 1969.

Elleman, Barbara. *Virginia Lee Burton: A Life in Art*. Boston: Houghton Mifflin Company, 2002.

Erkilla, Barbara H. *Hammers on Stone*. Woolwich, ME: TBW Books, 1980.

Erkilla, Barbara H. *Village at Lane's Cove*, Gloucester, MA: Ten Pound Book Island Book Company, 2008.

Kaplan, Wendy. *"The Art That Is Life": The Arts & Crafts Movement in America, 1875–1920*. Boston: Little, Brown and Company in collaboration with the Museum of Fine Arts, 1987.

Kenyon, Paul B. *Driftwood Captain*. Boston: Houghton Mifflin, 1954.

Kirkham, Pat, ed. *Women Designers in the USA 1900–2000: Diversity and Difference*. New Haven, CT: Yale University Press, 2000.

Koplos, Janet, and Bruce Metcalf. *Makers: A History of American Studio Craft*. Chapel Hill: University of North Carolina Press in collaboration with the University of North Carolina Center for Craft, Creativity and Design, 2010.

Lauria, Jo, and Steve Fenton. *Craft in America: Celebrating Two Centuries of Artists and Objects*. New York: Clarkson Potter, 2007.

Malcolmson, Anne, Grace Castagnetta, and Virginia Lee Burton. *Song of Robin Hood*. Boston: Houghton Mifflin, 1947.

Rayner, Geoffrey, Richard Chamberlain, and Annamarie Stapleton. *Artists' Textiles: Artist Designed Textiles 1940–1976*. Woodbridge, U.K.: Antique Collectors' Club, 2012.

Vail, June. *Folly Cove Sketches: Remembering Virginia Lee Burton*. Thomaston, ME: Custom Museum Publishing, 2022.

Weyl, Christina. *The Women of Atelier 17: Modernist Printmaking in Midcentury New York*. New Haven, CT: Yale University Press, 2019.

Wilgress, Jane. *Better Than Beauty: The Life and Work of Jeanne d'Orge*. Pacific Grove, CA: Park Place Publications, 2004.

EXHIBIT CATALOGS AND CONFERENCE PROCEEDINGS

Annual International Textile Exhibition. Greensboro: Weatherspoon Art Gallery, Woman's College of University of North Carolina, 1944. Exhibition catalog.

Caponigro, Jessica. "A Very Condensed History of Women Printmakers in America," in "Printing Social Justice: Past, Present and Future." *Mid America Print Council Journal, vol. 24*, Spring/Summer 2016), http://static1.squarespace.com/static/5279736fe4b06b69607f325d/t/57599e44ab48de6da1fa76ae/1465491012549/MAPCJournal2016SprSum.28-35.pdf.

Designer Craftsmen U.S.A. 1953. New York: American Craftsmen's Education Council, 1953. Exhibition catalog.

Eaton, Allen. "The New England Exhibition and the American Handicrafts Movement." In *An Exhibition of Contemporary New England Handicrafts*. Worcester, MA: Worcester Art Museum, 1943. Exhibition catalog.

Felsher, Lynn, and Joanne Dolan. *A Woman's Hand: Designing Textiles in America*. New York: The Museum at FIT, 2000. Exhibition pamphlet.

The Folly Cove Designers: 1941–1969. Gloucester, MA: Cape Ann Museum, 1996, amended and reprinted 2017. Exhibition catalog.

Kardon, Janet, ed. *Revivals! Diverse Traditions: The History of Twentieth-Century American Craft 1920–1945*. New York: Harry N. Abrams in collaboration with the American Craft Museum, 1994.

Langa, Helen. "Printmaking, Artistic Diversity, and Cultural Democracy in 1930s America." In *Ink, Paper, Politics: WPA-Era Printmaking from the Needles Collection*, ed. Belverd E. Needles, Jr., and Marian Powers. Chicago: DePaul Art Museum, 2014.

Lepionka, Mary Ellen. "Native American History." In Molly O'Hagan Hardy, *Unfolding Histories: Cape Ann Before 1900*, 14–21. Gloucester, MA: Cape Ann Museum, 2018. https://www.capeannmuseum.org/media/native_american_history_.pdf.

Mary Magna Maletskos. Gloucester, MA: Cape Ann Museum, 1995. Exhibition catalog.

Massachusetts Crafts of Today 5th Annual Exhibition. Boston: Society of Arts and Crafts, 1956. Exhibition catalog.

Sarni, Elena M. "Folly Cove Designers: A Time and Place." In *Dressing New England: clothing, fashion, and identity*, edited by Peter Benes and Jane Montague Benes. Deerfield, MA: Dublin Seminar for New England Folklife, 2014.

Seaton, Elizabeth G., ed. *Paths to the Press: Printmaking and American Women Artists, 1910–1960*. Manhattan: Marianna Kistler Beach Museum of Art, Kansas State University, 2006.

ARCHIVES, COLLECTIONS, AND ARCHIVAL MATERIAL

Demetrios, Virginia Lee. *Design and How!*, unpublished manuscript. Virginia Lee Burton Demetrios Papers (VLBDP), Cape Ann Museum, Gloucester, MA.

The Folly Cove Designers Collection (TFCDC), Cape Ann Museum, Gloucester, MA.

Gerda Peterich Papers. Syracuse University Archives, Syracuse, NY.

Gloucester Daily Times. Gloucester, Massachusetts. www.gloucestertimes.com.

Martin, Theodora, interviews, The Folly Cove Designers Collection, Cape Ann Museum, Gloucester, MA.

Periodical and Archival Collections, Henry Meade Williams Local History Department, Harrison Memorial Library, Carmel, CA.

Sandy Bay Historical Society, Rockport, MA.

Virginia Lee Burton Demetrios Papers (VLBDP). Cape Ann Museum. Gloucester, MA.

NEWSPAPER ARTICLES/ NEWSLETTER ARTICLES/ PERIODICALS

Carey, Walter. “Massachusetts's Designing Women.” *Magazine Digest*, December 1945.

Eaton, Ethel M. “Folly Cove Sets High Standards for Design and Achievement.” *Christian Science Monitor*, December 22, 1943.

Einik, Nurit. “Other Craft Organizations.” In Nurit Einik et al., “Collected Essays: Development in Post-War American Craft.” *Archives of American Art Journal* 50, no. 3/4 (Fall 2011).

“Folly Cove Designers: Yankee Prints Get National Recognition.” *Life*, November 25, 1945.

Furnas, J.C. “Braces Away: A Polio Victim Turns Bad Break into the Best of Good Fortune.” *Ladies Home Journal*, February 1947.

Hogarth, Grace Allen. “Virginia Lee Burton, Creative Artist.” *The Horn Book Magazine*, July–August 1943.

Howard, Robert West. “Designed in Folly Cove.” *Country Gentleman*, February 1949.

Maletskos, Mary. “The Folly Cove World of Jinnee and George Demetrios.” *Cape Ann Historical Association* 6, no. 3 (July–September 1986).

Nathan, Jean. “An American Original.” *Vogue*, May 2008, 156.

Neyman, Bella. “The (America) House that Mrs. Webb Built.” *Magazine Antiques*, July/August 2012. www.themagazineantiques.com.

Retailing Home Furnishings, August 27, 1945.

Roche, Mary. “New York Fabrics Make Debut Here.” *New York Times*, August 24, 1945.

Roth, Elizabeth M., and Mary L. Brandt. “How to Block Print.” *Woman's Day*, January 1945.

Sarni, Elena M. “Folly Cove Designers.” Uppercase 37 (April/May/June 2018): 74–81.

Scanlon, Jennifer. “The Space Between': Rediscovering the Folly Cove Designers.” *Massachusetts Review* 56, no. 2 (2015): 282–301. https://doi.org/10.1353/mar.2015.0056.

Views and Reviews: Retail Reporting Bureau. New York: Milton B. Conhaim, September 1945.

Winton, Alexandra Griffith. “Color and Personality: Dorothy Liebes and American Design.” *Archives of American Art Journal* 48, no. 1–2 (Spring 2009): 4–17.

ONLINE ARCHIVES AND OTHER RESOURCES

Brayton, Linda, David Masters, et al. “Toward an Oral History of Cape Ann.” Gloucester Oral History Collection, Sawyer Free Library, North of Boston Library Exchange, Inc., NOBLE Digital Heritage, https://digitalheritage.noblenet.org/gloucester/collections/show/1.

Craft Horizons. 1941–1979. American Craft Council, https://digital.craftcouncil.org/digital/collection/p15785coll2.

“Guide to the Dorothy Shaver Papers: Biographical History,” Smithsonian Online Virtual Archives, Smithsonian Institution. Accessed January 2021. https://sova.si.edu/record/NMAH.AC.0631.

ONLINE ARTICLES AND WEBSITES

Giaimo, Cara. “The Unlikely Story of the Folly Cove Guild, the Best Designers You've Never Heard Of.” Atlas Obscura, June 14, 2017, https://www.atlasobscura.com/articles/the-unlikely-story-of-the-folly-cove-guild-the-best-designers-youve-never-heard-of.

Hoffman, Andrea. “Designs out of the Depression: Block Prints from the Handicrafts Revival,” School of Human Ecology, University of Wisconsin-Madison.

Lepionka, Mary Ellen. “Erasure: The Forgotten Native American History of Cape Ann and Manchester-by-the-Sea.” *The Cricket*. February 27, 2020, updated March 27, 2022. https://www.thecricket.com/out_and_about/erasure-the-forgotten-native-american-history-of-cape-ann-and-manchester-by-the-sea/article_9b357d90-58c3-11ea-aae0-27f67f601c9f.html.

“Our History,” American Craft Council. https://www.craftcouncil.org/about/our-history.

Schweitzer, Jacqueline M. “Women's Work: The WPA Milwaukee Handicraft Project.” Milwaukee Public Museum. https://www.mpm.edu/research-collections/history/online-collections-research/wpa-milwaukee-handicraft-project.

Zaiden, Emily. “American Craft Council and Aileen Osborn Webb.” Craft in America, accessed May 2016, http://www.craftinamerica.org/profiles/american-craft-council-aileen-osborn-webb.

DOCUMENTARIES

Lundberg, Christine. *Virginia Lee Burton: A Sense of Place*. 2007; Red Dory Productions, DVD, 57 minutes.

Nogelo, Sinikka. *The Folly Cove Designers*. 1985; Cape Ann TV, CD-ROM, 55 minutes.

OTHER RESOURCES

Norton, Dorothy, binder of assorted Folly Cove Designers–related material, 1944–1969, collection of the author.

Sarni, Elena M., interviews, emails, and texts.

NOTES

INTRODUCTION

1 Dorothy Norton, list of "designs approved and shown under the Folly Cove name" in binder of assorted Folly Cove Designers–related material, 1944–1969, collection of the author.
2 In-house pamphlet, undated, in the collection of the author.
3 Eileen Boris, "Social Change and Changing Experience" in *Women Designers in the USA 1900–2000: Diversity and Difference*, ed. Pat Kirkham (New Haven, CT: Yale University Press), 36.

CHAPTER ONE

1 Muriel Lee Steele, interview by the author, May 29, 2010.
2 Mahlon Hoagland, interview by Theodora Martin, July 14, 1992, The Folly Cove Designers Collection, Cape Ann Museum, Gloucester, MA (hereafter cited as *TFCDC*).
3 Mary Ellen Lepionka, "Erasure: The Forgotten Native American History of Cape Ann and Manchester-by-the-Sea," *The Cricket*, February 27, 2020, updated March 27, 2022, https://www.thecricket.com/out_and_about/erasure-the-forgotten-native-american-history-of-cape-ann-and-manchester-by-the-sea/article_9b357d90-58c3-11ea-aae0-27f67f601c9f.html; Mary Ellen Lepionka, "Native American History," in Molly O'Hagan Hardy, *Unfolding Histories: Cape Ann before 1900* (Gloucester, MA: Cape Ann Museum, 2018), 14–21, https://www.capeannmuseum.org/media/native_american_history_.pdf.
4 Years of active granite industry (Barbara H. Erkilla, *Hammers on Stone* [Woolwich, ME: TBW Books, 1980], 3); Russian imperialism and conscription (Robert Natti, interview by Linda Brayton and David Masters, April 16, 1978, in "Toward an Oral History of Cape Ann: Robert Natti," Gloucester Oral History Collection, Sawyer Free Library, North of Boston Library Exchange, Inc., 4 sound files, digital, MPEG3 file, NOBLE Digital Heritage, https://digitalheritage.noblenet.org/noble/items/show/939).
5 Artist Walker Hancock recalled that one time when he got his hair cut in Cape Ann, a man came into the barbershop and asked what the chief industries were in the area. He was surprised when the barber replied, "Fish and artists" (Walker Hancock, interview by Linda Brayton and David Masters, April 25, 1978, in "Toward an Oral History of Cape Ann," https://digitalheritage.noblenet.org/gloucester/items/show/1253).
6 Hale and Clements being introduced to the area by their teachers ("A Little Community of Artists," Cape Ann Museum, https://www.capeannmuseum.org/lanesville-folly-cove); Clements studying with Parrish (Allen C. Abend, *Gabrielle DeVeaux Clements: Etcher, Painter, Muralist, Teacher: Late 19th and Early 20th Century Etchings of Baltimore Views* [Baltimore, MD: Abend Fine Art, 2012]).
7 *The Folly Cove Designers: 1941–1969* (Gloucester, MA: Cape Ann Museum, 1996, amended and reprinted 2017), exhibition catalog.
8 Dr. William D. Hoyt to Rev. Morris Reed Robinson, 19 April 1973, Cape Ann Museum Library and Archives, Gloucester, MA; Vera Seppala Olsen, interview by Theodora Martin, June 16, 1992, TFCDC.
9 Barbara H. Erkilla, *Village at Lane's Cove* (Gloucester, MA: Ten Pound Book Island Book Company, 2008), 107.
10 Barbara Elleman, *Virginia Lee Burton: A Life in Art* (Boston: Houghton Mifflin Company, 2002); self-conscious feeling (Jacqueline Darcy, "Mrs. Demetrios Has Full-Time Career in Designing, Books," *Gloucester Daily Times*, August 18, 1949).
11 Elleman, *Virginia Lee Burton*.
12 Elleman; Michael's birth year as 1935 ("Virginia Lee Burton: The Early Years," Houghton Mifflin Harcourt, http://www.houghtonmifflinbooks.com/features/mike_mulligan/arismike.shtml).
13 A history of the group in a timeline listed a Yankee swap of violin lessons in exchange for design lessons (Dorothy Norton, timeline in binder of assorted Folly Cove Designers–related material, ca. 1944–1969, collection of the author); years after the group disbanded, Aino Clarke said the lessons started because Virginia was worried about the high cost of illustration paper (perhaps Bristol board). Aino gathered other neighbors and they offered to pay fifty cents a session but Virginia ultimately refused payment. Aino recalled that in the initial years, lessons were informal and were taught in Virginia's kitchen (Aino Clarke to Harold Bell, 29 January 1989, TFCDC); Aino Clarke, interview by Theodora Martin, January 9, 1991, TFCDC; and Aino Clarke, interview by Sinikka Nogelo, *The Folly Cove Designers*, Cape Ann TV, 1985/1986, CD-ROM, 2010). Aristides and Michael Demetrios were unsure about the specifics of violin lessons but remembered taking various music lessons (Michael Demetrios, interview by Theodora Martin, June 25, 1993, TFCDC; Aristides Demetrios, interview by Theodora Martin, June 23, 1993, TFCDC); Libby Holloran said that Aino gave the boys piano lessons (Elizabeth [Libby] Holloran, interview by Theodora Martin, October 15, 1991, TFCDC). Other early members were unable to remember if they paid for lessons in the beginning (Vera Seppala Olsen, interview by Martin; Irja Jacobson Sheppard, interview by Theodora Martin, July 7, 1992, TFCDC).
14 There is also some discrepancy among former members interviewed about the exact year the first group lessons were started, 1938 or 1939. But an in-house timeline lists 1939 as the year Virginia taught the first community class in her studio/barn (Dorothy Norton, timeline in binder).
15 Aristides Demetrios, interview by Martin.
16 "Folly Cove Design Pupils Holding Display of Work," *Gloucester Daily Times*, July 15, 1940.
17 Dick Berkenbush is credited with coming up with the idea of having the main character, Mary Anne, convert from an aging steam shovel into a furnace in the cellar of Popperville's town hall (Elleman, *Virginia Lee Burton*, 3).
18 Eleanor Malmi, interview by Theodora Martin, October 8, 1991, TFCDC.
19 Vera Seppala Olsen, interview by Martin.
20 Irja Jacobson Sheppard, interview by Martin.
21 Erkilla, *Hammers on Stone*, 101.
22 Erkilla, 105.
23 St. Paul Lutheran Church, Gloucester, MA, "Our History," https://www.stpaulcapeann.org/who-we-are/history/.
24 Robert Natti, interview by Brayton and Masters; Vera Seppala Olsen, interview by Martin.
25 Olsen, interview by Martin; Irja Jacobson Sheppard, interview by Martin; "brains in their hands" comment (Aino Clarke, interview by Martin); Robert Natti, interview by Brayton and Masters; Dorothy Norton, interview by Linda Brayton and Martin Ray, May 25, 1978, in "Toward an Oral History of Cape Ann," Gloucester Oral History Collection, Sawyer Free Library, North of Boston Library Exchange, Inc., NOBLE Digital Heritage, 4 sound files, digital, MPEG3 file, https://digitalheritage.noblenet.org/noble/items/show/1025.

26 Erkilla, *Hammers on Stone*, 107.
27 Erkilla, 110; Lee Natti, interview by Theodora Martin, June 2, 1992, TFCDC.
28 Saunas were mostly offered on Saturday nights, but during the summer they were offered on both Wednesday and Saturday nights (Vera Seppala Olsen, interview by Martin).
29 Pottery mentioned ("The Folly Cove Designers New Cape Art Group," *Gloucester Daily Times*, 1940); Hestwood (Elleman, *Virginia Lee Burton*, 13); choice of linoleum block printing (Dorothy Norton, interview by Brayton and Ray).
30 Vera Seppala Olsen, interview by Martin; Dorothy Norton, binder.
31 Ilmari's *Kalevala* prints ("Folly Cove Design Pupils Holding Display of Work"); information on *Kalevala* (Books from Finland, accessed June 2016, http://neba.finlit.fi/booksfromfinland/bff/299/kalevala.htm).
32 Changing to hand-operated proof presses was a smart business decision since Dorothy Norton had to write the Lord & Taylor executive that an order couldn't be filled because Virginia had broken her ankle. Whether it was due to a printing accident or not, the break impeded production (Dorothy Norton to Charles Dimand, 14 December 1944, TFCDC).
33 Elizabeth (Libby) Holloran, interview by Martin, October 15, 1991.
34 Members Ruth Hendy and Barbara Bisbee Souza Hoffmann worked together (Barbara Bisbee Souza Hoffmann, interview by Theodora Martin, December 12, 1991, TFCDC).
35 Dorothy Norton, binder.
36 In-house history notes, TFCDC; Dorothy Norton, binder.
37 Elleman, *Virginia Lee Burton*, 75; Lee Natti, interview by Theodora Martin, October 17, 1991, TFCDC.
38 Dorothy Norton, rules and regulations in binder; "Notes taken during meeting with Mr. Roewer and Mr. Segal regarding Folly Cove trade-mark," August 23, 1946, TFCDC.
39 Victory gardens (Ethel M. Eaton, "Folly Cove Sets High Standards for Design and Achievement," "Today's Woman" section of *The Christian Science Monitor*, December 22, 1943); Virginia's ration book is part of the Virginia Lee Burton Demetrios Papers, Cape Ann Museum, Gloucester, MA (hereafter cited as *VLBDP*).
40 Grace Allen Hogarth, "Virginia Lee Burton, Creative Artist," *The Horn Book Magazine*, July–August, 1943, 224.
41 Mary Maletskos, interview by Theodora Martin, July 6, 1990, TFCDC; Aristides Demetrios, interview by the author, February 9, 2021.
42 Hogarth, "Virginia Lee Burton, Creative Artist."
43 Two of the designs have been attributed (one to Virginia Demetrios and one to Hetty Beatty), but no confirmation has been found, although Demetrios's illustration does appear to have her initials.
44 "Blood Bank Ads Draw Attention: Pictures, Layouts by Local Art Group Effective," *Gloucester Daily Times*, January 8, 1944.
45 "Folly Cove Design Pupils Holding Display of Work." A copy of this newspaper clipping was in a scrapbook that The Folly Cove Designers kept and later donated to the Cape Ann Museum when they disbanded. At some point "150 attendees" was crossed out in pen to say "472"; an in-house timeline lists the summer of 1940 as the year the group held its first exhibition (Dorothy Norton, timeline in binder, TFCDC); 1941 exhibit at Virginia's studio (Dorothy Norton, binder).
46 Dorothy Norton, binder; members Irina and Joshua Tolford owned Home Industries (Dorothy Norton, binder).
47 Dorothy Norton, binder.
48 Dorothy Norton, timeline in binder.
49 *The Folly Cove Designers: 1941–1969*.
50 It is not known who wrote the copy for the inserts. Dorothy Norton credited Lee Natti (Dorothy Norton, timeline in binder); Lee Natti credited Dorothy or Peggy Norton (Lee Natti, interview by Martin, June 2, 1992).
51 Barbara Bisbee Souza Hoffmann, interview by Martin.
52 Elizabeth and Anthony Iarrobino, interview by Theodora Martin, June 11, 1992, TFCDC.
53 Barbara Bisbee Souza Hoffmann, interview by Martin.
54 Elizabeth (Libby) Holloran, interview by Martin, October 15, 1991.
55 Lee Natti, interview by Martin, October 17, 1991.
56 Gertrude Griffin, interview by Theodora Martin, June 26, 1992, TFCDC.
57 Eleanor Curtis, interview by Theodora Martin, November 18, 1991, TFCDC.
58 Faith Harvey, interview by Theodora Martin, April 7, 1994, TFCDC.
59 Details about Saturday nights and musical entertainment (Aino Clarke to Harold Bell, 29 January 1989; Aristides Demetrios, interview by Martin; Michael Demetrios, interview by Martin); details on Aino Clarke's musical background (Aino Clarke, interview by Martin).
60 Art discussion and lively debate (Aristides Demetrios, interview by Martin); comment about George's singing voice (Aino Clarke to Harold Bell, 29 January 1989).
61 Lee Natti, interview by Martin, October 17, 1991.
62 Lee Natti, interview by Martin, October 17, 1991; Muriel Lee Steele, interview by Theodora Martin, June 1, 1992, TFCDC.
63 Irja Jadobson Sheppard, interview by Martin.
64 Michael Demetrios, interview by Martin; Aristides Demetrios, interview by Martin.
65 Michael Demetrios, interview by Martin.
66 Michael Demetrios, interview by Martin.
67 Aristides Demetrios, interview by Martin.
68 Michael Demetrios, interview by Martin.
69 Aristides Demetrios, phone conversation with the author, February 2011.
70 Michael Demetrios, interview by Martin.
71 Aristides Demetrios, telephone interview by Martin.
72 Lee Steele had a master's degree in social work (Muriel Lee Steele, interview by Martin).
73 Muriel Lee Steele, interview by Martin.
74 Aristides Demetrios, interview by Martin.
75 Muriel Lee Steele, interview by Martin.
76 Muriel Lee Steele, interview by Martin.
77 Muriel Lee Steele, interview by Martin.
78 In-house pamphlet, TFCDC.

CHAPTER TWO

1 Margaret Norton, interview by Linda Brayton and David Masters, June 14, 1978, in "Toward an Oral History of Cape Ann," Gloucester Oral History Collection, Sawyer Free Library, North of Boston Library Exchange, Inc., 3 sound files, digital, MPEG3 file, NOBLE Digital Heritage, https://digitalheritage.noblenet.org/noble/items/show/1085.
2 Virginia Demetrios, *Design and How!*, unpublished manuscript, Virginia Lee Burton Demetrios Papers, Cape Ann Museum, Gloucester, MA (hereafter cited as *VLBDP*).

3 Lee Natti, interview by Theodora Martin, October 17, 1991, The Folly Cove Designers Collection, Cape Ann Museum, Gloucester, MA (hereafter cited as *TFCDC*); Elizabeth (Libby) Holloran, interview by Theodora Martin, October 15, 1991, TFCDC.
4 Aino Clarke, interview by Theodora Martin, January 9, 1991, TFCDC.
5 Margaret Norton, interview by Brayton and Masters.
6 Demetrios, *Design and How!*
7 Barbara Elleman, *Virginia Lee Burton: A Life in Art* (Boston: Houghton Mifflin Co., 2002), 12; Jeff Gunderson, librarian and archivist at the San Francisco Art Institute, further clarified Burton's course of study: "In the fall of 1927 she studied painting with Otis Oldfield, 'costume design' with Lucienne [*sic*] Labaudt, Still Life painting with Constance Macky, and also a Life painting class with Lee Randolph and it looks like some sort of 'commercial art' class. In the Spring of 1928 Burton studied landscape painting with the legendary Giottardo Piazzoni" (Jeff Gunderson, email to the author, April 9, 2021).
8 Mary Maletskos, interview by Theodora Martin, July 6, 1990, TFCDC.
9 In this short article, Hestwood discussed his time in Mexico and mentioned spending time in Mexico City. "Robert Hestwood, Artist," *The Carmel Cymbal*, December 1, 1926, 9.
10 "Robert Hestwood, Artist."
11 Aino Clarke, interview by Martin.
12 Lee Kingman Natti, interview by Linda Brayton and David Masters, July 11, 1978, in "Toward an Oral History of Cape Ann," Gloucester Oral History Collection, Sawyer Free Library, North of Boston Library Exchange, Inc., 3 sound files, digital, MPEG3 file, NOBLE Digital Heritage, https://digitalheritage.noblenet.org/gloucester/items/show/1296.
13 Aristides Demetrios, interview by the author, February 9, 2021.
14 Folly Cove designers were given discounts on drawing lessons with George Demetrios (Elizabeth [Libby] Holloran, interview by Martin, October 15, 1991).
15 Demetrios, *Design and How!*; Aino "helped with the design instruction" beginning in 1941 (Dorothy Norton, timeline in binder of assorted Folly Cove Designers–related material, 1944–1969, collection of the author).
16 Demetrios, *Design and How!*
17 Elizabeth (Libby) Holloran, interview by Martin, October 15, 1991; Demetrios, *Design and How!*
18 Demetrios.
19 Demetrios.
20 Lee Natti homework, collection of Susanna Natti.
21 Peggy Norton, interview by Sinikka Nogelo, *The Folly Cove Designers*, Cape Ann TV, 1985/1986, CD-ROM, 2010; Margaret Norton, interview by Brayton and Masters.
22 Margaret Norton, interview by Brayton and Masters.
23 Margaret Norton, interview by Brayton and Masters.
24 Robert West Howard, "Designed in Folly Cove," *Country Gentleman*, February 1949; Dorothy mentioned types of ways to depict onions as "roped, peeled or fried" (Howard, "Designed in Folly Cove").
25 Demetrios, *Design and How!*
26 When working on this design in 1957, Virginia considered the alternate titles *Algae and Pisces* and *Fish in the Sea* (homework, VLBDP); existence of second *Fish Story* design (collection of Andrew Spindler and "Folly Cove Designers Get New Pattern Ideas from What's Around Them," *Gloucester Daily Times*, July 30, 1957, 10).
27 "Folly Cove Designers Get New Pattern Ideas from What's Around Them."
28 Virginia Lee Burton Demetrios, instructional poster, VLBDP.
29 Demetrios, *Design and How!*
30 Schools of fish ("Folly Cove Designers Get New Pattern Ideas from What's Around Them").
31 Demetrios, *Design and How!*
32 Demetrios.
33 Demetrios.
34 Demetrios.
35 Demetrios.
36 Demetrios.
37 Margaret Norton, interview by Brayton and Masters.
38 Margaret Norton, interview by Brayton and Masters.
39 Ruth Hendy and Barbara Bisbee Souza Hoffmann would sit at one of their kitchen tables to carve their designs (Barbara Bisbee Souza Hoffmann, interview by Theodora Martin, December 12, 1991, TFCDC).
40 Margaret Norton, interview by Brayton and Masters; Lee Natti, interview by Martin, October 17, 1991; Lee Natti, interview by Theodora Martin, June 2, 1992, TFCDC.
41 Tracing and applying the design to the block for carving (Elizabeth M. Roth and Mary L. Brandt, "How to Block Print" *Woman's Day*, January 1945); shoe polish/gesso detail (Lee Kingman Natti, interview by Brayton and Masters).
42 Demetrios, *Design and How!*
43 Elizabeth (Libby) Holloran, interview by Martin, October 15, 1991; Anthony and Elizabeth Iarrobino, interview by Theodora Martin, October 21, 1991, TFCDC.
44 Margaret Norton, interview by Brayton and Masters.
45 Roth and Brandt, "How to Block Print."
46 Standardization of blocks (Eleanor Dexter, "Even Foreign Visitors Come to Folly Cove Designers," *Gloucester Daily Times*, July 31, 1964, 2-A); plywood mounting (Barbara Stanton [*Woman's Day*] to Mrs. Demetrios regarding "Questions about enclosed photostats of Snively pictures of Block-Printing," October 1944, TFCDC).
47 Louise Kenyon, interview by Sinikka Nogelo, *The Folly Cove Designers*.
48 Lee Natti, interview by Martin, June 2, 1992.
49 Aino Clarke to Harold Bell, 29 January 1989, TFCDC.
50 Aino Clarke, interview by Martin, January 9, 1991.
51 Margaret Norton, interview by Brayton and Masters.
52 Roth and Brandt, "How to Block Print"; Boston Printer's Ink Company brand mentioned (Boston Printing Ink Company to Dorothy Norton, 19 December 1951, TFCDC).
53 Lee Natti, interview by Martin, June 2, 1992.
54 Damp material (Roth and Brandt, "How to Block Print").
55 Dorothy Norton, timeline in binder.
56 Louise Kenyon, interview by Theodora Martin, October 6, 1991, TFCDC.
57 Dorothy Norton to Leota Diesel (*Life*), "Folly Cove Designers" attachment, 7 October 1945, TFCDC.
58 Dorothy Norton, interview by Linda Brayton and Martin Ray, May 25, 1978, in "Toward an Oral History of Cape Ann," Gloucester Oral History Collection, Sawyer Free Library, North of Boston Library Exchange, Inc., 3 sound files, digital, MPEG3 file, NOBLE Digital Heritage, https://digitalheritage.noblenet.org/noble/items/show/1025).
59 Margaret Norton, interview by Brayton and Masters.
60 "Squash" (Margaret Norton, interview by Brayton and Masters).
61 Margaret Norton, interview by Brayton and Masters.

62 By the time the group disbanded there were approximately twelve presses owned by group members (Margaret Norton, interview by Brayton and Masters); by the late 1950s most designers had access to a printing press (Lee Kingman Natti, interview by Brayton and Masters); sharing (Elizabeth [Libby] Holloran, interview by Martin, October 15, 1991); printing done outside of meetings (Dorothy Norton, interview by Brayton and Ray).
63 Eino's press being moved to the barn (Dorothy Norton, timeline in binder).
64 Eino's press was an acorn press (Dorothy Norton, timeline in binder); acorn press ("1845 Adams Acorn Press," The International Printing Museum, https://www.printmuseum.org/1845-adams-acorn#:~:text=One%20of%20the%20most%2distinctive,house%20the%20press's%20toggle%20mechanism).
65 "Acorn Press, Tufts?," National Museum of American History, https://americanhistory.si.edu/collections/search/object/nmah_742170.
66 Roth and Brandt, "How to Block Print."
67 "Exciting thing" (Margaret Norton, interview by Brayton and Masters).
68 Roth and Brandt, "How to Block Print."
69 Dorothy Norton, binder; five days in advance (Dorothy Norton, rules and regulations in binder).
70 Dorothy Norton, binder.
71 Dorothy Norton said the jury was kept small because a "group of twenty people can't accomplish anything at a meeting" (Dorothy Norton, interview by Brayton and Ray).
72 Dorothy Norton, interview by Brayton and Ray; detail about non-jury members (Dorothy Norton, binder).
73 Lee Natti, interview by Martin, October 17, 1991.
74 Dorothy Norton, interview by Brayton and Ray.
75 Margaret Norton, interview by Brayton and Masters.
76 Margaret Norton, interview by Brayton and Masters.
77 Dorothy Norton, interview by Brayton and Ray; colors (Lee Natti, interview by Sinikka Nogelo, *The Folly Cove Designers*).
78 Dorothy Norton, rules and regulations, 1945.
79 Dorothy Norton, interview by Brayton and Ray.
80 Lee Kingman Natti, interview by Brayton and Masters.
81 Virginia Demetrios, sketchbook, VLBDP.
82 "Folly Cove Designers: Yankee Prints Get National Recognition," *Life*, November 1945.
83 Virginia Demetrios to Paul Brooks, 26 July 1954, VLBDP; the book's basic rules were the same principles she taught the Folly Cove Designers, including "Do it! (Don't talk about it.) Don't Copy!! Don't Give Up!!!" (Demetrios, *Design and How!*).
84 Paul Brooks to Virginia Demetrios, 16 December 1954, VLBDP.
85 Morton H. Baker (Houghton Mifflin) to Miss Virginia Lee Burton, 24 January 1955, VLBDP.
86 Paul Brooks to Mrs. George Demetrios, 4 January 1963, VLBDP.
87 Paul Brooks to Mrs. George Demetrios, 4 January 1963.
88 Paul Brooks to Mrs. George Demetrios, 4 January 1963.
89 Virginia Demetrios to Paul Brooks, undated, VLBDP.
90 Virginia Lee Burton, *Life Story* (Boston: Houghton Mifflin, 1962).
91 Demetrios, sketchbook.
92 Lee Kingman Natti, interview by Brayton and Masters.
93 Paul Brooks to Virginia Demetrios, undated, VLBDP. Paul initialed the artwork on the Christmas card and may have drawn the Christmas tree in the sketch as well.
94 Demetrios, *Design and How!*
95 Demetrios.
96 Demetrios.
97 Demetrios.
98 Demetrios.
99 Demetrios.
100 Demetrios.
101 Demetrios.
102 Demetrios.
103 Margaret Norton, interview by Brayton and Masters.
104 Aino Clarke to Harold Bell, 29 January 1989.
105 Lee Kingman Natti, interview by Brayton and Masters.
106 Cori Sherman North with Susan Teller, "Running the Presses: Women Printmakers As Teachers, 1945–1960," in *Paths to the Press: Printmaking and American Women Artists, 1910–1960*, ed. Elizabeth G. Seaton (Manhattan: The Marianna Kistler Beach Museum of Art, Kansas State University, 2006), 66.
107 Dorothy Norton, list of "designs approved and shown under the Folly Cove name" in binder.
108 North with Teller, "Running the Presses," 65; the Cape Ann Museum cites forty-four students/members (*The Folly Cove Designers: 1941–1969*, [Gloucester, MA: Cape Ann Museum, 1996, amended and reprinted 2017], exhibition catalog); Dorothy Norton cited forty-five (Dorothy Norton interview by Brayton and Ray).

CHAPTER THREE

1 Dorothy Norton, timeline in binder of assorted Folly Cove Designers–related material, 1944–1969, collection of the author.
2 Peggy Norton, interview by Sinikka Nogelo, *The Folly Cove Designers*, Cape Ann TV, 1985/1986, CD-ROM, 2010.
3 *Retailing Home Furnishings*, August 27, 1945, 12.
4 Dorothy Norton, interview by Linda Brayton and Martin Ray, May 25, 1978, in "Toward an Oral History of Cape Ann," Gloucester Oral History Collection, Sawyer Free Library, North of Boston Library Exchange, Inc., 3 sound files, digital, MPEG3 file, NOBLE Digital Heritage, https://digitalheritage.noblenet.org/noble/items/show/1025.
5 "Guide to the Dorothy Shaver Papers: Biographical History," Smithsonian Institution, Smithsonian Online Virtual Archives, accessed January 2021, https://sova.si.edu/record/NMAH.AC.0631.
6 "In the case of rugs, I know they have been unable to find any one [*sic*] to reproduce the designs in the proper price lines and quality" (David Williams to Dorothy Norton, 21 May 1945, The Folly Cove Designers Collection, Cape Ann Museum, Gloucester, MA [hereafter cited as *TFCDC*]); hand-printed table linen negotiating details (Dorothy Norton to Charles Dimand, 24 August 1944, TFCDC).
7 Dorothy Norton to David Williams, 29 September 1944, TFCDC.
8 Dorothy's business notebook listed five designs (Dorothy Norton, binder); a letter from Dorothy Norton to F. Schumacher lists the names of the six prints purchased by Lord & Taylor (Dorothy Norton to M.A. Dalton, 8 October 1945, TFCDC); a trade magazine cited six designs and described the displays (*Retailing Home Furnishings*); when negotiations started with Lord & Taylor, Louise Kenyon's *Head of the Cove* was called *Annisquam* and *New England (Wild) Flowers* was *Field Flowers* (Dorothy Norton to A.G. Howe, 6 September 1944, TFCDC).
9 *Retailing Home Furnishings*.
10 Milton B. Conhaim, *Views and Reviews: Retail Reporting Bureau*, September 1945.
11 William Grimes, "Karl Bissinger; postwar photographer of future cultural icons," *New York Times News Service*, November 30, 2008,

https://www.sandiegouniontribune.com/sdut-113008-karl-bissinger-2008nov30-story.html; Karl Bissinger papers, Special Collections, University of Delaware, https://library.udel.edu/special/findaids/view?docId=ead/mss0682.xml;tab=print.

12 David Williams asked for "twenty or so items which we will need for window and interior display" (David Williams to Dorothy Norton, 8 August 1945, TFCDC); Dorothy replied: "I sent to you yesterday by express a collection of materials, blocks, tools and paints, and sent by mail a group of photographs" (Dorothy Norton to David Williams, 10 August 1945, TFCDC); attribution of Bettine Nichols photo made by Nichols family.

13 Louise Kenyon and her husband visited New York City to see the window displays. Mention of the impending visit (Dorothy Norton to David Williams, 10 August 1945); mention of Louise having spoken to a Lord & Taylor representative, presumably while in New York City (Dorothy Norton to David Williams, 23 September 1945, TFCDC).

14 David Williams to Dorothy Norton, 12 September 1945, TFCDC.

15 *Retailing Home Furnishings.*

16 "Folly Cove Designers: Yankee Prints Get National Recognition," *Life*, November 25, 1945.

17 Dorothy Norton to Peter Leavitt, 28 November 1945, TFCDC.

18 Dorothy Norton to David Williams, 5 December 1945, TFCDC.

19 M.A. Dalton to Dorothy Norton, 14 September 1945, TFCDC.

20 Dorothy Norton to M.A. Dalton, 8 October 1945.

21 Dorothy Norton to M.A. Dalton, 8 October 1945.

22 Reason for reserving the right to print by hand (Norton to M.A. Dalton, 8 October 1945); Dorothy Norton to Peter Leavitt, 26 November 1945, TFCDC.

23 Norton to M.A. Dalton, 8 October 1945.

24 Peter Leavitt to Dorothy Norton, 9 November 1945, TFCDC.

25 $75 listed in attachment to letter (Peter Leavitt to Dorothy Norton, 9 November 1945).

26 Percentage listed in attachment to letter (Peter Leavitt to Dorothy Norton, 9 November 1945); screen print would have involved screen printing by hand. "Machine printed for fabric... is either rotary screen or possibly copper rollers. If it is machine printed wallpaper, it is either surface printed, gravure or rotary" (Pamela Marshall [creative director for design firm Patterson Flynn], forwarded by Katherine Kalapinski [Schumacher employee], email to the author, May 6, 2022).

27 Dorothy Norton to David Williams, 5 December 1945.

28 Dorothy Norton to David Williams, 5 December 1945.

29 Rene worked at F. Schumacher as the merchandising director according to his daughter (Nina Carrillo de Albornoz, email to the author, February 12, 2021); another letter listed Rene's position as "print buyer" (Peter Leavitt to Dorothy Norton, 25 January 1946, TFCDC); name of family company and date of sale as 1931 (Nina Carrillo de Albornoz, email to author); this article lists 1933 as the date Carrillo sold his family company to F. Schumacher (Jeffrey Simpson, "Fashionably Inspired: At F. Schumacher, a Tradition of Combining Couture and Interior Design," April 30, 2008, *Architectural Digest*, https://www.architecturaldigest.com/story/schumacher-article).

30 Avodica Ash [former curator of F. Schumacher], forwarded by Katherine Kalapinski [Schumacher employee], email to the author, May 16, 2018.

31 Vera Neumann detail from Avodica Ash email (Avodica Ash, forwarded by Katherine Kalapinski, May 16, 2018); Dorothy Draper detail from Nina Carrillo email (Nina Carrillo de Albornoz, email to the author, February 12, 2021); Frank Lloyd Wright line listed on F. Schumacher website ("Collaborators: Frank Lloyd Wright," https://fschumacher.com/collaborators/applied-architecture).

32 Rene Carrillo to Dorothy Norton, 17 January 1946, TFCDC.

33 "The Ricardos Change Apartments," episode of *I Love Lucy*, airdate May 18, 1953 (Avodica Ash, forwarded by Katherine Kalapinski, May 16, 2018).

34 Dorothy Norton to Rene Carrillo, 2 April 1946, TFCDC.

35 Dorothy Norton to Rene Carrillo, 5 June 1946, TFCDC.

36 Dorothy Norton to Rene Carrillo, 5 June 1946.

37 Rene Carrillo to Dorothy Norton, 18 June 1946, TFCDC.

38 Rene Carrillo to Dorothy Norton, 18 June 1946.

39 Undated royalty payment statements for 1946 and 1947, TFCDC; F. Schumacher list of Folly Cove Designers' prints (Rene Carrillo to Dorothy Norton, 11 February 1947, TFCDC).

40 Avodica Ash, forwarded by Katherine Kalapinski, May 16, 2018; Katie Rodger, "Back to the Future? Milk Fibers in the 21st Century," March 2019, *Splash*, International Milk Genomics Consortium, https://milkgenomics.org/article/back-to-the-future-milk-fibers-in-the-21st-century/.

41 Avodica Ash, forwarded by Katherine Kalapinski, May 16, 2018.

42 Samples of the six Lord & Taylor designs were received by the group (Dorothy Norton to Peter Leavitt, 8 February 1947, TFCDC); additional designs (Avodica Ash, forwarded by Katherine Kalapinski, May 16, 2018).

43 Agreement between F. Schumacher & Co. and Folly Cove Designers, November 30, 1945, TFCDC.

44 Rene Carrillo to Dorothy Norton, 3 August 1950, TFCDC.

45 Dorothy Norton to Rene Carrillo, 2 April 1946.

46 Rene Carrillo to Dorothy Norton, 30 November 1945, TFCDC.

47 Analysis that it was a little understood field (Pat Kirkham and Lynne Walker, "Context and Issues," in *Women Designers in the USA 1900–2000: Diversity and Difference*, ed. Pat Kirkham [New Haven, CT: Yale University Press, 2000], 72); from the outset designers requested that "the name or initials of the designer" be added (Dorothy Norton to Rene Carrillo, 10 December 1945, TFCDC); Carillo agreed to add designers' initials, as full names might "make the legend too long to print within the repeat" (Rene Carillo to Dorothy Norton, 12 December 1945, TFCDC); the initial samples also did not have the individual designers' initials so the group inquired again about "using the initials of the designer in the margin" (Dorothy Norton to Rene Carrillo, 2 April 1946).

48 A fabric sample of *Clover* by Louise Kenyon lists the design name and her initials in the selvedge (collection of Ann and Sue Kenyon).

49 Mary Brandt to Dorothy Norton, 18 September 1945, TFCDC; plans for a window display like Lord & Taylor's (Mary Brandt to Dorothy Norton, 11 October 1945, TFCDC).

50 Plants, photographs, slides, U.S. Forest Service material, listed on accounts payable receipt, dated October 27, 1945, TFCDC; description of items and Georgia architecture and iron grillwork photos mentioned (Mary Kistner to Mrs. Demetrios, 27 October 1945, TFCDC); on local color (Mary Kistner to Mrs. Demetrios, 27 October 1945).

51 Dorothy Norton to Mary Kistner, 12 December 1945, TFCDC.

52 Mary Kirstner to Dorothy Norton, 14 December 1945, TFCDC.

53 Howard Hughes to Dorothy Norton, 26 December 1945, TFCDC.

54 Dorothy Norton to Howard Hughes, 29 December 1945, TFCDC.

55 Memorandum samples, March 26, 1946, TFCDC; reference to spring style show (H.L. Holland, Jr., to Dorothy Norton, 21 June 1946, TFCDC).

56 H.L. Holland, Jr., to Dorothy Norton, 18 May 1946, TFCDC.

57 H.L. Holland, Jr., to Dorothy Norton, 18 May 1946; H.L. Holland, Jr., to Dorothy Norton, 21 June 1946.

58 George Gibson to Dorothy Norton, 18 March 1947, TFCDC.
59 George Gibson to Dorothy Norton, 11 July 1947, TFCDC.
60 George Gibson to Dorothy Norton, 11 July 1947.
61 George Gibson to Dorothy Norton, 11 July 1947.
62 Five out of ten of the Centennial Prints were created by members of the Folly Cove Designers (George Gibson to Dorothy Norton, 31 December 1947, TFCDC).
63 Eleanor Dexter, "Even Foreign Visitors Come to Folly Cove Designers," *Gloucester Daily Times*, July 31, 1964, 2-A.
64 The other two designs were *Centennial Promenade* by Maria Wilson and *Spirit of '48* (originally titled *1848–1948*) by Irina Tolford; Dorothy Norton listed the submission of *Centennial Promenade* by Maria Wilson (Dorothy Norton to George Gibson, 14 October 1947, TFCDC), but the Cape Ann Museum catalog cites this designer's name as Lili Wilson (*The Folly Cove Designers: 1941–1969* [Gloucester, MA: Cape Ann Museum, 1996, amended and reprinted 2017], exhibition catalog).
65 Chicago-based I. Doctor Dress Company purchased Irina Tolford's *Spirit of '48* and Famous Dress Company of Cleveland purchased Virginia's *Stitch in Time* design (George Gibson to Dorothy Norton, 28 January 1948, TFCDC).
66 R.H. Stearns as an "upscale" department store that "was well known for women's clothing and accessories" (Charles Boston, "Shopping Days in Retro Boston," [blog], January 25, 2011, https://shopping daysinretroboston.blogspot.com/search?q=stearns).
67 George Gibson to Dorothy Norton, 28 January 1948.
68 George Gibson to Dorothy Norton, 13 September 1948, TFCDC.
69 Dorothy Norton to George Gibson, 3 May 1948, TFCDC; George Gibson to Dorothy Norton, 13 September 1948.
70 Interest in using *Tiger* (George Gibson to Dorothy Norton, 13 September 1948); details of when *Tiger* was produced are not known; mention of billing for the design and intentions of using it "in the coming season's collection" (George Gibson to Dorothy Norton, 30 November 1948, TFCDC); still not released as of fall 1949 (George Gibson to Dorothy Norton, 26 September 1949, TFCDC).
71 Submissions (Dorothy Norton to George Gibson, 10 December, 1949, TFCDC).
72 George Gibson to Dorothy Norton, 8 February 1950, TFCDC.
73 George Gibson to Dorothy Norton, 8 February 1950.
74 George Gibson to Dorothy Norton, 8 February 1950.
75 George Gibson to Dorothy Norton, 8 February 1950.
76 "Folly Cove Design Pupils Holding Display of Work," *Gloucester Daily Times*, July 15, 1940.
77 Robert West Howard, "Designed in Folly Cove," *Country Gentleman*, February 1949.
78 Dorothy Norton, rules and regulations, 1945, in binder.
79 List of wholesale prices for 1956, TFCDC; list of wholesale prices for 1969, TFCDC.
80 Dorothy Norton, rules and regulations, 1945.
81 Dorothy Norton, rules and regulations, 1945.
82 List of wholesale prices for 1969.
83 Muriel Lee Steele, interview by the author, May 29, 2010.
84 Dorothy Norton to Leota Diesel (*Life*), "Folly Cove Designers" attachment, 7 October 1945, TFCDC.
85 Dorothy Norton to George Gibson, 14 June 1948, TFCDC.
86 Casual and practical style (Muriel Lee Steele, interview by the author); spinning recollection (Lee Natti, telephone interview by the author, May 28, 2010); skirts were available to order with gathered waists, box pleats, or knife pleats (Dorothy Norton, "skirt orders" in binder).
87 Frederick P. Lawrence to Dorothy Norton, 14 July 1950, TFCDC.
88 Frederick P. Lawrence to Dorothy Norton, 14 July 1950.
89 Frederick P. Lawrence to Dorothy Norton, 14 July 1950.
90 Dorothy Norton to Frederick P. Lawrence, 19 July 1950, TFCDC.
91 Dorothy Norton to Frederick P. Lawrence, 19 July 1950.
92 Dorothy Norton to Frederick P. Lawrence, 6 November 1950, TFCDC; Aino Clarke said that Virginia displayed an ash tree design of Aino's in her studio (Aino Clarke, interview by Theodora Martin, January 9, 1991, TFCDC).
93 Dorothy Norton to Frederick P. Lawrence, 20 November 1950, TFCDC.
94 Frederick P. Lawrence to Dorothy Norton, 21 January 1952, TFCDC.
95 Dorothy Norton to Frederick P. Lawrence, 2 February 1952, TFCDC.
96 Frederick P. Lawrence to Dorothy Norton, 21 January 1952.
97 Frederick P. Lawrence to Dorothy Norton, 21 January 1952.
98 Dorothy Norton to Frederick P. Lawrence, 14 March 1952, TFCDC.
99 Dorothy Norton to Frederick P. Lawrence, 14 March 1952.
100 The Iarrobinos said that Aino Clarke had used a magnifying glass to carve one of her music-related designs and Anthony said that he had used one for *Beach Ballet* (Anthony and Elizabeth Iarrobino, interview by Theodora Martin, October 21, 1991, TFCDC).
101 The process involved the group listing the products they produced, as well as providing samples and drawings ("Notes taken during meeting with Mr. Roewer and Mr. Segal regarding Folly Cove trade-mark," August 23, 1946, TFCDC); added protection ("Notes taken during meeting with Mr. Roewer and Mr. Segal regarding Folly Cove trade-mark"); final trademark paperwork for Wallpaper and Wrapping Paper with image of logo, U.S. Trademark 438, 011, TFCDC.
102 Trademarks received under the categories of: Class 38 Picture Prints, Christmas Cards and Calendars, Class 37 Wallpaper and Wrapping Paper, Class 42 Knitted and Textile Fabrics and Class 39 Clothing (Robert Segal to Dorothy Norton, 13 April 1948, TFCDC).
103 Dorothy Norton references the advice of Lord & Taylor's David Williams and F. Schumacher's Rene Carrillo advising Folly Cove not to copyright individual designs (Dorothy Norton to Dorothy Shaver, 20 June 1947, TFCDC); Rene Carrillo wrote, "I do not feel it worth while [*sic*] to copywrite [*sic*] your individual designs..." (Rene Carrillo to Dorothy Norton, 10 September 1946, TFCDC); the group's attorney mentioned that some "well known designers" opt to register for design patents but said that "little protection against infringement is really provided. Only slight variations will change a design patent" (Robert Segal to Dorothy Norton, 31 August 1946, TFCDC); Eino stated that the designs could not be copyrighted ("Eino Natti Tells Rotarians About Art as Craft, Business," *Gloucester Daily Times*, January 15, 1952).
104 Correspondence regarding Louise Kenyon's alleged infringement (Dorothy Norton to William Lord, 2 July 1947, TFCDC); correspondence regarding Peggy Norton's alleged infringement (Dorothy Norton to Cohn, Hall & Marx Co., 1 June 1955, TFCDC).
105 Libby recalled that it was Leon Kroll's wife who wore the copycat dress. She added "We always thought she did it on purpose..." (Elizabeth [Libby] Holloran, interview by Theodora Martin, June 11, 1992, TFCDC); Dorothy Norton's papers consisted of ads featuring the stolen designs, so it is possible it was brought to their attention via reading the publications (TFCDC); in a letter Dorothy wrote that "inquiries from both wholesale and retail customers asking if we had authorized the use of our 'Potpourri' design" had prompted them to reach out (Dorothy Norton to Cohn, Hall & Marx Co., 1 June 1955).
106 Dorothy Norton to Cohn, Hall & Marx Co., 1 June 1955.

107 Galey & Lord's response to the alleged Kenyon infringement specified that the design had been cleared through the Design Registration Bureau of the National Federation of Textiles (Galey & Lord to Dorothy Norton, 15 July 1947, TFCDC); Dorothy Norton responded by thanking them and saying "a firm cannot be expected to take any further precautions regarding a design if it has been approved the Design Registration" (Dorothy Norton to William Lord, 22 July 1947, TFCDC); Dorothy Norton received a response from Cohn, Hall & Marx Co.'s attorney regarding the alleged Peggy Norton infringement. They requested the "number of the design patent" (Lester Melzer to Dorothy Norton, 15 June 1955, TFCDC). Since they did not have one, this request seemed to put an end to the issue.

108 The group started this practice in 1956 (Dorothy Norton, timeline in binder).

109 Sally Ann Macfarlane to Dorothy Norton, 28 October 1947, TFCDC.

110 Sally Ann Macfarlane to Dorothy Norton, 28 October 1947; Aino Clarke did the lettering for some of the group's exhibit invitations, as well as an edition of *Song of Robin Hood* that Virginia illustrated; there are also references that designer Margaret Nelson was working on color overlays of her design for the book *With the Indians in the Rockies* (Sally Ann Macfarlane to Dorothy Norton, 26 November 1947, TFCDC); Margaret Nelson is listed as the illustrator for Houghton Mifflin's edition of *With the Indians* and the date recorded was 1947 (Dorothy Norton, list of "special designs" in binder).

111 Invoice from Houghton Mifflin, December 22, 1947, TFCDC.

112 It is not known for certain which designer was responsible for the cover illustrations for this series.

113 Attribution and observation regarding similarity to *The Emperor's New Clothes* illustration made by Susanna Natti (Susanna Natti, email to the author, May 6, 2022); sun observation by the author.

114 Lee's design is listed as 1966 in one accounting ledger. In the same ledger Peggy's design is handwritten (the others are typed) but crossed out (accounting ledger, 1963–1966, TFCDC); Dorothy Norton listed the date of 1964 for both Sturbridge designs (Dorothy Norton, list of "special designs"); the discrepancy in dates may be due to the design being an exclusive print for "about five years" so Natti did not debut it with the designers until 1966 (Eleanor Dexter, "New Design—Flowers, Plovers at Folly Cove," *Gloucester Daily Times*, August 12, 1966).

115 Lee's interest in historic items (Lee Natti, interview by Sinikka Nogelo, *The Folly Cove Designers*).

116 Exhibition catalog lists Lee Natti's *Grecourt* as 1954 and Louise's *Smith College* as 1955 (*The Folly Cove Designers: 1941–1969*); an accounting ledger also lists Lee's design as 1954 and Louise's as 1955 (accounting ledger, 1950–1955, TFCDC); Dorothy Norton cites 1954 for both designs (Dorothy Norton, list of "special designs"); both designs were commissioned in 1954 according to Cara White of the Cape Ann Museum (Nanci Young, forwarded by Susanna Natti, June 7, 2021).

117 Jean (Brown) Poole listed herself as a "sales agent for Folly Cove Designers" ("Class News," *Smith Alumnae Quarterly*, winter 1954, 121); the Smith agent was paid 10 percent of the Smith College sales by the designers in 1955 (accounting ledger, 1950–1955); the group once wrote to an interested agent, "Our policy has always been to deal directly with a company purchasing our designs...because as soon as someone acts for us in this capacity, we have no control over the placing and use of our designs" (Dorothy Norton to Mr. C.F. Bruno, Jr., 16 April 1952, TFCDC).

118 Ad in *Smith Alumnae Quarterly*, Fall 1955, 35.

119 Louise Kenyon, interview by Sinikka Nogelo, *The Folly Cove Designers*; mention of visiting campus (Louise Kenyon, interview by Theodora Martin, October 6, 1991, TFCDC).

120 Louise Kenyon, interview by Nogelo.

121 Louise Kenyon, interview by Martin.

122 Ad in *Smith Alumnae Quarterly*, Fall 1955, 35.

123 Louise Kenyon's submission was presumably her cow-based design *Thirty-four Cows*, which actually features thirty-five cows. The design wasn't released until 1954, but often submissions consisted of sketches and not a finished design (accounting ledger, 1950–1955); Dorothy Norton's binder cites 1951, Cape Ann Museum exhibition catalog cites 1952 as the year Peggy's design was released (Dorothy Norton, binder; *The Folly Cove Designers: 1941–1969*); napkins were also mentioned but the block is too big to be printed on a napkin so it is assumed that the napkins were plain, fringed fabric meant to coordinate with the printed place mats (Dorothy Norton to Mrs. Goyette [Guernsey Society], 20 February 1952, TFCDC).

124 Copy of undated letter from Peggy Norton to Mrs. Goyette, detailing her design research and elements of the design, TFCDC; in one interview Peggy said that she sketched a cow at Pingree Farm in Topsfield, Massachusetts (Margaret Norton, interview by Linda Brayton and David Masters, June 14, 1978, in "Toward an Oral History of Cape Ann," Gloucester Oral History Collection, Sawyer Free Library, North of Boston Library Exchange, Inc., 3 sound files, digital, MPEG3 file, NOBLE Digital Heritage, https://digitalheritage.noblenet.org/noble/items/show/1085).

125 Draft of in-house history in "Virginia Lee Burton Notes" folder, undated, TFCDC.

126 Accounting ledger, 1950–1955.

127 Accounting ledger, 1950–1955.

128 Lee Natti, interview by Theodora Martin, October 17, 1991, TFCDC.

129 Dorothy Norton, timeline in binder.

130 Dorothy Norton, rules and regulations.

131 Dorothy Norton, rules and regulations.

132 The ledger shows a 3 percent deduction and Massachusetts did not start charging sales tax until 1966 (accounting ledger, 1950–1955); by 1950 the group was also renting the Demetrios family's barn as their retail space so there was more overhead (accounting ledger, 1950–1955).

133 Accounting ledger, 1950–1955; the group bought fabric from the local Pequot Mills in 1950 (accounting ledger, 1950–1955); Lee Natti, interview by Theodora Martin, June 2, 1992, TFCDC.

134 Florence M. [*sic*] Pettit, "Hand blocking: an easy way to print fabrics," *Craft Horizons* 15, no. 2 (March/April, 1955): 39.

135 The Folly Cove Designers actually charged less for a wall hanging than a set of four place mats (list of suggested retail prices, April 1, 1966, TFCDC).

136 Lee Natti, interview by Theodora Martin, October 17, 1991.

137 "Summary of Amounts Paid to Individual Designers, December 31, 1950," in accounting ledger, 1950–1955, TFCDC; inflation calculated using January to January dates, "CPI Inflation Calculator," U.S. Bureau of Labor Statistics, accessed May 2022, https://www.bls.gov/data/inflation_calculator.htm.

138 Dorothy Norton, "record of accounts after the headquarters were established at 1269 Washington Street, Gloucester, MA," in binder; "CPI Inflation Calculator."

139 Individual sales ("Paid to Individual Designers for stock and completed sales," accounting ledger, 1956–1962, TFCDC); gross sales from wholesale and retail (Dorothy Norton, record of accounts after the headquarters were established at 1269 Washington Street, Gloucester, MA, in binder); "CPI Inflation Calculator."

140 Gross sales from wholesale and retail (Dorothy Norton, record of accounts after the headquarters were established at 1269 Washington Street, Gloucester, MA); individual earnings ("Summary of payments made to individual designers for the sale of their consignment stock and completed orders for January 1 to December 31, 1969" in accounting ledger, 1967–1972, TFCDC); "CPI Inflation Calculator."

141 Lee Natti, interview by Theodora Martin, October 27, 1995, TFCDC.

142 Dexter, "Even Foreign Visitors Come to Folly Cove Designers."

143 Dorothy Norton to Peter Leavitt, 28 November 1945.

144 F. Schumacher (M.A. Dalton to Dorothy Norton, 21 September 1945, TFCDC).

145 "Folly Cove Designers," *Life*.

146 Low overhead ("Babson Discusses: Folly Cove Designers: Their Enterprise and Achievements," *Gloucester Daily Times*, September 1945); Babson's syndicated article was presented in Congress and became part of the 1945 Congressional Record.

147 Documented in "Draft of in-house history"; two early articles do not mention Macy's specifically (Irene Alexander, "Noted Author Returns for Carmel Visit," *Monterey Peninsula Herald*, October 20, 1949; Walter Carey, "Massachusetts's Designing Women," *Magazine Digest*, December 1945); in a 1964 article the group said that they met with representatives of R.H. Macy in New York after meeting with America House (very early on) and this is when the infamous exchange took place (Dexter, "Even Foreign Visitors Come to Folly Cove Designers"); none of the business correspondence mentions this interaction, but there is mention of R.H. Macy representatives visiting Dorothy Norton with indication that the group felt they couldn't take on more department store orders due to war-related fabric shortages (Dorothy Norton to David Williams, undated but likely May 1945 due to context, TFCDC); Norton mentions not having acknowledged an inquiry by R.H. Macy's (Norton to Peter Leavitt, 28 November 1945).

148 Lee Kingman Natti, interview by Linda Brayton and David Masters, July 11, 1978, in "Toward an Oral History of Cape Ann," Gloucester Oral History Collection, Sawyer Free Library, North of Boston Library Exchange, Inc., 3 sound files, digital, MPEG3 file, NOBLE Digital Heritage, https://digitalheritage.noblenet.org/gloucester/items/show/1296; Aino Clarke said that Virginia had a meeting with Disney and that it did not go well, but that Virginia's brother, Justice Harold Burton, "read the contract and declared it to be the most legally binding document he could recall" (Aino Clarke to Harold Bell, 29 January 1989, TFCDC).

149 Dorothy Norton, letter to Virginia Demetrios, 19 October 1957, collection of the author.

150 Dorothy Norton to Virginia Demetrios, 19 October 1957.

151 Accounting ledger, 1956–1962; Dorothy made note that she "transferred the supplies of cloth, her office equipment and several pieces of antique furniture" to the barn in 1957 (Dorothy Norton, timeline in binder).

152 Dorothy Norton, timeline.

153 For many years, until the designers expanded their season in the late 1950s, Home Industries was still the local, year-round retail outlet for the designers (Dorothy Norton, timeline and *The Folly Cove Designers: 1941–1969*).

154 Tablescapes and flowers (Elizabeth [Libby] Holloran, interview by Theodora Martin, October 15, 1991, TFCDC).

155 The building (Alan Adelson, "They Demonstrate Good Design," *Gloucester Daily Times*, 1963; Eleanor Dexter, "500 View Old and New Works by Folly Cove Designers," *Gloucester Daily Times*, August 8, 1964).

156 Ethel M. Eaton, "Folly Cove Sets High Standards for Design and Achievement," *Christian Science Monitor*, December 22, 1943.

CHAPTER FOUR

1 Hildreth J. York, "New Deal Craft Programs and Their Social Implications," in *Revivals! Diverse Traditions: The History of Twentieth-Century American Craft 1920–1945*, ed. Janet Kardon (New York: Harry N. Abrams in collaboration with the American Craft Museum, 1994), 55.

2 York, "New Deal Craft Programs," 57.

3 Jacqueline M. Schweitzer, "Women's Work: The WPA Milwaukee Handicraft Project," Milwaukee Public Museum, https://www.mpm.edu/research-collections/history/online-collections-research/wpa-milwaukee-handicraft-project.

4 Schweitzer, "Women's Work."

5 Schweitzer, "Women's Work."

6 Schweitzer, "Women's Work."

7 Schweitzer, "Women's Work."

8 Schweitzer, "Women's Work."

9 Virginia studying printmaking in youth (Barbara Elleman, *Virginia Lee Burton: A Life in Art* [Boston: Houghton Mifflin Company, 2002]; inexpensiveness (Dorothy Norton, interview by Linda Brayton and Martin Ray, May 25, 1978, in "Toward an Oral History of Cape Ann," Gloucester Oral History Collection, Sawyer Free Library, North of Boston Library Exchange, 3 sound files, digital, MPEG3 file, NOBLE Digital Heritage, https://digitalheritage.noblenet.org/noble/items/show/1025).

10 Emily Zaiden, "American Craft Council and Aileen Osborn Webb," Craft in America, accessed May 2016, http://www.craftinamerica.org/profiles/american-craft-council-aileen-osborn-webb; Glenn Adamson, *Craft* (New York: Bloomsbury Publishing, 2021).

11 Zaiden, "American Craft Council and Aileen Osborn Webb"; Christine I. Oaklander, "Jonathan Sturges, W.H. Osborn, and William Church Osborn: A Chapter in American Art Patronage," *Metropolitan Museum Journal* 43 (2008), http://www.metmuseum.org/art/metpublications/jonathan_sturges_wh_osborn_and_william_church_osborn_the_metropolitan_museum_journal_v_43_2008.

12 Zaiden, "American Craft Council and Aileen Osborn Webb."

13 Zaiden, "American Craft Council and Aileen Osborn Webb."

14 Zaiden, "American Craft Council and Aileen Osborn Webb."

15 Zaiden, "American Craft Council and Aileen Osborn Webb."

16 Some sources cite her name as Caroë, others Caroé and others simply as Caroe.

17 Sandra Afoldy, *Crafting Identity: The Development of Professional Fine Craft in Canada* (Montreal: McGill University Press, 2005), 57.

18 Bella Neyman, "The (America) House that Mrs. Webb Built," *Magazine Antiques*, July/August 2012, http://www.themagazineantiques.com/articles/america-house/.

19 "History of Folly Cove Designers," undated, The Folly Cove Designers Collection, Cape Ann Museum, Gloucester, MA (hereafter cited as *TFCDC*); the designers developed a close relationship with Caroe; she even asked Virginia to design a logo for a basket business that she planned to start (homework, Virginia Lee Burton Demetrios Papers, Cape Ann Museum, Gloucester, MA [hereafter cited as *VLBDP*]).

20 Zaiden, "American Craft Council and Aileen Osborn Webb."

21 Afoldy, *Crafting Identity*, 56.

22 Afoldy, *Crafting Identity*, 58.

23 Neyman, "The (America) House that Mrs. Webb Built."

24 Zaiden, "American Craft Council and Aileen Osborn Webb."

25 This letter indicates that Hetty Beatty was handling at least some of the Folly Cove Designers' business dealings, prior to the group's hiring of Dorothy Norton. Hetty signed her letter "Hetty B. Beatty,"

for Hetty Burlingame Beatty. Hetty published books under this name ("What's New Under the Sun: News of American Craftsmen's Cooperative Council; Report to the Company," *Craft Horizons* 3, no. 5 [1944], 1).

26 "Timeline of Craft History: 1940s, March 26, 2017," American Craft Council, https://www.craftcouncil.org/post/timeline-craft-history-1940s.

27 Zaiden, "American Craft Council and Aileen Osborn Webb."

28 Afoldy, *Crafting Identity*, 59.

29 Lauria and Fenton, *Craft in America*, 27.

30 Statement about schools having to hire faculty (Cori Sherman North with Susan Teller, "Running the Presses: Women Printmakers As Teachers, 1945–1960," in *Paths to the Press: Printmaking and American Women Artists, 1910–1960*, ed. Elizabeth G. Seaton [Manhattan: The Marianna Kistler Beach Museum of Art, Kansas State University, 2006], 65); increase in educational opportunities in craft analysis (Nurit Einik, "Other Craft Organizations," in "Collected Essays: Development in Post-War American Craft," *Archives of American Art Journal* 50, no. 3/4 [Fall 2011], 24).

31 Lauria and Fenton, *Craft in America*, 27.

32 Lauria and Fenton, 29.

33 "Eino A. Natti, 66, artist-craftsman," *Gloucester Daily Times*, February 7, 1975; Eino's use of the G.I. Bill (Lee Natti, interview by Theodora Martin, October 17, 1991, TFCDC); "Ross Burton, Silversmith Dies in Salem, Aged 58," *Gloucester Daily Times*, March 15, 1970.

34 Eino's submission of *On Parade*, which is likely the same as his *Pass in Review* (list of samples sent to Miss Marjorie Mathias, Office of War Information, New York, NY, undated, TFCDC).

35 Marjorie D. Mathias to Mrs. George Demetrios, 3 October 1945, TFCDC.

36 Dorothy Norton, interview by Brayton and Ray.

37 Shaver served on Aileen Osborn Webb's board of directors, representing the purposeful blending of art and commerce behind much of Webb's work to make fine craft more accessible and for craft to become an economically viable profession. Author Glenn Adamson references Webb's "galaxy of Dorothys" for the fact that she also worked with textile designer Dorothy Liebes and interior decorator Dorothy Draper. (Adamson, *Craft*).

38 "Local Designers Exhibiting Work at Boston Show," *Gloucester Daily Times*, October 7, 1942; "Folly Cove Designers," *North Shore Breeze*, July 4, 1941; *Decorative Textiles, April 4–May 5, 1941* (Andover, MA: Addison Gallery of American Art, Phillips Academy), exhibition catalog.

39 "Folly Cove Designers Offer a Fresh Slant," *Philadelphia Record*, April 5, 1942, 7.

40 *An Exhibition of Contemporary New England Handicrafts* (Worcester, MA: Worcester Art Museum, 1943), exhibition catalog; a tree motif design by Ida Bruno is also included in the catalog, although she is not identified as a Folly Cove designer, probably due to an error in the catalog; Hetty Beatty and Aino Clarke were also in this exhibition; Hetty Beatty's participation in the Worcester exhibition mentioned (*Gloucester Daily Times*, January 3, 1944); Aino Clarke's participation mentioned (*Gloucester Daily Times*, January 17, 1944).

41 Allen Eaton, "The New England Exhibition and the American Handicrafts Movement," in *An Exhibition of Contemporary New England Handicrafts*, 5.

42 Jeannine Falino, "The Arts and Crafts Movement in America, 1890–1930," in Jo Lauria and Steve Fenton, *Craft in America: Celebrating Two Centuries of Artists and Objects* (New York: Clarkson Potter, 2007), 80.

43 Wendy Kaplan, "Introduction: Origins of the Movement," in Wendy Kaplan, *"The Art That Is Life": The Arts & Crafts Movement in America, 1875–1920* (Boston: Little, Brown and Company in collaboration with the Museum of Fine Arts, 1987), 52.

44 Eaton, "The New England Exhibition and the American Handicrafts Movement," 6.

45 Eaton, "The New England Exhibition and the American Handicrafts Movement."

46 Zaiden, "American Craft Council and Aileen Osborn Webb."

47 "News of the Educational and Cooperative Councils and of the Affiliated Groups: American Craftsmen's Educational Council Notes; Exhibitions," *Craft Horizons* 5, no. 13 (1946): 34.

48 Lynn Felsher, "Wesley Simpson: Designer, Stylist and Entrepreneur," in *Silk Roads, Other Roads: Proceedings of the 8th Biennial Symposium of the Textile Society of America*, 2002, Digital Commons at University of Nebraska–Lincoln, accessed June 2016, http://digitalcommons.unl.edu/tsaconf/383; Geoffrey Rayner, Richard Chamberlain, and Annamarie Stapleton, *Artists' Textiles: Artist Designed Textiles 1940–1976* (Woodbridge, U.K.: Antique Collectors' Club, 2012, reprinted 2014), 59–60.

49 Rayner, Chamberlain, and Stapleton, *Artists' Textiles*, 19–22.

50 *Annual International Textile Exhibition* (Greensboro: Weatherspoon Art Gallery, Woman's College of University of North Carolina, 1944), exhibition catalog.

51 Early member Ida Bruno also had work in this show (*Annual International Textile Exhibition*).

52 It is noted in the exhibition catalog that Dorothy Liebes was the "National Director Art and Skill Projects, American Red Cross" (*Annual International Textile Exhibition*).

53 Alexandra Griffith Winton, "Color and Personality: Dorothy Liebes and American Design," *Archives of American Art Journal* 48, no. 1–2 (Spring 2009): 6.

54 Exhibitors (*Annual International Textile Exhibition*); Marianne Strengell was listed as Marianne Strengell Dusenbury in 1944 (*Annual International Textile Exhibition*); background of Marianne Strengell ("Marianne Strengell Papers: History," Cranbrook Academy of Art, Cranbrook Archives, Cranbrook Center for Collections and Research, https://archives.cranbrook.edu/repositories/2/resources/130).

55 Zaiden, "American Craft Council and Aileen Osborn Webb."

56 "Craftsman's World: Exhibitions," *Craft Horizons* 11, no. 1 (1951): 42.

57 "Awards Made in Textile Show in Philadelphia," *New York Herald Tribune*, November 14, 1947.

58 "Mission and History," The Print Club, http://printcenter.org/100/mission-history/.

59 Janet Koplos and Bruce Metcalf, *Makers: A History of American Studio Craft* (Chapel Hill: The University of North Carolina Press in collaboration with University of North Carolina Center for Craft, Creativity and Design, 2010), 148.

60 Allen H. Eaton, *Handicrafts of New England* (New York: Bonanza Books, 1949), 139.

61 Einik, "Other Craft Organizations," 19.

62 Zaiden, "American Craft Council and Aileen Osborn Webb."

63 Traveling scheduling derived from online object description of *Designer Craftsmen U.S.A. 1953* (New York: American Craftsmen's Education Council, 1953), American Craft Council, accessed June 2016, http://digital.craftcouncil.org/cdm/compoundobject/

collection/p15785coll5/id/4150/rec/1; ten venues listed (Zaiden, "American Craft Council and Aileen Osborn Webb"); involvement of the American Federation of the Arts mentioned (Virginia Field to Miss Peggy Norton, 19 December 1955, collection of the author).

64 Afoldy, *Crafting Identity*, 65.

65 Zaiden, "American Craft Council and Aileen Osborn Webb"; number of craftsmen listed as 170 (Mrs. Vanderbilt Webb to Margaret [Peggy Norton], 2 October 1953, jury statement attachment, collection of the author).

66 *Designer Craftsmen U.S.A. 1953*; F. Schumacher provided the cash prizes for the woven upholstery and drapery fabrics category and the printed upholstery and drapery fabric categories (*Designer Craftsmen U.S.A. 1953*).

67 "Ruth Adler Schnee: Modern Designs for Living, December 14, 2019–March 15, 2020," Cranbrook Art Museum, accessed February 2021, https://cranbrookartmuseum.org/exhibition/ruth-adler-schnee/.

68 Dorothy Giles in *Designer Craftsmen U.S.A. 1953*.

69 Dorothy Giles in *Designer Craftsmen U.S.A. 1953*.

70 Einik, "Other Craft Organizations," 19.

71 *Dimension of Design: Second Annual Conference American Craftsmen's Council June 23–June 26, 1958* (New York: American Craftsmen's Council, 1958), exhibition catalog, https://digital.craftcouncil.org/digital/collection/p15785coll5/id/4416/rec/1.

72 "Applying the Theme: General Conclusions," in *Dimension of Design*, 159.

73 Robert W. Gray to Dorothy Norton, 1 September 1954, TFCDC; Dorothy Norton, binder of assorted Folly Cove Designers–related material, 1944–1969, collection of the author.

74 There were two venues, Fitchburg Art Museum (Fitchburg, MA) from March 28 to May 9 and Berkshire Museum (Pittsfield, MA) from June 1 to July 29 (*Massachusetts Crafts of Today—1954* [Boston: Massachusetts Association of Handicraft Groups, 1954], exhibition catalog); it is not known if the group participated in both, although Dorothy Norton listed Virginia's and her own designs and "Fitchburg Art Association" with the dates 1950 and 1954 (Dorothy Norton, binder); a letter mentions the hope of assembling "another portable exhibit," suggesting that the show continued to travel (Robert Gray to Dorothy Norton, 1 September 1954).

75 *Cross-Country Craftsman* 6, no. 5 (mid-November 1945), newsletter.

76 Possibly *Horse Chestnut* was not exhibited and Virginia's *Dance of the Hours* was instead (undated document in TFCDC).

77 Louisa Dresser to Dorothy Norton, 7 November 1955, TFCDC.

78 *Massachusetts Crafts of Today 5th Annual Exhibition* (Boston: The Society of Arts and Crafts, 1956), exhibition catalog.

79 Koplos and Metcalf, *Makers*, 255.

80 Koplos and Metcalf, 257.

81 Emily Zaiden, "The New Studio Crafts Movement," in Lauria and Fenton, *Craft in America*, 211.

82 Peggy mentioned that her first design for the Folly Cove Designers was actually a screenprint. She also mentioned designing her herb catalogs, but it is unclear if she printed those herself (Margaret [Peggy] Norton, interview by Theodora Martin, October 9, 1991, TFCDC); in her 1938 herb catalog she listed "herbal prints" for sale and described them as being "after the style of old woodcuts," although it does not say whether they were screenprints/silkscreens ("Herbs from The Little House," Winter 1938, collection of Peter and Bobbi Kovner); mention of sisters screenprinting together (Dorothy Norton to David Williams, 18 March 1946, TFCDC).

83 Dorothy Norton to David Williams, 18 March 1946.

84 The attachment to this letter lists "Cucumber Vine I & II" (Dorothy Norton to George Gibson, 10 December 1949, TFCDC).

85 Margaret (Peggy) Norton, interview by Martin.

86 Margaret Norton, interview by Linda Brayton and David Masters, June 14, 1978, in "Toward an Oral History of Cape Ann," Gloucester Oral History Collection, Sawyer Free Library, North of Boston Library Exchange, Inc., NOBLE Digital Heritage, 3 sound files, digital, MPEG3 file, https://digitalheritage.noblenet.org/noble/items/show/1085.

87 Examples of Eino's copper etching (Sandy Bay Historical Society, Rockport, Massachusetts).

88 Following teacher Stephen Parrish ("A Little Community of Artists," Cape Ann Museum, https://www.capeannmuseum.org/lanesville-folly-cove); Parrish as Clements's teacher (Allen C. Abend, *Gabrielle DeVeaux Clements: Etcher, Painter, Muralist, Teacher: Late 19th and Early 20th Century Etchings of Baltimore Views* [Baltimore, MD: Abend Fine Art, 2012]); Barbara H. Erkilla, *Village at Lane's Cove* (Gloucester, MA: Ten Pound Book Island Book Company, 2008).

89 *Mary Magna Maletskos* (Gloucester, MA: Cape Ann Museum, 1995), exhibition catalog; "Collographs: Anthony A. Iarrobino, 1913–2006," undated pamphlet, collection of the Iarrobino family.

90 Michael Demetrios, interview by Theodora Martin, June 25, 1993, TFCDC.

91 Robert West Howard, "Designed in Folly Cove," *Country Gentleman*, February 1949, 145.

92 Howard, "Designed in Folly Cove."

93 Dorothy Norton, interview by Brayton and Ray.

94 Aristides Demetrios, interview by Theodora Martin, June 23, 1993, TFCDC.

95 Neyman, "The (America) House that Mrs. Webb Built."

CHAPTER FIVE

1 The Cape Ann Museum cites forty-four (*The Folly Cove Designers: 1941–1969* [Gloucester, MA: Cape Ann Museum, 1996, amended and reprinted 2017], exhibition catalog); Dorothy Norton cited forty-five (Dorothy Norton, interview by Linda Brayton and Martin Ray, May 25, 1978, in "Toward an Oral History of Cape Ann," Gloucester Oral History Collection, Sawyer Free Library, North of Boston Library Exchange, Inc., 3 sound files, digital, MPEG3 file, NOBLE Digital Heritage, https://digitalheritage.noblenet.org/noble/items/show/1025).

2 Aino "helped with the design instruction" beginning in 1941 (Dorothy Norton, timeline in binder of assorted Folly Cove Designers–related material, 1944–1969, collection of the author).

3 Aino Clarke, interview by Theodora Martin, January 9, 1991, The Folly Cove Designers Collection, Cape Ann Museum, Gloucester, MA (hereafter cited as *TFCDC*).

4 Aino Clarke, interview by Martin.

5 The copyright was in Aino's name (Clarke, Aino Yrjola) and credited her with the arrangement. Joshua Tolford (a Folly Cove designer) was credited with design and words. The copyright entry is dated August 5, 1948, with a copyright number of EP29094.

6 Both Virginia and Aino are among those credited for help with the music of a book illustrated by Joshua Tolford (Robert Chase, comp., *Hullabaloo, and Other Singing Folk Games* [Boston: Houghton Mifflin, 1949]).

7 Aino Clarke, interview by Martin; Aino Clarke to Harold Bell, 29 January 1989, TFCDC.

8 Aino Clarke to Harold Bell, 29 January 1989

9 High school art classes and background (Aino Clarke to Harold Bell, 29 January 1989; Aino Clarke, interview by Martin).

10 "Childish looking" comment (Aino Clarke, interview by Sinikka Nogelo, *The Folly Cove Designers*, Cape Ann TV, 1985/1986, CD-ROM, 2010).

11 Elephant research process (Aino Clarke, interview by Martin); Aino's mother thought that the design was popular with Republicans, which was not Aino's intention (Aino Clarke, interview by Martin).

12 Aino Clarke, interview by Martin.

13 Lee Natti, interview by Theodora Martin, October 17, 1991, TFCDC.

14 Aino Clarke, interview by Martin.

15 Aino Clarke, interview by Martin.

16 Lee Natti, interview by Theodora Martin, June 2, 1992, TFCDC.

17 Aino Clarke, interview by Martin.

18 Aino Clarke, interview by Nogelo.

19 The Cape Ann Museum catalog lists this design as being created in 1943, which would have been before the United States dropped the atomic bomb on Japan (*The Folly Cove Designers: 1941–1969*).

20 This design was inspired by a local schooner named *Columbia* (Aino Clarke, interview by Martin).

21 Aino Clarke, interview by Nogelo.

22 Aino Clarke, interview by Martin.

23 Aino Clarke, interview by Martin.

24 Virginia credited Aino, although her name was printed as Vrjola (Anne Malcolmson, Grace Castagnetta, and Virginia Lee Burton, *Song of Robin Hood* [Boston: Houghton Mifflin, 1947]); Aino Clarke, interview by Martin.

25 Twins reference (Sally Ann Macfarlane to Dorothy Norton, 28 October 1947, TFCDC); exhibition invite credit (accounting ledger, 1956–1962, TFCDC).

26 Biographical details and working style (Aino Clarke, interview by Martin); Cape Ann Symphony ("Aino Y. [Yrjola] Clarke, 81," obituary, *Gloucester Daily Times*, August 24, 1995); while Aino mentioned being in a quartet, she did not mention being in the symphony when interviewed (Aino Clarke, interview by Martin).

27 Aino Clarke, interview by Nogelo.

28 Barbara Elleman, *Virginia Lee Burton: A Life in Art* (Boston: Houghton Mifflin Company, 2002), 7–8.

29 Virginia had an older sister named Christine and a younger brother, Alexander Ross. Her two siblings from her father's first marriage were Harold Burton and Felix Arnold Burton (Elleman, *Virginia Lee Burton*, 7, 9; Jane Wilgress, *Better Than Beauty: The Life and Work of Jeanne d'Orge* [Pacific Grove, CA: Park Place Publications, 2004], 31, 33).

30 1920 is the year both Demetrios's biographer Elleman and the author of a biography on Virginia's mother, Wilgress, cite as the year her mother moved with the children to California (Elleman, *Virginia Lee Burton*, 9; Jane Wilgress, *Better Than Beauty*, 39); reportedly Lena chose Carmel-by-the-Sea upon the recommendation of artist Marsden Hartley. Wilgress admits that she was not able to confirm that Hartley was the one to recommend Carmel to Virginia's mother (Elleman, *Virginia Lee Burton*, 9; Wilgress, *Better Than Beauty*, 39); incidentally, Hartley painted the area of Gloucester called Dogtown in the early 1930s; Demetrios's former editor Grace Hogarth cited 1916 as the year Virginia moved to California (Grace Allen Hogarth, "Virginia Lee Burton, Creative Artist," *The Horn Book Magazine*, July–August 1943); Virginia does not appear in local newspapers in Carmel until 1920.

31 Elleman, *Virginia Lee Burton*, 10.

32 Alfred Burton's participation in theater and community (Wilgress, *Better Than Beauty*, 40–42); Elleman and Wilgress cite 1925 (Elleman, *Virginia Lee Burton*, 11; Wilgress, *Better Than Beauty*, 43); it is not known whether Lena met Carl in Boston or in Carmel. Wilgress says a source recalled Lena meeting Carl at a painting class given by Lena's friend Robert Hestwood (Wilgress, *Better Than Beauty*, 47).

33 Elleman, *Virginia Lee Burton*, 10.

34 Wilgress, *Better Than Beauty*, 43.

35 Elleman and Wilgress's biographies state that Virginia was sent to live with a foster family and a neighboring family, respectively (Elleman, *Virginia Lee Burton*, 12; Wilgress, *Better Than Beauty*, 43); even her own sons never knew the identity of the family with whom she lived, but it is clear from articles in the Carmel newspapers that Virginia's mother knew the Hestwoods from teaching at summer school together (*Carmel Pine Cone*, July 11, 1925, 7) and later from writing a traveling puppet/marionette show based on Robert Hestwood and his brother's book *Gawpy* (*The Carmelite*, May 22, 1929, 6, and *Carmel Pine Cone*, January 16, 1931, 7); a 1925 newspaper announcement states, "Miss Virginia Burton will study art this winter with Robert Hestwood at Sonora. The Hestwoods and Miss Burton have already left" (*Carmel Pine Cone*, September 12, 1925, 5); both Robert Hestwood and his wife taught at Sonora High School (*Carmel Pine Cone*, June 13, 1925, 9); since Virginia moved to Sonora to continue her studies with Hestwood and attended the high school at which he and his wife taught, it seems to confirm that she lived with the couple during this time as she is not known to have had family in Sonora; when Virginia attended California School of Art, she took classes on the same day that the Hestwoods taught there so it is likely that she continued living with them until she moved to Boston to reunite with her father (Jeff Gunderson [librarian and archivist, San Francisco Art Institute], email to the author, April 9, 2021); on the Houghton Mifflin Harcourt website, Virginia mentions living with a friend from school named Mabel while attending classes at California School of Art but it is not sure for how long (Virginia Lee Burton, "Virginia Lee Burton: Early Years," http://www.houghtonmifflinbooks.com/features/mike_mulligan/earlyyears.shtml); after 1927 the Carmel newspapers made a point to write that Virginia was "formerly of Carmel" (*Carmel Pine Cone*, June 24, 1927, 3); by February 1929, Mrs. Hestwood had remarried, so Virginia's move may have been precipitated by the breakup of the Hestwoods' marriage.

36 Elleman, *Virginia Lee Burton*, 36; Wilgress, *Better Than Beauty*, 43; details about the Hestwoods' Saturday classes, Virginia's enrollment (fall 1927 and spring 1928) and coursework (Jeff Gunderson, email to the author).

37 Elleman, *Virginia Lee Burton*, 13.

38 Virginia Demetrios, *Design and How!*, unpublished manuscript, Virginia Lee Burton Demetrios Papers, Cape Ann Museum, Gloucester, MA (hereafter cited as *VLBDP*).

39 Elleman, *Virginia Lee Burton*, 14.

40 Elleman, 14; H.T.P.'s full name is cited in Irene Alexander, "Noted Author Returns for Carmel Visit," *Monterey Peninsula Herald*, October 20, 1949.

41 Aristides Demetrios, interview by the author, February 9, 2021; working from memory quote (Jacqueline Darcy, "Mrs. Demetrios Has Full-Time Career in Designing Books," *Gloucester Daily Times*, August 18, 1949).

42 Mary Maletskos said that Mary Greer had suggested Virginia take George's class (Mary Maletskos, interview by Theodora Martin,

July 6, 1990, TFCDC); Mary Greer is listed as being a member of the Folly Cove Designers (*The Folly Cove Designers: 1941–1969*); two-minute poses (Margaret Norton, interview by Linda Brayton and David Masters, June 14, 1978, in "Toward an Oral History of Cape Ann," Gloucester Oral History Collection, Sawyer Free Library, North of Boston Library Exchange, Inc., 3 sound files, digital, MPEG3 file, NOBLE Digital Heritage, https://digitalheritage.noblenet.org/gloucester/items/show/1286); Lee recalled sixty-minute poses (Lee Kingman Natti, interview by Linda Brayton and David Masters, July 11, 1978, in "Toward an Oral History of Cape Ann," https://digitalheritage.noblenet.org/gloucester/items/show/1296).

43 Elleman, *Virginia Lee Burton*, 14–15; Aristides told a story of his father fainting upon meeting his mother (Aristides Demetrios, interview by the author).

44 Elleman, *Virginia Lee Burton*, 17.

45 "Virginia Lee Burton: Aris & Mike," Houghton Mifflin Harcourt, http://www.houghtonmifflinbooks.com/features/mike_mulligan/arismike.shtml).

46 Elleman, *Virginia Lee Burton*, 17–18; Mary Maletskos, "The Folly Cove World of Jinnee and George Demetrios," *Cape Ann Historical Association* 6, no. 3 (July–September 1986); Aristides Demetrios, interview by the author.

47 Maletskos, "The Folly Cove World of Jinnee and George Demetrios"; Aristides Demetrios, interview by the author; Elleman, *Virginia Lee Burton*.

48 Aino Clarke to Harold Bell, 29 January 1989.

49 Aino Clarke to Harold Bell, 29 January 1989.

50 Aino Clarke to Harold Bell, 29 January 1989; Elizabeth (Libby) Holloran, interview by Theodora Martin, October 15, 1991, TFCDC.

51 Lee Natti, interview by Martin, October 17, 1991; Maletskos, "The Folly Cove World of Jinnee and George Demetrios."

52 Maletskos, "The Folly Cove World of Jinnee and George Demetrios"; Hogarth, "Virginia Lee Burton, Creative Artist"; Aristides Demetrios, interview by the author; Aino said that Jinnee worked from five to five daily (Aino Clarke to Harold Bell, 29 January 1989).

53 Dorothy Norton, interview by Brayton and Ray; intimidating perception (Anthony and Elizabeth Iarrobino, interview by Theodora Martin, October 21, 1991, TFCDC); Aino Clarke to Harold Bell, 29 January 1989; exact wording (Scrapbook, TFCDC).

54 Aristides Demetrios, interview by the author; Lee Kingman Natti, interview by Brayton and Masters.

55 Margaret Norton, interview by Brayton and Masters.

56 Murals (Aristides Demetrios, interview by the author, and Elleman, *Virginia Lee Burton*, 46–47).

57 Quote about "two alert little critics" as well as inspiration (Virginia Lee Burton, "Speech for June 14, 1943," VLBDP); inspiration and dedications (Elleman, *Virginia Lee Burton*).

58 The subtitle of *Calico the Wonder Horse* was changed from *Or the Saga of Stewy Slinker* to *Or the Saga of Stewy Stinker* likely when Virginia redid the designs in 1950 (Lee Kingman Natti, interview by Brayton and Masters); Aino Clarke said the publisher had originally protested the title *Stewy Stinker* so had changed the title in the first edition (Aino Clarke to Harold Bell, 29 January 1989).

59 Burton, "Speech for June 14, 1943."

60 Burton.

61 Lee Kingman Natti, interview by Brayton and Masters.

62 *Choo Choo* is part of the Cape Ann Museum collection or was listed as being in the collection in fall 2019 (Leon Doucette [Cape Ann Museum assistant curator], attachment to email to the author, November 9, 2019); *Steam Shovel* was mentioned in a letter to a Lord & Taylor executive (Dorothy Norton to David Williams, 23 September 1945, TFCDC). Neither design has been seen by the author.

63 Lee Kingman Natti, interview by Brayton and Masters.

64 Lee Kingman Natti, interview by Brayton and Masters.

65 Lee Kingman Natti, interview by Brayton and Masters; Malcolmson, Castagnetta, and Burton, *Song of Robin Hood*.

66 Eleanor Dexter, "New Design—Flowers, Plovers at Folly Cove," *Gloucester Daily Times*, August 12, 1966, 6A.

67 Lee Kingman Natti, interview by Brayton and Masters.

68 Lee Kingman Natti, interview by Brayton and Masters.

69 Elizabeth M. Roth and Mary L. Brandt, "How to Block Print," *Woman's Day*, January 1945.

70 Dorothy Norton listed three versions: "Swing Tree I, Swing Tree II and Swing Tree Calendar" (Dorothy Norton, list of "designs approved and shown under the Folly Cove name" in binder).

71 *Commuting* (accounting ledger, 1950–1955, TFCDC); all three designs (accounting ledger, 1956–1962, TFCDC).

72 In the collection of the Cape Ann Museum, Gloucester, MA; the block accession number 2019.10.22. The proof print is filed with Virginia's homework, VLBDP.

73 Accounting ledger, 1942–1945, TFCDC.

74 *An Exhibition of Contemporary New England Handicrafts* (Worcester, MA: Worcester Art Museum, 1943), exhibition catalog.

75 It seems that Aino's and Virginia's early designs were sometimes mistaken for each other's work, as an early article misattributed Aino's *Sauna* to Virginia ("Folly Cove Designers Offer a Fresh Slant," *Philadelphia Record*, April 5, 1942, 7).

76 Aristides Demetrios confirmed the attribution of this version of *Reducing* to his mother. It is not known what happened to the original block (Aristides Demetrios, interview by the author).

77 Dorothy Norton to George Gibson, "Designs submitted to William Skinner & Sons" attachment, 10 December 1949, TFCDC.

78 A display board with color swatches and the title of this design exists in the collection of Peter and Bobbi Kovner.

79 Homework, VLBDP.

80 Accounting ledger, 1950–1955.

81 She released two versions of *Fish Story* in 1957 ("Folly Cove Designers Get New Pattern Ideas from What's Around Them," *Gloucester Daily Times*, July 30, 1957, 10).

82 Zaidee was a gift of artist Leon Kroll, supposedly named after a woman George and Virginia met on their honeymoon (Aino Clarke to Harold Bell, 29 January 1989).

83 Virginia mentions a sixteen-piece set (Alexander, "Noted Author Returns for Carmel Visit"); Lee mentioned an eight-piece set (Lee Natti, interview by Sinikka Nogelo, *The Folly Cove Designers*).

84 Dorothy Norton, interview by Brayton and Ray.

85 Halftones (Lee Kingman Natti, interview by Brayton and Masters); Virginia's explanation of her design (Alexander, "Noted Author Returns for Carmel Visit").

86 Popularity of *Zaidee and Her Kittens* (Dorothy Norton, interview by Brayton and Ray).

87 Mary said that they were redone in zinc (Mary Maletskos, "The Folly Cove World of Jinnee and George Demetrios"); benefits of zinc versus linoleum (Frank Romano [President of The Museum of Printing, Haverhill, MA], email to the author, February 17, 2021).

88 Zinc block of *Spring Lambs II* in the collection of Andrew Spindler.

89 Elizabeth (Libby) Holloran, interview by Martin, October 15, 1991; "S. Elizabeth 'Libby' (Johnson) Holloran," Currentobituary.com, accessed 2016, https://www.currentobituary.com/obit/67292.

90 Elizabeth (Libby) Holloran, interview by Martin, October 15, 1991.
91 Elizabeth (Libby) Holloran, interview by Martin, October 15, 1991.
92 Elizabeth (Libby) Holloran, interview by Martin, October 15, 1991; Bob's service in South Pacific cited ("Robert T. Holloran," *Gloucester Daily Times*, https://www.legacy.com/amp/obituaries/gloucestertimes/116768993).
93 The placard specifically said to contact Folly Cove designer Ida Bruno (Elizabeth [Libby] Holloran, interview by Martin, October 15, 1991).
94 Elizabeth (Libby) Holloran, interview by Martin, October 15, 1991.
95 Elizabeth (Libby) Holloran, interview by Martin, October 15, 1991.
96 Elizabeth (Libby) Holloran, interview by Martin, October 15, 1991; Elizabeth (Libby) Holloran, interview by Theodora Martin, June 11, 1992, TFCDC.
97 Elizabeth (Libby) Holloran, interview by Martin, October 15, 1991.
98 Elizabeth (Libby) Holloran, interview by Martin, October 15, 1991.
99 Elizabeth (Libby) Holloran, interview, October 15, 1991; Libby also enlisted the help of her mother to fringe place mats (Elizabeth [Libby] Holloran, interview by Martin, October 15, 1991).
100 Design dates (*The Folly Cove Designers: 1941–1969*).
101 Elizabeth (Libby) Holloran, interview by Martin, October 15, 1991; Libby watched skiers and took photographs to work (Elizabeth [Libby] Holloran, interview by Martin, October 15, 1991).
102 Detail about ski lifts (Beth [Holloran] Bourguignon, email to the author, June 18, 2022).
103 Elizabeth (Libby) Holloran, interview by Martin, October 15, 1991.
104 Ken Davis's sugarhouse was located on the Sugarbush Trail in Jackson, NH, on Black Mountain (Elizabeth [Libby] Holloran, interview by Martin, October 15, 1991); it being a favorite ("Request for Biographical Information: Sarah Elizabeth Holloran," 1996, TFCDC).
105 Elizabeth (Libby) Holloran, interview by Martin, October 15, 1991; retirement (Beth [Holloran] Bourguignon, email to the author, June 3, 2021).
106 Elizabeth (Libby) Holloran, interview by Martin, October 15, 1991.
107 Elizabeth (Libby) Holloran, interview by Martin, October 15, 1991.
108 Louise Kenyon, interview by Theodora Martin, October 6, 1991, TFCDC.
109 Sue Kenyon (Louise Kenyon's granddaughter), email to the author, June 3, 2021; Paul knowing Virginia (Louise Kenyon, interview by Martin).
110 It is not entirely clear from the article whether the comment was made by Louise or Paul's mother, but Louise certainly admired her husband for his tenacity (J.C. Furnas, "Braces Away: A Polio Victim Turns Bad Break into the Best of Good Fortune," *Ladies Home Journal*, February 1947).
111 Louise Kenyon, interview by Martin; Paul started at *Gloucester Daily Times* in 1933 (Sue Kenyon, email to the author, June 3, 2021).
112 Louise Kenyon, interview by Martin.
113 Louise Kenyon, interview by Martin.
114 Louise Kenyon, interview by Martin.
115 Louise Kenyon, interview by Martin.
116 Louise Kenyon, interview by Martin.
117 Lee Natti, interview by Martin, October 17, 1991.
118 Aino Clarke, interview by Martin.
119 Dorothy Norton mentioned its popularity (Dorothy Norton, interview by Brayton and Ray).
120 Wall cloth (Louise Kenyon, interview by Sinikka Nogelo, *The Folly Cove Designers*); Lobster Cove (Sue Kenyon, email to the author, June 3, 2021).
121 Louise Kenyon, interview by Nogelo.
122 The original version of *Head of the Cove* exists in the F. Schumacher archives (Avodica Ash [former curator of F. Schumacher], forwarded by Katherine Kalapinski [Schumacher employee], email to the author, May 16, 2018).
123 In 1945 Dorothy Norton wrote a staff member at *Life* that Louise had used the design for "yard goods and as wallpaper," suggesting the block had not been used for printing place mats yet (Dorothy Norton to Leota Diesel [*Life*], "Folly Cove Designers" attachment, 7 October 1945, TFCDC), although the author owns a place mat printed in the original composition (collection of the author).
124 Dorothy Norton to Rene Carrillo, 2 April 1946, TFCDC.
125 Furnas, "Braces Away."
126 Louise Kenyon, interview by Nogelo.
127 Louise Kenyon, interview by Nogelo.
128 Louise Kenyon, interview by Martin.
129 Louise mentions not having put Hawaii in, but it is there (Louise Kenyon, interview by Nogelo); Betty Smith, "Blueberry Hill to Alaska," *The Cape Ann Countryman*, 1958; "Designer a Year Ahead of Congress on Alaska," *Gloucester Daily Times*, 1958).
130 "Ida Bruno and Louise Kenyon deal directly with Jays" (Dorthy Norton, rules and regulations, 1945, in binder, TFCDC); before Dorothy became secretary in 1944, different members of the group were involved with the business dealings and this seemed to be a business relationship that Louise had initiated and continued to maintain.
131 An undated ad featuring the bathing suit was kept in Louise's papers with this letter confirming the date (Ruth Broome [advertising manager Jays] to Mrs. Paul B. Kenyon, 9 June 1942, collection of Ann and Sue Kenyon).
132 Furnas, "Braces Away."
133 *Dogwood Leaf* had the original tag on it (collection of Ann and Sue Kenyon); *Grapevine* was featured in the January 1945 *Woman's Day* issue and the name of the design was mentioned in this letter (Dorothy Norton to Mrs. M.H. Souvaine, 30 September 1944, TFCDC).
134 Furnas, "Braces Away."
135 Paul B. Kenyon, *Driftwood Captain* (Boston: Houghton Mifflin, 1954); Louise Kenyon, interview by Martin.
136 Louise Kenyon, interview by Martin.
137 Furnas, "Braces Away."
138 Louise Kenyon, interview by Martin.
139 Louise Kenyon, interview by Martin; detail about frequency of cleaning woman (Furnas, "Braces Away").
140 Louise Kenyon, interview by Martin.
141 Louise Kenyon, interview by Martin.
142 Natti family tree, collection of Susanna Natti.
143 *The Folly Cove Designers: 1941–1969*; Sylvester Ahola was born in 1902 so was seven years older than Eino (Barbara H. Erkilla, *Village at Lane's Cove* [Gloucester, MA: Ten Pound Book Island Book Company, 2008], 86–87); "Eino A. Natti, 66, artist-craftsman," February 7, 1975, *Gloucester Daily Times*, 12; his nephew said that his uncle was stationed in Springfield, MA, and played the clarinet (Erik Natti, text communication to the author, November 7, 2021).
144 Susanna Natti (Lee Natti's daughter and Eino's niece), interview by the author, January 2021.
145 "Eino A. Natti, 66, artist-craftsman"; use of G.I. Bill (Lee Natti, interview by Martin, October 17, 1991).
146 Examples in the collection of Sandy Bay Historical Society, Rockport, MA; mention of sculpting and painting (Lawrence Dame, "Regarding Art," *Boston Sunday Herald*, July 29, 1951).

147 There is a possibility that Eino had started taking Virginia's courses before he left for the war since his younger brothers Ilmari and Robert Natti were all in the early classes—before the group had officially organized under the name "The Folly Cove Designers." But there is no evidence that he did.
148 Lee Natti, interview by Martin, October 17, 1991.
149 Mary Maletskos, interview by Martin.
150 Mary Maletskos, interview by Martin.
151 Anthony and Elizabeth Iarrobino, interview by Martin.
152 Accounting ledger, 1956–1962.
153 Demo at America House in New York City ("Craftsman's World: Exhibitions," *Craft Horizons* 11, no. 1 [1951]: 42); talks to the local Rotary Club ("Eino Natti Tells Rotarians About Art as Craft, Business," *Gloucester Daily Times*, January 15, 1952, and "Natti Talks on Design Group," *Gloucester Daily Times*, 1959).
154 Erik Natti, interview by the author, July 2020.
155 Eino Natti homework, collection of Susanna Natti.
156 Erik Natti, interview by the author, July 2020.
157 Including "Hen Party," for Edwin M. Knowles China Company.
158 Observation by art historian James A. Craig.
159 Frederick P. Lawrence to Dorothy Norton, 21 January 1952, TFCDC.
160 "Eino A. Natti, 66, artist-craftsman."
161 A. Ross Burton, *"GI": World War II* (Gloucester, MA: Richard C. Tarr, 1963).
162 Lee Natti, interview by Martin, June 2, 1992.
163 "Designs Created by Eino A. Natti During His Association with the Folly Cove Designers," TFCDC; meaning of *Tempu* ("Folly Cove Starts New Show," *Gloucester Daily Times*, August 1, 1952).
164 Aristides Demetrios, interview by the author; Lee felt that Eino may have negatively impacted his own work output due to his time spent printing for Virginia (Lee Natti, interview by Martin, October 17, 1991).
165 "Mary Lee Kingman Natti," May 31, 2020, *Gloucester Times*, https://obituaries.gloucestertimes.com/obituary/mary-lee-natti-1079309926.
166 Mother's background (Lee Natti, interview by Martin, October 17, 1991); Lee also said her mother worked at a library (Lee Natti, interview by Theodora Martin, October 27, 1995, TFCDC); father's career (Lee Natti, interview by Martin, October 27, 1995).
167 Lee Natti, interview by Martin, October 17, 1991; her desire to be a writer ("Mary Lee Kingman Natti").
168 "Mary Lee Kingman Natti."
169 Lee Natti, interview by Martin, October 17, 1991.
170 "Lee Kingman Papers: Biographical Sketch," de Grummond Collection, McCain Library and Archives, University of Southern Mississippi, https://www.lib.usm.edu/legacy/degrum/public_html/html/research/findaids/kingman.htm; "In Memoriam: Lee Kingman Natti (1919–2020)," The Horn Book, Inc., https://www.hbook.com/?detailStory=in-memoriam-lee-kingman-natti-1919-2020.
171 Lee Natti, interview by Martin, October 17, 1991.
172 Lee Natti, interview by Martin, October 17, 1991.
173 Lee Natti, interview by Martin, October 17, 1991.
174 This source says Lee worked at the insurance company briefly ("Lee Kingman Papers: Biographical Sketch") but Lee said she worked there for two years, which makes sense since she graduated in 1940 and started at Houghton Mifflin in 1942 (Lee Natti, interview by Martin, October 17, 1991).
175 Lee Natti, interview by Martin, October 17, 1991.
176 "In Memoriam: Lee Kingman Natti (1919–2020)."
177 One interview cites Lee as saying that Virginia was working on *The Little House* when they met, which would have been while Grace was Virginia's editor (Lee Natti, interview by Martin, October 17, 1991); other sources say that Lee met Virginia while she was working on *Katy and the Big Snow*, for which Lee served as editor (Lee Kingman Natti, interview by Brayton and Masters; "Mary Lee Kingman Natti"; Susanna Natti, interview by the author, January 2021).
178 Lee Natti to Dale (Johnson) DePeyster, 9 December 1943, collection of Susanna Natti; figure drawing detail (Lee Natti, interview by Martin, October 17, 1991); "In Memoriam: Lee Kingman Natti (1919–2020)."
179 Lee Natti, interview by Martin, October 17, 1991.
180 Detail about Army Air Forces (Susanna Natti, email to the author, July 24, 2021); Lee Natti, interview by Martin, October 17, 1991.
181 Lee Natti to Dale (Johnson) DePeyster; Lee Natti, interview by Martin, October 17, 1991.
182 Lee Natti to Dale (Johnson) DePeyster; Susanna Natti, email to the author, January 28, 2021.
183 Lee Natti, interview by Martin, October 17, 1991; Leonard S. Marcus, "Six Pioneers: Once marginal, children's books are now a huge presence in trade publishing, thanks in part to early innovators," *Publishers Weekly*, July 21, 2008, https://www.publishersweekly.com/pw/by-topic/childrens/childrens-book-news/article/9051-six-pioneers.html.
184 Lee described a daunting learning curve regarding business procedures, estimating costs, and dealing with the male-dominated business and sales side of the industry (Lee Natti, interview by Martin, October 17, 1991).
185 Lee Natti, interview by Martin, October 17, 1991.
186 Lee Natti, interview by Martin, October 17, 1991; Robert's brother Eino was the best man and Lee's friend Mary Maletskos was the maid-of-honor; both would become Folly Cove designers. They were married at the home of Ann Beatty, the sister of Folly Cove designer Hetty Beatty (Susanna Natti, email to the author, January 28, 2021).
187 Robert took all of the coursework, but never finished his dissertation (Lee Natti, interview by Martin, October 17, 1991).
188 Lee Natti, interview by Martin, October 17, 1991.
189 Lee Natti, interview by Martin, October 17, 1991; Lee mentions taking the course with Aino in 1947 but added "maybe 1949" ("Request for Biographical Information: Lee Natti," 1996, TFCDC).
190 *Mill Valley* was originally titled *Connecticut Valley* (Dorothy Norton to George Gibson, 5 September 1947, TFCDC).
191 Lee Natti, interview by Theodora Martin, October 27, 1995, TFCDC.
192 Lee Natti, interview by Martin, October 17, 1991.
193 Lee Natti, interview by Martin, October 17, 1991.
194 Lee Natti, interview by Nogelo.
195 Lee Natti, interview by Martin, October 17, 1991.
196 Lee Natti, interview by Nogelo; Lee Natti, interview by Martin, June 2, 1992.
197 Lee Natti, interview by Martin, June 2, 1992.
198 Lee Natti, interview by Martin, June 2, 1992.
199 Lee Natti, interview by Nogelo.
200 Lee Natti, interview by Martin, June 2, 1992.
201 "Lee Kingman Papers: Biographical Sketch."
202 Lee Natti, interview by Martin, October 17, 1991.
203 Lee Natti, interview by Martin, October 17, 1991.
204 Lee Natti, interview by Martin, October 17, 1991.
205 Lee Kingman Natti, interview by Brayton and Masters.

206 Lee Kingman Natti, interview by Brayton and Masters; Lee says that *Snowflake* took eighty hours (Lee Natti, interview by Nogelo).
207 Lee Kingman Natti, interview by Brayton and Masters.
208 Lee Natti, interview by Nogelo.
209 Lee Natti, interview by Martin, October 17, 1991.
210 Lee Natti, interview by Nogelo.
211 Lee Natti, interview by Martin, October 17, 1991.
212 Lee Natti, interview by Martin, October 17, 1991.
213 "Mary Lee Kingman Natti"; "She also wrote and assembled *The Illustrator's Notebook*, published by the Horn Book. That would make the books she's authored 30. She also produced, with two other authors, the Horn Book compilations of *Illustrators of Children's Books*, one covering the period from 1957–1966, and the other covering the period from 1967–1976" (Susanna Natti, email to the author, May 30, 2022).
214 Lee Natti, interview by Martin, October 17, 1991.
215 Susanna Natti, interview by the author, July 2020.
216 Lee Natti, interview by Martin, June 2, 1992.
217 "Dorothy Norton, designer," *Gloucester Daily Times*, October 16, 1989; Dorothy Norton, resume, TFCDC; some family history (Margaret [Peggy] Norton, interview by Theodora Martin, October 9, 1991, TFCDC).
218 Amy Sacker also designed book covers for Houghton Mifflin in the early 1900s (Mark Schumacher, "Amy Sacker [1872–1965]: Boston Book Designer," The Amy Sacker Site, http://www.amysacker.net/documents/sacker.htm); "Artist Biography & Facts: Amy M. Sacker," askArt, accessed January 2021, http://www.askart.com/artist/Amy_M_Sacker/100032/Amy_M_Sacker.aspx; the name of the school is listed as Miss Amy Sacker's School of Design and alternatively Amy Sacker's School (Schumacher, "Amy Sacker [1872–1965])"; the school was called the School of Miss Amy Sacker (David Pankow, "Fields of Gold: American Decorated Trade Bindings and Their Designers, 1890–1915," Cary Graphic Arts Collection, Rochester Institute of Technology, https://www.rit.edu/carycollection/fields-gold); the school was called Sacker School of Design and Interior Decoration ("Artist Biography & Facts: Amy M. Sacker"); Dorothy's resume listed A.M. Sacker School of Design and Interior Decorating (Dorothy Norton, resume).
219 Dorothy Norton, resume; "Dorothy Norton, designer."
220 Margaret (Peggy) Norton, interview by Martin, October 9, 1991.
221 Dorothy Norton, resume; Dorothy's resume cited the term "executive secretary."
222 The business records at Cape Ann Museum reflect her organizational skills (business records, TFCDC); duties and contributions (Dorothy Norton, timeline in binder); full-time commitment (Dorothy Norton to Virginia Demetrios, 19 October 1957, collection of the author).
223 Elizabeth (Libby) Holloran, interview by Martin, October 15, 1991.
224 Lee Natti, interview by Martin, June 2, 1992; approximate dates Susanna worked at the barn (Susanna Natti, email to the author, July 19, 2021).
225 Lee Natti mentioned that Dorothy never had much stock because she was so involved with the "business end of it" and that this was upsetting to her, in part because she wasn't able to earn money through her designs and yet wasn't earning that much as business manager (Lee Natti, interview by Martin, October 17, 1991); *Village Green* submission (Dorothy Norton to George Gibson, 5 September 1947).
226 Dorothy Norton often received praise or requests for her work in exhibitions. "P.S. May I add I particularly like 'Bird in the Hand,' (Louisa Dresser [Worcester Art Museum] to Dorothy Norton, 19 October 1948 [TFCDC]).
227 Dorothy Norton, interview by Sinikka Nogelo, *The Folly Cove Designers*.
228 Dorothy Norton, notebook, TFCDC.
229 Dorothy Norton, interview by Nogelo; Dorothy Norton, interview by Brayton and Ray.
230 Lee Natti, interview by Martin, October 17, 1991; Lee Natti, interview by Martin, June 2, 1992; Elizabeth (Libby) Holloran, interview by Martin, October 15, 1991; Louise Kenyon, interview by Martin.
231 Lee Natti, interview by Martin, October 17, 1991.
232 The poem erroneously cites the inspiration poet as "Henry Ogden Longfellow" (Lee Natti, "Dorothy Rides Again," undated, collection of Susanna Natti).
233 Elizabeth (Libby) Holloran, interview by Martin, October 15, 1991.
234 Elizabeth (Libby) Holloran, interview by Martin, October 15, 1991.
235 Margaret (Peggy) Norton, interview by Martin, October 9, 1991.
236 Dorothy Norton, interview by Brayton and Ray.
237 Dorothy Norton, interview by Nogelo; Dorothy Norton, interview by Brayton and Ray.
238 Margaret (Peggy) Norton, resume, TFCDC; Margaret (Peggy) Norton, interview by Martin, October 9, 1991; regarding the uncertainty of the Sacker School of Design and Interior Decoration, see note 218; her mother was a portrait painter (Margaret [Peggy] Norton, interview by Martin, October 9, 1991).
239 Margaret (Peggy) Norton, resume.
240 Margaret Norton, interview by Brayton and Masters; rehabilitation detail (Margaret [Peggy] Norton, interview by Martin, October 9, 1991; 1939 (Margaret [Peggy] Norton, resume).
241 Peggy cited 1937 as the date she started her business (Margaret [Peggy] Norton, resume); her mother's background as founder of what Peggy referred to as the "herb society" (Margaret Norton, interview by Brayton and Masters); Frances (Torrey) Norton ("History," the Herb Society of America, https://www.herbsociety.org/about/history.html); Peggy herself belonged to The Herb Society of America (Margaret [Peggy] Norton, resume).
242 Margaret Norton, interview by Brayton and Masters.
243 Margaret Norton, interview by Brayton and Masters.
244 Margaret Norton, interview by Brayton and Masters; Libby Holloran described Peggy as being "stuck together with sticky tape that girl" (Elizabeth [Libby] Holloran, interview by Martin, October 15, 1991).
245 Margaret (Peggy) Norton, interview by Martin, October 9, 1991.
246 Lee Natti, interview by Martin, October 17, 1991.
247 Margaret Norton, interview by Brayton and Masters.
248 Charles Norton (nephew of Peggy Norton), forwarded by Susanna Natti, email to the author, May 19, 2021; the design was listed as *The Little House* by Dorothy (Dorothy Norton, list of "designs approved and shown under the Folly Cove name" in binder).
249 Charles Norton, forwarded by Susanna Natti, email to the author; Margaret (Peggy) Norton, interview by Martin, October 9, 1991.
250 "Herbs from The Little House," Winter 1938, collection of Peter and Bobbi Kovner.
251 "Peggy Norton could put them down beautifully…" (Lee Natti, interview by Martin, June 2, 1992).
252 "Denis L. Batcheller," August 27, 2016, https://www.currentobituary.com/member/obit/197553.
253 Margaret (Peggy) Norton, interview by Sinikka Nogelo, *The Folly Cove Designers*.
254 Dorothy Norton, interview by Brayton and Ray.

255 1950 and 1952 being two years (accounting ledger, 1950–1955).
256 Margaret [Peggy] Norton, interview by Martin, October 9, 1991; it is not entirely clear from the transcript, but it appears Peggy silk screened this first design because she did not have a press yet (Margaret [Peggy] Norton, interview by Martin, October 9, 1991).
257 1950 (accounting ledger 1950–1955); returning to the subject on a smaller scale, but as a linoleum block print (Margaret [Peggy] Norton, interview by Martin, October 9, 1991).
258 Attribution of the floral design to Peggy was made through a printed card with the same design and Peggy's name (Gregory Van Boven Collection); this design was not listed on Peggy's resume, which may indicate that she did not print it as a Folly Cove designer, although at least one of her other designs was missing from her resume as well (Margaret [Peggy] Norton, resume).
259 Arthritis and weaving (Margaret Norton, interview by Brayton and Masters); Lee Natti and Faith Harvey, interview by Theodora Martin, June 24, 1996, TFCDC; Peggy listed 1966 (Margaret [Peggy] Norton, resume); Dorothy listed 1967 as Peggy's retirement (Dorothy Norton, timeline in binder).
260 Lee Natti and Faith Harvey, interview by Martin; Margaret (Peggy) Norton; year of Haystack class (Margaret [Peggy] Norton, resume); instructor information (Paul Sacaridiz [executive director, Haystack Mountain School of Crafts], email to the author, February 24, 2021).
261 Margaret Norton, interview by Brayton and Masters.
262 Margaret (Peggy) Norton, interview by Nogelo.
263 Margaret Norton, interview by Brayton and Masters; Margaret (Peggy) Norton, interview by Martin, October 9, 1991.
264 Margaret (Peggy) Norton, interview by Martin, October 9, 1991.
265 Margaret (Peggy) Norton, interview by Nogelo.
266 "Ross Burton, silversmith dies in Salem, aged 58," *Gloucester Daily Times*, March 18, 1970; Ross (Sandy) Burton (son of Ross and Hilja Burton), in discussion with author, May 17, 2022.
267 A. Ross Burton, *"GI": World War II.*
268 Virginia Lee Burton to Paul Brooks, 6 March 1963, VLBDP.
269 Ross (Sandy) Burton, interview by the author, May 17, 2022.
270 "Hilja S. Burton, Owned Rockport Shop," *Gloucester Daily Times*, November 15, 1993; "Folly Cove Design Pupils Holding Display of Work," *Gloucester Daily Times*, July 15, 1940.
271 Ross (Sandy) Burton, email to the author, May 8, 2021.
272 Walter Carey, "Massachusetts's Designing Women," *Magazine Digest*, December 1945.
273 Ross (Sandy) Burton, email to the author, May 17, 2021.
274 Ross (Sandy) Burton, email to the author, May 8, 2021; Ross (Sandy) Burton, email to the author, May 9, 2021.
275 Ross (Sandy) Burton, email to the author, May 9, 2021; "Hilja S. Burton, Owned Rockport Shop."
276 "Request for Biographical Information: Zoe Eleftherio," 1996, TFCDC.
277 Zoe said that she was a member from 1950 to 1952 ("Request for Biographical Information: Zoe Eleftherio"); in this article Zoe says she joined in 1952 (Joy N. Wieder, "Artist Zoe Eleftherio Is Harvard's For Art's Sake Artist of the Month," WickedLocal.com, March 5, 2012, https://www.wickedlocal.com/story/archive/2012/03/05/artist-zoe-eleftherio-is-harvard/39334024007/).
278 Wieder, "Artist Zoe Eleftherio Is Harvard's For Art's Sake Artist of the Month."
279 "Request for Biographical Information: Zoe Eleftherio"; Wieder, "Artist Zoe Eleftherio Is Harvard's For Art's Sake Artist of the Month."
280 "Request for Biographical Information: Robert Timothy Holloran," 1996, TFCDC.
281 Family history ("Request for Biographical Information: Robert Timothy Holloran"); degree in architecture ("Robert T. Holloran"); he also studied at Boston Architectural College and Tufts University ("Request for Biographical Information: Robert Timothy Holloran").
282 "Robert T. Holloran."
283 "Request for Biographical Information: Robert Timothy Holloran."
284 "Robert T. Holloran."
285 Anthony A. Iarrobino eulogy, written and presented by Anthony Iarrobino, Jr., March 2006, collection of the Iarrobino family; Elizabeth Iarrobino eulogy, written and presented by Anthony Iarrobino, Jr., March 2009, collection of the Iarrobino family.
286 This source lists Anthony as earning an MFA in 1936 ("Collographs: Anthony A. Iarrobino, 1913–2006," undated pamphlet, collection of the Iarrobino family); this source also lists MFA (Anthony A. Iarrobino, resume, undated, Collection of the Iarrobino Family); this source said that they both earned BFAs, with Elizabeth receiving hers in 1937 ("Request for Biographical Information: Iarrobinos," 1996, TFCDC); meeting in college (Anthony A. Iarrobino eulogy).
287 Anthony A. Iarrobino eulogy.
288 Elizabeth Iarrobino eulogy.
289 Anthony A. Iarrobino eulogy; Anthony Iarrobino, Jr., email to the author, May 14, 2022.
290 Elizabeth Iarrobino eulogy.
291 Anthony A. Iarrobino eulogy; Anthony A. Iarrobino, resume; classes (Anthony Iarrobino, Jr., email to the author, May 14, 2022).
292 "Collographs: Anthony A. Iarrobino, 1913–2006."
293 Elizabeth Iarrobino eulogy.
294 Salem State and Massachusetts College of Art and Design (Elizabeth Iarrobino eulogy); Elizabeth only listed Massachusetts College of Art and Design but listed 1961 as the year she received her education degree ("Request for Biographical Information: Iarrobinos"); Elizabeth says that she returned to school in 1960 (Anthony and Elizabeth Iarrobino, interview by Martin).
295 Teaching career ("Request for Biographical Information: Iarrobinos"); subjects she taught (Elizabeth Iarrobino eulogy).
296 "Request for Biographical Information: Iarrobinos"; Anthony and Elizabeth Iarrobino, interview by Martin.
297 Anthony and Elizabeth Iarrobino, interview by Martin.
298 "Request for Biographical Information: Iarrobinos"; Elizabeth says she studied with Aino privately (Anthony and Elizabeth Iarrobino, interview by Martin).
299 Anthony and Elizabeth Iarrobino, interview by Martin; Anthony said that "being an artist I think sometimes was a handicap," indicating that the design principles might have felt restrictive to him (Anthony and Elizabeth Iarrobino, interview by Martin); it is not known whether men were exempted from the course or whether their schedules did not allow them to take the course. In many instances where the wife was already a member, maybe it was assumed that their wives would teach them the course.
300 Anthony and Elizabeth Iarrobino, interview by Martin; Elizabeth wrote that she took drawing and sculpture with George ("Request for Biographical Information: Iarrobinos").
301 Elizabeth listed 1960 as their end date ("Request for Biographical Information: Iarrobinos"); Elizabeth cited 1963 (Anthony and Elizabeth Iarrobino, interview by Martin); 1962 cited (Dorothy Norton, timeline in binder).
302 Dorothy Norton to Aris Demetrios, 9 February 1969, TFCDC.
303 Elizabeth Iarrobino eulogy.
304 Anthony A. Iarrobino, resume; Anthony Iarrobino, Jr., email to the author, May 14, 2022.

305 Anthony A. Iarrobino, resume; this group might have been affiliated with the deCordova Sculpture Park and Museum in Lincoln, MA (Anthony Iarrobino, Jr., email to the author, May 14, 2022).
306 Anthony and Elizabeth Iarrobino, interview by Martin; donation (Elizabeth Iarrobino eulogy).
307 Studio versus kitchen table (Anthony and Elizabeth Iarrobino, interview by Martin).
308 Anthony and Elizabeth Iarrobino, interview by Martin.
309 Interests (Anthony A. Iarrobino eulogy); Anthony and Elizabeth Iarrobino, interview by Martin.
310 Elizabeth described the work as figurative (Anthony and Elizabeth Iarrobino, interview by Martin).
311 Anthony also commented, "I think they were a little kind to me when they passed that" (Anthony and Elizabeth Iarrobino, interview by Martin).
312 Humor comment (Anthony and Elizabeth Iarrobino, interview by Martin).
313 Turtles (Alice B. Beer to "Gentlemen," 15 December 1954, TFCDC).
314 "Fanciful Linens," the *New York Times Magazine*, September 22, 1957.
315 Elizabeth Iarrobino eulogy.
316 Hilda Kaihlanen, resume, undated, TFCDC; *The Folly Cove Designers: 1941–1969*.
317 Jim Kurtti, "Hilda Kaihlanen—Happily Colorful," *The Finnish American Reporter*, January 2010.
318 Kurtti, "Hilda Kaihlanen—Happily Colorful."
319 "Hilda S. Kaihlanen," *Gloucester Daily Times*, October 22, 2013, https://obituaries.gloucestertimes.com/obituary/hilda-kaihlanen-772493981).
320 Hilda Kaihlanen, telephone interview by the author, May 28, 2010.
321 "Request for Biographical Information: Mary Ann Lash," 1996, TFCDC; *The Folly Cove Designers: 1941–1969*.
322 "Request for Biographical Information: Mary Ann Lash."
323 "Mary Updike Magna Maletskos, Artist," *Gloucester Daily Times*, March 1, 1993.
324 Mary Maletskos eulogy, written by Lee Natti, presented by Robert Natti, March 1993, TFCDC.
325 *Mary Magna Maletskos* (Gloucester, MA: Cape Ann Museum, 1995), exhibition catalog.
326 "Mary Updike Magna Maletskos, Artist."
327 Lee Natti, interview by Martin, October 17, 1991.
328 *Mary Magna Maletskos*.
329 Reference to her taking the course in 1946 (Mary Maletskos, interview by Martin); Lee Natti not sure whether Mary studied with Aino or Virginia (Lee Natti, interview by Martin, October 17, 1991).
330 Mary Maletskos, interview by Martin.
331 Mary Maletskos eulogy.
332 *Mary Magna Maletskos*.
333 Aino Clarke, interview by Martin.
334 Aino Clarke, interview by Martin; Lee Natti thought Mary studied with Aino before she studied with Virginia (Lee Natti, interview by Martin, October 17, 1991).
335 Aino Clarke, interview by Martin.
336 Lee Natti, interview by Martin, October 27, 1995.
337 Mary Maletskos, interview by Martin.
338 Mary Maletskos, interview by Martin.
339 Mary said that she printed "mostly runners" (Mary Maletskos, interview by Martin).
340 This piece was purchased by a private collector at a Maletskos estate sale.
341 Mary Maletskos, "The Folly Cove World of Jinnee and George Demetrios."
342 He both spelled his name and was referred to alternatively as Ilmar and Ilmari (Erik Natti, text communication to the author, November 7, 2021).
343 Natti family tree.
344 "Folly Cove Design Pupils Holding Display of Work."
345 Natti family tree.
346 "Ilmar" Natti mentioned as being "the lone man of the group" (Ethel M. Eaton, "Folly Cove Sets High Standards for Design and Achievement," *Christian Science Monitor*, December 22, 1943); naturalist lectures (Vera Seppala Olsen, interview by Theodora Martin, June 16, 1992, TFCDC); Dorothy Norton cited "Jimo Natti and Virginia" as having given "lectures on special subjects" in the winter of 1941 (Dorothy Norton, binder); Libby Holloran joined in 1942, but does not remember him being a member (Elizabeth [Libby] Holloran, interview by Martin, October 15, 1991).
347 "Folly Cove Design Pupils Holding Display of Work."
348 Erik Natti, text communication to the author, May 17, 2022; "History," The Medallic Art Company, https://medallicartcollector.com/medallic-art-company.shtml).
349 Anthony and Elizabeth Iarrobino, interview by Martin.
350 Elizabeth (Libby) Holloran, interview by Martin, October 15, 1991.
351 "Isabel A. Natti, December 12, 2011," Currentobituary.com, https://www.currentobituary.com/obit/103722.
352 "Folly Cove Design Pupils Holding Display of Work."
353 Military detail (Susanna Natti, email to the author, July 24, 2021).
354 Lee Natti, interview by Martin, October 17, 1991.
355 "Robert Natti Fund," Gloucester Stage, https://gloucesterstage.com/robert-natti-fund/.
356 Theater and chorus (Lee Natti, interview by Martin, October 27, 1995); pottery (Lee Natti, interview by Martin, June 2, 1992).
357 Jane Nichols-Ecker, interview by the author, September 2015; article about Kenyon family home and the "house's small ell apartment that was rented during the war to a friend" (Furnas, "Braces Away"); branch of service (Jane Nichols-Ecker, text communication to the author, July 28, 2021).
358 Bettine was living there by June of 1942 since there are photos of her and her son Peter at what appears to be the Kenyon home with dates on the back (collection of the Nichols family); in 1945 Dorothy Norton wrote, "Mrs. Nichols came to live in Annisquam about three years ago with her young son..." (Dorothy Norton to Leota Diesel [*Life*], "Folly Cove Designers" attachment, 7 October 1945).
359 Jane Nichols-Ecker, interview by author; "Arthur Ames Nichols," Family Search, https://ancestors.familysearch.org/en/L6FD-HD9/arthur-ames-nichols-1912-1966.
360 Jane Nichols-Ecker, interview by the author; detail about starting practice (Dorothy Norton to Peter Leavitt, 8 February 1947, TFCDC).
361 Jane Nichols-Ecker, interview by author.
362 Dorothy Norton to Peter Leavitt, 8 February 1947.
363 Dorothy Norton to Peter Leavitt, 8 February 1947; Bettine passed away on January 16, 1947 ("Bettine R. Bradish," Family Search, https://ancestors.familysearch.org/en/L6FD-HZD/bettine-r-bradish-1911-1947).
364 Roth and Brandt, "How to Block Print."
365 Collection of the Nichols family.
366 Notebook, collection of the Nichols family.
367 Natti family tree.

368 "Request for Biographical Information: Anna Natti Stephanio," filled out by unidentified person, 1996, TFCDC; meeting her husband (Ellie Fleet [Anna's daughter], email to the author, May 27, 2022).
369 "Request for Biographical Information: Anna Natti Stephanio."
370 Modeling (Genevieve [Mrs. Leon] Kroll, interview by Linda Brayton and David Masters, March 21, 1978, in "Toward an Oral History of Cape Ann," Gloucester Oral History Collection, Sawyer Free Library, North of Boston Library Exchange, Inc., NOBLE Digital Heritage, 2 sound files, digital, MPEG3 file, https://digitalheritage.noblenet.org/gloucester/items/show/1234); Ellie Fleet, email to the author, May 27, 2022.
371 "Request for Biographical Information: Anna Natti Stephanio."
372 "Request for Biographical Information: Mary Ann Mangan," filled out by unidentified person, 1996, TFCDC.
373 Birthdate (*The Folly Cove Designers: 1941–1969*).
374 Art and musical background (Muriel Lee Steele, interview by the author, May 29, 2010); degrees (Kelly Knox, "Folly Cove Designer Shares Her History" *Gloucester Daily Times*, May 27, 2016).
375 Husband's name (*The Folly Cove Designers: 1941–1969* and Susanna Natti, email to the author, May 14, 2022); Muriel Lee Steele, interview by the author.
376 She carved two different size blocks with a geranium design, likely the smaller one for tea towels and the 11x17–inch for place mats and larger items (collection of Muriel Lee Steele).
377 Muriel Lee Steele, interview by the author.
378 Knox, "Folly Cove Designer Shares Her History."
379 There is some discrepancy regarding her birth year; 1907 listed at University of Oregon, which houses her papers and in her obituary ("Hetty Burlingame Beatty Papers," University of Oregon Libraries, scope and contents note, https://scua.uoregon.edu/repositories/2/resources/732 and "Hetty B. Whitney dies, wrote children's books," obituary, *Gloucester Daily Times*, August 27, 1971); the Cape Ann Museum lists 1906 as her birth year (*The Folly Cove Designers: 1941–1969*).
380 "Hetty B. Whitney Dies, Wrote Children's Books"; "Hetty Burlingame Beatty Papers," University of Oregon Libraries, scope and contents note.
381 "Hetty B. Whitney Dies, Wrote Children's Books"; years of study and University of Maryland detail ("Hetty Burlingame Beatty Papers," University of Oregon Libraries, scope and contents note).
382 Listed in first article on the group ("Folly Cove Design Pupils Holding Display of Work").
383 "Hetty B. Whitney Dies, Wrote Children's Books."

CHAPTER SIX

1 Michael Demetrios, interview by Theodora Martin, June 25, 1993, The Folly Cove Designers Collection, Cape Ann Museum, Gloucester, MA (hereafter cited as *TFCDC*).
2 Dorothy Norton, interview by Linda Brayton and Martin Ray, May 25, 1978, in "Toward an Oral History of Cape Ann," Gloucester Oral History Collection, Sawyer Free Library, North of Boston Library Exchange, Inc., 3 sound files, digital, MPEG3 file, NOBLE Digital Heritage, https://digitalheritage.noblenet.org/noble/items/show/1025.
3 Dorothy Norton, interview by Brayton and Ray.
4 Cara Giaimo, "The Unlikely Story of the Folly Cove Guild, the Best Designers You've Never Heard Of," Atlas Obscura, June 14, 2017, https://www.atlasobscura.com/articles/the-unlikely-story-of-the-folly-cove-guild-the-best-designers-youve-never-heard-of.
5 *Retailing Home Furnishings*, August 27, 1945, 12.
6 Top sellers (Dorothy Norton, interview by Brayton and Ray).
7 Aristides Demetrios, interview by Theodora Martin, June 23, 1993, TFCDC.
8 Margaret Norton, interview by Linda Brayton and David Masters, June 14, 1978, in "Toward an Oral History of Cape Ann," Gloucester Oral History Collection, Sawyer Free Library, North of Boston Library Exchange, Inc., 3 sound files, digital, MPEG3 file, NOBLE Digital Heritage, https://digitalheritage.noblenet.org/noble/items/show/1085.
9 Dorothy Norton, interview by Brayton and Ray.
10 Lee Natti, interview by Theodora Martin, June 2, 1992, TFCDC.
11 Lee Natti, interview by Martin, June 2, 1992.
12 Louise Kenyon, interview by Theodora Martin, October 6, 1991, TFCDC.
13 Mahlon Hoagland, interview by Theodora Martin, July 14, 1992, TFCDC.
14 Anthony and Elizabeth Iarrobino, interview by Theodora Martin, October 21, 1991, TFCDC.
15 Dorothy Norton, interview by Brayton and Ray.
16 Anthony and Elizabeth Iarrobino, interview by Martin; Lee Natti, interview by Theodora Martin, October 17, 1991, TFCDC.
17 Mahlon Hoagland, Robert Holloran, and Anthony Iarrobino (Mahlon Hoagland, interview by Martin; Robert [Bob] Holloran, interview by Theodora Martin, December 3, 1991, TFCDC; Anthony and Elizabeth Iarrobino, interview by Martin).
18 Robert (Bob) Holloran, interview by Martin.
19 Mahlon Hoagland, interview by Martin.
20 Anthony and Elizabeth Iarrobino, interview by Martin.
21 Anthony and Elizabeth Iarrobino, interview by Martin.
22 Susanna Natti, email to the author, January 29, 2021; Beth (Holloran) Bourguignon, email to the author, June 3, 2021.
23 "Collographs: Anthony A. Iarrobino, 1913–2006," collection of the Iarrobino family.
24 Eleanor Curtis, interview by Theodora Martin, November 18, 1991, TFCDC.
25 Louise Kenyon, interview by Martin.
26 Faith Harvey, interview by Theodora Martin, April 7, 1994, TFCDC.
27 Margaret (Peggy) Norton, interview by Sinikka Nogelo, *The Folly Cove Designers*, Cape Ann TV, 1985/1986, CD-ROM, 2010.
28 Dorothy Norton, list of "designs approved and shown under the Folly Cove name" in binder of assorted Folly Cove Designers–related material, 1944–1969, collection of the author.

INDEX

O

P

Q

R

S

T

U

V

W

Y

Z

CREDITS

Note: The following abbreviations are used after first mention: Cape Ann Museum (CAM), The Folly Cove Designers Collection (TFCDC), Virginia Lee Burton Demetrios Papers (VLBDP), Sandy Bay Historical Society (SBHS)

COVER

Front cover (clockwise from the top): *Down on the Farm* by Louise Kenyon. Photograph by Gary Lowell. Courtesy of the author; *Home Port* by Louise Kenyon. Photograph by Gary Lowell. Courtesy of SBHS; *Finnish Hop* by Virginia Lee Demetrios. Photograph by Gary Lowell. Courtesy of Sandy Bay Historical Society (hereafter *SBHS*); Spring Lambs by Virginia Lee Demetrios. Photograph by Gary Lowell. Courtesy of SBHS; Photograph by Harold Carter. The Folly Cove Designers Collection (hereafter cited as *TFCDC*), Cape Ann Museum (hereafter cited as *CAM*).
Spine: *Violets* by Eino Natti. Photograph by Gary Lowell. Courtesy of SBHS.
Back cover: *Smith College* by Louise Kenyon. Photograph by Peter Morse. Courtesy of Peter and Bobbi Kovner.

PREFACE

p. 8: TFCDC, CAM. **p. 11:** Photograph by Gary Lowell. Courtesy of Kathryn Soucy.

CHAPTER 1

p. 14: Photograph by Gary Lowell. Courtesy of SBHS. **Fig. 1:** Courtesy of Peter and Bobbi Kovner. **Fig. 2:** Library & Archives, CAM. **Fig. 3:** Virginia Lee Burton Demetrios Papers (hereafter cited as *VLBDP*), CAM. Gift of Aristides Burton Demetrios and Ilene H. Nagel Demetrios. **Fig. 4:** Photograph by Peter Morse. Courtesy of Dan and Evan Shay. **Fig. 5:** Photograph by Gary Lowell. Courtesy of Alex and Angela Subach. **Fig. 6:** Photograph by Harold Carter, *Life*, November 25, 1945. Courtesy of Dan and Evan Shay. **Fig. 7:** Photograph by Peter Morse. Courtesy of Peter and Bobbi Kovner. **Fig. 8:** Courtesy of the Estate of Ilmari Natti. **Fig. 9:** Photograph by Gerda Peterich. TFCDC, CAM. **Fig. 10:** Photograph by Gerda Peterich. TFCDC, CAM. **Fig. 11:** Photograph by Harold Carter. TFCDC, CAM. **Fig. 12:** Photograph by Peter Morse. Courtesy of Peter and Bobbi Kovner. **Fig. 13:** *Gloucester Daily Times*, January 5, 1944. Courtesy of Sawyer Free Library. **Fig. 14:** *Gloucester Daily Times*, January 14, 1944. Courtesy of Sawyer Free Library. **Fig. 15:** *Gloucester Daily Times*, January 15, 1944. Courtesy of Sawyer Free Library. **Fig. 16:** Unattributed, Folly Cove Designer Box, undated, painted wood. CAM. Gift of the Folly Cove Designers, 1970 (2004). **Fig. 17:** Courtesy of the author. **Fig. 18:** Photograph by Eric Roth. Courtesy of Susanna Natti. **Fig. 19:** TFCDC, CAM. **Fig. 20:** Photograph by Gary Lowell. Courtesy of SBHS.

CHAPTER 2

p. 34: Courtesy of the author. **Fig. 21:** TFCDC, CAM. **Fig. 22:** Photograph by Eric Roth. Courtesy of Susanna Natti. **Fig. 23:** Photograph by Gary Lowell. Courtesy of SBHS. **Fig. 24:** VLBDP, CAM. Gift of Aristides Burton Demetrios and Ilene H. Nagel Demetrios. **Fig. 25:** Courtesy of Carl Cherry Center for the Arts, Carmel, CA. **Fig. 26:** VLBDP, CAM. Gift of Aristides Burton Demetrios and Ilene H. Nagel Demetrios. **Fig. 27:** CAM. Gift of Christine Kahane, 2016 (2016.078). **Fig. 28:** Photograph by Peter Morse. Courtesy of Anne Morin. **Fig. 29:** CAM. **Fig. 30:** Photograph by Gary Lowell. Courtesy of SBHS. **Fig. 31:** Photograph by Gary Lowell. Courtesy of SBHS. **Fig. 32:** VLBDP, CAM. Gift of Aristides Burton Demetrios and Ilene H. Nagel Demetrios. **Fig. 33:** Photograph by Gary Lowell. Courtesy of SBHS. **Fig. 34:** Photograph by Eric Roth. Courtesy of Andrew Spindler. **Fig. 35:** Photograph by Peter Morse. Courtesy of the Iarrobino family. **Fig. 36:** Photograph by Peter Morse. Courtesy of the Iarrobino family. **Fig. 37:** Photograph by Gary Lowell. Courtesy of SBHS. **Fig. 38:** Photograph by Peter Morse. Courtesy of Erik and Theresa Natti. **Fig. 39:** VLBDP, CAM. Gift of Aristides Burton Demetrios and Ilene H. Nagel Demetrios. **Fig. 40:** CAM. Gift of Christine Kahane, 2015 (2015.082). **Fig. 41:** VLBDP, CAM. Gift of Aristides Burton Demetrios and Ilene H. Nagel Demetrios. **Fig. 42:** CAM. Gift of Christine Kahane, 2015 (2015.082). **Fig. 43:** VLBDP, CAM. Gift of Aristides Burton Demetrios and Ilene H. Nagel Demetrios. **Fig. 44:** Photograph by Gerda Peterich. TFCDC, CAM. **Fig. 45:** Photograph originally taken for *Ladies' Home Journal*, February 1947. Courtesy of Ann and Sue Kenyon. **Fig. 46:** Photograph by Gary Lowell. Courtesy of SBHS. **Fig. 47:** Photograph by Gary Lowell. Courtesy of SBHS. **Fig. 48:** Paul B. Kenyon Papers, CAM. **Fig. 49:** Photographs by the Snivelys. TFCDC, CAM. **Fig. 50:** Folly Cove Designers, Massachusetts (Gloucester), active 1941–1969, *Woman's blouse*, Linen, Center back: 49.5 cm (19½ in.), Museum of Fine Arts, Boston, Gift of Andrew Spindler, 2012.844. **Fig. 51:** VLBDP, CAM. Gift of Aristides Burton Demetrios and Ilene H. Nagel Demetrios. **Fig. 52:** VLBDP, CAM. Gift of Aristides Burton Demetrios and Ilene H. Nagel Demetrios. **Fig. 53:** VLBDP, CAM. Gift of Aristides Burton Demetrios and Ilene H. Nagel Demetrios.

CHAPTER 3

p. 52: Photograph by Gary Lowell. Courtesy of Ann and Sue Kenyon. **Fig. 54:** Photograph originally published in *Views and Reviews* (now Visual Profile Books, Inc.), September 1945. Courtesy of WindowsWear. **Fig. 55:** Photograph originally published in *Views and Reviews* (now Visual Profile Books, Inc.), September 1945. Courtesy of WindowsWear. **Fig. 56:** TFCDC, CAM. **Fig. 57:** Photograph by Gary Lowell. Courtesy of Susana McDonnell and Angus Smith. **Fig. 58:** Photograph by Kevin Kerr. Courtesy of F. Schumacher & Co. **Fig. 59:** *House and Garden*, September 1946. TFCDC, CAM. **Fig. 60:** Photograph by Esther Pullman. Courtesy of the Perry family. **Fig. 61:** Photograph by Peter Morse. Courtesy of Ann and Sue Kenyon. **Fig. 62:** Photograph by Gary Lowell. Courtesy of Ann and Sue Kenyon. **Fig. 63:** CAM. **Fig. 64:** Photograph by Eric Roth. Courtesy of private collection. **Fig. 65:** Photograph by Eric Roth. Courtesy of private collection. **Fig. 66:** Photograph by Gary Lowell. Courtesy of Ann and Sue Kenyon. **Fig. 67:** CAM. Gift of the Folly Cove Designers, 1970. **Fig. 68:** Photograph by Peter Morse. Courtesy of Ann and Sue Kenyon. **Fig. 69:** CAM. **Fig. 70:** Photograph by Eric Roth. Courtesy of Susanna Natti. **Fig. 71:** TFCDC, CAM. **Fig. 72:** CAM. **Fig. 73:** CAM. **Fig. 74:** Lee Kingman Natti, *In Clover*, 1964, cotton, 37½ × 33 inches (95.25 × 83.82 cm), Gift of Lee Kingman Natti, 2009, 138746, Courtesy of the Peabody Essex Museum.**Fig. 75:** Folly Cove Designers, Massachusetts (Gloucester), active 1941–1969, *Day ensemble*, American, Cotton, Center back (skirt): 73.7 cm (29 in.), Center back (shirt): 55.9 cm (22 in.), Museum of Fine Arts, Boston, Gift of Andrew Spindler, 2012.845.1–2. **Fig. 76:** CAM. Gift of Paul Littlefield, 2000 (2000.39). **Fig. 77:** Photograph by Eric Roth. Courtesy of Andrew Spindler. **Fig. 78:** Photograph by Gary Lowell. Courtesy of SBHS. **Fig. 79:** CAM. Gift of Sylvia M. Pingree, 2019, in memory of her mother, Barbara Pingree (2019.018.2). **Fig. 80:** Photograph by Eric Roth. Courtesy of Susanna Natti. **Fig. 81:** Photograph by Peter Morse. Courtesy of Peter and Bobbi Kovner. **Fig. 82:** Photograph by Eric Roth. Courtesy of Andrew Spindler. **Fig. 83:** Photograph by Eric Roth. Courtesy of Andrew Spindler. **Fig. 84:** Photograph by Eric Roth. Courtesy of Andrew Spindler. **Fig. 85:** Photograph by Eric Roth. Courtesy of Andrew Spindler. **Fig. 86:** CAM. Museum purchase, 2014 (2014.019.35). **Fig. 87:** Courtesy of the author. **Fig. 88:** Library & Archives, CAM. Gift of Arthur Ryan, 2017 (2017.006). **Fig. 89:** Photograph by Gary Lowell. Courtesy of Kathryn Soucy. **Fig. 90:** CAM. Gift of the artist (Lee Kingman Natti), 1996 (1996.8.1). **Fig. 91:** Photograph by Peter Morse. Courtesy of Peter and Bobbi Kovner. **Fig. 92:** Photograph by Peter Morse. Courtesy of Peter and Bobbi Kovner. **Fig. 93:** Photograph by Gary Lowell. Courtesy of SBHS. **Fig. 94:** Courtesy of the author. **Fig. 95:** Photograph by Peter Morse. Courtesy of Ann and Sue Kenyon. **Fig. 96:** TFCDC, CAM. **Fig. 97:** TFCDC, CAM.

CHAPTER 4

p. 84: Photograph by Gary Lowell. Courtesy of SBHS. **Fig. 98:** TFCDC, CAM. **Fig. 99:** Photograph by Leslie Bartlett. Courtesy of Matthew Babson. **Fig. 100:** Photograph by Peter Morse. Courtesy of Ann and Sue Kenyon. **Fig. 101:** Photograph by Gary Lowell. Courtesy of SBHS. **Fig. 102:** Photograph by Gary Lowell. Courtesy of the author. **Fig. 103:** Photograph by Peter Morse. Courtesy of the Iarrobino family. **Fig. 104:** Photograph by Peter Morse. Courtesy of Anne Morin. **Fig. 105:** Photograph by Peter Morse. Courtesy of Peter and Bobbi Kovner. **Fig. 106:** Photograph by Peter Morse. Courtesy of Peter and Bobbi Kovner. **Fig. 107:** Photograph by Gary Lowell. Courtesy of the author. **Fig. 108:** Photograph by Gary Lowell. Courtesy of the author.

CHAPTER 5

p. 100: Photograph by Gary Lowell. Courtesy of SBHS. **Fig. 109:** TFCDC, CAM. **Fig. 110:** Photograph by Peter Morse. Courtesy of private collection. **Fig. 111:** CAM. **Fig. 112:** Photograph by Gary Lowell. Courtesy of SBHS. **Fig. 113:** Photograph by Peter Morse. Courtesy of Peter and Bobbi Kovner. **Fig. 114:** Photograph by Eric Roth. Courtesy of private collection. **Fig. 115:** CAM. **Fig. 116:** Photograph by Peter Morse. Courtesy of Peter and Bobbi Kovner. **Fig. 117:** Photograph by Gary Lowell. Courtesy of Kathryn Soucy. **Fig. 118:** TFCDC, CAM. **Fig. 119:** VLBDP, CAM. Gift of Aristides Burton Demetrios and Ilene H. Nagel Demetrios. **Fig. 120:** Clipping from *Boston Evening Transcript*, Wednesday, October 15, 1930. VLBDP, CAM. Gift of Aristides Burton Demetrios and Ilene H. Nagel Demetrios. **Fig. 121:** Photograph by Eric Roth. Courtesy of Susanna Natti. **Fig. 122:** Photograph by Gary Lowell. Courtesy of SBHS. **Fig. 123:** TFCDC, CAM. **Fig. 124:** Photograph by Peter Morse. Courtesy of Peter and Bobbi Kovner. **Fig. 125:** VLBDP, CAM. Gift of Aristides Burton Demetrios and Ilene H. Nagel Demetrios. **Fig. 126:** CAM. **Fig. 127:** Photograph by Gary Lowell. Courtesy of SBHS. **Fig. 128:** Photograph by Gary Lowell. Courtesy of SBHS. **Fig. 129:** Photograph by Gary Lowell. Courtesy of Gregory Van Boven and David Beck. **Fig. 130:** Photograph by Gary Lowell. Courtesy of Gregory Van Boven and David Beck. **Fig. 131:** Photograph by Gary Lowell. Courtesy of Gregory Van Boven and David Beck. **Fig. 132:** CAM. Gift of Aristides Burton Demetrios and Ilene H. Nagel Demetrios, 2019 (2019.010.22). **Fig. 133:** CAM. Gift of Aristides Burton Demetrios and Ilene H. Nagel Demetrios, 2019 (2019.010.21). **Fig. 134:** Photograph by Gary Lowell. Courtesy of SBHS. **Fig. 135:** VLBDP, CAM. Gift of Aristides Burton Demetrios and Ilene H. Nagel Demetrios. **Fig. 136:** CAM. **Fig. 137:** Photograph by Gary Lowell. Courtesy of SBHS. **Fig. 138:** VLBDP, CAM. Gift of Aristides Burton Demetrios and Ilene H. Nagel Demetrios. **Fig. 139:** Photograph by Peter Morse. Courtesy of Peter and Bobbi Kovner. **Fig. 140:** Photograph by Peter Morse. Courtesy of Peter and Bobbi Kovner. **Fig. 141:** Photograph by Eric Roth. Courtesy of Andrew Spindler. **Fig. 142:** Photograph by Gary Lowell. Courtesy of SBHS. **Fig. 143:** VLBDP. CAM. Gift of Aristides Burton Demetrios and Ilene H. Nagel Demetrios. **Fig. 144:** VLBDP, CAM. Gift of Aristides Burton Demetrios and Ilene H. Nagel Demetrios. **Fig. 145:** Photograph by Gary Lowell. Courtesy of Gregory Van Boven and David Beck. **Fig. 146:** CAM. **Fig. 147:** Photograph by H.C. Williams. Courtesy of Beth Holloran Bourguignon. **Fig. 148:** Photograph by Gary Lowell. Courtesy of SBHS. **Fig. 149:** Photograph by Peter Morse. Courtesy of Peter and Bobbi Kovner. **Fig. 150:** Photograph by Eric Roth. Courtesy of Beth Holloran Bourguignon. **Fig. 151:** Photograph by Gary Lowell. Courtesy of SBHS. **Fig. 152:** Photograph by Eric Roth. Courtesy of Beth Holloran Bourguignon. **Fig. 153:** Photograph by Gary Lowell. Courtesy of Susana McDonnell and Angus Smith. **Fig. 154:** Photograph by Eric Roth. Courtesy of Beth Holloran Bourguignon. **Fig. 155:** TFCDC, CAM. **Fig. 156:** Photograph by Esther Pullman. Courtesy of Mark and Valentine Oldham. **Fig. 157:** Photograph by Peter Morse. Courtesy of Ann and Sue Kenyon. **Fig. 158:** TFCDC, CAM. **Fig. 159:** TFCDC, CAM. **Fig. 160:** TFCDC, CAM. **Fig. 161:** Photograph by Peter Morse. Courtesy of Peter and Bobbi Kovner. **Fig. 162:** Photograph by Leslie Bartlett. Courtesy of Mark and Valentine Oldham. **Fig. 163:** Photograph by Peter Morse. Courtesy of Ann and Sue Kenyon. **Fig. 164:** Photograph by Peter Morse. Courtesy of private collection. **Fig. 165:** CAM. **Fig. 166:** Photograph by Peter Morse. Courtesy of Peter and Bobbi Kovner. **Fig. 167:** Photograph by Peter Morse. Courtesy of Ann and Sue Kenyon. **Fig. 168:** Photograph by Eric Roth. Courtesy of Second Glance Thrift Store. **Fig. 169:** Photograph by Gary Lowell. Courtesy of Ann and Sue Kenyon. **Fig. 170:** Photograph by Gary Lowell. Courtesy of Ann and Sue Kenyon. **Fig. 171:** CAM. Museum purchase, 2010 (2010.39.04). **Fig. 172:** Photograph by Peter Morse. Courtesy of Ann and Sue Kenyon. **Fig. 173:** Photograph by Peter Morse. Courtesy of Ann and Sue Kenyon. **Fig. 174:** Photograph by Peter Morse. Courtesy of the Nichols family. **Fig. 175:** Courtesy of SBHS. **Fig. 176:** Photograph by Eric Roth. Courtesy of Susanna Natti. **Fig. 177:** Photograph by Gary Lowell. Courtesy of SBHS. **Fig. 178:** Photograph by Gary Lowell. Courtesy of SBHS. **Fig. 179:** Photograph by Eric Roth. Courtesy of private collection. **Fig. 180:** Photograph by Eric Roth. Courtesy of Susanna Natti. **Fig. 181:** Photograph by Gary Lowell. Courtesy of SBHS. **Fig. 182:** Photograph by Gary Lowell. Courtesy of SBHS. **Fig. 183:** Photograph by Gary Lowell. Courtesy of SBHS. **Fig. 184:** Photograph by Eric Roth. Courtesy of private collection. **Fig. 185:** Courtesy of the author. **Fig. 186:** Photograph by Eric Roth. Courtesy of Susanna Natti. **Fig. 187:** Photograph by Gary Lowell. Courtesy of SBHS. **Fig. 188:** CAM. **Fig. 189:** Photograph by Leslie Bartlett. Courtesy of SBHS. **Fig. 190:** Photograph by Gary Lowell. Courtesy of SBHS. **Fig. 191:** Courtesy of Susanna Natti. **Fig. 192:** Photograph by Eric Roth. Courtesy of Susanna Natti. **Fig. 193:** Photograph by Gary Lowell. Courtesy of SBHS. **Fig. 194:** Photograph by Eric Roth. Courtesy of Susanna Natti. **Fig. 195:** Photograph by Gary Lowell. Courtesy of SBHS. **Fig. 196:** Photograph by Eric Roth. Courtesy of Susanna Natti. **Fig. 197:** Photograph by Peter Morse. Courtesy of Susanna Natti. **Fig. 198:** Photograph by Peter Morse. Courtesy of Susanna Natti. **Fig. 199:** Photograph by Gary Lowell. Courtesy of SBHS. **Fig. 200:** Photograph by Peter Morse. Courtesy of Susanna Natti. **Fig. 201:** Photograph by Eric Roth. Courtesy of Susanna Natti. **Fig. 202:** TFCDC, CAM. **Fig. 203:** Photograph by Peter Morse. Courtesy of Peter and Bobbi Kovner. **Fig. 204:** Photograph by Peter Morse. Courtesy of Anne Morin. **Fig. 205:** Photograph by Peter Morse. Courtesy of private collection. **Fig. 206:** Photograph by Gary Lowell. Courtesy of Gregory Van Boven and David Beck. **Fig. 207:** Photograph by Eric Roth. Courtesy of private collection. **Fig. 208:** Photograph by Gary Lowell. Courtesy of Alex and Angela Subach. **Fig. 209:** TFCDC, CAM. **Fig. 210:** Photograph by Peter Morse. Courtesy of Peter and Bobbi Kovner. **Fig. 211:** Photograph by Peter Morse. Courtesy of Anne Morin. **Fig. 212:** CAM. **Fig. 213:** CAM. Gift of Christine Kahane, 2015 (2015.082). **Fig. 214:** CAM. Gift of Christine Kahane, 2015 (2015.082). **Fig. 215:** CAM. Gift of Christine Kahane, 2015 (2015.082). **Fig. 216:** CAM. Gift of Christine Kahane, 2015 (2015.082). **Fig. 217:** CAM. Gift of Christine Kahane, 2015 (2015.082). **Fig. 218:** Photograph by Gary Lowell. Courtesy of Gregory Van Boven and David Beck. **Fig. 219:** Photograph by Gary Lowell. Courtesy of Kathryn Soucy. **Fig. 220:** Photograph by Peter Morse. Courtesy of Susanna Natti. **Fig. 221:** Photograph by Gary Lowell. Courtesy of the author. **Fig. 222:** Photograph by Eric Roth. Courtesy of Faith Ronan. **Fig. 223:** Photograph by Eric Roth. Courtesy of private collection. **Fig. 224:** Photograph by Peter Morse. Courtesy of Peter and Bobbi Kovner. **Fig. 225:** Photograph by Gary Lowell. Courtesy of Kathryn Soucy. **Fig. 226:** CAM. **Fig. 227:** Photograph by Gary Lowell. Courtesy of SBHS. **Fig. 228:** Courtesy of Ross (Sandy) Burton. **Fig. 229:** CAM. **Fig. 230:** CAM. **Fig. 231:** Photograph by Peter Morse. Courtesy of Peter and Bobbi Kovner. **Fig. 232:** VLBDP, CAM. Gift of Aristides Burton Demetrios and Ilene H. Nagel Demetrios. **Fig. 233:** CAM. **Fig. 234:** Photograph by Eric Roth. Courtesy of Beth Holloran Bourguignon. **Fig. 235:** Courtesy of Beth Holloran Bourguignon. **Fig. 236:** Photograph by Peter Morse. Courtesy of the Iarrobino family. **Fig. 237:** Photograph by Peter Morse. Courtesy of the Iarrobino family. **Fig. 238:** CAM. **Fig. 239:** Photograph by Peter Morse. Courtesy of the Iarrobino family. **Fig. 240:** Photograph by Peter Morse. Courtesy of the Iarrobino family. **Fig. 241:** CAM. **Fig. 242:** CAM. **Fig. 243:** Photograph by Gary Lowell. Courtesy of Susanna McDonnell and Angus Smith. **Fig. 244:** Photograph by Eric Roth. Courtesy of private collection. **Fig. 245:** Photograph by Gary Lowell. Courtesy of Kathryn Soucy. **Fig. 246:** Photograph by Gary Lowell. Courtesy of Kathryn Soucy. **Fig. 247:** CAM. **Fig. 248:** Photograph by Eric Roth. Courtesy of Susanna Natti. **Fig. 249:** Courtesy of the Estate of Ilmari Natti. **Fig. 250:** Photograph by Peter Morse. Courtesy of Susanna Natti. **Fig. 251:** Photograph by Peter Morse. Courtesy of the Nichols family. **Fig. 252:** Courtesy of the Nichols family. **Fig. 253:** Photograph by Peter Morse. Courtesy of the Nichols family. **Fig. 254:** Photograph by Peter Morse. Courtesy of the Nichols family. **Fig. 255:** Photograph by Peter Morse. Courtesy of the Nichols family. **Fig. 256:** CAM. **Fig. 257:** CAM. **Fig. 258:** Photograph by Peter Morse. Courtesy of Peter and Bobbi Kovner. **Fig. 259:** Photograph by Peter Morse. Courtesy of the Nichols family.

CHAPTER 6

p. 188: Photograph by Peter Morse. Courtesy of the Iarrobino family. **Fig. 260:** Courtesy of the author.